The Economic Development of Ceylon

MAP I

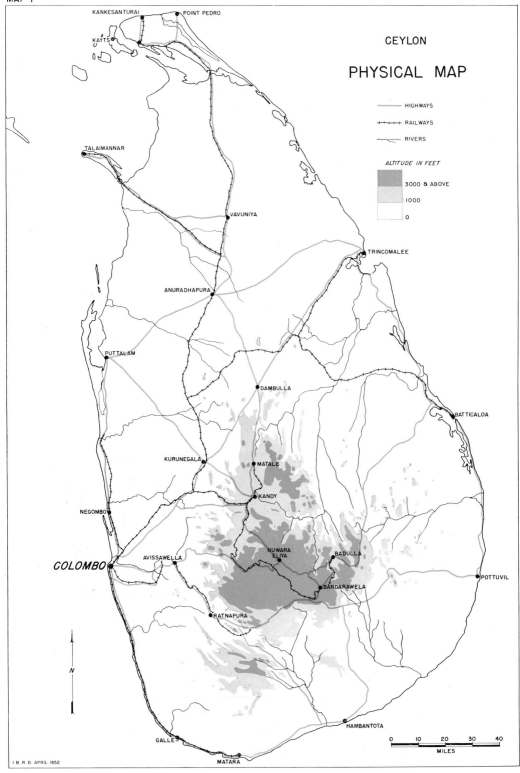

CEYLON

PHYSICAL MAP

HIGHWAYS
RAILWAYS
RIVERS

ALTITUDE IN FEET

3000 & ABOVE
1000
0

KANKESANTURAI
POINT PEDRO
KAYTS

TALAIMANNAR

VAVUNIYA

TRINCOMALEE

ANURADHAPURA

PUTTALAM

DAMBULLA

BATTICALOA

KURUNEGALA
MATALE
KANDY

NEGOMBO

NUWARA
ELIYA
BADULLA

COLOMBO
AVISSAWELLA
BANDARAWELA
POTTUVIL

RATNAPURA

HAMBANTOTA

N

0   10   20   30   40
MILES

GALLE

MATARA

I.B.R.D. APRIL·1952

THE ECONOMIC DEVELOPMENT OF

CEYLON

Report of a Mission organized by the

INTERNATIONAL BANK FOR RECONSTRUCTION
AND DEVELOPMENT *at the request of the*
GOVERNMENT OF CEYLON

Published for the International Bank for
Reconstruction and Development by
THE JOHNS HOPKINS PRESS

The Johns Hopkins Press: Baltimore

Oxford University Press

Geoffrey Cumberlege: London

Copyright 1953, The Johns Hopkins Press

The Mission

SIR SYDNEY CAINE, K.C.M.G.
Chief of Mission

LEOPOLD BARANYAI	*Adviser on Finance*
ERIC BEECROFT	*Assistant to Mission Chief*
FRANCANTONIO BIAGGI	*Adviser on Power*
JEAN R. DE FARGUES	*Adviser on Irrigation and Water Resources*
PAUL T. ELLSWORTH	*Chief Economist*
WILLIAM M. GILMARTIN	*Economist*
FRANCIS W. GODWIN	*Adviser on Industry and Mineral Resources*
ARIE KRUITHOF	*Agricultural Economist*
JOHN D. M. LUTTMAN-JOHNSON	*Adviser on Transportation and Communications*
AMOLAK R. MEHTA	*Adviser on Public Health*
JOHN F. V. PHILLIPS	*Adviser on Agriculture*

Secretaries:

ELIZABETH P. DALLAS
MYRTLE C. TIMMINS

INTERNATIONAL BANK FOR
RECONSTRUCTION AND DEVELOPMENT

WASHINGTON 25, D. C.

OFFICE OF THE PRESIDENT

July 3, 1952

The Honorable J. R. Jayewardene
Minister of Finance
Colombo 1, Ceylon

My Dear Mr. Minister:

I take pleasure in transmitting the report of the Mission to Ceylon organized by the International Bank for Reconstruction and Development at the request of the Government of Ceylon.

The Bank hopes that the Report will help to extend and accelerate Ceylon's progress in economic development and that it will be widely read and discussed. You will understand, of course, that the Executive Directors and the Management of the Bank have not reviewed the Mission's recommendations in detail, and that they are therefore transmitted to you as the views of the Mission, not those of the Bank itself. We believe, however, that the Mission's Report deserves serious consideration and can help the Ceylon Government substantially in determining the general lines of the country's future development program and the economic policies and administrative arrangements necessary for carrying out that program.

The Bank will follow with interest the action taken in connection with the Report, and will be prepared, if desired by the Ceylon Government, to discuss any questions arising from it, and to consider how the Bank can best help in the future development of Ceylon.

It is my sincere hope that the Report may be of positive and lasting benefit to your country.

Sincerely yours,

Eugene R. Black

INTERNATIONAL BANK FOR
RECONSTRUCTION AND DEVELOPMENT
1818 H STREET, N. W.
WASHINGTON 25, D. C.

June 10, 1952

Mr. Eugene R. Black
President
International Bank for Reconstruction and Development
Washington 25, D. C.

Dear Mr. Black:

I am pleased to submit herewith the Report of the Mission to Ceylon organized by the International Bank at the request of the Government of Ceylon. Our conclusions and recommendations are based on studies made by the Mission in Ceylon during the later months of 1951.

On behalf of the Mission I should like to express our thanks for the cooperation and assistance which the Mission received from Ministers and officials of the Ceylon Government and from private persons everywhere in Ceylon. We are particularly grateful for the assistance received from Mr. J. R. Jayewardene, the Minister of Finance, under whose auspices the Mission was arranged, and the staff of the Ministry; and for the great interest which was taken in the work of the Mission by the late Prime Minister, Mr. D. S. Senanayake, and Mr. Dudley Senanayake, at that time Minister of Agriculture and now Prime Minister.

I must also express my great personal appreciation of the work done by the individual members of the Mission, who displayed the greatest keenness and industry in applying the wealth of their varied experience in other parts of the world to Ceylon's special problems. The Mission also owes a debt of gratitude to the many members of the Bank's staff who have assisted us with information and comment during the preparation of the Report, and, not least, to those members of the staff who have borne the burden of typing successive drafts. While in Ceylon we benefited from frequent contacts with members of the FAO team now in the country and other specialists serving there under technical assistance schemes.

It is the sincere hope of the Mission that the recommendations of the Report will help the Government of Ceylon in its great task of ensuring the further development of the country's economy, and of improving the standard of living of its growing population.

Yours sincerely,

Sydney Caine

Introduction

On May 9, 1951, the Government of Ceylon requested the International Bank for Reconstruction and Development to send an over-all mission to Ceylon to survey the development potentialities of the country with special consideration to be given to the following fields of economic activity:—

I. Agriculture, particularly rice cultivation, mixed farming, dairying, colonization and resettlement.
II. Irrigation.
III. Fisheries.
IV. Forestry.
V. Minerals.
VI. Power.
VII. Industrial Development.
VIII. Inland Transport and Shipping.
IX. Vocational Training.
X. Health, including Housing and Water Schemes.
XI. General Economic and Financial Survey, including—

    (a) Public Finance.
    (b) Money and Banking.
    (c) Savings and Investment.
    (d) Balance of Payments.

In particular the Government desired to have advice on the development program to be drawn up for the six-year period after the expiration of the current six-year plan, that is, commencing October 1, 1953 and ending September 30, 1959.

After discussion the Bank agreed to organize such a mission. Two other international agencies cooperated in the selection of the personnel. The principal agricultural member of the Mission was nominated by the Food and Agriculture Organization of the United Nations, which also undertook to pay a portion of his salary and expenses. The World Health Organization nominated the specialist in health.

The Mission arrived in Ceylon on October 6, 1951, and remained in the country until the second week of December. During their stay the members of the Mission travelled widely about the country, and every important area, including all the principal development projects, was visited by at least one member of the Mission. Local staff were provided by the Ministry of Finance, under whose general auspices the Mission worked. Extensive use was made also of the resources of many other government departments and agencies, whose cooperation was generously given, and the Mission benefited particularly from the help of the special liaison officers who were appointed by each of the departments mainly concerned. The Mission takes this opportunity to express its gratitude not only to government officials in Ceylon but to the many people in private positions who helped them in their work.

This Report is presented in two parts. Part I reviews the basic problems of Ceylon's economy and sets out the main lines which economic development may be expected to follow, together with the problems besetting such development. It puts forward definite conclusions both as to the size of the investment program for which Ceylon can afford to budget in the six years 1953–59 and suggests specific allocations in the various fields. Finally it indicates, with brief explanations, the chief practical recommendations of the Mission whether as to innovations in organization, changes in government policies or particular development projects.

Part II analyzes in considerably greater detail the background and the problems arising in specific fields of development. It not only reviews more fully the reasoning, conclusions and recommendations of Part I, but also makes many additional suggestions of individual importance but more limited application.

Contents

CONTENTS

xiv

CONTENTS

CONTENTS

CONTENTS

CONTENTS

CONTENTS

CONTENTS

CONTENTS

CONTENTS

CONTENTS

Tables

TABLES

TABLES

Charts and Graphs

Maps

UNIT MEASURES

NOTE ON CERTAIN UNITS USED IN THIS REPORT

Currency

    1 Ceylon Rupee = 1s. 6d. sterling = $0.21 U.S.
    1 £ sterling = $2.80 U.S.
    (Rs. 1,000,000 = £ 75,000 = $210,000)

Weight

    Unless otherwise stated, English long tons and corresponding units are used throughout.
    1 hundredweight (cwt.) = 112 lb.
    1 ton = 20 cwt. = 2240 lb.

PART ONE

A Program of Development

1. The Problem in its Setting

The Challenge

Ceylon today is passing through a very significant period of her history. Four years ago, after more than four centuries of rule successively by Portuguese, Dutch and British, she obtained political independence. Almost simultaneously there emerged a new economic problem.

This problem is not one of correcting maladjustments already become critical, but rather of forestalling a clearly seen threat of such maladjustments in the future. For some generations past Ceylon's productivity has maintained a lead in the race with population. Now the odds in the race are shifting. There is grave doubt whether increasing production in the old patterns can any longer keep up with a greatly accelerated population growth. Government and people therefore face the task of expanding and diversifying the country's sources of production fast enough to maintain the tempo of progress.

In the past 75 years the population of Ceylon has trebled. Yet typical living standards, while low in comparison with the West, have been maintained and almost certainly improved; at present they are among the highest in Southern Asia. This advancement of the levels of national well-being has been achieved by a virtual revolution in Ceylon's agriculture over the past century, accompanied by a limited industrialization. The revolution has lain in organized large scale production and processing of agricultural commodities for export—specifically tea, rubber, and coconut products. A hundred years ago only the last of these was of real significance in the island. Today the three utilize about two thirds of the developed agricultural land of Ceylon, and contribute over three quarters of the total value of agricultural production.

1

Important as these export crops are, they are no more vital than the rice and diverse crops consumed locally. These, indeed, are the principal means of livelihood for a large part of the population and meet a major share of Ceylon's food requirements. Their present cultivation, however, lacks the dynamic elements necessary to support the steady population increase; for this, an ever greater recourse to the export sector of agriculture has been necessary. Thus Ceylon has become increasingly dependent upon imports for food and other goods, while the means to pay for these has been supplied by the rising output of export crops.

Today's most active currents of economic life and income flow from production of the main exports, together with their associated industries and services, and the domestic and import trade which they finance. Yet the old momentum in this sector is unlikely to be maintained. Although tea and rubber output has actually expanded over the past decade, the first is approaching the limit of available land suitable for its cultivation, and the second faces an uncertain world market which could easily make part of the present production unprofitable. Aging palm groves threaten to diminish coconut production.

To be sure, opportunities remain for further improvements in production and yields of the main export crops. The less important export crops, too, can be more fully developed, and new ones introduced. Export agriculture must certainly continue as the mainstay of Ceylon's economy; but while it may not be threatened with absolute decline, its future growth will be slower than heretofore.

Meanwhile the island continues to add to its population—not at the earlier pace, but at a rate which is now one of the highest in the world. This accelerated growth is mainly attributable to a lowered death rate, accomplished by the virtual elimination of malaria during and since the war. As a result, an annual population increase of about 2.4% must be assumed as a basic factor for the coming decade.

2

The danger of population growing faster than total output is all the more serious because of Ceylon's food situation. Well over half of her rice supplies are imported, mainly from Burma and Siam. Apart from possible political disturbances, there has, ever since the war, been a serious deficiency in world rice supplies. Ceylon's supplies of food of all kinds per head of population are, in fact, already lower than prewar, and the world shortage is likely to continue for many years.

Thus, while science and medicine have opened up new vistas of better health and living standards, they have, against a background of adverse world developments, brought a serious economic challenge to the people and government of Ceylon. The country can no longer rely upon expansion of its traditional exports to keep production and population on a parallel course and to enable it to go on importing a high proportion of its food. The government has accepted the challenge and is vigorously seeking greater productive efficiency and a wider range of economic activity in order to preserve the progressive force formerly supplied by the spread of estate cultivation.

PHYSICAL ENVIRONMENT

Ceylon is a tropical island of 25,000 square miles just off the southeastern tip of the Indian subcontinent. Its location, topography and climate have played unusually influential roles in the dramatic story of its development.

A topographic map [1] of the island suggests the shape of a hat. The crown of mountains, rising to peaks of seven or eight thousand feet in the south-central region, is surrounded on all sides by a brim of level coastal lands which are narrow to the east, south, and west but which extend out like a visor into a large tapering plain pointing toward India in the north. The rivers flow in a radial pattern from the mountains to the sea.

The central highlands jut into the moisture-bearing winds, and

----

[1] See Map No. 1.

3

cause the southwest monsoon to spill most of its generous supply of rainfall on the windward slopes and lowlands in the southwest quarter of the island. Here the abundant moisture and steady tropical temperatures have fostered the agricultural development which has been the foundation of Ceylon's economy in modern times.

In the remaining three quarters of the island, including the long, level northern plains, the combination of winds and mountains has been less benevolent. This region, while often called the "Dry Zone," is actually dry only by comparison with the "Wet Zone" in the southwest corner. But its rainfall, which reaches 50 to 75 inches a year, is mainly concentrated in the season when the milder winds from the northeast and convectional rains dominate the island's climate. At other seasons there are long dry periods when the flow of water drops sharply in the larger rivers and disappears entirely in the smaller streams and reservoirs. Then evaporation is heavy, and soils dry out.

HISTORY AND POLITICAL DEVELOPMENT

Except in a few areas, this so-called Dry Zone has been largely neglected in modern times. Its difficult physical environment plus its endemic malaria have been forbidding barriers to settlement and cultivation. Yet the northern plain of this region was the logical avenue for the earliest migrations into the island from India. It was here, rather than in the more inviting climate of the Wet Zone, that Ceylon developed the highly advanced ancient civilization whose ruins still testify to the remarkable levels of development in the arts, religion, technology and civil organization first achieved more than 2,000 years ago.

This ancient culture was built on rice production, which flourished in the unfriendly environment of the Dry Zone by means of complex, ingenious and extensive irrigation works whose remains are still to be seen over wide areas of the island. How far these old engineering achievements constituted a unified system and how many actually functioned during any one period are not known, since the ruins seen today are the accumulation of various times and stages in the development of ancient and mediaeval Ceylon. Nevertheless, these irrigation works and the rice economy which they supported represented a striking victory over the natural disadvantages of the drier region.

The tides of this ancient kingdom, founded by the Sinhalese of North Indian Aryan origin, ebbed and flowed for centuries. Periods of peaceful accomplishment were interrupted by successive invasions from the Tamil kingdoms of South India, and by prolonged times of internal rivalry, conflict and disorder. War and neglect gradually took their toll of the irrigation works and the society which they supported and, after a last great revival of Ceylon's early culture toward the end of the twelfth century, decay was uninterrupted. The Sinhalese retreated finally to the protective mountains and the southwest, abandoning the rest of Ceylon, save for a few pockets of settlement, to the jungle and the anopheles mosquito.

Ceylon in this era of decay was an easy conquest when the peoples of the West began to open up sea-borne trade with the East. Its situation at the southern tip of India, about midway between the African coast and the great East Indian Archipelago —the famous Spice Islands across the Bay of Bengal—gave it obvious importance as a port of call. It was occupied, partly or wholly, first by the Portuguese in the early 16th century, then by the Dutch in the 17th century, and finally by the British at the close of the 18th century.

During the periods of Portuguese and Dutch administration the economy of Ceylon was essentially one of small peasant agriculture, concentrated largely on rice and other foodstuffs; some additional crops were traded with the outside world, such as coconuts, cinnamon, and to a lesser extent tobacco and cotton.

Development of Ceylon's agricultural resources for export on an extensive scale began only within the past century. Coconut production, which increased sharply during this period, was

5

primarily a Ceylonese undertaking and was mostly in small holdings. Other major developments were carried out principally by British capital and enterprise. The earliest large individual agricultural investments were in coffee, which flourished until the 1880's when production was virtually destroyed within a few years by the spread of a fungus blight. Interest of the large planters quickly shifted to tea estates. Tea cultivation soon exceeded the acreage formerly in coffee and continued to expand, to become by far Ceylon's most valuable crop. The rubber estates have been a development of the past fifty years.

During the interwar period the economic history was one of consolidation rather than of new enterprise. That period and the later years have been more significant for Ceylon's political development.

By a series of changes spreading over more than a generation and accomplished with remarkably little violence or ill feeling, Ceylon has advanced from a purely colonial status to one of complete political independence within the Commonwealth. Even before the final step in 1948, internal affairs had been almost wholly under the control of Ceylonese Ministers for a number of years; in fact the group which formed the first cabinet of the new regime, under the late D. S. Senanayake, had been associated since 1931 as the effective leaders of the government. There is, therefore, a record of stability unrivalled in southern Asia. The peaceful changeover meant also that the new regime inherited unimpaired a soundly based, competent and honest administrative machine.

The same standards of orderliness in politics are still maintained. Political life in Ceylon is not dull: there are a number of active parties, more than one of them professing Marxian views of one variety or another. But their disputes are conducted without physical violence, and there seems little disposition to attempt any major social revolution. There are conflicts and strains between the different racial and religious groups but they have not hitherto led to mass violence.

6

THE PEOPLE

Ceylon's population is an interesting mixture of various racial and religious groups, who have preserved a substantial measure of cultural distinctiveness while living side by side with an unusual degree of communal tolerance.

More than two thirds of the people are Sinhalese descendants of the early Aryan migrations from northern India. They speak Sinhalese and their predominant religion is Buddhism. The largest minority group, about 20% of the total population, are the Tamils of South Indian Dravidian ancestry who speak Tamil and by and large are Hindu in religion. Origins of the predominant Tamil population of the extreme north of the island go back to the early invasions from South India. Another large bloc of Tamils are laborers on the tea and rubber estates who came in when those estates were being developed.

The group known locally as "Moors" constitutes about six percent of the population. Mostly Moslems, these people stem from the Arab traders who were active in Ceylon even before the arrival of the Portuguese. The remaining population includes Eurasians, Malays, Europeans and the aboriginal stock of the island, the Veddahs.

While racial and religious groupings correspond closely in Ceylon, there is also a substantial Christian population, mainly Roman Catholic, which cuts across ethnic lines. Almost 10% of the population are Christians mostly living along the west coast of the island.

Map No. 2 shows how Ceylon's population is concentrated in the southwest quarter of the island. This includes the city of Colombo and most of the country's other important urban centers. It contains about two thirds of the total cultivated area, and most of the industry. Residents of this area represent about 70% of the total population and the density reaches over 700 per square mile. Here the pressure of numbers on the lands of the country-side is severe, especially in peasant agriculture.

Outside of this southwest section there are only two pockets where agricultural conditions have encouraged concentrated settlement. These are the Jaffna peninsula at the extreme northern tip of the island, and a narrow belt along the center of the east coast, particularly in the vicinity of Batticaloa. Together they include perhaps 10% of the total population.

Broadly, about 80% of Ceylon's people occupy only around a third of the area of the island. The remainder are scattered thinly over the Dry Zone. They are found in small settlements near rivers and artificial lakes or "tanks"; in isolated villages where they earn a meager livelihood on the fringes of the jungle, or from shifting clearings; or increasingly, and more hopefully, in the new organized settlement areas now being built up.

The rate of growth of Ceylon's population in recent years is strikingly high. At the time of the most recent census of 1946 the population was 6,657,000. Since then it has grown to an estimated 7.75 million at the end of 1951, or at the extremely rapid pace of about 2.8% a year. Between the census years 1931 and 1946 the average annual rate was only about 1.7%. The startling change reflects a drop of almost 40% in the average death rate, while annual births have remained at the normally high level of between 35 and 40 per 1,000 persons. As mentioned earlier, the remarkable success in reducing mortality is largely attributable to the achievements of the recent anti-malarial campaign; reported malaria cases have been reduced from an average of 2,660,000 during 1937-1946 to about 700,000 in the past few years.

In the next decade or so the crude birth rate is expected to fall a little owing to changes in the age composition of the population. But allowing for that and assuming continuance of the present low death rates, population is expected to increase at an average annual rate of about 2.4%, reaching about 10,000,000 by 1962 and 12,700,000 by 1972.

Ceylon's people are predominantly rural. Urban residents represent only about 15% of the total. Among the gainfully occupied (Table I) more than half are engaged in agriculture,

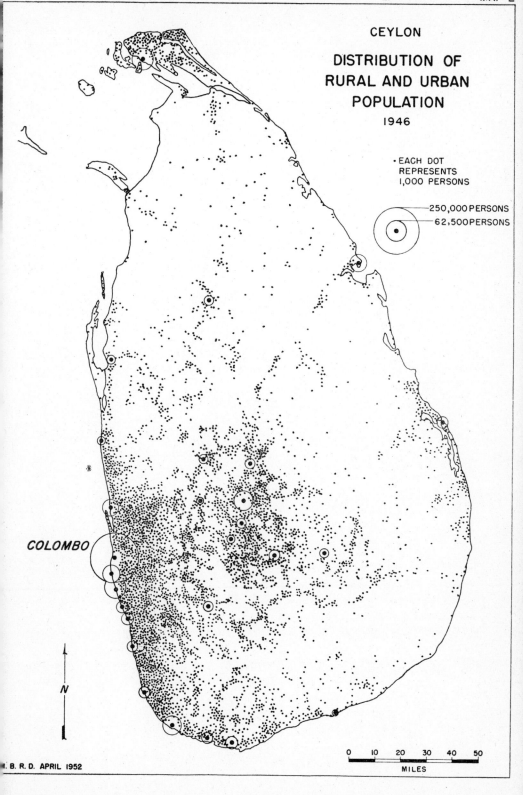

MAP 2

CEYLON

DISTRIBUTION OF
RURAL AND URBAN
POPULATION
1946

• EACH DOT
REPRESENTS
1,000 PERSONS

250,000 PERSONS
62,500 PERSONS

COLOMBO

N

0   10   20   30   40   50
MILES

I. B. R. D. APRIL 1952

and the proportion would be still larger if the wives and minors of peasant families who make a subsidiary contribution to farm income were included.

TABLE I

OCCUPATIONAL GROUPING OF GAINFUL WORKERS, 1946 CENSUS

	Number (thousands)	Percent
Agriculture	1,339.1	51.3
Forestry and fishing	42.3	1.6
Industry and mining	286.5	11.0
Trade, transport, banking, etc.	552.5	21.1
Professions and public and domestic services	390.9	15.0
Total	*2,611.3*	*100.0*

Actually, the agricultural population may be separated into two broad categories according to the fairly distinct segments into which agricultural activity in Ceylon is divided. In the first group are the employees on the large estates, mainly tea and rubber. The second consists of the small-scale peasant cultivators. Workers on estates of over 20 acres and with more than 10 employees may be estimated at about 45% of the gainfully employed in agriculture. The greater part of farm employment is in the cultivation of small holdings. These produce rice, fruits, vegetables and a variety of other foodstuffs for domestic use; they also cultivate by far the largest part of the coconut acreage, about 40% of the rubber lands, and grow practically all of such lesser cash crops as cinnamon, citronella, tobacco, and cacao. The importance of small-scale cultivation to the agricultural population is even greater than census figures indicate, since those enumerated in the peasant sector consist for the most part only of the principal household earners, whereas the estate worker category covers all paid employees, including many wives and minors as well as family heads.

9

OUTLINES OF THE ECONOMY

The National Product

Official estimates of Ceylon's gross national product are necessarily inexact, since reliable statistical information is scanty. Recent data made available by the Central Bank indicate a figure for 1950-51 of approximately Rs. 4,450 million. Table II shows the components of this estimate.

TABLE II

GROSS NATIONAL PRODUCT, JULY 1, 1950 — JUNE 30, 1951

(in millions of rupees at market prices)

1.	Net value of exports		1,855
2.	Rice produced and consumed in Ceylon		154
3.	Other foods produced and consumed in Ceylon		480
4.	Industrial products produced and consumed in Ceylon		263
5.	Personal services		246
6.	Trade and transportation in imports and in food, non-government handled		463
7.	Earnings in other trade and manufactures		69
8.	Public utilities		43
9.	Professions		22
10.	Private education		25
11.	Rents of houses		112
12.	Gross domestic investment:		
	Housing		67
	Business		202
	Government		233
13.	Current government expenditures		232
14.	Interest and bank services		57
15.	Factor incomes from abroad		35
16.	Indirect taxes		45
17.	Minus imports of investment goods:		
	Tools and implements	6	
	Building and engineering supplies	145	–151
	Total		4,452

Note: Strictly speaking, this table portrays gross expenditure on national product rather than gross national product. But since the two

10

come to the same thing if properly calculated, we use the shorter and more familiar term. Most of the individual items in this table are based on recorded data or upon sample surveys, and are probably reasonably accurate. Exceptions are the figure for domestic rice, which reflects a very rough estimate, that for rents of houses and the components of domestic private investment. No data directly reporting this activity are available, so indirect estimates had to be employed. The figure for business investment is the outcome of deducting certain assumed percentages from the original gross figures for the various types of business activity. These are: 5% of items 1, 7, 8 and 10, 2% of item 2 and 8% of items 4 and 6. Investment in housing reflects estimates of the number of houses and of the average life and rents of different categories.

With gross national product at Rs. 4,452 million, the per capita figure is Rs. 570 (equivalent to U. S. $120). Next to Malaya, this is the highest in Southern Asia, and compares favorably with any country in Ceylon's stage of development. The level of investment, at 11.3% of gross national product, is likewise highly creditable. The average for Southeast Asia does not exceed 5%, for Latin America it is about 8%, and in Western Europe in 1938 it was 12%. Nor is investment by any means solely governmental. More than half of the total is private, and this sector comprises an important element in Ceylon's present and future prospects for progress.

Together, peasant and estate agriculture constitute the core of Ceylon's economy. Not only are they the mainstays of employment, but the production, processing and distribution of agricultural products furnish directly about half of the island's income —and even more if we consider the varied economic activity indirectly related to or supported by these pursuits. Much of such industrial development as has taken place has been in the factories and mills preparing tea, rubber, coconuts and rice for exports or domestic consumption.

Of total gross national product, about Rs. 2,400 million or 55% represents the estimated value of output attributable to the production and handling of agricultural commodities grown in

11

Ceylon. Table III shows how different sectors of the economy contribute to the total.

TABLE III

GROSS NATIONAL PRODUCT BY SOURCES, 1950-51

	Percent
Production, Processing and Distribution of Domestic Agricultural Products	
For export	42.1
For domestic consumption	12.9
Other Domestic Goods and Services	
Factory and cottage industry, fisheries, construction, etc. (including government investment)	17.2
Trade and transport (other than in domestic agricultural products)	11.3
Professions, finance, personal service	7.9
Government services	5.3
Rents	2.5
Income from Abroad	0.8
Total	*100.0*

Agriculture

These figures demonstrate not only the prominence of agriculture, but also its high degree of concentration upon export crops. Out of a total developed agricultural area of about 3.5 million acres, tea accounts for more than 560,000, rubber about 660,000, and coconuts around 1,000,000 acres. As seen in Map 3, cultivation of export crops dominates the Wet Zone and spreads from the coast up into the highlands in a fairly well defined pattern. There is a belt of coconut groves nearest the sea, tea at the higher elevations and rubber in the intermediate levels. Tea is grown almost exclusively on extensive estates, largely foreign owned and operated. Such estates also produce over half the rubber and some of the coconuts. Probably two thirds of the value of agricultural exports comes from large-scale cultivation.

While the remaining rubber and most of the coconuts are

cultivated on small holdings, the most characteristic crop of the small-scale peasant sector is rice. Most of the rice and other peasant crops are also grown in the Wet Zone, but in hundreds of thousands of small patches scattered among the estates, especially in the well-watered valleys. This is true up to elevations of about 3,000 feet; the lands above this altitude really form a separate sector of the Wet Zone, cultivated almost entirely by the tea planter because growing conditions do not suit the small scale cultivator.

The ubiquitous tiny rice plots add up to a total of over 600,000 acres which, after allowance for double cropping, provide a total effective rice area of about 900,000 acres a year. The average peasant rice holding is less than a single acre, and only 8,000 rice farms are larger than 10 acres.

Such "postage stamp" cultivation prevails over the wide assortment of other typically peasant crops. Most of these are foodstuffs for domestic consumption, but a few like cacao, cinnamon, citronella, and tobacco are cash crops. Excluding rice and the principal exports, in the aggregate these varied products occupy around half a million acres. About half of this acreage consists of individual plots so small as to be classified in official statistics simply as "town and village gardens." These are nevertheless important, furnishing reliable local sources of such tropical foodstuffs as jak fruit, bread fruit, coconuts, plantains, and a variety of other fruits, vegetables, pulses and small grains.

The pressure of population on the land—becoming steadily more acute in the Wet Zone in the absence of substantial agricultural opportunities elsewhere in the island—is reflected in the fractional scale of Ceylon's peasant farming. The land has been minutely sub-divided among successive generations of peasant families, until today typical holdings are far below an economically satisfactory size. The consequences are chronic underemployment and poverty, heavy indebtedness, absentee ownership and insecurity of tenure, and the presence of a large element of landless agricultural laborers among the peasant population.

13

These circumstances, coupled with the extreme conservatism of the smallholder, tend to perpetuate the inefficiency and low productivity of peasant cultivation and raise formidable obstacles to the introduction of improved farming techniques.

It would appear that the land hunger of the small cultivator has been somewhat aggravated by the absorption of agricultural lands into the large estates; but this is perhaps more fancied than real. By far the greater part of the tea land is at elevations beyond the reach of typical peasant crops. Much of the rubber land is otherwise unsuited to rice. Hence no more than a part of the estate development can have been a real obstacle to extension of peasant farming. The expansion of rubber, and even more of coconuts, has in fact involved participation of the small cultivator. Almost certainly, such additional pressure on the land as may have arisen from the growth of estates has been more than offset by increased employment in nonagricultural occupations directly or indirectly connected with the development of estate production.

Industry

Outside of agriculture, the fields of activity whose economic importance has grown most rapidly during Ceylon's recent history have been those associated with foreign and domestic commerce and the professions, government and domestic service. These now provide about a third of the island's employment and at least as large a share of its national income.

Industrial production, other than the processing of the leading agricultural commodities, accounts for most of the remaining employment and output in Ceylon, but its development to date has been quite limited. Probably more than half of the income and employment classified as industrial represents essentially handicraft activity. Manufacturing, aside from the preparation of tea, rubber, coconut products and rice, is confined to a few moderate-sized plants producing salt, cement, cotton textiles, soap, shoes, cigarettes, machinery for the tea and rubber estates, glassware, beverages, matches and plywood, together with numerous

14

but quite small establishments making such things as pottery, bricks, cigars, rope, nets and miscellaneous handicraft products.

While it is no guide to ultimate possibilities, the list of readily apparent and easily exploitable industrial raw material resources is quite short and the research and investigation necessary to uncover promising additions have been negligible. The island has no known deposits of coal or petroleum. The first step in the development of hydroelectric potentialities has only just been completed. Iron ore deposits are substantial but badly scattered. Promising ilmenite and monazite sands are as yet unutilized. The only minerals of commercial significance at present are graphite, limestone, precious and semiprecious stones, glass sand and various ceramic clays; small quantities of mica are also mined haphazardly. In the most favorable area for timber resources, the Wet Zone, much of the exploitable forest has been replaced by cultivation. In the Dry Zone, natural growth covers much of the area but a great deal of it is low growing jungle and small, poorly developed evergreen and deciduous timber, by nature and location not attractive as a commercial possibility.

The island has a small fishing industry along most of the coastline, but its resources are poor and provide a most meagre livelihood. The continental shelf of the Indian subcontinent surrounds the island, and the consequent shallow waters offer only a limited catch within the short off-shore distances within reach of the primitive techniques of the fishing community.

Foreign Trade and Finance

Essentially, then, most of the economic eggs of Ceylon are in a very few baskets. The fortune of a few agricultural export commodities in world markets has become the most important single determinant of the year-to-year material well-being of the island. Fluctuations in the prices of tea, rubber and coconut products have a major effect not only on Ceylon's balance of payments but on the national income as a whole, including government as well as private income. The high degree of specialization

15

in agriculture has brought large foreign earnings but with them corresponding risks of instability.

This participation in foreign trade has of course involved a parallel growth in Ceylon's overseas expenditures. The population relies on imports for more than half of its rice, practically all of its flour and sugar, and a large volume of other foodstuffs as well as manufactured goods, raw materials and fuels. On a per capita basis the volume of imported consumer essentials has remained fairly constant, and this has meant a steadily rising level of imports to supply the minimum needs of the growing population.

Nevertheless, the economy of Ceylon has normally functioned on an even keel. Prices of tea, by far the most important export, are less erratic than those of rubber and coconut products and they exert a steadying influence on export earnings. And a rising export volume has usually left enough margin to take care of price fluctuation and still maintain a foreign trade surplus, despite growing import requirements and adverse terms of trade in the war and postwar period. Imports for consumption fluctuate in sympathy with export earnings, and total imports exceeded exports in only two of the past 25 years. The trade surplus has generally been about adequate to cover the normal net invisible payments arising from investment income and personal remittances, with only minor plus or minus deviations from a balanced international payments position.

Ceylon's internal finances have been similarly kept in balance. In the postwar world of lopsided budgets the Government of Ceylon has consistently covered its ordinary expenditures from revenues, leaving a surplus to meet at least part of the capital expenditures for development.

PATTERN OF DEVELOPMENT

The Postwar Programs

Immediately after the end of the war, the Ceylon Government commenced a program of accelerated capital investment and

16

development. On the attainment of political independence in 1948, this was given more precise form in the Government's first six-year program, designed to cover the years 1947-53. The aims of that program were sound. Valuable work already done under it includes completion of the first stages of the large multi-purpose development in the Gal-Oya valley, much other irrigation work, improvement of Colombo Port and many new schools, village dispensaries, etc.

This accelerated development has been paid for without in any way threatening the financial stability of the country. That this is so is due to the sound policies pursued by the Central Bank of Ceylon in the monetary field and to the prudent and skillful handling of the government budget by the Minister of Finance. Thanks to their policies and to reasonably favorable export markets, the development expenditure has been entirely covered by net surpluses of revenue over ordinary expenditure plus receipts from internal loans; and the external costs of development have been met without significant reduction of external exchange reserves.

Objectives

In Ceylon as everywhere the primary object of development is higher average real income and therefore higher output per head. Previous discussion has shown how large a task it is to attain a rate of production increase higher than—not merely in step with—the rate of population increase.

But we must not yield to the temptation of thinking that higher material standards are the answer to all social problems and override all other objectives. True, the social stresses which exist in Ceylon appear to be primarily the simple stresses of poverty. If the Ceylonese worker or peasant is discontented he thinks in terms of better opportunities to earn a living on the land or in urban employment, not of social revolution. It has been the basic object of all recent government policies to provide those opportunities for better living. The individual in Ceylon has, however,

17

other objects besides material advancement. Though he may think somewhat enviously of the higher material standards of the West, he does not want to attain these standards by sacrificing other values inherent in his own social traditions, customs and culture. We shall have many occasions to point out where material and cultural objectives clash. It does not follow that cherished cultural traditions and long standing social habits must always give way. On the contrary, it is essential that the way of life to be built up in Ceylon shall be not merely a better one materially, but one spiritually satisfying to the Ceylonese people.

Basic Assets

What has Ceylon got to work with in trying to increase her output? And what does she chiefly lack?

Her first asset—and overwhelmingly the most important in the long run—is her people themselves, whose very increase is an opportunity as well as a threat. There is an old saying that "with every mouth the Lord sends a pair of hands"; but the aphorism is deceptive and dangerous if it generates complacency. Additional hands are useless without land and raw materials to work upon; without tools, equipment and power to work with; and without trained technical guidance and organization to direct their work.

Ceylon has something of these other necessary factors of production. She has substantial, if not unlimited, unused land and some raw materials. There is a basis (though no more than a basis) of social capital—transport network, ports, schools and hospitals—and a modest amount of industrial plant. There is substantial hydroelectric power capacity still to be developed. There is a sound framework of government. And there is at least a rudimentary technical knowledge of the country and its potentialities and of the best skills and techniques of production.

These facts point clearly and obviously to the main channels for the fuller use of the natural resources of the country, following and extending the work of the past and the present. In existing agricultural production the high standards of the best estates must be maintained and the efficiency of the less well run estates and especially of the smallholders greatly improved. The unused lands of the Dry Zone must be opened up by irrigation, jungle clearance, settlement of colonists, and provision of transport and other necessary services. Every encouragement should be given to the growth of sound manufacturing industry and to the effective utilization of the raw materials available in the island. As an essential basis and supplement to these improvements of production, the hydroelectric potential needs to be harnessed, and transport and other general services improved and expanded.

Special Features and Problems

These lines of development have special characteristics which we believe have very important effects on the nature of the plans to be made. The changes to be looked for in Ceylon, although obvious, are not simple. It is not a mere matter of installing capital equipment and transport facilities to develop rich mineral deposits already known to exist; or of throwing open new lands to settlers who need only a skeleton of communications to develop those lands with well-established techniques. Nor is the task of improvement of agricultural methods a simple matter of importing superior techniques which have been perfected and proved elsewhere. In many cases, especially in the farming of the drier areas, techniques suited to the peculiar conditions of Ceylon have still to be discovered by experimentation and research. Even where it is reasonably clear what improvements in technique are desirable, conservatism and complexities of the social structure (e.g. the system of land tenure) may obstruct their adoption by peasant cultivators. On the industrial side, both the proper utilization of raw materials already known and the introduction of newly discovered ones require research, survey and, in the case of many agricultural materials, a period of practical experimentation.

19

The first consequence of these characteristics is the necessity of preliminary survey and research in nearly all fields and our detailed recommendations contain a series of specific proposals for physical and social surveys and for a large expansion of research activity.

A second consequence is that education in its broadest sense must play a very important role. Not only is there today a serious deficiency of technically trained men and women at all levels; a change is required in the whole bias of education in order to encourage receptivity to the new ideas and improved methods essential to increased output. Included in the general field of education is the large task of the Department of Agriculture, assisted by Cooperative and Rural Development Societies, of spreading knowledge of new methods among the hundreds of thousands of peasant farmers.

Thirdly the role of Government has special importance. The tasks of survey, research and education already mentioned mainly fall to the government. Similarly, the basic structure of social capital, including the general communications network, is in Ceylon primarily a government responsibility. In the development of the Dry Zone, irrigation and jungle clearance are fundamental and can only be undertaken by an agency with wide authority. It is conceivable that these tasks could be executed by a private corporation receiving large grants of land, but such a method of operation would certainly not today be thought tolerable in Ceylon, and the main task of organization therefore rests with the government. It follows that the closest attention is needed to the machinery of government for planning and execution of development work.

But although there is so much to be done by the government in providing the basis of progress, it is perhaps nowhere more evident than in Ceylon today that development cannot proceed in detail without a great deal of private activity and a true partnership between government and private enterprise. The extent of current private investment has already been noted. We believe it needs to be increased. In agriculture and indeed in rural activities as a whole, there is large scope for private corporate activity through cooperatives and rural development societies as well as continuation of the present roles of commercial companies; and the development of new industries offers an equally large scope for private energy and ingenuity.

With these problems in mind we have grouped our detailed examination of development prospects under the headings of material resources, human resources and organization.

2. Development of Material Resources

True economic development comes about through balanced, parallel achievement in various departments. A few spectacular projects in one field or another will not accomplish it.

The different lines of creative endeavor are like so many draft oxen hitched together. Each must help the others. Some lead, others follow; some are bigger and stronger and can pull harder than the others. If half want to go a different way, we can unhitch them; if one wants to outdistance the others, we can let him; but then the remaining ones cannot move the wagon as fast—or perhaps not at all.

In our analogy the main lines of productive development, agriculture, industry and their associated activities, are the oxen. Monetary and fiscal policies, organization, and the like are the wheels of the wagon. One wheel out of order can stop the wagon, or at least slow it down. But a full set of good wheels will not make it go; the oxen do that.

Elsewhere we discuss the wheels. In this chapter the Mission attempts to indicate, in general, its observations on Ceylon's principal avenues of material development and what might be done in each for a balanced program of progress during the six-year period 1953-59. Wherever possible we suggest quite specific goals; these—though they may disappoint the most optimistic—are what we believe to be possible, though not easy, of achievement. Where precise targets of achievement cannot be set because progress depends upon the unforeseeable results of research or survey, reaction of private enterprise or other unpredictable factors, we suggest what we believe will be the most profitable direction of development.

For actual accomplishment, of course, general observations

are not enough. All of the subjects dealt with here are treated in far greater detail in the individual chapters of Part II, whose hundreds of practical recommendations on specific matters may in the aggregate constitute most of the value of this report.

Agriculture

Agricultural advancement is essential, first to relieve Ceylon's dangerous dependence upon external sources of food. But it also offers the greatest avenue to an increase of total national wealth in any near future. It must set the pace in tomorrow's development, even if other activities may in the more distant future come to rival it.

With some overlapping of interest, Ceylon's agriculture divides itself into three fairly distinct sectors. First is the cultivation looking solely to export, dominated by tea and rubber and mainly a plantation or "estate" economy in the higher lands of the southwest. The second might be termed the wet farming sector, consisting typically of peasant agriculture and concentrated especially in the lower lands of the southwestern quadrant. Rice and other food crops are its mainstays; but it includes the bulk of the coconuts, about half of which are exported directly or indirectly. The third sector is the dry zone, largely uncultivated, where the problem remains one of winning the land back from the jungle.

Of Ceylon's total area of about 16.25 million acres, 6.75 million are considered suitable for agriculture in some form. Tea, rubber and coconuts occupy 2.25 million acres of this; rice and miscellaneous crops now use another 1.25 million. About 3.25 million acres await development.

Export Agriculture

The value of the three export crops, tea, rubber and coconuts, can hardly be overstated. Without the foreign exchange which they earn Ceylon could not buy the food she imports to feed half her population. She could not buy the wide range of manufactured goods which are an integral part of the higher standard

23

of living to which her people aspire, and she could not buy the capital goods on which her plans of future development depend. Of the three, tea is the most important—well exceeding in export earnings the other two combined—and is most completely an estate industry. Coconuts, the smallest of the "big three," are predominantly a product of small holdings.

Main emphasis in this sector should be placed on maintaining and improving efficiency and output. Technical improvements are proceeding well at the hands of the estate managements. Continued support of the excellent Tea Research Institute is urged, and this institution could profitably extend its studies toward the processing side of the industry. Although the market would justify increased acreage, there is little chance of it since most of the suitable tea land is already planted.

For rubber the outlook is different. On the one hand there is much more room for improvement in technical efficiency, by planting higher yielding types and by greater attention to tapping techniques and water conservation. On the other hand, a net expansion of acreage, for which land could no doubt be found, is not recommended. Natural rubber is likely to be faced with increasingly hard market conditions in the future, as both production and competition from synthetic increase, and Ceylon will need to concentrate on lowering her costs if she is to retain even the present export sales. On many of the estates interplanting with cacao is recommended.

Transfer of foreign-owned tea and rubber estates to Ceylonese control has been going on for the last ten or fifteen years. Such growth of local interest is natural, and in the long run beneficial. Ceylonese observers point out, however, that it has often resulted in lowered efficiency, as well as later deterioration through subdivision of the estates. It is in one sense regrettable, too, that this local capital is not used in new productive ventures to benefit the island's output instead of merely transferring ownership of what is already there. Accordingly we urge that the government refrain from any action designed to force such transfers. They

24

should be allowed to occur naturally, but not in a way to discourage the continued interest of those non-Ceylonese firms to whose enterprise and energy their creation was due.

Coconut products come next, as they are the third largest export; but domestic consumption is equally important and, as population grows, appears destined to take more and more of the output. Coconut products of all kinds enter intimately into the traditional domestic economy, contributing both foodstuffs and fiber as a basis for various village industries. However, a large proportion of the planted area is in very poor condition—owing, we fear, to the improvidence of the cultivators in failing to replace their trees. Extensive replanting is necessary. This should be given a measure of government assistance, but more important are education and propaganda to bring home to the growers the need for replanting. Extension of area is both possible and desirable. Improvements in fertilization and cultivation practices are very necessary. In all these matters a special effort is needed to persuade the numerous growers to improve their holdings. A major difficulty is the tiny size of many of the "plantations," resulting from excessive subdivision of ownership and representing one facet of Ceylon's critical land tenure problem.

Apart from the three main export crops, Ceylon has a number of much smaller agricultural exports such as cacao, cinnamon and citronella. Development of these and others should certainly be encouraged. Cacao is promising and among many other possibilities reviewed by the Mission are groundnuts, sesame, pineapples, cotton and hard fiber plants. With more resistant varieties a revival of the once-important coffee is also not impossible, although it should not occur at the expense of tea.

General Wet Zone Agriculture

In relation to the staple exports, the main reliance is still on private action and, in the case of tea, it is almost true that the only action required of the government is inaction.

In the second main sector of Ceylon's agriculture, however,

a great deal of vigorous action from the government is required. Here must be made the main effort to reduce reliance upon external food supplies. Rice is at once the staple food and the dominating crop in wet zone agriculture. The output is estimated at some 200,000 tons of paddy a year, but a substantially greater quantity, nearly 400,000 tons, is imported. There has been some increase of output in recent years but, in spite of it, the total cereal supplies per head of population are almost certainly lower than prewar. A greatly increased output from existing rice acreage is both urgently necessary and possible if improved methods are adopted.

No observer can fail to be impressed by the low average yields campared with those of other rice-growing areas of Asia. Much of the blame must be placed on poor cultivation practices, failure to transplant, inadequate or improper fertilization, and a prodigal use of water which is often wasteful and sometimes harmful. The Mission believes that proper practices in all these matters could double the reported yield of 14 bushes per acre from present rice lands. If that could be done today, it would go far to dispense with the need for the present huge rice imports.

The necessary changes in traditional methods will not, however, be brought about quickly or easily among the normally conservative peasantry. There is a tremendous task of education and persuasion here for the agricultural extension officers, the cooperative and rural development societies, the village schools, and all other agencies able to influence the small rice-grower. The force of trained extension officers needs to be greatly expanded, and that, in turn, requires much larger facilities for training. There should be expansion at the university level and a multiplication of the numbers of training schools for all grades of the agricultural department.

Although the education of the cultivators themselves in improved methods is primarily a task for the local leaders of the rural population, external technical aid could play a key part in the whole process, by providing staffs for the training of the expanded force of field workers. That would be particularly appropriate work for outside technical aid since, by helping to relieve Ceylon's own dependence upon external sources of food, it would help also to improve the basic world food situation.

We believe the minimum target to be achieved by these and other measures by 1959 is a 10% increase in average rice yields. Similar increases can be made in the yield of other food crops, and new food crops can be added. In this program more money would be needed for the agricultural extension service and for agricultural research and education. The cooperative societies can also render more help in the financing of improvement, the purchase of equipment and fertilizers and the like. But the measures required here make but a modest call on finance. The main responsibility for achieving the very important objective of a much higher percentage of home food supplies must lie with the personal effort of all those concerned in Ceylon, supported, we hope, by generous technical assistance from outside.

Dry Zone Agriculture

It is the third sector of agriculture—the development of unused lands—that offers the most scope for government action and for outside technical aid, and that will make the greatest claims on financial resources.

The area of potential development is nearly as great as the total acreage now under cultivation. But it must not be inferred that bringing it all under crops will by any means double the current agricultural output. Most of the unused lands are in the dry zone. Their soils are poorer than in the wet zone. They need irrigation to develop their full output; and the Mission's preliminary calculations suggest that not more than 600,000 additional acres can be irrigated. Therefore a large part must be developed through dry farming, with much lower yields per acre. As for any unused portions of the wet zone, these naturally tend to be marginal lands in point of fertility or accessibility. Very broadly, the combined crop potential of all unused agricultural

27

land may be put at roughly half that of the island's lands now producing for domestic consumption.

Such an addition to the country's output would be a major achievement. It is in the foreground of the present governmental program, and we give it equal prominence in the basic development program we envisage for Ceylon. But to realize this potential output will be a long task. It requires careful organization by government and much enterprise from individuals. It requires intense study of soils, water resources and new agricultural methods. And it requires large capital expenditures, especially for irrigation and colonization (discussed in more detail below). It will take at least another generation to do the job fully, and it will need much patience, as hasty action for quick results can bring heartbreaking setbacks and irremediable damage to the soil. What can be done in the next six years is to make a further good bite into the undeveloped area and to lay a sound foundation for more rapid progress later.

Opening up the Dry Zone is no new project. It has been going on for many years—slowly at first, but much faster recently with the subjugation of malaria. There is therefore a rapidly growing volume of experience to guide future action. The Mission is nonetheless convinced that much fuller knowledge is needed to avoid tragic mistakes and that a first requirement is much more survey work on topography, soils and land-use potential. These should be island-wide, with more detailed treatment of selected areas. Of prime urgency is aerial topographic mapping on which soil, land-use and water surveys can be based. Experienced commercial help would be most valuable for the initial mapping, as there are private companies unusually skilled at this work; technical assistance through the Colombo Plan and United Nations agencies should be available for the other studies.

Much remains to be learned of the adaptability of new crops to these areas, and we suggest a wide variety for experimental trial. On the irrigated portions rice will undoubtedly predominate as usual; but starting from scratch should make it easier to introduce improved methods, and such practices as the cooperative use of modern farm machinery. Dry farming on the scale required raises problems novel in Ceylon. Study of the necessary techniques will be greatly aided by the special FAO team now engaged in this work, but establishment of the right practices will depend finally on continuous experimental and educational work by the Department of Agriculture. All this development raises problems of soil conservation of the first importance for Ceylon's long-term future, and we recommend greatly expanded effort in that field.

Sugar is being considered as a major Dry Zone crop. According to latest information, the Government intends to proceed with a factory and 6,000 acres of cane at Maha Illuppallama; but in addition various other projects have been mentioned, including one at Gal Oya of 20,000 acres. From inspection of the impressive (although inconclusive) experiments in cane production, we share the general belief that Ceylon should be able to grow cane with satisfactory yields. We believe also that this industry should be established on the island, and that it will contribute directly to an improved balance of payments by lowering the imports of sugar. But we are aware of the complexities of the industry as experienced elsewhere, in both field and factory, and therefore recommend that expansion beyond the initial project at Maha Illuppallama should await the results of experience there.

Livestock

Development of animal husbandry on the island has been retarded, partly through religious considerations. The consequences are loss of potential production, prevalence of dietary deficiencies, and failure to secure the benefit to soil fertility which would come from a proper integration of stock farming with crop-raising.

Present policies of the Department of Agriculture, reinforced by the suggestions of the FAO team, are in the right direction. The Mission supports these, and has added specific suggestions in Chapter 11 on the improvement of cattle breeding, development of dairying (including more extensive use of buffalo milk), and other matters. One fault, however, is that most measures to date have been designed for immediate needs and have lacked consistent direction. Fundamentally, policy for livestock development must be framed on a very long term basis, with perhaps a 25-year target; and as groundwork for such a policy, a thorough regional survey of livestock potentialities is urgently needed.

Forestry

As a result of government attention over many years, at the end of 1950 there were about 2,760,000 acres of forest land set aside for production or protection and 897,000 acres of national parks and wild life preserves also under Forest Department control, representing in all about 23% of the total land area of the island. By careful exploitation, improvement and replanting, these forests can supply a fair portion of Ceylon's needs for timber and domestic firewood, while at the same time serving their functions in flood control and soil conservation. But excessive cutting must be avoided; in particular, there is not enough timber to permit large-scale industrial consumption of wood fuel, or the operation of railroads on firewood.

Basic objectives of the Forestry Department are sound, but to carry out the necessary research, development and forestry education the Department does not yet have the personnel required. The staff should be strengthened as rapidly as trained men can be found or produced. This applies especially to field officers. In forestry, as in other matters of land use, there is need for a survey based on aerial photographs and supplemented by ground inspection.

We recommend that the government give the fullest weight to the cautious views of its forest officers when considering further appropriations of forest land for other purposes. On the other hand, we doubt that the present ban on removal of any indigenous forest above the 5,000-foot level need be so rigid; it might be advantageous to replace some such areas by new forest plantations of potential commercial value. Other such plantations should be encouraged also, including an extension of teak in the Dry Zone.

General Policies

Additional personnel is urgently needed at nearly all levels of the Department of Agriculture. Extension work, education and research should be strengthened in virtually every division. In many fields we believe that the employment of outside advisers on a long-term basis would be more valuable than the comparatively brief visits of experts for superficial study.

Progress cannot stop while awaiting the results of the basic surveys which are so badly needed. However, until fuller knowledge of the topography and soil is at hand, we believe that the consequences of error can be limited best by concentration on numerous small schemes rather than big, impressive ones. Collectively, in fact, the achievement of these smaller schemes should be just as great as that of the large projects.

For broad benefit to agriculture, serious study should be given to reforms in the land tenure system. These should be designed to discourage excessive fragmentation, and to provide greater security of tenure and better titles (possibly Torrens titles) so as to facilitate borrowing. Such modifications would give cultivators greater security and incentive to improve their land.

COLONIZATION

Commencing some twenty years ago under the guidance of the late Prime Minister and with increasing intensity in recent years, the Ceylon Government has sought to resettle families from the congested areas on "new" Dry Zone lands opened up and provided with irrigation. This is undoubtedly one of the major avenues of economic development and one of the soundest uses of available resources.

It is symptomatic and appropriate that Ceylon's largest and most dramatic single development project to date is a colonization scheme—the Gal Oya Development. This is a multi-purpose project, based on the Gal Oya Valley in the east of the island, and operated by a government-created but independent board. Construction methods and clearing techniques have been much more highly mechanized than in any other settlement project. Over a ten-year period it is hoped to settle in the area some 250,-000 people, about half of whom will be smallholders and their families. It involves irrigation of over 100,000 acres, mostly reclaimed from virgin jungle, and installation of a 25,000 KW hydroelectric power station. Also contemplated are some large-scale farming units to be operated by the Board itself, and ultimately some industrial development. The dam upon which the whole scheme depends was completed in 1951; construction of irrigation channels and the clearing of jungle by rapid mechanical methods are proceeding, and some colonists are already on their holdings.

Elsewhere smaller projects are in progress, and others are being studied. If the irrigation works contemplated by the Mission[1] are carried out, the period 1953–59 should see the colonization—through a number of individual schemes—of about 125,000 acres of irrigated land plus perhaps 75,000–100,000 acres of dry land; these projects will involve resettlement of more than 250,000 people, including the nonagricultural populations of the new villages and towns which will be created. About two thirds of these will be in Gal Oya.

All the colonization schemes, big and little, throw a great burden onto the various departments concerned with the many activities incidental to their success: clearing jungle from the new land; preparing it for cultivation; building houses for the colonists; laying out and building roads, schools, village centers and medical facilities and other community needs; providing financial aid to the colonist until his crops begin to yield; and

---

[1] Chapter 13.

32

furnishing continuing advice and assistance in the operation of his holding. The greater part (in the Gal Oya scheme virtually the whole) of this work is undertaken by government. It is axiomatic, therefore, that in each individual scheme there should be the closest collaboration between the various agencies concerned, and as extensive preliminary survey, study and planning as is possible. We hope that our various proposals for the coordination of central economic planning and administration, for the planning of water use, and for topographical and soil surveys will contribute to these essentials.

The Mission believes that these most valuable resettlement activities could be made even more beneficial by certain changes in policy. First, we suspect that the government is spending more on the individual colonist than is needed to attract him. Earlier, when the areas for colonization were inaccessible and malaria-ridden, large inducements had to be offered. Now that these conditions have been so largely corrected there are more people anxious to move into the settlements than can be accommodated. We therefore suggest some reduction in the provision of free services and assistance, and a reduction in the standard amount of land offered at less than an economic rental. If such changes can be made they will permit settlement of more people for the same cost, on the same amount of irrigated land.

Secondly, we believe it would help to speed economic development if part of the new land were leased in larger blocks to financially responsible individuals or to corporations, instead of being wholly reserved for allotment to smallholders in uniform plots. This would bring in private capital and energy and would relieve the government of at least some of the burden of clearing, building and the like. Workers employed in such larger units would, of course, need assurance of fair treatment and the existing legislation applying to estate laborers should provide a basis for control with that object. In addition there might be greater elasticity in allotments to smallholders, and more opportunity for successful colonists to take up extra acreage. With the report of an Interdepartmental Committee on the disposal of Crown lands under consideration, the time is opportune for careful reconsideration of these procedures.

Study of the Gal Oya Development suggests some special precautions, based on lessons learned in the Tanganyika ground-nuts scheme of the United Kingdom Overseas Food Corporation. We feel that the Gal Oya project is excellent; but we fear that undue haste, coupled with the absence of adequate preliminary surveys, may easily result in waste and permanent damage to the land. Apart from a number of specific suggestions on technical points, the Mission recommends that the Gal Oya Board and the Ministry of Agriculture carefully review the targets of achievement set for the early years. It is also our recommendation that no new large-scale schemes should be undertaken until further experience has been gained through the Gal Oya Development, and, in any case, until the further surveys recommended are available. Meanwhile we believe that the available technical and administrative resources should be concentrated on a series of smaller schemes, which we are confident can be done without reducing the number of people actually settled in the six-year period.

WATER AND POWER RESOURCES

Ceylon has substantial water resources not yet fully utilized for irrigation, power generation or other economic purposes. Rainfall is heavy: the island's average is over 75 inches, and even in the Dry Zone only a few places receive less than 50 inches per year. Much of this is already turned to agricultural use, directly or through irrigation; but there remain millions of acre feet, now running to waste, which could be used to irrigate land still uncultivated or not fully productive. Moreover the physical configuration of the island, with its central highlands and the descent to the coastal plain in successive steps, offers obvious possibilities for utilizing the fall of the rivers to generate power.

Nonetheless these resources must not be exaggerated. The rainfall is unevenly distributed, and in the Dry Zone especially the rivers alternate between high flood and a mere trickle. The hill country has few sites for large-capacity reservoirs, so that storage for flood control, irrigation or the regulation of flow for steady generation of electric power is sometimes difficult. For the same reason, in many of the rivers there is no practicable alternative to allowing a high proportion of the flood waters in the rainy seasons to run off. Where reservoirs can be built (and thousands of small reservoirs or tanks exist in the lower parts of the river valleys) they are shallow, and the loss of water by evaporation and seepage is high. The large variations in flow, and the need to draw water at times and rates governed primarily by irrigation requirements, make it impossible to realize the full theoretical hydroelectric potential.

It has been observed that the water which can actually be made available should suffice to irrigate roughly 600,000 acres, or about as much land again as is now under irrigation and about 16% of the present cultivated area. This substantial acreage, with associated dry-farming areas, can take care of something like 1.5 million people. But looking to the probable population of Ceylon in another two decades, the water supply is not so large that the resources can be treated as inexhaustible. Nor is the utilization of that water a simple matter. There must be careful selection of the most suitable land for irrigation, and careful planning of the irrigation works.

Accordingly the first need is to insure that the water available is used to the best advantage. For this the Mission proposes a Water Resources Planning Unit attached to a central economic planning organization (not to any individual department) and responsible for the planning of all major uses of water. The unit will need not only regular hydrological records but also the basic topographical and soil surveys which have been recommended for more general purposes.

Irrigation

The Irrigation Department has been at work since 1900. Its first operations were concerned with repair and maintenance of some of the ancient tanks, whose rehabilitation had begun on a small scale 40 years earlier. Since 1931 the Department has not only extended this work widely, but has initiated entirely new schemes. The largest of these is the Gal Oya Development already described. Upon completion of the first six-year program in 1953, it is expected that over 75,000 acres of newly irrigated land will have been provided under 24 major schemes including the first stages of Gal Oya.

For the second six-year program the Mission has drawn up a set of suggested works which it believes offer the most rapid progress feasible with present knowledge and available technical staff. It includes the completion of Gal Oya and other schemes now in progress, together with a number of new ones, and calls for a total 1953–59 expenditure on irrigation works of Rs. 190,-000,000. Among the new schemes, we recommend giving priority to those of small or medium size pending the preparation of a general water-utilization plan. Especially recommended are the Padawiya and Pavatkulam projects.

One new large scheme comparable to Gal Oya, in the Walawe Ganga valley in the south, has been strongly supported locally. The Mission has concluded, on the information submitted to it, that this scheme is quite uneconomic as now planned. The cost, per acre of land irrigated, would be over three times the cost in Gal Oya and about five times the average cost in other schemes. The Mission cannot recommend the use of an estimated Rs. 200,-000,000 out of Ceylon's limited resources for so poor a return, and believes that the money would be much better spent on a series of smaller projects.

The Irrigation Department itself, which has done much excellent work, is inadequately staffed to meet the still heavier tasks before it. There is need of more trained engineers and more technically trained men at all levels. Our suggestions for strengthening the professional staff include more recruitment from outside Ceylon as well as increased provision for training, both overseas and local. Meanwhile, to secure some immediate relief for the

Department, and also as a contribution to local training, we suggest employing more outside contractors for specific works.

Flood Control and Drainage

Floods are a periodic threat in many places, especially in the Colombo area and elsewhere in the southwest. Unfortunately the topography and the very concentrated rainfall make control by reservoir construction or other standard methods exceedingly expensive. Indeed, the cost would far outweigh the actual damage done by floods. Therefore the Mission can recommend only a moderate provision for local protective works.

There are a few areas, most obviously the Jaffna Peninsula and the southwest coastal strip, where drainage and salt water exclusion may be particularly useful in reclaiming land or protecting present cultivated areas. At this time the Mission proposes more intensive study of these possibilities and a small provision of funds to carry out existing schemes.

Power

Over most of the densely populated southwestern area, including Colombo, electric power is supplied by the Government Electrical Undertakings Department. In addition there is substantial private generation by the many tea and rubber factories, and a number of municipalities have their own supplies.

Thermal plants formerly provided nearly all the EUD power, but since 1950 the southwestern area has been served by the new hydroelectric plant at Aberdeen-Laksapana. However, consumption is already nearing the limit of installed hydroelectric capacity; pending its enlargement, and as the load increases further, the older thermal plants in Colombo will almost certainly have to be reactivated. At the end of 1951 the island's total installed capacity was 35,300 KW hydroelectric and about 108,-000 KW thermal, of which 10,000 KW of the hydro power and 77,000 of the thermal (diesel) capacity were in private plants.

Recent official policy has been designed both to replace the existing thermal plants by hydroelectric power—so saving imports of fuel—and to make a great deal more power available for industrial and other uses. These are good objectives in principle, but they cannot both be realized in any near future. It will be many years before hydroelectric production can even reach the island's present level of consumption. On technical grounds, furthermore, the experience of countries with a high hydroelectric development has shown that it is desirable to retain a percentage of thermal plants as a means of regularizing output and as standby capacity. Hydroelectric development in Ceylon should therefore be regarded primarily as the means of meeting the increased power demands certain to arise in the future, rather than as a substitute for any major part of the existing thermal capacity.

We are fully satisfied that the extension of the existing hydroelectric installation at Laksapana is justified and should be pressed on as rapidly as possible. Through the developments known as Laksapana Stages II-A and II-B, involving new dam construction and additional generating capacity, the hydroelectric output can be doubled by 1957 and trebled by 1959 or earlier. Well before the completion of these works, say by the end of 1955, there should be a new and more precise investigation of hydroelectric potentialities. This should be made in conjunction with the proposed Water Resources Planning Unit, and from the studies a decision should be taken on the best place for still further development, whether by extensions at Laksapana or elsewhere. We have set out[2] a 10-year program which we believe represents as rapid progress as the inevitable delays of planning, construction and deliveries will permit, and which will provide by 1961 a capacity of 125,000 KW and an estimated annual output of 500,000,000 KWH. Within the period 1953–59 capacity would reach 75,000 KW at an estimated expenditure of Rs. 120,000,000. During the same period extensive developments in the main grid and distribution network would be needed, costing another Rs. 100,000,000.

It will not be possible during 1953–59 to look for the extension

---

[2] Chapter 14, Table VII.

of hydroelectric supplies all over the island. Outlying areas should continue to rely on thermal plants. In Jaffna a continued supply from the cement factory plant is assumed. In Trincomalee arrangements should be made to get increased supplies for the town from the British naval installations there. In smaller towns the supplies might be improved by transferring to them some of the small diesel plants which will become redundant in the southwestern area as hydroelectric output increases. A new source of hydroelectric power will enter service during 1952 when the plant being installed at Gal Oya is completed, with a possible output up to 25,000,000 KWH per year. But the Mission doubts seriously whether the very high costs of the necessary transmission line will make it economic to link this plant with the main grid in the near future. It would be better to utilize its output in the Gal Oya Development area itself and in neighboring villages and towns, including Batticaloa.

At least within the period up to 1959, the increase in output is likely to be absorbed by natural increases in demand, by extensions of supplies to new areas (including a substantial switching of rubber and tea factories to the public supply system) and by service to new industries of types making only modest demands for electric power. Thus within that period the Mission sees no reasonable prospect of really large amounts of hydroelectric power for such heavy users as electric furnace steel-making or railway electrification; and, as it does not appear economic to supply the power requirements of such developments by construction of new thermal plants, we have not provided for them in our general development program in that period.

The Mission believes the Electrical Undertakings Department ought to be converted into a statutory authority with a reasonable degree of independence, on the lines of the British Electricity Authority. It should be strengthened by employing a high-level technical adviser responsible to the manager; and a scheme of overseas training of Ceylonese personnel is proposed.

Rates charged for electricity by the EUD should be reviewed, with the dual objectives of achieving more uniformity and of increasing revenue at least to a point where it equals the cost of supply under a proper commercial accounting of both capital and running costs. If a revenue surplus can be secured, so much the better, as it will provide a fund for further electricity improvements.

INDUSTRY

Diversified industrial growth, while not as urgent as increased agricultural production, is essential to Ceylon's ultimate development. It is true that for some time to come both the additional population and the major investment of capital can most profitably be applied to the development of new lands and the improvement of cultivation; but before many years, as the empty lands fill up, Ceylon will need to seek other means of using new additions to population and available capital, and especially uses in the manufacturing field.

Labor and capital are not enough for industrial development; there must also be raw materials, technical knowledge, skill and experience, and enterprise. An industrial community cannot be created overnight. Especially complex is the growth necessary to make available the "external economies" of a diversified industry. Efforts must be started immediately to widen the base for industrial growth, even if the major developments are expected to arise much later.

The Mission's proposals for industry are inspired, therefore, by two principles. First, considering the narrow limits of Ceylon's available capital resources, the time is not yet ripe for really large investment in individual industrial projects unless they have unusually secure prospects of paying their way. Second, this is the time to lay the foundations of later development by close and systematic scientific study of raw material possibilities, by promoting as wide a variety of small projects as possible, and by facilitating the acquisition of technical skills, managerial experience and a habit of industrial enterprise.

Present Industry

It should not be inferred from this that the country is entirely devoid of industry today. On the contrary, in a sense most of the big exports are industrial products made from agricultural crops. The total operating plant for these and lesser industries employs hundreds of thousands of workers and consumes annually an estimated .156,000,000 KWH, about two thirds of all the electricity generated on the island. There are 950 tea factories alone.

But until recently Ceylon's industries, like her agriculture, have been concentrated upon the three main export commodities, supplemented only by some minor production of consumer goods and handicrafts. Of these, the three principal industries are too specialized, and the others too small, to have built much in the way of broad industrial experience, general technical know-how or skilled labor for expansion into new fields. Meanwhile, preoccupied with tea, rubber and coconuts, the country has done little or no research to disclose its possible industrial raw materials, and not many important ones have been self-evident. Partly for these reasons, and partly for others, private industrial capital has been shy.

Governmental efforts to fill this gap began with the creation of nearly a dozen small emergency factories to meet World War II shortages. Most of these later proved uneconomical and were closed, perhaps belatedly, in or about 1950–51. More recent attempts are on a larger scale, and began with a Rs. 21,000,000 cement plant opened in August, 1950. Today, in various stages of preparation, are projected factories for textiles, coconut oil, sugar, steel, paper, fertilizer, caustic soda, DDT, concentrated ilmenite, ceramics and some others, at an investment which will aggregate at least Rs. 150,000,000.

Unfortunately the government has tried to do the whole job itself, building and operating factories under full public ownership and bureaucratic administrative procedures. The results have been so unsatisfactory as to call into being a special com-

41

mittee to investigate the huge financial losses of these and other governmental commercial undertakings.

Future Developments

While the need for government assistance in industrial development remains, it has become clear that it should take the form of initiative and financial participation rather than actual operating control. A recent local proposal to set up publicly-owned industrial corporations suggests, we fear, nothing more than continuation of the present unsatisfactory system under a new name; for in its details this proposal fails to transfer effective control and operating authority to the corporations themselves, and this is the real heart of the problem.

We believe that the solution will be found in the creation of an autonomous Ceylon Development Corporation, with capital participation of the government, the commercial banks, and the investing public.[3] This will call into play private as well as public resources, and will permit joint financing of industrial projects under competent and profitable commercial management. Under appropriate conditions it might also provide a suitable mechanism for industrial financing through the International Bank for Reconstruction and Development, should this become desirable later.

Typical of the important industries which such an institution could help to establish is a flour mill. Although Ceylon is not a wheat-growing area, our studies show that considerable advantage would accrue from local milling, and that private capital is prepared to participate in such an enterprise. The Mission recommends an initial flour mill to meet about a third of the island's flour requirements, at a probable capital cost of about Rs. 9,-200,000.

A review of current industrial schemes of the government indicates that some are technically and economically sound, while others are not. Success of the projected fertilizer and paper fac-

---

[3] For a fuller discussion see Chapter 4.

tories is doubtful. Some of the others—such as the caustic soda, DDT and coconut oil projects—call for relocation or revision in the light of more careful economic study.

We feel that the government's Rs. 24,000,000 steel mill project is at least premature, for technical reasons quite apart from the government's earlier unfortunate experience in this field. The plan is to employ the expensive electric furnace method, which is customarily reserved for special steels and is not used for ordinary steel even in Sweden where power is cheap. The project will demand fully half the new hydroelectric power available by 1956, and this cannot be spared. Moreover, the local ore deposits are scattered in such a way that mining costs will be higher than anticipated, and we believe that the future supply of scrap has been overestimated. Not even the capital investment figure is firm, as the technical preparation for the project has been superficial; in any event the sum can be better spent elsewhere at this time. We strongly recommend deferring this scheme, meanwhile calling for its review by an experienced commercial steel company.

Criteria for Industries

Our conclusion is that, for the present, Ceylon's main industrial growth should be centered on the development of numerous small or medium-sized industries, rather than a few large ones. These should be widely scattered and diversified, to take advantage of labor and raw materials in various parts of the island. Government help, in addition to participation in the Development Corporation, should include technical advice, tax incentives, marketing aids and similar measures to encourage the private sector to do its share. On the other hand the Industrial Products Act, compelling purchase of local manufactures, is harmful to sound development and should be repealed.

Ceylonese conditions define certain criteria for selecting new industries. Dependence upon local raw materials offers distinct advantages, but need not always be the rule. Available wastes and by-products should be utilized if feasible; in this and other ways industries should become mutually helpful and inter-related for greatest economic benefit. Where possible, industries requiring abnormal amounts of fuel, power or fresh water should be avoided; local fuel supplies are limited to firewood, potential hydroelectric power is not excessive, and water supplies are irregular. Trained labor can be developed, but it is scarce now; hence new industries in the next few years should be those whose skills are not too difficult to master. As always, there will be exceptions in the use of such broad criteria.

From its brief field studies the Mission has been able to suggest a substantial number of potential new industries. Among them is the production of acetic acid (once before started), machine-made bottles, bottle caps, prepared animal feeds, fiber bags (other than coir), new types of furniture, meat by-products, rope-soled shoes, tannins, tooled leather goods, tobacco by-products, new vegetable oils, and various light manufactures in metal or wood including turned woodenware. We must emphasize that these are only the most obvious ones, and that modern methods of applied technical research [4] hold the key to many more of even greater significance.

The same is true of those existing industries which can be expanded or improved. Among these we note especially canning, clay products, coir goods, cooking fats, tanned leather, rubber goods, salt, soft drinks and textiles. Mining improvements are indicated for graphite, and new market studies should be made of thorianite, monazite and flaked or ground mica. Other mineral developments may result from intensification of the geological survey, for which we recommend an annual budget of at least Rs. 500,000 over its present funds. Expansion of the fishing industry would be desirable, but can proceed but slowly until there are more trained seamen and fishermen. Meanwhile ocean research and various marketing aids will be valuable.

Continued attention to cottage industries is recommended, al-

---

[4] See Chapters 4 and 19.

ways keeping in mind their primary purpose of utilizing the part-time labor of underemployed agriculturalists. Cottage industries cease to be cottage industries when their handwork methods are brought to centralized plants offering full-time employment; they then become nothing more than inefficient factories incurring industrial overhead, and in this form are uneconomical. Hence the government is urged to resist such conversion if it hopes for success in this field.

TRANSPORT AND COMMUNICATIONS

Ceylon has a fair basic system of internal transport and good sea and air connections with other countries. Colombo is a main port of call for the shipping lines to the Far East and Australia. There is also a very fine harbor at Trincomalee, at present undeveloped commercially, and three or four other small ports handling mainly local trade. The island has regular international air services to Europe, India, Singapore and Australia, as well as domestic flights. Internally a government railway connects all the larger towns and centers of population and there is a good system of roads, bringing nearly all townships of any size within 24 hours of the capital. A telephone and telegraph network of moderate efficiency has been built up.

Thus there is no question of major and dramatic transport developments. Nevertheless, a great many improvements are needed, some of them more of the character of long-deferred maintenance, and much remains to be done in extending the local rail and road network into more of the Dry Zone lands which are being opened up. Almost every current development project brings new transport problems. Every agricultural settlement scheme needs at least new minor roads, and every new factory puts heavier—sometimes even specialized—demands on roads, railways and ports. As more things are produced they must be moved to market.

Better transport is thus an underlying need of agriculture, industry, and indeed of all development. Hence the total amount which has to be spent on communications of all kinds is large. In the development program recommended by the Mission[5] for the next six years it amounts to Rs. 430,000,000, or over 25% of the total capital expenditure proposed. A summary of the major needs in the several categories will indicate the general directions of this investment.

Seaports

Almost all external trade flows through the port of Colombo, and today the facilities are inadequate to handle the volume of traffic efficiently. A major defect is the absence of deep water quays, other than oil tanker piers. All ordinary ocean-going ships have to load and unload by lighter. The port suffers chronically from congestion, and the consequent delays have led the shipping lines to impose a freight surcharge.

A program of improvement, including the building of about 7,000 feet of deep water quays, is already in progress and scheduled for completion in 1953. The Mission urges that this and its various auxiliary works be pushed on as rapidly as possible, and also that road and rail access to the port be improved. Further extension schemes have been projected and we feel that their study should be continued; but construction should be deferred until fully justified by prospective traffic.

Trincomalee, on the northeast coast, is a first class natural harbor. Its large area of deep water is almost entirely landlocked yet open to shipping at all seasons. Today its surrounding country is undeveloped, but, as settlement of the area proceeds, Trincomalee will be the obvious channel for much of the resultant trade. Accordingly it is not too soon to plan the installation of commercial shipping facilities there. As a British naval base, the harbor is now controlled by the United Kingdom Admiralty under agreement with Ceylon, and it is understood that the Admiralty would be cooperative. Engineering studies should be completed at a site which has been designated at Cod Bay, in

---

[5] See Chapters 6 and 16.

the inner harbor. Actual construction should be timed to correspond with developments in the hinterland region, but we have suggested financial provision within the 1953–59 program.

There are also proposals for development of some of the lesser ports. At Galle (once Ceylon's main port) we feel that major development at this time would be premature; but limited improvements are recommended now as part of a master plan for the future. Facilities should be provided here for importation of the rice requirements of the extreme southwestern part of the island, relieving Colombo of this cargo. In the north, additional port facilities may be needed eventually on the Jaffna peninsula, and we suggest an engineering survey at Kankesanturai; but we do not contemplate any port construction work there during the six-year period, as development of Trincomalee should come first.

On the organizational side the Mission believes it would be desirable to create an independent Ceylon Ports Authority, replacing the Colombo Port Commission and having charge of all Ceylon's ports.

A local proposal has been made to establish a Ceylonese international shipping line. But Ceylon today has hardly any personnel with experience in either the operation or management of ships; there are not even any domestic coastal services between Colombo and the outports. Nor has the Mission seen any evidence that operation of a nominally national service, through any form of agreement with foreign shipping interests, would be profitable to the government or beneficial to the country's economy. We therefore recommend no allocation of funds for such a development. Some effort might be made at first to develop coastal services between Ceylon's own ports and possibly the neighboring ports in India, and this would be a suitable project for the proposed Development Corporation.

Railways

Built and operated by the government, the island's railway system serves most of the major areas and today includes 809 route-miles of broad gauge (5 ft. 6 in.) together with one section of 86 route-miles of narrow gauge (2 ft. 6 in.) track.

At one time the railways earned large working surpluses. Since 1930, however, the growing competition of road transport and other factors have caused losses which the government has made up from general revenue. A contributing cause has been the badly neglected maintenance of both track and rolling stock, beginning with the depression of the thirties and aggravated by supply difficulties in some later years. Some lines have been abandoned since 1937.

The system remains essential to the country's economy. Until now the government has attempted to assist it through financial support and some legislative protection from road competition in the longer hauls. But the deficit on current operation is a heavy charge on general revenue, and of course reduces the surplus available for development expenditure. While recognizing that subsidization of an indispensable railway may be unavoidable if its users clearly cannot pay rates high enough to cover costs, the Mission is not satisfied that this is true in Ceylon. Fares and freight rates have risen much less than other prices since 1939; we recommend increases at least to balance operating expenses.

For railway capital works as a whole we propose a six-year allocation of Rs. 150,000,000. First call on these funds should be for the current rehabilitation of facilities where upkeep is in arrears. For the balance, certain key construction projects are recommended. A section from Bangadeniya to Puttalam, where the track was taken up during the war for other uses, should be relaid; and the Panadura-Alutjama section should be double-tracked. A new extension should be built from Eravur to Amparai, to serve the Gal Oya Development; another new line between Vavuniya and Trincomalee should tap the land to be opened up in the north. The Kelani Valley narrow-gauge line should be converted into a special motor road, on which the railway could operate a faster and cheaper bus and truck service; much of the old track and rolling stock could be used in various contemplated industrial projects, as in the transport of cane to the sugar factory.

Electrification of at least the Colombo suburban rail services has been much discussed. If cheap hydroelectric power were plentiful it is probable that this would be sound, although the traffic density is still on the low side for economic electric operation. But as has been shown above, there is little prospect that hydroelectric power will be available for such major new uses before 1960, if then. This project should therefore be deferred. It might be reconsidered towards the end of the six-year period 1953–59, if warranted by the growth of traffic and the power outlook by that time.

Some suggestions are made in Chapter 16 on matters of railway administration, but the Mission believes that the Railway Department would find it profitable to engage a firm of management consultants to review all phases of management and operation.

Roads

Although nominally Ceylon has 30,000 miles of roads, about 60% are mere trails and bridle paths. The major and minor roads maintained by the Public Works Department total 11,000 miles, and village committees control another 8,000 miles. Nevertheless, the network of motorable roads covers the present populated areas fairly well.

Only a few sections, mainly in and near Colombo, approach modern trunk highway standards; the majority are narrow and surfaced only for a single lane of traffic. Many stretches, especially in the Dry Zone are subject to flooding in the rainy season. There is real need for widening, surfacing, and straightening many roads, building or rebuilding certain bridges, and other general improvements. Several new main links[6] are needed to

---

[6] See Map 20.

remedy gaps in the primary network, and various additional minor roads will be required either now or later. Because the timing of these developments depends upon the progress of other schemes, the Mission has not attempted a detailed schedule of road construction, but has proposed an annual allocation of Rs. 17,500,000 for all such extensions and improvements. This would be in addition to maintenance costs of about Rs. 20,000,000 per year.

Measured by expenditure, such a rate of construction is higher than the Public Works Department has been able to achieve to date. To accomplish it the Department's supply of modern construction equipment should be increased substantially. At the same time greater attention to the training of staff of all kinds is required. More use could be made of private engineering firms and contractors, both local and foreign; contracts with the latter might include provisions for extensive training of local men.

We do not suggest any changes in the basic regulations of the 1951 Motor Traffic Act. Continued operation of road passenger services by controlled private concerns is seen as the most satisfactory procedure. These companies provide a very extensive network of services, although many of the buses leave much to be desired in standards of comfort and reliability. We believe that a limited fare increase would encourage some improvement in bus services.

Airways

Ceylon has one international airport at Ratmalana near Colombo and various airfields and landing strips for internal services.[7] Ratmalana is used regularly by BOAC, Air India, Quantas Empire Airways and Air Ceylon which together provide reasonably frequent services to Europe, India, Australia and Singapore.

A national air line, Air Ceylon, has been promoted by the

---

[7] See Map 19.

government to supplement the international lines and to provide internal service. Commencing in December 1947 with a Colombo-Kankesanturai-Madras route, Air Ceylon now runs daily to Madras and Trichinopoly, weekly to London via Bombay, Cairo and Rome, and fortnightly to Sydney via Singapore and Djakarta. It was first organized as a wholly governmental undertaking, but the services to London and Sydney are now operated on behalf of the government by Australian National Airways under a ten-year agreement. Internal services, apart from the Colombo-Kankesanturai run, at present operate somewhat irregularly to Minneriya, Trincomalee, Asparai (for Gal Oya) and Galle. In the aggregate these various services show a financial loss, although the division between different categories is not known.

For the moment we do not look to any large developments in the civil aviation field. Some expenditure will be necessary on the smaller local airfields, and to improve Ratmalana to full international standards. We believe that Ceylon would do well to encourage other foreign airlines to include a stop at Ratmalana; in this way she would capitalize on her geographic position on a natural route from the Eastern Mediterranean to Australia and the Far East, building air traffic and tourist trade. Effective Ceylonese participation in international air transport will be best secured by concentrating first on interregional services to India and Pakistan with possible extensions to Burma and Thailand, and on the development of internal lines; when these establish a popular reputation, longer extension will be easier.

Telecommunications

No new developments are proposed for international telephone and telegraph services. However, the internal services of both need extensive improvement. Today neither offers the coverage, speed or reliability which modern standards require. A six-year program of extension and improvement to cost about Rs. 90,-000,000 has been prepared locally, and is supported in principle by the Mission. Such rapid expansion will be difficult, however,

51

as progress will be slowed by delays in procuring equipment and by shortage of staff. We recommend spreading the program over 10 to 12 years instead, with an investment of only Rs. 35,000,000 during 1953–59. In any event additional technical assistance from outside will be needed.

3. Development of Human Resources

The Labor Supply

Ceylon's rate of development will be determined very largely by the efficiency with which the human resources of the country can be applied to the natural resources within it. Therefore it is essential to look at the quantity and adaptability of those human resources.

Concerning the quantity of labor available for development work, there is at present no significant unemployment; that is, there is no substantial body of workers normally dependent on wages who are without work for any extended period. As in most countries in Ceylon's stage of development, however, there is a high degree of.underemployment, especially in the rural areas. The village population is certainly much larger than is necessary for the efficient use of presently cultivated lands, and it is steadily increasing. This is, of course, a facet of the pressure of population; it is reflected again in the "postage stamp" cultivation plots. Here is a growing reservoir of labor which could be more effectively utilized through the improvement of cultural practices on existing lands, the opening of new lands for settlement and cultivation, and the creation of additional employment outside the agricultural sector.

In mere numbers, then, Ceylon's labor supply is large enough for a substantial expansion of production. The real problems in the field of human capacities lie in the efficiency and mobility of the labor force, and in the enterprise, knowledge and organization required for the job.

Attitudes

The chief difficulties in the way of effective use of human capacities for economic development are to be found in the wide and complex field of interests, motives, aptitudes and cultural background.

Economic interests and motivations are of course important in Ceylon as elsewhere, but there expression has largely followed well-defined paths established by tradition and heredity. As in most underdeveloped areas, the economy has been too specialized to favor a diffusion of attitudes of curiosity in the scientific sense, or to give scope for a general habit of business enterprise and innovation.

Nor have influences other than the actual state of economic development acted as correctives. Religious forces are powerful and have undoubtedly exerted a conservative pressure. The influence of the caste system, which Ceylon long ago discarded as a formal social structure, has lingered in a continuing disinclination to enter many non-agricultural occupations and a tendency to avoid job-changing. Political subordination to foreign powers for over three centuries inevitably led to a habit of expecting major decisions to be taken thousands of miles away, and to a corresponding lack of responsibility and initiative except in the strongest minded.

Opportunities to break away from these limitations—to foster attitudes of technical curiosity and business enterprise through experience gained in new fields of production—have been limited by the small domestic market, scarcity of the basic raw materials, shortages of finance and the handicap of inadequately developed "social capital" installations.

Past development of the export sector of agriculture and its related commercial activity offers a significant exception in this general background. But this development has been directed and financed mainly by non-Ceylonese enterprise with an essentially external orientation, and such commercial or technical experience and outlook as has seeped into the streams of the Ceylonese culture has been limited.

Adherence to the traditional viewpoints and lines of activity is characteristic of the economic life of Ceylon. As an obstacle to the adoption of new techniques and methods in peasant agriculture it has already been noted. It means also that village improvements such as minor irrigation works, improved water supplies, community building programs, road works and many other possible community ventures have depended on outside stimulus.

A similar dominance by tradition is reflected outside the field of agriculture in a conspicuous shortage of ordinary business initiative. There is a widespread reluctance to depart from established routines, not only in the development of new productive ventures but even in existing enterprises. The few individuals who might be willing to pioneer new lines of production are often thwarted by lack of adequate technical guidance and by a reluctance of private and institutional capital to join in a departure from beaten paths.

Technical Knowledge and Skill

Finally, the acute shortage of trained personnel, which has been brought out in many sections of Chapter 2, is one of the main obstacles to rapid progress. This deficiency extends all the way from manual skills through supervisory abilities, to managerial and engineering talents. Agriculture has too few high level men for research and also too few extension officers in the field. The Public Works Department has neither the architects to design the buildings, the draftsmen to draw up detailed plans, nor the masons and carpenters to do the building for all the structures they are requested to erect.

The failure to fill these gaps is due to the lack of variety in productive activity with the consequent limitations on practical training and absence of incentive to learn more complex techniques.

In the family the children are excessively sheltered, especially among the more prosperous classes. Parental discipline is generally unquestioned and submission to the decisions of parents in all matters is taken for granted. Initiative, self-confidence, experimentation, inquiring habits of mind are thereby discouraged from early childhood. Traditions of caste which disparage occupations such as carpentry, pottery-making and fishing breed a distaste for manual skills. Children are seldom encouraged to develop hobbies such as woodworking, model building and the like which foster a respect for fine workmanship and a facility with tools.

This same neglect of the technical aptitudes and enterprising side of childhood development continues into the educational system. According to the testimony of leading Ceylonese, the schools stress the encyclopaedic and purely academic aspect of education, rather than skills and independent solution of new problems. This is true even of the postprimary grades, where one might expect a considerable leavening of the typical academic subjects with vocational studies that would assist the pupil in preparing for life as he is actually going to live it.

How these influences can affect national growth is suggested by the contrast between occupational preferences among adolescent school children and actual opportunities of employment. A recent survey[1] exhibits a glaring disparity between ambitions and opportunities among secondary school pupils in Ceylon. Only a quarter show an interest in such productive activities as farming, handicraft work, and skilled labor, whereas nearly two thirds of the gainfully employed are engaged in these fields. On the other hand, over half the pupils questioned aspire to service occupations, while only 15 percent of the population find employment therein.

Although school children of this age group in any country

---

[1] In an unpublished study by Professor T. L. Green of the University of Ceylon. This study canvassed the preferences of 1,365 pupils of senior secondary schools in all nine provinces of Ceylon in 1950.

may be expected to express unwarranted optimism in their preferences and to set a goal somewhat above their capacities, such a great disparity between aims and prospects is certainly extreme and probably significant. Among other things, it would seem to reflect a strong desire for the security and status of government employment, which predominates among service occupations in Ceylon. Equally, perhaps, it reflects a dislike of work involving direct contact with the soil or the exercise of manual skills. For too many young Ceylonese, the ideal job consists in sitting at a desk and telling others what to do.

AVENUES OF PROGRESS

All the various phenomena we have surveyed—traditionalism, the underemployment of rural labor, the lack of scientific curiosity or of enterprise, and the dislike of occupations demanding manual skill—constitute a set of social obstacles which stand in the way of Ceylon's progress. Most of them add up to a social attitude which, if it persists, will inevitably reduce the benefits of improved physical resources. Fortunately, there are many ways in which this attitude can be modified. Some of them will be considered in the following pages.

Rural Development Societies

We have indicated the extensive underemployment of labor in Ceylon's rural areas. To harness the interest and enthusiasm of the villager, and to make productive use of his labor in periods of comparative inactivity, is a real challenge. If successfully met, much could be done to improve village conditions in scores of ways.

The Department of Rural Development has made a good beginning. Its staff works closely with over 5,000 Rural Development Societies scattered throughout the island. Together, they have succeeded in channeling the energies of local people into many types of useful work, including construction of roads, wells, school and other buildings and the provision of various services such as voluntary police patrols and conciliation boards. Such joint endeavors also help to break the habit of excessive reliance on the central authorities, and to generate a spirit of self-reliance and communal initiative.

Work of this type is accomplished at minimum cost, since materials and labor are provided locally and are generally free or available for a nominal sum. Certain projects, however, require skilled labor or materials from outside, and these call for financial assistance. During the past two years the government has made a beginning in the provision of such assistance.

The promise of accomplishing much with relatively little gives a strong appeal to the rural development movement. While clearly needing to synchronize its activities with those of other government departments, the Department of Rural Development is doing excellent work which should continue to receive support. Financial help should increase in step with the demonstrated capacity of the movement to get things done.

Cooperative Societies

Ceylon is fortunate in possessing a well-developed and vigorous cooperative movement. It furnishes leadership and guidance in the solution of many agrarian problems, such as effective utilization of existing resources and the introduction of improved methods of cultivation. Cooperatives provide a large share of agricultural credit on reasonable terms. They also perform an important educative role, both in the training of local leaders and in quickening the awareness of the peasant to the opportunities that are open to him. Perhaps best of all, they promote local organization for a joint attack on the problems of the community.

Cooperatives are of many types; the main divisions comprise retail stores societies, credit societies, and marketing and production societies. These provide small cultivators, fishermen and other small-scale producers with a welcome alternative to the exactions of the ubiquitous village trader and moneylender. Yet in spite of rapid growth within the past decade the island is still not adequately covered, especially by credit cooperatives and by marketing and production societies. Perhaps a doubling of the numbers of these agencies will be necessary to make their facilities available to all who need them.

Although the individual loans made by the societies are small and might advantageously be increased, it does not appear that lack of financial resources seriously hampers the further growth of the movement. For in addition to the funds that come from stock subscriptions and deposits of members, these societies are able to borrow from nine Provincial Cooperative Banks and a central Cooperative Federal Bank. The supplementary funds made available through these institutions should provide adequate financing in future years.

In truth, the factor which significantly limits the expansion of cooperatives is the shortage of local people who are sufficiently literate, honest and forceful to furnish competent and responsible officers for the local societies. Solution of this difficulty can come only gradually with educational and cultural advancement. Meanwhile progress can be somewhat expedited by wider use of trained and paid executive secretaries. For the Agricultural Production and Sales Societies these men are now furnished by the Department of Land Development. A further extension of the training facilities of the School of Cooperation would also be helpful.

Lack of acceptable security makes it impossible for the average peasant to obtain long-term loans for improvement, expansion, or consolidation of debt. Probably a complete solution to the lack of long-term credit must await clarification of titles to land, perhaps through a system of registration of titles. Pending this, the Mission recommends that Credit Cooperatives be authorized to make long-term loans on the personal credit of carefully selected borrowers, at first on an experimental basis in localities where strong credit societies exist.

Education

Although cooperatives and rural development societies can contribute greatly to changing conservative habits of thought and to generating alertness and initiative, we must look principally to the schools for progress in altering social attitudes that obstruct Ceylon's economic development. Children are more malleable than adults, and while the school is not the only force shaping their outlook, it is one of the most important. In the past it has been an influence on the side of conservatism, especially in reinforcing the prejudice against the acquisition of manual skills. Today it is on the threshold of important change. A glance at its inheritance will serve to bring out the significance of impending reforms.

Ceylon offers all its children an education up to the age of 14, with accommodation for a fair proportion at the secondary school level and a growing number at the University. Tuition is free throughout.

Educational development has been haphazard, not systematically planned. Shaped during its formative years according to a 19th century model, the school system from the beginning corresponded but poorly to the needs of a preponderantly agricultural population. For most pupils destined to work on the land or in occupations closely related to it, the curriculum has been excessively academic. Practical training has been almost nonexistent: even in village schools the emphasis has been on "book learning." In nearly all schools memory is stressed rather than reasoning ability. Two thirds of the teachers have little or no specific preparation for their work, but go directly from secondary schools to the front of a classroom of pupils.

Reforms now in progress promise to go a long way toward remedying some of these shortcomings. Training in the arts and crafts is to be introduced throughout the primary and secondary grades. For those who drop out at the eighth standard, special vocational work will be available. At a somewhat more advanced level, the present Ceylon Technical College will be reinforced by the establishment of four additional technical schools in different parts of the island. The supply of trained teachers is being increased by the admission of greater numbers to the training colleges.

Improvement still has a long way to go. Classroom equipment is deficient. The available arts and crafts teachers are only a fraction of the total needed, and at scheduled rates of training it may be decades before there are enough. Even with the stepped-up training of primary and secondary school teachers, most of the additional supply will be absorbed in replacing ordinary losses by retirement, etc., and in keeping up with the growing number of school children.

Every effort therefore needs to be made to speed up the training of additional staff. Facilities should be provided for the training of 2,300 teachers per year. This will mean probably a 25% addition to buildings and equipment and 50% more staff. Training selected Ceylonese teachers abroad and appointment of additional foreign educators to training college staffs would help. However, except for the much greater stress on practical work, these remedies are mainly quantitative. The most needed reform is essentially qualitative—a shift from emphasis on memory and the accumulation of facts to stress on reason and the marshalling of information for purposeful use. Along with this reform will come a change in the role of the teacher, from that of unquestioned authority to that of leader in the shared experience of learning. Realization of these goals must be a slow process which will require constant emphasis, first on the training of teachers, then on their daily activities in the classroom. For specifically vocational training a valuable institute already exists in the Basic Technical Training Institute at Ratmalana. Additional similar institutes, with adequate equipment of tools and plant, should be established.

University education will be of increasing importance, for it not only trains the higher technical staff but must deeply influence the intellectual background of the whole educational system and the community at large. Ceylon has had a university of its own only for ten years and it is still in its first growth, with the major emphasis on medical training and arts courses. Students number something over 2,000—about one in every 3,500 of total population. The ratio is not only lower than in Western countries (in the United Kingdom it is about one to 600, in the United States better than one to 100) but also a good deal lower than in India where it is about one to 1,400. Continued expansion of university facilities is therefore necessary, with emphasis on such studies as engineering and agriculture.

Technology

The inability of Ceylon's own technology to meet the needs of a broad development program has already been shown. Accordingly, for its many recent projects in agriculture, industry, irrigation, health and other fields, the government has relied heavily upon imported specialists. Some have been engaged directly; others have been obtained through the Colombo Plan and the various United Nations agencies. On the whole they have been helpful. It must be said, however, that there is a good deal of confusion in this field. Government officials have been too ready to ask for "experts" without a clear-cut definition of the real needs; and the international agencies have perhaps been insufficiently exacting in asking for more precise definitions before trying to meet the demand.

This has resulted in duplication and overlapping, waste or poor use of specialists once obtained, sometimes procurement of the wrong type of specialist or even, occasionally, of an incompetent or completely unnecessary one. We are convinced that there is great need for coordination here, by a qualified and locally-based body which can give Ceylon "technical help in selecting technical help." Means for supplying this are discussed in Chapter 4.

We believe that in many cases foreign technical experts could be of greater value to the country if they could remain to offer guidance over a period of years. Too often they are brought for a short visit only, to prepare a report and depart. This may suffice when all that is wanted is the expert's general impressions, but it rarely leaves behind any permanent addition to the nation's technology. In particular, it trains no Ceylonese; for a man cannot convey to another in a few months what it took him many years to learn.

Like even the most advanced countries, Ceylon must expect always to draw useful new techniques from all over the world. But she should not look forward forever to sole reliance upon external sources of competent technicians. The Mission urges that Ceylon increase and improve her own technical training facilities, from the University at one extreme to the vocational and lower schools at the other. To provide a larger training nucleus, more Ceylonese should be sent abroad for advanced technical education and practical experience.

As for the research upon which all progress depends, Ceylon has almost none. Special institutes exist for studies in tea, rubber and coconuts, but they are too limited in scope or staff to contribute much toward new lines of development. Research in other agricultural fields, and in the special institutes, too, requires more funds and experienced personnel. We recommend this, as well as larger support of the Geological Survey mentioned earlier.

Applied industrial research is present in name only—that is, in the name of one of the ministries. So-called industrial research laboratories are maintained by the government, but operate mainly as routine analytical laboratories. The conditions under which they function are definitely unsuited to the conduct of research, and they are inherent conditions which cannot easily be changed. We believe that these facilities should be designated as the government's bureau of standards and customs control laboratories, and reorganized for those important purposes. Genuine applied research should be organized on a more independent basis, as described in Chapters 4 and 19.

Social and Economic Surveys

Naturally associated with the scarcity of technical training and scientific curiosity is the lack of knowledge of the resources and background of the country itself which has led us to recommend a number of surveys of physical resources.

Much work also needs to be done in the fields of social and economic surveys. Here is an area of study which in Ceylon is almost untapped, but whose exploration could yield information of high value to the country's development. Village surveys could provide information of direct value to rural development and to the conduct of cooperatives, as well as to any attack on the problem of land tenure. Studies of psychological attitudes and of social habits could suggest what government measures would be welcomed and what opposed, in what areas public education is needed, and how the needs of economic efficiency can best be reconciled with the noneconomic values which are important to the community. Some work of this kind has already been started with assistance from UNESCO and it should be extended. Conspicuously lacking are data as to the annual value of industrial and agricultural production outside the major export crops. Little is known of the value of existing capital installations, while the volume of current savings and investment can only be guessed. Data such as these are vital to the intelligent formulation of national plans.

Public Health

Like many of the social traits discussed earlier, health is another aspect of the social environment having a distinct bearing upon efficiency. Good or poor health will always affect the quality of human resources, and will influence what they can accomplish.

Before examining what needs to be done to improve Ceylon's health conditions, we may look at some substantial facts on the credit side. Ceylon has virtually no cholera, plague or smallpox. A major victory has been won since the war in the fight against malaria. The population is in the main moderately well fed. A fundamentally sound medical and health administration has been built up; and real progress has been made in an ambitious effort to make medical service available, free or at a nominal cost, to every inhabitant of Ceylon. The benefits of the work of the last decade are to be seen in the dramatic fall in the death rate, from a prewar average of over 20 to 12.6 per 1,000 in 1950. Infant and maternal mortality rates have fallen similarly.

Yet much remains on the debit side. The rate of sickness has not fallen with the death rate; on the contrary, if we judge by recorded attendances at hospitals, it is rising. As malaria has been reduced, its place as public health enemy No. 1 has been taken by tuberculosis, cases of which are believed to have doubled since 1941. The debilitating hookworm is believed to affect nearly nine people out of ten. Mortality among children from one to five years old seems not to have shared fully in the general decline in death rates. The hospitals, and especially their outpatient departments, are badly overcrowded. Trained medical personnel of all kinds—doctors, dentists, apothecaries, nurses—are insufficient in numbers even to run existing services. Many obvious cases of malnutrition are to be seen. Water supplies and drainage are woefully inadequate, the general sanitary standard is low, and there is much overcrowding and bad housing.

Finally there hangs over the island the threat of serious over-population. Since 1871 population has trebled, partly by natural increase, partly by immigration; this represents an average cumulative increase of 1.25% per annum. In the last few years the rate of natural increase has been greatly inflated by the decline in the death rate, unaccompanied by any decline in the birth rate, and in 1950 reached nearly 3% per annum.

Up to now the development of new agricultural land has kept pace with the increase in population. It is very doubtful whether it can do so much longer. Mr. Dudley Senanayake, the present Prime Minister and former Minister of Agriculture, has emphasized publicly that the birth rate is "well ahead of the food production drive" and has pointed out the consequences to living standards if the rate of population growth is maintained. The expansion of the agricultural area which now appears possible, for instance, will fall short of providing for the population increase which may be expected at present rates within a single decade. In actual figures, this population growth may be of the order of 2-2.5 millions; the 600,000 acres we believe can be developed over a much longer period as irrigated land, together with complementary dry farming land, can hardly support more than 1.5 million.

The Mission's first important recommendation in the field of health is, therefore, an earnest plea that Ceylon follow the example of her neighbor, India, in a bold effort to convert her people to the principle and practice of family planning. The individual must be persuaded to act by propaganda and by making available advice and facilities. This is not a policy which requires large financial resources, but rather one calling for great courage and tact. It is a measure which can do more to raise the living standards and well-being of the Ceylonese of the future than any other action or influence within the power of the government.

When we examine the other debit items in Ceylon's health balance sheet, one common feature emerges; overwhelmingly, the problems are those of environmental conditions and sanitation. The main diseases are no longer ones such as cholera or smallpox or even malaria which can, in principle at any rate, be completely eradicated by simple specific precautions and preventive vaccinations and inoculations. The threats of today have more complex origins and need more comprehensive answers. Tuberculosis, notoriously, is the product of poor housing and nutrition; hookworm is the product of generally low sanitary conditions; the same is almost certainly true of those ailments which sustain the high death rates among the children. Only by getting at the indirect causes can these diseases be attacked successfully. Such things as housing, water supply, sewage disposal and so on, are the very basis of a healthy environment.

Accordingly, the Mission's second recommendation is that the weight of effort in the government's health activity should be shifted away from curative work toward prevention of disease and improvement of the surroundings. We can mention here only a few of the specific changes which this involves.[2] First is the extension throughout the Medical and Sanitary Department of the amalgamation of curative and preventive organization, introduced several years ago in the headquarters staff. This means bringing each of the provincial and regional units under the control of a single officer responsible for government health work. To improve the standard and morale of medical officers of health, we propose reform of the methods of selection and allocation; and we suggest that they devote more of their time to field work. We have examined the interesting development of the comprehensive Local Health Unit; we consider it valuable and support its continuance substantially as now organized, but have made suggestions for specific changes to increase the effect of its preventive work. A special survey of the causes of the high child mortality should be made.

Our next recommendation in the preventive field is to continue improvements in housing, water supply and drainage. There are limitations of funds and technical capacity, but we have included what we believe to be reasonable provision for those items in the suggested program of expenditure. Study and planning of further schemes in these fields should be undertaken as part of the over-all planning of water utilization. To coordinate the housing activities of various agencies a Housing Commissioner should be appointed under the Ministry of Local Government.

Close attention to malaria is still required. We hope also to see a strengthened campaign against tuberculosis and greater attention to nutrition, including especially a joint effort with the Agricultural Department to increase the present very low consumption of milk and other animal proteins.

On the curative side, the shortage of hospital buildings and staff results in overcrowding up to as much as 100 percent. We have attempted to suggest realistic targets for increases in hospital beds and in personnel, bearing in mind the inevitably slow processes of training and the certainty of having to care for a larger

[2] For other suggestions see Chapter 17.

population. The major requirements are a second medical school to double the output of doctors, enlargement of other training facilities, and a program of hospital construction designed to add 50% to the bed capacity within 10 years. We estimate that those improvements will cost Rs. 80,000,000 in the six-year period 1953-59. Suggestions are also made for changes in administrative practice, designed to lessen the pressure on hospital beds and staff caused by the increasing demand for accommodation.

A word must last be said about the indigenous or Ayurvedic medicine, a venerable system of medical practice founded on ancient Indian tradition. This has had a revival in popularity and some recognition from government in late years, connected no doubt with the strengthening of national sentiment. Modern medical opinion recognizes that there may be value in some of the traditional practices. By the same token, it can hardly be right for the Ayurvedic practitioners to deny themselves the opportunity of adding to their traditional knowledge the proven fruits of modern research. Three measures which seem to be required are: a raising of the standards of training in the School of Indigenous Medicine by incorporation of some "Western" medicine; further study of Ayurvedic drugs and practices with a view to absorbing what is proved to be good in them into modern medical practice; and inclusion of the government's activities in the field of indigenous medicine under the control of the Director of Medical and Sanitary Services, like any other medical matters.

There is no easy road to health. Any general program of national capital expenditure should include provision for increased medical facilities, for increased training facilities and for further government assistance to other basic health needs. But the Mission is convinced that the most fundamental improvements can come only from changes in individual conduct—whether in the sphere of family planning, in hygienic habits, or in the thousand and one administrative actions of every member of the medical and public health service.

4. Organization and Stimulus

COORDINATED GOVERNMENT ACTION

The nature of the developments required in Ceylon throws upon the government increasing responsibility for a very wide range of activities, encompassing land clearance, agricultural re-settlement, irrigation, railway and highway improvement, the expansion of industry and electric power, port development and advances in health and education. All these are closely inter-related and must be kept properly in step with one another.

This calls for careful advance planning. Also, in view of the limitations of finance, manpower, and technical skills, it calls for the establishment of priorities so that total effort neither exceeds nor falls short of available resources. In such circumstances, to insure a balanced program, other countries engaged in similar development have found it necessary to establish a specific planning organization.

No such coordinating mechanism exists in Ceylon. The various aspects of development are undertaken by individual ministries, each with a justifiable pride in its work and anxious to make a good showing. There may be some general interchange in the Cabinet, but many projects meet each other for the first time on the floor of Parliament, in the course of that body's regular and voluminous business. Inevitably, decisions rest upon such extraneous factors as the skill and vigor with which a particular minister presents his case, the relative strength of the various claimants for funds, and the like. The information upon which a specific project is based may be sketchy; there is no provision for critical professional review, such as might bring to light objectionable or doubtful features which the advocates of the project either do not stress or do not know. Projects may thus be approved which are doomed to failure—wasting the country's resources and preventing more beneficial projects from being undertaken. Specific cases have been noted already in Chapter 2.

Ultimately, the effectiveness of any planning and coordinating process will depend upon the integrity and ability of the men who make the final decisions, and upon the quality of the information furnished them as a basis for reaching these decisions. The form of the machinery itself cannot guarantee the results. But at least by centralizing the decision-making authority, by facilitating the free flow of information, and by providing for a critical review of plans, good organization can insure that decisions are responsible, informed, and checked by professional judgment. Ceylon needs this kind of organization. We suggest below how it could be created.

Alternative Methods

Coordinating mechanisms which have been used variously elsewhere include Cabinet Committees, autonomous General Development Organizations, and independent National Planning Boards. In Ceylon the Mission favors the Cabinet Committee system, for reasons which are clear from inspection of the main alternatives.

Under the method of the General Development Organization[1] both planning and execution of all major development projects are handed over to an autonomous corporation. In our view this would involve too great an invasion of the well-established responsibilities of existing government agencies—particularly as the most important development projects in the near future will need close integration with the regular administration of government. Also, such a broad development corporation would be a large one, and it would be almost impossible to staff it locally without taking away valuable personnel from existing agencies. Even

---

[1] Not to be confused with the more specific Ceylon Development Corporation recommended later in this chapter, primarily for industrial development with private capital participation.

if this could be done, there would be much wasteful duplication of organization.

The alternative establishment of an independent Planning Board implies complete separation of the task of planning from that of execution. This we believe to be undesirable in Ceylon's circumstances. Such a Board would either become a mere advisory body with very little real power, or would come to challenge the authority of the Cabinet itself.

Ceylon's development program involves many ministries, each of which will continue to have contributions to make in its own sphere. It is desirable that detailed planning of these individual projects be done in the separate departments, both for the sake of decentralization of work and because each department is presumably best acquainted with its field. Projects and suggestions must continue to come forward with the backing of the appropriate minister. And under the established governmental responsibilities the decision as to which proposals shall be adopted, which trimmed and which dropped must rest, as now, with the Cabinet.

Cabinet Economic Committee

As the coordinating device best suited to the government structure of Ceylon, therefore, we propose an Economic Committee of the Cabinet. This has worked well in the United Kingdom, with a similar form of government, and concentrates authority where it belongs—in the hands of those most directly concerned.

Such a committee is customarily composed of those few ministers whose fields cover the broadest aspects of economic development. It is recognized that the work of all agencies is in some way ultimately connected with progress, and that other ministers must be drawn in from time to time for special assistance. But the aim is to conserve the time of these, and to focus general responsibility upon a smaller group.

In view of the character of Ceylon's development we recommend that such a Committee consist of the Ministers of Agriculture, Industry, Transport and Works, Rural Development, and

Finance. It would be advantageous if the Prime Minister were also a member, and would serve as chairman; but it is equally possible that he would prefer not to be involved in the detailed work of this committee, in addition to his many other responsibilities. In such event the obvious chairman would be the Minister of Finance, because of his necessarily central role in all matters of economic development.

This committee would undertake to examine all proposals for development and significant capital expenditure, to consider the interrelationship and division of available funds between such proposals, to recommend to the Cabinet as a whole which projects should be carried out, and to keep informed on the execution of development programs once they are approved and started.

While those Ministers suggested above would be the only regular members of the committee, the Ministers of Health, Food and Cooperative Undertakings, or others would attend its meetings on occasions when proposals of their own were under consideration. The chairman might also invite them to attend discussions of some projects in other fields which could have an indirect influence upon their work. At other times these remaining members of the Cabinet would be free to devote their full attention to the progress of work within their respective ministries.

Economic Planning Secretariat

Creation of a coordinating Cabinet Committee by itself would be only a partial solution. To make its decisions such a committee needs a great deal more information than time permits the members to gather for themselves. It also needs continuous professional advisory services in a number of fields, to aid in critical review and evaluation of proposals as well as to conduct special studies, make suggestions, answer questions, and in all other ways assist the work of the committee.

For these purposes the Mission recommends the appointment of an officer of status equal to that of Permanent Secretary to a Ministry, to serve as Secretary to the Economic Committee and chief economic planning officer. He should be assisted by a small staff which should include specialists in both economic and technical subjects and might initially be partly recruited from outside Ceylon.

This planning secretariat should receive all proposals with respect to economic development together with their supporting data. It should be authorized to consult freely with all persons or institutions able and willing to give pertinent information, and to employ special experts for temporary help when needed. It should not duplicate existing services, but should call upon such agencies as the Central Bank and the Department of Census and Statistics for all possible aid and information.

The planning secretariat should arrange to receive regularly sufficient information on the execution of current projects to insure continuous familiarity with their progress. It should in particular attempt to reconcile any issues or misunderstandings arising between different departments in the execution of projects; and where this is not feasible, should refer the differences to the Economic Committee of the Cabinet for settlement. Coordinated execution of development plans will, we believe, be facilitated by the creation of certain special executive bodies such as the proposed Ceylon Ports Authority and Electricity Authority and those bodies as well as the various Ministries should keep in close contact with the planning secretariat.

The work of economic planning, although by no means a purely financial matter, must always be closely involved with budgetary finance. It will therefore be essential that the planning secretariat consult regularly with the budget section of the Ministry of Finance.

Technical Consultation

For the further assistance of the planning secretariat and the Economic Committee of the Cabinet, a Development Advisory Board should be set up under the chairmanship of the Secretary to the Economic Committee. This should not be a large body but should include persons with outstanding practical knowledge of agriculture, industry, labor problems and economics. The members would, of course, be part-time but might well be partly drawn from among the senior officers of such agencies and institutions as the Department of Agriculture, the Central Bank, the University of Ceylon and the two new institutions proposed later in this chapter—the Ceylon Institute for Applied Research and the Ceylon Development Corporation. Besides giving valuable advice on general issues, such a Board would help to insure a wider understanding of the practical problems of economic development.

Statistics

Both the Department of Economic Research of the Central Bank and the Department of Census and Statistics are doing good work in attempting to compile reliable figures on Ceylonese conditions, and both have much more to do in this direction. In this they should be given the necessary financial support and the full cooperation of other departments involved. Neither the Cabinet Committee nor its secretariat will be able to do their best work without good statistics, especially in matters of national income and population trends. In return, the planning groups should remember their obligation to supply the statistical agencies with any useful data that come to hand.

Surveys

In a number of places in this report the Mission recommends that certain physical and social surveys be undertaken for specific purposes. We feel that in all these cases it will be essential that the central planning organization keep in close contact with the progress of such studies.

Where the nature of the work takes it very far outside the sphere of any one ministry, it is probable that the survey itself should be under the direct supervision of the central planning staff. We have definitely proposed this for the suggested Water Resources Planning Unit, and doubtless the government will find other cases where the procedure will be useful.

Technical Aid from Abroad

For a long time to come, while her own technical personnel is being built up, Ceylon will need much technical help from outside. There is already much activity in this field and the Mission's own recommendations contain many new proposals for such foreign aid. Yet, as we have seen, the present tendency toward duplication, lack of definition and waste of the experts obtained points to a clear need for some coordination here also; and it would seem very appropriate that the task should be undertaken by the central planning secretariat.

This secretariat would not have the final say in all requests of this kind, nor would it have any power of veto. We suggest merely the adoption of a rule that all requests for international technical aid should be passed through the Secretary to the Cabinet Economic Committee and that he should have the right to make suggestions to the originating department. This would first be a precaution against overlapping and duplication; secondly, it would give an opportunity for scrutiny of the form of the request, to insure that the task in view and the kind of expert knowledge required were adequately definied; and thirdly, in time it would enable the planning secretariat to advise in the light of experience on the best source to approach for any particular assistance.

If given this additional function, the secretariat would, of course, keep in close contact with the local representative of the UN Technical Assistance Board and the Director of the Technical Assistance Bureau of the Colombo Plan, this affording them a central point of liaison with the Government.

ENLISTMENT OF PRIVATE INITIATIVE

The Government and Private Activity

Important as is the improvement of the government planning machinery, the Mission believes that it is equally important to recognize that the task in view is not one which can be done by government alone. Every resource of private initiative and energy, both Ceylonese and foreign, is needed if the country is to mobilize its latent resources, to discover new lines of production and to increase its total output faster than its population. A real effort is needed to create an atmosphere conducive to genuine and fruitful partnership between government and private initiative in all its forms.

Specific measures to assist or stimulate private activity working through cooperatives and rural development societies have already been discussed; and we have suggested that more opportunities might be afforded to larger scale agriculture in the development of the Dry Zone. We believe that it would also be beneficial to offer incentives to private capital and enterprise to enter desirable lines of development, especially (but not exclusively) in the industrial field. The most suitable incentives would probably be found in modifications of taxation, e.g., reduction of duties on imports of machinery and raw materials not locally available, more generous income tax allowances for depreciation and obsolescence of machinery, and tax deductions for income spent on technical developments. Such tax concessions should be general, not reserved to new enterprises, as that might merely induce businessmen to develop new factories while neglecting old ones without adding to the total industrial effort.

Apart from such measures the Mission feels there is need to demonstrate that government policy is not, as some fear, permanently inimical to private initiative. This fear is greatest among non-Ceylonese firms. We believe it is still of great value to Ceylon to maintain their interest in the country, considering their potential contribution in management, know-how and finance. We could not escape the conclusion that in recent years they had felt the attitude of the government to be antagonistic toward them and that, although formal discrimination may be insignificant, there is an undefined but pervasive atmosphere which dampens new enterprise and prevents the investment of external capital in the economic development of the country.

76

The most specific and direct manifestation of this is in the policy of Ceylonization. Its object is to increase the proportion of Ceylonese employed in a given enterprise; in particular to foster an increase in the number of Ceylonese in the better managerial and technical positions of the island's business; and to reserve certain fields of business and commercial activity for Ceylonese. Though not embodied in major legislation, the policy is expressed partly in official regulations, but much more in administrative measures and constant public pressure from certain ministries.

It is understandable that the people of Ceylon should wish to see employment opportunities, and especially positions of importance, filled as much as possible by Ceylonese. There is no real substitute for actual practical experience in building a broader base of technical and business abilities among Ceylon's citizens, and some degree of compulsion or pressure to create openings where such experience can be obtained may be justified.

There are, however, two main dangers in such a policy. First, it means a net loss of manual, technical and managerial skill available for the service of the country's economy. Even if the Ceylonese who replaces a "foreigner" is equally well qualified for that particular post, Ceylon loses by that operation the services of one qualified man. In most cases the Ceylonese is, at the time of the changeover, less well qualified; the loss to the general pool of qualified personnel is all the larger and the loss of efficiency to the firm concerned may be vital. The whole atmosphere is, furthermore, calculated to discourage trained men from outside Ceylon from taking posts in the country because of the basic insecurity it creates.

All this would be less serious if we could treat the economy as entirely static, so that the problem was merely one of giving Ceylonese as large a share as possible of a fixed number of jobs. But Ceylon must strive for a dynamic economy in which the number of jobs, and especially of the better-paid skilled jobs, will increase. Exclusion of non-Ceylonese personnel will give Ceylonese a better chance of filling all the existing jobs but will make it harder to increase, or even to maintain, their total number.

The second danger is that Ceylonization will still further discourage investment from outside. Non-Ceylonese interests wishing to bring capital into the island will normally want also to bring their own technicians and managers. If they are artificially restricted in their freedom to do so, they will seek elsewhere for opportunities of investment. On the other hand, once an enterprise is firmly established and local men have gained experience in its operations it will be to the investor's own advantage to substitute equally competent Ceylonese for non-local staff who are certain to be more costly.

Both the Ceylonese community as a whole and the overseas businesses thus have interests on both sides of this issue. The Mission believes that, if a dynamic outlook is adopted by all concerned, it should be possible to work out mutually acceptable principles which will recognize both the importance of training Ceylonese on the one side and of continuing good management on the other.

We have thought it worth discussing this particular problem because it is typical of numerous aspects of the relationship of government to private business and because we are deeply convinced of the necessity for a great joint endeavor by the Ceylon government and private enterprise, both Ceylonese and non-Ceylonese. No visitor who makes a dispassionate survey of Ceylon can fail to be impressed by the best work of private enterprise, mainly non-Ceylonese, in developing the great industries on which the country now depends. Equally impressive is the more recent drive and initiative of the government in promoting other forms of economic development. We see no reason why these two forces should not work together, acting in friendly rivalry rather than in opposition. The detailed recommendations made later in this chapter are designed to provide an institutional framework for mutually helpful activity; but that framework will be ineffective unless both government and private enterprise put into their joint task all their resources of intelligence, knowledge, industry and, above all, mutual forebearance.

STIMULATION OF NEW PRODUCTION

Although Ceylon's industrial prospects are not extraordinary, there are very real possibilities for the introduction of industries and special related agricultural pursuits beneficial to the economy. Some of these are elaborated in Chapter 15. It is urgent that such opportunities be exploited, both for the immediate gain to the national income and with the broader objective of increasing and diversifying productive experience and local techniques for future growth. But to accomplish this, two major obstacles must be removed. The first is lack of knowledge about the real potentialities of local materials and about the necessary adaptation of modern techniques in local circumstances. The second is lack of enterprise, managerial capacity and finance.

Applied Research

To remedy the lack of knowledge, Ceylon needs an effective organization for applied technical research. Nothing of the sort exists now; we have seen that such laboratories as are operated by the government serve other valuable ends, but are not suited to the conduct of original investigation. For Ceylon's purposes what is required is a special type of institution, enjoying governmental cooperation but free of outright governmental control, which can do the following:

(1) Study local productive activities—industrial or otherwise—with a view to solving technical problems, improving production techniques, finding by-products, and instituting better methods of quality control.

(2) Study local raw materials, propose and develop processes for new industries, build and operate pilot plants, and at the same time design simple cottage industry equipment.

(3) Advise on the technical aspects of projects seeking financial support, on the need for and selection of foreign specialists,

and on similar matters at the request of various institutions or the Development Advisory Board.

(4) Collaborate in the preparation, publication and dissemination of technical information in practical form for local (especially small) producers.

(5) Train practical Ceylonese research workers for the future, and in all ways encourage applied research as a dignified and profitable career.

It is the opinion of the Mission that these requirements can be satisfied most effectively in Ceylon by a semi-independent research organization, created along the lines of a prototype of proven success in Mexico and described fully in Chapter 19. Ceylon's problem in this respect is remarkably parallel to that which confronted Mexico in 1944.

The Mexican research program was started, with skilled foreign assistance, under the sponsorship of the *Banco de Mexico*. Combining practical research and training, it served the needs of both government and private industry. At the end of five years it had not only solved many important technical problems, but had developed a permanent national institution able to continue the same course after withdrawal of the foreign specialists. Moreover, at that stage it was reckoned that the annual value of new exportable products alone, resulting from its work, was sixty times the total five-year cost of the program. Today the *Instituto Mexicano de Investigaciones Tecnológicas* has become a recognized center of technical development, and its own earnings for private service will soon make it self-supporting.

Ceylon Institute for Applied Research

We recommend immediate establishment of a Ceylon Institute for Applied Research in this same pattern, with minor modifications to fit Ceylonese conditions. We believe that it would be most suitably sponsored initially by the Central Bank, as in Mexico, and in specific fulfillment of one of the stated objectives of the Central Bank of Ceylon. It should not in any case be attempted under direct operation by a government department, for experience shows that such a program requires a flexibility and freedom which cannot be expected under direct government control.

It is not generally appreciated that applied research of this kind is a profession in itself, to be distinguished from the more academic fundamental scientific studies. We must emphasize that neither money alone nor the mere creation of scientific councils and organizations will solve any research problems, either now or in the future. The entire success of this program, with its intangible training aspects, will depend upon the most skillful selection of personnel. Next to this in importance is the freedom of the research men to pursue their investigations to a practical conclusion without interference; it has been wisely said that "the main job of a research director is to protect the research men from those who who want to direct them."

Properly experienced outside technical assistance for this work is available but the requirements are unusually critical and cannot be defined in terms of academic qualifications. For this reason we suggest joint action with the interested international agencies and have discussed it with the International Bank for Reconstruction and Development which we believe to be in closest touch with the field involved.

Costs of such a program are not high. Assuming outside technical help to be supplied as outlined in Chapter 19, the total annual investment and operating expense to Ceylon would be only about Rs. 750,000, exclusive of a Rs. 375,000 laboratory building. This outlay may be diminished gradually as various forms of independent income for the institution are developed. Were it necessary for Ceylon to bear the entire cost including hire of outside specialists, the total would approximate Rs. 1,000,000 per year.

Stagnation in Investment

While the foregoing offers a solution to the lack of technical knowledge, the other obstacle, shortage of enterprise and managerial capacity, is a more complex matter. It stems from a multitude of social and economic factors, and is not confined to any one productive field. Ultimately the remedy may be in the field of education, but that must be a slow process. Meanwhile a review of the circumstances suggests a means for some earlier relief, through a direct attack on the joint problems of enterprise, management and finance.

We have already observed how both Ceylonese and British business firms have concentrated on traditional lines, with comparatively little interest in new enterprises and with consequent stagnation on the manufacturing side.

In the financial field, the banks have been concerned primarily with financing the movement of goods into or out of the country by short-term advances. The Bank of Ceylon, which has expanded rapidly since its creation some 15 years ago by the Ceylon government, has undertaken a wider range of business but still on too short a term to suit much industrial financing. In general the banks have not provided facilities for the kind of medium-term borrowing which would be helpful to a new factory venture, such as advances secured on plant to be paid off over five to ten years. Still less do they provide any regular channels for the supply of funds in equity form. Of course, it has to be borne in mind that a large factor in shaping the operating policies of the banks is that Ceylon law has made it unusually difficult for them to get satisfactory security (e.g. land) for long-term loans.

It is also to be noted that, although Ceylon has an orthodox Companies Act, the possibilities of the joint-stock form of business organization have been very inadequately realized. One advantage of the joint-stock company is that it permits undertakings of a size which no individual or small group of individuals could finance; another, especially great in Ceylon, is its value as a form of organization eminently fitted to take the long view which industrial management requires—and which the individual is tempted to sacrifice to short-term profit. Thus any approach to this problem should be one which will facilitate and encourage the acquisition of industrial shares by Ceylonese.

Government can help in this. On the other hand, the record of government in the promotion of industrial enterprises is not encouraging. We believe that there is need for new institutional machinery through which government initiative based on the broad social needs of the country may play its part alongside private business interests; but we are convinced that, if efficient enterprises are to be created, this initiative must take a form other than direct operation of factories by government departments. Moreover, although government may play a useful role in getting such enterprises started, once they are launched they should be given maximum freedom to develop by themselves. If they are constantly subject to arbitrary interference, either by removal of officers or dictation of policies, they will never achieve that independence of decision and action so essential to successful enterprise. What is needed is a mechanism permitting government to participate in capitalization, ownership and profits, while leaving operation strictly in the hands of well-chosen corporate management personnel.

A Community of Interests

Involved in this problem are numerous separate interests. The government wants development in the industrial as well as in the agricultural sector. It is to its interest that such development should be efficiently managed, and that the burden on its own human and financial resources should be minimized by the cooperation of private enterprise and ability. Private enterprise, for its part, needs improved access to capital, help in overcoming its inexperience, and assurance that once started it can keep going. Banks and going business concerns would benefit if there were additional profitable outlets for their surplus funds; moreover, they could protect their existing interests by participating in the further development of the country. The investing public would gain from a wider range of choice for the investment of its savings, and the possibility of higher returns. The general public would profit from the larger national income made possible by industrial growth, and from the increased opportunities of employment. Similar benefits would accrue, too, if there were a corresponding stimulus to corporate development in general business and in certain branches of agriculture.

Clearly these interests are all essentially harmonious and convergent. Some catalyst, some new institutional arrangement, is needed to bring them together for mutual benefit.

Ceylon Development Corporation

To this end the Mission recommends the establishment of a Ceylon Development Corporation, whose main purposes would be: (1) to provide the finance necessary to initiate new projects in industry, agriculture, or miscellaneous business, and to assist the progress of promising ventures already started by individual enterprise; and (2) to furnish or arrange for managerial and technical assistance to new ventures, or to others in need of it. From these objectives it will be seen that the Corporation would be a pioneering agency, charged with giving the primary impulse to economic expansion in productive fields where private enterprise was lacking or laggard.

If its purposes are to be fully realized, certain features of the Corporation are clearly implied. First, it must have freedom of initiative. This means that its staff must be able to explore, without binding restrictions of any kind, all likely avenues of economic development. Secondly, its finances must be independent and secure. This follows from the fact that, since many of its projects will require considerable time before they can be brought to maturity, the Corporation, as the responsible agency, must have adequate funds and independence in their use. Finally, and above all, it has to be imbued with a spirit of vigorous enterprise. This is a "must" for any kind of pioneering work.

To insure that these features are embodied in the Corporation, the Mission makes the following recommendations:

(1) The corporation should be an autonomous body with an independent management, free from the inflexibility of government financial and civil service regulations, as well as from arbitrary interference with management.

(2) Its capital—amounting to a total, say, of Rs. 100 million—should be raised by the joint participation of the government, the Central Bank, the commercial banks, and possibly the investing public. No single participant or group should hold a controlling interest. Further funds, if and when they become necessary, might be raised by the sale of bonds to the public or to overseas institutional lenders.

(3) Officers and staff of the Corporation should be appointed and promoted solely on the basis of competence. This should be a permanent policy, which means that the administration should enjoy complete freedom to hire and fire without outside interference. Furthermore, to attract a capable staff, salaries should be adequate and conditions of work superior.

An autonomous corporation has the advantage of a fresh start, free from the bureaucratic burdens of established government departments. For this fresh start to lead to movement in the right direction, it is vital that the Corporation begin with an able staff. Reputation and tradition are important. Vigorous, intelligent and clear-headed conduct of the affairs of the new organization at the start will help it to establish continuity and to maintain a high standard over the years. A second consequence of a fresh and independent start is that the Corporation will have a better chance than an ordinary government department, subject to the direct influence of politics, of making objective judgments on new projects.

Various methods for carrying out the purposes of the Corporation suggest themselves. First and most essential would be a careful study of possible lines of development. For the technical aspects of such studies, reliance should be placed upon the proposed Institute for Applied Research. For information on the creditworthiness of potential clients, use could be made of the extensive knowledge in the possession of the commercial banks. Economic data needed to evaluate market prospects and related problems could be obtained from the research staff of the Central Bank, and from the various specialized agencies of the Government.

After preliminary study had disclosed promising lines of development, new enterprises might be initiated in either of two ways. Preferably, the Corporation should encourage local business men to undertake a project, offering them the technical and economic information at its disposal and its assistance in finding managerial staff. If the Corporation's financial participation is needed it might take the form of the purchase of shares in the new venture, underwriting of its security issues, or a medium to long-term loan secured by a mortgage on equipment or plant. Alternatively, if private capital were unwilling to inaugurate the new enterprise, the Corporation might do so itself by setting up a subsidiary corporation and subscribing as much as necessary (even the whole) of its capital stock, but encouraging maximum private participation.

In either case, once the new enterprise had established confidence as a going, profitable concern, the Development Corporation should sell its stockholdings to the public. To continue to hold them would add to its resources, to be sure. But this would be inconsistent with its primary purpose, which is not to earn maximum profits for itself but to stimulate the country's economic development. Selling its investments as they proved successful would replace its capital as a revolving fund for continuing operations, while at the same time the country's private industrial activity would be increased.

In addition to setting new enterprises on their feet, the Development Corporation should be prepared to aid new enterprise started independently, or older establishments wishing to expand their activities. As in the case of the Corporation's own projects such aid could take the form of loans, underwriting, stock participation, or managerial and technical advice. The Development Corporation would naturally replace the existing Agricultural and Industrial Credit Corporation. This should then be dissolved, and its agricultural mortgage business transferred to the State Mortgage Bank.

The Corporation would provide an obvious channel for external borrowing from the International Bank for Reconstruction and Development or other sources, following precedents in Turkey and elsewhere. Even if no outside borrowing were envisaged, the IBRD might well be requested to advise on details of the Corporation's establishment, based on its similar experience, and might also be prepared to assist in the staffing of the Corporation.

This, then, is the third of three new organs which the Mission considers necessary to complete the structure Ceylon already has for the planning and execution of development. The first is a body with the clearly defined task of pulling together the planning of development as a whole, supervising the necessary general surveys, and coordinating requests for external technical advice; for these functions we have proposed an Economic Committee of the Cabinet aided by an economic planning secretariat. The second is a competent organ of technical research and enquiry— the proposed Ceylon Institute for Applied Research. Finally, there is need for an executive financial arm to promote and carry out, in partnership with private interests, specific projects of a commercial nature. That will be the task of the Ceylon Development Corporation.

We cannot emphasize too strongly the importance of careful selection of the staffs which will run these organizations. There is no magic in the mere establishment of a new institution, no matter how well designed for its task. An institution is no more than a set of powers conferred upon men together with the men who exercise them. How these powers are used—whether with imagination and understanding, or in a dull, routine fashion— depends upon the quality of the men to whom their exercise is entrusted.

5. Financial Resources Available

Ceylon is in a position to undertake a substantial government-financed development program out of current income and resources presently available to her. The calculations set out below suggest that, at recent levels of prices and incomes, the government should be able to finance investment averaging Rs. 250 million to Rs. 275 million a year. This is somewhat higher than the rate of expenditure on such activities during 1949-50 and 1950-51—the third and fourth years of the current Six-Year Plan—and also higher than the current rate of expenditure in the fiscal year 1951-52.

Domestic Financial Resources[1]

About Rs. 100 million of this sum may be expected to come from a surplus of revenues over net current expenditures. This level was closely approximated in 1949-50. Although in the following year the surplus slightly exceeded Rs. 150 million, it would be unrealistic to base plans upon this record figure, since it reflected the post-Korean boom level of world prices which has already receded. Except for a recurrence of boom conditions, it appears that an annual surplus greater than Rs. 100 million would depend upon changes in government fiscal policies.

To maintain a continuing surplus of Rs. 100 million, it will

---

[1] The calculation of available domestic finance has not been based on national income analysis, because of the present inadequacy of national income figures. There is not enough information to deduce any standard ratio of personal savings to national income, still less the ratio of that part of personal savings which will be available to government. Those figures, and similar relevant quantities, can be better estimated directly than by attempting to deduce them from national income figures which are themselves built up from such estimates.

of course be essential to keep current expenditures under firm control and to seek additional sources of revenue; for there is always pressure to increase current outlays, especially for welfare purposes. Current expenditures are bound to increase in any event as an inevitable accompaniment of an investment program. All the new investment projects will require maintenance and in some at least, roads, hospitals, perhaps some irrigation projects, the expense will fall on current revenue.

Some of the obvious ways of improving the budget position include: increasing income tax rates and reducing the exemption limit; adjusting electricity rates and railway transport charges on a commercial basis as we have recommended elsewhere; following the lead of the United Kingdom government in cutting food subsidies—a move which might be expected to yield net benefit, even after making necessary compensating adjustments by way of salary and wage increases and tax relief to the export industries, and transferring additional financial responsibilities and powers of taxation to local authorities. The machinery of budget control over expenditure should be strengthened and the collection of taxes expedited. By such means, in our view it would not be difficult to improve the budgetary position by 50 million or even 100 million rupees per year. If the government wishes to move ahead rapidly with development, changes of this kind will be essential.

To supplement investment funds derived from a budget surplus, the accumulation of savings in excess of what is required to cover private investment expenditure furnishes a source from which the government can borrow. At the rate of accumulation prevailing in the second half of 1951 the special local savings institutions could purchase government securities to the extent of some Rs. 40 million a year, although at the lower rate obtaining in 1949-50 this sum would not exceed Rs. 10-15 million a year. In addition, investors such as insurance companies and commercial banks might be expected to provide out of current savings enough to absorb another Rs. 20 million or 30 million of such securities. As a mean total figure for government borrowing of current savings, Rs. 50 million corresponds to recent experience. Adding this to the budget surplus, then, domestic resources available for public developmental purposes on reasonable assumptions total approximately Rs. 150 million a year.

Private saving must obviously be maintained and if possible increased. It should be encouraged by the offer of a suitable range of government securities and by continuation of the propaganda of the National Savings Committee. But perhaps the most effective means of stimulating private saving, and in particular of channeling it into constructive avenues, would be the proposed Ceylon Development Corporation. It might well mobilize for productive ventures in the private sector substantial sums now going into the purchase of tea and rubber estates from nonresident owners, into speculative operations, or into idle balances.[2]

The figures suggested here are based on what are believed to be realistic assumptions, which rule out inflationary methods of financing. It would be possible, of course, for the government to borrow sums greatly in excess of current savings, by selling its securities to the banks. But this would increase the money at the disposal of the government and enable it to outbid competing buyers of goods and services. It would thus acquire resources at the expense of the general body of consumers, without their consent and indeed without their realizing precisely what was happening to them.

Such inflationary methods are always dangerous, since they upset the balance of a country's economy. Once started, they are difficult to stop. They are especially hazardous for Ceylon, because of its heavy dependence upon foreign trade. Imports would increase sharply as money incomes rose, while rising export costs would handicap the country's export trade. The resultant gap in the balance of payments if unchecked, would soon drain

---

[2] The purchase of foreign-owned investments and assets in 1950 alone resulted in the export of about Rs. 35 million of capital which might have been used productively.

the nation's foreign exchange reserves, requiring that inflationary financing stop or that the currency undergo a substantial devaluation. More likely, the government would check exchange losses by introducing or extending import and exchange controls. Though perhaps arresting the decline in reserves, these measures would intensify inflationary pressures in the domestic and export sectors, leaving the underlying problem essentially unchanged. For all these reasons inflationary methods of attempting to speed up development would be self-defeating and should be avoided.

External Financial Resources

External finance might be obtained in any of three ways: (1) by borrowing abroad; (2) by receiving grants of aid from other countries; or (3) by using external assets.

External borrowing may be useful later, and is considered elsewhere in this chapter. It will in any case depend upon the prospects of Ceylon's ability to service external loans. With respect to grants, we have assumed substantial technical assistance from abroad, and it is to be hoped that further useful contributions for specific purposes will be received under the Colombo Plan, such as those of Rs. 3.2 million already promised by Australia and Rs. 3.3 million by New Zealand. But reliance should not be placed on the uncertain prospects of new grants, and if larger ones are received they should be regarded as windfalls enabling the speed of development to be stepped up.

In the immediate future we must concentrate on the possibilities of using for development the large volume of external assets now held by Ceylon. These arose because of large trade surpluses during the war and again during the export boom of 1950–51. Mainly in the form of sterling balances, these assets totaled Rs. 1.185 million in December 1951.

What proportion of these assets could be used to pay for the needs of development, and at what rate, depends upon their ownership and upon the extent to which they might be needed

91

for other, more urgent, purposes. Their ownership is shown in Table I.

Of the Rs. 367.4 million owned or controlled by the government, approximately Rs. 100 million are earmarked for sinking funds against external debt or consist of the unpaid balance of the United Kingdom war loan. Some Rs. 15 million of the Central Bank's balance are also represented in the United Kingdom loan. The commercial bank's holdings of Rs. 147 million are privately owned and needed by these banks as operating balances in London. This leaves roughly Rs. 267 million in the hands of the government and about Rs. 656 million belonging to the Central Bank, or a total of Rs. 923 million available in the first instance as a reserve against contingencies.

TABLE I

EXTERNAL ASSETS, DECEMBER 1951

(million rupees)

Government	76.1
Government agencies and institutions	291.3
Central Bank	670.8
Commercial banks	147.0
Total	*1,185.2*

For a number of reasons, the Mission believes that some Rs. 450 million should be held for this purpose, leaving Rs. 473 million which might be used during 1953–59 for financing the external requirements of the development program. Although, as we shall see, the country's balance of payments has been relatively stable, there was a large if exceptional deficit of Rs. 180 million in 1947. The trend of both imports and exports is unfavorable; sudden changes in the market for rubber, and to a lesser degree for coconut products, are possible. As a reserve against dangers of this sort, the Mission feels that enough should be set aside to cover a deficit of Rs. 150 million in each of two years: Rs. 300 million for this purpose should be adequate protection for the period 1953–58.[3] A further sum of Rs. 150 million should be reserved as a cushion for the requirements of further development, after plans now being formulated have been carried out.

In round numbers, about Rs. 80 million could be drawn from external assets and added to domestic resources for development each year. But if export markets slumped badly, without a corresponding drop in imports, it might be necessary to divert exchange from development purposes to meeting large payments deficits. In this case the exchange available for development might not exceed Rs. 50 million annually. Moreover the rate at which Ceylon can use her accumulated sterling is not determined solely by what would be prudent from her individual point of view. As a member of the sterling area she has an obligation not to draw down her balances at a rate which would be embarrassing to the area as a whole, and that consideration might impose narrower limits on the amount to be used.

It may help to focus our discussion if we now draw together the estimates of financial resources available on different assumptions. Table II sets forth minimum and maximum figures for possible investment programs.

TABLE II

POSSIBLE INVESTMENT PROGRAMS
(million rupees)

	Minimum	Maximum
Budgetary surplus	100	170
Borrowing, domestic	30	70
External assets	50	80
Total	*180*	*320*

[3] Ceylon's quota in the International Monetary Fund is $15 million, or approximately Rs. 70 million. Ceylon might draw foreign exchange from the Fund if the Fund were satisfied that drawings were appropriate. Without the use of a special waiver, Ceylon could not draw in excess of 25% its quota in any one 12 months period.

The minimum column assumes continued good budgetary practice, but no attempt to increase the resources available to the government; it also assumes a low rate of saving, and early balance of payments difficulties or a necessity to limit sterling balance withdrawals. The maximum column, on the other hand, postulates such favorable elements as a budget policy designed to increase government revenue and curb ordinary expenditure, 1951 levels of saving, and continued balance of payments stability. Neither column, however, makes allowance for any new overseas loans which Ceylon could if necessary raise, as discussed later. The table brings out clearly how the size of the development program that can be financed depends directly on the kind of policies that are adopted. We have taken a figure of Rs. 250–275 million—between the two extremes—as the annual development investment which Ceylon can safely manage.

Balance of Payments Considerations

It may seem that earmarking half the available external assets for a contingent reserve bespeaks an overcautious attitude. But because of the character of Ceylon's balance of payments, and because of uncertainties as to the future, we do not believe this is so. The analysis in this chapter explains our view, while at the same time indicating some of the relevant external aspects of the development program.

Over the past 25 years Ceylon has enjoyed a consistent trade surplus. Instability in earnings from rubber and coconuts, caused by short-term fluctuations, has been moderated by the steady price and volume of tea exports. Moreover, there has been some further automatic stabilization of the trade balance because of the close relation between exports and income. Falling exports induce a decline in income, and, with lower incomes, people have less to spend on imports. In 15 of the past 20 years, imports have moved with exports, the average variation in imports being about three fourths of the change in exports. In only

three years of the 20 did imports increase while exports fell—
the worst possible combination for the balance of payments.

The trend of the two sides of Ceylon's foreign trade has been
only moderately unfavorable so far. Imports of consumer goods
have risen in close correspondence with the growth of population. Exports have also increased, though somewhat more slowly. The net result has been a continuing surplus of exports over
imports, turning into a deficit only in 1932 (at the bottom of the
depression) and in 1947 when postwar re-stocking contributed
heavily to the largest net deficit on record, Rs. 180 million. Except for these two years, too, there has been no significant over-
all deficit. The trade surplus has otherwise been about sufficient
to cover invisible payments such as personal remittances and
investment income.

The record of Ceylon's balance of payments is thus one of
fair stability and only occasional difficulty. Such instability between payments and receipts as there has been, which shows up
in deficits and surpluses, has resulted principally from fluctuations in the demand for and prices of exports. Imports of consumer goods, in particular, have since the 1920's been remarkably stable, remaining (except for the war years) very close to
Rs. 100 per capita in 1950 prices. Other imports, to a lesser
degree consumption imports, have varied together with exports,
thus furnishing a considerable element of automatic adjustment
in the balance of payments.

Balance of Payments Prospects

In relation to future plans, however, it is prospects that count.
Considering first the receipts side, this will be determined mainly,
in the years to come, by movements in the prices and volume of
exports. The years 1949–50 and 1950–51 were unusually favorable for exports, and some decline in earnings from this source
must be expected. As to volume, we estimate that recent levels
for tea and rubber (approximately 300 million and 215 million
lbs. respectively) will be continued. Because of increasing domestic consumption, as well as the declining yield of overage

trees, coconut products available for export appear likely to decline by the equivalent of 20–30 million nuts a year; exports will probably average the equivalent of less than 800 million nuts, but as the highest value exports will no doubt be continued to the extent that demand is maintained, the fall in their value should be less serious.

Prediction of price trends is risky; the best we can do is to try to avoid either undue optimism or excessive pessimism. For tea, in view of the relative stability in both price and markets, continuation of the average 1950 price of Rs. 2.5 per lb. does not seem unreasonable. The export price of rubber in 1950 averaged Rs. 1.50 per lb., rose much higher in the following year, and stood at Rs. 2.10 in December 1951. On the basis of recent world price levels, we assume an average world price of U.S. $0.30, or about Rs. 1.35 in Ceylon for the next few years. Coconut products, though higher in 1951, have recently been selling around the 1950 average. Since market prospects are fairly good, it seems reasonable to take the 1950 level as a basis for forecasts.[4]

According to the foregoing assumptions, export earnings during 1953–58 may be estimated to average roughly as follows:

		Million rupees
Tea:	300 million lbs. at Rs. 2.50	750
Rubber:	215 million lbs. at Rs. 1.35	300
Coconut products:	say 750 million nuts, concentrated in more valuable products	200
Other exports at approximately 1950 level:		150
Total		*1,400*

This total is lower than the 1950 figure of Rs. 1.563 million because of the assumptions of lower rubber prices and a reduced

[4] These price expectations assume, of course, no marked change in the general level of international prices. If such a change should occur it would be reasonable to expect approximately similar changes in import prices also.

96

volume of exports of coconut products. It will almost certainly be augmented by additional exports resulting from development policies in operation or proposed. Among other possibilities, cacao, canned fruits and preserves, concentrated ilmenite, tannins, certain vegetable oils and coir manufactures might add to export receipts sums gradually rising to Rs. 100–200 million annually. A close estimate is out of the question at this stage. In any event, in the near future such additions to exports are unlikely to affect Ceylon's external earnings to any major degree.

Payments to be made abroad will depend mainly upon the demand for imports. This may for convenience be divided into two categories—imports for consumption, and imports required for the development program. We shall consider the latter shortly. Imports for consumption, the principal component of the country's ordinary imports,[5] will be determined principally by the trend and composition of income. Aside from changes in public taste, which are slow to occur and cannot be predicted in advance, income must rise if imports are to increase above recent levels. For without the larger purchasing power provided by rising income, people will lack the means to buy additional imports.

As Ceylon's population increases, aggregate national income should also increase. Additional workers will seek and find employment and will add their production to the total. Whether per capita incomes rise or fall will depend upon the amount and quality of the productive resources with which these workers are provided. It is the purpose of the development program to raise standards of living by improving Ceylon's productive resources, and the new workers, as well as those already in employment, should therefore be supplied with tools and equipment and instructed in methods superior to those already in use. While this process will take time and cannot be expected to proceed perfect-

---

[5] Over the past 20 years, imports for consumption have averaged fairly consistently around 70% of total imports.

ly smoothly, the end result should be an increase not only in total national income but also in per capita incomes.

Is this likely to mean such a rise in imports as to exceed substantially earnings from exports, and thus to cause continuing and mounting balance of payments deficits? Granted the assumptions within which we are working, it is our opinion that this outcome is not only unlikely but impossible on any large scale. This is apparent if we consider the forms which the expected increase of national income may take. If the increase results from larger production for export, foreign exchange will automatically be available to pay for imports. If, as seems more likely, the increase of national income results from a specially large increase in the output of goods which can be directly substituted for imports, the need for additional imports will be reduced. Finally, if the increase results from a more than proportionate rise in the output of goods for purely local use, such production can only be continued for any length of time if there is a change in the pattern of demand, involving the expenditure of a smaller proportion of total income on imports.

In other words, so long as increased production corresponds to the pattern of demand, and thus provides both the income with which to buy goods and the kinds of goods wanted, there can be no disproportionate increase in import demand. Such an increase could only occur and be long maintained if the spending power of the public were supported by inflationary measures, which we have assumed will be avoided. That is, if national expenditure is not increased faster than national output, there should be no more than transitional or frictional disturbances in the balance of payments. Equilibrium will be maintained, however, only if the Central Bank and the Finance Ministry continue their present sound policies in monetary and budgetary management. For us "non inflationary finance" is an assumption —one of our most important assumptions; for the Ceylon finance authorities it is an objective and a task to be achieved only by constant vigilance.

The evidence suggests that production for export, and therefore the means to pay for imports, will not increase as rapidly as population. If, however, population, employment and income all rise, how is the demand for the kinds of goods which in the past have been imported to be met? The answer is, by home production of substitutes for imports. Even in the absence of prearranged plans for reorienting a country's productive structure, a shift that corresponds to marketing possibilities will be brought about automatically, though doubtless with friction and lags which might cause temporary balance of payments deficits. Thus Ceylon, in the past, has faced increasing demands for her major export products and has possessed the physical resources to expand them. Part of her growing population has found employment in producing a rising volume of these products. Another part has devoted its energies to producing goods and services for purely local use, and still another to producing substitutes for imports. Each of these lines of production has grown in close correspondence with the demand for its output. The income earned in such production has furnished the purchasing power to absorb the goods produced. That part earned in producing exports has made possible expenditure to an equivalent value on imports.

Suppose that from now on, exports were to cease expanding altogether. No additional employment would be offered in the export industries. If producers of domestic goods and of existing substitutes for imports were to employ all the new workers added by the growth of population, while these workers desired to spend part of their earnings on imports, imports would rise temporarily while the markets for domestic goods and import substitutes became clogged. Too many of the latter types of goods would have been produced, production would decline, and workers would become unemployed. Gradually, the competition of the unemployed workers for employment would reduce wages. This would make profitable the production of certain additional substitutes for imports, whose production could not be undertaken

99

earlier because wages were too high. Slowly, employment would increase, until all the addition to the working population was employed producing domestic goods and services or new as well as previous substitutes for imports.

We do not contemplate relying on the slow and harsh operation of these market forces in Ceylon. The prospects for further growth of exports and therefore of employment in export industries are not bright; plans for development are deliberately pointed toward augmenting the production of substitutes for imports for which there is a ready and growing demand. Especially significant is the increase of local food production to replace part of the very heavy food imports. We may cite colonization in the dry zone, which should produce a rice crop worth at least Rs. 30 million, to say nothing of currystuffs, hard fibers, and other crops. By 1959 the island should be producing 20,000 tons of sugar annually, worth about Rs. 10 million. Nearly all the expected industrial production will displace imports, while the increase in the ratio of hydroelectric to thermal power will reduce dependence on imported fuel.

In these directions, as in increased production of such domestic goods and services as housing, education and entertainment, the additions to be expected to the working population will find employment, earn incomes, and find suitable objects on which to spend them from domestic sources.

If the development program allocates investment so as to increase the production of goods and services wanted by the Ceylonese people, the country should incur no ordinary deficits in the balance of payments. We believe that the program envisaged does correspond to the needs and desires of the people, as expressed either in their demands in the market place or in their willingness to support government expenditure on education, improved housing, better health services and the like. If any disparity between types of production and avenues of expenditure should arise, it would appear in an excess of imports over earnings from exports, supported by an expansion of credit. Its

UNIVERSITY COLLEGE OF WALES LIBRARY ABERYSTWYTH

correction would require a revision of investment plans to accord with the direction of expenditure—that is, a curtailment of production unable to find a market and an increase in the output of goods and services which were in demand.

Thus the present outlook is that ordinary deficits are unlikely, except possibly those which might result from frictions, and these would be small in size and non-recurrent. But, even if this general argument is correct, we cannot rely on a "normal" surplus to meet the foreign exchange costs of the development program. We have therefore to consider how these may be covered.

Investment and the Balance of Payments

How much external expenditure is likely to be caused by the development program? We have estimated a reasonable public investment outlay to be Rs. 250–275 million a year. The foreign exchange element in such a program appears likely to be about 35%.[6] On a total program of Rs. 1.6 million this would be Rs. 560 million for the period 1953–59.

Against this direct external impact of the government investment program, we have that portion, some Rs. 480 million, of existing foreign exchange resources which we suggest might be used for development. Moreover, the raising of internal finance by higher taxation and private saving, which must be accompanied by some reduction of private consumption expenditure, will itself

---

[6] Various approaches all give a figure of about this magnitude. Imports of investment goods in 1950-51 stood at Rs. 151 million, while gross investment was about Rs. 502 million. The import content of investment in that year was thus 30%. In the Bank's report on Colombia, a country with requirements and prospects not too dissimilar to Ceylon's, the weighted average ratio of investment goods imports to total investment is 33.5%. Application of similar calculations to our own estimates of the components of Ceylon's development program gives a weighted average of 36%. Finally Ceylon's own Colombo Plan estimates a figure of 35 to 40%.

have some beneficial effect on the balance of payments. On the other hand, even with the program financed out of public and private savings, there are likely to be inflationary "fringe" effects. Thus if success attends the effort to stimulate private investment, some savings which in the past have gone into idle balances may be diverted into the active circulation. The resultant increased expenditure would tend to raise the demand for imports above the calculated level. Delays in getting increased domestic production under way would have a similar impact. The net effect on the balance of payments is not exactly predictable, as the foreign component of the investment expenditure is itself only an approximation. But the total deficit of the six years might exceed the Rs. 480 million of exchange reserves earmarked by as much as Rs. 100 million.

To meet this need for external funds, Ceylon should consider overseas borrowing. Loans totalling Rs. 200 million would not appear excessive, and would suffice not only to prevent an undue lowering of external reserves, but to maintain these at a somewhat higher level than the Rs. 450 million minimum we have suggested. Alternatively, such loans would provide the foreign resources which would be needed should it become possible to expand the program in its later years.

The Development Program and Standards of Living

Ceylon's development plans are designed to improve the nation's productive resources and therewith to raise the standards of living of the people. Some may feel that the program we advance is too modest in size to realize this objective. It is only half as large, in terms of the outlay projected, as that set forth at the recent Karachi meeting of participants in the Colombo Plan. As we point out more fully in the next chapter, however, Ceylon's Colombo Plan estimate is an expression of what it would be desirable to do if resources beyond those now in sight could be made available. Our proposals, on the other hand, are intended as a statement of what can actually be accomplished with the financial, technical and physical resources upon which one can reasonably count.

This chapter has considered in some detail the finances which might be mobilized in support of economic development. Even to achieve an annual outlay of Rs. 250–275 million will require an increase in the budget surplus and institutional saving somewhat above recent averages.

Limitations on the speed of development also arise because of technical and physical factors. We have stressed the need for preparatory work such as land surveys, agricultural experiments and industrial research to lay a firm foundation for progress. Unless this work is undertaken and completed before large expenditures are made, precious resources will run to waste in uneconomic ventures. Again, Ceylon's stage of technical advancement will not permit the immediate introduction of the latest equipment and the most modern methods to increase her productivity. Much investment is needed to improve the technical skills of her people before they can make effective use of these means to greater production. Tractors without skilled operators are just so much rusting metal.

For all these reasons, we have tried to "cut the suit according to the cloth." We do not deny that a larger program could be undertaken. It would necessitate, however, either (a) even more substantial increases in taxation and in private savings available to the government; or (b) inflationary financing; or (c) the use of authoritarian methods. The first of these is not ruled out, but is unlikely. The second we believe would be harmful, for reasons given earlier in this chapter. The third is impossible for a people dedicated to parliamentary government and democratic methods.

Albeit limited in scale because of circumstances, the program suggested is, we believe, large enough to bring important benefits in the form of greater output of goods and services, particularly in its later years. Public and private investment together should total from Rs. 500–600 million during the six

103

years, averaging about Rs. 550 million.[7] This would represent about 11 to 12% of gross national product, a figure that exceeds the rate of investment in most underdeveloped countries and compares favorably even with that in western Europe.

How great an effect such a volume of investment would have upon income depends upon the increase in output to be expected from a given amount of investment. In economically advanced countries like the United States, the ratio of new capital investment to annual additions to gross output is approximately three to one. For underdeveloped countries it is probably higher, since the comparatively heavy investment in social overhead capital (roads, utilities, etc.) yields its return only indirectly and over long periods. A conservative figure for Ceylon might be four to one. With such a capital-output ratio, annual increments to income should start at Rs. 125 million and increase steadily to around Rs. 150 million. Just to maintain living standards for the growing population will require that income increase by 2.5% or about Rs. 106 million a year. If we allow for less favorable returns in the early years, in the later ones there should be a margin that is increasingly favorable. Moreover, there is much scope for a rise in output from the spread of improved methods among producers not directly affected by the investment program.

Such a hoped-for increase in income will not come about automatically, even with rising investment. Investment must be

---

[7] Such recent data as are available suggest that private capital formation is fairly close to the level of government investment. Thus the Central Bank's estimate for private gross investment in 1950-51 is Rs. 269 million, compared with Rs. 233 million for the Government. Our own calculations incline us to put the figure for private investment some Rs. 50 million lower, at about Rs. 217 million. Nonetheless, if during coming years action is taken to discover new outlets for private capital and to stimulate private savings and channel them into productive investment, we feel it not unreasonable to expect private investment to keep pace with investment by the government.

of the right kinds. The capital-output ratio in the advanced countries is low and per capita income rises steadily because new capital is embodied in ever more productive equipment and methods. The same must occur in Ceylon; it will not happen if additions to capital are of the same types as have been employed in the past. To insure that the development program will raise productivity, there must be constant attention to the careful selection of better tools, equipment and methods. This means that, with aggregate resources for investment limited, the margin for waste and inefficiency will be very narrow.

It is also to be remembered that much of the investment will bear fruit only at a later date. This is notably true of outlays on education, technical training and public health. Finally, development is a continuing process. It is not to be expected that Ceylon's development will cease with the completion of the next six-year program. That program, while in itself improving the country's productive resources and permitting some rise in living standards, can best be regarded as laying a solid foundation for future advance.

6. Programs and Priorities

Existing Programs

Two broad development programs, both for six-year periods, are customarily spoken of as being in operation in Ceylon today. The first, to which we have referred already, was adopted when Ceylon attained its present national status and runs from October 1, 1947 to September 30, 1953. It covered the major new projects which the government intended to carry out during that period, and has been very largely followed, but it was not designed to comprehend the government's total developmental or capital investment activities as completely as the program this Mission has prepared.

The second current plan is the Colombo Plan, originally drawn up as a consequence of the Commonwealth meeting held in Colombo in January 1950; this plan runs from July 1, 1951 to June 30, 1957. This may be regarded as more rather than less comprehensive than the Mission's proposals, as it represents an assessment or compilation of the works it would be desirable to undertake in its six-year period if the necessary internal and external resources could be found. It forms part of a larger effort to assess the needs of the whole area of Southern Asia for both financial and technical assistance, in the provision of which the Colombo Plan organization is already doing valuable work.

The Mission has tried to present a program for the six years following the first six-year plan. It is designed to cover all capital expenditure by the government and is based on the financial and technical resources in fact likely to be available. Our aim has been a schedule of projects which can provide a firm program of work for the government departments concerned, one on which they can make their own plans for staff recruitment and training,

106

for purchase of equipment and for all the other activities which need foresight and careful preparatory work.

It is of interest, nevertheless, to note the main outlines of the expenditures envisaged for Ceylon when the Colombo Plan was drawn up[1], as well as the revised figures reported by Ceylon's representative at the recent conference held in Karachi to review the progress of the Plan. These are set forth in Table I.

TABLE I

PROPOSED SIX-YEAR DEVELOPMENT EXPENDITURES
OF CEYLON UNDER THE COLOMBO PLAN
(millions of rupees)

Field of Development	First Estimate 1950	Revised Estimate 1952
Agriculture	503	900
Transport and Communications	297	600
Power	109	150
Industry	75	200
Housing	47	175
Health	132	300
Education	196	275
Rural Development	—	400
Research	—	25
Miscellaneous	—	175
Total	*1,359*	*3,200*

The Mission's Approach

We have discussed in earlier chapters the most urgent and promising lines of development of both material and human resources. As always, not all the desirable things can be done in any given time. Funds, technical personnel and technical facilities are all limited. Some processes cannot be accelerated, no matter how desirable. Difficulties in acquiring specialized capital equipment for development projects might also delay progress,

[1] *The Colombo Plan;* Cmd. 8080, H.M.'s Stationery Office, London, Nov. 1950, p. 29.

107

although this should not be a serious problem if no new international disturbance arises and if advance requirements are properly programmed, since the projects actually recommended do not in the main depend heavily on imported equipment.

Given a number of desirable projects and the financial and technical resources on which one can reasonably count, it is next necessary to choose which of the many projects should be undertaken. The process of selection necessarily involves rejecting many attractive schemes, some of which we have discussed individually. In making a selection we have first looked to those lines of development which will produce the greatest permanent benefits and secondly have aimed at an integrated program in which progress in each of the several fields of action will balance and support the rest.

Priorities

The application of those principles has been guided by our conclusions about Ceylon's basic economic potentialities. For the sake of clarity we summarize these conclusions here.

(1) Ceylon has the good fortune to have resources immediately available which, if properly used, can meet the needs of the inevitable population growth of the next decade, improve the average standard of living and add permanent strength to the economy. But her resources, in land, materials and money are limited and it is imperative that they should not be wasted by impetuous or ill-considered action. The developments of the next six years must provide a springboard for further advance and leave the economy better able to meet the situation which emerges as the reserves of empty land and unused resources diminish.

(2) Priority must be given at the present time to the maximization of agricultural production. This means maintaining or improving the efficiency of existing agriculture and opening up new lands. Education, research and agricultural extension are the keys to the first. Irrigation, jungle clearance and coloniza-

tion are the keys to the second. But besides the direct investment in agriculture itself, higher output from the land will be vitally helped by investment in transport improvements and in power and industry. Moreover, while agricultural development deserves priority in the allocation of funds, the optimum rate of progress is unfortunately slower than might be expected because of the need to take extreme care not to damage the soil—the most irreplaceable of Ceylon's assets.

(3) Industry is the second string. For many years manufacture will contribute much less than agriculture to the national wealth; but in the more distant future, when the vacant lands are occupied and the possibilities of irrigation fully exploited, the further growth of national income and living standards will depend on a much larger application of Ceylon's remaining labor resources to industrial processes. The next six-year period must build the foundations for that development by research and education, and by fostering a variety of new industries not individually involving too heavy investment of capital and resources.

(4) Power is a basic service and an essential to industrial growth. The ultimate possibilities of hydroelectric power in Ceylon are smaller than is sometimes supposed and the work of harnessing them is necessarily slow; but it should be pressed on as rapidly as possible without prohibitive expense.

(5) Improvements in transport and communications are essential, both to enable other developments to be undertaken and to enable the increased produce planned for to be moved to either internal or overseas markets. Individual road and railway extensions and new port developments are directly related to the opening up of new lands. More generally, experience in other countries demonstrates the enormous contribution of easy communications with urban centers to the quickening of thought and improvement of techniques among the cultivators. Similarly, the educational "output" of agricultural extension officers and others is dependent on easy access to the villages. Hence the large allocation of funds to transport.

(6) Improvements in public health and education, quite apart from their direct contribution to welfare, are necessary on purely economic grounds, to secure a fitter and more competent working population; but expenditure on the curative side of public health must, for the time being, be kept within rather narrow limits.

(7) Much further survey and investigational work is needed in many fields and until it is completed new large-scale schemes should be put aside in favor of a larger number of smaller projects. Development must certainly not be brought to a standstill while studies proceed. Some of the risks which are inevitable when knowledge is incomplete must be taken; but the risks should be individually small.

(8) Everything should be done to enlist the spontaneous energies of the population as well as the drive and broad views of the government. Help should therefore be given to the work of cooperative societies and of the rural development organizations, and more scope afforded to the play of private enterprise.

The Size of the Program

The preceding chapter has shown that, with proper mobilization of her internal financial resources, both public and private, and with prudent use of her external assets and external borrowing power, Ceylon can afford a capital expenditure on public account of a little more than Rs. 250,000,000 per year. Any additional funds provided by international grants would of course be very useful, but we cannot assume that such grants will be forthcoming on a scale big enough to affect our figures. We assume that expenditure in the earlier years will be somewhat less than the average contemplated and that as the preliminary surveys and researches recommended bear fruit, the rate of expenditure will rise. The suggested level of expenditure probably comes near to the maximum which the administrative and technical staffs of the government can manage efficiently and economically in the next few years. We hope that the recommended organizational and educational improvements will make a higher rate of investment technically feasible in later years. To provide for the possibility that sufficient finance and technical facilities will be available to permit more rapid progress, we have included suggestions for supplementing the initial program we have drawn up.

This initial or basic program contemplates a total investment in the government sector of Rs. 1.6 million in six years. It includes all those government expenditures which are distinguishable as capital, without differentiating between what has hitherto been financed from general revenue or from loan funds. We have not, however, attempted to cover all the minor improvements which will no doubt continue to be covered by "recurrent expenditure" votes.

Investment in the private sector will, we hope, continue and increase under the stimulus of the measures we have suggested to interest and encourage private capital. Thus, if the government, as recommended, puts up Rs. 50 million, representing half the total capital, as its contribution to the capital of the proposed Development Corporation, the sum immediately available would actually be Rs. 100 million. Similarly, the funds actually available for land development would be greater if some land were leased in the form of large farms and estates.

A program of this size is basic, we believe, in the sense that, barring only a major collapse of her export markets or some other severe world-wide economic disturbance, Ceylon can be reasonably confident of carrying it through. It is basic, too, in that if increased resources become available the program can be enlarged or expedited on the lines of the Mission's suggestions for supplementation.

Timing

The starting date of the period we are concerned with—October 1, 1953—is still some distance ahead. We have assumed that during 1952–53 development will continue along the general lines of the existing program. We recognize, furthermore, that by the time the Mission's recommendations have been considered in Ceylon many decisions determining the 1952–53 activities will

111

already have been taken. Yet what is done in this year will affect what can be done in the next. In drawing up an orderly second six-year program, we must base it on the assumption that insofar as our recommendations are accepted there will be some modifications in present activities. For example, where we have advised deferring or abandoning one or two specific projects proposed earlier, we hope that they will not be started and therefore will not consume funds needed elsewhere. In other matters, especially in organization, survey and research, we most strongly hope that action will be taken at once, without awaiting the new period.

The Recommended Program

Based on all these considerations, Table II sets out the allocation of development funds recommended by the Mission for the 1953–59 period. Tables II–A to II–C give further breakdowns of the larger allocations. A worthwhile allocation of the total expenditures to individual financial years is not possible so far ahead, but proposed schedules are presented under some of the headings in appropriate chapters of Part II of this report.

The program should not be regarded as an inflexible plan to be followed slavishly to the end, but rather one which can and inevitably will be modified from time to time in the light of new information and new needs. The surveys and investigations which the Mission considers so important are likely to disclose improvements in existing projects, and to uncover new possibilities deserving higher priority than some now included.

TABLE II

RECOMMENDED DEVELOPMENT PROGRAM, 1953-59

(million rupees; all estimates at 1952 prices)

Agriculture and Allied Activities

Irrigation	187
Land development, including settlement of colonists	200
Flood control, drainage, reclamation, etc.	18
Agricultural extension, research, surveys, etc.	30
Development of cooperatives	25
	——
	460

Power
  Development of new resources, hydroelectric and
    thermal plants   110
  Distribution network   99
                                                            ─────   209
Industry
  Government contribution to Ceylon Development
    Corporation [1]   50
  Institute for Applied Research   5
  Other developments, including existing commitments   20
                                                            ─────   75
Transport
  Ports and harbors   118
  Inland waterways   2
  Railways   150
  Roads   105
  Civil Aviation   20
  Telecommunications   35
                                                            ─────   430
Health
  Training   13
  Hospital extensions   80
  Government assistance to housing   30
  Water supplies   60
  Miscellaneous   12
                                                            ─────   195
Education
  School buildings, equipment, etc.   72
  Training of teachers   8
  Primary and secondary education   20
  University buildings and equipment   40
  Miscellaneous   5
                                                            ─────   145
Rural Development   60
Administration and Miscellaneous   26
                                                            ──────────────────
                                                                        1,600

[1] It is assumed that private investment through the Development Corporation will, within the six-year period, exceed the government's.

113

TABLE IIA
DEVELOPMENT PROGRAM 1953-59
Agriculture

(million rupees)

Irrigation

Completion of schemes started under 1947-53 program	59	
Pavathulam scheme	7	
Padawiya scheme	10	
Other schemes to be completed in period	20	
New schemes to be begun but not finished by 1959 [1]	30	
Village works	36	
Improvements included in major works	10	
Irrigation works incidental to other water developments	15	187

Land Development (including settlement of colonists) (approximately 125,000 acres at Rs. 1,600 per acre [2]) 200

Drainage, etc.

Drainage, reclamation and salt water exclusion	6	
Flood control	12	18

---

[1] Including possible commencement of work on a modified Walawe Ganga Scheme if justified by further investigations.

[2] Rs. 1,600 is the present average on the basis of allotment of five acres per settler. Adoption of the Mission's recommendations on colonization policy would (i) reduce total expenditure on housing and other aid to each colonist; (ii) increase the number of colonists settled per 1,000 acres, by reducing the standard allotment of land; and (iii) reserve some land for supplementary allotments and some for allocation to "capitalists" who would themselves meet most of the costs now borne by government. These changes would have divergent effects on total cost to government. If aid per settler were reduced by 10%, i.e. to Rs. 7,200 and if 10% of the land were reserved for supplementary and "estate" allocations, the cost to government per irrigated acre, on a basis of four acres standard allotment per settler would work out to Rs. 1,620.

114

Agricultural Extension, Research, etc.

Additional technical staff (to maximum of 50) including assistants and incidental expenses	6	
Soil conservation (staff to maximum of 20, equipment and assistance to farmers)	14	
Advisers (12 at Rs. 55,000 each, assuming half are met by international technical aid)	2	
Experts for university education in Ceylon and overseas	2	
Research, additional staff and facilities	2	
Land-use survey	4	30
Development of Cooperatives		25
Total		*460*

TABLE IIB

DEVELOPMENT PROGRAM 1953-59
Power
(million rupees)

New Generating Capacity

Completion of Laksapana Stages IIA and IIB	65	
Commencement of new hydroelectric 50 MW installation (for completion in 1960)	40	
Commencement of new thermal 25 MW plant (for completion in 1962)	5	110

Distribution

132 KV grid	60	
33 KV system	27	
11-33 KV system	12	99
Total		*209*

115

TABLE IIC

DEVELOPMENT PROGRAM 1953-59
Transport and Communications
(million rupees)

Ports and Harbors

Colombo Port development	65	
Colombo Port, access improvements	13	
Galle, improvements and equipment	4.8	
Trincomalee	25	
Port equipment, general	10	
Engineering surveys (Colombo further works and Kankesanturai)	.2	118

Inland Waterways		2

Railways

General improvements	65	
Kelani valley replacement	4.3	
Extensions, etc.	80	
Colombo electrification (commencement only)	.7	150

Roads

General improvements and new construction		105

Civil Aviation

Ground facilities	13	
Communications equipment	3	
Aircraft	2	
Training	2	20

Telecommunications

Part of long-term program of improvements		35

Total	*430*

Nonetheless, the program as a whole reflects policies which, if approved, will govern development work far beyond 1959. Many individual projects involve planned expenditure over a number of years, extending in some cases into that later period. Firm decisions on these must be taken now, to avoid later delays in related programs. It is essential that at all times the government should have a clear program of work before it. It is equally essential that the program be reviewed systematically every year in the light of changing conditions and greater knowledge gained. The central planning organization we have proposed is designed to do precisely that.

Possible Supplementary Program

As already mentioned, the Mission has studied what additions might be made to this program if more finance than now anticipated becomes available. This would be one of the most important matters for consideration in the annual review of the program; hence additional suggestions are highly tentative.

It is very unlikely that the total funds available over the six years would in any event exceed Rs. 2 billion. For even if there were a much greater improvement in the financial situation of Ceylon, it would certainly be prudent to take advantage of the opportunity to preserve the external exchange reserves at a high figure rather than to draw them down as much as we have assumed —or as an alternative, to avoid any external borrowing. Below are the Mission's views as to the division of supplementary allocations totalling Rs. 400 million.

Agriculture: Some additional development work would be possible, but there are technical and administrative obstacles. It would not be physically possible to speed the irrigation work very much more except with a quite disproportionate increase of cost per acre irrigated, and the pace of colonization is determined by the pace of irrigation. A further Rs. 50 million might be allocated to irrigation and land development jointly.

Power: The present program for development of new hydroelectric resources could not be greatly expedited without greatly increasing costs, and extension of distribution is dependent on increase of generation; but it should be possible to start the sug-

117

gested new 50,000 KW hydroelectric installation a little earlier if funds permit. A supplementary allocation of Rs. 20 million is suggested.

Industry: If (but only if) projects develop with sufficiently good prospects, an additional Rs. 25 million or even Rs. 50 million could be allocated to building up industrial capital; actually, we doubt that the larger of these sums could be used economically. More and better industrial training facilities would be profitable. In all, another Rs. 30 million is suggested.

Transport: Subject to technical limitations in the departments concerned and to availability of imported equipment, the programs of extensions and improvements in this field could be expedited. Greater use of foreign contractors could help in this case. If 20% were added to the railway provision, 33.3% to roads, 50% to civil aviation and Rs. 10 million to telecommunications, a further Rs. 85 million would be required.

Health and Housing: Obviously the hospitals program could be enlarged, subject to technical limitations on the rate of building and to the capacity of training facilities to provide the necessary additional staff. A supplementary allocation for this, including also some enlargement of preventive medical activities, might be Rs. 25 million. In housing, a bigger drive would be technically easier and could usefully absorb another Rs. 50 million.

Education: If more funds were available, faster progress could be made in this basic service. An extra Rs. 10 million per year might be envisaged.

Rural Development: It has been urged on the Mission that if funds were available a great number of small but valuable village works could be carried out through the local Rural Development Societies. We strongly favor the stimulation of self-help by this means, and would allocate an additional Rs. 80 million to it if funds become more plentiful.

Therefore, if altered circumstances made possible a six-year expenditure of Rs. 2 billion, instead of Rs. 1.6 billion, the suggested supplementary allocations would be as shown in Table III.

TABLE III

PROPOSED DISTRIBUTION OF SUPPLEMENTARY DEVELOPMENT FUNDS
UP TO RS. 400 MILLION IF AVAILABLE LATER

(million rupees)

Irrigation and Land Development	50
Power	20
Industry	30
Transport	85
Health	25
Housing	50
Education	60
Rural Development	80
	—
Total Additions	*400*

7. Summary of Recommendations

In this chapter are gathered together the most important of the Mission's practical recommendations. Many other recommendations and suggestions will be found in the text of the Report and especially in the more detailed discussion of special topics in Part II. The recommendations only are set out here, without any elaboration of reasons. They are grouped, for convenience of presentation, under subjects rather than according to the chapters in which they occur.

General Policies, Organization and New Institutions

1. To provide for properly coordinated planning and supervision of government capital investment programs, an Economic Committee of the Cabinet should be created comprising the Ministers of Agriculture, Industry, Transport and Works, Rural Development, and Finance, and possibly presided over by the Prime Minister. This Committee should be assisted by an Economic Planning Secretariat headed by an official of high standing who would serve as Secretary to the Committee, and by a part-time Development Advisory Board. The planning secretariat should be the central point for the examination and collation of development projects and for gathering information about their practical progress.

2. Existing policies of active assistance to the Cooperative and Rural Development Societies should be continued, and funds should be provided to enable them to extend their activities.

3. Government policies should be such as to encourage further investment of private capital, both Ceylonese and non-Ceylonese.

4. A Ceylon Development Corporation should be established by joint action of the government, the Central Bank, the com-

mercial banks and other private interests, to promote and assist in the financing of new commercial ventures in industry, agriculture or other business fields. Its initial capital might be Rs. 100 million of which government should contribute not more than half, and no single participant should own a controlling share. It should have full independence in management and the widest freedom in method of operation and mode of financing projects.

5. A Ceylon Institute for Applied Research should be created under the sponsorship initially of the Central Bank of Ceylon, with appropriate specialized help from international agencies concerned with development. It should undertake systematic research into the potentialities of raw materials available in Ceylon, creation of new industries and other productive activities, and means for improving the efficiency of existing ones. To encourage private support and for related reasons it should be free of direct governmental control.

6. A Water Resources Planning Unit should be established under the proposed economic planning secretariat, to study and program all aspects of water utilization and control.

7. The management and development of all the harbors of the country handling ocean traffic should be placed under a Ceylon Ports Authority.

8. The Electrical Undertakings Department should be transformed into an authority comparable to the British Electricity Authority, with responsibility for all electrical development and operations in the southwestern area of the island.

Surveys

9. As an essential preliminary to other studies and to the detailed planning of water and irrigation development, a large-scale aerial topographical survey should be arranged as early as possible.

10. The work of geological survey already in progress should be intensified with the aid of an annual budget at least Rs. 500,000 larger than at present.

11. As soon as the detailed topographical survey is available as a basis it should be supplemented by full land use, soil and forest surveys, for which expert advice from outside should be called in.

12. A complete survey of available water resources, including potential sites for development of hydroelectric power, should be undertaken under the supervision of the Water Resources Planning Unit. Records of the flow of water in the principal rivers should be maintained and extended.

13. Specific engineering studies, in preparation for possible works to be undertaken towards the end of the period 1953–59 or later, should be made in the field of drainage, water supplies for Colombo suburban areas, sea water exclusion projects and further harbor development at Colombo, Galle and Kankesanturai.

14. Increased use should be made of detailed social surveys, for which further assistance might be sought from UNESCO.

15. The efforts of the Department of Census and Statistics and other agencies to improve the general statistics of the country, which are an essential basis for the rational planning of development, should be fully supported.

MONETARY AND FISCAL POLICIES

16. The policies and measures hitherto adopted by the Central Bank, in the discharge of its statutory duty of maintaining internal monetary stability, should be continued.

17. Assuming the continuation of these policies, the programming of development work over the six-year period commencing October 1, 1953, should initially envisage a total sum of Rs. 1.6 billion to be available for public capital expenditure.

18. Every effort should be continued to maximize private saving and promote its investment, directly or indirectly, in government securities.

19. The machinery of budget control should be strengthened, in order to insure that as large as possible a surplus of revenue over recurrent expenditure is available for capital investment.

MAP 4

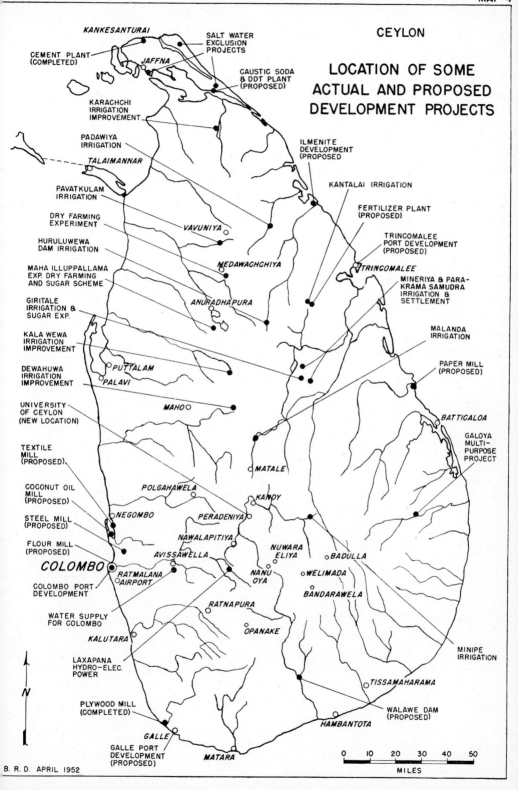

CEYLON

LOCATION OF SOME
ACTUAL AND PROPOSED
DEVELOPMENT PROJECTS

KANKESANTURAI

CEMENT PLANT
(COMPLETED)

SALT WATER
EXCLUSION
PROJECTS

JAFFNA

CAUSTIC SODA
& DDT PLANT
(PROPOSED)

KARACHCHI
IRRIGATION
IMPROVEMENT

PADAWIYA
IRRIGATION

TALAIMANNAR

ILMENITE
DEVELOPMENT
(PROPOSED

KANTALAI IRRIGATION

PAVATKULAM
IRRIGATION

DRY FARMING
EXPERIMENT

VAVUNIYA

FERTILIZER PLANT
(PROPOSED)

TRINCOMALEE
PORT DEVELOPMENT
(PROPOSED)

HURULUWEWA
DAM IRRIGATION

MEDAWACHCHIYA

TRINCOMALEE

MAHA ILLUPPALLAMA
EXP. DRY FARMING
AND SUGAR SCHEME

ANURADHAPURA

MINERIYA & PARA-
KRAMA SAMUDRA
IRRIGATION &
SETTLEMENT

GIRITALE
IRRIGATION &
SUGAR EXP.

MALANDA
IRRIGATION

KALA WEWA
IRRIGATION
IMPROVEMENT

PAPER MILL
(PROPOSED)

DEWAHUWA
IRRIGATION
IMPROVEMENT

PUTTALAM

PALAVI

MAHO

BATTICALOA

UNIVERSITY
OF CEYLON
(NEW LOCATION)

GALOYA
MULTI-
PURPOSE
PROJECT

TEXTILE
MILL
(PROPOSED)

MATALE

COCONUT OIL
MILL
(PROPOSED)

POLGAHAWELA

KANDY

STEEL MILL
(PROPOSED)

NEGOMBO

PERADENIYA

FLOUR MILL
(PROPOSED)

NAWALAPITIYA

NUWARA
ELIYA

BADULLA

COLOMBO

AVISSAWELLA

NANU
OYA

WELIMADA

RATMALANA
AIRPORT

COLOMBO PORT
DEVELOPMENT

BANDARAWELA

WATER SUPPLY
FOR COLOMBO

RATNAPURA

KALUTARA

OPANAKE

MINIPE
IRRIGATION

LAXAPANA
HYDRO-ELEC.
POWER

N

TISSAMAHARAMA

PLYWOOD MILL
(COMPLETED)

WALAWE DAM
(PROPOSED)

GALLE

HAMBANTOTA

GALLE PORT
DEVELOPMENT
(PROPOSED)

MATARA

0   10   20   30   40   50

MILES

B. R. D.   APRIL 1952

20. Income tax revenue should be increased by introducing lower exemption limits and allowances as well as higher tax rates, and by tightening the machinery of collection.

21. Additional financial responsibilities and powers of raising revenue should be delegated to local authorities, with the dual object of giving greater scope to local initiative and relieving the central government budget of some expenditure.

22. Food subsidies should be eliminated gradually over the next few years, the necessary adjustments being made in wage rates, including government salaries, and in the tax burden of the export industries.

23. Passenger fares and certain freight rates on the government railways should be raised with the object of eliminating the operating deficit.

24. Charges for electricity supplied by the Government Electrical Undertakings should be revised on a more exact calculation of costs, with the object of yielding a revenue surplus to help finance further electrical developments.

25. The Department of Agriculture, working with Cooperative and Rural Development Societies, should further increase its efforts, through education, propaganda demonstration and assistance to growers, to improve yields of rice and other food crops in existing cultivated areas. Special attention is required to methods of cultivation, greater use of transplanting of rice, use of fertilizer and more economical use of irrigation water.

26. Development and settlement of uncultivated lands in the Dry Zone are and should continue to be major objectives of policy. Existing schemes, including the Gal Oya development, should be completed and a number of new schemes commenced. Preference should be given to smaller irrigation schemes comparable to those at Minneriya, Polonnaruwa, and Kantalai rather than to further large-scale multi-purpose projects.

27. The Mission is firmly convinced that the proposed irrigation and general development in the Walawe Ganga Valley would absorb too large a proportion of the available development re-

sources for the returns expected and recommends against its being undertaken.

28. The costs of colonization on the newly irrigated lands should be reduced; possible means are a reduction in the standard or minimum allocation of land to each colonist, leaving the colonist to do rather more preliminary work for himself, and less expensive housing.

29. A more flexible policy should be pursued in the selection of colonists and the allocation of newly irrigated land and consideration should be given to the possibility of allocating a small proportion of the land in larger blocks to individuals or companies to develop on a middle-class farming or estate basis.

30. Investigation of improved methods of dry farming should be continued with the assistance of the FAO team now working in Ceylon.

Specific Development Policies

Agriculture, Irrigation and Colonization

31. In the export industries—tea, rubber and coconuts—government policies should be directed to encouraging and facilitating the maintenance of maximum efficiency—including the full maintenance of present research activities.

32. While net extension of rubber acreage is undesirable, the replanting of some of the existing acreage with higher yielding clones should be facilitated.

33. Extensive replanting of coconuts is necessary; the government should intensify its advisory and propaganda work on this, as well as give practical assistance.

34. Existing minor export crops should be further developed; one promising possibility is cacao, which could be widely interplanted with rubber.

35. Investigation of possible new crops both for local consumption and for export (as to which detailed suggestions are made in Part II) and, where favorable prospects appear, encour-

agement of their cultivation should be vigorously prosecuted by the Department of Agriculture.

36. Sugar cultivation offers sufficiently promising prospects to justify the proposed construction of a sugar mill and the development of some 6,000 acres in sugar cane. More extensive developments should await experience with this scheme.

37. Improvements in land tenure, toward greater security of title and less fragmentation of land into uneconomic plots, should be carried into effect as soon as practicable. While this complex subject requires more detailed study before a firm recommendation can be made, the Mission calls attention to the possible advantages of the Torrens system of registration.

38. To remedy the present backward state of animal husbandry, a very long-term policy, covering say 25 years, is required; a survey of existing livestock population and potential should be undertaken and special attention should be paid to the breeding of cattle and the development of milk supply.

39. In order to carry out the present soundly conceived policy of forest conservation and prudent exploitation, the staff of the Forestry Department should be strengthened, and forest education and research encouraged. Planting of teak is recommended and a modification of the present absolute ban on the removal of indigenous forest above 5,000 feet is proposed.

Power

40. Development of further hydroelectric capacity is recommended on a program of work calculated to increase public-owned capacity from 25,000 KW to 125,000 KW by 1962 and beginning with the completion of Stages IIA and IIB of the Laksapana development plan. Thermal capacity should be retained and indeed enlarged towards the end of the period to provide standby plants and to supplement hydroelectric output in dry periods.

41. Parallel to the increase of generating capacity, a main transmission grid on 132 KV basis should be completed in the southwestern area and the detailed distribution network extended.

42. The Jaffna area and Trincomalee should not at present be connected to the main grid; the former should continue to rely on the thermal plant at Kankesanturai cement plant and the latter should arrange for supplies from the station attached to the British Naval installations. Other outlying townships might be given increased supplies by transfer to them of small thermal plants rendered surplus by the extension of the hydroelectric grid in the southwest.

43. Power developed in the Gal Oya scheme should be used locally until the amounts of power needed by the main grid justify the connection of a 132 KV link.

44. Since the probable increase of hydroelectric capacity is not expected to yield power in excess of the normal growth of domestic and industrial demand before about 1960, schemes of development involving exceptionally heavy power demands should be deferred for some years at least.

Industry

45. Present industrial development policy should aim at the promotion of initially small industries which will contribute to the spread of industrial techniques and know-how as a basis for later growth, rather than at the undertaking of single large projects making heavy demands on the still restricted capital, technical and managerial resources available.

46. In the selection of industries to be promoted the prime consideration must be the prospects of commercial success. Among other criteria, it appears, always subject to exceptions, that industries deserving prima facie consideration are those which use local raw material, including wastes and by-products already available but unused; which do not require abnormal amounts of fuel, power or fresh water; and whose labor requirements involve the development of skills comparatively easy to acquire.

47. While active government sympathy and encouragement of industrial development is of the first importance, direct government management of factories should be avoided. A genuine

partnership with private enterprise should be the objective. If circumstances require the government to be the major or the only shareholder in an individual concern the management should be given the independence which is normal in commerical practice.

48. The Mission supports the projected caustic soda, DDT, ilmenite and sugar plants, subject in some cases to relocation or technical revision and in all cases to the transfer of the projects to sufficiently independent management. Government assistance to improve existing coconut oil plants is preferable to erection of a new and redundant plant. Among new suggestions for additional industrial projects the most promising is for a flour mill.

49. The proposed steel, fertilizer and paper projects should be deferred for more careful study.

50. Further investigation of the current markets for thorianite, monazite and mica is suggested.

51. Although development of fisheries is handicapped by scarcity of experienced seamen and fishermen, the government should try to expedite it by ocean research, and by continuing the various aids in marketing and other phases which are now parts of its program.

52. Encouragement of sound cottage industries should continue; but their operations should retain the true character of cottage industries, and not be transformed into uneconomical factory units.

Transport and Communications

53. Colombo Harbor developments now in progress and scheduled for completion in 1953 should be accelerated, along with the various ancillary works, to relieve port congestion. Schemes for later extension of this development should be deferred at present except for engineering studies. Meanwhile, plans should be drawn up for improved rail and road access to the port.

54. Small harbor improvements (including new equipment and facilities for handling of rice imports), should be undertaken at Galle; and commercial facilities at Trincomalee (as specified

127

in Chapter 16) should be developed so as to synchronize with the expected development of the surrounding countryside.

55. Existing programs of rehabilitation and improvement of railway track and rolling stock should be carried out, at a total cost of Rs. 125 million but this will have to be spread over more than six years.

56. Track on the Bangadeniya-Puttalam section of the railway should be relaid, the Panadura-Alutgama section should be double-tracked, and extensions built from Eravur to Amparai (serving the Gal Oya area) and between Vavuniya and Trincomalee. Whether these can all be undertaken by 1959 will depend on the availability of funds and technical staff.

57. The Kolani Valley narrow-gauge rail track (Colombo to Opanake) should be taken up; the line converted to a modern highway on which the Railway Administration should organize road transport services; and the track and equipment used in one or more of the projected industrial ventures requiring extensive local transport facilities, e.g. the sugar project and the ilmenite development.

58. Electrification of Colombo suburban rail services should be deferred until surplus power is available from future hydro-electric developments.

59. Rs. 17.5 million per year should be provided for road improvements and development over and above current maintenance. To facilitate this the Public Works Department should acquire more modern road and bridge construction plant and equipment.

60. Civil aviation ground facilities should be modernized. Ceylonese international air transport should be developed by concentrating first upon good regional and internal services, and by encouraging foreign lines to stop at Ratmalana in order to build traffic and tourist trade.

61. Improvements and extensions to the internal telecommunications system should be made on the basis of a 10- or 12-year

128

program envisaging total expenditure of Rs. 89.6 million of which about 40% may fall within the period 1953–59.

Public Health

62. The government should initiate a campaign to popularize and facilitate the planning of parenthood in order to check the rapid increase of population.

63. Preventive rather than curative work should be the primary object of public health policy. The integration of the Department of Medical and Sanitary Services already effected at headquarters should be carried through in the provincial and regional organization as well. Selection and allocation for duty of Medical Officers of Health should be reformed and the weight of emphasis in the work of the local Health Units thrown more on the preventive side. A special survey should be made of the conditions responsible for the still very high rate of mortality among children aged one to five.

64. Hospital extensions should be undertaken with a view to a 50% increase of beds within 10 years and corresponding provision made to increase hospital staffs (see recommendations 78 and 79 as to training).

65. Water supply schemes for both towns and villages should be undertaken in accordance with an island-wide master plan to be drawn up.

66. To coordinate the work of various agencies concerned with housing a Housing Commissioner should be appointed under the Ministry of Local Government and additional funds should be provided for assistance to housing construction.

67. Close attention to malaria should be continued, to consolidate the great advances made; among other diseases tuberculosis should now be regarded as Public Health Enemy No. 1 and all energies, public and private, united in fighting it.

68. Intensive educational work using all media of publicity, should be undertaken in the importance of a well-balanced diet; and special efforts made in conjunction with the Agricultural

129

Department to increase the availability of milk and other animal proteins.

EDUCATION AND TECHNICAL ASSISTANCE

69. Present plans for expansion of practical work in primary and secondary schools and for the modernization of teaching methods and objectives, aiming at the development of reasoning power rather than of memorized facts, should be pushed vigorously. This will involve special teacher training, including some overseas training, as well as expenditure on equipment and possibly revision of salary scales.

70. Additional vocational training institutes similar to that at Ratmalana should be established, with adequate provision for their equipment with tools and plant.

71. The planned development of the University of Ceylon should be continued, with special attention to the expansion of the departments of engineering and agriculture.

72. Outside specialists will be required on a long-term basis in the Agriculture Department, Irrigation Department, Electrical Undertakings Department and the proposed Economic Planning Secretariat, Development Corporation, Institute for Applied Research and Water Resources Planning Unit.

73. The help and advice of international and national technical assistance organizations should be sought in connection with recommendation 72 and other needs for expert assistance on a long- or short-term basis. In order to avoid duplication, to select the most appropriate agency in each case and to secure the most accurate definition of requirements, all requests to such outside agencies should be channelled through the economic planning secretariat.

74. More extended use of outside contractors should be made by the Public Works Department and Irrigation Department both in planning and executing works, so as to relieve pressure on the departments' own limited staffs and to increase facilities for training through contact with outside specialists.

75. More men should be sent overseas for engineering training. Simultaneously, extended provision should be made for local
training of engineers.

76. A second Medical School should be established as soon
as possible, so as to double the annual output of doctors not later
than 1960.

77. Comparable increases should be made in the training of
dentists, nurses, midwives and other medical personnel.

78. Physical and human facilities of teachers' training colleges should be enlarged to provide for the graduation of 2,300
trained teachers per year; this will require about a 25% addition
to buildings and equipment and about 50% more staff.

PART TWO

Selected Fields of Development

8. Foreign Trade and Commercial Policy

THE STRUCTURE OF CEYLON'S TRADE

Summary

Ceylon's foreign trade pattern is relatively simple. Exports of tea, rubber and coconut products provide nearly all of the island's export earnings, while two thirds or more of imports consist of grains, textiles and other essential consumer goods. Over the past quarter century Ceylon has maintained a consistent export surplus with the exception of only two abnormal years. Its trade surpluses, earned primarily with the U. K. and the dollar area, more than offset deficits arising largely in trade with India, Burma and the Middle East.

Marked short-run fluctuations in rubber export earnings—and to a lesser extent in receipts from coconut products—create a considerable element of year-to-year instability in Ceylon's export position. The extent of such swings is kept within limits, however, by the comparatively steady price and volume of the predominant tea exports. Furthermore, because such a large share of Ceylon's national income is contributed directly or indirectly by the export trade, a fairly stable trade balance is automatically maintained through movements in income (and therefore in import demand) which tend to follow the course of export earnings.

Nevertheless, long-term trends have been gradually narrowing the favorable margin between the real value of exports and imports. Growth of imports, especially in consumer goods, has corresponded fairly closely with the rate of population growth. Export volume has risen too, over the past 20 years, but somewhat behind the long-term trend in imports. Price relationships between exports and imports have also been less favorable to Ceylon in the

135

postwar period. The major adverse price movements have been the lag in the price of rubber behind general world price trends and the high postwar price of rice. While the export boom of 1950 and early 1951 brought an improvement in Ceylon's terms of trade, the favorable position proved only temporary, and by late 1951 export-import price relationships had again moved against Ceylon.

Exports

Tea is by far the most important of Ceylon's exports; it usually accounts for well over 50% of total export value. Rubber and coconut products, including coconut oil, copra, desiccated coconut, fresh coconuts and coir fiber, have each provided about 15 to 20% of export receipts in postwar years. Among minor exports the most important are cinnamon, cinnamon oil, citronella oil, cacao, plumbago (graphite) and arecanuts.

Over the past decade the value of Ceylon's exports has increased from the prewar level of around Rs. 300 million to more than Rs. 1,000 million in 1948 and 1949, Rs. 1,560 million in 1950, and to Rs. 1,900 million in 1951. The gain reflects not only price increases but also a larger volume. In the past three years the volume of tea exports has been around 25% above prewar levels, while rubber shipments have run about 50% greater. Exports of coconut products, expressed in nut equivalents, have dropped in volume about 15% below the prewar figure partly because of increased home consumption, partly because of the advanced age and declining yield of a large proportion of coconut palms. But this has been somewhat compensated by a continuous shift in the nature of coconut exports toward the higher unit-value form of coconut oil.

The general average of Ceylon's export prices has followed a postwar course fairly similar to that of world primary commodity prices. Individually, however, the price patterns of her principal products have shown marked divergencies from the composite picture. Tea prices maintain a reasonable degree of year-to-year stability, with a postwar trend approximately in line with world price movements. Rubber and coconut product prices are much more volatile and, especially in the case of rubber, are subject to strong short term fluctuations. After the war the price of rubber lagged far behind general world price trends until 1950; then it soared rapidly and by early 1951 was more than five times higher than the 1949 level. Postwar prices of coconut oil and copra have been consistently high in relation to most other primary products. They too advanced sharply in the boom conditions of 1950 and early 1951, but the increase was far less than in the case of rubber. All of the principal export prices have sagged since the spring of 1951; by April 1952, rubber, tea and coconut products had dropped back to about their pre-Korea price position.

Imports

Much of Ceylon's imports are consumer goods, which represented about 65% of the total value of imports before the war and around 70% in the past few years. As seen in Table I the bulk of these consumer items is made up of rice, flour, other foods and drink, textiles and clothing.

TABLE I
SELECTED IMPORTS: PERCENT OF TOTAL IMPORTS

	1938-39	1949	1950	1951
Rice	24.0	23.0	23.8	15.2
Other Grains and Flour	3.0	8.9	9.0	9.8
Other Foodstuffs	17.0	17.3	17.1	19.2
Textiles and Clothing	11.5	14.8	16.1	14.4
Raw Materials	14.4	10.7	10.2	10.5
Other Manufactures	28.5	24.1	22.6	30.7

Source: *Statistical Abstract of Ceylon*, 1950; *Monthly Customs Statistics*, December 1950, 1951.

Compared with prewar there has been a rise in the relative position of foodstuffs and textiles, some shift in grain imports from rice to flour and other grains, and a small decline in the percentage of imports which are raw materials. The importance of "other manufactures" also declined until 1951 when there was a sharp increase, largely in capital goods.

Since the late thirties but excluding the war years, the rise in volume of consumer goods imports has corresponded closely with the growth of Ceylon's population. Expressed in constant prices, per capita imports of consumption items have been maintained at a fairly uniform level, except for a decline during the war, in spite of a 25% increase in population since 1938. With no really substantial increase in domestic production of consumer goods, maintenance of this per capita rate tends to create a rising floor under import requirements.

Balance of Trade

In spite of the fluctuating character of export earnings and the great dependence on imports for essential consumer goods, Ceylon has maintained a steady export surplus. Her only trade deficits in the past 25 years occurred in 1932 at the depth of the depression, and in 1947 when there was heavy restocking following wartime restrictions. While the average volume of imports in 1948-50 was about a third larger than in 1926-30, a steady, though somewhat smaller, rate of growth in the volume of exports has been sufficient to sustain the trade surplus. In these past two decades the growth in rubber export volume has more than kept pace with the rise in import volume, but the rate of increase in tea shipments has been smaller than that of imports, while the quantity of coconut exports has declined. The value of Ceylon's imports and exports and the indices of volume during the last two decades are shown in Table II.

TABLE II
FOREIGN TRADE

| | Imports | | Exports | | |
Year	Value (m.Rs.)	Volume Index (1934-38=100)	Value (m.Rs.)	Volume Index (1934-38=100)	Trade Balance (m.Rs.)
1926-1930 av.	381	91	435	105	+ 54
1931	218	84	233	106	+ 15
1932	196	84	189	102	— 7
1933	177	81	200	99	+ 23
1934	217	95	264	109	+ 47
1935	228	94	253	94	+ 25
1936	214	96	268	92	+ 54
1937	243	104	332	102	+ 89
1938	236	98	285	103	+ 49
1939	242	103	328	103	+ 86
1940	283	103	387	113	+104
1941	287	93	424	111	+137
1942	296	65	531	127	+235
1943	447	69	570	124	+123
1944	518	67	680	124	+162
1945	621	78	666	111	+ 45
1946	696	87	765	127	+ 69
1947	963	108	889	118	— 74
1948	994	110	1011	129	+ 17
1949	1029	119	1063	128	+ 34
1950	1167	133	1563	142	+396
1951	1559	149	1904	144	+345

Source: Ministry of Finance, *Economic and Social Development of Ceylon, 1926-1950*, July 1951; *Ceylon Customs Returns*, Dec. 1951; Central Bank of Ceylon, *Bulletin*, February 1952.

Terms of Trade

During World War II there was a severe deterioration in Ceylon's terms of trade. According to official statistics import prices rose threefold between 1940 and 1946, while the rise in export prices was only about 90%. Thus the terms of trade turned adverse in this period, declining from 100 to 63. Although some overstatement of the rise in import prices in the official index exaggerates the deterioration, nevertheless it is clear that Ceylon's exports had a lower import purchasing power per unit after the war than in the prewar period. Even with a relative rise in export prices during 1946-49, the terms of trade remained below prewar by 20 to 25% on the average. Chiefly responsible for this adverse movement was, on the export side, the lag in rubber prices behind general world price trends; on the import side the main cause was a six fold jump in the price of rice.

The world-wide raw material price boom of the last half of 1950 and early 1951 carried the terms of trade for a brief period to the most favorable level in two decades. Since April 1951, however, sagging export prices plus firm or rising import prices have again reduced the purchasing power of exports below the prewar position. Terms of trade data for the past few years are shown in Table III.

TABLE III
Price Indices and Terms of Trade
(1934-38=100)

Year	A Export Price Index	B Import Price Index [1]	C A/B
1946	226	316	71
1947	300	370	81
1948	305	398	77
1949	324	371	87
1950	439	395	111
1951 (Dec.)	473	541	87

[1] Approximate. Involves a rough adjustment of the official import price index to allow for what appears to be an overstatement of import price increases compared with the base period.

Source: Central Bank of Ceylon, *Annual Report*, 1951.

140

Direction of Trade

More than half of Ceylon's import and export trade is with Commonwealth countries and British possessions. The United Kingdom is the largest single trading partner, accounting for about a third of total exports and about 20% of imports. Other principal countries of export destination are the United States, Australia, Egypt, Canada, Germany, South Africa and Italy. The principal sources of imports, other than the United Kingdom, are Burma, India, Australia, the United States and Japan.

With few exceptions, the recent directional pattern of trade remains about the same as before the war. The most notable change has been a drop in the percentage of exports going to the United Kingdom, from about half the total in 1938 and 1939 to about a third in the late 1940's. This is largely the result of a sharp reduction in the proportion of Ceylon tea shipped to the United Kingdom and an increase in tea exports to the United States and to Canada, Australia and other Commonwealth countries. On the import side the principal change has been some growth in the proportion of goods from Australia and the United States and smaller increases from Japan, Indonesia, India and Pakistan.

In the postwar years Ceylon has maintained a consistent trade surplus with the United Kingdom, with other countries of western Europe and also, except in 1947, with the dollar area. Its principal deficits have been incurred with India, which is the source of a wide variety of imports of which textiles are most important; with Burma as the principal source of rice imports; with Iran as the main supplier (until recently) of petroleum products; and with Japan whose cloth and other products have spread rapidly in the Ceylon market during the past two years.

The dollar surplus (Table IV) is maintained by shipments of about 20% of total tea exports and around half of rubber exports to the United States and Canada. Since the war dollar exports have averaged more than twice the value of dollar imports. In spite of potential weaknesses in the dollar rubber market, there

141

seems little doubt of Ceylon's continued ability to maintain a net surplus position with the dollar area.

TABLE IV

TRADE WITH THE U.S. AND CANADA [1]

(million rupees)

	Exports			Imports			Balance		
	U. S.	Canada	Total	U. S.	Canada	Total	U. S.	Canada	Total
1939	60.3	11.8	72.1	5.1	.6	5.7	+ 55.2	+11.2	+ 66.4
1947	119.4	56.6	176.0	112.4	66.9	179.3	+ 7.0	+10.2	+ 3.3
1948	165.3	40.0	205.3	75.4	8.2	83.6	+ 89.9	+31.8	+121.7
1949	114.6	44.0	158.6	73.0	10.7	83.7	+ 41.6	+33.3	+ 74.9
1950	332.7	93.5	426.2	34.8	20.8	55.6	+297.9	+72.7	+370.6
1951	198.2	73.3	271.5	82.7	17.2	99.9	+115.5	+56.1	+171.6

[1] The U.S. and Canada represent about 95% of Ceylon's dollar trade.

Source: *Statistical Abstract of Ceylon*, 1950; Ceylon Customs Returns, December 1951.

BALANCE OF PAYMENTS

On international transactions other than merchandise account Ceylon normally runs a substantial net deficit. The major invisible payments items on current account are for transfer of income on foreign investments and for personal remittances, the latter mainly to India. Principal invisible receipts are for services furnished to foreign shipping by the Port of Colombo.

Generally, the balance of payments pattern in the past has exhibited a trade surplus about sufficient to cover the invisible deficit. Such over-all current deficits as have been incurred have been small, excluding a very few exceptional years.

The figures of Table V summarize the net position on current account in 1938 and during recent years. It will be noted that the large jump in export earnings in 1950-51 has given Ceylon a substantial over-all current surplus.

TABLE V

NET BALANCE OF PAYMENTS POSITION ON CURRENT ACCOUNT,
1938 AND 1947-1951

(*million rupees*)

	1938	1947	1948	1949	1950	1951[1]
Merchandise [2]	+38	—118	+44	—16	+231	+253
Invisibles:						
Transportation	+19	+ 38	+53	+51	+ 29	+ 35
Investment income	—47	— 68	—49	—29	— 55	— 65
Private remittances	—24	— 25	—68	—58	— 69	— 76
Other	—14	— 7	+44	+22	+ 1	— 30
Total invisibles	—66	— 62	—20	—14	— 94	—136
Net Balance	—28	—180	+24	—30	+137	+117

[1] Preliminary

[2] Merchandise credits which are published on a c.i.f. basis have been converted to an f.o.b. basis by deducting the figure for transportation debits.

Source: *Statistical Abstract of Ceylon,* 1950; Central Bank of Ceylon, *Annual Report,* 1951.

Long-term capital movements were generally inward until the past few years, when there was a reversal representing withdrawal of foreign capital from Ceylon. In the latter half of 1948 the recorded net outward capital transfers amounted to about Rs. 16 million in 1949, Rs. 22 million in 1950 and Rs. 38 million in Ceylon amounted to about Rs. 29 million, in 1950 to about Rs. 48 million and in 1951 to about Rs. 67 million. These were gross movements; the net outflow of private capital amounted to Rs. 22 million in 1949, Rs. 22 million in 1950 and Rs. 38 million in 1951. As yet the rate of capital withdrawals has not been large. Repatriation of foreign capital on a major scale is a potential danger for the future rather than a present reality.

From the end of World War II through mid-1951, Ceylon's net dollar receipts amounted to about $138 million (Rs. 658 million). Almost two thirds of these receipts were earned during 1950 and

143

the first half of 1951. The recent balance of dollar payments was as shown in Table VI.

TABLE VI

CEYLON'S NET BALANCE OF DOLLAR PAYMENTS ON CURRENT ACCOUNT, 1949-51

(million rupees)

	1949	1950	1951[1]
Merchandise	+78	+320	+157
Current Invisibles	—12	— 23	— 16
Total	+66	+297	+141

[1] Preliminary.

Source: 1949—International Monetary Fund, *Balance of Payments Year-book,* Vol. 3, 1951. 1950-51—Central Bank of Ceylon.

External Assets

As a result of large trade surpluses during the war, Ceylon accumulated external assets—mostly in sterling—which by the end of 1945 amounted to Rs. 1,260 million. Balance of payments deficits reduced the figure to Rs. 934 million by the end of 1949. With the export boom in the latter part of 1950 and the first part of 1951, external assets again jumped to Rs. 1,187 million at the end of June 1951 (Table VII). They were still at this level at the end of December 1951.

Part of these assets represent investments of sinking funds abroad and the outstanding principal due to Ceylon from the United Kingdom on a loan of Rs. 100 million extended to the United Kingdom during the war. The remainder in Ceylon's No. 1 and No. 2 sterling accounts and in short term U. S. dollars, Indian rupees, and other currencies amounted on June 30, 1951 to about Rs. 978 million.

Some of the sinking funds shown in Table VII are held against internal obligations payable in Ceylon rupees. They might, therefore, be included as available external reserves, bringing the total at the beginning of 1952 to about Rs. 1,000 million. While this

TABLE VII

EXTERNAL ASSETS, JUNE 30, 1951

(*million rupees*)

Sinking Funds	142.0
World War II Loan	67.9
Liquid External Assets	977.5
Total External Assets	1,187.4

Source: Central Bank of Ceylon.

total includes blocked sterling balances, Ceylon and the United Kingdom have agreed upon the transfer of these to the unblocked account over the seven years ending on July 30, 1957.

COMMERCIAL POLICY

In preceding pages we have considered Ceylon's trade and balance of payments without reference to the framework of commercial policy within which they operate. Until the outbreak of World War II this might have been summarized rather simply as one of moderate protection, with participation in imperial preference. Although there have been modifications since then, the basic outlines remain the same.

The Tariff

Today, Ceylon has a fairly elaborate list of dutiable imports. As of August 1951, it comprised 1,910 distinct items. All but 109 of these were subject to ad valorem rather than specific duties. By the crude measure of actual count of ad valorem rates, 407 duties were 20% or less, being primarily for revenue purposes. Another 280 items carried moderate protection, with duties from 21 to 40%. Those subject to fairly heavy protection, with duties from over 40% up to a maximum of 100%, totalled 114 items. But many of these duties could hardly be called protective, since they were levied on luxuries and liquors. Among the more im-

145

portant commodities subject to substantial protection were rubber and coir manufactures, baskets and mats, wooden furniture, matches and certain types of paper manufactures.

In addition to import duties which afford both revenue and protection, Ceylon has for many years imposed export duties on her three principal products, as well as on paper, cardamoms and citronella oil. Originally these were fixed in amount, but in September and October of 1951 a sliding scale replaced the fixed duties on rubber and tea, and in December a similar tax was applied to coconut products.

Since the war, import and export duties together have supplied about 60% of Ceylon's government revenue, in approximately equal proportions. (See Table XIV, Chapter 9.)

Exchange Control

Until the outbreak of World War II, such control as was exercised over foreign trade was limited to import and export duties, with preferential treatment of certain empire products. In September and October of 1939, various Acts of the United Kingdom Parliament introduced restrictions on foreign exchange which became effective in Ceylon by proclamation of the Governor. These applied only to non-sterling area transactions. They required the surrender to the Controller of Exchange of holdings and earnings in specified non-sterling currencies, after which such foreign currencies would be released for international payments only by his authorization. In effect all foreign resources of the sterling area were pooled, and all needs of members were met out of this common pool on agreed principles. The control aimed to minimize foreign expenditures and to conserve scarce cargo space. Surrender of foreign exchange was enforced by a system of export licenses, which has remained in operation without fundamental change ever since.

Through the Sterling Assets Agreement of May 18, 1948 with the United Kingdom, the use of accumulated sterling balances was regulated, an agreed limit of £ 3.5 million being set for the remainder of 1948. Such a sum, plus £ 4 million for a working balance, was credited to Ceylon's No. 1 sterling account, in which all current receipts were also to be deposited. The remainder of Ceylon's sterling assets were blocked in her No. 2 account. In order to limit drawings as agreed, exchange control was extended to transactions within the sterling area. The regulations by which control was enforced embodied the usual provisions, such as restriction of dealings in foreign exchange to authorized dealers, prohibition of the export of currency, gold and securities, and of any other transfer of payments or creation of debts outside Ceylon.

During the first six months of 1949, an additional £ 1.75 million was released from the No. 2 to the No. 1 account, and in the following year a further £ 7 million. Because of the crisis which led to sterling devaluation in September 1949—a step in which Ceylon participated by devaluing the rupee by 30.52%—Ceylon agreed to cut dollar imports by 25% in common with other members of the sterling area.

Upon its establishment in late August 1950, the Central Bank took over exchange control, but without any change in policy. Exchange control regulations originally enacted under United Kingdom legislation have been continued in temporary operation by Act of the Ceylon Parliament, pending new permanent legislation.

In actual administration of the controls, the authorities imposed a fairly rigorous restriction on personal remittances and remittances for travel; this was especially true during 1948 and 1949, when the balance of payments was rather tight. In 1950, because of improved prices for Ceylon's exports, the pressure was eased and allocations were somewhat more liberal. Control over the exchange available for imports was exercised through a modified system of licensing.

Control of Imports and Exports

Ceylon established quantitative control over foreign trade simultaneously with exchange control, and promptly merged the

147

administration of both in a common office. This merger continued until April 1947, when the Controller of Imports and Exports became a separate office.

The control first restricted imports only from non-Empire sources; licenses were issued for such goods quarterly, on the basis of the quantity brought in by each importer during the base period January 1, 1937 to June 30, 1939. As the war intensified and shipping space became scarcer, control was extended to imports from all sources. Export licenses began to be used restrictively, to keep strategic raw materials from getting into enemy hands. These policies continued until the war ended.

During the ensuing two and a half years the authorities relaxed the restrictions on trade rapidly, substituting open general licenses for individual licenses from specific sources and granting applications with comparative liberality. This proved to have gone too far in 1947, when the balance of payments became seriously adverse. This fact, together with the implications of the sterling assets agreement, led to a tightening of restrictions in the following year. The cabinet imposed an over-all ceiling of Rs. 850 million on imports and limited dollar imports to Rs. 100 million. To enforce these limits some non-essential imports were prohibited altogether, individual licensing was reintroduced and dollar imports were held to the minimum. At this time heavy import duties were imposed on luxuries, and even on some essentials. An improvement in the balance of payments permitted an upward revision of the import ceiling to Rs. 1,031 million in September.

Again in the first six months of 1949, an adverse balance of trade of Rs. 75 million led the government to set a low ceiling on the next year's imports, but the unpredicted rise in export prices made its enforcement unnecessary. Sterling area and "soft currency" imports were eased by the decontrol of many foods and building materials and by more liberal treatment of licensed goods. Restriction of dollar imports to the minimum by more restrictive licensing became obligatory, however, by the agreement of the Commonwealth Finance Ministers to cut this source of foreign exchange drain by 25%. At the beginning of 1952 the government was considering whether it would be necessary to tighten its import controls once more—this time because of the generally weakened sterling area position and Ceylon's own declining dollar earnings.

It was in 1949 that the government took the first steps toward a new policy of "Ceylonization" of trade, aimed to divert more of the island's trade into the hands of Ceylonese. At the end of March, citizen-traders were invited to register as Ceylonese newcomers. Over 2,000 responded. The control authorities followed this up by issuing them licenses to import certain consumer goods.

With the continued rise in export prices and concomitant improvement in the balance of payments, it became possible to decontrol a long list of imports from sterling and other easy currency areas. These consisted mainly of foods, building materials, and some consumer items. For goods still licensed, liberal ceilings were fixed; a percentage was reserved for Ceylonese newcomers, while larger quotas were given to established importers. In addition, both groups had reserved to them numerous consumer imports from Japan, Germany, and other sources. By the end of 1950, some 1,208 Ceylonese registered importers had reserved to them approximately 60% of licensed trade with non-dollar sources. In late 1951 the policy of Ceylonization was extended further, when all imports from Germany and Japan were allocated to Ceylonese traders.

Export licensing has continued, except for exports by official agencies and a short list of commodities going to Empire destinations. At the war's end the system ceased to be applied in a restrictive manner, but it has since been used at various times to assist traders and producers to get a "fair price"—notably for cocoa, cinnamon and coir fiber.

Industrial Products Act

Included under the head of import control is an unusual piece of legislation dating from May, 1949. This is the Industrial Products Act, which aims "to facilitate the sale of the industrial products of Ceylon by regulating the importation of industrial commodities from abroad." It does so by naming "regulated products", whose importation thereupon becomes subject to license by the Controller of Industrial Products. Such license can be obtained only by undertaking to purchase local products, supposedly of similar character, in a specified ratio to the imported quantities.

The law was applied during 1951 to four categories of products. Rolled steel sections must now be purchased locally in the ratio of one local unit to five of imports (for a time the ratio was one to three). Importers of towels must buy five domestic towels for each one imported. An identical ratio applies to rubber footwear while for each glass tumbler bought locally, three may be imported.

The most significant effect of this law has been to raise the resale price of imported articles, especially in the case of rolled steel and glass tumblers. The only domestic rolled steel available is the stock remaining from the earlier operation of a government mill. It is so poor in quality that no purchaser can use it; hence he merely adds its cost to that of the imported article. Glass tumblers, also the product of a government factory (a private producer in the island finds the legislation of no benefit), are similarly of poor quality and can seldom be resold. Hence their price, too, is added to that of imports. Domestic towels come from small cottage producers. They are not as uniform in quality as the imported article, but are saleable. As for rubber footwear, the law benefits one relatively high-cost local plant, but is not needed by another competitor.

By introducing an element of compulsion into trading, this legislation is even less satisfactory than excessive straightforward protection. It creates waste, and seeks to perpetuate uneconomical activities which contribute little to national development. It sets a premium on inefficiency, and tends to raise the cost of living. The Mission recommends that the Industrial Products Act be repealed, that the remaining stock of rolled steel be sold for scrap, that the obsolete government glass factory be abandoned, and that encouragement to the handicraft production of towels be in the form of technical assistance to improve production methods and quality with perhaps some assurance of a market through purchases for government use.

9. Money, Banking and Public Finance

Background

Since the end of the war, besides going through the transition to peacetime conditions, the economy of Ceylon has been greatly influenced by two important events. The first was the announcement by the government of the "Six Year Plan" in 1947, and the second was the establishment of a Central Bank in 1950.

The Six Year Plan changed the budgetary pattern from an approximately balanced position to one of substantial deficits, financed partly from borrowing and partly from reserves built up during the war. No inflationary creation of credit was involved and an exceptional inflow of foreign exchange in the last two years has largely restored the exchange reserves; but internal prices have risen sharply as a result of the shortage of imported goods in the early postwar period and in sympathy with the recent rise in international prices.

Prior to the establishment of the Central Bank, the rupee was on an exchange standard operated by the Board of Commissioners of Currency. Under the new monetary system the rupee is now defined in terms of gold, with a par value fixed at 2.88 grains of fine gold and an official exchange rate equivalent to one Indian rupee. The new currency is operated by the Central Bank, created by the Monetary Law Act of 1949. The task of the Bank, as defined in this Act, comprises: the stabilization of domestic monetary values; the preservation of the par value and the free use of the rupee for current international transactions; the promotion and maintenance of a high level of production, employment and real

152

income; and the encouragement and promotion of the full development of productive resources.

To achieve these objectives, the Bank was given wide powers to control the banking system and to regulate the supply of money. In addition to the traditional means of control—such as discount rates, minimum reserve requirements and open market operations —a series of new techniques enable it to use quantitative as well as qualitative or selective methods in implementing its monetary policies.

Equipped with all the modern weapons of a strong monetary authority, the Bank established itself as a leader and controller of the banks. These, though their liquidity position was very strong, immediately realized the necessity and advantage of acting in line with general policies directed toward preserving the country's monetary equilibrium.

In its relations with the government, the Bank enjoys a considerable measure of autonomy, enabling the Board and the Governor to work in close and unconstrained cooperation with government offices. Advances to be made by the Bank to the government are restricted to legitimate short-term needs of the Treasury, and the government is required by the law to consult the Bank before floating new loans in the market.

As a financial adviser to the government, the Bank is in a position of influential aid in bringing about a close coordination of fiscal policies with monetary and general economic considerations. It is the duty of the Central Bank to keep a watchful eye on the country's economic health, to take appropriate remedial measures in its own field whenever they are needed, and to recommend corresponding measures by the government in the field of fiscal policies. In the event of a conflict of opinion, the law requires the Minister of Finance and the Bank to negotiate for an understanding and, if they are unable to reach an agreement, the government has to assume full responsibility for the adoption of its own views by the Bank.

Though an institution of recent origin, the Bank has rapidly acquired high prestige and influence, and its establishment has opened a new chapter in Ceylon's monetary history.

Money Supply

Ceylon emerged from the war with a money supply more than five and a half times greater at the end of 1945 than at the end of 1939, and with a price level twice the prewar. The cost-of-living index was held down by price and wage controls and by a system of food subsidies, still in existence and considerably extended since the end of the war. Moreover, the Treasury converted budget surpluses and proceeds of war loans into foreign assets, and the banks continued to hold a considerable part of their funds abroad. This sterilized, in the form of exchange reserves, a substantial proportion of inflated incomes derived from record exports and Allied military expenditures. At the end of 1939, the money supply had amounted to Rs. 129.7 million and exchange reserves totalled Rs. 275.1 million; whereas at the end of 1945, the money supply stood at Rs. 729.4 million and exchange reserves totalled 1,259.9 million. [1]

Changes in the supply of money [2] and its components in the post-war period are shown in Table I.

Changes in the money supply during the postwar years show three distinct phases: in 1946 and 1947, a substantial decrease occurred both in currency circulation and demand deposits; in the following two years currency circulation remained fairly stable, whereas demand deposits showed a marked increase; during the third period, covering 1950 and 1951, demand deposits continued to rise sharply and the supply of currency expanded at about the same rate. An analysis of the factors responsible for these changes is given in Table II.

---

[1] This includes war loans of Rs. 102.1 million re-lent to the United Kingdom.

[2] Defined in the Monetary Law Act of 1949 to include currency and demand deposits exclusive of those held by commercial banks or the government.

TABLE I

MONEY SUPPLY

(*million rupees*)

Period Ended	Currency Circulation	Demand Deposits	Money Supply	Ratio of Currency to Money Supply
1945	330.4	399.0	729.4	45.2%
1946	274.7	392.1	660.8	41.2%
1947	238.1	324.4	562.5	42.3%
1948	241.1	365.7	606.8	39.7%
1949	243.9	395.1	639.0	38.1%
1949*	243.9	405.5	649.4	37.6%
1950	325.5	585.3	910.8	35.7%
1951	377.3	628.8	1,006.1	37.5%

* Change in series.

Source: Earlier data from *Statistical Abstract of Ceylon,* 1950; later data from Central Bank of Ceylon, *Annual Report,* 1951.

It is immediately obvious that, throughout the three periods, changes in foreign balances represented the largest of the factors determining the supply of money. In the first period, extension of credit to the government and to private enterprise was overcompensated by a very large outflow of exchange and other contractive factors. Lending to the government continued to be a small factor throughout the second and the third periods. The expansion in lending to private enterprise was small in the second period; but, subsequently, rapidly rising export prices sharply increased the demand for new credit.

Changes in the foreign exchange held by the monetary authority and the commercial banks do not correspond as closely to changes in the balance of payments as one might expect. Neither do variations in the Treasury's cash balances check with changes in the government's financial position. Both these statistical discrep-

TABLE II

CHANGES IN MONEY SUPPLY BY SOURCES

(*million rupees*)

Factors Having an Expansive (+), or Contractive (−) Influence on the Money Supply	1946-47	1948-49	1950-51
Exchange Balances Held by the Currency Board (or Central Bank) and Commercial Banks	−168.1	+58.1	+223.8
Commercial Banks			
Credit to private enterprise	+ 69.6	+11.2	+116.3
Time and savings deposits plus balance of other liabilities and other assets	− 3.0	− 0.4	− 38.6
Government securities and Treasury bills held in portfolio	+ 22.9	+28.1	+ 31.2
Central Bank, Net Domestic Assets	—	—	+ 0.5
Changes in Government Cash Balances; Increase (−)	− 81.8	−19.6	+ 32.4
Adjustments (for untraceable items in 1946-47 and 1948-49, and for transit items in 1950-51)	− 6.5	− 0.9	− 8.8
Total	*−166.9*	*+76.5*	*+356.8*
Changes in money supply	−166.9	+76.5	+356.8

Source: *Statistical Abstract of Ceylon,* 1950; Central Bank of Ceylon, *Annual Report,* 1951.

ancies are explained by the fact that the government, itself, held large external assets at the end of the war, and has used much of those assets, either directly or after conversion into rupees, to cover budget deficits and extra-budgetary outlays.

Changes in prices and wages, as compared with changes in the supply of money, are shown in Table III.

TABLE III

CHANGES IN MONEY SUPPLY, PRICES AND WAGES

| | Percentage Changes | | |
	1946-47	1948-49	1950-51
Money Supply	—22.9	+13.6	+54.9
Cost of Living Indices:			
Colombo working class	+14.0	+ 2.4	+11.6
Estate workers	+ 7.6	+10.5	+12.1
Estate Workers Wages Index:			
Nominal wages	+20.0	+ 9.2	+44.4
Real wages	+10.9	— 0.9	+28.9

Source: Central Bank of Ceylon, *Bulletin*, Feb. 1952.

Although the money supply contracted considerably during the first two postwar years, the excess purchasing power carried over from the war continued to force prices upward. In the following two periods, prices rose considerably less than the money supply expanded, because food subsidies continued to moderate the increase in food prices.

Wages of estate workers rose more rapidly than prices, and the trend of the real-wages index suggests that wage-earners in the plantation sector improved their income considerably; there were two successive upward revisions of rates—after devaluation and again in December 1950. Though there is no reliable index showing the position of other categories of workers, wage rates in various trades indicate that a general improvement in real wages occurred during the last years.

Operations of the Central Bank began in August 1950, at a time when the inflationary pressure resulting from high export earnings was growing rapidly.

157

In order to counter the effect of a large exchange inflow on domestic prices, the Central Bank enjoined private banks to refrain from financing nonessential or speculative transactions and to reduce the conversion of exchange receipts to a strict minimum compatible with their business. Moreover, the Bank decided to raise the minimum reserve requirements against demand deposits from 10% to 14%. These measures helped to reduce the impact of a booming world market on internal prices. The money supply, after steadily increasing from 1948 to about Rs. 1,000 million in February 1951, fluctuated around this level in the first nine months of the year; cost-of-living indices registered a decline of five index points during the period March to September 1951.

As the inflow of exchange is no longer exerting pressure on the country's monetary equilibrium, the Central Bank is now confronted with a new situation, where the most important factor determining the supply of money rests in the government's fiscal policy. If budget estimates of a sizeable over-all deficit are realized, the government's cash balances—which stood at Rs. 168 million at the end of September 1951—will decline and lead to a renewed expansion in the money supply, followed by an increase in prices.

The Banking System

Ceylon's banking system comprises a set of commercial banks, a number of long-term finance institutions and two savings banks.

Commercial Banks. The foundations of Ceylon's commercial banking system were laid around the middle of the last century, when British and Indian exchange banks began to establish branches in Ceylon. Of the major foreign-owned commercial banks operating in the country, six are incorporated in the United Kingdom and three in India. Their activity is concentrated almost exclusively on financing the country's export and import trade.

The only indigenous commercial bank is the Bank of Ceylon, established by the government in 1939. Its growth was greatly fostered by the rapid expansion of the country's exports during the war; in 1951, the assets of the new bank represented about one third of all commercial banking assets. Though the Bank of Ceylon is doing the same kind of banking as the British and Indian banks, its position is somewhat different; some of its funds, especially those obtained from the government, can be utilized to finance transactions which would be considered unsuitable for the traditional type of exchange banking.

The consolidated balance sheet of the commercial banks is presented in Annex A. Its main items are summarized in Table IV.

It will be seen that the volume of bank credit to private enterprise is small in comparison with the volume of deposits. The gap, between the large amount of money held in bank accounts and the comparatively low demand for credit, suggests that private enterprise is operating to a large extent on a self-financing basis. On the other hand, the wide use of the overdraft and foreign bills, or trade acceptances, is an indication that the banks are concentrating primarily on short-term operations. Loans play a subordinate role, and about two thirds of the total amount of loans were held by the Bank of Ceylon. Though the banks are generally reluctant to make long-term loans, they hold a sizeable amount of government securities. These, in fact, represent about 38% of the outstanding amount of government loans floated in the domestic market. Thus in addition to financing the country's foreign trade, the commercial banks provide a large source of funds for investment by the government.

In spite of a comparatively large portfolio of government securities, the liquidity position of the commercial banks is very strong. Though the ratio of cash resources declined during the last few years, at the end of September 1951 all banks held reserves of 52% against their demand deposits and 47% against their total deposits. An ultimate explanation of the high liquidity lies in the fact that business in Ceylon depends so largely on the fate of a few export crops. Sharp fluctuations in the world market during a single generation created an atmosphere of insecurity,

159

TABLE IV

SELECTED BALANCE SHEET ITEMS OF COMMERCIAL BANKS
(*million rupees*)

	End of Period		
	1949	1950	1951
Demand Deposits (excluding interbank deposits)	558.7	719.7	717.1
Time and Savings Deposits	66.7	77.1	91.1
Total Deposits	*625.4*	*796.8*	*808.1*
Credit to Private Enterprise:			
Foreign bills	29.9	52.6	72.0
Local bills	0.3	0.2	0.9
Overdrafts	75.1	97.9	146.2
Loans	26.2	31.5	37.7
Total Credit to Private Enterprise	*131.5*	*182.2*	*256.8*
Credit to Government:			
Treasury bills	16.5	54.4	14.4
Securities	187.3	216.5	220.7
Total Credit to Government	*203.8*	*270.9*	*235.1*
Liquid Reserves Including Cash on Hand, Deposits with Central Bank and Readily Available Net Assets Abroad	335.5	406.0	380.2*
Ratio of Liquid Reserves			
To demand deposits	60%	56%	52%*
To total deposits	54%	51%	47%*

* September 1951.
Source: Central Bank of Ceylon, *Bulletin*, Feb. 1952.

and it is understandable that business firms and banks, alike, developed the tradition of relying on plenty of liquid reserves.

Demand deposits, as shown in Table IV, include cash balances of the government. Deducting these balances from the total, business deposits appear to be as follows:

December 1949	Rs. 405.5 million
December 1950	Rs. 585.3 million
December 1951	Rs. 628.8 million

It is generally believed that the large volume of sight deposits held by business firms, and to a certain extent by private individuals, includes a considerable amount of inactive funds which could be used to finance new investments. This view is confirmed by the strong liquidity position of the banks, as well as by the low turnover of sight deposits. These show a monthly ratio of about two to one during the first six months of the year 1951. This is very low, considering the essentially short-term character of current banking transactions. For earlier years, only bank clearings are available; their ratio to sight deposits was about 0.8 in the month of December in the years 1947-50.

Statistics available in Ceylon are insufficient to make an estimate of gross and net savings. There can be no doubt, however, that the bulk of savings out of current income come from retained earnings and reserves of various kinds accumulated by those engaged in growing, processing and trading the three export crops. Most of these savings pass through the channels of the commercial banks, and an unknown portion of them is sterilized in the form of idle balances held in anticipation of another depression in the world market.

Our general conclusion is that the banking system is in a strong financial position, and that it represents an important source of liquid funds and potential savings which could be utilized to expand agricultural and industrial production. The problem is to get these funds and savings to finance new enterprises and new employment instead of leaving them as idle emergency reserves. An answer is seen in the establishment of a Development Corporation along the lines recommended in Chapter 4 of the present report.

Long-term Finance Institutions. Lack of private capital for investment and the cautious attitude of the commercial banks have led to the establishment of four long-term finance institutions: the Ceylon State Mortgage Bank, the Agricultural and Industrial Credit Corporation, the Local Loans and Development Fund and the Housing Loans Board.

All four institutions are controlled by the government and, with the exception of the State Mortgage Bank, draw their funds entirely from public sources. The State Mortgage Bank sells its own government-guaranteed debentures but a considerable portion is held by government-controlled funds and organizations. The Local Loans and Development Fund makes loans primarily to local communities for developing public utility services. The Housing Loans Board, designed to finance low-cost housing, began its operations in April 1950 with an initial fund of Rs. 5 million provided by the government and has not yet published its first balance sheet. The position of the other three institutions is shown in Table V.

Activities of the Mortgage Bank and the Credit Corporation reveal a great deal of overlapping. Although the latter was intended to provide capital mainly for industrial development, both in fact concentrate on loans to agricultural borrowers for the acquisition and improvement of land. The principal difference seems to be that the Credit Corporation is less rigorous in requirements but the Mortgage Bank is stricter in examining the borrower's title to the land offered as security.

Agricultural Credit. Special problems of agricultural credit are discussed under the heading of Cooperation and Rural Development in Chapter 10.

Savings Institutions. Institutions for collecting personal savings include the Ceylon Savings Bank, the Post Office Savings Bank and the National Savings Movement which issues savings certificates. Larger savings and time deposits are held with the commercial banks and especially with the Bank of Ceylon.

162

TABLE V

POSITION OF LONG-TERM FINANCE INSTITUTIONS

(*million rupees*)

	1950	1951
Ceylon State Mortgage Bank		
Debentures issued	9.7	11.2
Loans outstanding	9.9	11.5
Agricultural and Industrial Credit Corporation		
Funds provided by the government	14.1	19.8
Loans outstanding	14.0	19.7

	1949	1950
Local Loans and Development Fund		
Funds provided by the government	7.9	12.4
Loans outstanding	10.1	11.5

Source: Ministry of Finance, Ceylon State Mortgage Bank, Agricultural and Industrial Credit Corporation.

At the savings institutions the monthly rate of accrual, as shown in Table VI, has been irregular. From Rs. 4.2 million in 1946, it dropped gradually to Rs. 0.6 million in 1949, reached a record level of Rs. 4.5 million in the first half of 1951 and dropped slightly to Rs. 4.3 million in the last quarter of 1951. Deposits at the savings institutions are considerably larger and the process of accumulation has been much faster than at the commercial banks. Since the savings institutions are controlled by the government, funds collected by them represent a readily available source for government borrowing.

Insurance

Statistical information on insurance is limited; it is known, however, that the most important companies are foreign-owned.

163

Data covering 34 out of a total of about 80 life insurance companies are summarized in Table VII.

TABLE VI

SAVINGS AND TIME DEPOSITS
(*million rupees*)

Period Ended	Savings Institutions	Commercial Banks	Total	Average Monthly Rate of Accrual	
				Savings Institutions	Total
1945	142.3	63.6	205.9		
1946	192.2	61.0	253.2	4.2	3.9
1947	204.5	63.6	268.1	1.0	1.2
1948	215.1	67.5	282.6	0.9	1.2
1949	222.3	66.7	289.0	0.6	0.5
1950:					
June	226.7	66.2	292.9	0.7	0.6
December	244.9	77.1	322.0	3.0	4.8
1951:					
June	271.7	81.6	353.3	4.5	5.2
September	282.2	84.1	366.3	3.5	4.3
October	285.8	85.4	371.2	3.6	4.9
November	289.1	86.3	375.4	3.3	4.2
December	295.0	91.1	386.1	5.9	10.7

Source: Central Bank of Ceylon, *Bulletin*, Feb. 1952.

TABLE VII

POLICIES, PREMIUMS AND ASSETS OF 34 LIFE INSURANCE COMPANIES
(*million rupees*)

	1947	1948	1949
Ordinary Life Insurance:			
Policies at the end of the year	297.7	316.6	347.8
Premiums collected during the year	16.7	18.6	20.7
Assets in Ceylon at the end of the year	26.1	32.4	45.0

Source: *Statistical Abstract of Ceylon*, 1950.

Insurance funds invested in government securities amounted to Rs. 14.2 million in 1949, Rs. 21.7 million in 1950 and Rs. 30.2 million in 1951. There is no law regulating the activity of insurance companies and, consequently, the companies are under no obligation to hold their assets in Ceylon. At present, however, under the system of exchange control now in force, special licenses issued by the Exchange Controller are required to transfer and invest funds outside Ceylon.

It has been disclosed recently that the government is planning the establishment of a limited social insurance system. The scheme under consideration is intended to provide unemployment, health and retirement benefits, and will promote savings by the accumulation of contributions from workers, employers and the government.

Other Savings Mechanisms. Besides the savings institutions and the insurance companies, there are a number of various minor institutions and organizations—the Public Trustee, private trusts, provident and benevolent funds and cooperative societies—which contribute towards the accumulation of institutional and personal savings.

Capital Market

Ceylon has an organized stock market operated by the Colombo Brokers' Association, with a membership of eight brokers who deal both in stocks and produce. The number of shares listed is around 200, including practically all plantation companies and about 30 industrial and commercial enterprises. The absorptive capacity of the market is low and the volume of transactions is small, since most of the companies are closely held.

As regards the market for government bonds, the Central Bank floated loans of Rs. 150 million during the fiscal year 1950-51, which coincided with a period of exceptionally high earnings from booming exports. Two previous loans subscribed in 1949-50 totalled Rs. 77.5 million.

Commercial banks hold about 38% of government bonds out-

TABLE VIII

GOVERNMENT BONDS BY TYPE OF OWNERSHIP
(*million rupees*)

	End of September		
	1949	1950	1951
Commercial Banks	199.7	207.5	249.1
Savings Institutions, Including Government and Local Government Institutions	169.4	155.6	222.0
Public Trustee, Private Trust Funds, and Cooperative Societies	46.9	56.4	68.6
Insurance Companies	14.2	21.7	30.2
Other Companies	32.5	34.9	46.7
Individuals	26.1	24.9	30.1
Federated Malay States	3.1	3.1	3.1
Total	*491.9*	*504.1*	*649.8*

Source: Central Bank of Ceylon.

standing at the end of September 1951; savings institutions, various trusts and funds, insurance companies and cooperative societies had absorbed another 50% whereas other companies and individuals accounted for about 12% of all holdings.

Current transactions in government securities are small, because there is no general market for government issues other than the institutional market just mentioned. Institutional savers consider their holdings as permanent investments; the commercial banks, in view of their strong liquidity position, are also inclined to hold a large amount of government securities in their portfolios. Therefore, though the market is comparatively narrow, there is a permanent demand for government issues.

Provided savings continue to accumulate at the rate prevailing in the second half of 1951, their annual accrual available for investment in government securities is likely to be of the order of Rs. 40 million per year. Other investors, including insurance companies and commercial banks, may be expected to be in a position to absorb annually another Rs. 20 or 30 million of government securities.

The structure of capital yields and interest rates is shown in Table IX. Share yields of the plantation companies are subject

TABLE IX

STRUCTURE OF CAPITAL YIELDS AND INTEREST RATES
(*percent*)

	1951
Share Yields, October 5	
Tea Companies	
Uplands	13.6
Tonocombe	15.3
High Forest	14.3
Rubber Companies	
Kalutura	25.0
Udapolla	25.0
Miscellaneous Companies	
Hunter and Co.	12.5
Cargills	10.0
Ceylon Brewery	6.0
Ceylon Investment Co.	5.3
Bond Yields, end of August	
National Loan 3% (1953)	2.93
National Development Loan 3% (1965-70)	2.91
Treasury Bills, November 15	0.40
Loan Rates	
Mortgage Bank	4 to 5½
Credit Corporation	5 to 6½
Savings Deposits	2 to 2½
Commercial Banks	
Advances, unsecured, to first class firms	3
Overdrafts, secured	3 to 5
Trade Acceptances	4

Source for Share Yields: Yield tables issued by Forbes and Walker, Ltd., Colombo.

to frequent changes, reflecting fluctuating export prices and, therefore, cannot be considered as a representative measure of the cost of capital. The yields of various other companies are probably closer to reality. Transactions in such shares, however, are much too small to permit any general conclusion as to the rate at which capital would be available in the market. In the absence of a general market for government issues, government bond yields cannot reflect the true market rate. It will be noticed, however, that insurance companies are generally reluctant to invest in government securities, since they can obtain higher yields abroad than in Ceylon. The rates on Treasury bills are lower than those in the United Kingdom; nevertheless demand for short-dated issues is generally larger than offerings by the Treasury. Loan rates charged by the Mortgage Bank and the Credit Corporation are fixed on an arbitrary basis, and so are the rates paid on savings deposits. Loan rates at commercial banks indicate the price at which money is available for financing short-term transactions.

In order to establish a broader market in government securities, public loan issues should be made more attractive to investors. Through cooperation of the Central Bank and the Treasury, an effort should be made to issue such types of securities as would meet the needs of various groups of investors. As regards the supply of long-term funds to private enterprise, it may be hoped that the proposed Development Corporation will be able to create a market for private investments.

PUBLIC FINANCE

General Structure

With the announcement of the Six Year Plan in 1947, the government engaged the country's financial resources in a program of development involving a sharp increase in the annual volume of capital outlay and a rapid expansion in current expenditures.

Data showing the financial position, as it was in the last prewar year and as it changed in the years after the war, are presented in Annex B. From these it will be seen that, in addition to "loan

168

expenditures" as shown in the Treasury's accounts, a substantial amount of new capital investment has been included every year in the category of ordinary current expenditures. Actual capital outlay is, therefore, considerably larger than the amount of loan expenditures. To approximate the true picture, in the accompanying tables capital expenditures exceeding Rs. 100,000 (so far as identifiable) have been segregated from current expenditures and

TABLE X

PUBLIC EXPENDITURES AND REVENUES
(*million rupees*)

	1947-48	1948-49	1949-50	1950-51 Provisional Accounts
Current Expenditures As Shown in the Budget Accounts	602.7	625.9	642.2	814.5
Less				
Capital Expenditures Included in Current Expenditures	33.7	37.3	44.0	63.0*
Net Current Expenditures	569.0	588.6	598.2	751.5
Current Revenues	600.5	640.0	691.4	904.7
Surplus on Current Account	+ 31.5	+ 51.4	+ 93.2	+153.2
Capital expenditures:				
"Loan expenditures"	70.3	122.5	155.5	159.3
Plus				
Capital Expenditures Segregated from Current Expenditures	33.7	37.3	44.0	63.0*
Total Capital Expenditures	*104.0*	*159.8*	*199.5*	*222.3*
Over-all Deficit	*— 72.5*	*—108.4*	*—106.3*	*— 69.1*

* This figure has been taken from the estimates for 1950-51 and is used here on the assumption that actual outlay was equal to the estimated amount of expenditure.

Source: *Estimates of the Revenue and Expenditure of the Government of Ceylon*, Ceylon Government Press.

transferred to the category of capital outlay. The most significant changes brought about by the Six Year Plan are summarized in Table X.

As seen from this table, capital expenditures more than doubled during the first four years, reaching Rs. 222.3 million in 1950-51 as against Rs. 104 million in 1947-48. An increasing amount of capital investment was financed from current surpluses. This fact, together with a greater rise in revenues than in expenditures, traceable to inflated export prices and higher taxes, caused the over-all deficit to drop to Rs. 69.1 million in 1950-51. The sharp rise in expenditures resulted mainly from a very large increase in food subsidies.

Current expenditures other than food subsidies (Table XI) increased more gradually; their rise was about 26% between 1947-48 and 1950-51. Since prices—as measured by the cost-of-living index—went up by 11%, the real increase in current expenditures (exclusive of subsidies) was about 13%.

TABLE XI

CURRENT EXPENDITURES AND FOOD SUBSIDIES

(million rupees)

	1947-48	1948-49	1949-50	1950-51
Current Expenditures	569.0	588.6	598.2	751.5
Food Subsidies	77.8	53.7	35.8	133.0
Current Expenditures Exclusive of Subsidies	*491.2*	*534.9*	*562.4*	*618.5*

Source: Central Bank for 1947-48; Department of Food Supplies for other years.

The distribution of capital expenditures (Table XII) demonstrates the emphasis which the government places upon improvement of public health and education. Outlays for these purposes increased from 15.4% in 1947-48 to 22.4% in 1949-50. But the largest portion of expenditures went into irrigation, land reclamation, colonization, industries and trade. Next in importance were utility services, whose share dropped from 37.8% in the first year to 28.2% in the third year.

TABLE XII

DISTRIBUTION OF CAPITAL EXPENDITURES*
(million rupees)

	1947-48	1948-49	1949-50
Development of National Wealth			
Irrigation, land reclamation, colonization, industries and trade	44.0	76.0	77.9
Percent	(42.3)	(47.6)	(42.8)
Social Services			
Mainly public health and education	16.0	26.2	40.6
Percent	(15.4)	(16.4)	(22.4)
Utility Services			
Public Works, transportation, ports and harbors, electrical plants, post services	39.3	49.7	51.2
Percent	(37.8)	(31.1)	(28.2)
Other Investments			
Administration, defense, external affairs and miscellaneous items	4.7	7.9	12.0
Percent	(4.5)	(4.9)	(6.6)
Total	*104.0*	*159.8*	*181.7***

* The classification follows that adopted in *Economic and Social Development in Ceylon*, with the difference that this table includes, in addition to loan fund expenditures, investments financed from ordinary current revenues.

** Excluding Rs. 17.8 million as subscription to the International Monetary Fund and the International Bank for Reconstruction and Development.

Source: *Estimates of the Revenue and Expenditure of the Government of Ceylon*, Ceylon Government Press.

Over-all deficits incurred in the first four years of the Six Year Plan aggregated Rs. 356.3 million; net cash operating deficits, which include balances of extra-budgetary operations, totalled Rs. 341.3 million. Deficits were financed, as seen from Table XIII, partly from cash balances and partly from new loans.

TABLE XIII

NET CASH OPERATING DEFICIT
(million rupees)

	1947-48	1948-49	1949-50	Three Years' Total	1950-51
Deficit	—59.9	—113.1	—156.1	—329.1	—12.2
Net Receipts from Borrowing and Repayment of Advances	+43.3	+ 42.5	+ 79.6	+165.4	+90.8
Cash Balances	—16.6	— 70.6	— 76.5	—163.7	+78.6

Source: *Estimates of the Revenue and Expenditure of the Government of Ceylon*, Ceylon Government Press.

Considering the first three years together, borrowing and cash balances shared equally in financing deficits, whereas in 1950-51 funds raised by borrowing exceeded the deficit of the year and resulted in a substantial increase in cash holdings. [3]

Ceylon's internal funded debt (excluding war loans re-lent to the United Kingdom) amounted to Rs. 582 million at the end of 1950-51. [4] Sinking fund accumulations aggregated Rs. 113 million, leaving a net internal debt of Rs. 469 million. In addition,

---

[3] Cash balances include balances held abroad plus domestic rupee balances as shown in the Treasury's accounts; therefore, they are not comparable with government deposits as shown in bank statistics.

[4] About 70% of this was long-term with interest rates ranging from 2.25% to 3.5%, whereas about 23% was medium-term with interest rates from 2.5% to 3.25%; one Rs. 40 million loan issued in 1950, bearing interest at a rate of 1.5%, is due for redemption in 1952.

Rs. 30 million of Treasury bills were outstanding at the end of the fiscal year.

The external debt was entirely in long-term sterling bonds, and amounted to Rs. 125.4 million with interest rates from 3% to 5%; deducting sinking funds of Rs. 53.8 million, the net debt was Rs. 71.6 million.

Taking internal and external debt together, the net amount of the funded debt was Rs. 540.6 million, representing about 60% of budget revenue in 1950-51. Service payments on the debt required Rs. 38.5 million, or 42% of revenue in the same year.

A percentage distribution of the main revenue categories is given in Table XIV. (Revenues from railway, postal, electrical, aviation and harbor services are not shown.) The general structure of public revenue reflects the island's economic concentration on exports and the ensuing dependence on the world market.

TABLE XIV

DISTRIBUTION OF REVENUES
(*by percent*)

	1947-48	1948-49	1949-50	1950-51 Estimates	1950-51 Provisional Accounts
Import Duties	34.4	33.1	32.2	31.5 ⎫	68.3
Export Duties	26.6	27.3	28.5	36.3 ⎭	
Excise and Sale	9.1	8.5	7.5	8.0	5.6
Direct Taxes	20.3	22.3	22.6	18.3	19.3
Licenses	0.8	0.9	1.1	0.9	1.0
Fees	0.8	0.8	1.0	0.6	0.8
Medical Services	0.7	0.6	0.6	0.4	0.5
Other Revenues	7.3	6.5	6.5	4.0	4.5

Source: *Estimates of the Revenue and Expenditure of the Government of Ceylon*, Ceylon Government Press.

One element that is immediately apparent is the growing importance of export duties. Since they are now levied on the basis of a sliding scale related to prices, their yield is automatically determined by the volume and value of exports. The sliding scale is a useful mechanism to skim off excess purchasing power arising out of booming prices. In a period of declining prices, however, it tends to intensify the decline in revenue.

It is a remarkable feature of the revenue structure that while export duties rose from 26.6% of total revenue in 1947-48 to 36.3% in 1950-51, the percentage share of all other categories either remained stationary or tended to fall. The decline in the relative importance of direct taxes in the last year is explained by the fact that taxes collected in 1950-51 were assessed on the lower incomes earned in 1949.

Although available statistics do not disclose how far direct taxation depends upon the income from exports, the general income structure leaves no doubt that the bulk of the yield derives from export profits. Export duties and direct taxes together represented 54.6% of the revenue total in 1950-51 indicating the extent to which public revenue is associated with the prosperity of export industries.

Budget estimates for 1951-52, as compared with the provisional accounts of the preceding year, are shown in Table XV. Provisions for current expenditures are 19% higher than last year's actual expenditures, whereas revenues are expected to exceed last year's actual receipts by 9% only. As regards capital expenditures, estimates are based on the assumption that the government will be able to spend Rs. 433.2 million on development as against Rs. 222.3 million in 1950-51.

Those concerned with drawing up the annual revenue estimates are confident that actual receipts from direct and indirect taxes will attain the level forecast in the budget. Nevertheless, even if revenues continued to run at high levels throughout the year, it would still be necessary to finance an over-all deficit of Rs. 346.3 million, which is nearly as large as the combined deficit of the last four years.

There can be little doubt that various physical and adminis-

TABLE XV

Budget Estimates 1951-52

(*million rupees*)

	Provisional Figures 1950-51	Budget Estimates 1951-52
Current Expenditures	751.5	897.5
Current Revenues	904.7	984.4
Surplus on Current Account	+153.2	+ 86.9
Capital Expenditures (including those segregated from current expenditures)	222.3	433.2
Over-all Deficit	— 69.1	—346.3

Source: *Estimates of the Revenue and Expenditure of the Government of Ceylon,* Ceylon Government Press.

trative limitations—shortages of raw materials and equipment, delays in their delivery and lack of trained staff—will prevent capital expenditures from reaching the estimated level. For this reason alone the actual deficit will probably not exceed the country's financial capacities. As regards current expenditures, actual outlay in the first four months of the fiscal year was considerably smaller than one third of the total scheduled.

Future Prospects

It is apparent from the foregoing analysis that Ceylon's resources are sufficiently strong not only to sustain a fairly high level of current government services, but also to provide sizeable funds for development purposes. Experience of the last four years has shown that the government has been able to increase its revenues from taxation and float loans without undue difficulty.

Annual surpluses on current account, while comparatively small in the first two years, reached Rs. 93.2 million in 1949-50 and attained an all-time peak of Rs. 153.2 million in 1950-51. Since this last fiscal year was one of exceptionally high export

175

receipts, it can hardly be considered as a basis for appraisal of future surpluses. A more realistic measure is provided by the year 1949-50, following the devaluation of the rupee but preceding the period of high world market prices. Considering that tax rates now are higher than in 1949-50, the surplus obtained in that year justifies the conclusion that the government should be able to budget for an annual surplus of at least Rs. 100 million.

In analyzing the country's liquid savings and the government's borrowing opportunities, we conclude that the annual amount available for investment in government securities might reach a level of Rs. 70 million.

In addition to budget surpluses and current savings, Ceylon enjoys the advantage of large exchange reserves, built up during the war and again in 1950-51. External assets represent savings, and can be utilized to meet foreign exchange requirements of capital development. If spent abroad on requirements arising out of the development program, they would have no inflationary effect in Ceylon. The extent to which it will be advisable to run down exchange reserves has been discussed in the preceding chapter where we suggest a possible range of Rs. 30 to 80 million a year.

Taking into account an annual budget surplus of Rs. 100 million on current account, savings of Rs. 70 million a year, and perhaps Rs. 80 million to be drawn annually from external assets, funds available for capital development are likely to aggregate Rs. 250 million a year. This would enable development expenditure to go on at a rate moderately higher than during the last two years, at least as long as the market position of exports continues to be favorable.

If progress is to continue, it is essential that development be financed as much as possible from budgetary surpluses—especially as the capital market is undeveloped and savings available for government borrowing are limited. But surpluses large enough to match the needs of development cannot be achieved without continuous efforts to increase the flow of revenue and to keep the growth of expenditure under tight control.

General Taxation

Direct Taxes. Ceylon's direct taxes include an income tax imposed on net income, as well as a profits tax charged on profits in excess of Rs. 50,000, or over 6% of the capital employed, whichever is larger. Income from employment is exempt from the profits tax, and no account is taken of dividends in computing profits tax liabilities.

The personal income tax is progressive, with an exemption limit of Rs. 4,800. For resident companies the income tax rate is 30%; for companies incorporated outside Ceylon it is 36%. The profits tax is levied at a uniform rate of 25%, and is allowed as a deduction from income in the assessment of income tax.

Income of resident individuals is computed after making the following deductions: personal allowance of Rs. 2,000; earned income allowance equal to one fifth of the income, but not exceeding Rs. 4,000; wife allowance of Rs. 1,500; children allowances of Rs. 1,500 for the first child and Rs. 1,000 for each additional child up to a maximum of Rs. 4,500.

Scheduled rates are 9% on the first Rs. 6,000 of taxable income, 19% on the next Rs. 10,000, 24% on the following bracket of Rs. 20,000 and reach a rate of 76% at the top bracket of income in excess of Rs. 100,000. Where the deduction of allowances reduces the tax liability to less than 1% the taxpayer is subject to a 1% charge on his income before allowances.

Though the scale is fairly progressive, the actual tax liabilities are very low. Table XVI shows the liability of a married man with two children, under the present system of allowances, at various earned income levels. It will be seen that even incomes of Rs. 100,000, of which there are only about 200 in the country [5], pay a rate of only 37.6%. The comparatively low level of the actual rates charged on incomes ranging from Rs. 5,000 to Rs.

---

[5] In 1948 when export prices were substantially lower, there were 97 incomes in the Rs. 100,000-150,000 bracket, and a total of 135 incomes in excess of Rs. 100,000.

TABLE XVI

TAX LIABILITY ON EARNED INCOME OF A MARRIED MAN WITH
TWO CHILDREN

(*in rupees*)

Income	5,000	7,500	10,000	20,000	50,000	100,000
Allowances	7,000	7,500	8,000	10,000	10,000	10,000
Taxable income	nil	nil	2,000	10,000	40,000	90,000
Tax Liability	50	75	180	1,300	8,960	37,585*
Tax in percent of income	1%	1%	1.8%	6.5%	17.9%	37.6%

* This includes Rs. 12,500 as profits tax.

50,000 indicates that the lower and middle range income groups are carrying a surprisingly small share of the financial burden.

In coming years additional taxes will undoubtedly be needed, and these should be drawn primarily from higher taxation of personal incomes. Since Ceylon can hardly afford a system of taxation under which large sections of the population are either exempt or pay no more than a token rate, it seems inevitable that rates will have to be raised and the exemption limit and allowances reduced eventually.

Incentive Taxation. To encourage new ventures, temporary exemptions are granted to new enterprises established before the end of March 1954. Corporations established with contributions by the government are exempt from the tax during the first three years of their existence, as are the dividends paid by such corporations. New private industrial undertakings employing more than twenty-five persons and using electricity or mechanically transmitted energy are entitled, for the first three years of their operations, to an exemption in respect of profits not exceeding 5% of the share capital; it is understood that dividends paid out of such profits are also exempt from taxation.

Besides these exemptions applicable to new undertakings, all sorts of agricultural and industrial enterprises are allowed (in addition to the usual depreciation allowances) to make an initial deduction of 33.3% on new buildings used for the housing of

178

employees, 10% on business buildings and 15% on machinery, provided such buildings or machinery are installed before the end of March 1954.

Since Ceylon's basic problem consists in promoting and expanding production, it is desirable to make more liberal tax concessions in all fields where they can reasonably be expected to encourage higher output and productivity. Therefore exemptions granted to new industrial undertakings, whether established with or without government contributions, should be of a considerably longer duration than three years; and in the case of private undertakings, the percentage of exempted profits should be somewhat higher than 5%. In addition, it should be made a general principle of taxation that all sorts of undertakings, whether new or not, be allowed to deduct from their taxable income any part of profits reinvested for productive purposes, including research and development in the national interest. The initial loss in revenue would be more than compensated by the gain in taxable income resulting from the operation of more and better capital equipment.

Tax Collection. Under the present administrative system, taxes assessed on the income of a particular year are collected in two installments; the first is payable in September or October of the next year, and the second in January or February of the following year. The profits tax is paid in full with the first installment of the income tax. Taxes on salaries are deducted by the employer in 12 monthly installments—the first of which is due in September, nine months after the end of the income year.

In a time of rising prices, delayed tax collection may involve considerable losses in terms of purchasing power. There are various ways to avoid such losses, by eliminating or reducing the time lag between the income period and the date of payment. Thus, it would be quite easy to oblige employers to compute tax liabilities on current salaries and to deduct the tax immediately as an advance payment on the employee's total liability. Similarly, all other taxpayers could be required to compute and pay their liabilities at the end of the income year. Such simplifications

179

would enable the revenue administration to improve its efficiency and reduce the number of unsettled files, which stood at 70,000 in October 1951.

Indirect Taxes and Other Revenue. Leaving aside export and import duties, indirect taxes (Table XIV) represent only a very small and diminishing proportion of public revenue. Though it is desirable to place emphasis increasingly upon direct taxation, a system of selective indirect taxes might be helpful in strengthening the general revenue structure and also in reducing luxury consumption. The customary pattern of private expenditure in Ceylon includes a good deal of conventional luxuries which are comparatively cheap and, therefore, suitable for excise taxation.

Suggestions are made elsewhere for increases in electricity rates (Chapter 14) and railway charges (Chapter 16), as well as for revised management of government-owned industries to eliminate recurrent losses (Chapters 4 and 15). All of these will be of benefit to the national budget.

Local Taxation. Available information indicates that total current revenue of all types of local governments recently stood at an annual level of around Rs. 35 million, including recurrent government subsidies. In comparison with the central government's revenue of Rs. 600-900 million during the same period, financial resources available to local governments are very small. They are obviously insufficient to secure even a minimum standard of communal services.

In 1950 the country's 400 village committees had a revenue of little more than Rs. 3 million, and 85 of these had revenues of less than Rs. 2,000 a year. It is not surprising that under such circumstances most of the local communities have to rely on the central government for grants and contributions—which totalled Rs. 29.6 million in 1949-50 and are estimated at Rs. 33.5 million for 1951-52. We believe that every effort should be made to improve the financial position of local communities, with the ultimate aim of reducing the central government's expenditures for local purposes and allowing it to concentrate more fully on the broader national program of development.

Local governments have the right to impose various taxes, of which the property rate and the acreage tax represent the most important sources of revenues. The property rate is subject to a ceiling of 6% for smaller towns and villages, whereas in larger communities it varies from 10 to 15%. The maximum in Colombo is 30%; this, however, is a consolidated rate including various other rates in addition to that on property. The acreage tax is imposed on cultivated land at a maximum rate of half a rupee per acre. Tax liability starts at five acres; all lands under paddy or chena cultivation, however, are exempt.

A committee was appointed in 1948 to study the structure of local taxation and to submit proposals for consideration by the government. For the property tax, the committee suggested replacing the present flat rate by a graduated system, in order to shift the burden to properties with higher valuations and to provide an incentive for investment in low-cost housing. As to the acreage tax, the committee recommended the reduction of the exemption limit from five acres to one half acre, and the inclusion of paddy lands in the category of taxable property. It supported an increase in the rate from the present maximum of one half rupee to a new maximum of two rupees, but suggested that small holdings not exceeding an acre should have the benefit of a lower maximum rate of one rupee.

The committee considered and rejected the idea of imposing an increment tax on such increases in value of real properties as are brought about by public investment. It recommended, however, the establishment of a differential tax on nonutilized or underutilized land in urban as well as in rural areas. Moreover it debated the merits of a local income tax. The committee decided against this last measure, and instead recommended a tax on trades and professions modelled after that of Madras, where the tax is on a progressive scale with a half-yearly top rate of Rs. 25 for individual taxpayers and Rs. 1,000 for companies.

We feel that the approach made by the committee towards improving and extending the present structure of local taxation is essentially constructive and deserves full support. Toward this end we would suggest a few modifications worth further thought.

Land being the most important source of income, the tax on land should be an abundant financial resource of local governments. Therefore, the maximum rate of two rupees as proposed by the committee seems to be too low and should be raised to three rupees. Also, since the bulk of the burden of a higher land tax would fall on the estates, most of the benefit would normally accrue to villages settled in the estate area. To bring about a more equal distribution of revenues from land taxation, one rupee of the tax should be collected as a national tax and distributed by the government among the villages situated outside the estate area.

Establishment of a differential tax on nondeveloped or underdeveloped land, as suggested by the committee, would open a practical and equitable way to promote better and more economical use of land. As regards a special increment tax, we believe that a tax of this kind would provide a suitable means of financing communal investments and suggest that it receive further consideration.

The arguments brought forward by the committee against a local income tax are not convincing—particularly the committee's opinion that a local income tax would be inconsistent with the property rate. Since the system of property rates is already practiced side by side with the national income tax, there is no reason why it should not be compatible with a local income tax.

One decisive practical argument in favor of a local income tax is that revenue from property rates and other local resources is obviously insufficient to enable even the larger towns to finance an adequate level of communal services. Thus the central government has to undertake many functions which could be discharged more efficiently by local communities. A much wider decentralization of powers to local governments is desirable in order to reduce the financial burden of the central government, and to develop a stronger sense of local responsibility. This, however, can be achieved only by giving local authorities an opportunity to increase their revenue through new taxes.

For some communities, therefore, we recommend the adoption of a local income tax with a flat rate and a low exemption limit. This should be applied in the city of Colombo, and in those larger towns where its introduction would seem to be justified by the level and structure of incomes. In all other areas, a tax on trades and professions should be established as suggested by the committee.

Financial Control

It is in the nature of things that a rapidly growing volume of investment and an equally rapid expansion in public services tend to create disturbances in the administrative mechanism. It takes time for the departments to adjust their activities so as to put expenditure and benefit in a sound relation. The general impression is that the departments have no opportunity to base the administration of their functions on carefully studied and clearly defined plans. Instead of concentrating in their own fields of activity, they tend to compete with each other and would appear to believe that the more they spend, the greater the service they render. The major departments seem to have no doubt that they would be able to increase their individual budgets at an annual rate of 10 to 15%.

Little attention is paid to the interrelation between investment and cost of operation. In many instances the question of whether next years' revenue will be sufficient to meet current expenses resulting from this year's investments goes unanswered. The departments are unduly willing to spend money in all sorts of ways, and there is no guarantee that the money will be used efficiently. To illustrate the point, reference may be made to the postal services, which have been running a growing deficit over the past four years. With an estimated revenue of Rs. 24.7 million in 1951-52, expenditures are expected to amount to Rs. 41.6, leaving a deficit of Rs. 16.9 million. This seems to be due to an overexpansion of services for which there is no demand. In spite of this precarious financial position, the postage rate for domestic letters was reduced from six to five cents last year.

Clearly, the existing control mechanism is insufficient to cope with the problem. The Audit Office is concerned only with seeing that public funds have been spent with proper authority and for purposes voted by Parliament. In earlier days, when the administrative mechanism was simple, there was not much danger in postponing the supervision of expenditures until after the end of the fiscal year. Today the functions of the departments are much more complicated, and the work of supervision should go well beyond a mere revision of accounts. What is wanted is a continuous process of financial control by an active and independent body, with the aim of securing strict economy in all fields of public services.

A new authority should be created for the purpose, preferably on a parliamentary basis, with a small number of members selected in proportion to the representation of the various parties and with a chairman elected from the opposition. On detailed administrative and accounting procedures the task requires a great deal of expert assistance, which could be drawn from a secretarial office provided by the Auditor General's staff. With an independent supervisory committee of this kind making frequent efficiency audits, it should be possible to establish adequate safeguards against waste and to develop economical, efficient financial administration.

Food Subsidies

Ceylon's problem of food subsidies is of the greatest importance not only because of its adverse effect on the budget, but also from the general economic point of view. In its annual report for the year 1950, the Central Bank commented on the problem at length, concluding that ". . . a widespread system of subsidies has a tendency to hide real costs, to distort the country's economy, and sometimes to act as a serious barrier to efficiency. Even before the decision to increase the subsidy on rice as of December 11, the cost of subsidies was so large as to be a heavy and seemingly unending drain upon the exchequer. Government policy could now be directed toward reducing subsidies." The substance of this recommendation was repeated in the Bank's 1951 report.

During the first four years of the Six Year Plan, expenditure on food subsidies aggregated about Rs. 300 million. From Rs. 35.8 million in 1949-50, these subsidies increased to Rs. 133 million in 1950-51 and the budget estimates for 1951-52 provide another Rs. 160 million, absorbing more than 16% of the government's revenue. Food subsidies impose an unending drain on the country's financial resources.

The price of imported food is the most influential of the factors indirectly determining costs of production. If the price of food rises, the only natural solution is to match the rise by an effort to increase the productivity of domestic industries and, particularly, the efficiency of the export industries.

Food subsidies are no more than a palliative, concealing the necessity of adjustment by keeping food prices at an artificially low level. By doing so, subsidies create a profit margin which is larger than it would be if prices and wages were allowed to find their natural level. Larger profit margins enable the government to impose higher export duties, which in turn provide the funds from which food subsidies are financed. This is the way the system of subsidies is working. If there were no subsidies, food prices and wages would be higher, whereas profit margins and consequently the yield of export duties would be smaller.

From the viewpoint of national progress, a twofold disadvantage is inherent in the subsidy system. By concealing the real level of food prices and the real cost of production, they destroy the producer's incentive or need to achieve higher productivity. At the same time, they tend to confirm the widespread belief that any further rise in food prices is to be compensated automatically by higher subsidies.

Food subsidies have established an unreal equilibrium between

185

export prices, wages, cost of production and profits, apparently on the assumption that the relation between export prices and prices to be paid for imported foodstuffs will return to its prewar pattern within a few years. Since price tendencies in the world market do not confirm this assumption, it would be sound policy to abandon the system of subsidies and allow food prices to find their expression in wages and costs of production.

Therefore the Mission concurs in the view of the Central Bank, that food subsidies should now be reduced. As a first step, it should be made a principle that no further increase in subsidies will be granted, even if prices of imported foodstuffs should continue to rise.

Although the immediate abolition of subsidies might threaten to throw the present structure of prices into confusion, we believe that a gradual removal of the system, if carefully planned and spread over a period of two or three years, can be carried out without any major disturbances. The rise in the cost of living which will take place in each stage must be compensated by an equivalent increase in wages and salaries including those of government employees. On the other hand, the margin between export prices and cost of production must be preserved by a reduction in export duties, corresponding to the rise in wages and salaries. Calculations along these lines indicate that the removal of food subsidies would result in a net gain to the government.

Budget System

A weakness of the present budget system is its lack of a clear distinction between current expenditure and capital investment. Consequently the budget accounts do not give as complete a picture of the government's development activities as they should. It is essential to know past performances with exactness—what has been spent for capital development on the one hand and for current services on the other. Without detailed information on the interrelation between investment and cost of operation, execution of a major development program is extremely hazardous. The danger is that current expenditures may be driven up to a level where they absorb the government's revenue completely, leaving no surplus for further capital development. Estimates for 1951-52 already foreshadow this danger, since they provide for an increase of almost 100% in capital investment. This large volume of new investments—if it were carried out—would undoubtedly require a higher level of current expenditure in 1952-53; but, so far as we know, no attempt has been made to draw up detailed estimates in this respect.

To improve the existing practice of budgeting, it is suggested that the accounting system be revised to present separately ordinary current expenditures and new capital investment, and to show capital expenditures on various projects as distinct categories.

Each year's budget should be accompanied by a realistic general survey of prevailing economic conditions, including a detailed analysis of the financial position, and drawn up in consultation with the proposed economic planning secretariat. The financial part of the survey should be based on properly arranged data showing projects carried out in the past and planned for the next year, emphasis being placed on the amount of current expenditures required to maintain completed and planned projects in operation. The survey should give detailed information on all types of budgetary and extra-budgetary transactions, indicating the sources from which expenditure was financed in the last year. Moreover, it should contain an estimate of the over-all deficit likely to be incurred in the coming year, and should show how the expected deficit is to be financed.

Conclusions

From this review of the government's revenues and expenditures it is clear to the Mission that the structure of Ceylon's public finances, though less flexible than that of more advanced countries, offers opportunities both for considerable savings in expenditure and for an equally substantial increase in revenue. With a studied policy of taxation and a system of efficient financial control, coupled with a serious effort to keep current expenditures within proper limits, it should be possible to achieve annual surpluses in excess of Rs. 100 million for developmental purposes.

Our conclusion that Ceylon is able to finance an annual Rs. 250 million of new investment is based on the assumption that exports will continue to enjoy a favorable position in the world market. As against this assumption, Ceylon may have to face two possible alternative situations in the next few years, each depending on international conditions.

If international tension is further aggravated, there may be another rise in export prices, combined with another shortage of such consumer and capital goods as Ceylon has to import from abroad. Since 1950, when a similar situation arose, both the government and the Central Bank have gained experience in how to deal with increasing incomes and rising prices: the government by improved methods of taxation—especially its sliding-scale export duties—and the Central Bank by floating government loans and restricting the money supply. With a Central Bank controlling the market and with a flexible system of export duties, it may be said that Ceylon is fairly well equipped to prevent high export incomes from driving up prices and wages to a level where they would threaten to upset the equilibrium of the country's economy.

Alternatively, if international tension is eased substantially, Ceylon may be confronted with a decline in the prices offered for her exports. If this situation arises, export incomes will fall and employment may tend to decline. The cost of living will depend largely on the rice market, since rice may still be scarce and sell at prices comparatively higher than those obtainable for Ceylon's export products.

A temporary recession of this kind resulting in a moderate decline in incomes would not justify either the use of inflationary measures or the tightening of direct controls on imports and consumption. Declining incomes would automatically decrease the effective demand for imported goods. Monetary and fiscal measures intended to cope with falling incomes should be combined with measures promoting further development. There would be an opportunity for the Development Corporation to expand its activity, and for the Central Bank to support the Corporation in its efforts to utilize available labor and increase the supply of domestically produced goods. Fortunately, Ceylon still has a substantial amount of exchange reserves which may be drawn upon in bad times in order to enable the government to continue its developmental activities.

A decline in public revenue, and in savings available for borrowing, is inevitable in a period of falling prices. But this does not necessarily mean that the government would have to run a deficit. With strict economy in current expenditures, and with serious efforts to make the revenue structure more resistant, there is no reason why the government should not be able to balance its budget and still carry on a flexible program of development without resorting to the expedient of inflationary methods.

RECOMMENDATIONS

1. The commercial banks are in a position to participate in a Ceylon Development Corporation as defined in Chapter 4, and to extend credit facilities to enterprises operated or controlled by the Corporation. They should be prepared to do so for mutual benefit.

2. The commercial banks are also in a position to absorb government securities and Treasury bills. These investments, however, should be kept within such limits as might be determined from time to time by the Central Bank with regard to the general monetary position.

3. In floating new public loans, the Central Bank should recommend to the government such types of bonds as will meet the needs of various investors—particularly those of the insurance companies, the commercial banks and the prospective social insurance system.

4. The State Mortgage Bank and the Agricultural and Industrial Credit Corporation should be merged into one institution.

5. Considering that savings available for investment in government securities are limited and that external assets will probably be spent within a few years, the government should make a continuous effort to finance as much of its capital expenditures as possible from current budgetary surpluses and to encourage private savings for investment in government loans.

6. Additional taxes which will be needed in coming years should be drawn primarily from higher taxation of personal incomes. To increase the yield of the income tax, the Mission recommends a reduction of the exemption limit and allowances and an upward revision of the rate schedule.

7. Income tax collection should be improved so as to reduce the time lag between the period of income and the dates of payment.

8. Although it is desirable to place emphasis on direct taxation, a system of selective indirect taxes should be developed also.

9. The structure of local taxation should be reorganized, and local governments should be given wider powers to increase their revenue from existing taxes and to impose new taxes.

10. Present tax incentives to encourage production should be enlarged, and more liberal exemptions and allowances should be granted to promote new productive investment.

11. A system of efficient financial control should be established by creating a permanent supervisory committee.

12. Food subsidies should be removed gradually in order to restore a more natural relationship between prices, wages and cost of production. As the initial step, further increases in subsidy rates should be stopped. All groups should be advised that the removal of subsidies will necessitate adjustments in wages and export duties.

13. The accounting system and the method of budget presentation should be improved so as to provide a complete picture of the financial position every year.

14. The policies and measures hitherto adopted by the Central Bank, in the discharge of its statutory duty of maintaining internal monetary stability, are effective and should be continued.

Annex A

TABLE XVII

YEAR-END CONSOLIDATED BALANCE SHEET OF COMMERCIAL BANKS
(*thousand rupees*)

Liabilities	1949	1950	1951
Paid-up Capital, Reserve Funds and Undistributed Profits	11,639	15,338	21,147
Deposits			
Demand deposits	558,665	719,690	712,983
Interbank deposits			
Domestic	176,205	3,581	13,378
Foreign	5,625	10,654	10,241
Time and savings deposits	66,739	77,139	91,071
Borrowings			
Domestic	—	2,000	3,000
Foreign	13,131	7,669	8,230
Other Liabilities	20,600	22,444	22,572
Total Liabilities	*852,604*	*858,515*	*882,622*

Source: Central Bank of Ceylon, *Annual Report,* 1951.

TABLE XVII

(*continued*)

YEAR-END CONSOLIDATED BALANCE SHEET OF COMMERCIAL BANKS
(*thousand rupees*)

Assets	1949	1950	1951
Cash on Hand	227,980	35,973	33,827
Bank Balances			
Central Bank	—	163,153	191,734
Other banks	173,210	2,638	4,267
Foreign Currency and Bank			
Balances Abroad	101,529	180,398	137,356
Investments			
Treasury bills	16,494	54,403	14,383
Government securities	187,278	216,539	220,696
Loans and Advances			
Locals bills	315	241	902
Foreign bills	29,879	52,564	72,008
Overdrafts	75,147	97,859	146,168
Loans	26,175	31,495	37,723
Items in Process of Collection	1,604	10,269	10,401
Other Assets	13,993	12,982	13,158
Total Assets	*852,604*	*858,515*	*882,622*

Note: Bank statistics relating to previous years, published in the *Statistical Abstract of Ceylon*, 1950, are not comparable with the above series of statistics started by the Central Bank as from the end of 1949.

Source: Central Bank of Ceylon, *Annual Report*, 1951.

Annex B

TABLE XVIII

CURRENT GOVERNMENT EXPENDITURES
(*million rupees*)

Fiscal Year	Expenditures			Capital Expenditures Included in Current Expenditures	Net Current Expenditures
	As Shown in the Accounts	Railway and Electrical Department	Total		
1938-39	127.1	21.8	148.9	6.5	142.4
1946-47	405.4	68.1	473.5	25.2	448.3
1947-48	525.3*	77.4	602.7	33.7	569.0
1948-49	547.8	78.1	625.9	37.3	588.6
1949-50	563.2	79.0	642.2	44.0	598.2
1950-51 Provisional Accounts	814.5	**	814.5	63.0***	751.5
1951-52 Estimates	982.8	**	982.8	85.3	897.5

* Expenditures as shown in the accounts amounted to Rs. 621.9 million, including food subsidies of Rs. 96.6 million expended in previous fiscal years.

** From 1950-51, expenditures of Railway and Electrical Department have been included in the general budget accounts.

*** This figure has been taken from the estimates for 1950-51 and is used here on the assumption that actual outlay was equal to the estimated amount of expenditure.

Source: *Statistical Abstract of Ceylon*, 1950; *Estimates of the Revenue and Expenditure of the Government of Ceylon for the Financial Year 1st October, 1951 to 30th September, 1952.*

THE ECONOMIC DEVELOPMENT OF CEYLON

TABLE XIX

GOVERNMENT REVENUES AND NET CURRENT EXPENDITURES
(*million rupees*)

Fiscal Year	As shown in the Accounts	Railway and Electrical Department	Total	Net Current Expenditures	Surplus or Deficit
		Revenues			
1938-39	116.9	18.4	135.3	142.4	− 7.1
1946-47	461.3	54.2	515.5	448.3	+ 67.2
1947-48	540.6	59.9	600.5	569.0	+ 31.5
1948-49	576.1	63.9	640.0	588.6	+ 51.4
1949-50	623.3	68.1	691.4	598.2	+ 93.2
1950-51 Provisional Accounts	904.7	*	904.7	751.5	+153.2
1951-52 Estimates	984.4	*	984.4	897.5	+ 86.9

* Since 1950-51, revenues of Railway and Electrical Department have been included in the general budget accounts.

Source: *Statistical Abstract of Ceylon*, 1950; *Estimates of the Revenue and Expenditure of the Government of Ceylon for the Financial Year 1st October, 1951 to 30th September, 1952.*

MONEY, BANKING AND PUBLIC FINANCE

TABLE XX

GOVERNMENT CAPITAL EXPENDITURES AND OVER-ALL SURPLUS OR DEFICIT
(*million rupees*)

| Fiscal Year | Capital Expenditures | | | Surplus or Deficit on Current Account | Over-all Surplus or Deficit |
	"Loan Expenditures"	Capital Expenditures Included in Current Expenditures	Total		
1938-39	7.6	6.5	14.1	− 7.1	− 21.2
1946-47	32.1	25.2	57.3	+ 67.2	+ 9.9
1947-48	70.3	33.7	104.0	+ 31.5	− 72.5
1948-49	122.5	37.3	159.8	+ 51.4	+108.4
1949-50	155.5	44.0	199.5	+ 93.2	−106.3
1950-51 Provisional Accounts	159.3	63.0	222.3	+153.2	− 69.1
1951-52 Estimates	347.9	85.3	433.2	+ 86.9	−346.3

Source: *Statistical Abstract of Ceylon, 1950; Estimates of the Revenue and Expenditure of the Government of Ceylon for the Financial Year 1st October, 1951 to 30 September, 1952.*

TABLE XXI

Revenue of the Government of Ceylon

(thousand rupees)

	1938-39	1946-47	1947-48	1948-49	1949-50	1950-51 Estimates	1950-51 Provisional Accounts	1951-52 Estimates
1. Customs								
Import duties	51,931	166,662	177,015	180,212	188,296	243,784	—	201,000
Export duties	3,345	83,067	136,740	148,667	167,196	281,016	—	351,606
Sundries	32	273	300	412	413	200	—	300
Total	55,308	250,002	314,055	329,291	355,905	525,000	535,924	552,906
2. Port, Harbor, Wharf, Warehouse and Other Dues	6,401	8,925	10,086	13,848	17,655	17,910	20,757	17,910
3. Excise and Salt Taxes	10,087	40,776	46,771	46,207	43,690	61,713	44,326	46,119
4. Other Revenues								
Income tax	17,342	55,071	61,798	74,920	78,463	85,000	—	146,500
Contribution by Electrical Department	73	89	4	35	285	600	—	300
Estate duty	1,112	2,531	3,895	2,637	6,197	4,000	—	3,500
Stamps	2,779	8,008	7,853	8,338	8,782	9,500	—	8,000
Excess profits duty	—	30,651	21,457	15,412	14,148	14,000	—	9,500
Profits tax	—	—	9,088	18,375	24,395	28,000	—	50,000
Miscellaneous	—	—	182	1,715	184	296	—	1,291
Total	21,306	96,350	104,187	121,432	132,454	141,396	151,281	219,091

TABLE XXI

REVENUE OF THE GOVERNMENT OF CEYLON
(continued)

5. Licenses and Unclassified Internal Revenues	1,746	2,781	4,005	4,770	6,310	6,831	7,740	6,848
6. Court and Specific Service Fees	2,080	3,816	4,355	4,540	5,983	5,165	6,471	5,571
7. Medical Services	1,993	3,181	3,367	3,224	3,573	3,519	3,729	3,522
8. Reimbursements	4,003	6,752	7,459	9,144	9,151	9,446	8,100	10,241
9. Postal and Telecommunication Services	5,811	15,206	16,341	17,622	19,801	22,200	21,451	24,650
10. Interest and Annuities	4,074	9,046	5,590	6,130	4,030	4,127	4,174	4,314
11. Miscellaneous Receipts	2,755	19,601	19,755	15,667	19,711	12,210	18,229	13,860
12. Land Revenue	1,122	1,840	2,023	1,958	2,708	2,564	3,528	2,445
13. Land Sales	204	210	224	312	399	368	491	441
14. Colonial Development Fund	38	—	—	—	—	—	—	—
15. War Loan Interest	—	2,687	2,386	1,920	1,912	1,912	553	1,905
Total	*116,928*	*461,173*	*540,604*	*576,065*	*623,282*	*814,361*	*826,754*	*909,823*
16. Railway Revenue	15,441	48,349	52,468	55,078	57,650	65,000	66,074	65,000
17. Electrical Department revenue	3,013	5,896	7,409	8,799	10,432	10,737	11,858	9,550
	135,382	515,418	600,481	639,942	691,364	890,098	904,686	984,373

Source: *Estimates of the Revenue and Expenditure of the Government of Ceylon*, Ceylon Government Press.

197

10. Cooperatives and Rural Development

Cooperatives

It is the setting of the village economy of Ceylon which gives its well-developed cooperative movement meaning and importance. The typical paddy cultivator, tilling his small plot of land, has such slim resources that he must borrow to cover his expenses and his living costs during the periods of planting and harvesting. For long, his only recourse was the village trader and money-lender, who advanced funds at exorbitant rates of interest. With a good crop the peasant would normally pay off his loan at harvest time. But if the crop failed or were poor, he might have to extend the loan and add to it, with the frequent result that he became permanently indebted to the money lender and, in the worst circumstances, lost his property through inability to meet his obligations. Even in good crop years, the trader had another opportunity to mulct the peasant, for he was generally the sole purchaser for the crop. With competition between traders virtually nonexistent, he could stipulate a price that enabled him to resell at a handsome profit in the central markets. On top of these exactions, the boutique keeper also levied a toll as seller of supplies to the village cultivator.

It was to furnish to the peasant some relief from the monopolistic lender, buyer and supplier that the cooperative movement in Ceylon came into being.

In 1912 the first of a series of Credit Cooperatives was established. Down to the outbreak of World War II their growth was steady though unspectacular. In the earlier years, unfortunately, these cooperatives fell under the control of the richer peasants, and so gave little aid to those for whom they were intended. But

as time went on this fault was corrected and, today, the cooperatives are staffed and managed by democratically elected personnel.

By 1939-40, there were 1,302 Credit Cooperatives with a membership of 34,404. Today there are 2,149 Credit Societies, with
a membership of nearly 70,000. These societies cover the island
fairly completely and, as the doubling of membership in the
last 11 years shows, they are rapidly extending their services.
Loans are advanced to members on the basis of character and
need and on reasonable terms—not exceeding 9% per annum,
and often at 6%. Each society puts a limit on the amount of
such individual advances—usually in the neighborhood of Rs.
200-300. Most loans are "productive"—that is, for cultivation or
harvesting; but there is a small proportion (less than 4%) of
"unproductive" loans for ceremonials, repayment of old debts,
and the like.

Stores Societies, to compete with the local boutique keeper in
supplying curry stuffs, other foods and simple household neces-
sities, got under way shortly before the last war. In 1939-40
there were only 26 of these, with 12,566 members. But in 1943,
when they were given the task of administering the government's
food rationing program, their numbers and their membership shot
up rapidly, rising to 4,004 societies and over a million members
in 1944-45. For a year or two longer there was a small growth;
then, with the relaxation of rationing, the number of societies contracted (3,430 in 1950-51) and membership fell to just under
900,000. This is accounted for by the liquidation of uneconomical
village stores, the indifference of members of some of the more
inefficient stores, and the inability of the stores to sell on credit.

Were rationing of rice to be abolished, it is probable that there
would be a further substantial shrinkage in the membership of
Stores Societies. In such an event the societies would still cover
about half the family units of the country. Officials in the movement contend, with some justice, that even though the cooperative
stores have limited stocks, and may not even have scarce articles at
times, nonetheless the fact that they sell standard items at reason-

able prices is enough to justify their existence. They benefit much larger numbers than their actual customers, because their competition keeps down the prices of traders. Also worthy of note is a recent stirring on the part of the central cooperative authorities, who have undertaken to weed out inefficient managers and improve the administration of the stores.

One of the most interesting and fruitful of the various types of cooperatives in Ceylon is the Marketing and Production Society. The great majority of these—337 out of 542—are the Agricultural Production and Sales Societies, which cater to the needs of the small peasant cultivator; there are also small numbers of societies engaged in marketing coconuts, fish, dairy products and the products of cottage industries. Starting shortly before World War II, by 1939-40 there were 36 societies. By 1942-43 they numbered 111, with nearly 11,000 members. For the next five years growth was steady and fairly rapid, with membership more than doubling (23,165 in 1947-48). Phenomenal expansion has occurred in the last three years: membership has risen to just over 100,000, and the number of societies to 542.

In communities where all three types of societies exist side by side, the peasant can hope to become independent of the private trader. This is especially true where Credit, Production and Marketing, and Sales Societies are linked into a coherent system. In such communities, the Agricultural Production and Sales Society furnishes implements and other farming requisites in kind and on credit; the Credit Cooperative arranges a line of credit which can be used at the Stores Society to purchase needed goods between harvests; and either the Credit or the AP & S Society advances the costs of planting and harvesting. When the harvest comes in, the cultivator sells it to the Sales Society at a fair price, and the advances he has received are recouped out of the proceeds. Under such ideal circumstances, the peasant can improve his methods, raise larger crops and increase his income. This leaves him with a margin for the settlement of old debts to

UNIVERSITY COLLEGE OF WALES LIBRARY ABERYSTWYTH

traders, reduces interest claims on his income, and thus still further accelerates his progress.

Such full-scale and adequate arrangements exist, however, in only a part of the areas served by cooperatives. In many—for example, where only a Credit Society has been established—the tendency to set a low individual credit limit means that the peasant must still have recourse to the private trader for part of his financial needs. He remains in debt, and may even get in deeper and deeper. Some help from the Credit Society is better than none; yet if he is to begin getting out of debt, he must have available to him financial resources which are adequate to meet *all* his needs.

A brief survey of the scope of the various cooperative societies will give some indication of the degree to which the ideal—the provision of complete credit, marketing, and supply services—is approached. In 1946 there were some 20,508 villages and towns in Ceylon, and 350,000 cultivators of paddy, chena and market garden products. To serve these localities and people, somewhat more numerous five years later, there were 2,149 Credit Societies, 3,430 Stores Societies, and 337 AP & S Societies. (A few of the Credit and a sizeable number of the Stores Societies were in Colombo and the other larger towns, but we will not be far from the mark if we ignore this qualification.) The ratio of Credit Societies to villages is approximately 1:10, of Stores Societies 1:6, and of AP & S Societies 1:60. The ratio of society memberships to small cultivators is, for Credit Societies 1:5, and for AP & S Societies one to about four. Membership of Stores Societies comprises about one in eight of the total population, or about one for every two family units.

Ceylon's villages and towns had an average population of 283 in 1946. Many so-called villages, however, are mere hamlets, quite incapable of supporting even a small store. A ratio of one Credit Society to five villages, as against the present 1:10, would appear to be reasonably adequate, and would imply a doubling of their numbers. AP & S Societies can serve a wider area, but it would be difficult to guess how many additional units would be needed before the agricultural districts were reasonably well served. Certainly their numbers should be doubled, and probably even more than that will be needed.

In sum, Ceylon's cooperative movement is well advanced and doing most useful work yet it falls far short of providing most peasant farmers an effective alternative to the exactions of the trader-lender. If it offers as much to the peasant as its leaders claim, then why, with nearly 40 years of experience for the Credit Societies and some 15 for the Stores and for the Marketing and Production Societies, does it still fail to reach at least a majority of those it is designed to serve?

It is true that both the resources and the volume of loans of individual societies are small. At the end of the financial year 1950-51, total assets of the 2,149 Credit Societies [1] amounted to Rs. 5.3 million, or an average of only Rs. 2,450 per society. Loans advanced during this year totalled Rs. 4.5 million; the average size of loans was less than Rs. 100. Loans granted by AP & S Societies totalled Rs. 2.13 million with the average loan apparently also less than Rs. 100. But each of Ceylon's nine provinces now has a Provincial Cooperative Bank, of which the various local individual societies are members and from which they borrow. Of the total working capital of Credit Societies, some 23% comes from Provincial Bank loans, 31% from deposits (mainly of members), the remainder from share capital and surplus. The working capital of Marketing and Production Societies is derived 13% from Provincial Bank loans, 44% from government advances, the rest from capital, reserves and undivided profits.

---

[1] These were societies of unlimited liability, which cater primarily to the small farmer and producer. There were also 129 societies of limited liability, with capital of Rs. 2,166,000 and loans extended (1950-51) of Rs. 1,567,000. These, however, are of relatively small importance to the peasant; nearly 35% of their advances were trade loans, while only 13% were for agricultural purposes.

Apparently then the growth of cooperatives is not held back by lack of funds. Loans from Provincial Banks could provide additional amounts as required. If these institutions exhaust their immediately investible funds, they can borrow from the central Cooperative Federal Bank in Colombo.

The real and effective limitation on the expansion of cooperatives is human, not financial. Proper local personnel to staff the individual societies are difficult to find. In administration, the societies are voluntary, autonomous local bodies, with president, secretary and any other officers recruited from the local populace. Although district agents, divisional revenue officers, and food production officers all join their efforts in seeking to find suitable local people to inaugurate and staff additional cooperatives, progress is limited by a shortage of individuals who are sufficiently literate, honest, forceful and responsible to be trusted with these tasks.

There is no immediate means of removing this obstacle. It can be fully overcome only as the educational system improves, and as more and more of the rural population attain the necessary level of literacy, arithmetic competence and of self-discipline. A partial solution has been found in the AP & S Societies, each of which is provided with a paid, full-time administrative secretary in the person of a food production officer appointed by the Department of Land Development. Progress will also be aided by the training facilities of the School of Cooperation at Polgalla, where not only inspectors of the Registrar of Cooperatives but also stores managers and administrative secretaries of the AP & S Societies receive training in various relevant subjects. Making the facilities of this unique school available to the local officers of the various cooperatives might pay good dividends in increased efficiency of the local societies.

A second factor which restricts the scope of cooperative lending is the extremely small size of the majority of peasant holdings, which average less than an acre. Even the best production on

203

such plots can yield little margin for debt service and generous lending could lead only to bankruptcy.

The only apparent solution to this problem is a gradual transfer of the least well-endowed peasants to colonization areas and of their holdings into the hands of others. Cooperative long-term credit could assist the latter process.

It is, indeed, in the field of long term credit that cooperatives have so far made no contribution. The need for loans of long duration comes from several sources. Some cultivators have become heavily in debt to traders, either because of bad harvests, illness or other causes; it would be a great boon to them if they could fund such debt for a term of several years at reasonable rates of interest, retiring it gradually. Other farmers may wish to extend their small holdings by purchase, or to make permanent improvements to their property. Theoretically, such individuals can borrow from the State Mortgage Bank; but in practice the claims to title are so confused, especially with respect to small holdings, that mortgages are ruled out.

No complete solution to this problem will be found until titles to land are clarified, perhaps by a registration system. [2] Some progress could be made, however, by making long-term credit available to individuals of probity and energy, on the basis of their character. Such knowledge of potential borrowers exists only within the local communities; this fact makes unrealistic any attempt to deal with the problem through a new national institution operating out of Colombo. Even a new decentralized arrangement such as a system of cooperative land mortgage banks [3] would be of dubious merit, since it would place additional demands for competent but scarce staff upon local communities.

All the facts seem to indicate, as the preferred remedy, an extension of the lending power of existing Credit Cooperatives

---

[2] For a discussion of this topic, see Land Tenure, Chapter 11.

[3] Such a solution has been suggested; see Appendix V to the Report of the Kandyan Peasantry Commission.

into the long-term field. The officers of these institutions reside in the villages; they know their people, and they already possess a great deal of information about their creditworthiness. The Mission therefore recommends that authority be given to Credit Cooperatives to make long-term loans on the personal credit of carefully selected borrowers, up to a maximum term of say 20 to 25 years, and that funds for this purpose be provided by such increase in the lending capacity of the cooperative banking system as is necessary. First operations under this procedure should be confined to experiments in a few localities where strong and well-run Credit Cooperatives are known to exist. Only if these trials were successful should the system be extended over a wider area.

A useful accompanying step would be to require the deposit of all evidences of debt in village communities with the nearest Credit Cooperative Society, with the added proviso that all debt not so registered would be nonenforceable in the courts. This would have the double advantage of making the debt of peasants to traders a matter of public record, and of bringing debtors into contact with the officers of the Credit Cooperatives. Such contact might lead, in suitable cases, to the substitution of the short- or long-term credit of the cooperative for that of the trader.

Rural Development

A high proportion of the projects and activities of the government operate, directly or indirectly, to improve the condition of that typical citizen of Ceylon, the villager. Irrigation works, resettlement schemes, demonstrations and technical advice by officers of the Department of Land Development, are only the more obvious ones. The building and improvement of roads, the extension of the electrical power network, the spread of educational and health facilities, are also clearly to the villager's advantage. Much benefit comes to him, too, from the credit facilities of the cooperatives, and from the efforts of the Production and Sales Societies to encourage the use of fertilizer, improved seed and better agricultural implements. Indeed, it would not be too much to say that every effective measure of economic development, by increasing the abundance of goods and services generally, favorably affects the villager's position.

Most of the developmental activities under way, however, appear to the village resident as something brought to him from outside his local community. They make little or no demands on him, and neither require nor attempt to enlist his cooperation. A new road is built, a new school erected, by outside labor and supervisors and with funds from the central government. When completed, it is there for him to use, and he is doubtless appreciative; but it embodies none of his own labor, his own enthusiasm, his own planning.

Yet in the person of the villager there is an immense and relatively little used resource of labor. It is not that he is unemployed —for the amount of unemployment of any kind in Ceylon is comparatively small—but he is underemployed. During the planting and harvest seasons, he is generally very busy. Between these periods of peak activity, however, there are many days when the village cultivator has little to do. If his interest could be enlisted in a cooperative effort to do things he himself would like to see done in his community, it would harness a very substantial amount of energy that now runs to waste.

The Ministry of Home Affairs and Rural Development has made an excellent beginning in tapping some of this energy and interest. Its Department of Rural Development now possesses a staff of over 100 rural development officers and 20 supervisors who work closely with more than 5,000 local Rural Development Societies (4,477 men's societies and 665 women's in 1950), complemented by another 500 independent women's welfare societies (Lanka Mahila Samiti). These organizations, under the guidance and direction of rural development officers, undertake a wide variety of activities which enlist the efforts of the local populace. They range from the construction of roads, wells, school buildings, dispensaries and recreation facilities, through the organization of handicraft industries and milk feeding centers, to the formation of volunteer rural police patrols and conciliation boards to settle disputes in the villages. Members of the Mission have discussed these activities with the leaders of various societies and have seen the keen interest which they generate.

In addition to providing advice, guidance and organizing assistance through its rural development officers, the Department has undertaken to train village headmen and village workers at various training centers. During 1952 this work is to be greatly expanded, with the aim of training some 5,000 this year. In the past, owing to limitations of time and staff, the information furnished has been rather superficial; for the future, it is to be hoped that greater stress will be laid on imparting knowledge of *how to do* some of the things that need doing in every village.

A great advantage of this approach, which appears to have been met with enthusiasm, is that it enlists the voluntary participation of local villagers. Labor that might have gone to waste in idleness is turned into productive channels, to the lasting benefit of the community. While major projects requiring sizeable amounts of capital and the use of skilled labor obviously cannot be carried out by such local organizations, there is an immense number of tasks they can do. Moreover, both the available manpower and the financial resources of the central government will for many years be needed elsewhere for developmental work which must be organized on a relatively large scale.

Until recently, the Rural Development Societies have had to operate entirely on the basis of voluntary labor supplemented by such funds as could be raised locally. But in the fiscal year 1951, the government began to help in a small way in the financing of undertakings involving the use of skilled labor or relatively costly materials. Parliament then authorized a grant of Rs. 500,000. It is gratifying to see that this was increased to Rs. 3 million in the following year. Through moderate grants-in-aid, much can be accomplished (e.g., in the construction of wells, latrines, culverts, bridges, and even buildings) that might have to wait a long time before it could be tackled by the appropriate Ministry. Besides, the cost of these projects is held to a minimum, since local materials (often donated) are used wherever possible and most of the labor is unpaid or paid only a nominal wage.

The Mission feels that the activities of the Rural Development Societies should continue to receive encouragement, without losing sight of the original objective of utilizing village labor rather than national funds. Financial aid may be expanded gradually, as the number of societies increases and as their capacity and willingness to undertake additional tasks grows. Divisional and District Committees should keep other agencies of government informed of tasks actually accomplished, especially in the field of construction, so that they may revise their plans accordingly. Meanwhile other agencies should consider how they can work with the societies, making the maximum use of their members' energies in carrying out the smaller local works for which they may be responsible.

At this stage the larger development projects are given priority in the allocation of the limited money available. Yet if additional funds are forthcoming, from Ceylon's own resources or from external aid, rural development should take a high place among the claimants for supplementary allocations—subject of course to the ability of the societies to use more money effectively.

11. Agriculture

Today's Problem

More than half of Ceylon's working population work on the land, and six out of seven of its people are directly or indirectly concerned with agriculture or related activities. It is the island's life.

But Ceylon's agriculture is highly specialized. Production, preparation and distribution of the three main export crops, tea, rubber and coconut occupy two thirds of the working population. These crops provide about 90% of the island's exports and their market prices are a barometer of local prosperity.

Meanwhile, for a fast growing population, over half the food supply is imported. For rice, the staple diet of the people, the import proportion is about 60%; for pulses, currystuffs and dried fish, about 90%; and for sugar and wheat, 100%. What this means in terms of quantity and expenditure is shown in Table I. Food imports in 1951 amounted to Rs. 683,700,000 out of the total import bill of Rs. 1,558,700,000.

Nor is this all. There are frequent difficulties in obtaining adequate supplies of such staples as rice, wheat flour and sugar and the rise in world prices has induced the Ceylon Government to subsidize the price of rice and other commodities to the public, adding an ever-increasing financial burden to the treasury.

There is, then, need for greater agricultural diversification and especially for all possible increase in domestic food production.

Present crop yields are below the potentialities of the land and the cultivator, but a dramatic improvement in farming ability, which would quickly rehabilitate lands that have been wastefully worked and rapidly improve lands that have been maintained but not agriculturally enriched, is unlikely. To look for a remarkable increase in production from existing areas during the next 5 to 10 years would be to court disappointment.

Rough estimates indicate that of the 3.25 million acres under cultivation, about 90% is under the four main crops—tea, rubber, coconut and rice—while the undeveloped land still available for agricultural production might total at most another 3.25 million acres. Of this, little has been cleared of jungle or otherwise prepared for the growing of crops or the more extensive carrying of livestock. After deducting areas which must be set aside for conservation, water supply, aesthetic, residential, transportation and other purposes, these residual 3.25 million acres are likely to be reduced appreciably. Moreover most of this land is much less well watered than the existing cultivated areas and it is estimated (see Chapter 13) that only about 600,000 acres can be irrigated.

To plan and to clear, prepare, develop and cultivate either irrigated or dry land sufficient to produce a really significant contribution to the country's home grown food supplies demands time, experience and an abundance of money. Given experience and the money, the development to a state of productive return still would take many years. There is no short-cut.

Recent History and Development

Until the nineteenth century Ceylon was concerned almost wholly with subsistence agriculture.

During the Portuguese period (1505-1658) and rather more in the Dutch period (1658-1796) there was some export of spices, notably *cinnamon* and *cardamoms*. A supply of cinnamon indeed had been one of the principal commercial objectives in the search of the Portuguese for a seaway to India and further east. Obtained largely from wild trees, its export was a state monopoly from 1656 till 1833. Small cultivated acreages were established by the Dutch from 1770 onward and for a time the crop attained considerable significance. Later it declined and today Ceylon has about 33,000 acres of planted cinnamon, ranking still as the main producer, with Java and the Seychelles following far behind.

Cardamom (*Elettaria*), first collected from wild plants, was also later cultivated. The present acreage is said to be about 6,000 acres; maximum exports are understood to have reached 850 thousand lbs. of capsules per year in the past but they have since fallen considerably.

Coffee, of the *arabica* variety, although introduced in 1690 by the Dutch, was not planted commercially until 1825 and not given really serious attention until about 1845. By 1874 the export had approached one million hundredweights. But in the year following the maximum crop of 1882, a most serious infection by *Hemeleia vastatrix* (coffee rust fungus) practically put an end to the coffee industry in Ceylon.

Tea (China tea) was introduced in 1824 and Assam tea in 1839, but as late as 1873 the total export for the year was a sample of 23 lbs. Fortunately from 1867 onward rather more attention was given to this crop, and as coffee collapsed the British planters commenced a systematic conversion of many of the coffee plantations to tea. Naturally, it was not possible to convert all the coffee land to the new crop; hence many plantations perforce reverted to natural vegetation, remaining to this day in various stages of grassy and mixed *patana* and scrub. The present tea acreage is over 555,000.

Cinchona, introduced to the Botanic Garden at Hakgala in 1861 by the Royal Botanic Garden, Kew, was given more serious attention from 1870 onward. Acreage rose from 500 in 1872 to 64,000 by 1883. At this stage the export of bark attained 16 million lbs. Subsequent overproduction caused a fall in price and general abandonment of the crop.

Rubber (*hevea*) was tried experimentally at both the higher elevation of Peradenyia and at the lowland elevation of Henaratgoda in 1876, utilizing seed collected by Wickham from the Amazon and obtained through Kew. By 1900, however, this crop had been planted to only a few hundred acres. Demand for rubber was much stimulated at the turn of the century by the rapid evolution of the motor industry. From then on the area extended rapidly, reaching 500,000 acres in 1930 and 656,000 acres in 1951.

In 1819 the British introduced *cacao* but by 1878 the export was still confined to a few sample hundredweights. Slowly but steadily Ceylon's crop has expanded in acreage and yield and has won a good name, especially for a particular type imported by the Philippines. Official records give roughly 19,000 acres as the area under cacao today, but this probably does not take account of the quite extensive use of cacao as a protective understory in rubber plantations.

The existing area of over one million acres of *coconut* is the outcome of centuries of work by the small agriculturalists of the country, there being comparatively few large plantations or estates. Coconut products today account for nearly one fifth of the island's exports and for some time Ceylon has been the principal exporter within the British Commonwealth. European influence on coconut production has been slight except in the development of exports and in the earlier scientific investigation of the various aspects of the crop.

Paddy, the staple diet of the country, covers today somewhat over a million acres and yields a reported 15 million bushels of grain. Early European influence, with its major emphasis on the production of tea, rubber and cacao, tended to give too little attention to the extension of the acreage of paddy and to the improvement of yields. At a later stage, however, the British did direct some attention to the scientific investigation of the crop and to its better management. Their work on the renovation of ancient tanks, commenced in the sixties of the last century, also assisted locally to increase the acreage under paddy.

Maize and *sorghum*—potentially important food crops, especially for use in the Dry Zone—have until very recently excited little scientific interest or attention in agricultural extension work.

212

MAP 5

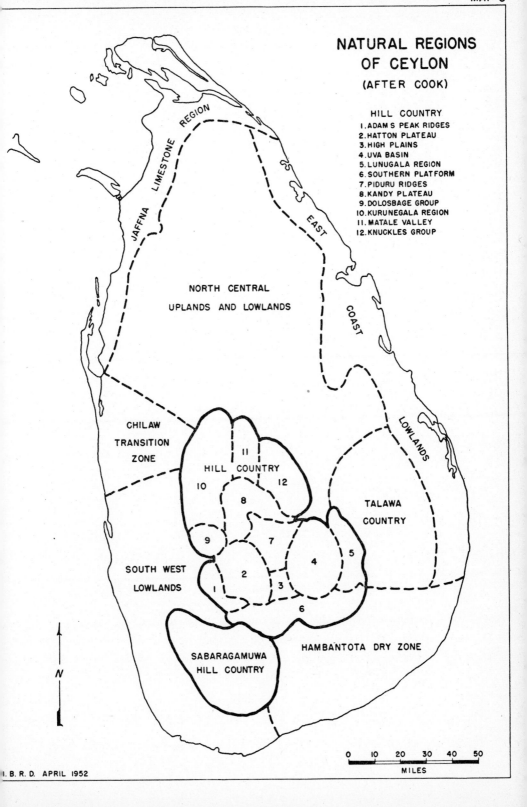

NATURAL REGIONS
OF CEYLON
(AFTER COOK)

HILL COUNTRY
1. ADAM'S PEAK RIDGES
2. HATTON PLATEAU
3. HIGH PLAINS
4. UVA BASIN
5. LUNUGALA REGION
6. SOUTHERN PLATFORM
7. PIDURU RIDGES
8. KANDY PLATEAU
9. DOLOSBAGE GROUP
10. KURUNEGALA REGION
11. MATALE VALLEY
12. KNUCKLES GROUP

JAFFNA LIMESTONE REGION

EAST

COAST

NORTH CENTRAL
UPLANDS AND LOWLANDS

CHILAW
TRANSITION
ZONE

HILL COUNTRY

LOWLANDS

TALAWA
COUNTRY

SOUTH WEST
LOWLANDS

HAMBANTOTA DRY ZONE

SABARAGAMUWA
HILL COUNTRY

N

0   10   20   30   40   50
MILES

A millet grown for a very considerable period in the Dry Zone and showing increasing promise as more is learned about it, *Eleusine coracana* (*kurakkan*) has by no means had the agronomic attention it deserves.

Tobacco has long been grown for local use and exported in crude forms to India, particularly from the Jaffna region. There has been little attempt at scientific improvement. Indications are that much better quality leaf suitable for cigarette tobacco could be produced in the north central region, in the Dumbara Valley and probably elsewhere.

More recently *chillies*, the crop so popular in Ceylon, India and elsewhere in the East, have been belatedly accorded somewhat better scientific and agricultural attention, as have a number of other crops in varying degree. The introduction, nutrition, selection and management of *livestock* have received neither scientific investigation nor attention to management technique commensurate with their importance.

In general it should be said that European and particularly British agricultural influence, in the past century, has been directed more particularly to the following:

a. Establishment of the *tea, rubber* and, to a less extent, *cacao* estates and industries, with all that this has ultimately entailed for the general economic development, welfare, financial strength and political status of the country.

b. Introduction and increased application of improved methods of plant management of these crops, to reduce soil erosion and deterioration. While much remains to be learned and very much more to be achieved in practice, some useful work in this field has been accomplished down the decades.

c. Introduction of scientific investigation and better management technique in *coconut* and *paddy*.

d. Laying the foundations of an agricultural service, advisory executive and scientific, that has done some very valuable work since its inception.

e. Through the influence and facilities of tea and rubber

estates and the Government Department of Agriculture, the training of a very large number of men educated in varying degree
in the principles and practice of specialized or general agriculture;
they include superintendents, foremen and skilled laborers.

It is largely upon this base that Ceylon will build her future
agricultural development by whatever course is chosen after careful inventory of her natural endowment and needs.

NATURAL ENDOWMENT

Climate

The main rainfall and temperature distribution is shown in
Maps Nos. 5, 6 and 7. Traditionally the Ceylonese speak of
their island as divided into a Wet Zone and a Dry Zone. The
terms are merely relative and apt to mislead an outsider as
there is no truly dry area. Nevertheless, the difference between
them is marked.

Climatically the Wet Zone has a relatively satisfactory integration of temperature, humidity and rainfall (in amount, effectiveness and distribution) and is therefore well endowed for the production of the major export crops, tea, rubber, coconut and cacao,
and for a fair range of other crops of lesser significance. It represents, however, only about one quarter of the land area of the
island. Of this area, portions of the montane region are at present
excluded from economic production by a combination of topography, boisterous climatic conditions and the natural covering of
dense, stunted montane jungle.

The Dry Zone extending over about three quarters of the island,
is climatically far less favored. Here the amount, effectiveness and
distribution of rainfall vary considerably according to the particular region[1], while the degree of unreliability of the effective
rainfall is high and, with present knowledge unpredictable. The
interplay of high temperature, low humidity, poor and uncertain
rainfall creates a high rate of evaporation which acts severely on

---

[1] Some details of these variations are given in the discussion of Natural
Regions in later pages of this chapter.

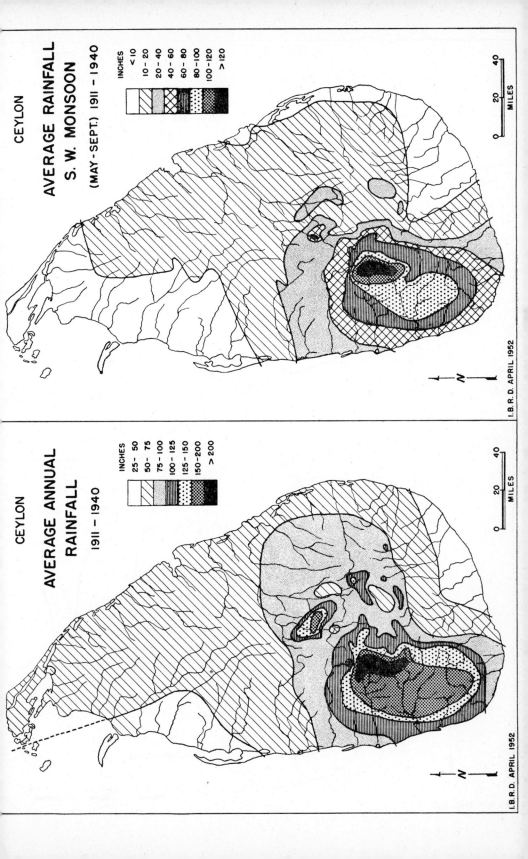

CEYLON

AVERAGE RAINFALL
S. W. MONSOON
(MAY-SEPT.) 1911-1940

INCHES
< 10
10 - 20
20 - 40
40 - 60
60 - 80
80 - 100
100 - 120
> 120

N

0   20   40
MILES

I.B.R.D. APRIL 1952

CEYLON

AVERAGE ANNUAL
RAINFALL
1911 - 1940

INCHES
25 - 50
50 - 75
75 - 100
100 - 125
125 - 150
150 - 200
> 200

N

0   20   40
MILES

I.B.R.D. APRIL 1952

MAP 8

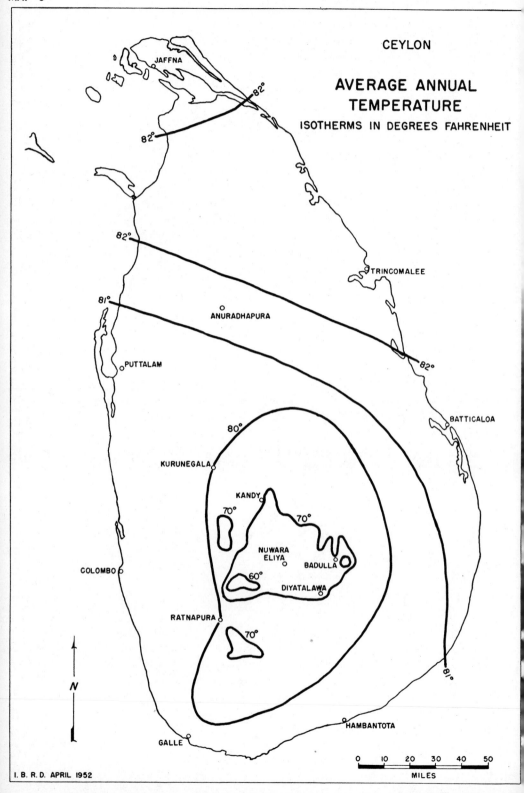

CEYLON

AVERAGE ANNUAL
TEMPERATURE

ISOTHERMS IN DEGREES FAHRENHEIT

JAFFNA

82°

82°

82°

81°

TRINCOMALEE

ANURADHAPURA

PUTTALAM

82°

BATTICALOA

80°

KURUNEGALA

KANDY

70°

70°

NUWARA
ELIYA

BADULLA

COLOMBO

60°

DIYATALAWA

RATNAPURA

70°

81°

N

HAMBANTOTA

GALLE

0   10   20   30   40   50

MILES

I. B. R. D. APRIL 1952

both natural vegetation and cultivated crops. These conditions plus
the limits to the extension of irrigation and the comparatively poor
and readily erodible nature of much of the soil, add up to no
mean hazard for large-scale agricultural development and settlement in the Dry Zone.

Soils[2]

While the soils range all the way from good to poor according to locality, topography and history of their working,
their capacity for production could be appreciably improved
by correct soil husbandry, wise application of organic matter and
fertilizers and proper methods of soil conservation. In most localities of the Wet Zone, water conservation would be less important
than drainage to improve physical, chemical and biological conditions. In the Dry Zone, however, soil and water conservation
practices should march hand in hand and are of the greatest practical significance.

In the Wet Zone organic matter is normally fairly well represented but in the Dry is generally deficient. Available nitrogen
ranges from very fair to below average in the Wet Zone but is
more deficient in the Dry. Lime is usually wanting in the Wet
Zone but is better represented in the Dry. Replaceable bases, on
the whole, are more abundant in the Dry Zone than in the Wet.

While the soils of the Dry Zone are somewhat richer chemically
than those of the Wet Zone, they are not rich or even above average in plant nutrients. Physically they present many problems and
are readily erodible. Their management for agricultural production—notably for dryland farming—is likely to call for improvement of texture, enhanced water retaining capacity, protection
against surface erosion and increase in fertility.

Although the soils of the Wet Zone generally deteriorate more
rapidly when exposed to the sun, the Dry Zone soils also seem to
suffer greatly in this respect. The difficulty is, of course, characteristic of all tropical and subtropical soils.

Problems of erosion and reduction in fertility are significant
[2] See Map No. 8.

throughout the island. Despite the long continued efforts of both tea and rubber planters and the skill of many Ceylonese farmers in the Wet Zone in terracing their paddy fields, erosion is nevertheless serious. In the Dry Zone the capacity of the peasantry to grow paddy and to maintain reasonably good soil conditions may take care of the irrigated areas; but the special climatic and soil characteristics and the novelty of dryland farming in the island are likely to bring more than ordinary difficulties in working the non-irrigated soils. Inexperienced colonists coming from urban areas or elsewhere are less likely to make an immediate success of soil maintenance whether on irrigable or dry land.

Water Supply

Where rainfall is irregular or inadequate, subsoil water for primary and limited irrigation purposes would of course be of great value. But a flooring of extensive, ancient crystalline rock over the greater portion of the Dry Zone argues against the possibility of large underground water supplies. Exceptions do occur, as in the Jaffna Peninsula and in a narrow zone running along the northwest coast, where the nature of the underlying rocks permits accumulation of telluric water. But apart from the larger or smaller fissures that contain local supplies, the ancient rocks are impermeable and cannot hold any appreciable volume. While a mantle of variable depth of decayed rock, detritus and soil covers the extensive ancient rocks, the total amount of water this holds is comparatively small[3].

For future development this circumstance is indeed significant. It means that in the absence of sufficient and suitably distributed surface water supplies, colonization of the Dry Zone will call for special and expensive provision of water.

It might be argued that the existence of upwards of 10,000 to 11,000 ancient "tanks" or dams throughout the Dry Zone indicates that it would be possible to hold very large volumes of surface water by renovating and enlarging many of these ancient tanks and constructing a number of large modern dams.

---

[3] See Map No. 9 for the main geological structure.

MAP 9

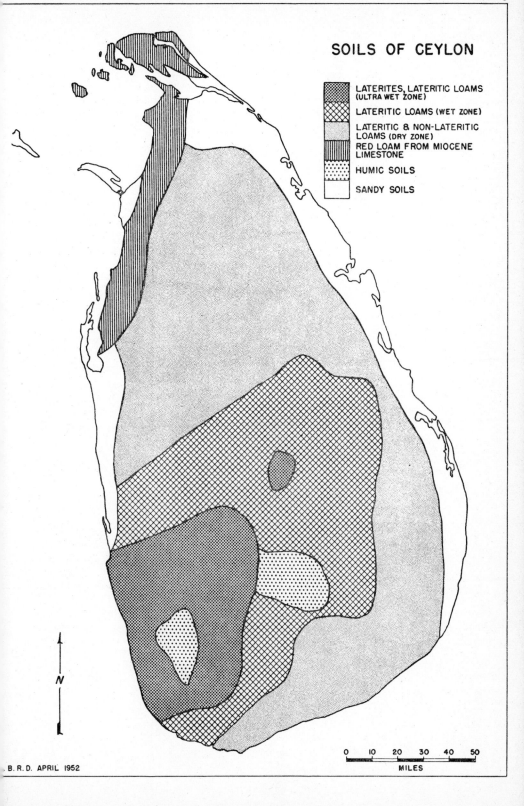

SOILS OF CEYLON

LATERITES, LATERITIC LOAMS
(ULTRA WET ZONE)

LATERITIC LOAMS (WET ZONE)

LATERITIC & NON-LATERITIC
LOAMS (DRY ZONE)

RED LOAM FROM MIOCENE
LIMESTONE

HUMIC SOILS

SANDY SOILS

N

0 10 20 30 40 50
MILES

B. R. D. APRIL 1952

A study of the known facts [4], however, suggests the less optimistic conclusion that the expansion of surface water supplies has definite limitations. The torrential floods that occur in the Dry Zone threaten destruction of all but the most robustly constructed irrigation dams and cause a rapid rate of siltation in certain areas. Moreover, the rate of evaporation is very high, particularly in relation to the volume of the shallower tanks; hence there is great loss of water during the drier seasons.

The ancient tanks are the inheritance of several successive stages of history, and it is unlikely that all of them carried water at the same time. Reconstruction or renovation would not by any means imply the restoration of the whole number. If this were done their distribution in relation to the larger and smaller catchments would probably interfere with the water regime, and it is likely that there would not be enough water to fill and maintain every tank.

Natural Regions

Agricultural potentialities are closely correlated with the characteristics of natural regions, as determined by a complex of geological and physiographic features, annual seasonal distribution of rainfall, temperature, evaporation, natural vegetation and indigenous population. Some comments on these criteria may help explain the classification of Ceylon's natural regions in the pages that follow[5].

Geological Structure. Geologically the island is remarkably uniform in its ancient crystalline rocks. The one major exception is the limestone plain of the Northwest and the Jaffna District. Here the difference is reflected in the approach made to the working of the soil and a combination of Tamil population and really severe environmental conditions, edaphic as well as climatic, has

---

[4] Presented in more detail in Chapter 13.

[5] In this study the Mission is indebted to the work of the late Miss E. K. Cook, *Ceylon, Its Geography, Its Resources and Its People;* Mac-Millan & Co., Ltd., London, 1951.

produced a remarkably efficient and intensive form of arable agriculture.

Elsewhere the outstanding geological feature of the island is its bed of crystalline rocks, with a mantle of detritus and soils derived directly therefrom. Thus, in general, there is a similarity in soil, in mineral and other resources, and in water regimen that tends to override and cancel out racial differences in the local population.

Physiography. The land relief naturally subdivides the country into: (1) coastal lowlands; (2) lowlands and uplands of the interior; and (3) hill or montane country. Ranges or ridges divide the last into a number of sub-regions with differences in rainfall, temperature and accessibility.·

Mean Annual Precipitation. Differences in the mean annual rainfall and, in the Wet Zone, in the condensation of hydrometeoric mists and the rate of evaporation, divide the country into certain major divisions:

(1) *Dry Zone*
  - (a) A region of deficient rainfall in the Puttalam District;
  - (b) A similar region in the Hambantota District—the mean annual rainfall being less than 50 inches;
  - (c) The northern and eastern uplands and lowlands, with a rain fall less than 75 inches.

(2) *Wet Zone*
  - (a) A region of abundant rain and high humidity within the 75 inches isohyet;
  - (b) A small region of excessive fall and very high humidity within the 150 inches isohyet.

Again, these major divisions may be further divided according to local differences in fall, humidity, temperature and evaporation.

Seasonal Rainfall Distribution.

(1) *Dry Zone*
  - (a) North and east coast regions experiencing rain mainly

218

in one season only: during the intermonsoon and
N.E. monsoon periods ranging from about October
to about January, (Trincomalee and coast stations
from Mannar to Potuvil);
- (b) The remainder of the Dry Zone with two seasons of
increased fall: one from about February or March
to about April or May; another from about October
to about January.

(2) *Wet Zone*
- (a) Lowlands experiencing two maximum periods, about
April to June and about October to November.
- (b) Uplands experiencing rain during the southwest monsoon, say about June to August;
- *(c) Uplands experiencing rain during the N.E. monsoon,
say December to February;
- (d) Uplands of the southwestern hill country, as at Kandy,
experiencing three periods of increased rainfall, on
about April, the second from June to July, and the
third from October to December.

Temperature.
- (1) The warm to hot lowlands;
- (2) The moderately warm intermediate elevations;
- (3) The cooler uplands and montane regions, with mean temperatures below 75°F.

Natural and Induced Vegetation. The country can today be
divided into broad vegetation zones by reference to what is known
of the forest climaxes, subclimaxes and transition zones, but
detailed survey of ecological land potential should enable a more
refined subdivision to be based on both natural and induced vegetation and its related physical features.

Race Distribution. Some natural subdivision is implied in the
main racial distribution:
- (1) The Jaffna limestone area, mainly the home of the indus-

219

trious and agriculturally minded Ceylon-Tamils, forms a distinctive region with its own racial, sociological, agricultural and economic features and idiosyncrasies.

(2) Development of the upland and montane regions for tea estates, etc., in the last 60 years, has led to the introduction of immigrant and semi-immigrant Indian and other labor, which has given a particular characteristic to portions of these regions.

The remainder of the country is roughly divisible into the regions principally inhabited by:

(3) The Lowland Sinhalese; and

(4) The Upland Sinhalese.

Utilizing the foregoing criteria, the natural regions defined by Cook and shown in Map No. 10 are described briefly below.

(i) *Southwest Lowlands.* This lies from sea level to about 600 feet, much of it just above sea level. Influenced by the southwest monsoon, rainfall ranges from 75 to 150 inches, increasing at the equinoxes; accordingly it is very wet, with flood and drainage problems. Its crystalline rocks are covered by laterite and lateritic loams, with alluvial soils along river flood plains. Almost the whole area is cultivated, largely under coconut especially on the littoral and blown sand, with some cinnamon and, in suitable sites, paddy. The population density is the greatest in the island and is evenly distributed except around Colombo. Lowland Sinhalese predominate but there is a mixture of peoples in the vicinity of the major ports. The main littoral centers are Colombo, Negombo and Galle.

(ii) *Sabaragamuwa Hill Country.* Appreciably wetter than the southwest lowlands because of condensation of the southwest monsoon on the hills, this has been preserved as a distinct natural unit throughout history by its isolation and inaccessibility. It is made up of a series of almost parallel ridges running roughly southeast to northwest, usually not exceeding 1,500 feet; but at the southern end there is a compact massif over 3,000 feet, known as the Rakwana Hill Country. The rivers flow between the ridges, sawing through at lower points, and forming at the northern end the Kalu Ganga. From the Rakwana area a number of streams radiate in various directions on the southern side and ultimately form the rivers Walawe, Nilwala and Gin Ganga. The population is sparse and localized. Much of the region is still under little-disturbed wet evergreen forest, some of it reportedly of very fine quality as at Sinaraja. Tea estates have been developed at Deniyanya and Rakwana. Along the alluvial valleys some paddy is grown. Probably appreciable portions are suitable for rubber, cacao and, at higher elevations, tea.

(iii) *Hambantota Dry Zone (Southeastern Dry Zone)*. Within the 50 inches isohyet, this area experiences some rain at most times of the year. Owing to the high rate of evaporation, however, the lighter falls are of no agricultural value. The natural vegetation is thorn scrub and dry jungle although toward the North there is better, taller dry mixed forest containing satinwood and ebony. In early times a limited number of tanks provided irrigation. The present population is sparse and is localized along the Walawe Ganga.

The littoral area has patches of saline soil of little agricultural value. Salt pans provide salt for export from the zone. The government has made some effort to grow cotton but, except on experimental plots, the yields so far have been low. Some groundnuts are produced. Livestock tend to fall off in condition in the drier seasons.

(iv) *Eastern Coast Lowlands*. This is a zone 10 to 30 miles wide extending roughly from Pottuvil northward to Mullaittivu. It is flat, with many lagoons and swamps for the first five miles inland. The Mahawli Ganga enters the sea approximately in the center of the region. Trincomalee is an important natural port with great promise, but its hinterland has had little development because of its swampy nature. Rainfall is low, with a single maximum in the northeast monsoon. Temperature is high, especially during the southwest monsoon when it is the hottest in Ceylon; severe drought is experienced during the same period.

Standing water in various parts permits the growth of paddy. This and coconut are grown near the lagoons, but much of the region is still under dry mixed evergreen forest. Numerous abandoned tanks indicate a onetime much larger population, as at Batticaloa and along the coast. During the southwest monsoon, west coast fishermen live in temporary camps. The population consists mainly of Tamils and Tamil-speaking Sinhalese; there are small settlements of Moors along the coast.

(v) *Jaffna Limestone Region.* The rough boundaries of this area extend from Puttalam to Madhu, a little south of Elephant Pass, across to Hullaittivu. A superficial limestone covers the crystalline rocks, thinning out toward the south. There is a single rainfall maximum during the northeast monsoon, except south of Mannar where there are two periods of increased fall and a somewhat lower mean temperature; between Mannar and Puttalam is a narrow zone with increased rainfall at the equinoxes. This is a dry region; temperatures are high during the southwest monsoon but not quite so high or lasting as long as in the eastern coast lowlands.

The Jaffna Peninsula is densely inhabited, principally by Tamils. Population on the mainland is sparce; in the vicinity of Puttalam, Moors and some African negroid types are found. The agriculture is intensive and the standard of practice high. Limestone outcrops at the surface in many places and has had to be removed to free the soil for cultivation. Large amounts of organic matter, both animal and plant, are returned to the soil. The foliage of the tulip tree (*Thespesia populnea*) is widely used for this purpose, being applied at the rate of several tons per acre per annum.

Somewhat better soil conditions are found on the western side of the Peninsula, near Jaffna. Paddy, tobacco, chillies and vegetables are grown as well as coconut and palmyra palm. Some livestock are carried, principally as producers of manure; spread-

222

ing is accomplished by moving the tethered stock from point to point in the fields. Wells in the limestone provide fairly adequate supplies of water for primary and small scale irrigation. The region presents a spectacle of industrious and efficient arable agriculture in marked contrast to the remainder of the Dry Zone.

(vi) *Chilaw Transition.* A small region with intermediate conditions links the southwest lowlands with the Jaffna limestone region on the coastal side, and with the north central uplands and lowlands region further inland. Abandoned tanks are found on the northern boundary, along the Deduru Oya. Coconut is grown extensively on the blown sand; in some localities these stands are fair, but in others they suffer from either inundation during heavy floods or periodic drought.

(vii) *North Central Uplands and Lowlands.* From the line Mankulam to Dambulla (on the edge of the hill or montane region) this well-marked region extends far to the southeast to include a great proportion of the valley of the Mahaweli Ganga. Much of it lies at just over 100 feet elevation and is flat to undulating. Numerous low buried hills project through the sediments of the plains; on the southern side, ridges project 600 to 1,000 feet from the same sediments. The soils are lateritic and non-lateritic red loams. Maximum rainfall occurs at the equinoxes, alternating with two periods of ineffective rainfall and very high evaporation. The fall is greatest during the northeast monsoon. Total annual rainfall is generally from 50 to about 70 inches. Ancient tanks abound, indicating dense population in the past. Present population, partly Tamil and partly Sinhalese, is sparse and localized near irrigation areas. This region contains most of the colonization schemes commenced in recent years.

Paddy production in this region requires irrigation. Subsurface water is limited, being far less than in the Jaffna limestone area. Dry farming may in the future produce sorghum, eleusine (kurrakan), drought-resistant maize, Deccan hemp (*Hibiscus*), sisal and other crops in fair amount, but the colonists and villagers have slight experience in efficient dryland farming practice.

223

(viii) *Talawa or Savanna Region.* Climatically this has much in common with the north central lowlands, but the rainfall is somewhat higher—rather more than 75 inches per year. Drought in this area is normally less severe. Hills and ridges with an elevation over 1,000 feet alternate with flat stretches with some alluvial soil suitable for paddy. The region is drained to the east by tributaries of the Gal Oya, Maha Oya and Maduru Oya. On the north, east and south the country is poorly inhabited. Until the road from Badulla to Batticaloa was built the region was not readily accessible, hence it has been comparatively little developed.

Here the natural vegetation is tree or tree-group and grass savanna. There is very little irrigation, the staple food of the few Veddhas at Migala and of the Kandian Sinhalese being not so much paddy as kurrakan. Little cash cropping is possible; production is largely for subsistence only. Grazing is coarse and, in the drier seasons, poor. Grass fires are an annual feature. Rotational grazing and other pasture management probably would improve the grazing in time.

(ix) *Hill or Montane Country.* This is a most important natural unit, with a high rainfall, high humidity and low evaporation. Numerous subdivisions can be distinguished [6] on the basis of relief, amount, distribution and intensity of rainfall and vegetation type. The climax of subtropical evergreen forest shows a number of types related to local climatic and relief conditions.

Portions of this region carry the well-known and valuable tea estates; others carry rubber, underplanted with cacao at the lower levels. Higher elevations are still densely clad in montane forest or jungle of poor, stunted type. In some localities, such as the Uva Downs and certain of the higher plains, man has brought about a fairly extensive replacement of forest by grassland.

The Man on the Land

In every sector of Ceylon's agriculture—on the estates, the middle-class properties and the smaller farms, plots, and colon-

---

[6] Cook, E. K.; *loc. cit.* See also Map No. 10.

MAP 10

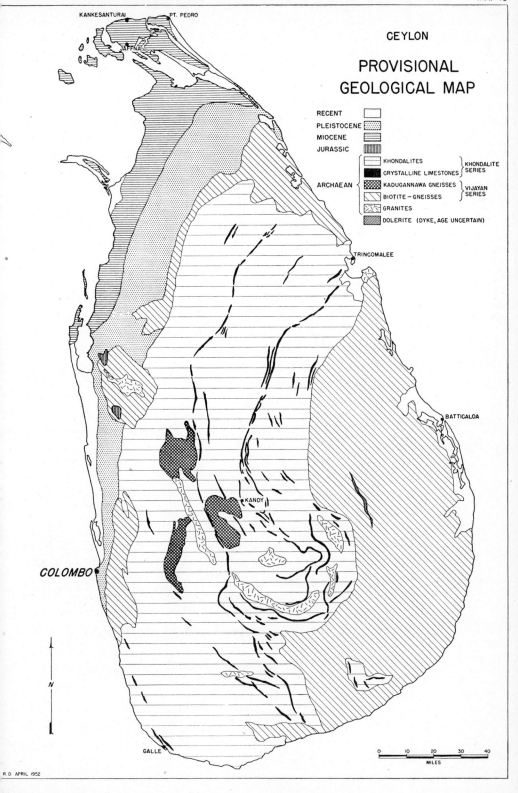

CEYLON

PROVISIONAL
GEOLOGICAL MAP

RECENT
PLEISTOCENE
MIOCENE
JURASSIC

ARCHAEAN
KHONDALITES ⎱ KHONDALITE
CRYSTALLINE LIMESTONES ⎰ SERIES
KADUGANNAWA GNEISSES ⎱ VIJAYAN
BIOTITE – GNEISSES ⎰ SERIES
GRANITES
DOLERITE (DYKE, AGE UNCERTAIN)

KANKESANTURAI   PT. PEDRO
JAFFNA

TRINCOMALEE

BATTICALOA

KANDY

COLOMBO

GALLE

N

0   10   20   30   40
MILES

R.D. APRIL 1952

ist holdings—there are men experienced in farming and capable of getting good results from the land while at the same time improving it. On the whole, however, a tremendous amount needs to be done to raise the general standards of farming, production and conservation. On the average the estates are far and away more efficient. The middle-class farmers, with some range of variation, come next, but will require considerable guidance and help for a long time. Finally, the "small" men—farmers villagers and colonists—still show an overwhelming proportion of inefficient producers. The task for the Agricultural Extension Service is a big one.

Estates. On the larger estates there appears, with inevitable variations, to be a good deal of administrative, commercial and agricultural ability.

Of late there is evidence of some change—perhaps only temporarily. Too rapid replacement of experienced European staff by Ceylonese employees, not usually as well trained and experienced, is reducing efficiency. Transfer of the ownership of estates has often meant less attention to good field and soil husbandry and conservation, with consequent deterioration in yield and in the value of the soil.

Middle-class Farmers. Although there is a wide range in efficiency and in yields, the agricultural sense of the middle-class farmer, when basic information is available to him, is fair to good. He should increasingly be brought in to assist the government in improving the agricultural practices in the island and should receive particular attention from government and Research Institute extension staff.

Small Farmers, Villagers and Colonists. The agricultural skill of small farmers, villagers and colonists varies widely. Some show considerable natural ability in terracing and similar practices, especially in the cultivation of paddy. Others still use primitive methods and produce smaller yields than could readily be achieved.

Among colonists there is equal range in ability. Those drawn from farming communities, particularly those who have grown up with the tradition of paddy growing, have shown marked aptitude for adjustment to the conditions on the colonization schemes. Others who have not farmed, but have either worked around urban areas or had limited laboring experience with special crops on the estates, must gain experience over some years before they can be expected to farm satisfactorily.

Extension work by the government departments will, in time, appreciably change the attitude of this extensive class of small producers toward the fundamental tenets of good soil and field husbandry and soil and water conservation. And especially it is hoped that their practical handling of farm animals can be much improved, for often there appears to be little or no understanding of how to care for, manage and get the best work from livestock.

PRESENT AND FUTURE AGRICULTURAL PRODUCTS

The following pages contain the Mission's observations on the potentialities of a number of individual agricultural products. The list does not pretend to be exhaustive. Included are the main crops now grown, as well as some undergoing experimentation and others which might be profitably introduced.

The products are divided under the following heads:

> Major export crops
> Other commercial crops
> Food crops
> Forest products
> Pasture and fodder
> Livestock

Within the larger groups the Mission has discussed together groups of related products such as cereals, fibers, spices, etc., fitting in the isolated items as appropriately as possible. The reader is referred to the Index for finding any commodity quickly. Map No. 11 shows the main distribution of existing crops.

Major Export Crops

(i) Tea

Market Outlook. World production of black tea in recent years has fluctuated around 1,000 to 1,100 million lbs. per year. Of this Ceylon provides about 300 million lbs. (305,171,168 lbs. in 1951), exceeded only by India with an annual output of about 575 million lbs. While tea production is fairly elastic in the short run (the output can be regulated to a certain extent by varying the methods of plucking), longer-period changes in production are slow because they involve heavy expenses for new planting or for depreciation on land going out of production.

Although world absorption has somewhat increased over the prewar level, tea has suffered less fluctuations in demand than other commodities. This steadiness exists partly because nearly half of the demand originates in the United Kingdom, where tea consumption is still rationed. The effect of de-rationing would be either a larger consumption or a general rise in the quality of teas consumed, or both. Ceylon, whose teas are above average in quality, would find either effect to her advantage.

The market in the near future is also protected by the International Tea Agreement between India, Ceylon, Pakistan and Indonesia which runs until April 1955. Excessive supply can, if necessary, be curtailed by means of export regulations.

The general market outlook thus seems to offer a fairly stable basis for tea cultivation unless changing local production conditions adversely affect Ceylon's competitive position.

Tea Growing Areas. Exacting requirements of soil, rainfall and elevation confine tea cultivation to the Wet Zone of the island and particularly to the mountainous region. However, low-grown tea is found at elevations lower than 2,000 feet, mainly in the southern part of the island in the Districts of Galle, Matara (about 41,500 acres) and Kalutara (10,500 acres).

High-grown tea (over 4,000 feet elevation) and medium-grown tea (2,000-4,000 feet) constitute the bulk of the crop. These types are cultivated principally in the region west of the line

227

Matale-Ratnapura, with the lines Matale-Badulla and Badulla-Pelmadulla as the other sides of the triangular producing area. It will be seen that tea cultivation is highly concentrated within a few districts; in fact, 35% and 19% of the total acreage is situated in the Districts of Kandy and Nuwara Eliya respectively.

Acreage. Of the three big export crops, tea with 561,031 acres covers the smallest part (about 17%) of the Island's total cultivated area.

No important changes in the acreage under tea have occurred since 1933, nor are to be expected in the near future, because of the expansion provisions in the International Tea Agreement. Under its latest terms the total permissible area is 588,227 acres, with possible extension during the regulation period not exceeding 5%. Within the same period replacements (to be accompanied by simultaneous uprooting in the area replaced) are allowed to the extent of 10% of the permissible acreage. Should Ceylon make full use of her extension rights, the area under tea might total 617,638 acres on March 31, 1955.

Changes in the division between the estate area and small holdings have also been negligible since 1933. At the end of March 1951 the total estate area amounted to 496,060 acres, while small holdings covered only 64,971 acres or 11% of the total tea acreage.

New Acreages. Expansion of the crop is limited to the Wet Zone where a very high percentage (about 80%) of the land is already occupied. Moreover, the danger of soil erosion, especially great in tea cultivation, offers a further limiting factor. One of the few expansion possibilities seems to exist in the *patana* (grass) lands. However, costs of preparation of this land are reported very high because of the long unproductive period preceding the actual preparation and planting.

Over and above this scarcity of suitable land and the existing statutory control, the need for highly skilled agricultural and technological personnel and the high investment costs for both

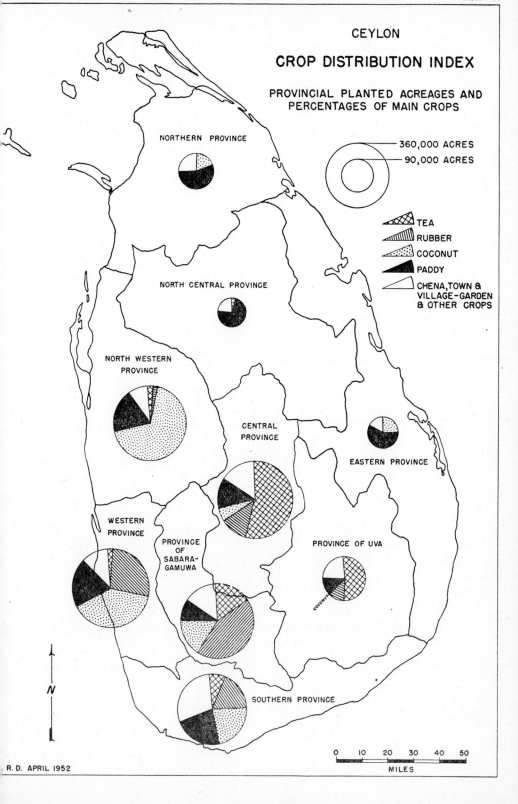

MAP II

CEYLON

CROP DISTRIBUTION INDEX

PROVINCIAL PLANTED ACREAGES AND
PERCENTAGES OF MAIN CROPS

360,000 ACRES
90,000 ACRES

TEA
RUBBER
COCONUT
PADDY
CHENA, TOWN &
VILLAGE-GARDEN
& OTHER CROPS

NORTHERN PROVINCE

NORTH CENTRAL PROVINCE

NORTH WESTERN
PROVINCE

CENTRAL
PROVINCE

EASTERN PROVINCE

WESTERN
PROVINCE

PROVINCE
OF
SABARA-
GAMUWA

PROVINCE OF UVA

COCONUT

SOUTHERN PROVINCE

N

0   10   20   30   40   50
MILES

R. D. APRIL 1952

cultivation and processing contribute to make substantial increase in tea acreage unlikely.

Composition of Area and Replanting. The small proportion of the tea acreage cultivated by small holders includes many extremely small plots with sometimes no more than a few tea bushes per holding. There are reported to be 78,000 small holders, indicating an average of only about 0.8 acres. Yields are very low—in some cases not more than three lbs. of dry tea per year. The wet leaf crops of these small properties are processed either in neighboring estate factories or in "bought leaf" factories; of the latter there were 42 operating in 1951.

Number, acreage and average size of tea estates are given in the following table:

TABLE I

TEA ESTATES IN 1951

	Number	Acreage	Average Size
10-100 acres	1,511	42,443	28.0
100-500 acres	592	166,413	281.1
Over 500 acres	344	287,204	834.8
	2,447	496,060	

High capital costs, occasioned by the expensive processing phase of tea production, demand fairly large areas to supply the wet leaf to the factories. One of the targets, therefore, should be to prevent any further splitting of acreage into smaller production units; amalgamation of small stands to more economic producing units would be advantageous.

Land requisitioning by the government, although not actually large, has become a point of great concern among tea cultivators. The government policy in this respect will have to be clear and limited if a high level of tea production is to be maintained. The tendency to fragmentation, caused by prevailing inheritance laws and customs, has been encouraged by the recent transfer of tea estates from European to Ceylonese owners, although the acreage

229

transferred is as yet only 1% of the total. The Mission suggests that, if practicable, such transfers should be made subject to provisions designed to prevent uncontrolled division into small plots in the future.

TABLE II

TRANSFER OF TEA ESTATES [7]

	From Europeans and Indians to Ceylonese		From Ceylonese to Indians	
	Acres	Value (000 Rs.)	Acres	Value (000 Rs.)
1948	1,203	1,450	—	—
1949	1,370	1,600	—	—
1950	978	3,310	26	5
1951	1,769	5,936	136	160

Although replanting is restricted by the International Tea Agreement, actual applications for replanting permits have been far below the permissible percentage. While in large measure attributable to high costs, this is also influenced by the uneasy feeling about the future engendered in tea cultivators by cases of land requisitioning.

In some cases new or replanted areas are not planted on the contour, despite the provisions of a recent law requiring such practice in specific circumstances. The tea industry would benefit greatly from a stringent application of this act, since soil deterioration caused by planting along the hill slopes, combined with inadequate soil protection, is one of the main long-term problems facing the industry.

Production. Under the stimulus of wartime and postwar shortages, tea production increased from a prewar average of 229 million lbs. per year to 298 million lbs. in 1950. It must be assumed

---

[7] In addition to the acreages listed, an estate area of 2,250 acres has changed proprietorship, but of this no details are immediately available.

that for a number of years the island's tea stands have produced at near maximum capacity. Since rejuvenation has been hampered by high costs of new planting or replanting, this high level of production may not be sustainable for a further long period.

This production has been maintained in spite of serious attacks in recent years of "blister blight," a disease which in some cases in certain locations has reduced output of wet leaf from 30 to 50%. Successful control is tending to eliminate this adverse factor.

On balance the Mission does not foresee in the near future any reduction in output for technical reasons, although temporary market fluctuations may affect actual production.

Tea cultivation is an intensive user of labor. About 70% of the costs of production are wages. As wages rise, the industry must seek economies to keep costs in balance. One method is to amalgamate small units, especially in the factory phase. For the processing of about 300 million lbs. of "made tea" there are not less than 950 factories operating in Ceylon, divided among the different types as follows:

	Estate Factories	Bought Leaf Factories	Total
High grown	316	3	319
Medium grown	357	17	374
Low grown	235	22	257
	908	42	950

The ratio to output is high by comparison with some other areas. In Indonesia before the war for example about 300 factories processed an aggregate of 160 million lbs. of tea. Thus, concentration toward optimum-size units may become a competitive necessity. Meanwhile, further economy through improvement of methods of cultivation such as pruning, fertilizing and shade growing in the tea stands will have to be a continuing subject of study.

231

Home Consumption. Domestic consumption before the war amounted to about 10 million lbs., but has increased to an estimated 14 million lbs. Until recently the tea sold and consumed on the island was of the poorer grades; more recently the Ceylon Tea Propaganda Board has launched a campaign to improve both its quantity and quality.

Naturally the home consumption, at about 5% of total production, does not represent a substantial support for the market as a whole; yet it is a part of the market deserving a continuing and increasing activity of the Propaganda Board. Although local per capita consumption of about two lbs. per year is rather low in comparison with, for instance, the United Kingdom (7.8 lbs. per year per head) and Australia (6.5 lbs. per year per head), recent trends indicate that the population is prepared to drink more tea than before.

This suggests possibilities for further expansion, especially if standards of living improve. At present, because of the lack of uniformity in quality, the small holdings output is at a disadvantage in the international market. A permanent increase in home consumption, therefore, should form a sound outlet for this part of the production, provided continuing attention is paid to the improvement of quality. In this connection legal measures to protect and identify the quality in retail trade are apt to have a favorable influence, and should be considered at an early date.

Tea Research Institute. The Tea Research Institute is devoted to technical studies toward strengthening Ceylon's competitive position in the world market. Its principal station is at St. Coombs in the center of the main upland tea country. Here it operates a complete experimental estate and factory. In addition there are two low country substations—one at Kalutara about 30 miles south of Colombo, and the other at Passara in the center of Uva Province—where problems of low-grown tea are studied.

The Tea Research Institute has a well established reputation for useful work. It is financed by means of a tax on exported tea, the rate of which has been raised from 14 cents per 100 lbs. to

30 cents, including 5 cents specifically allocated to the operation of a Smallholders Advisory Service, which is charged with helping the 78,000 small tea producers.

Some of the more significant features of the work of the Institute are:

(a) The depredations of *blister blight* (a yield-reducing fungus disease caused by *Exobasidium vexans*, which attacks the young leaves in particular) known to reduce the yield by a considerable amount and often by as much as 20 to 30%, have been reduced by systematic application of a metallic copper compound spray, either cuprous oxide or copper oxychloride. This is very important because the blight together with the effects of severe pruning took a heavy toll until comparatively recently. The costs are reported to be about Rs. 2.76 per acre per pound, the round of spraying being at 10 day intervals, and the seasonal costs about Rs. 50 to 60. The tea appears to be tolerant of reasonable amounts of copper.

(b) *Pruning* has been carefully studied, the prevailing view being that better recovery and yield and a greater resistance to blight are associated with milder pruning. Earlier reshooting after milder pruning is also influenced by systematic fertilizing of the soil and the mulching of the soil surface with the pruned material and grass. Planters are advised to prune more lightly than many of them did previously.

(c) *Shade.* A wide range of upper and lower shade trees and shrubs has been tried over the years. Some of the shade trees are used also as lopping material for the mulching of the surface or for organic material to work into the soil. Some of these also act as useful agents for the better holding of the soil, their roots forming a good mat. Certain pest and disease organisms are known to be associated with particular shade species, e.g., Calonectria, a fungal leaf-spot with *Acacia decurrens* and eel-worm with the common Erythrina.

(d) *Soil husbandry. Fertilizer* studies reveal a response to potash but little to phosphate above a certain level of application;

233

response to nitrogen is less marked than to potash. No response to "Trace" elements has been demonstrated but sulphur in ammonium sulphate form is thought to have a tonic effect.

No prostrate "soiling" crops have been found really satisfactory. Loppings of certain leguminous trees and shrubs (e.g., Crotalaria, Gliricidia and others) have been found effective when used as mulch or worked into the soil.

Mulching by means of prune-trash and grass (notably *Tripsicum laxum* and Napier Fodder, *Pennisetum purpureum*) is reported to induce soil improvement and an earlier recovery from pruning. Mulching also reduces run-off of water on steeper slopes.

(e) *Vegetation propagation* is being given serious study, with the object of producing blight-resistant clones giving a good yield; some encouraging results are being obtained.

(f) *Root studies* aimed at throwing light on several physiological and management of soil problems have been commenced.

(g) *Soil conservation* and *water conservation* have been sought through less severe pruning and the consequent provision of a better and earlier cover to the soil, fertilization of the soil and mulching, but contour planting is being studied along with associated water control methods.

(h) The *factory* side—processing and so forth—is receiving only limited attention (see Chapter 15).

In proportion to the volume of tea produced, expenditure on assistance to the smaller growers is necessarily high. A number of tea instructors of the Agricultural Assistant grade administer to their technical needs. Publications in the vernacular are supplied gratis; holders of more than 15 acres receive the more advanced literature in English. The staff does its best, but is too small to reach the multitude of these small holders personally and should be expanded.

Conclusions and Recommendations.

    1. Although there is a slight excess of supply over demand in the world tea market, possibilities for increased con-

sumption are present (e.g., derationing in United Kingdom), so that prices are not expected to differ widely from the 1951 level.

2. Reduction of costs of production on existing acreage will be the main problem rather than expansion of acreage.

3. To ensure a continuous rejuvenation and prevent harmful fragmentation, the tea industry needs a clear government policy in regard to land requisition and preservation of estates transferred to Ceylonese ownership.

4. In the long run, some concentration of processing facilities seems to be necessary.

5. Continuing research on and application of soil conservation methods, fertilizing and pruning are necessary.

6. An expansion of the small holder extension service is recommended.

7. Propaganda for domestic tea consumption is essential for the future of the small-holders industry.

(ii) *Rubber*

Market Conditions. Development of synthetic rubber makes any comparison with the prewar situation of limited value. This is clearly demonstrated by Table III.

TABLE III

WORLD PRODUCTION AND CONSUMPTION OF RUBBER
(thousand long tons)

	Production			Consumption		
	Natural	Synthetic	Total	Natural	Synthetic	Total
Average 1934-38	965	—	965	1,025	—	1,025
1949	1,490	440	1,930	1,440	450	1,890
1950	1,850	535	2,385	1,705	580	2,285
1951 [a]	1,860	910	2,770	1,530	895	2,425

[a] Estimates

Production of natural rubber is exceeding consumption at an increasing rate, the predicted difference for 1951 being about 18%, but it appears that stock-piling demand has so far bridged the gap. Indeed, demand was so strong after Korea that prices rose from 17.5 United States cents per lb. at the end of 1949 to 78 cents in December 1950, subsequently falling to a little under 35 cents in March 1952.

The market has been largely dominated by "artificial" forces— government regulations regarding consumption of natural and synthetic rubber, government buying of natural rubber and reactivation of the synthetic plants in the United States. These measures and the continuing increase in production (especially the revival of Indonesian production) caused the drop in prices during 1951.

Recently regulations affecting consumption have been relaxed, government monopolization of imports into the United States has ceased and the New York market has been re-opened. The market is more under the influence of the permanent trends of production and consumption and less affected by special stock-piling demand. It is, however, too soon to say whether the sharp fluctuations, which have characterized rubber almost throughout its history, will cease. Much will depend on whether the underlying reasons for stock-piling retain their strength.

Actual consumption—the other part of the demand—has increased reassuringly in the postwar period and can undoubtedly be further increased, though some of the increase will be filled by synthetic rubber. Consumption of natural rubber will depend largely on the United States policy on synthetic production, which is not likely to be reduced as sharply as in the years immediately after World War II.

Natural rubber prices will therefore remain subject to at least three depressing factors: (a) the large capacity of natural rubber production; (b) continuing production of synthetic rubber; and (c) existence of large, "nonconsumption" stockpiles. Bearing in mind the price of 23½ cents per lb. at which general purpose synthetic is now sold in the United States, natural rubber prices may fluctuate around 30 to 35 cents in the next few years.

Ceylon provides about 5% of the total world production, and has therefore only a small influence on price levels. Ceylon's policy should be to concentrate on improving methods of production so as to achieve the best possible competitive position in a market where supply is likely for a long time to outrun demand.

Rubber Cultivation. Rubber cultivation is limited by soil and climatic requirements to the Wet Zone. Rubber flourishes on lands of low and medium elevation (up to about 2,000 feet) where precipitation is over 80 inches per year. The main region of rubber cultivation is roughly in the middle of the Wet Zone, in an area defined by Kurunegala, Matale, Kandy, Ratnapura and Kalutara, but there is some rubber as far east as Badulla and as far south as Matare.

Acreage. At the end of 1950, 655,225 acres or 20% of the total cultivated area were planted with rubber. Of this area 83% is wholly planted with rubber, while over 72,000 acres or 11% are interplanted; the remaining 51,400 acres consist of budded rubber. According to the figures from the Rubber Controller (Administrative Report, 1950), of the total budded area not less than 23,373 acres or 46% is classified as small holdings of less than 10 acres each. Small estates (10 to 100 acres) account for 15,565 acres or about 30%, while in the category of large estates (100 acres and over) only 12,500 acres were budded.

After 1938 up to 1945, there was an appreciable (9%) increase in the recorded rubber acreage; from then on a slight decrease has occurred. Part of the apparent increase is probably due to different methods of recording, but Ceylon's position as the only important supplier of natural rubber for the Allies from 1942 to 1945 also contributed to expansion.

A noteworthy shift has taken place in the division of the acreage among the various classes of holders (see Table IV).

TABLE IV

RUBBER ACREAGE OF CEYLON BY CLASSES OF HOLDINGS
(thousand acres)

	Large Estates	Small Estates	Small Holdings	Total
1938	349.6	124.0	130.5	604.1
1941	356.5	135.0	146.1	637.6
1944	356.8	139.5	161.2	657.5
1947	354.3	139.7	165.0	659.0
1950	344.5	141.9	168.8	655.2

All the expansion has occurred in the smaller units, the increases over 1938 for small estates and small holdings being 13.5% and 29% respectively.

Here we meet a factor which is affecting Ceylonese agriculture in general and which demands an early solution. In rubber, as in tea, the fragmentation of properties already caused by the existing laws of inheritance is aggravated by the government policy of land acquisition. For various reasons large estates or parts of such estates have been requisitioned and either put under cooperative management or divided into small plots. No accurate figures on the consequence of these measures are available but it has been reported that losses of 25% in output are not exceptional.

The fact that Ceylonese owned holdings increased between 1949 and 1950 from 58% to 61% indicates the speed of transition.

The average size of small holdings (total number in 1950: 122,911) in Ceylon is 1.4 acres as against an average of 26 acres for small estates (5,434) and of 400 acres for large estates (860).

New Acreages. Policy should concentrate on the improvement of that part of the existing rubber area which can already produce the quantity expected to be marketed in the future. The total area under rubber should not be increased and might even be reduced. There is accordingly no need to search for new lands suitable for rubber cultivation.

Composition of Area and Replanting. At the end of 1950, 453,263 acres of Ceylon rubber (69% of the total) were registered as seedling rubber planted before 1922. 6,260 (1%) acres were

seven years old or younger; 84,900 acres (13%) were from 8
to 20 years old, and 110,802 acres (17%) were aged from 20
to 29 years. The greatest rate of new planting takes place in
periods of rising rubber prices as is demonstrated by the following
table:

	New York Price Per lb. cents	Newly Planted Acres
1922-24	24.32	17,400
1925-28	47.99	92,900
1929-33	9.23	30,200
1934-43 [a]	18.01	54,700
1949-50	29.20	6,300

[a] During 1934-38 and 1941-42 new planting was prohibited.

Newly planted trees normally come into production six to seven
years after planting, when there is no reason to expect the
price situation to be as favorable as when planting took place.
Indeed, the effect of simultaneous heavy planting in other areas is
likely to cause depression of prices when all the new trees come
into bearing. It might therefore be argued that it would pay
Ceylon to be "out of phase" with the common trend and that the
Rubber Controller should use his powers to withhold permits
when prices are attractive. Since, however, this is precisely when
rubber growers are best able to finance new planting such a policy
could hardly be enforced. What does emerge from consideration
of the basic economics of rubber is that new planting policy ought
to be based on long-run considerations and not on ephemeral
market situations. The government should certainly use its influence and legal powers to see that a steady long-run policy is
pursued.

This can be done the more easily in view of the existence of
a large uneconomic rubber acreage. Based on assumptions in
regard to wages, yields and net selling prices, this uneconomic
acreage in 1947 was estimated by the Ceylon Rubber Commission
to be about 175,000 acres. By its own calculations the Mission is

239

inclined to agree with this figure. But present average yields of Ceylon rubber are about 375 to 400 lbs. per acre per year, while improved production methods should increase the yield to about 500 lbs. per acre annually. Thus a quantity of about 100,000 tons of rubber, for probable disposal in the future world market, can be produced on about 500,000 acres, leaving an excess of 150,000 acres in the present acreage.

Probably the most important contribution to increase yield would be the replacement of the old seedling rubber by high-yielding clones. The Rubber Rehabilitation Scheme, in operation since May 1950, has this item as one of the points of its program. Unfortunately the present price of rubber does not encourage replanting; accordingly it may pay to intensify the propaganda for replanting, particularly through the office of the existing Rubber Smallholders Propaganda Office.

Production. Rubber output, which amounted to 60,000 tons in 1939, was greatly stimulated during World War II, when extraordinary production methods were applied to fulfill the requirements of the Allies. From a peak of 105,500 tons in 1943 there was a gradual decline to 89,500 tons in 1949, but in 1950 the rubber shortage raised the level to an all-time record of 113,-500 tons. Of this total, 85,500 tons (75%) were produced on estates and 28,000 tons by smallholders. [8]

The effects of slaughter-tapping, both under government orders in the war years and in response to high prices in 1950-51, can be widely seen in the rubber stands and will undoubtedly influence future production. Moreover, investigations of the Mission indicate that normal methods of tappings are desperately in need of improvement. The number of trees tapped per tapper (175-200)

---

[8] This tonnage for smallholders is an estimate based on export and estate production figures. It is open to doubt because it would indicate an average annual production of about 500 lbs. per acre for smallholders as against about 450 lbs. per acre for estates. This is contrary to what is observed in other crops, although it is possible that slaughter-tapping by smallholders would account for it.

is low compared with similar conditions in other countries. Implements used in tapping are of rather poor quality (very few aluminum cups are used) and the hours of tapping seem to be too late in the day. The necessary adjustments in these matters would, we believe, be rewarded by a lasting increase in production.

Ultimately, increase of yields will require not only higher yielding material but also clones resistant to various diseases. The widespread *Oidium* disease, which affects the leaves of the trees during the wintering time decreases the output of latex from 20 to 40%, hence effective control would bring a marked increase in production.

The newly established system of latex-collection centers in smallholding areas is highly commendable. It should be expanded as much as possible, to avoid waste through scattered processing and to improve the quality of the product.

Consumption. It is very probable that future natural rubber consumption will be mainly of high-quality types and special forms (e.g., latex). Therefore the general policy should be to prepare for this market as soon as possible. Research on the physical properties of rubber and latex should be carried out at an increasing rate, preferably in accordance with the programs laid out by the International Rubber Research Board.

Local consumption, some 150 tons annually, is negligible to date. Admittedly, in relation to the export market, attempts to increase the local consumption are of only minor importance. On the other hand, in view of Ceylon's industrialization program it is noteworthy that rubber is a suitable and available raw material for numerous additional small-scale industries. These include automobile tires, garden hose, batteries, toys, rubber shoes, and various articles made from latex by the dipping process.

Rubber Research Institute. Sponsored by the Department of Agriculture, rubber research from 1927 to 1951 was carried on by the Rubber Research Scheme. In 1951 this was renamed the Rubber Research Institute. At present the organization is financed from a tax on exported rubber of 55 cents per 100 lbs., and from income derived from 500 acres of rubber it manages. As to policy,

241

the Institute is directed by the Rubber Advisory Board, of whose members more than half are nominated by the government or are government officials. The Board is responsible to the Ministry of Agriculture and Lands.

Among its various activities the Institute has concerned itself with vegetative propagation, oidium control methods, root-rot fungus, fertilization ground cover, cacao underplanting, tapping technique, and the production of budded material for small holders. In addition it supplies instruction, advice and propaganda to small rubber producers.

At the moment the organization is somewhat short of technical staff to handle its work. Ceylonese citizens are to be appointed to the staff as rapidly as suitable men become available.

Organizational Control. Not one, but several government organizations are now dealing directly with rubber cultivation and trade. In addition to the Rubber Research Institute, there is the Office of the Rubber Controller (collection of statistics, registration of rubber lands, permits for planting, etc.) as well as that of the Rubber Commissioner (created during World War II to purchase and ship rubber).

It would help the industry if these functions could be centralized under one organization in which government, producers and the trade would have equal representation. The work could then be coordinated along lines of general policy laid out by the government on recommendation of this organization. Moreover, under centralized control the levying and distribution of the total tax (now including the 0.55 cents per lb. for the Rubber Research Institute, 0.10 cents per lb. for the office of the Rubber Controller and 0.75 cents for the Medical Aid Fund) would be more flexible to meet changing needs in the various activities.

Conclusions and Recommendations.

1. Improvement of Ceylon's competitive position in an apparently declining world market for natural rubber should be the main objective of the government rubber policy.

2. Measures to increase yields per acre should prevail over any attempt to increase the existing acreage.
3. Assistance in replanting, not only with rubber but also with other crops, should be expanded along the lines of the existing Rubber Rehabilitation Scheme.
4. Recognition, in determining the measures to be adopted, that saleable production for the world market will probably fluctuate around a level of 100,000 tons annually.
5. Expansion of propaganda services among smallholders deserves high priority, not only in the field of replanting and agricultural production methods but also in regard to methods of processing, amalgamation of small plots and organization of producers.
6. Among yield-increasing methods, attention should be paid to improvement of tapping and conquest of yield-decreasing diseases.
7. Centralization of general control, research and advisory work will contribute toward the recommended long-term policy of producing high-quality and special types of rubber, and will unify objectives for the benefit of the industry.

(iii) *Coconut*

Ceylon is one of the world's leading producers of coconut. Apart from the large export of copra, oil and coir fiber, the crop is important to the island for food and a multitude of secondary uses. Exports in 1951 were:

		Value (Rs.)
Copra (cwt.)	386,927	27,059,451
Desiccated coconut (cwt.)	795,719	65,686,845
Coconut oil (cwt.)	2,195,640	227,061,213
Fresh coconuts (no.)	6,621,425	3,019,871
Total value		*Rs. 322,827,380*

Although there are no accurate figures, it is sometimes estimated that as many nuts are consumed locally as enter into the processing and export trades.

World Situation. Present world production of oils and fats is about 5% to 10% above prewar levels. Because of world population growth, however, per capita output is probably no greater than it was. At the same time, increased consumption in producing countries has kept per capita world exports actually below the prewar figure.

With the supply relatively tight, the demand side of the fats and oils market meanwhile shows a fairly strong position in the face of high consumers' incomes and lively industrial activity. True, one of the price incentive factors in recent years—buying for stockpiling—is no longer influential; yet under existing conditions it is hard to imagine that Ceylon's share in world production would meet a very weak market in the forthcoming years.

Ceylon's contribution to the net exports of fats, oils and oilseeds from the principal exporting countries was about 2.5% in 1950 (about the same as before the war), but its importance in a particular section of this market, copra and coconut oil, was much higher and amounted to 9% in 1950 as against 12% in 1938. From Table V it will be seen that Ceylon ranks third in exports of copra and coconut oil, after the Philippines and Indonesia.

Barring unpredictable events such as war or a heavy slump in the world's economy, conditions indicate that the Ceylonese production can be disposed of in a fairly stable market. Ceylon should reinforce this important branch of its economy in the forthcoming years, so as to be prepared for the time when the market conditions require a better competitive position.

Location of Coconut Groves. Most of the coconut palm area lies within a triangle whose corners are approximately at Colombo, Puttalam and Kurunegala—with sides about 80, 50 and 55 miles in length respectively. Coconuts are found extensively also in a narrow coastal strip, 5 to 10 miles in width, from Colombo to Matara in the extreme south and in scattered plots elsewhere, especially on the Mannar peninsula on the west coast and in the Batticaloa and Trincomalee districts on the east coast. In the

TABLE V

WORLD EXPORTS OF OILS AND OILSEEDS BY LEADING PRODUCERS

(Net Exports in Terms of Oil)

(thousand long tons)

Exporting Countries	Fats, Oils and Oilseeds			Copra and Coconut Oil		
	1938	1949	1950	1938	1949	1950
Argentine, Brazil and Uruguay	630	326	576			
British West Africa	384	570	571			
French West Africa	291	252	256			
Belgian Congo	108	181	184			
China	630	87	174			
Philippine Republic	374	407	504	374	407	504
Indonesia	630	358	325	365	240	209
Malaya	128	94	101	92	45	59
Ceylon	123	110	87	123	103	87
India & Pakistan	512	19	88			
Australia & New Zealand	209	175	196			
Antarctic	557	339	341			
New Guinea and Mozambique				71	54	60
Total	*4,576*	*2,918*	*3,403*	*1,025*	*849*	*919*

Source: FAO Commodity Report, October 1951.

Jaffna province, in the north of the island, the main palm cultivation is not coconut, but palmyra.

Acreage. Accurate figures of coconut acreage are not available. In current statistics 155,000 acres in town and village gardens is added to the 1946 census figure of 920,942 acres, giving a total of roughly 1,075,000 acres or nearly 33% of the total cultivated area.

From the official figures it is hard to draw a conclusion in regard to the sizes of the holdings. The 1946 census figures as quoted in the report of the Coconut Commission [9] would lead to the following division:

A-estates	107,400 acres
B-estates	812,600 acres
Town or village gardens	155,000 acres
Total	*1,075,000 acres*

In this breakdown, an A-estate is one of 20 acres or more employing 10 or more resident laborers and giving its census information in English. B-estates are those of 20 acres or more but with less than 10 resident laborers and managed by a person not well acquainted with English. Further on this subject, the Coconut Commission states:

"Most of the coconut lands in Ceylon fall within the B-estates and the town and village gardens. The coconut plantations are mostly holdings of over 20 acres. The extent of those below 20 acres is approximately 155,000 acres. It is possible that there are a larger number of smallholders claiming the 155,000 acres than there are owners of the 920,093 acres. To that extent only is the coconut industry a smallholders' industry. We consider that it is reasonable to define a coconut small holding as one below 20 acres in extent."

Analysis of data from other sources tells a different story. Starting with the official census figures as reported in the Statistical Digest, Volume I, Part II, under Section 15, Tables 63-66 there is the following breakdown:

(a) Total acreage under coconut, excluding cultivation in town and village gardens   920,942 acres

(b) Areas other than A-estates and town and village gardens   812,653 acres

(c) A-estates   108,289 acres

(d) Agricultural holdings other than A-estates (all crops except paddy lands and chena)

---

[9] Sessional Paper XII, 1949.

B-estates		Small Holdings	
Number	Acres	Number	Acres
9,021	369,604	394,782	903,191

Although no separation according to crops is given for the last-mentioned figures, reliable data for tea and rubber can be found in the administration reports of the Tea Controller and Rubber Controller. These show the following acreages as held in small holdings (smaller than 10 acres) at the end of 1950:

Tea	64,970	acres in	78,841 holdings
Rubber	170,020	acres in	122,911 holdings
Total	*234,990*	*acres in*	*201,752 holdings*

These figures refer to 1950; other information suggests that in 1946, to which year the census figures relate, tea and rubber small holdings occupied about 225,000 acres in 200,000 holdings.

Assuming 20% of the total acreage of small holdings to have been occupied by other crops, an acreage of about 722,000 acres held by about 315,000 smallholders would be divided among rubber, tea and coconut small holdings. Subtracting the above figures for tea and rubber would leave roughly 500,000 acres of coconut cultivated by 115,000 smallholders or an average holding of about five acres.

The foregoing computation, as well as the impression gained by visiting parts of the coconut area, leads the Mission to disagree with the statement of the Coconut Commission. The Mission considers the coconut palm cultivation as being overwhelmingly a small-holders' industry, and suggests that the division of the total acreage is more nearly as follows:

(a) Small holdings (less than 10 acres):		
(1) Town and village gardens	155,000	acres
(2) Commercial small holdings	500,000	"
(b) Small estates	310,000	"
(c) Estates of more than 20 acres	110,000	"
	1,075,000	acres

It is, however, important that these deductions be checked in order to secure a correct approach to the problems of the industry. The Mission recommends that the departments and organizations concerned should gather definite data on this subject as soon as possible.

New Acreage. Supposing expansion of the area under coconut to be economically desirable, is suitable land available, and if so where?

Coconut cultivation is restricted to areas where there is a temperature of about 70 to 80°F. Rainfall, which is of primary importance, should be over 50 inches yearly, preferably equally distributed throughout the year. Moreover, soil conditions are a critical factor for economic production. Flat, well-drainable light soils suit the growing of the palms best, while the water table also plays an important role.

In August, 1951, the Coconut Research Institute made a survey of land suitable for coconut cultivation, but it was not sufficiently full for definite conclusions to be drawn. Out of about 183,000 acres investigated (actually or theoretically), 110,000 acres were thought to be "probably or possibly" suitable for coconut cultivation. This land was, however, stated to be of the lower grades. Further detailed surveys should be made to appraise the suitability of these lands more accurately, regardless of whether an expansion program is actually started at this time.

As a second source, parts of the 175,000 acres of the rubber lands defined by the Rubber Commission (in 1947) as uneconomic for rubber production may be suitable for coconuts. It would be valuable to examine and map out those areas which fulfill the basic requirements for coconut cultivation as early as possible. Even if only a small part of this area is suitable, a definite plan for conversion will be of great help when rubber production on those lands becomes uneconomic.

Finally, it has been suggested that coconut cultivation should be tried out in the government colonization and land-settlement schemes. Although it seems technically feasible to grow this crop under irrigation, the Mission doubts that the government should spend valuable time and money on this project. The main objection to such a scheme is that it would lead to a number of very small holdings which at best could make only a minor contribution to local consumption in those communities—and this probably to the detriment of other crops.

Composition of Acreage and Replanting. The coconut palm passes its optimum yield at the age of about 60 years. Since planting in Ceylon started not later than the middle of the 19th century, an appraisal of the present age-composition of the acreage is important. Here again, no detailed figures are available and conclusions have to be based on partial data and rapid field observations.

The 1946 census figures supply the following classification for trees on A-estates.

Years Old	Percentage
over 60	9.7
30-60	52.8
10-30	28.8
under 10	8.7

These figures cannot be representative of the situation as a whole, since replanting and underplanting has been undertaken mainly by the larger estates. According to the Coconut Research Institute, since the replanting program was started about 5,000 acres have been replanted by private enterprise, in addition to 10,000 acres rejuvenated with government help. Obviously the 5,000 acres fall in the category of A-estates, thus representing about 5% of the total acreage from this group. Even assuming all of the rest to have been accomplished on B-estates and small holdings, this would represent not more than 1%.

The rate of replanting and underplanting seen during visits to the various areas was very low, and probably would not account for more than 1%. Taking into consideration the large number of old trees observed by the Mission, and the knowledge that replacements in the groups of B-estates and small holdings have been very low, it is estimated that over one third of the total acreage must have passed the 60-year mark, and that another large proportion is very near that age.

A well-planned replanting program, with special attention to the rejuvenation of small estates and small holdings, is therefore necessary to maintain production capacity. With increasing home consumption per capita, and an expanding population representing an additional demand of about 30 million nuts per year, about one million seedlings will have to be planted each year to maintain even the present export level and meet the increased home demand.

Since 1948 the Coconut Replanting Scheme—a separate divison of the Coconut Research Institute—has carried out the actual work of rehabilitation with the help of government grants. The grant for 1951-52 amounts to Rs. 520,500, and is spent on advisory work as well as on the production of selected seedlings from high-yielding palms. Costs of production of one selected seedling are said to be one rupee. They are sold for Rs. .50 to individual cultivators and for Rs. .25 to cooperative societies, who then raise the seedlings in their own nurseries and resell them at their own prices.

Despite the strong need for rehabilitation, the Mission doubts that such a heavy subsidy on these seedlings is necessary under present circumstances. Nut prices received by small producers at the time of the Mission's visit ranged between 9 and 15 cents; an average of 10 cents per nut would be conservative. For the two acre plots (which are probably most numerous and need rehabilitation most urgently), gross income may be calculated as 2 (acres) $\times$ 70 (trees per acre) $\times$ 20 (nuts per tree) $\times$ Rs. .10 or Rs. 280 per year. It is the Mission's opinion that from this return 10% could easily be spent on replanting material. Coconut growers, like other agriculturalists, must be provident enough to allow for seed; actually they are more fortunate in that their need for replanting is so infrequent. Government financial help

250

would more usefully be applied in soil conservation, fencing, and other aspects of rehabilitation.

The main difficulty in the replanting program is to convince the smallholders of the importance of rehabilitation and the benefits which they themselves will derive. It is this lack of appreciation of the finite life of a coconut tree which has led to the present situation. Therefore, continuous educational propaganda would be more helpful than mere financial assistance in the provisions of seedlings.

Accordingly, the Mission recommends that the Coconut Research Institute be requested to submit a plan for an extensive propaganda service, including the training of a large number of coconut-propaganda assistants to be stationed later throughout the coconut areas.

Production. Whether there has been a long-term downward trend in total production has been questioned repeatedly. Statistics are available for exports only, and the crop fluctuates with seasonal weather conditions from year to year. Table VI gives a series of 5-year averages of production, based on published estimates by the Coconut Commission.

TABLE VI

ESTIMATED COCONUT PRODUCTION, 1925-50

(*million nuts per year*)

1925-30	1,810
1930-35	1,795
1935-40	1,725
1940-45	1,605
1945-50	1,800

These figures suggest that, despite the fall in production between 1925 and 1945, potential production is high in good market conditions despite the aging cultivation.

Yields per acre vary widely with local rainfall and soil, size of holdings and type of management. The reported range is from 4,000 nuts or more for the first class holdings per acre per year to 1,400 for low-class sites, with an island average of 1,700 to 1,800.

Even if large-scale rehabilitation could start very early, production will not be affected for some years. Weather conditions and the state of the market will no doubt cause fluctuations, but it is reasonable to assume that production will average about 1,600 million to 1,700 million nuts a year for the next decade.

From various tests and the Mission's own observations it is clear that production of the present acreage could be maintained and even be increased by : (a) improvement in the use of fertilizers; (b) better soil husbandry; and (c) better water conservation or drainage. The staff of the Coconut Research Institute is already working along these lines. In this, as in the replanting program, the major difficulties lie in getting the information over to the smallholders and securing their cooperation.

Consumption. Coconuts and their derivatives constitute the most widespread branch of the island's economy, and home consumption and export demand are in permanent competition for the output. Home consumption will be affected both by the regular increase in population of nearly 2.5% per year and by the rise in living standards.

At present consumption per head of all kinds of coconut products is equivalent to 130 to 140 nuts per year. Increase of population at the rate of 200,000 per year will add over 25 million nuts to annual consumption every year, and changes in living standards might add another four million. Thus in the forthcoming decade annual consumption will hardly average less than 1,000 million nuts, leaving around 600 to 700 million nuts to be exported in one form or another; it may reach 1,300 million nuts at the end of the decade, leaving only 300 to 400 million for export. Even this residue may be further reduced if domestic production of soap and other manufactured products absorbs more coconut oil.

It may be taken as certain that home consumption will absorb an increasing part of the crop. This must be recognized in any plan for the benefit of coconut cultivation.

Coconut Research Institute. Established by an ordinance of 1928, the Coconut Research Institute is governed by a Board of Management in which both the government and producers' associations are represented. Various phases of its work have been mentioned. Operating funds are derived from:

(a) cess levied on exports, at the following fixed rates (1950):

    (1) Copra—6.25 cents per cwt.

    (2) Coconut oil—9.25 cents per cwt.

    (3) Desiccated coconut—8.75 cents per cwt.

    (4) Nuts—25 cents per 1,000.

(b) government grants (in 1950 amounting to Rs. 180,000);

(c) income from estates (in 1950 amounting to nearly Rs. 160,000);

(d) miscellaneous income (in 1949 amounting to about Rs. 17,000 from investments).

Situated at Lunuwila, 32 miles north of Colombo, the Institute possesses two estates, Ratmalagara (Madampe) of 230 acres and Bandirippuwa (Lunuwila) of 150 acres. Experimentation is also carried out on many private estates and elsewhere. The staff is made up of five senior officers, 28 junior staff, 12 minor staff and about 90 daily-paid laborers. There is also a Planting Division, concerned with the coconut replanting program and financed separately; this Division has a staff of about 24 and operates some 30 nurseries.

Apart from replanting, the principal work of the Institute at present concerns the following subjects:

(a) Soil management and water conservation;

(b) Soils and fertilizers; NPK at various levels;

(c) Trace elements in nutrition;

(d) Plant hormones;

(e) Nursery studies in support of the replanting projects;

(f) Plant breeding and genetics;

(g) Seed studies;

(h) Interrelations of coconuts and animal husbandry;

(i) Estate costing and accounts;

(j) Educational and advisory services;

Major problems facing the Institute are those of securing additional properly trained personnel and adequate financial support. In connection with the latter, particularly, the Mission feels strongly that year-to-year dependence upon uncertain grants is not satisfactory. In an institution of this kind, concerned with long-term studies, budgeting with confidence is essential to intelligent planning of work. Even more, for good results it is necessary to create an atmosphere in which the scientific staff can concentrate on their tasks without an extraneous fear for their financial future.

For these reasons it is urged that the research tax be placed at such a level that both operating and capital costs will be covered, and that these costs be shared by all producers. Similarly, it is urged that, unless there are exceptional circumstances, the Board of Management refrain from upsetting the work by making later revisions in budgets already approved. Finally, better work could be achieved through more effective delegation of power to the executive officers of the Institute.

Recommendations. Principal points in the Mission's recommendations for coconut development, arranged in order of priority, include the following:

1. Surveying, classification and mapping of existing coconut area.

2. Outlining a rehabilitation (replanting and underplanting) program based on replacement of at least 15,000 acres per year, or preferably 30,000 acres.

3. Intensive surveying of new areas suitable for coconut cultivation.

4. Imposing a tax, based on either acreage or production, sufficient to meet the financial requirements of a well-planned 10-year program of research and rehabilitation.

5. Intensifying the educational work designed to overcome the "natural resistance" of smallholders toward the continuous application of new cultivation methods and necessary replanting of their holdings.

Other Commercial Crops

Cacao (Theobroma). For 1951 the export of cacao reached 50,638 cwts., the largest since 1943. The export value in 1951, Rs. 10.2 million, was the highest on record—Rs. 149.40 per cwt. for No. 1 grade in 1948 to Rs. 110.29 in 1949. A good proportion (40% in 1951) is exported to the Philippines mostly for use as "chewing" cacao. Although prices are now lower than the postwar peak, the general market prospects are good and Ceylon should have no difficulty in selling any probable increase in her output at fair prices.

The variety now widely grown is *Forastero* (actually a hybrid of *Forastero X. Elongated Criollo*); there is also a small amount of *Criollo*. The quality of "bean" is good—due largely to the care taken in its picking, cleaning and preparation. Yields range from over six cwts. per acre (on the very best sites under the best management) to as low as two or three cwts. Two crops per year are obtained.

This crop does best at elevations up to 2,000 feet, with fairly well distributed rainfall of not less than 60 to 80 inches and high and consistent temperatures. Sensitive to the physical "blowing" as well as to the drying or cooling effects of wind, the crop demands protection from this element. It is also sensitive to insolation and is grown under some form of canopy to reduce light intensity, sun temperature and rate of evaporation. The shade may be provided either by indigenous trees or by those used for shading tea. In recent years, however, it has become common to plant cacao under rubber stands in the drier districts. This has provided a reasonable yield of a second crop, while at the same time protecting the bark of the rubber against the desiccating effects of hot, dry air.

Best results are produced by deeper soil, sufficiently water-retentive but at the same time well drained, with good organic content and a good supply of the principal chemical nutrients. These ideal conditions are rarely met in Ceylon, but some moderately good localities for the crop exist in parts of the Kandy and Matale sub-regions of the hill and montane region.

About 55% of the cacao acreage in the island is said to be in Kandy district and about 33% in Matale district, but acreage figures are defective and unreliable. The official estimate of about 19,700 acres for the whole country can scarcely be correct, as the Rubber Research Institute estimates that there are upwards of 20,000 to 30,000 acres of rubber underplanted with cacao in stages ranging from newly established plants to those long in bearing.

The following conclusions may be drawn regarding the present and future status of the crop:

(1) There may be a limited acreage of relatively suitable soil within climatically congenial portions of the Kandy and Matale sub-regions that could be brought under cacao. Systematic field survey would be required to confirm this, but informed opinion is that the potential area is not more than 20,000 to 30,000 acres. So far as entirely new sites are concerned, possible expansion is thus very limited.

(2) The vigor and yield of cacao under rubber in the more suitable localities have justified the establishment of this second crop, and the policy of extension of underplanting on other good sites appears sound. Underplanting on the marginal estates is, however, dubious and should not be encouraged. Also, there is a possible hazard in all underplanting in that Phytophthora is common to the two species.

A systematic survey of the rubber sites is needed to define the relative suitability and extent of the areas worth underplanting to cacao. It should be conducted by persons combining scientific knowledge and practical experience of the crop both in Ceylon and elsewhere.

(3) As practically no consistent scientific work has been done on this crop in Ceylon, there is a clear need for the government to inaugurate such work. The advice of experienced cacao research officers on the Gold Coast and in other large cacao producing areas should be sought, as experience in those areas should be instructive in spite of differences in the varieties grown and methods employed.

Cinnamon (Cinnamomum zeylanicum). About 33,000 acres of this one-time highly prized crop are grown. The majority of plantations are from 10 to 25 acres each, with only a few above 100 acres. All are Ceylonese owned and worked. The larger ones tend to be rather more systematically coppiced and barked than the smaller.

The crop does best in the southwest lowlands and lower hill regions up to about 2,000 feet, under fairly well distributed rainfall of not less than 80 inches. Some of the best sites are on the deep, alluvial sandy loam soils near the sea. The plant is established from seed sown *in situ* in circular clusters, usually spaced about 10 feet from center to center; long, upright clean shoots are thus obtained. About 50 to 60 lbs. of bark quills per acre are yielded from the first crop after three to four years, and until about the 10th season. Thereafter good crops will be from 150 to 200 lbs., provided the husbandry has been satisfactory.

Ceylon is the principal producer of cinnamon. In 1951 the export of quills totalled 38,655 cwts. valued at Rs. 6.2 million, while chips totalled 5,503 cwts. worth Rs. 173,000; however, the amount was somewhat higher than normal due to the clearing of accumulated stocks. Mexico is the chief importer of quills, taking 42% of all exports in 1951; for the same year the chips were exported principally to Australia, South Africa and the United Kingdom.

Cinnamon leaf oil exports for 1951 totalled 2.1 million oz., valued at Rs. 1.2 million. Cinnamon bark oil exports for 1951 were 17,000 oz. valued at Rs. 96,000. The main importers in 1951 of leaf and bark oil were the United Kingdom (42%) and the United States (23%).

257

There is no reason to expect demand for cinnamon to vary greatly and no reason to stimulate any expansion of acreage. To maintain the quality and quantity of yield, seems the right policy. The crop will remain a product for small to medium holdings.

Arecanut (Betelnut: Areca Catechu). Indigenous to Malaya, this palm has been extensively cultivated in Ceylon and elsewhere in Asia for the sake of its "nuts" (seeds). These are about the size of a fowl egg, and are widely used as a masticatory. They find use also as the source of a vermifuge for dogs, and in the preparation of dyeing, tanning and dentifrice materials. The stems furnish poles for simple construction.

In Ceylon the palm is widely grown in several varieties, both in the Wet Zone and in suitable sites in the Dry, but rarely at altitudes above 3,000 feet. Yield ranges from about 200 to 250 nuts per palm or about 6 to 12 cwt. per acre; bearing normally begins at about six to eight years and ceases at 30 to 40. Fairly extensive pure stands are found at Kegalla, but commonly it is a village garden product. It is estimated that there are some 69,000 acres of this palm in the island.

Arecanuts are sold locally and also exported to India and the Maldives. In 1951 the exports totalled 128,000 cwts. valued at Rs. 5.9 million. Indian imports are now under restrictive control.

While expansion may occur as village settlements and colonization schemes progress and as these provide suitable climatic or irrigation conditions for this peasant crop, it is unlikely that there would be any interest in the establishment of larger pure stands. Attention to improved varieties, however, would be worth while so that quality and yield may be improved in time.

Citronella (Cymbopogon nardus). Distillation of this tall, coarse grass yields an aromatic essential oil used mainly for medicinal purposes, in soaps and cosmetics, and as an insect repellent.

Native of Africa and Asia, the grass occurs in Ceylon on a wide range of soils under warm, moist climatic conditions from sea level to about 2,000 feet. Commercially, however, it is confined to suitable sites in the southern province. Here there are about 30,000 acres, half in the Matare District and the bulk of the remainder near Hambantota. Two cuttings are obtainable per year under good conditions, about 40 lbs. of marketable oil per acre being considered an average yield. It is established vegetatively.

For 1951 the export was approximately 1.6 million lbs., and its value of Rs. 12.9 million was the highest on record. The United Kingdom took the greater amount (35%) and the USA, 13%. For 1950 about 1.6 million lbs. were exported, valued at Rs. 8.3 million.

Citronella is an easily established crop and one requiring merely the elements of good husbandry for its satisfactory growth and development. There are several varieties, some being more robust, others better oil bearers.

That this will remain a peasant crop in Ceylon seems probable. The use of better varieties and the application of fertilizers likely to increase the yield of oil might be worth the attention of the Department of Agriculture. The crop would make a good soil improver for perennial plantings such as tea and cacao. In Guatemala the waste grass after distillation is used successfully for making paper. Possible similar use in Ceylon appears to have been disregarded but might be considered.

Pepper (Piper nigrum). The so-called "black" and "white" pepper of commerce is yielded by one and the same plant, the black being the product resulting from drying and grinding with the outer cover of the peppercorn left in position, the white from the berries from which the covering has been removed.

Indigenous to Southern India and Ceylon, pepper is grown in the island in the moist lowlands and up to about 2,000 feet elevation. It requires moist, warm to hot conditions together with suitable shade. As a climbing or ranking plant it is normally grown with common shade trees as support, either along roads or on plantations such as tea. Erythrina, mango, jak and especially kapok (non-spined variety) make excellent supports.

Propagation is by terminal cuttings. The plant may bear well

259

for 20 to 25 years—the first yield coming in the third year but with higher production about the sixth year. There may be a larger crop in March-May and a small one in August-September; from 800 to 1,500 lbs. may be produced per acre at a 7 x 7 feet espacement—a distribution and abundance that is rarely found. A mature, well grown vine yields from 3 to 6 lbs. of dried pepper annually, depending on locality and management factors.

In 1951 Ceylon exported a total of 4,690 cwts. of whole pepper valued at Rs. 3,870,550. The principal importers were the United States (1,150 cwts.), Italy (1,130 cwts.), the Netherlands (920 cwts.), United Kingdom (560 cwts.) and Canada (470 cwts.). Before the war from 1,500 to 3,500 cwts. per year were exported.

Malaya, Java, Sumatra, Malabar and Ceylon have been the leading producers for export, but the war disturbed production in both Malaya and the former Dutch possessions. While present circumstances are unusual, therefore, Ceylon might nevertheless take more interest in this significant crop. The growing of pepper on suitable shade trees in tea and possible cacao plantations and along estate roads could be practiced more consistently than in the past. Also, it is recommended that investigations of variety and fertility factors be undertaken.

Nutmeg and Mace (Myristica fragrans). The medium to small tree bearing the seed (nutmeg) and covering aril (mace) so well-known as spices and flavoring media was introduced in 1804, probably from the Moluccas where it is indigenous. It has been exported from the one-time Dutch East Indies and from Grenada in the West Indies; Penang nutmegs are said to command the highest prices.

In Ceylon the crop is produced in gardens in the moist lowlands more particularly, but can also be grown at elevations up to about 2,000 feet in the hill country. It does best in deeper, better drained soils; in youth it does better under such common shade trees as Erythrina and Gliricidia. Because it is dioecious (the trees being of distinct sexes) plantings are so arranged that about one male is left to ten to fifteen female trees. This is done as soon as the first flowering has occurred and the sexes of the planted trees can be determined; excess males are then cut out. Bearing takes place in about the seventh to ninth year and increases until the tree is about 30 years old, when the crop may be from 3,000 to 8,000 nuts per tree. Two main crops are yielded per year. Bearing may continue for many years, some of the century-old trees in Peradeniya being reported as still giving heavy annual crops in June-July and October-December.

Production for export has declined considerably since rubber became an important crop. For 1950, 781 cwts. of nutmegs valued at Rs. 216,428 were exported to various Commonwealth and other countries; the USA purchased 394 cwts. Mace exports for the same year were 117 cwts. valued at Rs. 67,913. There are from 60 to 100 nuts to the lb., and mace normally is yielded at about 10% of the weight of the nut.

As the production can be so readily worked in with ordinary gardening, it probably would be worth while for the Department of Agriculture to encourage establishment of a limited number of trees in the better localities. More careful attention to the quality of nutmeg and mace would result in an enhanced name and competitive position for these Ceylon products.

Cardamoms (Elettaria Cardomum). A native of Southern India and Ceylon, this spice has long had a place as an export crop. The aromatic fine seed, produced in small capsules, is used for flavoring of confectionery and curry; in pharmacy it has been used as a carminative. There is a wide market for it on the island itself.

In Ceylon it occurs at levels from 2,500 to 4,000 feet in native forest, in steep valleys where the canopy is sufficiently light. It is also grown as a crop in relatively small areas, the total extent being about 6,000 acres. It does best within a rainfall range of 100 to 150 inches, in light shade on sloping ground, well protected from boisterous wind. Several varieties are commonly grown, the upright being preferred to the trailing forms because their capsules are less likely to be damaged by wet soil conditions.

The principal producing districts are Kandy, Matale and Nuwara Eliya in the hill and montane region.

Establishment is by seed or rhizome, three to four plants per hole, the holes at 10 feet espacement. The plant usually yields in the second or third year, an acre producing from 150 to 250 lbs. of capsules. Heavy rain at the flowering period may cause a poor crop as seed setting is likely to be impaired by the dampness. Chief bearing seasons are February-March and August-September, but there is some production in other months.

At one time as much as 850,000 lbs. of capsules were exported per year; this had dropped to 343,000 lbs. in 1933. For the year 1950, the export totalled 3,074 cwts. valued at Rs. 4.6 millions, of which Commonwealth countries took 1,911 and the United States 151 cwts.

Unless new outlets appear it is obvious that any policy of expansion of the acreage should be studied cautiously in relation to the likely markets. Meanwhile it would be well to continue the search for higher yielding, upright varieties.

Cloves (Eugenia caryophyllata). Introduced in 1796 from Moluccas, the clove is grown in gardens and elsewhere in the warm, moister districts from sea level to about 2,000 feet. It does best on the higher, deeper and better drained soils.

The tree, although long-lived, is comparatively slow growing and usually does not bear until about the tenth year. An average yield of mature trees in good condition may be from 5 to 10 lbs. of dried cloves per year. At 20 feet espacement with about 60% of the trees in bearing, a yield of 500 to 700 lbs. per acre is to be expected. The unexpanded flower buds are picked green about January and dried for several days in the sun.

Ceylon's export for 1951 is reported as 408 cwts. valued at Rs. 105,318. The bulk of the world's crop (about 90%) comes from Zanzibar and Pemba, with some additional supply from Indonesia and Madagascar. The East African crop, however, is in serious danger of reduction through the ravages of the so-called "Sudden Death" disease, believed to be a virus. To date this disease has not shown itself outside of the islands of Zanzibar and Pemba. In Ceylon the records of disease include a root-rot fungus *(Fomes caryophylli)* and an alga causing some leaf disturbance *(Cephaleuros parasiticus)*, but these are not serious.

Bearing in mind that production in East Africa may well decline, and that demand is fairly steady, it should be profitable to extend plantings. The tree could be produced in larger groves or small holdings in the southwest lowlands and the intermediate elevations of the hill country.

Extension of acreage should be made only after careful selection of suitable localities, and with provisions to assure good husbandry and grove hygiene. It would be advisable to obtain the advisory and executive services of an experienced clove officer or planter from Zanzibar.

Tobacco. Tobacco has been grown for a long time; chewing, pipe, cigar, cheroot and cigarette types are produced. Emphasis in earlier years has been on chewing tobacco, largely for export to India. Present Indian restrictions on its import, together with growth of the local cigarette industry, are now shifting attention to the cigarette types.

Total acreage under tobacco, principally in the Jaffna area, is variously estimated at from 10,000 to 15,000 acres. About 2,000 acres in 1951 produced approximately one million pounds of cigarette tobacco, representing a third of the island's local requirements of this type. Exports for 1951 included 1,006,990 lbs. of unmanufactured tobacco valued at Rs. 1,595,424 (mostly chewing types to India), 1,602 lbs. of cigars worth Rs. 3,072 (mainly to the Maldives), and a few cigarettes destined for ships' stores.

Much of the Jaffna tobacco has been grown under partial irrigation from wells. The shift in demand toward the lighter varieties means a reduction in output from that area, unless the present chewing types can be replaced successfully in the region. Present production of cigarette tobacco is mainly in the Central Province, although more recently trials have been undertaken in portions of the North Central and Northern Provinces. About 6,000 acres will be needed to produce the island's present requirements of this type.

In collaboration with major cigarette companies, the Department of Agriculture has encouraged the wider trial of cigarette tobacco by cultivators, more particularly at Ganewatte, Wariyapola, Katupotha, Mailapitiya, Unantenne and Hanguranketha; less extensive plantings have been made elsewhere, including Jaffna. Yields of cured leaf per acre are reported to have ranged from 371 (Ganewatte) to 595 lbs. (Mailapitiya, Unantenne, Hanguranketha); production was encouraging in both the *Maha* 1949-50 and in the *Yala* 1950 seasons. Plantings for Maha 1949-50 totalled 507 acres, for Yala 1950, 726 acres, and for Maha 1950-51, 805.

Cigarette tobacco trials in the Jaffna Peninsula promise well. The trials have been carried out mainly in cooperation with growers on their own land. Seven localities have been reported on for the Maha 1949-50 season, with acreages ranging from 0.14 to 2.0 acres. The result from the 4.62 acres on the seven farms gave an average yield per acre of 6,815 lbs. of green leaf with an average value of Rs. 1,286.20 as green leaf and of Rs. 1,723.14 when flue-cured. The burning quality is reported as having been good on three farms, poor on one, very poor on another and bad on two others.

The Department of Agriculture is attending to the fundamentally important matter of the use of tobacco in crop rotation. For example, a recent report shows that at Ganewatte, Pelwehera and Ridiyagama farms, the following rotation on high (nonirrigable) ground was tried, the tobacco being a Maha crop dependent on monsoon rain:

1.	Maha	*Tobacco*	5.	Maha	Maize or sorghum
2.	Yala	Legume	6.	Yala	Fallow
3.	Maha	Mustard	7.	Maha	*Tobacco*
4.	Yala	Legume			

Results for the 1949-50 season showed: at Ganewatte, on 10 acres, a yield of 441 lbs. per acre; at Pelwehera, on five acres,

515 lbs. per acre; and at Ridiyagama, on five acres, 1,921 lbs. per acre—the island's highest recorded yield for Virginia type tobacco. Rotation trials at Budamuttawa and elsewhere in the Dry Zone indicate fair prospects for cigarette tobacco in rotation with paddy.

As regards other types of tobacco, there is an increasing demand for the local Dumbara and mild cigar tobacco types for the manufacture of cheaper brands of cigarettes, mild cigars, cheroots and pipe tobacco. Trials have been conducted with the local Dumbara and American Broadleaf varieties in the Dry Zone at Hingurakgoda and Maha Illuppalama; at the former station yields up to 900 lbs. per acre were obtained from both varieties.

The Ceylon Tobacco Company has established buying depots for this class of tobacco at important growing points such as Melsiripura, Kudawewa and Hanguranketha. Minimum prices paid for the 1950 Dumbara leaf were: Grade 1, Rs. 1.36, Grade 2, Rs. 1.15 and Grade 3, Rs. 0.85 per lb. For 1951 an additional five cents per lb. was agreed upon.

On the whole, however, the best promise lies in the growing of well cured, good colored and satisfactorily textured cigarette tobacco. Trials initiated by the Tobacco Officer include the Virginian varieties of Cash, Virginia Bright, Yellow Mammoth, Mammoth Gold and Harrison's Special. Particular attention has been given Harrison's Special, seed of this variety being collected for development work from specially selected and self-fertilized plants.

Three leading local tobacco manufacturers, in cooperation with the Department of Agriculture, have worked out purchase schemes for green leaf and flue-cured tobacco to encourage production. Major details of these forms of aid, which are still evolving through experience, are as follows:

(a) The Department selects suitable areas for the operation of the schemes, assisting the companies in persuading cultivators to grow tobacco in rotation with other crops. This is a most valuable provision aimed at maintaining food production while at the same time producing a valuable cash crop.

(b) The companies advance the seedlings and fertilizers, the cost thereof being recovered at the time of final payment for the green or the cured leaf.

(c) The companies purchase the green or the cured leaf at agreed prices. In the green leaf purchase scheme, the companies concerned cure the leaf at their own cost in flue-curing barns erected by them at different development centers.

(d) The Department and the companies provide advice and guidance on the best methods of production.

(e) At least one company is reported to be willing to supply middle-class growers and cooperative societies with certain requirements for the construction of their own flue-curing barns, such as furnaces, flue piping and roofing material. The cost of these is to be recovered over 12 seasons against suitable quality leaf produced.

As an indication of results, during 1950 the Ceylon Tobacco Company is reported to have established 114 flue-curing barns at six development localities, and 22 such barns were built by middle-class growers at five points. New barns are being established in the Jaffna Peninsula as well as in the Central Province.

All of the tobacco companies are reported to be prepared to purchase whatever quantity of tobacco is produced, at the agreed new prices, provided only that the crop is grown in areas designated as suitable. Revised prices, estimated to give the producer an average price of Rs. 1.80 per pound of flue-cured leaf, are shown below:

	Grade	Price per lb.
Green leaf	1	Rs. 0.20
	2	0.08
Flue-cured leaf	1	2.75
	2	2.50
	3	2.20
	4	1.35
	5	1.20
	scrap	1.00

Very useful work is being done by the government tobacco officer and his small staff of three agricultural assistants, as well as by the tobacco companies, in instructing and generally aiding growers in various parts of the island. The following observations are intended for their help.

Some very serious erosion is taking place in the tobacco growing country of the Central Province, owing to the lack of simple soil conservation practices. Such erosion takes the form of sheet wash, but there is some incipient gully erosion developing even after a single season of tobacco. Further delay in commencing conservation measures will soon result in serious deterioration of arable land. The tobacco officer's staff is quite inadequate in numbers, training and experience to combat the growing wastage. The staff should be increased and, under the guidance of the conservation officer, be given practical field instruction in soil conservation in this area of broken topography and erodible soils.

The great dependence of the valuable tobacco crop upon details of field practice and barn preparation justifies the appointment of a specialist officer to assist the tobacco staff in the technical aspects of production.

Further experimental work both in the field and in the curing barns is needed before significant extension of Virginia type cigarette tobacco in the Jaffna region is encouraged, although there can be little doubt that this class of tobacco could be produced successfully there, once the more suitable varieties and the most effective technique have been determined.

A further point is that while disease so far has been restricted to a certain amount of loss in quality of leaf from Frogeye (Cercospora) and to damage by stem-borer in the earlier stages of growth, more serious pests and diseases are likely to show themselves should the acreage be too rapidly increased. Mosaic so far has not appeared, but is an ever-present danger.

267

Kapok (Ceiba pentandrah [10] or earlier *Eriodendron anfractuo-sum).* This tree has been widely grown from sea level to about 2,000 feet in Ceylon, but is cultivated more extensively in Java and the Philippines and to some extent in various other tropical countries. The silky fiber is used for stuffing life-saving equipment, mattresses and pillows; it is also mixed with other fine fibers for textiles, although it is too brittle for spinning by itself. In earlier years the export from the island was rather less than 10,000 cwts. per year; in 1950 the amount had risen to 16,800 cwts. valued at Rs. 2.8 million, while the 1951 figures fell to 8,167 cwts. valued at Rs. 1.7 million. Java formerly exported as much as 240,000 cwts. per year.

Although it comes readily from seed, the plant is often raised from cuttings or truncheons. When grown in plantation form it is usually espaced about 15 x 15 feet. It normally yields in the fourth to sixth year, first at about 1.5-2 lbs. of fiber per tree, later at about 6-10 lbs. Bearing continues for many years.

The plantations usually are small, the tree often being grown along roads or as a shade tree to other crops, or as a support for pepper. No record of total acreage is available. It does best in hot to warm, moist conditions such as those of the southwest lowlands and in the intermediate elevations of the hill and montane regions.

A spined variety which has been introduced is giving unnecessary additional difficulty in collecting the pods. Moreover, it presents a troublesome problem in picking pepper grown with these spined stems as support. Any extension should be limited to the better smooth-boled varieties grown in Java and elsewhere (e.g. *C. pentandra var. indica*).

While it is unlikely that there would ever be a really large demand for kapok, it is nevertheless the kind of simple tree crop

---

[10] This should not be confused with the Red Cotton Tree: *Bombax nalabaricum,* a heavy spined tree bearing an inferior floss or kapok, also grown in Ceylon.

well worth keeping in the larger gardens and holdings in localities with sufficient rainfall and a sufficiently high temperature. Furthermore, its seed yields a semi-drying oil of value for the manufacture of soap and margarine; this oil is sometimes in demand by Ceylon's largest soap factories.

Cotton. True cotton so far has been produced in Ceylon to a very limited extent, the largest recorded area being 3,280 acres established in 1950-51. Most of this was grown on the *chena* [11] system, in the Southern Province, except for 350 acres on rotation areas at Wirawila and Maha Illuppallama. An Uganda variety has been shown to be the most successful to date. At Maha Illuppallama a yield of 5.5 cwts. per acre of seed cotton was produced on the experimental areas. A more common local yield in practice is about 3 cwts., but in poor seasons when drought strikes hard as it did in 1949-50, a greatly reduced harvest follows; 3,700 acres in that season returned only 2,800 cwts. of seed cotton.

In some quarters much reliance is placed upon cotton production in the development of the Dry Zone—as a high or dry land crop, in chena and in colonization schemes alike. The yields recorded under favorable conditions—with the right variety established, well-tended and free of disease—give ground for hope of successful development. Fifteen acres at the Hambantota Cotton Station in 1949-50 gave an average of 15 cwts. per acre and chena cultivators have obtained yields of from 4-6 cwts. per acre in favorable seasons—a very encouraging result with cotton selling at Rs. 48 per cwt.

---

[11] Under the *chena* system of cultivation, secondary jungle land is cleared by peasant cultivators by burning. Stumps are not removed and the soil is only roughly prepared. After taking a few crops (mainly maize, kurakkan and other food crops) the land is abandoned and the cultivator shifts to another plot to repeat the process. Such cultivation is in theory controlled by a system of government permits but enforcement is difficult.

Nonetheless too much hope should not be built on these highly favorable but sporadic yields and expansion should proceed with some caution. A proposal to get 2,500 acres of chena cultivation under cotton in the current season may, for instance, be over-optimistic. There are possible threats from the numerous diseases and pests of cotton and the uncertain rainfall distribution in both the Hambantota area and north central uplands and lowlands region is a serious hazard.

Selection, agronomic and field husbandry trials (work on which has already begun at several Agricultural Department stations) should be accomplished over say five years in chena, on various colonization schemes and at Gal Oya, so as to gain more information, over a wider range of conditions, about the details of the economic production of this valuable but uncertain crop.

Aid of the Empire Cotton Growing Corporation certainly should be sought. The presence in Ceylon, for some years, of an experienced cotton officer would help the solution of a number of pressing problems. Such an officer could train local staff and cultivators in the various aspects of the art, science and practice of the production of cotton.

Jute or Gunny-fiber (Corchorus capsularis and C. olitorius). Jute is indigenous to Ceylon, India, Pakistan and Malaya, but the great bulk of production is from several million acres in Bengal. The fiber is of outstanding significance as the preferred material for the manufacture of burlap and gunny-bags. *C. capsularis* is the more widely cultivated species, but requires an abundance of water for the flooding of the alluvial land; it may be harvested in four or five feet of water. *C. olitorius,* on the other hand, is produced on higher land and does not tolerate flooding; it is slower in maturing and its fiber is somewhat less valuable. Both species need fertile soil.

The crop is broadcast-sown at 8 to 15 lbs. per acre, the seedlings being thinned out when about 12 inches high to an espacement of about four to six inches. Branching must not take place. Maturity

270

is within three to four months, the crop being cut while the plants are partly in flower and partly in fruit.

Jute stems attain a height of 6 to 12 feet. These are cut, bundled, and stooked for some days to allow shedding of the foliage. They are then retted for periods of about a fortnight to two months. The labor requirement is heavy: up to 30 men may be necessary for the cutting, bundling and stooking of one acre in one working day. One skilled laborer strips 80 to 100 lbs. of dry, clean fiber in a working day; this may amount to about 5% of the total weight of the stems. An average economic yield is about 1,000 to 1,200 lbs. of fiber per acre.

It would be beneficial if Ceylon could produce some of the gunny cloth which she now imports to meet local requirements of gunny bags. No history of experimentation with jute in Ceylon has been available to the Mission. If extensive and well regulated trials have not been carried out over a reasonable period, for both varieties, it would be wise to arrange them. With the future increase in irrigation in the Dry Zone, it might be possible to produce a limited amount of this most valuable fiber. Because of its lower water requirement, *C. olitorius* may prove more satisfactory. Under irrigation jute could be grown in rotation with paddy.

Deccan Hemp, Kenaf or Bimlipatam Jute (Hibiscus cannabinus). This fiber has come into more prominence since true jute has been difficult to obtain; it is produced to a limited extent in Southern India, with a very much smaller export from Nigeria. Interest in its production has developed in South and East Africa, Cuba and Central America in recent years. The fiber is yielded by the inner bark, at a rate of 500 to 1,000 lbs. per acre. The proportion of fiber to dry stalk is about 16%.

Deccan hemp requires fertile, well-drained soil and from 25 to 35 inches of rainfall (or equivalent irrigation) during the growing season. Seed is broadcast, and may be sown mechanically with a standard rice planter. Stalks may be cut from 100 to 150 days after planting, depending upon variety and growing conditions;

271

in some areas two crops per year are obtained. Harvesting may be done by hand, or by using an ordinary hay mower equipped with a heavier sickle-bar. Decortication of the fiber is accomplished by retting, as for jute, but rapid advances are being made in its mechanical decortication in the West Indies where labor costs are high.

When harvested for fiber, Deccan hemp is cut in the bloom stage. If grown for seed for extension of acreage—as in Cuba at present—the plant yields between 500 and 800 lbs. of seed per acre.

Deccan hemp is likely to prove of value in the Dry Zone of Ceylon, as a dryland crop. Trials commenced in the north central and eastern agricultural divisions so far have indicated that the better responses are coming from the strain HC2 (Vizianagram, which in 1950 yielded on experimental plots up to 750 lbs. of fiber per acre). The Delhi strains NP3 and NP6 have also been under trial, the former giving the better response at Karadian Aru in the eastern agriculture division.

As fairly considerable quantities of hemp cables, rope and twine are imported into the island annually (the figures for 1951 are 2,129 cwts. valued at Rs. 360,372) and as the fiber of Deccan hemp actually is now widely used as a jute substitute, there could be no doubt about the value of the crop both for local use and for export in due course. American manufacturers consulted by the Mission report the fiber operates perfectly in existing jute-handling machinery, both spinning and weaving.

Rozelle (Hibiscus sabdariffa, var. altissima). Closely related to Deccan hemp, rozelle is also a well known jute substitute, yielding much the same quality and quantity of fiber. There is a record (R. C. Wood: 1947) that a yield of 1,120 lbs. per acre has been obtained in Ceylon. Like Deccan hemp, this crop also is worthy of careful field trial in the Dry Zone. Apparently a variety of NP5 has been given some attention at Unnichchai in the eastern agriculture division.

This crop has been found simple to establish when once the

responses to the local conditions of climate and soil are understood. Should any special difficulty be experienced, advice from Southern India might be sought.

Sunn-hemp (Crotalaria juncea). This "soft" hemp, yielding a fiber prepared from the bast of the stem, is extensively grown in India; in recent years it has been grown elsewhere but more especially as a soil improving crop. Rope, canvas, twine and fishing nets are made from the fiber, which represents 8-10% of the dry stalk weight.

The crop is in use in Ceylon as an "improver." Should its response be good, it might also be grown for its fiber. A yield of from 500 to 1,000 lbs. of dry fiber per acre is to be expected, according to locality factors. The crop will withstand a good deal of drought, but for the best yield it should have an annual rainfall of not less than 30 inches, fairly well distributed. Under irrigated, semi-irrigated and better dry land conditions in the Dry Zone its response should be satisfactory.

Seed is broadcast at the rate of 50 to 100 lbs. per acre, if for fiber production; for seed production the sowing is usually 20 to 30 lbs. only. The yield of seed per acre is from 350 to 700 lbs. according to conditions. In Rhodesia difficulty has been experienced in raising satisfactory seed, owing to the ravages of an insect.

In light of the value of the crop as a green manure and its potential additional usefulness as a fiber producer, it is recommended that the Department of Agriculture give it careful field study under a wide range of conditions.

Sisal (Agave sisalana). Sisal hemp—a "hard" hemp fiber in very great demand—is produced in large quantity in Tanganyika Territory, Kenya, Mexico where it is indigenous, Indonesia and elsewhere in the tropics. Its main uses are for rope, cordage and baler twine. Hot, medium moist conditions favor the growth, a summer rainfall of about 40 to 50 inches in East Africa producing the best response.

The plant appears to have been introduced into Ceylon about

273

1890 but, from available accounts, has not been given serious attention. In various parts of the island several varieties are used along road sides and for hedges; it has also "escaped" locally. From the climatic and soil factors reported for the Dry Zone, it appears that there is a fair chance of producing sisal economically.

In plantation practice, the bulbils produced by the mother plant are set out in nurseries. At the end of about six months these are transplanted to the field at an espacement of about 8 x 6 feet with at least seven feet between rows if hand cultivated, at least 10 or 13 feet if mechanically cultivated and depending on whether the rows are single or double. Espacement in the rows depends on climatic and soil factors. In the third to fourth year leaf cutting commences. Between first production and the falling off, an economic yield may be obtained for three to five years if the plantation is kept well weeded, the yield of fiber being up to four to five tons per acre. Where the plantation is not so well tended the extension of cutting life may be up to 10 years, the yield being appreciably less. Fiber recovery may range from 2 to 5%, depending on local climatic and soil conditions. In drier areas the percentage return is higher but the total yield is lower owing to the poorer production of leaf. The fiber is not retted, but is removed mechanically by large power-driven decorticators.

Much experimental work has been carried out in Tanganyika over the past 20 years and various improvements in soil preparation, espacement, establishment, tending, reaping and preparation of the fiber have been introduced, with satisfactory economic results. Were the government to undertake intensive and extensive trials in the Dry Zone, the government of Tanganyika and the East African Sisal Growers' Association might be approached to provide the advisory services of an experienced sisal grower, to guide local staff in the selection of the more suitable sites and in the detailed techniques of growing and mechanical preparation.

Pawpaw, or Papaya (Carica papaya). Papain—an enzyme used in beverages, medicine, beer clarification, meat tenderizing, degumming of silk and softening of wool—is obtained from the thin, whitish latex in the unripe fruit of the well-known pawpaw. The export of papain for 1951 was 153,219 lbs. valued at Rs. 2,605 million; of this the United States took 101,018 lbs.

Indigenous to the West Indies and Central America, the pawpaw is now cultivated in many tropical countries. The plant is capable of growing under a wide range of subtropical and tropical conditions. Its acreage in Ceylon could be greatly extended, more particularly on colonization schemes in the Dry Zone, where irrigation water is available. The average yield of fruit is about 40 to 60 per tree, and of dried papain about 3 to 8 oz. per tree per year or about 150 lbs. per acre. Bearing is usually from about 12 to 18 months of age, continuing to be good until about the third or fourth year. The present price of papain in East Africa is one pound fifteen shillings per lb. but a good return can be got at prices from one pound upward. It is essential to attend to purity and general quality of the product, otherwise buyers become shy, as happened some years ago in several parts of Africa.

Remembering that the plant is readily grown, that the fruit is an excellent food and that papain is likely to remain in demand, it would be well to encourage colonists in the Dry Zone to grow a good quality of pawpaw. Much of the present production is wanting in vigor, in quality and in promise for the future. Attention to better varieties, to the nature of the response to soil requirements and to tapping and preparatory methods should result in improved quality and quantity of production and the development of a market reputation.

Tumeric (Curcuma domestica or C. longa). The bright orange-yellow rhizome of this perennial herb belonging to the ginger family are used in the preparation of curry powder, for dyeing silk and wool and for inclusion in varnishes. The plant is extensively grown in various parts of Asia and to a limited degree in tropical Africa. While some tumeric is now being grown by colonists and settlers in Ceylon for use in cookery and in the making of curry, import figures for 1951 (16,723 cwts. valued at Rs. 650,127) indicate an ample market for local production. In

275

time there should be no difficulty in exporting a reasonable excess over the country's own requirements.

Tumeric is readily grown from rhizomes, from 1,000 to 1,800 lbs. being required to plant an acre. This in turn should yield from 10,000 to 20,000 lbs. of fresh rhizome, which should dry down to about a quarter or a fifth of the weight. The crop yields 9 to 12 months after establishment.

In Ceylon it could be grown in warm to hot, moist localities from sea level to about 3,000 feet, in well drained soil and in light shade. It is considered suitable for some extension in acreage in village gardens, small holdings and on the colonization schemes.

Ginger (Zingiber officinale). West Africa is now the principal exporter of ginger, important additional suppliers being Jamaica, India, China and Formosa. In 1951 Ceylon exported the small amount of 37 cwts. valued at Rs. 10,668. This export could be considerably greater as the crop could readily be raised in the warmer portions of the island up to about 3,000 feet, where good yields (from 1,000 to 2,000 lbs. of dried rhizome per acre, or say five times the amount of "green" or fresh) could be produced on soils containing enough organic matter. It should be a valuable additional crop for villagers, settlers and colonists.

Chillies or Red Peppers (Capsicum spp.). Ceylon, in 1951, exported 307 cwts. of dried chillies valued at Rs. 44,136, the bulk of this going to the Maldive Islands (248 cwts.).

The Department of Agriculture for some time has aided in the selection, establishment, and general field husbandry of this important crop. A variety of Tuticorin chilli, for example, is reported to be giving encouraging yields. The Department has also encouraged considerable additional planting, the acreage for 1950 being reported as 6,000. Had the monsoon rains in both the Maha 1949-50 and the Yala 1950 seasons not failed or been late, 20,000 acres would have been planted from material issued by the Department, for about 48 million seedlings were raised.

The crop lends itself to production by settlers and colonists, and should form an important aspect of farming in the Dry

Zone. In all probability it will be worked into various useful rotations. It may be grown in elevations up to about 3,000 feet, but does not thrive under humid conditions. Yields are from 500 to 800 lbs. dried chillies per acre, the fresh pods weighing roughly rather more than twice the amount.

Considering the local as well as the export demands, the policy of the Department of Agriculture in furthering the production of better and more chillies is to be commended. By all means the useful preliminary field experimental work should be carried further.

Coffee (Coffea). Knowing the catastrophic history of *C. arabica* in Ceylon, it might seem foolhardy to encourage further growth of coffee. *Hemeleia vastatrix* destroyed the industry in 1883; yet it is probable that limited acreages could be grown by using the less susceptible *robusta (C. canephora,* formerly *C. robusta)* and possibly other species, as well as by utilizing information and experience regarding fungus control not known at the time of the great rust epidemic. As a matter of fact a very small amount of coffee has been grown continuously on the island since then. But imports of coffee are appreciable: totals for 1951 showed 1,371,000 lbs., mostly unroasted, valued at Rs. 3.275 million.

Of special interest to the Department of Agriculture will be the field trial of *C. canephora (robusta)* at the lower elevations; although of less value than *C. arabica,* under suitable conditions it would give a somewhat higher yield.

While breeding, selection and field trial work should be attempted and while application of the most modern knowledge of disease control should be exercised throughout, the planting of extensive acreages would be most unwise until after a decade of thorough trial.

Gingelly (Sesame Beni-seed; Sesamum indicum). Sesame or gingelly is indigenous to parts of Africa and Asia, including Ceylon. India is the main producer, with over four million acres in 1948. The oil is widely used for cooking, margarine, soap-making and as a lighting oil.

In Ceylon gingelly is grown largely in chena and is highly suitable for production on the colonization schemes. Under normal conditions of rainfall and soil and with ordinary care, a colonist could expect a yield of 300 to 600 lbs. per acre. It is capable of good growth under moderate rainfall but does best when the distribution is fairly even; it gives best response on the lighter, · better drained soils.

The Department of Agriculture has taken commendable interest in the selection of suitable strains and in field trial of their management; a selection "B 3" for instance, is reported a good yielder of high oil content. Effort to find a nonshattering variety is being exerted. The seed may be produced in black, yellow, red and white, of which the last is generally preferred and most valuable.

Exports of gingelly oil for 1951 were 5,315 cwts. valued at Rs. 531,482; 5,002 cwts. went to Burma. In 1951 exports dropped to only 130 cwts. This crop could in time become of very real export value to the island. It is, in addition, an excellent product for home use.

Pineapple (Ananas sativa). Pineapple has long been grown in the island at elevations ranging from sea level to 3,000 feet or even more. Production has been limited to individually small areas, gardens and small holdings.

Recently there has been more interest shown because the government Marketing Department has been purchasing the fruit for canning. In 1949, 62,510 cans of pineapple were preserved and 2,603 tins of jam made. Action taken to encourage production has included the introduction of machinery for slicing and removing the core—reducing costs to raise local demand—and the payment of a minimum price of 7 cents per lb. for Smooth Cayenne pineapples weighing over 3 lbs. including top and stem.

The fruit is grown very extensively in Hawaii, Malaya, Sarawak, South Africa, Cuba, Mexico and elsewhere, but demand from the United Kingdom, the Continent and the United States for both fresh and canned pineapple continues to grow. Within the

278

past few years very large acreages have been planted and several big canning factories established in South Africa. Judging from the conditions under which the fruit is being grown, Ceylon has much more favorable climatic and soil factors for a large-scale production.

The crop may, however, be subject to a serious wilt (root rot) caused by a toxin introduced by a mealy-bug. Ways and means for controlling this vector are feasible today through proper plant protection and hygiene.

As the crop responds to a wide range of climatic and soil conditions, economic plantations of fairly large size could be developed both in parts of the southwest lowlands region and in the Dry Zone. Smooth Cayenne (Kew) and Ripley Queen are among the varieties that should be given attention. The plant requires light soils, good drainage, and a reasonable amount of moisture. It responds well to fertilization, using either organic matter or chemical fertilizers or both. In South Africa a rainfall not less than 25-30 inches per year produces good results. In Ceylon, with its higher temperatures, this would mean a fall of about 45-55 inches; regular occurrence of a dryish spell toward the end of the season is an advantage for ripening. Planting would take place just before the rains (say from early September to late November); maturity would occur about 20 to 22 months later, in the drier portion of the year.

Pineapple has been urged as one of the more important "catch" crops in coconut stands. The Mission feels that this and other aspects should be studied by a suitably constituted technical committee, aided by experienced pineapple growers and canners from outside areas. Canneries should be considered from the economic aspect of continuous operation with supplementary crops.

What is to be avoided, above all, is too rapid extension of pineapple acreage which might result in poor production, high incidence of disease, flooding of the present limited canning facilities, financial loss and consequent disappointment.

Groundnuts (Peanuts, Monkeynuts; Arachis hypogea). Excellent climatic and soil conditions are believed to exist in various portions of the Dry Zone for a fairly large production of this valuable food and export crop. Yet at the present time Ceylon depends upon imports for the groundnut oil used in soap manufacture.

The crop is grown in gardens and on small holdings in various parts of the island and in recent years has been encouraged in the Dry Zone by the Department of Agriculture. The Department quite rightly has directed attention to the trial of varieties, fertilizer responses, espacement and other aspects of the husbandry of groundnuts. Figures quoted by departmental officers suggest that, given suitable variety and conditions, commercial production could range from 300 to 600 lbs. of kernels per acre, with yields up to 800 lbs. in the better locations under good management.

At the Maha Illuppalama Station in the North Central Agriculture Division, for example, best responses have been shown by Uganda Erect, TMV 2, Peradeniya, Wirawila, Imperial Spanish Bunch, Small Spanish, and Virginia Bunch. At this station the crop of the last season was reported to have averaged 800 to 1,000 lbs. of pods (say 500 to 700 lbs. of kernals) per acre, without the use of fertilizer. This may be considered a good yield, which with improved soil management and the addition of NP fertilizer or organic matter, could be raised appreciably.

Groundnuts fit very well into dryland farming rotations. From experience in South and East Africa it is clear that there are encouraging possibilities of production on the high or dry land portions of the colonization schemes. While responses under even partial irrigation would be excellent, it is obvious that normally it would not be feasible to grow this crop under irrigation except where the groundnut forms part of the rotation with paddy. Some of the sites and soil at Gal Oya, for instance, would grow very good groundnuts provided the elementary precautions regarding soil and water conservation, fertilization, establishment, cultivation and ridging were taken.

While the crop would fit into the ordinary small-scale farming operations on the colonization schemes, larger-scale mechanized production would have advantages. In Tanganyika experience has demonstrated that the operations can be done satisfactorily by machine, with the exception of the "combining"—entailing the digging, lifting, shaking, picking and bagging of the nuts. Even this may soon be mechanized by new equipment under development in the United States. The digging itself does not present problems unless the soils bake very hard, which is less likely in the Dry Zone of Ceylon than in the more severe, compacting soils of Tanganyika. Lifting can be done by hand until a really satisfactory "pick-up" becomes available. The stationary combine can be used for picking and cleaning. Small portable decorticators of fair efficiency are available.

Considering the value of the nut as a food, the demand for the oil and the cake both for local use and for export, and the value of the crop for rotational purposes on dry ground, the Mission advises:

(a) That the Department's selection, field husbandry and other trials be continued and be extended over a wider range of conditions.

(b) That the experience of the Overseas Food Corporation (East Africa Groundnuts Scheme) regarding soil preparation, equipment, field husbandry and related matters, be sought for guidance—both in what to do and what not to do. (Application should be made to the Chairman of the Board, Dar es Salaam, Tanganyika, or the Secretary of State for the Colonies, London.)

(c) That a policy of careful extension of the crop at Gal Oya and other suitable colonization schemes be applied.

(d) That when satisfactory results have been shown by these activities, the crop be considerably extended in suitable localities.

African Oil Palm (Elaeis guineensis). Introduced in 1850 this stately and useful palm, a native of West Africa, grows vigorously

281

from sea level to about 2,000 feet elevation where the rainfall is not less than about 70 inches. It withstands drought somewhat better than the coconut.

As the outcome of local studies in West Africa, the Belgian Congo and elsewhere, several varieties and sub-varieties are known. The commonest type with a thick-skinned trunk is *E. guineensis var dura;* a better, thin-skinned type is *E. guineensis var tenera;* in *dura* the average proportion of shell to fruit is about one third by weight, whereas in *tenera* the proportion is about one tenth only. On the other hand, *dura,* in addition to being adaptable over a wider range of habitat conditions, is likely to bear slightly more oil. Unfortunately *tenera* produce progeny that are not true, and may revert to a comparatively useless small, thin skinned *pisifera* type.

In the East Indies an outstanding type is the well-known Deli form of a *dura* type. Seedlings are usually ready to lift at from 6 to 18 months of age. Planting is usually at espacements from 25 ft. upwards. Artificial pollination may be practised— the palm being monoecious. Production from the fruit is of the following order:

Pericarp	40-50% of the fruit
Nut	50-60% of the fruit
From the Pericarp:	oil 40-50%; moisture 20-40%; residue 14-16%.
From the nut:	shell 75-82%; kernel 18-25%.

The yields per acre naturally depend on the precise habitat conditions and on the variety and age of the palms, but at 26 ft. x 26 ft. production may be of the following order:

	5-10 years	11-30 years	30-50 years
Total weight of fruit in tons	1.5	4.5	1.5-2
Total weight of pericarp in tons	1.0	2.75	1.0
Total palm oil in tons	.5	1.5	.5
Total kernels in tons	.1	.4	.1
Total kernel oil in tons	.06	.2	.06

Pericarp oil is used principally for the manufacture of lubricants, soaps and candles. As the kernel oil is more stable, kernels may be shipped overseas for oil extraction. Oil cake is valuable stock feed. The oil is rich in protein fat and vitamin A. It is useful in household economy as well as for export.

The oil from properly established and managed palms shows less than 2% free fatty oil but that from the crude African presses may possess as much as 8 to 10%. There is usually a 90-95% oil extraction by modern presses but from primitive presses the percentage is much lower; about 40 to 50% only.

An intoxicating drink, palm wine or toddy, is obtained by tapping the tender upper portion of the stem.

The palm could be grown more extensively than at present. There is room for it under a light irrigation in severe seasons on the colonization schemes in the Dry Zone.

Better varieties should be obtained from the West African Oil Palm Research Institute, Benin, Nigeria, and from Malaya for trial. The palm would be valuable as a food crop but later could also provide an export commodity.

Cashew Nut (Anacardium occidentale). Native of the tropics of America and the West Indies, this plant has become naturalized in coastal portions of tropical Africa and Asia. It occurs along the littoral of Ceylon, on poor sandy and sandy-loam soils but also ranges up to 3,000 feet elevations on better soils. The nut is in great demand in Europe and the United States for dessert. Decortication is difficult as the shell is very hard and possesses an acrid and toxic property making decortication by hand an unpleasant task. One decortication plant exists in Calicut, also a small one is probably by now in operation in Portuguese East Africa (Mozambique). It is worth considering whether plantations of well established and cultivated trees would be economically productive. Work on the nut commenced a number of years ago and was allowed to fall away in Ceylon, but is now being resuscitated to a limited degree.

The tree supplies several additional products such as an indelible ink, an insect repelling gum and long-chain alcohols, but their production is scarcely likely to arouse any interest in normal circumstances.

Illuk (Imperata arundinacea). Much publicity has been given to a decision of the government to establish a mill north of Batticaloa on the east coast, for the preparation of paper from illuk grass and paddy straw. Technical reports supplied to the Mission by the Ministry of Industries indicate the intention of using a soda process to make 2,500 tons of writing and printing paper per year; in addition, two million cement bags are to be made from imported kraft pulp. Contractors, already starting construction, estimate that the project will cost Rs. 17 million. An area has been set aside for cultivation of the illuk grass.

Illuk is a common tropical and subtropical grass indigenous to the island. It is a troublesome weed in other cultivation, and is a poor grazing grass except when very young. Its growing characteristics are not too well known; available evidence indicates that it would require careful management, irrigation and probably heavy nitrogenous and phosphatic fertilizer, for the production of a reasonable volume or weight of leaf, on a sustained yield basis. There is no known industrial experience with it in paper manufacture.

Some work has been commenced at Karadian Aru in the Eastern Agriculture Division, bearing on the establishment, the irrigation and the response to phosphate of this grass. For 1950 it is reported that irrigation had to be done by hand owing to some difficulty in irrigating normally, an increase in yield of 27% being recorded in contrast with non-watered controls. The basic slag and ammonium phosphate used in the fertilizer trials failed to show any positive response, perhaps because of heavy rain at the time of application. Propagation by means of root division showed better results in establishment trials in the Maha 1950-51 season, than did stolons and seed.

Some investigations have also been undertaken at the Illuk Farm at Punanai. Here it has been found that the light-textured

284

soils give the best yields under ordinary rainfall, whereas under irrigation the better yields are given by loamy types.

In the Mission's opinion the attempt to establish large acreages of rapidly grown illuk, expected to withstand a sustained series of cuttings over the year, is unsound. The grass is not likely to give high sustained yields unless the soil is well prepared, irrigated and fertilized. This all means expensive production. It is doubtful that paper manufacture can stand such high costs in a country like Ceylon, where the total demands are not large.

Before embarking on the expense of establishing the mill or of attempting to put down large acreages of this uncertain source of supply, it would be wiser at least to await the outcome of more extensive and scientific field trials of illuk, as well as more practical pilot-scale tests with it in commercial paper making. Meanwhile, despite one adviser's rejection of citronella grass as unsuitable, it is suggested that a delegate from Ceylon visit the Guatemalan paper factory now using that material. Species of Cymbopogom and other similar grasses are used in South Africa.

In addition, the possibilities of utilizing other sources of supply should be sought. It is worth noting that in South Africa, where supplies of grass and other rapidly grown materials are difficult to maintain, the mills have had to fall back on expensive exotic timbers such as *Eucalyptus saligna* and other gums, paying high prices in competition with the mining groups requiring the same timbers for pit props. Research on the possibility of obtaining pulp from some of the Dry Zone jungle species and appropriate varieties of bamboo is worth undertaking. Admittedly, dependence upon jungle forests is not to be preferred, and sustained-yield cutting could be justified only where clearing was the objective. The use of bamboo is not new, and should be considered on a crop basis as is done elsewhere.

Food Crops

Paddy (Rice: Oryza sativa). Consistent and wholly reliable figures for paddy acreage and production are difficult to obtain.

285

Various estimates for recent years are shown in Table VII, from which a steady increase is seen. Yet, encouraging as this may seem, there remains a vast shortage to be made up before the island even approaches the production needed by its population.

TABLE VII

PRODUCTION OF PADDY IN SELECTED YEARS

Years	Season	Acres	Bushels
1944-45	Total	895,660	10,800,000
1948-49	Maha*	635,987	—
1949	Yala*	436,817	—
1948-49	Total	1,072,803	—
1949-50	Maha	665,019	9,701,257
1950	Yala	425,892	5,571,503
1949-50	Total	1,090,911	15,272,760
1951-52	Total	1,115,561	17,996,882

Source: 1944-45, 1949-50, 1950 Yala, 1951-52 (estimate)—Ceylon Government Annual Report to FAO October, 1950; 1948-49, 1949 Yala—Ceylon, *Year Book*, 1950.

* The *Maha* season is the main paddy growing season; sowing is about August to October and the crop is harvested at the end of the North-East monsoon, about February-March. The *Yala* season is shorter; crops are sown in March-April and harvested towards the end of the South-West monsoon in July-September. Occasionally a *Maha* crop is grown between the two ordinary seasons.

Using basic figures taken from the government's report to FAO, the production of paddy is estimated at about 280,000 tons per year, or a mean yield of only 14 bushels per acre. It is possible that this figure is too low because of the difficulty in getting satisfactory statistical returns from the vast number of small producers. [12] Be that as it may, recent annual importation

[12] The 1951 Annual Report to FAO, since made public, contains a revised estimate, based on new sampling techniques, of about 25 bushels per acre.

of paddy is reported to be about 390,000 tons, so as to maintain the 5.7 oz. ration per head per day.

It was estimated that with an additional 15,000 acres of paddy land (by September 1949) the crop increase would be only 42,000 tons. If an additional 24,650 acres were brought into production in 1951-52 the total area would approximate 1,115,561 acres, from which an anticipated yield of about 17,996,882 bushels might be harvested—*if* the hoped-for increase of two bushels per acre were indeed achieved.

Present paddy production would have to be at least doubled to overtake the requirements of the existing population, to say nothing of an annual 2.5% increase in numbers. Such a yield is theoretically possible, but cannot be achieved quickly. Arrayed against it are such factors as the uncertainty of water supply in certain areas, the wastage of water in others, the vagaries of season, the biological vicissitudes, the still too low fertility of much of the paddy land, the low efficiency and natural conservatism of many small producers, and the shortage of better, higher yielding strains.

Even under the best guidance, with a good supply of improved seed, with the most satisfactory fertilizers and with the issue of suitable plows, harrows, livestock and other facilities, the task is formidable. Out of a total of about 771,908 holdings only 8,260 are over 10 acres in extent. The multiplicity of "small" workers with their inherently conservative attitude toward new ideas and methods, the complications arising from the small dimensions of their holdings, the peculiar land tenure systems tending to increase fragmentation of the land, and their inability to improve methods beyond a certain point owing to lack of capital, certainly present a constellation of problems.

The Mission believes that by consistent effort on the part of the government departments, the CAP & S Societies and other organizations, the paddy growers might be induced to raise the average yield by as much as seven bushels per acre within the next ten years; but that is an ambitious target requiring tremendous efforts. It can be expected that on the colonization schemes, where

287

more aid and guidance are available than elsewhere, the colonists will react more readily to efforts made to help them.

Commendable progress is being made by the above mentioned agencies in disseminating information and in helping the peasantry to obtain supplies of seed, fertilizers, equipment, livestock and other requirements on reasonable terms. Meanwhile investigations extending over a number of years have been conducted by the Department of Agriculture, which now has several special paddy experimental centers.

Transplanting of paddy has been the subject of considerable study and trial. The results to date indicate that when accompanied by wise use of manures and fertilizers, satisfactory soil preparation and good cultural practices, transplanting is a highly important means of producing higher yields. Increases ranging from 20% to near 175% have been shown under experimental plot conditions, while on a larger scale also appreciable percentage gains have been demonstrated. In the shorter-season varieties (three or four months and shorter) there is still some doubt as to whether transplanting is justifiable, but with the longer season varieties (ranging from four and a half to six months) evidence points strongly toward its value. Studies of comparative costs of production of transplanted and broadcast paddy in Ceylon show only slightly higher costs for transplanting. Yield returns from transplanted areas, however, show a very considerable increase.

Fertility requirements of rice have been studied. While an abundance of the right form of organic matter probably brings the best response, application of a heavy tonnage is often impossible. Very fine responses are said to be given to two to three tons per acre—an amount far in excess of what the average villager or colonist would be able to supply.

Nitrogen and phosphorus are the principal requirements to be obtained from chemical fertilizers. Nitrogen in the ammonia form is the most satisfactory, whereas phosphorus may be applied in any suitable soluble form; the ratio should be about 18% N: 18% P. Suitable mixtures of N and P (e.g. ammonium phosphate) should be applied at rates from one half to two cwts. per acre, according to the fertility of the soil and whether organic materials are also used. It is good practice to apply the dressing either before the last preparatory harrowing, or as a top dressing after harrowing the standing crop. As Rhind [13] has pointed out, there is no objection to ammonium sulphate provided it is used in conjunction with a compatible phosphate fertilizer. Basic slag, calcium cynamide and lime are incompatible with sulphate of ammonia; potash should not be mixed with it unless for immediate application. The response to potash is less certain: in some circumstances a good response is shown, in others very little.

Improved varieties have been studied with much care. The aim is to obtain varieties giving a combination of such desirable features as increased yield, strong straw, grain size and shape, absence of grain shedding, absence of awns, high milling turn-out with low grain breakage, free tillering, and disease resistance. Cooking qualities should be an important consideration. Some attention has also been given to saline-resistant varieties. Some 18 improved varieties are now listed by the Department of Agriculture, suitable either for the Maha or Yala seasons or for both.

It will, of course, take a number of years for the production of varieties combining the most desirable qualities. Even then, unless improved soil preparation, general husbandry and provision of fertility march hand-in-hand with the production of improved varieties, such varieties will be of little value.

Introduction of the light single-furrow plow and the spiked or so-called Burmese harrow has produced much improvement in soil preparation, levelling and weeding. Harrowing both before sowing and as a later weeding operation has given excellent results. Control of the important pest, the Paddy Bug *(Leptocorisa acuta)*, by dusting with about 10 lbs. of Gammaxene per acre or by using aqueous DDT, has proven a great advance. So also has the more

---

[13] Rhind, D., formerly Director of Agriculture in Burma and later Ceylon.

cautious use of water, where it has been practiced at all, for it is clear that far too much water is used by the average grower.

Areas of uncertain water supply as well as very appreciable acreages of hill or highland paddy decrease the average yield for the island appreciably. It has been argued that properly such areas should not be under paddy at all. Yet obviously, until much more irrigable land is made available elsewhere the precariously supplied areas will continue to be worked. And to take highland paddy out of cultivation would entail so much social unrest and so great an expense (in attempted compensation) that it would be inadvisable for the government to consider it—at all events, for a long time to come. The proximity of the highland paddy terraces to the homes of the people is one of the conveniences that no ordinary compensation could ever cover.

The government's objectives in relation to an increase in the production of paddy are sound, but they cannot be achieved in a short period. The more significant are: (a) cultivation of the maximum extent of land now available; (b) bringing into cultivation as much new land as possible by means of jungle clearance, provision of irrigation water and colonization schemes; (c) restoration and improvement of minor irrigation works; and (d) improvement of yield through the propagation of information on the benefits of improved strains, use of organic matter and fertilizers, the timeliness of operations in relation to the seasons, good soil preparation and husbandry, transplanting, weeding and other progressive practices.

So far as the dissemination of information is concerned, a shortage of practical agricultural extension staff to demonstrate on the peasant's own plot the efficacy of such improved seed, implements and practices is one of the great handicaps in implementing this very wise policy.

In summary, the Mission believes that for continued increase in paddy output the following points should be stressed:

(1) Intensification of the work on strains, fertilizers, implements, transplanting, weeding, reaping, threshing and ro-

tation, so that yields on existing and new lands may be raised. This entails a strengthening of the Department of Agriculture's investigatory staff. It might be worth investigating the influence of the length of day upon the yield, because it has been said often that the low yield in Ceylon, Java and Malaya may partly be due to this factor. Very much higher yields are obtained in both tropical and temperate regions where the growing day is longer, as in Japan and Italy.

(2) Dissemination of knowledge and practical demonstration of technique for better management of the crop and of the soil. Need for a larger and more efficient extension service is the natural corollary of this. All results of the work on yield increase obtained by the government stations should be made known to every producer in the island, through extension staff, Rural Development Societies and the Cooperatives. Practical demonstration on the plots owned by villagers and colonists should be a major aim of all concerned, so that the small men may see that the means of gaining an increased yield is not a secret of the fortunate, well equipped government stations. Too often the work stops short of this step. Demonstration must go hand in hand with consistent efforts to capture the interest and the imagination of the villager and the colonist, for they in the last analysis are the men who are going to do the job.

(3) An acceleration of effort aiming at restoration and improvement of a large number of the small tanks and irrigation schemes. This presupposes a good survey (including aerial photographs), of the river regime and the distribution of the ancient irrigation areas, for careful planning of such restoration as may be deemed desirable. Any effort to hasten such restoration or renovation, in the absence of a synoptic view of the whole distribution of the tanks in a given catchment, probably would lead to

failure, heavy expenditure and possible damage by erosion following the breaching of tanks.

(4) Study of the water supply in relation to the needs of the crop, area for area, so that maximum use may be made of the supply available. It should be possible to reduce the amount of water consumption well below the present figures. As much as 14 acre feet are said to be used— largely wasted—on many paddy lands. The water saved may not in every case be usable for increased acreages because of local topographic, soil and other conditions, but in many instances extension would be feasible.

Collaboration between the Department of Agriculture, the Irrigation Department and the other government staff is necessary so that the essential studies may be made without delay, and so that information obtained can be passed on promptly in practical form to the users of the water: colonists, settlers and villagers.

Kurakkan; Finger millet; (Eleusine coracana). Widely grown in the semi-moist to drier portions of Asia and Africa, kurakkan has been produced for local consumption for a long time in Ceylon. A recent record shows that in the 1948-49 Maha, 64,383 acres were under this crop and that in the 1949 Yala the extent was 19,850 acres. The Government Report to FAO for 1950 shows that for the year 1944-45 the acreage was 81,474 and the yield 374,085 bushels for both Maha and Yala seasons; it includes an estimate for 1951-52 of 89,621 acres for an expected yield of 411,493 bushels, or an increase of 10% on the 1944-45 returns. The great bulk of this production is in chena.

The average yield shown, of about four and a half bushels or 270 lbs. per acre, is low. In Africa, under conditions no less severe than those of the Dry Zone, an average range of from 500 to 1,200 lbs. per acre may be expected, according to locality factors and efficiency of husbandry. With rainfall of 35 to 40 inches reasonably distributed over the growing season, and reasonably fertile soils, the yield may attain 1,500 lbs. per acre.

There can be little doubt that with better soil preparation, the use of better strains and of better seed, the application of fertilizer containing nitrogen and phosphate, and more attention to weed control, the yields could be raised very much above the present low average figures.

In Africa damage from birds is one of the hazards with kurakkan, and doubtless this has been the experience in Ceylon. However, the crop has good keeping qualities and a capacity to withstand periodic drought, as well as a distinct utility in rotations. It is of definite value in the various dry land colonization schemes, and is worthy of very much wider use.

The Department of Agriculture is to be commended for its attention to this crop. Work has been done on the selection of better varieties, and some success is reported on strain E-43, of which 497 bushels of seed have been issued for sowing.

Sorghum spp. (Sorghum; Guinea corn; Kaffir corn; Dura). The Mission can readily agree with the view of the Department of Agriculture that sorghum should, in time, become an important substitute for paddy in the Dry Zone. Its capacity for withstanding periodic drought, its resistance to adverse soil factors and its tendency to produce some sort of yield even in the severest seasons make it a far more reliable crop than maize. It is a useful rotation crop, and moreover, if later desirable, can be mechanized readily for large-scale production.

Yields may be expected to vary considerably in relation to climatic conditions, rainfall amount and distribution, soil fertility and espacement of the crop. In favorable circumstances 2000 lbs. may be returned per acre; more frequently yields from 600 to 1200 lbs. are to be expected.

At first little known and rather suspect so far as the colonists and others of the Dry Zone are concerned, the white-grained sorghums have begun to be accepted. Apparently their cultivation and popularization were commenced seriously only in 1949. By the 1950-51 Maha there were 2,100 acres of sorghum, raised from seed produced on the Department's farms. For the 1951-52

Maha the estimate is that about 10,000 acres should be sown. This progress in overcoming prejudice is attributable not only to the good trial work accomplished by the Department of Agriculture in various parts of the Dry Zone, but also to the strenuous efforts of this Department and other government officers to demonstrate by actual grinding, milling, and cooking that the grain is both palatable and useful.

The Department has worked not only with the grain sorghums of tall and dwarf kind, but also with the fodder and dual types. Among the better responding of the grain types have been Hegari, Tambagalla and A.S.475, all with white grains. Good responses have been noted from the fodder types, Kavirondo, R 2 S 4, Sweet Honey, and Sweet Sugar Drip. A dual purpose (grain and fodder) variety of interest is said to be San Pyaung. The fodder and dual types are most valuable as stock food if certain precautions are taken against development of cyanogenetic toxic substances.

It is important that emphasis has been placed on the varieties producing the white grains. It was found in East Africa that these were readily accepted whereas the red grained varieties were generally considered bitter, sour, or dry. The red types are liked for the making of beer. In Ceylon the same critical attitude toward the red types for food is reported.

Much good use has been made of various sorghums in the drier portions of Australia, and either a suitable officer from there or a member of the staff of the Queensland-British Overseas Food Corporation (an organization with extensive experience in raising sorghum by mechanized means) might usefully be invited to spend some time in Ceylon.

Maize; Corn; Indian Corn; Mealies (Zea mays). This well known plant has had a long history of casual use in Ceylon but not until recently has it been considered a crop worthy of serious consideration.

Recent advice of the Director of Agriculture indicates that maize (along with Kurakkan) has become a very popular crop in the villages of most of the provinces outside the very wet regions, and that it is grown as a substitute food crop on paddy lands which may be out of cultivation seasonally through lack of water. The Department of Agriculture states that in the 1948-49 Maha the acreage under maize was 25,750 and that in the 1949 Yala it was 4,382. In the Government Report to FAO for 1950, the total acreage for 1944-45 is given as 27,860 and the total Maha and Yala yield as 199,821 bushels. The estimate for 1951-52 is 31,633 acres, expected to yield 239,785 bushels or an increase of 10% over 1944-45. Most of this production has been in chena. According to a recent report 1,440 bushels of selected seed were issued for sowing purposes, from the official farms of the Department of Agriculture.

In marginal regions maize is, however, an uncertain crop. In a number of other countries efforts to produce large acreages in any but the regions endowed with satisfactory rainfall have been fraught with disaster or disappointment. Maize is capable neither of withstanding long periods of drought, nor of making use of the smaller amounts of effective rainfall that may break the longer droughts. In these matters it is far less adaptable than either kurakkan or sorghum.

As experience with strains and local factors grows, gradual extension of acreage in certain portions of the Dry Zone would be safe; but general extension throughout colonization schemes and throughout chena would be unduly risky. Poor yields or even complete failure would undoubtedly be the outcome of planting maize in the drier areas with a highly unreliable moisture distribution.

Maize is not a good crop for conserving either water or soil. In fact, growing it on slopes should be avoided, for, unless careful contouring and terracing are practiced, its cultivation tends to encourage run-off and erosion.

It is also a "hungry" crop, rapidly depleting soil nutrients. It should never be grown except in rotation with leguminous crops, and even then to grow large acreages without addition of chemical fertilizers (nitrogen and phosphorus) is likely to prove uneconomical.

Other Cerals

Among other cereals already grown to a limited extent in chena, or suitable for trial both in chena and on the colonization schemes of the Dry Zone are the following:

Indian Millet (Panicum miliaceum; Meneri, Wal-meneri), a hardy drought-resistant millet yielding from 400 to 800 lbs. per acre of grain according to conditions; responds well to good preparation of soil and NP fertilizer. A good rotational crop.

Little Millet (Panicum miliare; Heen-meneri), also hardy and drought-resistant; yields at much the same rate as *P. miliaceum*. This is also a good rotational crop.

Cockspur Millet (Panicum crus-galli var. frumentaceum; Wel-marukku), a hardy drought-resistant, fast-maturing crop yielding at much the same rate as the other millets noted above.

Italian Millet (Setaria italica; Boer manna; Tana-hal), a relatively hardy, drought-resistant millet. This is a useful soil-improving and rotational crop. The grain is usually in high demand for bird seed mixtures, but is also used as a food in various parts of the subtropics and tropics. Its use on colonization schemes is certainly worth a serious trial.

Bulrush Millet (Pennisetum spicatum P. typhoideum; Pollu). Grown extensively in parts of Asia and throughout the drier parts of Africa, this very hardy and strongly drought-resistant millet may be expected to return some yield even under severe conditions. Under good conditions up to 800 to 1,000 lbs. per acre may be returned; under severe conditions up to 500 lbs. It is an excellent stand-by crop in areas where rainfall is unreliable. Its wider use in drier portions of the Hambantota east coast Lowlands and north central Lowlands regions is recommended, both in chena and on the colonization schemes.

Miscellaneous Minor Millets. Other minor cereals either produced to a limited degree in the Dry Zone or capable of being

296

grown there include: *Digitari exilis* (Hungry rice), *Paspalum scrobiculatum* (Koda millet; Amu)—with a grain liable to be slightly poisonous and requiring preparation before use; and *Coix lachryma-jobi* (Job's tears), a larger seeded cereal. The Mission does not recommend extension of these cereals or even their use.

Although none of the foregoing crops approach sorghum in value as a food crop, the *Panicums* and *Setaria* are valuable soiling crops bearing moderately useful grain, while the *Pennisetum* is a particularly useful "reserve" crop for severe or unreliable localities. Most of them have some place to fill in the pattern of both chena and dry land colonization farming.

Sugar (Saccharum officinarum). Imports of sugar total over 100,000 tons per year—the figures for 1949 being 116,450 tons valued at Rs. 47.4 million. Local production of sugar, therefore, has been much discussed and a limited amount of actual field experimentation and study has been undertaken.

Earlier field trials were somewhat lacking in clarity of objective, scientific planning, and careful execution. They showed, however, that cane would grow well vegetatively in certain parts of the Dry Zone if it were given adequate irrigation and they drew attention to the greater promise of certain varieties, especially Co. 349, Co. 419, Co. 421 and P.O.J. 2878.

Recently, through the joint activities of an FAO sugar expert and the Department of Agriculture, more precise field trials have been initiated at Polonnaruwa. These appear to be well planned, well executed and well managed but firm conclusions cannot yet be drawn from them since they were only established during 1951. However, the growth appears to be excellent and the preliminary sugar tests are encouraging. In these trials the strains Co. 419, Co. 421 and P.O.J. 2878 were showing the greatest promise at the time of the Mission's visit.

Opinions of the FAO sugar expert, as expressed to the Mission after his eight months study of climatic and soil conditions in several parts of the Dry Zone (Giritale and Gal Oya more particularly) and of the existing stands of sugar at Polonnaruwa and elsewhere, might be summarized as follows:

1. Generally speaking, conditions for the growing of sugar are good; soil and climatic conditions are suitable in the areas inspected.

2. A preliminary estimate of an average of 40 tons cane per acre, yielding about 4 tons sugar, seems reasonable under suitable locality factors and efficient management.

3. Costs of production would be reasonable, chiefly because of the comparatively high yields of sugar and the spread of the labor over the year (utilization of labor in the dry season being important). Furthermore he thought there would eventually be income from the ancillary products such as bagasse, molasses, cane spirit and so forth. He also envisaged the use of the cane tops as a useful ensilage or green feed material for livestock of colonists. Finally, in comparison with paddy, sugar provides about three times the food value per unit of water.

4. A sugar and rice rotation is feasible and would be a suitable means of subdividing the ground with one half being under rice and the other under sugar.

5. The responses of some of the varieties tried earlier, and again being tested under his direction at Polonnaruwa, have been promising. On these and the general conditions of climate and soil he based his estimates of yield. The outstanding variety so far is the well known P.O.J. 2878, but Co. 419 and Co. 421 also promise well. At Polonnar-uwa 35 varieties are under test.

6. Disease did not appear to be significant; mosaic-resistant varieties are being used and no other disease or pest have given any trouble.

7. Good responses are being shown to suitable fertilizers.

8. A trial unit of 8,000 to 10,000 acres would be warranted.

Such trials, he thought, could be carried out at Giritale near Polonnaruwa and at Gal Oya.

9. Records of some 300 acres planted at Polonnaruwa in June 1950 show the following response for the three important varieties:

Variety	Planted	Analyzed	Tons of cane per acre	Rende-ment	Tons of sugar per acre
POJ 2878	1 June 1950	5 June 1951	20.9	12.10	2.54
Co. 421	10 ″ ″	6 ″ ″	28.5	7.97	2.27
Co. 419	26 ″ ″	7 ″ ″	21.4	8.81	1.89

These had been fertilized with: 20 lbs. per acre of nitrogen as ammonium sulphate; 9 lbs. phosphorus pentoxide as superphosphate; and 10 lbs. potash as potassium muriate. Planting had been in the form of three-budded setts, with espacement between rows four and a half feet, along the contour.

The somewhat low yields on the 300 acres could be explained, the FAO expert thought, by the fact that the crop had had little attention, since it had been raised for multiplication purposes, not for yields.

10. In contrast are the results of some recent monthly planting experiments:

Variety	Planted	Analyzed	Tons of cane per acre	Rende-ment	Tons of sugar per acre
POJ 2878	15 June 1950	20 June 1951	45.5	10.01	4.55
Co. 421	″ ″ ″	21 ″ ″	49.0	7.98	3.88
Co. 419	″ ″ ″	22 ″ ″	38.7	8.35	3.23

The experimental plantings received better attention and better fertilizing. There had been five tons of cattle manure applied per acre at the time of planting, 471 lbs. ammonium phosphate six weeks after planting, and 471 lbs. of ammonium sulphate 12 weeks after planting.

11. A method of preparing and propagating planting material so as to save cane and yet produce equally strong plants, had been demonstrated at Polonnaruwa and could be advocated for general use in large scale plantings. The field demonstration of this method was impressive; much less material was used than in normal practice, and very vigorous rooted material resulted.

12. A small sugar laboratory, which had been established at Polonnaruwa during the year, was making progress with various innovations in laboratory and field techniques that had been introduced by the FAO specialist.

The Mission's investigations included field visits to all major locations and installations then connected with contemplated sugar projects, as well as discussions with the various officials and specialists concerned. Our views are based on examination of areas at Gal Oya and Giritale, near Polonnaruwa, but would apply generally to other possible sites for sugar development, including the one at Maha Illuppallama which we understand is now favored by the government.

There can be no doubt that good sugar can be grown in suitable localities in the Dry Zone provided that enough irrigation water becomes available, and the Mission supports the effort to establish a sugar industry. The planting of large areas within a short time would, however, carry serious dangers. Among the hazards are the insufficiency of existing knowledge regarding the response of the crop to the varying types of soil over the intended areas, uncertainty of fertilizer requirements and water relations in the several localities, lack of experience on the part of local staff and labor in the establishment and general field husbandry of cane, and the complete absence of experience as to the reaction of individual cultivators to the growing of cane on land they traditionally would plant to paddy.

The suggested rotation of sugar with paddy needs to be tried out further so as to test not only the agronomic aspects but also

UNIVERSITY COLLEGE OF WALES LIBRARY ABERYSTWYTH

the reaction of the cultivators. To embark on large-scale planting of sugar on smallholders' plots, on the assumption that the sugar paddy rotation is an assured practice, involves too great a risk at this stage. Smaller scale, but nevertheless "practical," trial not only of this rotation but of other possibilities is first needed.

Additional survey and testing of the areas scheduled for large plantings of cane are also necessary to provide a solid basis for rapid, extensive cultivation of the crop. Water usage for sugar cultivation needs fuller investigation. The statement that sugar requires only one third as much water as paddy has to be proved locally under the hot, high-evaporating power of the air in the Dry Zone.

While the yields of four tons of sugar per acre from 40 tons of cane may be feasible on carefully controlled experimental plots, an extensive acreage, broken down into individually small areas managed by a large number of colonists, cannot be relied upon to produce so high a return. The estimates should be set much lower, say at one and a half to two and a half tons of sugar instead of four, for the first planting and two ratoon cuttings. Overestimation would lead to disappointment both for the government and for the colonist.

What is first of all required—and what is now reported to be the intention of the government—is to establish a single practical trial area of say 6,000 acres and a factory of corresponding size.

In such a trial careful study would be directed to the economics of establishment, management, supply of fertilizers and water, and operation of a small trial factory, against the resulting value of sugar molasses and any other materials produced. Since it is unsafe to rely on data gained in other countries where labor costs and other conditions for calculating the costs of large-scale local undertakings may be very different.

On the basis of such experience, expansion on a larger scale can be considered in a few years' time. Meanwhile, although small-scale field trials in promising localities could be continued, developed on the scale which has been contemplated at Gal Oya (some 20,000 acres) should be deferred.

At least a part, perhaps the greater part, of the acreage should be cultivated initially on an estate basis. It may be considered desirable, at any rate in the long run, to grow a proportion of the cane on colonists' plots but the returns, yields and costs on the estate acreage will be a valuable standard by which to measure the smallholders' efficiency. A substantial proportion of "mill" cane serves moreover to give the mill some assurance of scheduled operation if smallholders fail to harvest on time.

Problems concerning the possible utilization of molasses, bagasse and other by-products are discussed in Chapter 15. There will also be problems of transport, both of the manufactured sugar and other products and of the cane. The first should not be serious if the mill is located at Maha Illuppallama which is close to the railway, but would be more difficult in any present development at Gal Oya. On any site, the movement of cane will be a considerable problem, as the tonnage to be moved will be large and the movement must be exactly timed to avoid deterioration of cut cane or interruption of mill working. A suggestion has been made in Chapter 16 for the use of part of the track of the Kelani Valley narrow gauge railway line to provide transport in the sugar cane area.

Details of the government's current plans are available only through press reports. As stated there [14] the main features are:

(1) As the first step 6,000 acres under the Maha Illuppallama Augumentation Scheme have been allocated by the Minister of Agriculture for the growing of cane; a sugar mill is to be erected there.

(2) Of the 6,000 acres, 1,500 are to be planted and placed under the Sugar Factory Administration—presumably to be run as an "estate" production area—while the remaining 4,500 acres are to be alienated to "middle-class" farm-

---

[14] Ceylon Daily News, January 18, 1952.

ers in blocks of 50 to 100 acres for sugar cultivation. The government is said to expect a good response to this from farmers capable of employing mechanized cultivation methods. "On this basis the proportion of individual allotments under the Ceylon Sugar Cultivation Scheme is thought to be quite capable of proving an economic proposition to farmers."

(3) The Ministry of Agriculture and Lands will be responsible for the agricultural aspects and for investigational work bearing on selection of varieties, mapping out of allotments, the supply of water and so forth. The Ministry of Industries, Industrial Research and Fisheries "will concern itself with the successful working of the factory—the manufacture of sugar and byproducts such as power-alcohol."

(4) "The Sugar Factory will be a self-contained unit . . . with its own power plant, water supply, repair shops and other essential features." It is estimated that the capital cost of the factory together with the necessary plant for making power-alcohol will be between Rs. 16 million and Rs. 17 million.

In many respects, for example, the size of the initial scheme and the reservation of a substantial estate acreage, these proposals accord with the Mission's own conclusions. Other aspects which the Mission hopes will be considered in working out the details of the development are discussed in Chapter 15 as well as in this chapter. In particular the Mission urges that a full survey of soil, water supply and transportation problems be made, if it has not already been done, before actual plantings are made. If the sugar project is tackled with adequate preparation and care, it should become the foundation of a most valuable new agricultural and manufacturing enterprise.

Beans and Pulses

Apart from leguminous trees and crops to improve the soil,

some leguminous crops can add substantially to the food supply of the island. These include the following:

Groundnut—already discussed and recommended for extension of acreage, under Commercial Crops.

Dhal (Cajanus cajan, C. indicus; Congo pea) is a perennial shrub attaining six to ten feet in height; it may be interplanted with other crops or grown pure; normally the Dhal is cropped for two seasons only, then resown. Pods are produced within six months, with yields ranging from 500-750 lbs. of seed per acre per year. Apart from the value of the seed as a human food, the pods and foliage form a good stock food. The plant is also valuable in rotations as a soil improver. The Department of Agriculture reports the development of a strain that produces a heavy yield of pods in four to five months; seed of this variety has been distributed to the Dry Zone for trial.

Sword Bean (Canavalia ensiformis) is suitable for growing where it can be irrigated from time to time. As it is a trellis plant, its extension over large acreages is not feasible, but it is a useful home garden legume. The Department of Agriculture has made selections for trial and later distribution.

Chick Pea (Cicer arietinum; Bengal gram; Konda-kadala) produces small angular peas commonly used in Ceylon as a fried or roasted legume, for inclusion in curries and as an ingredient in coffee substitutes. The crop is fairly drought-resistant. The yield is usually not more than 350-500 lbs. per acre. Care must be taken in disposal of the straw to livestock, owing to its poisonous oxalic acid content.

Bonavist-bean (Dolichos Lablab) is grown in gardens in the island, and yields edible pods, immature and dry beans. The Department of Agriculture has made selections for distribution for use in gardens. A white-flowered, green-podded variety has recently been sent out for trial.

Green Gram (Phaseolus aureus; Mung; Muneta) is a well-known bean widely grown in India, parts of Africa and to some extent in the Dry Zone. The 1950 Government Report to FAO gives the 1944-45 acreage as 7,600 with a yield of 28,474 bushels (bushel weight is about 66 lbs.), and estimates that for 1951-52 the acreage will rise to 9,119 and the yield to 34,168 bushels, an increase of 20%.

The principal product is the dried seed, which is used in much the same way as dhal; the pods are also edible, while the straw is a useful fodder for livestock. This is a valuable rotational or soil improving crop. It is drought hardy, but gives its best yields under well-distributed rainfall. A yield of 300-450 lbs. may be expected under the more severe conditions of the Dry Zone, where its use should certainly be encouraged. Glossy-seeded varieties are preferred. The Department of Agriculture has recently distributed 230 bushels of seed of "B3" to Dry Zone cultivators.

Black Gram (Phaseolus Mungo; Urd) is said to be more highly considered in India than green gram. The seed is larger, but is yielded at much the same rate per acre. It is ground to produce a meal for making bread, wafer biscuits and spice balls. If investigation by the Department of Agriculture proves favorable, its trial in suitable sites on colonization schemes would be worth while.

Lima Bean (Phaseolus lunatus; Butter, Java or Madagascar bean). While more suited to higher elevations, this climber could be grown in gardens in the Dry Zone if some irrigation were possible during dry periods. Under unusually good climatic and soil conditions its yield may range from 1,000-1,500 lbs. per acre. Good quality Lima beans would find a ready market outside the island.

Princess Bean (Psophocarpus tetragonolobus; Winged bean; Daradhambala) is a vigorous climber bearing long, four-angled pods. The pods may be eaten in their immature state; the fleshy, tuberous roots are also edible. The Department of Agriculture has made selections for trial in the Dry Zone and elsewhere. As a home garden crop this bean has much to commend it.

Cow Pea (vigna catiang V. sinesis; Me-karal) is a well known soil improver and fodder plant. In addition to its edible beans, it produces a good spinach from the young, tender shoots and leaves. Some of its many varieties are remarkably drought-resistant. Wide use could be made of it in the Dry Zone colonization schemes.

Velvet Bean (Stizolobium (Mucuna) spp. Florida bean; Mauritius bean) is now being tested as a cover crop at Maha Illuppallama. *S. deeringianum* and *S. niveum,* well known as green manure and stock feed legumes, probably could play a significant role in the rotation in the Dry Zone. In addition to providing cover and useful material for "plowing in," they produce edible pods for home consumption. A yield of up to 1,000 lbs. of bean and 8 to 10 tons of green matter may be expected. The crop is worthy of more attention than it has been accorded in the past.

Yams and Tubers

Included here for convenience and discussed separately below, are the true yams (Dioscorea yams) as well as the two aroid yams *Colocasia antiquorum* and *Alocasia* (Xanthosoma) *indica,* the sweet potato *(Ipomea Batatas),* the ordinary potato *(Solanum tuberosum)* and the manioc *(Manihot utilissima).*

Except for the ordinary potato, these form an increasingly important item of diet in the peasant and colonist communities of the island, and offer much promise for the future. They are all of tropical ancestry and respond well in Ceylon. The true potato, however, is not really at home in the tropics, even at higher elevations; yields are poor, quality is low, and the rate of deterioration both through virus and physiological discomfort is rapid.

All but the ordinary potato have steadily increased in acreage during the past few years, largely through the activities of the Department of Agriculture in issuing planting material of suitable varieties. Available figures indicate nearly 24,000 acres established in the Kurunegala, Chilaw and Puttalam districts and the Sabaragamuwa Division in 1950-51, as well as 250,000 setts of Dioscorea yam, 145,000 manioc cuttings and lesser amounts of others distributed in the Western Division.

Dioscorea Yams (Velala). These are widely cultivated in the

West Indies and tropical America generally, where they form an important item of the diet. In recent years they have become somewhat more popular in West Africa, Ceylon and the eastern tropics. In Ceylon they do well from sea level to about 3,000 feet, in good, loamy soils. The yield under favorable circumstances may attain five to six tons per acre.

There are numerous varieties. Among those being distributed by the Department of Agriculture are Kirikondol, Baeton and Rattivalli. These are reported to have responded well to the local conditions. In time yams should play a much greater role in the home gardens of settlers, colonists and the peasantry as a whole.

Colocasia and Alocasia (Coco-yams; Dasheen; Kiri-ala). Of these the former (peltate-leafed) is the preferred one, said to be more palatable than the latter (hastate-leafed). This kind of yam is more popular in the West Indies and parts of Africa, less so in the East and in Ceylon. Six or more varieties have been grown in the island. Some short-period varieties mature in three to four months, in contrast with the usual nine months in most others. The yield may be from two to five tons per acre, under favorable rainfall conditions. It is gratifying that the Department of Agriculture is attempting to popularize them by means of improved varieties for they should find a ready place in Dry Zone and other gardens.

Sweet Potato (Ipomea Batatas). The sweet potato is common in most tropical countries, and has been grown in Ceylon for a long time in half a dozen or more varieties. Its extensive use by colonists and others in the Dry Zone should be pushed strongly. The yield ranges from two to five tons per acre, according to conditions. The crop prefers a light loam, well drained but with plenty of moisture and a moderate fertility. With addition of fertilizer or organic matter, the quality and yield improve greatly.

Manioc (Cassava; Tapioca; Manyokka; Manihot utilissima). Grown extensively throughout the tropics, manioc is said to have been introduced to the East by the Portuguese in the seventeenth century. Of the two forms "bitter" and "sweet" (perhaps corresponding to *M. utilissima* and *M. palmata* respectively) there are very many varieties. Work has been done in various parts of the tropics to develop varieties more resistant to disease (mosaic is a common disease in some parts of Africa), more palatable, less toxic (cyanogenetic glucosides) and earlier maturing.

Recently the Department of Agriculture has distributed a four-months Philippine variety. Should this prove to be a good, hardy plant bearing satisfactorily, it should be an improvement on the normal nine-months maturity forms. Yields of two to six tons per acre may be expected, according to conditions; but with really favorable rainfall, soil texture, and fertility, a good variety may yield up to 10 tons.

Although manioc possesses only about 2% proteid, it is in great demand on account of its heavy (over 60%) carbohydrate yield and the great tonnage per acre. The crop is used both as a home food and as a carbohydrate stock feed. It is also an important source of starch (tapioca) for commercial purposes; this may form about 30% of the total weight of the tuberous roots.

The crop is a "hungry" one, taking a heavy toll of the major soil nutrients. It should not be grown for more than two or three years on the same ground. To a limited extent it has been used by the Forest Department as a nurse crop in the *taungya* system of raising teak and mahogany trees in jungle clearings. For this the crop must be kept open lest its strong competition for moisture and nutrients inhibit growth and development of the young trees.

With issuing of the better varieties, and with a sound rotation so that the crop will not impoverish the soil, extension of this crop is to be advocated. In time the crop may be large enough to warrant the establishment of a small starch factory.

Potato (Solanum tuberosum). The country in the vicinity of Nuwara Eliya and in the drier district of Udapussellawa has produced limited quantities of potatoes. For the tropics, they are of fair quality but by temperate zone standards they are decidedly poor. Numerous varieties have been tried by the Department of Agriculture and the European estates.

More recently the Department of Agriculture has considered production of potato in the Jaffna district. It is reported that demonstrations laid down on cultivators' plots, using a variety from Holland commonly found in the market, have given "very promising" results. More intensive trials are being conducted at the Farm School, Jaffna, so as to obtain suitable varieties.

Investigations should certainly continue of the production of more suitable early and late varieties, for both the moister and the drier hill and montane region and for the Jaffna subregion of the Dry Zone. "Ring Blight" *(Bacillus solanacearum)* and other diseases and pests also require study.

Onions and Shallots (Allium cepa and A. ascalonicum). Onions, and particularly shallots (red onions) form a most important and valued item of food, particularly for use in curries and for pickling. Imports for 1950 (mainly from India) totalling 703,885 cwts. and valued at Rs. 10.8 million indicate the significance of the crop in the life of the people.

While a certain amount has been grown for home consumption, the Department of Agriculture has only recently taken an active part in investigating varieties, espacement, fertilization and disease control in this crop. The latest Government Report to FAO shows that in 1944-45, 5,206 acres produced 24,613 cwts.; estimated figures for 1951-52 are 19,104 acres to yield 98,872 cwts.—an increase of 400%.

For 1950 it is reported that there was an increase of 1,600 acres in the North, Central and Uva Provinces alone, as well as 600 acres in the Jaffna District which had a total of 2,250 acres under the crop. In explanation of this, the Department of Agriculture reports that an incentive of 18 cents per lb. led cultivators to plant at any season of the year. While this did increase acreage at Jaffna it also contributed to the high incidence of "tip burns" caused by thrips, which called for control by application of sulphur.

Experimental work conducted at Polonnaruwa recently has thrown some interesting light on espacement, response to fertilizers, and storage. Espacement of 6 x 1.5 inches is said to have increased yields by 49% in comparison with the 6 x 6 inches, but the bulbs were smaller; fertilizer applied in the form of ammonium sulphate at 100 lbs. per acre (i.e. 30 lbs. nitrogen) produced a 26% increase, whereas 200 lbs. gave no further significant increase; the larger bulbs stored for three months better than the smaller, the keeping power not being affected by the fertilizer.

At Jaffna, seven parts of ammonium sulphate plus five parts superphosphate, at the rate of 1.5 cwts. per acre have been used in experiments with manure on cultivators' plots. Comparison of Indian and local "seed" has also been conducted in this area.

On the colonization schemes as well as elsewhere in the Dry Zone, where some water is available and where good drainage and some fertility exists, reasonable yields could be obtained. Suitable varieties and espacement should produce up to several tons per acre.

Fruit

It is not possible to attempt more than a very brief statement here on the broad subject of fruit—a source of food that could be greatly increased in both quantity and quality under the good growing conditions offered in various parts of the island. However, the more important fruits to which the Department of Agriculture has given attention are mentioned, and some others which offer special possibilities.

Sapodilla (Achras sapota) is grown more particularly in Galle and Kalutara districts and other damp to wet lowland areas where it is suitable for increased propagation. It is slow growing and bears two crops per year; improved varieties may be propagated by grafting as well as by seed.

Pineapple (Ananas sativa) has already been discussed in earlier pages.

Bread-fruit (Artocarpus incisa rata-del) is a much prized fast-growing fruit introduced about 1796 from the Pacific islands; it does well from sea level up to about 2,000 ft., with best results in warm, moist sites.

Jak-fruit (Artocarpus integrifolia; Kos), producing one of the largest fruits known, is also one of the most highly favoured trees in Ceylon; the fruit and seeds are widely used in curries and as a vegetable. In addition, this tree yields an excellent timber for furniture and building needs. The Department of Agriculture has encouraged its propagation on the colonization schemes, while the Forest Department has planted it as a useful timber tree in the southwest lowlands and elsewhere.

Pawpaw (Carica papaya) has been discussed. The "Solo Hawaii" variety, of superior quality and a good yielder, is being encouraged.

Watermelon (Citrullus vulgaris) in a number of varieties is suitable for medium-dry areas on light, sandy loams. This plant could receive more attention than it has in the past, as it lends itself to preparation for canning as well as being of value as a fresh fruit; it could be grown more widely on the colonization schemes and elsewhere in the Dry Zone.

Citrus, including orange, lime, sweet lime, grapefruit, lemon, citron and tangerine, has been studied by the Department of Agriculture as to stock varieties, disease resistance and locality responses. On the whole the texture, flavor and general appearance of the citrus seen by the Mission appeared below standard; likewise, the few citrus groves seen required better management. So far as orange is concerned, a seedless Bibile Sweet Orange is being propagated on a large scale in preference to other varieties.

There is considerable scope for improvement in quality and quantity of citrus. Hardy, disease-resistance stocks should be sought and given careful trial. Soil and climatic conditions are suitable in many localities in the hill and montane region, the Sabaragamuwa hill region, the Chilaw transition zone, and the Hambantota and north central uplands and lowland regions. While it is doubtful that really top grades of fruit worth exporting could be produced in large amount, much could be done to provide more and better fruit for local demand.

Durian (Durio zibethinus) has received some attention from the

311

Department of Agriculture. It grows very well in the southwest lowlands and other moister, warmer sites up to about 2,000 feet, but is being grown to a limited extent in the Dry Zone. As a useful food for home use it is worth planting on the colonization schemes.

Mangosteen (Garcinia mangostana) does reasonably well in the southwest lowlands and the adjacent humid and warmer regions, up to about 2,000 feet. It does best on the better classes of soil; within the limits of the wet and hot to warm portions of the island it is worth more attention.

Mango (Mangifera indica) has been given much study by the Department of Agriculture in recent years, with the object of selecting and distributing better fruited and better yielding varieties. A large amount of planting material was being distributed by the Horticultural Division, Peradeniya. There is a comparatively large stand of mango at the government farm at Hingurakgoda in the Dry Zone.

The Horticultural Division, in addition to issuing suitable grafted varieties, has assisted in the conversion of inferior trees to more profitable ones, by means of "top working" sour and fibrous-fruited trees. The varieties distributed include Karuthai, Kolumban and Willard. Useful work has also been done on stock and scion relations and responses.

Being able to withstand dry periods if there is a satisfactory soil moisture content, the mango could play a much greater part in the Dry Zone than it does today. It has obvious use on the colonization schemes. Now that canned mango is being produced in the island there should be little difficulty in extending this activity to the Dry Zone at a later stage, when supplies of fruit justify new canneries.

Banana (Musa spp.; Plantain) has been grown in several varieties in the island for a long time. Although in the West Indies there is a fairly clear distinction between "plantain" or cooking bananas and "banana" or dessert varieties, this distinction does not hold in Ceylon, where the name plantain includes both kinds.

312

As to botanical nomenclature, recent work by Creeseman shows that *M. sapientum* probably is an interspecific hybrid, that *M. paradisiaca* (once thought to include the cooking varieties only) contains both dessert and cooking varieties, and that *M. Cavendishii* (the name given to the "Chinese" or "Canary" banana) is invalid.

Lately the Department of Agriculture has given serious attention to selection and distribution of this valuable fruit. According to recent information it has decided to issue for extensive planting the well known Gros Michel or Martinique variety. While this is undoubtedly the best of the edible and exportable varieties, it must be remembered how prone it has been in Jamaica, Central and South America and the old world to the dread Panama Disease, caused by the soil-borne fungus *Fusarium oxysporum cubense*. Another threat to the same variety is *Cercospora musae*, causing a serious leaf-spot, loss of vital leaf surface and defoliation. The Ceylon variety known as Kol-Kuttu is said to bear a resemblance to the Gros Michel. The submerging of land for over a year to a depth of several feet as a means of killing out Fusarium, and the expensive spraying of Bordeaux mixture as a means of controlling the Cercospora (methods adopted in Central and South America by the great fruit companies), would not be feasible in the small stands of banana and plantain grown on either high or irrigable ground in Ceylon.

On the whole, however, the Department's policy of extension of the small sweet Chinese or Canary (formerly *M. Cavendishii*) banana, other dessert varieties and a range of cooking varieties is a very wise one. On the colonization schemes much additional food could thus be made available, both for home consumption and for sale.

Litchi (Nephelium Litchi) is grown in several varieties in the moister, warmer areas but only in small quantities. With a view to home consumption and export, its trial in some of the less severe areas of the Dry Zone would be worth the attention of the Department of Agriculture.

Avocado-pear; Alligator-pear (Persea gratissima) of tropical American origin, is grown to a limited degree in the island. It does well in the moderately warm, moister areas but also should be tried in the less severe parts of the Dry Zone. The Department of Agriculture is investigating the performance of recently introduced varieties on certain well-known stocks of West Indian origin; these varieties include Gotfried, Pollock, Puebla and St. Anne. Owing to its high nutritional value (among other desirable points its fat content is 10% to 27% of its fresh weight) this is a fruit worth extending.

Guava (Psidium guayava), abundant in vitamin C, is growing in favor dietetically. In one or another of its many varieties this species should do well in Ceylon, especially in the range from about 1,500 to 3,500 feet. As it is drought- and heat-hardy, however, efforts should be made to grow it more abundantly on the Dry Zone colonization schemes. There are now several varieties that yield large, fine-flavored and almost seedless fruit.

Cape Gooseberry (Physalis pubescens; P. peruviana; Peruvian Cherry), of Peruvian origin but naturalized in parts of South and East Africa, is grown in the higher regions of the island. It produces a fruit highly prized for preserving and for jam-making. In Africa it does well under hot and dry climatic conditions, so long as there is enough soil moisture; accordingly it should respond well on Dry Zone colonization plots where a certain amount of water could be spared from time to time for irrigation. The fruit transports quite well if left in the papery cover or "cape," hence its shipment to a central preserving factory would be feasible.

Fruits for the Higher Elevations. While a wide range of subtropical and temperate fruits are grown at the intermediate to higher elevations, only a few are really promising for such altitudes and conditions. Among these are the custard apple or cherimoya *(Anona cherimola)*, the persimmon *(Diospyros Kaki)*, the strawberry *(Fragaria vesca)*, the passion-fruit *(Passiflora edulis)* and the cape gooseberry *(Physalis)*. Generally speaking

314

the temperate or subtropical genera Prunus, Pyrus, Malus (peaches, plums, apricots, pears, apples) are not at home and produce poor quality fruit.

Vegetables. Marked encouragement of the cultivation and marketing of vegetables has been given by the Department of Agriculture, especially through Rural Development Societies and other village agencies. In addition to collecting information and providing extension services, the Department produced on its farms and at its vegetable seed station (Katugastota) 3,070 lbs. of seed for distribution during 1950.

Vegetable collecting depots, established at Negombo, Kandy, Newara, Eliya, Bandarawela, Batticaloa, Jaffna, Kurunegala, Anuradhapura and Ratnapura, have assisted the cultivator or the Cooperative Societies in the sale of their products, and have thus reduced wastage and encouraged production. For 1949 the vegetables thus collected totalled 3,900,288 lbs. These were disposed of locally, at various other Marketing Department Outstations and in Colombo. In Colombo itself there are several selling points for vegetables (and fruits) received from the collecting depots; hospitals in the area are supplied, and house delivery services and street sales are arranged.

At the lower elevations, in addition to the various cereals, beans, chillies, pulses, yams and onions, already mentioned, the following vegetables are of importance and their increase certainly would be beneficial to the welfare of the island; gourds, pumpkins, squashes and melons of a number of species and varieties; okra *(Hibiscus esculentus)*; horse-radish tree *(Moringa pterygosperma)*; brinjal *(Solanum melongena)*; spinach *(Amaranthus, Basella, Boussingaultia, Chenopodium, Portulaca, Talinum,* etc.); kohlrabi; tomatoes; and radishes.

At the higher elevations a range of subtropical and temperate vegetables is produced. Among these are; artichoke (Globe and Jerusalem); beans of several kinds; beetroot; spinach-beet; brussels sprouts; cabbage in a number of varieties; carrot; cauliflower (but not without special care); celery; cho-cho *(Sechium edule)*;

315

cucumber; leeks and onions; lettuce; parsnip; peas; radish; rhubarb; true spinach *(Spinacia)*; New Zealand spinach *(Tetragonia)*; turnip; and marrow.

PASTURES AND LIVESTOCK

Pasture and Fodder

Before discussing the animal husbandry and veterinary sides of livestock production a brief examination is necessary of the principal types of natural grazing and browsing, problems of establishing certain pastures, and the role to be played by selected crops in the production of livestock feed.

Natural Grazing and Browsing. The more important types of natural grazing and browsing, determined by the natural regions already described, are:

1. The hill and montane patanas of high rainfall, high humidity and lower temperature, where European cattle generally are more at home than at lower elevations. (There may perhaps be exceptions to this; for example, the Jersey is said to be happier under the drier conditions of the somewhat lower patanas.) The grazing is green, often lush, yet rather poor by comparison with hill and montane grazing elsewhere with lower rainfall.

2. The drier, warmer patanas at intermediate elevations. The grazing and browsing here are rough and poor.

3. The grass-and-tree or grass-and-bush savannah of the typical Talawa country, where rainfall and humidity are lower, evaporation greater. Grazing and browsing here is even less palatable and nutritious than that of the lower elevation patanas.

4. The grass glade grazing and the browse of the Dry Zone. This varies according to local climatic factors, and is better toward the south and west than in the east and the north. In the dry season it offers poor, unpalatable and innutritious grazing; some browse is obtained from the shrubs and trees.

5. Incidental grazing in coconut plantations and elsewhere in the southwest lowlands, the Chilaw transition zone and in the more developed parts of the Sabaragamuwa hill region. There is a certain amount of this throughout the medium-sized and small holdings in these regions and also on the large rubber and coconut estates, but of limited volume and poor quality.

Natural pasturage throughout the island is deficient in nutriment. It tends also, especially in the drier regions, to lack palatability except when young, short and fresh. Even the grazing in the montane region, though better than elsewhere, leaves much to be desired. The intermediate patanas provide poor, coarse grazing for the greater part of the year. In the Dry Zone the grazing is palatable and nutritious for a very short time—during the wet season and sometimes just after.

Dependence on natural grazing and browsing for the carrying of livestock during the green season may indeed be found possible in better parts of the Dry Zone and in the Talawa and intermediate patana; but during the transitional and the dry seasons supplementary feeding would be essential if stock were to retain anything like a satisfactory condition. At the higher elevations, where rainfall and humidity are actually in excess, the nutritional value is low; hence here too supplementary feed is necessary.

Even from the limited observations of the Mission it is apparent that careful attention will have to be given to grazing rotation, seasonal regulation of grazing intensity, and control of encumbering woody growth. Otherwise Ceylon can expect a fairly rapid deterioration in the already low-grade grazing—with either erosion of the surface or development of impenetrable, useless scrub in the course of years.

Established Pastures. The Department of Agriculture has, over the past few years, given much time and thought to the possibilities of finding and establishing suitable grasses and legumes as pastures. Efforts have been made at the two montane stations as well as at several in the Dry Zone. So far as the Mission is aware, nothing serious yet has been attempted for the drier patanas and the Talawa. In the intermediate and lowland plantation regions there has been some recent establishment of pasture under stands of coconut.

Unfortunately, for carrying out this work no specialist officer is available whole-time. The studies, trials and practical field applications have been the duty of the already overworked Botanist and Senior Agricultural Research Officer at Peradeniya, and of the Divisional Agricultural staff. It is to their credit that progress has been made in the assembly, selection and preliminary trial of a wide range of grasses and legumes at the various stations.

Among the grasses that are showing signs of usefulness at the montane stations are *Paspalum dilatatum*, *Paspalum Urvillei*, *Pennisetum clandestinum* (Kikuyu), *Melinis minutiflora* (Molasses grass), *Axonopus compressus* (carpet grass), *Chloris gayana* (Rhodes), and—for feeding fresh or as ensilage—*Pennisetum purpureum* (Napier). For the reclamation of swampy land, following drainage, Napier and *Paspalum Urvillei* (for ensilage and green fodder) have been established.

Locally the legumes, on the whole, are not readily established and soon disappear owing to competition with the grasses or as a result of grazing and trampling by livestock. Species of *Trifolium*, *Stylosanthes*, *Medicago* and some local species of *Desmodium* and *Smithia* have been established.

One of the outstanding pasture species so far is held to be *Melinis minutiflora*. Supplies of seed for sowing in the Dry Zone and elsewhere have been obtained from the *Melinis* at the Bopatalawa farm. It remains to be seen, however, whether this species will withstand much grazing and trampling.

Kikuyu is not favored locally as much as *Melinis*. Yet the Mission believes that with the right management—which would include periodic vigorous harrowing, discing or even plowing up the heavy sward and dense rhizome mass—this grass would be found to withstand very much heavier trampling and grazing than would any other that could be established in this kind of environ-

318

ment. Fertilizing would be essential, as Kikuyu is a gross feeder. It is, of course, somewhat susceptible to frost. There have been doubts expressed about its feeding value, but again this is probably a matter of providing the correct management and fertility so that the grass is kept in a really vigorous, lush condition. A combination of fertilizing, rotational grazing, spreading of cattle droppings by means of simple drags, and periodic spike or disc harrowing or plowing is likely to produce more vigorous, taller, more palatable and more nutritious grass.

At the Dry Zone stations earlier reports indicate some faith in the ability of *Melinis minutiflora* and the legume *Stylosanthes gracilis* to withstand the rigors of the dry seasons. Actually, there is room for doubt that either of these would be able to withstand severe drought, especially in combination with grazing and trampling pressure. Yet while the more recent observations at the Polonnaruwa and Kilinochchi stations raise questions as to the suitability of *Melinis,* they suggest that *Stylosanthes* may prove capable of holding its own. Under the somewhat less severe conditions at the Karagoda Uyangoda station near Matara (in the transition from the southwest lowlands region to the Hambantota Dry Zone), recent reports indicate both *Melinis* and *Stylosanthes* are likely to withstand the test of drought and of grazing. At Aradian Aru, *Melinis* and *Stylosanthes* are said to provide "plenty of grazing during the period September to April, but not afterwards unless the pasture is irrigated." It is an expensive pasture that has to be irrigated to carry cattle of such low productivity as Zebu.

From Polonnaruwa comes a report for 1950 that the African *Urochloa mosambicensis* and *Panicum coloratum* responded well; again it is doubtful whether these will be found capable of withstanding, on a field scale, severe drought combined with trampling and grazing.

For the southwest lowlands, not enough actual work has yet been done to indicate any reliable grass or legume that could be established readily and could resist the trampling and puddling by

319

stock in the prevailing wet conditions. Selections from *Axonopus compressus,* tropical *Brachiaria* and *Panicum* species might be tried as grazing grasses. Some attention might be given to the African species of *Setaria* and upright *Pennisetum.*

The possibilities of obtaining established pastures in the wet, cool montane regions may be summarized as fair, given more experience. For the southwest lowlands and transitional regions, where the conditions are hot and wet, there are some possibilities but very little information. In the Dry Zone, except for the less severe localities, the difficulties in obtaining readily-established, drought-hardy species, to provide even light grazing in the dry season, are great; no really practical solution along this line can be expected until very much more field study has been done.

Fodder Plants. In all the regions of Ceylon more food for cattle is essential. In the wet, cool upland and montane regions green fodder, hay or ensilage, and concentrates are required in addition to the grazing, particularly for cattle of European origin. In the drier regions, with the very poor grazing and browse of the dry season, even the Zebu stock need green fodder, hay or ensilage. Roughage may be adequate in the natural pasture where the growth is particularly luxuriant, but even this is below requirements in the dry season in the Dry Zone.

Annual and perennial fodder crops should therefore be grown wherever possible. These cover a wide range, but the more valuable and more readily established ones may be selected for use as green feed, stover, ensilage or hay according to kind, season and locality.

Of the annuals, maize (for green feed, stover, ensilage and grain) does better where rainfall conditions are more reliable; yet in all but the most severe localities in the Dry Zone it should give some yield of green, dry or ensilage feeding even if little or no grain is produced. Sweet sorghum (green feed, stover, ensilage) is more suitable for the Dry Zone than at higher elevations; some good varieties have been introduced by the Department of Agriculture. Various millets such as *Panicum miliaceum, P. mili-*

are, and *Setaria italica* are useful for feeding green or dry; these would do better at the lower elevations and in reasonable rainfall conditions in the Dry Zone. Velvet bean and cowpea may be grown in the Dry Zone for hay and ensilage, the upright forms of the latter being preferable for this purpose. At the high elevations oats, barley, rye, rape, kale, chou moullier, turnips, lupins and other temperate and subtropical species grow moderately well if given reasonable treatment.

Of oustanding value among the perennials are *Panicum maximum* (Guinea grass) and *Pennisetum purpureum* (Napier grass). Both have a fairly wide range, growing from sea level to the montane regions, and respond well to NP fertilizers. Given suitable soil moisture, drainage and fertility, both may be cut a number of times per season and yield tonnages ranging from 20 to 40, according to the locality and length of the growing season. Exceptional yields ranging from 50 to 80 tons may be expected in really good sites and seasons, and where some irrigation is provided. There are, of course, many varieties of both these grasses —some more rapid, more productive, more palatable and more resistant than others. While a number of the varieties observed in Ceylon seem vigorous and palatable, additional material for test could be obtained from South, East and West Africa.

Para or Mauritius grass *(Brachiaria mutica stapf; Panicum barbinode)* is naturalized in Ceylon at various elevations in wet or damp situations. It yields a fair quality of green feed and hay if cut while still young; the yields are said to be from 20 to 30 tons per acre, and even more. Rhodes grass *(Chloris gayana)* is probably suitable over a wide range of elevation, provided there is adequate soil moisture but at the same time a fair drainage; this provides hay and ensilage, and is also a good grazing grass. Lucerne *(Medicago sativa)* is also capable of good growth over a wide range of altitude and soils, provided depth, drainage and moisture content are satisfactory.

Important leguminous fodder trees include *Leucaena glauca* and the pigeon-pea *(Cajanus indicus)*. Other fodder trees worthy

321

of trial in the Dry Zone are *Ceratonia siliqua* (carob), *Prosopis spp.* (mesquite and *Gleditschia triacanthos* (honey locust).

For good production, all fodder plants require just as much careful attention to the tenets of good husbandry as do other crops —a point often overlooked. The cereals, grasses and legumes, for best output, often call for application of chemical fertilizers or organic matter.

Feed Supplements. Roughage and nutriment supplied by the fodder plants would require fortification by means of certain concentrates—in the feeding of dairy stock particularly. Where possible, use should be made not only of the trade-compounded concentrates but also of such valuable items as coconut poonac, gingelly or sesame poonac, groundnut poonac, rice meal, maize meal, fish meal, bone meal, dhal husks and kurakkan (Eleusine). Molasses—if and when available—may be mixed with feeds or fed directly as in Cuba. Salt blocks containing trace elements should be placed where the stock can lick them if they wish, as this may affect their useful intake of nutritious foods.

Livestock

There are no full records of Ceylon's livestock population, but estimates made for 1950 showed 1,105,447 beef cattle, 522,418 water buffalo, 370,091 goats, 43,627 sheep, 74,198 pigs and 353 horses. Livestock appear comparatively scarce and of generally poor quality.

A number of general studies relating to Ceylon's livestock problem were made available to the Mission. Of special value are the recent publications of Wright, Turbet and R. Phillips. [15]

---

[15] Wright, N. C., *Report on the Development of Cattle Breeding and Milk Production in Ceylon;* Ceylon Govt. Press (1946).

Turbet, C. B., *Development of Cattle Farms;* Ceylon Govt. Press (1949).

Phillips, R. W., *Breeding Livestock Adapted to Unfavorable Environments;* FAO Agricultural Studies No. 1 (1948).

The records of the Division of Animal Husbandry and Veterinary Services contain much detailed information on the work of the seven main cattle farms and the smaller stations administered by the Division. Also, some useful unpublished memoranda were prepared during 1951 by the FAO animal husbandry expert appointed to investigate the possibilities of improving the livestock production.

So far as the University's contribution is concerned, studies have been few. A Professor of Veterinary Medicine was appointed several years ago but so far has been able to do virtually no training because of a dearth of student candidates. A Professor of Animal Husbandry was about to be appointed at the time of the Mission's visit. Prior to the establishment of local facilities for the training of veterinarians, the majority of the staff recruited to the service were educated in Europe and India. In recent years both veterinary and senior animal husbandry training has been taken almost entirely in India.

Government Activities. Livestock development is the general responsibility of the Division of Animal Husbandry and Veterinary Services. Under the Director of Agriculture, this Division is headed by a Deputy Director and has a staff of 95, including 19 in animal husbandry and 76 in veterinary services.

Broadly, the objectives of the Division are: (1) to improve the breeds of livestock reared in the country; (2) to improve the quality and usefulness of the livestock by means of proper care and feeding as well as by preventive and curative treatment of disease; and (3) to extend the use of livestock in the agricultural economy, for food and motive power. Along these lines a good beginning has been made in numerous diverse aspects of the problem, within the limitations of available staff and the difficulties inherent in a multitude of short-range programs.

Breeding stations have been established at various localities for Khillari and Kangayam draft bulls, Murrah buffalo, and cattle of the Scindi, Tharparkar, Black Sinhala and Red Sinhala breeds. Two stations are breeding with European types, including Holstein-

Friesian, Red Poll, Shorthorn, Jersey and Ayrshire—chiefly with stock introduced from Australia. Culling, progeny testing and artificial insemination are parts of the programs.

So as to intensify the breeding of livestock, 93 Government stud points and 100 subsidized private stud points have been established about the island, with special attention to the Dry Zone. These centers are intended as demonstration points for improved methods considered to be within reasonable reach of the average colonist or villager. Four hundred and ninety stud bulls are maintained. Through village committees, Cooperative Societies and Rural Development Societies another 92 stud bulls have been lent for purposes of local improvement of cattle.

Dairies at various government farms give elementary, practical training in cattle management and dairy routine to young men in the vicinity and to students in the agricultural schools; they also produce milk for hospitals and milk feeding centers.

An effort is being made to find a suitable milch goat for the use of colonists and villagers, especially in the Dry Zone. Goat husbandry has been seriously set back by the susceptibility of most of the exotic breeds to Goat Paralysis—a disease of unknown cause now under study at the Veterinary Research Laboratory. Trials of Jamnapari goats from India, Saanens from Australia and other hardy breeds are in progress.

Pig breeding is very popular in the coconut growing districts and in upcountry estates. It is being encouraged by the issue of young breeding stock at low rates from government stations, where purebred Berkshire and Large Blacks are maintained.

Government poultry stations are working for the development of a village poultry industry, in three ways: firstly, by the introduction of good poultry in so-called "pioneer" villages, in which there has been little or no poultry keeping; secondly, by upgrading poultry in "established" villages, where poultry rearing is already an established industry; and thirdly, by casual assistance to poultry keepers. In "pioneer" villages all issues are free for a period of about six months; thereafter such villages may become "established" ones. In this last class of village no poultry is issued free, but good cockerels are issued in exchange for village cockerels which are then sold at market prices.

At Peradeniya the Veterinary Hospital and Laboratory offers a range of services to estates, villagers and farmers. Artificial insemination is being popularized. The laboratory undertakes examination of all types of specimens (blood-smears, faeces, urine, internal organs and carcasses) for identification and report on animal disease. Advice on desirable or legally enforcible preventive and curative measures is given to the veterinary officer or to the general public, as the case may be. Vaccines are prepared for the control of anthrax, black quarter, contagious abortion, calf pneumonia, ranikhet disease and fowl pox.

Qualified veterinary surgeons are stationed in various parts of the country, each aided by a veterinary conductor or vaccinator who is trained to carry out routine inoculation and to help in various other ways. The veterinary officer concerns himself with enforcement of the Contagious Diseases (Animals) Ordinance, and is responsible also for developmental work in animal husbandry.

Assistant veterinary surgeons organize mass vaccination against rabies and ranikhet disease. They also attend to matters of animal husbandry under the direction of the divisional agricultural officers. In addition they are expected to organize and carry out the castration of unwanted bulls and weeding out of unprofitable animals, and to give advice and guidance on better methods of breeding, feeding, management of livestock, marketing of dairy and meat products, and the production of fodder. They also advise, without charge, on the treatment of minor ailments of livestock. They are very busy.

Long-range Policy. As to the main features of a proper livestock development program the Mission is in general agreement with the FAO animal husbandry expert. Most of the principles involved are also in general accord with the present aims of the Division of Animal Husbandry and Veterinary Services, and are restated here only to express the Mission's concurrence.

325

It is essential that there be a long-term policy covering perhaps 25 years, broken into, say, four periods of about six years each. Details of general aims, programs and practical working plans should be reviewed at the end of each of the periods and, where necessary, revised in the light of experience gained by that time. This procedure should take the place of the all-too-frequent, disoriented, short-run and stop-gap formulation of policies in the past. A study of the cattle in the intermediate and montane parts of the country illustrates the result of working toward no clearly defined distant goal; here we see a range of poorly productive stock, much of it of unknown intermixed European and other cattle.

Better integration of livestock into agricultural practice is clearly required if the fertility of the soil is to be maintained. All crops, whether for local consumption or export, would benefit from such a policy.

Imports of livestock, livestock products and feeding materials make a heavy demand on the finances of the country, and provide opportunity for the introduction of pests and diseases. To reduce them requires expansion and improvement of local production, processing and marketing methods.

An aim should be to produce types of livestock to suit the requirements of the various classes of owners in the various climatic regions. Such requirements embrace not only hardy draft cattle but also animals capable of supplying milk economically to villager or colonist owners. The development of suitable higher-production dairy stock is, of course, an objective in itself and should not be confused with the more general requirement of hardy stock for dual-purpose use by the rural communities.

Government stations and farms concerned with improvement of the livestock industry require a careful study, drawing upon all available knowledge and experience, for the purpose of clarifying objectives, improving the quality and increasing the number of the staff, and introducing the most adaptable modern methods essential to progress. This observation is not intended as criticism of the men now on the stations; but today there is much unnecessary overlapping, and at the same time a number of serious gaps in the coverage of particular aspects of animal husbandry and veterinary science.

Good work has been done in controlling rinderpest and certain other diseases and pests. Yet preventive and curative veterinary work requires more support than it has ever had in the past, both in research and in provision of aid throughout the countryside. Integration of sound animal husbandry methods with those of livestock hygiene and health is a primary need. An increased extension service of men with animal husbandry and veterinary medicine experience, working in the closest harmony, is therefore an essential part of a long-range policy.

Policy for the Immediate Future. Until fuller and better information is available on the livestock potentialities of the country and on the reactions of the different breeds of livestock in the various regions, it would be wise to continue the general lines of policy already being followed by the Division of Animal Husbandry and Veterinary Services on the government stations and farms. However, the Mission cautions against the understandable but undoubtedly perilous aspiration of the Department of Agriculture to bring about a very rapid improvement and numerical increase in the island's livestock, without taking due account of the rigors of the various regions or the inexperience, natural approach and poverty of the people concerned. To produce livestock beyond the immediate possibilities of the food supplies and management experience of farmers has produced dire results in other lands—an outstanding example for many years being the Union of South Africa.

Among the subjects requiring early attention are: (1) provision of a supply of good cross-bred cattle for the urban dairies, pending the development of Zebu milk breeds; (2) development of the milking properties of water buffaloes, toward encouraging the use of buffalo-curd in rural areas; (3) supplementing urban milk supply by more intensive dairying in urban districts, through modern large-scale methods; and (4) production and distribution

327

of sires likely to produce progeny of good survival rate and economic response in particular regions. This last involves more castration of unsuitable sires and the organized introduction of better sires from districts of similar climatic and other natural features.

Survey of Livestock Potential. There should be an island-wide survey of livestock potential, to provide a sound basis for formulating long-range policy. It would include: (a) classifying country into regions and subregions with respect to ecological factors, population, transportation and other conditions; (b) determining the size, age of maturity, and level of productivity of the existing livestock in relation to the available feed, water and other requirements; (c) making a detailed appraisal of animal husbandry potentialities in each region or subregion, with due regard for any regional policies already established; and (d) reviewing the information gained on the survey together with that gained by the Department of Agriculture and by some of the more advanced private dairies and livestock enterprises.

A satisfactory survey of this kind would probably require about a year of work. It must inspect in detail, travel widely and intensively and make a thorough examination of local experience and records. The survey group would probably comprise: (1) a survey leader widely experienced in animal husbandry with special reference to the tropics, and with an ecological approach (such an officer might be obtainable through FAO or other international organization); (2) a local livestock officer with good knowledge of cattle; (3) a local livestock officer specializing in small livestock—especially pigs, goats and poultry; (4) a local agronomist experienced in plant ecology, field crops and soil conservation measures; and (5) a local economist with a sound knowledge of local marketing, cooperative enterprise, extension work and, if possible, processing of the major animal products.

Coordination. The Mission emphasizes the need for the closest coordination between the three major facets of livestock production: animal husbandry, animal health, and distribution of animal products. Thus, there should be established a Livestock Produc-

328

tion Section of the Division—concerned with production, slaughter and distribution—but it should be integrated with the two existing Sections. Although there is already a common head for these, there are many points at which there must be even closer connection if overlapping, inefficiency and conflicts of purpose at lower levels are to be avoided.

Livestock Research Station. Three stations should be established—one in the lower Wet Zone, one in the Dry and one at high elevation in the Wet Zone—for the investigation of: (a) the influence of local habitat on the growth, reproduction and productivity of buffalo and European and Zebu breeds of cattle; (b) the digestibility and palatability of local hay, fodder, ensilage and other foods; (c) manufacture and preservation of livestock products; (d) the economics of livestock production under extensive, semi-intensive and intensive systems suited to the particular zone in which each station is situated; and finally, (e) the raising of small livestock.

In view of the great importance of the lower Wet Zone and the need for improving the supply of livestock products for Colombo and certain other larger centers, it is suggested that a station in this zone should come first.

Probably some local officers will need to be specially trained overseas for the work of such stations. It may also be useful to call in the temporary aid of some senior officers from outside the island, to assist in organizing the program of studies and to contribute experience gained elsewhere in similar undertakings.

Extensive Animal Husbandry in the Dry Zone. Small special pilot schemes are desirable to collect both scientific and management information about the running of cattle, sheep, goats and poultry over a range of climatic and soil conditions in the Dry Zone.

The need for this practical information is shown, for example, by some slight divergence of opinion between the Mission and certain other investigators regarding the likely role of the goat in the Dry Zone. Some hold the view that if the undergrowth of jungle were to be removed and goats turned in to browse on the resultant coppice, sucker and seedling regeneration of undergrowth and tree species, the effect would be to produce a vegetation community resembling parkland. The Mission, recalling earlier experience with goats in attempting to control undergrowth in the African tree and grass savanna, is skeptical. The goats are unlikely to exercise a sufficient control; moreover, if such a control were to be attempted on any major scale, it might well produce conditions of soil erosion and deterioration that would present major problems for the future. While the introduction of milk and slaughter goats has much to commend it, their number must be limited, for the goat is a good servant but a bad master.

Dairying at High Elevation. From the work at Bopatalawa and Ambawela stations it seems that some success could be achieved by the intensive management of European dairy herds at higher elevations, say from about 5,000 feet upwards. Despite the desire to avoid disturbance of montane forest, certain localities have much poor, unproductive jungle that could be removed carefully without impairing the water conserving factors. Sites for pilot dairy schemes should be chosen on the joint advice of the Conservator of Forests, the Forest Research Officer, the Soil Conservation Officer and members of the Agricultural Department.

Poultry Keeping. Government should encourage poultry production on a large scale by the estates and others able to invest in it, as well as by smaller units, by furnishing technical advice and a supply of foundation stock at cost. The suggestion of the late Prime Minister for producing nonfertile eating eggs for the Buddhist community might be implemented through a scheme of registration and inspection service.

Small Livestock on Estates at High Elevation. To augment home supplies of meat and milk, production of stalled pigs and tethered goats by estate laborers at the higher elevations might prove possible. As it would be necessary to prevent wandering, trespass and damage on tea and other estates, housing would be of importance. Exploratory discussions between estate operators and official representatives should be arranged.

Dissemination of Knowledge Through Youth Clubs. There is much value in the suggestion that the Department of Agriculture assist in organizing youth clubs, for the purpose of encouraging the interest of young people in the maintenance of good livestock. This would involve giving some elementary training in the theory and practice of livestock management and production. Formation of such clubs probably could best begin on the colonist settlement schemes, where the presence of guiding staff would be assured.

FORESTS

History. From the passing of the first Forest Ordinance until 1905, Ceylon's forests were under the unsatisfactory dual control of the Government Agents and a Conservator, the latter having advisory powers only.

In 1905 the forests were placed under the control of the Forest Department, and two years later the authority of the Conservator was strengthened considerably by ordinance. This ordinance redefined state ownership of the forests, "waste" crown land, chena, uncultivated and unoccupied land. It framed rules for the protection of crown land, for the declaration of reserves, for village forests, for the control of all timber in course of transport, and for the checking and punishment of forest offences. The management of reserved forest was vested in the Forest Department. Definite royalty rates on timber and minor products were fixed.

Following retrenchment in 1934, the forests were subdivided into two classes for purposes of administration: (a) forest land dedicated to systematic management; and (b) forest areas which would ultimately be utilized for agricultural development. The Forest Department was charged with the administration of land in the first class, while the government agents administered lands in the second.

331

In 1947 the forests were reclassified into the following three groups:

(a) Protection forests, maintained for climatic, topographic, water conservation and aesthetic reasons.   (507,000 acres)

(b) Commercial forests, maintained for timber and other forest products for the demands of the general public.

(1,900,000 acres)

(c) Domestic forests, maintained for the supply of timber and other forest products primarily for local needs. (195,000 acres)

By the end of 1950 the total area of forest land set aside for production as well as protection was 2,762,705 acres, representing 17.04% of the total land area of the island. In addition 894,773 acres had been declared national parks, intermediate zones and nature reserves for the preservation of wild life. All this acreage falls under the administration of the Conservator of Forests.

Utilization. In accord with a general policy that the state forests should supply the timber needs of state departments and the public, a number of reserve forests and proposed reserves have been exploited since 1945. Exploitation has been on the basis of annual contracts—the contractors tendering for the felling, logging, transportation and delivery of the logs to a depot. At such central depots the logs are sawn to the requirements of the indenting departments, the surplus of sawn timber being then sold to the public. The volume of timber thus extracted from the crown forests in recent years has been as follows:

1947:	1,135,694	cubic feet
1948:	1,416,206	” ”
1949:	2,891,428	” ”
1950:	2,625,627	” ”

Export of timber is comparatively small. For 1950 the details were:

Melia dubia (lunu-midella)........................615 tons valued at Rs.   45,643
Mimusops hexandra (palu)...........................3 tons valued at Rs.   1,040
Chloroxylon swietenia (satinwood)..........252 tons valued at Rs. 178,791
Other ....1,071 tons valued at Rs. 235,253

Protection Forests. Of the original montane subtropical wet ever-green forests, only about 100,000 acres remain, concentrated in the central montane region above 5,000 feet. About 3,000 acres were clean-felled between 1914 and 1940, the ground so cleared being planted with exotics such as cyressus and Australian gum (eucalyptus). Since 1940, however, conversion of the indigenous forest above 5,000 feet to exotics has been stopped on ministerial order, for aesthetic reasons. Planting of the wet patana grassland from 5,000 feet upward with exotics such as *Eucalyptus saligna, E. microcorys,* and *Acacia mollissima* (sometimes incorrectly called *A. decurrens*) is being continued.

Wind and fire belts have been established in the dry patana grassland between 3,500 and 5,000 feet, to an extent of about 3,200 acres. The species planted (in pits) have been eucalyptus and callitris. So good has been the apparent soil amelioration, and so helpful the improvement in living conditions for man and beast in the locality, that large scale afforestation schemes are contemplated for the next 10 years in areas of this type. In addition, areas subject to landslip and accelerated erosion are being planted, notably in the Kotmale Oya catchment and in the Walapona Harasbedde patanas.

Commercial and Domestic Forests. From 1937 to 1939 sys-tematic working plans were prepared for the more valuable for-ests, particularly the plantation areas of teak *(Tectona)* in the Dry Zone, jak *(Artocarpus)* and mahogany *(Swietenia)* in the intermediate zone, and eucalyptus and cypress in the montane zone; these plans covered 1,500 acres. Working plans for the wet evergreen forests were completed in 1939, based on intensive mapping and classification into economic types such as hora, hardwood, softwood and fuel, and a one percent cruising enum-eration of all trees.

For the dry mixed evergreen forests a similar one percent enum-eration of trees was accomplished, working plans being prepared separately for commercial exploitation and for firewood improve-ment fellings. The latter were particularly intended to meet emergency railway requirements during the War. Unfortunately, except in the plantation areas, the working plans could not be strictly adhered to under the emergency pressures; this was particularly true in the wet evergreen forests, from which material was taken for urgent military and civil needs.

Simple exploitation plans are now being followed for the forests of the Wet and Dry Zones. In late 1950 a special Working Plans Division was created for the purpose of preparing plans for all the more important forests, commencing with a five percent enumeration study of the most valuable wet evergreen forests in the south. Working plans for the montane, teak and jak plantations are being revised. Inventories of all other forests are being prepared, so as to ensure continuity of management and a permanent record of operations.

Dry Zone Forest Management. Fellings in the dry mixed evergreen forests are of both selective and intensive types. The selective fellings are worked on the basis of a girth limit, reserving "support" trees of the valuable hardwood species. The intensive fellings are of a more comprehensive kind, including the removal of inferior species, particularly in areas where there is a ready demand for firewood and poles. So far 6,200 acres have been given some such form of management. No rotation for these very slow growing forests has yet been worked out; an empirical felling cycle of 25 to 40 years has been adopted tentatively.

Cooperative Afforestation. Since about 1890 the Burmese *taungya* system has been applied, using shifting cultivation to raise forest plantations. About 6,700 acres of teak, chiefly near the eastern seaboard, have been raised in this manner. Although these teak plantations are of only third class value by standards of the Indian Forest Service Yield Tables, they nevertheless are an improvement on the indigenous forests in the locality.

In the intermediate zone the same system has been adopted to raise about 4,000 acres of jak and mahogany. The older plantations have already produced some good quality timber, of great value during the War. The yields have included some high grade timber, poles for hutments, and firewood. These plantations are now being brought under systematic thinning practices.

Plantings in Gaps in the Forest. In commercially exploited forest in the Dry Zone some success is attending the planting of gaps with stump Halmilla *(Berrya cordifolia)* plants which will give useful timber in about 80 years. In contrast other hardwood species of the Dry Zone would take from 200 to 300 years. The trenches for the stump plants must be at least 24 inches deep. About 2,700 acres have been so treated to date.

Wet Zone Forest Management. The wet evergreen forests have been worked on the basis of regeneration fellings of the Malayan "seeding felling" kind, modified through local experience since 1939. Natural regeneration thus obtained is said to be satisfactory. Subsequent treatment consists of cleanings such as liane cutting, slashing back the rank undergrowth, and felling or ringbarking unwanted poles and trees of inferior species. (Ringbarking is used where the disposal of firewood is either uneconomic or impracticable.) A total of about 56,500 acres is under regeneration felling, of which about 6,300 acres may be considered as fully regenerated.

Forest Research. Silvicultural research—commenced seriously only in 1937—has consisted of: (a) basic studies, including identification and phenological behavior of timber and other species of forest trees, identification of pests and diseases, and the elements of forest ecology; and (b) special purpose studies. Among the latter have been: the collection of information about nursery practice and behavior of the important tree species; growth, yield and volume statistics; responses of indigenous and exotic species in gardens and arboreta; natural regeneration of the different types of forests; grassland afforestation; artificial reforestation with teak in the Dry Zone; mixed Eucalyptus species and selected conifers in the subtropical zone of the hills; mixed plantations of *Artocarpus integrifolia, Swietenia macrophylla* (Honduras Mahogany), *Melia composita, Vitex pinnata,* and *Aericapsis mooniana* in the Wet and Intermediate Zones; Teak seed

335

origin trials; weed control of indigenous forests and plantations; and soil erosion in plantations.

For utilization research, just recently organized, the necessary workshops, laboratory and other buildings are now nearing completion. It is intended to investigate the structure, working, seasoning, finishing, bending properties and methods of preservation of Ceylon woods. Laboratory and other facilities for entomological and mycological investigations will also be available shortly.

Education. Gazetted grades of forestry personnel are trained either in India or at Oxford. Up to the current year the small percentage of the Forest Ranger grade actually trained had been sent to the Forest Ranger College, Coimbatore. The remainder of the Forest Rangers and all the Forest Guards hitherto have been without any form of training.

To rectify an obvious want, a Forestry Field Training School has recently been set up with two camps for instructional purposes, one in a Wet Zone forest and the other in a Dry Zone forest. The present class has about 30 trainees, consisting of 10 Forest Rangers and 20 Forest Guards. There is a permanent teaching staff of two officers, assisted by 11 visiting lecturers and demonstrators. The three-months' course is conducted on a practical basis. By this means it is hoped to provide all junior staff with at least some form of training during the next three years.

Future Objectives. According to the Conservator of Forests the present timber requirements in cubic feet may be assessed roughly thus:

Timber for construction purposes	2,000,000
Poles and fence sticks for villages	750,000
Railway sleepers	650,000
Industrial needs: boxes, cases, shooks, etc.	2,000,000
Furniture woods	500,000
Telegraph poles	100,000
Total	6,000,000 cubic feet

Allowing for increasing population and a rising standard of living, it is estimated that a forest yield of about 10,000,000 cubic

336

feet per year will be necessary if Ceylon is to be self-supporting in timber. This would require about one million acres of Dry Zone forest and from 500,000 to 800,000 acres in the Wet Zone under intensive management.

The additional land required to produce this amount of timber annually would be difficult to obtain today owing to the intensive development of agriculture. In return for areas of Dry Zone forest already expropriated from the forest estate for colonization schemes, the Forest Department feels that an equal area of land of low economic forest growth should be restored to forestry use. To free still further land for nonforestry projects, it argues, would be quite impossible if the large yield of 10,000,000 cubic feet per year is ultimately to be attained.

The Department is furthermore clear that the task of producing exploitable stands of timber in the shortest possible period requires suitable silvicultural systems. It is suggested, for example, that teak and halmilla will have to be planted in the Dry Zone on chena land, employing the taungya system already mentioned. Such plantings would require careful raising of the necessary stump plants, and above all a sufficient number of suitable chena planters willing to cooperate with the Department. Failing the latter, the Department might have to undertake the taungya work on a departmental basis, which would mean a greatly increased staff of junior officers for the necessary field inspection duties.

Because of earlier overexploitation and the original low stocking percentage (2-3%) of valuable species, the Dry Zone forests yield little valuable timber. The better types of Reserve would be improved on the "Hamilla-gap" system, with gaps extended to half-a-chain square. The species fortunately regenerates rapidly.

Planting is to be extended in the upcountry dry patanas, utilizing fast-growing eucalyptus species. Ten thousand acres extension is the target during the next 10 years. Useful timber for boards is expected from these gums.

With land in the Intermediate Zone in great demand for agricultural purposes, the valuable jak and mahogany plantations

337

established there cannot be extended. The total available in this region would be about 5,000 acres.

Because of overexploitation in the past, the future welfare of the accessible forests in the Wet Zone will probably demand a progressive reduction in the amount felled. On account of the heavy rainfall and danger of erosion, these forests will not be worked by "clear felling and planting," but will have to be managed on a "shelterwood" or a "partial cutting" system. Either system will require the attention of qualified forest officers.

In order to keep the cost of timber as low as possible, modern logging methods should be adopted. FAO has sent out a forest technologist-engineer to advise on this matter. If, as is hoped, suitable roads are built, forests now inaccessible will become available for exploitation. Installation of more suitable sawmills is being considered; and for the treatment of railway sleepers and other timbers exposed to the soil and weather, an impregnation plant is to be installed.

The possible uses of forest products and research with them are further considered in Chapter 15.

Staffing for the Future. With the expanding work of the Department, the present staff is unable to fulfill satisfactorily all the duties expected of it. Further, in all grades the rate of recruitment of new officers is too low.

Such a state of affairs is bound to be detrimental to the management of both the indigenous forests and the new plantations. There is danger in working with an inexperienced, untrained and far too small staff, for in forestry practice mistakes may not show up for years. The Conservator estimates that during the next five years the staff required will be approximately double the present size, distributed somewhat as follows:

Superior Staff	1 Conservator
	1 Deputy Conservator
Controlling Staff	3 Senior Asst. Conservators
	1 Administrative Secretary
	5 Accountants

338

Research and Education	1 Silviculturist
	1 Utilization Research Officer
	2 Research Assistants
	1 Principal of Forest School
Divisional Staff	10 Asst. Conservators
	1 Working Plans Officer
	4 Divisional Assistants
Subordinate Staff: Technical	25 Foresters
	185 Forest Rangers and Range Assistants
	40 Head Forest Guards
	350 Forest Guards
	200 Clerks
	10 Draftsmen

General Observations. The Forest Department has been struggling for a long time with an increasing volume of responsibilities —administrative, executive and research—and, for one reason or another, has not received the support it requires. Among the causes may have been the slow realization by the earlier colonial government of the full significance of forests in the life of the country, as well as the staff retrenchment following the great depression of the thirties and the emergency of the Second World War.

The weaknesses in carrying out forest policy are largely traceable to the lack of sufficient gazetted forest officers and the scarcity of trained, experienced, permanent junior executive officers. It is unfortunate, for example, that so little had been done earlier to learn more about the ecology, silvicultural requirements and management of the forests. Such basic information could have been obtained over the past 30 or 40 years by the employment of several officers specifically assigned to the task. The knowledge would be invaluable today, when so much improvement and extension are desired in a short time.

The Mission's inspection of the forests of the montane subregion, the Intermediate Zone and the Dry Zone, although necessarily brief, was sufficient to show that both the senior and the junior staff should give much more time to field work. Many instructive details that could be learned from more frequent inspections and field studies by divisional officers are being either lost or only partially appreciated. Apparently this is due, not to any lack of interest on the part of the officers concerned, but to preoccupation with administrative and executive duties at the expense of the professional and technical aspects of their responsibilities.

Ignorance of the importance of forests and forestry in the life and welfare of the country is not confined to the public at large, but is found also in political and administrative circles. Frequently, for example, an even greater reduction in the forest estate is suggested in order to provide more land for crop production and colonization. That such a diminution may be detrimental to the real interests of the community seems to be dismissed as merely academic. The true role of forests should be made the subject of an intensive educational campaign throughout the island.

Suggestions. A good forest survey should be made, based on aerial photographs and maps supported by adequate foot inspection and description. By ingenuity and experience, forest officers responsible for the survey would readily develop their own technique for interpreting the photographs and filling in the maps. Such a survey would yield information that would prove most valuable in delimiting forest types, planning silvicultural treatment, arranging for exploitation and presenting suggestions for extension.

In view of the heavy timber requirements now and in the future, the Forest Department should be supported in its efforts to improve the increment of the indigenous forests, to regenerate these wherever desirable and to extend them on appropriate sites within the existing forest estate. This will entail additional staffing at all levels and an improvement in the form of forestry education given to the junior ranks. It will also require more adequate funds for the development of nurseries and for other phases of the work.

Consistent efforts will be made to persuade the government to part with additional portions of the forest estate. The demands will range from those wishing to extend the acreage of cacao or coconut to those anxious to see more colonization schemes. This will be particularly marked in the Intermediate Zone but will become increasingly serious elsewhere. While it is true that the government may find it advisable to expropriate certain areas from the forest estate for particular purposes, it is urged that this be done only after the fullest study has been made in cooperation with the Forest Department. In general the Mission's advice would be to resist expropriation except in the most pressing circumstances or where marked national advancement is likely to accrue.

Formation of plantations of indigenous and exotic trees should be intensified. The response of the exotics in the wet portions of the montane subregion has been encouraging, despite the comparatively little skilled attention they have received. Better practice would appreciably improve the rate of increment and the quality of the timber that could be grown in these wet montane sites.

There is a strong feeling against the removal of indigenous forest or jungle above 5,000 feet, because of its aesthetic beauty and because it is feared that removal would jeopardize water and soil conservation. Yet probably there is little danger of such deterioration so long as the removal is careful and is accompanied by all necessary conservation measures and proper establishment of exotic stands. Replacement of some of the less attractive, less accessible montane forest by good plantations would make a useful contribution to the timber supplies of the future.

While the growth of eucalyptus and other exotics has been much less spectacular in the lower, drier patanas (3,500 to 5,000 feet), extension of such plantations would aid in the production of rough timber for farming needs and in protection against wind. Thorough plowing and cross-plowing rather than the existing method of planting in pits should, however, produce stronger, faster growing plants. Also, there has apparently been a tendency

341

to plant the trees too close for the best growth responses in the prevailing climatic and soil conditions.

Teak promises well enough in portions of the Dry Zone to justify extending it on the taungya system. Perhaps the Department should be permitted to carry out some of this work on a departmental basis.

Provision of fuel forests for the use of the population on the colonization schemes is essential. Their management should be placed in the hands of the Forest Department so that knowledge and experience may be brought to bear upon the maintenance of these important resources. While in most instances fuel forests would be indigenous jungle, the establishment of fast growing fuel stands may be necessary in some areas. However, the planting of wet patana with exotics of the kind of *Acacia mollissima* (Black Wattle), is not recommended for this purpose. Although fast growing, there is a strong possibility that this species will build up thickets of seedlings and suckers that will impoverish the soil and impair the conservation of water.

Forestry education should be stimulated. It is salutary that the government has commenced again to send certain of its prospective officers to be trained in Britain. The ideal probably would be to follow the basic training in Britain with a special postgraduate year in one of the Indian Forest Service training centers. For the junior staff, the government should lengthen, enlarge and improve the camp courses it has already begun. While more trained staff is needed at all levels, the most pressing requirements are in the junior grades for the day-to-day executive and protective duties.

For a long time forestry research languished, but recently it has been stimulated and some of the work being done is of promising quality. These studies, as well as the strengthening of links with research interests in India and elsewhere, should be given every possible support. An exchange of forestry research officers would be an advantage to the services concerned.

Outside technical assistance is needed on the exploitation,

342

extraction and milling aspects of production. The presence of officers with experience in these lines of work would be of great value to the country. Further assistance of FAO or other international organizations may be sought in this matter.

SPECIAL PROBLEMS AND POLICIES

While it is apparent that Ceylon has many natural assets favoring the successful expansion of her agricultural production, there are also certain broad problems whose conquest will determine the ability of the country to make use of these assets. In addition to those applying generally to the whole island's development and dealt with in other chapters, a number of these problems more specifically related to agriculture are discussed below.

Pests and Diseases

Estate farming in Ceylon, as well as research experience, has confirmed the presence of the intricate web of pathological, entomological, physiological and ecological relations that is ordinarily associated with tropical agriculture. Ceylon presents no unique disease or pest, nor any peculiar ecological relationships. It is evident, however, that there are enough problems of a biological nature to demand that research into the means of overcoming them must not only continue but must be intensified.

General Indigenous Fauna. At one time Ceylon was well populated with a fairly wide range of mammals, birds, reptiles and invertebrates. Increase in human population, removal of much of the original forest in the Wet Zone, increased disturbance of the cover in the Intermediate Zone and the opening up of parts of the Dry Zone have reduced the numbers of the larger mammals. Indeed, some forms have become very rare.

The fauna has much in common with that of South India, but several indigenous species such as the sambhur (Ceylon elk) and the poisonous snake, the polonga, are endemic to the island. Conversely the tiger, hyena, fox and wolf, occurring in parts of India, are absent.

A government Department of Wild Life provides for the conservation of wild fauna and flora. The total areas proclaimed under a 1949 Ordinance for the preservation of plant and animal life are 200,000 acres of Sanctuaries and 665,000 acres of National Reserves. In certain of these the wild elephant, water buffalo, deer, leopard, cheetah and other animals exist in varying proportions. Throughout the island there is still a large and interesting avi-fauna, a number of birds being migrant from the temperate zone during the northern winter.

Creation of sanctuaries and reserves for wild game is not the end of the story of conservation. Careful study of the dynamics of population growth, food supply and so forth is essential to the proper management of such reserves. Otherwise unbalanced multiplication, wandering, destruction of crops of adjacent villagers—and, in some cases, loss of life—may follow. Monkeys, which are numerous over the island both in and out of sanctuaries, already do considerable damage to standing cereal crops in the Dry Zone.

Malarial Mosquito. The prevalence of malarial mosquito, which at one time rendered large areas of the Dry Zone virtually uninhabitable, is now very much reduced. The use of DDT and other control measures, introduced by the British during the last war and continued with vigor by the present government, promises in the near future to stamp it out altogether.

Ticks. Ticks *(Ixodidae)*, occurring in both the Dry Zone and in portions of the Wet Zone, serve as vectors of various tick borne diseases in livestock, such as tick fever, piroplasmosis (red-water) and anaplasmosis in cattle, and bilary fever in dogs.

Termites. Termites, or white ants, are often responsible for destruction of living plants as well as rapid deterioration of timber. While certain species are highly destructive, they have undoubtedly done some good to soils in the Dry Zone. Termites are known to bring about both chemical and physical amelioration of soils in various parts of the world.

Tea Pests and Diseases. Blister Blight, which is caused by

344

Exobasidium vexans, an obligate parasite attacking the younger foliage, has been discussed earlier in this chapter.

Other diseases and pests of tea, discussed by C. H. Gadd in his book *The Commoner Diseases of Tea,*[16] include: physiological disturbances; root, stem and leaf diseases; diseases of young plants in the nursery; virus diseases; root-knot caused by nematodes; galls and burrs; sun scorch; and non-infectious variegation.

Impressive as the list may seem, it is as true of tea in Ceylon as of many other crops elsewhere that control of pests and disease can be very substantially aided by affording the best possible growing conditions and management to the host crop. Blister Blight is a case in point, for the production of vigorous plants and correct practices in picking and pruning appear to play an important part in its control.

Rubber Pests and Diseases. While rubber suffers several root, stem and leaf diseases, the organism responsible for the greatest trouble and loss of vigor and yield in this crop in Ceylon is *Oidium heveae.* This fungus causes loss of assimilating surface and premature fall of leaf as well as damage to the flower and seed. According to the Rubber Research Institute of Ceylon, up to 40% decrease in latex yield might follow a severe infection. Control by means of sulphur spraying appears effective; it is expensive, however, and sulphur of the correct specification has become difficult to obtain.

Oidium-resistant clones are being sought. Clone LCB 870, reported to be showing very satisfactory resistance qualities, unfortunately shows low yield capacity. Cross-pollination of the oidium-resistant clone by a high yielding one has been tried in an endeavor to obtain a resistant high yielder. Crown budding of the resistant clone on high yielding "tapping panels" has also been done with the same objective. Budwood of the resistant clone is being distributed by the Rubber Research Institute.

A root-rot caused by a species of Fomes is a troublesome

---

[16] Monograph No. 2, Tea Research Institute, Ceylon (1949).

disease, because on removal of trees showing the fungus the associated roots and soil have to be carefully fired. Such drastic treatment entails a great deal of labor, time and money. Unless it is done, however, *Fomes lignosus* may remain dormant in root material left behind and infect new plantings in the vicinity.

There is some fear that new disease problems may develop in cacao underplantings in rubber stands, by reason of the fact that *Phytophthora* diseases of rubber are also diseases of cacao. In rubber *Phytophthora Faberi* is the cause of leaf fall, stem canker and fruit-rot.

Coconut Pests and Diseases. Various fungus diseases and insect pests of the palm, at its several stages, are recorded in the files of the Coconut Research Institute of Ceylon. The three most troublesome today are the tapering disease, the coconut caterpillar and the black beetle.

"Quick tapering" of palms has been recognized since about 1875, when it was recorded in Travancora. Originally thought to be caused by an organism, this phenomenon is now held to be some physiological discomfort—possibly due to malnutrition, deficiency of certain minor elements, restricted root growth or extensive root injury and decay. It is suspected that magnesium deficiency may be partly responsible, causing inability of the palm to synthesize sufficient chlorophyll, which in turn reduces the formation of wood. This theory may explain the yellowing and necrosis of the lower foliage and the tapering and softening at the apex of the stem.

Coconut caterpillar *(Nephantis serinopa)*, which causes serious damage to the foliage from time to time, is now controllable biologically by means of the Eulophid parasite *Trichospilus pupivora*. During 1950 the Coconut Research Institute bred and liberated seven million of these on infested areas in the eastern, north western and western Provinces.

Eating out the tender portions of the crown of the palm, the black beetle *(Oryctes rhinoceros)* at times does much local damage.

346

Cacao Pests and Diseases. The fungus diseases more commonly encountered in cacao include: *Botryodiplodia Theobromae,* causing a die-back of the stem; *Phytophthora Faberi,* causing stem canker and a pod rot of the fruit; and *Fomes cf. lamaoensis,* said to be responsible for the brown root disease.

Among insect pests are the pod borer *(Dichrocis punctiferalis)* doing damage to the fruit and the mosquito blight *(Helopeltis antonii)* which harms fruit and young foliage.

As yet not fully understood, the sickle leaf disease in 1950 occurred in a large number of trees at Kundasale and Pallekelle in the Kandy subregion. So far soil conditions are suspected to play a part in this discomfort. Whether the finding of unusual amounts of potash in the soil and affected leaf has any bearing on the cause of the disease has still to be proven.

Paddy Pests and Diseases. While various fungi and insects are known to take a toll of paddy, the outstanding loss in the island is brought about by the notorious paddy bug *(Leptocorisa acuta),* which attacks the flowering portions. Rhind [17] states that this pest is more serious in Ceylon than anywhere else in Asia, probably because there is always a paddy crop on the land somewhere, or a growth of alternate host plants on which it can feed. Absence of a long, dry period (which would tend to reduce the population) also works in favor of the pest. Fortunately DDT and Gammaxene have provided almost complete remedies which can be profitably applied. Gammaxene commonly is applied in the form of a dust, at the rate of 10 lbs. per acre, when the leaves are wet but when rain and wind are lacking. In windy weather a DDT water spray has been found easier to apply.

The paddy swarming caterpillar *(Spodoptera mauritia)* may do very serious and extensive damage to paddy. In 1950, for example, much loss was caused in young paddy around Batticaloa, Trincomalee, Anuradhapura, Hingurakgoda and in four other

---

[17] *Notes on the Improvement of the Yields of Paddy in Ceylon:* Government Printing Office, Colombo (1950).

347

districts. Not only paddy but also grass, young kurakkan *(Eleusine coracana)* and young maize were attacked.

Paddy stem-borer *(Schoenobius bipunctifer)* in some years takes a heavy toll. In 1950, for example, considerable damage was incurred through its ravages in the districts of Alawwa, Mirigama, Kegalla, Kagame, Embilipitiya and in several others.

Thrips, although not usually a serious pest, does damage in some seasons and localities. In 1950 it was particularly abundant and troublesome in the Ganewatte range, where all varieties of long duration paddy sown late in the year were attacked. Gammexene dusting, flooding of fields, and also harrowing or rolling of the older plants helped to reduce the pest.

More recently a Fusarium species, possibly related to the *F. moniliforme* causing root-rot disease elsewhere in Asia, is suspected of causing death of young paddy plants.

Biological Problems in Livestock. Apart from the general biological problems which have already been discussed, there is a wide range of organisms that have to be investigated and controlled if the health of livestock is to be improved. Only a few of the more significant ones can be mentioned here.

Rinderpest was a serious disease in the island earlier but by strenuous effort on the part of the veterinary staff it has now been stamped out. As the disease is enzootic in India and as Ceylon perforce imports livestock from that country, firm measures must be exercised to prevent reintroduction of infection. Central control of quarantine is thus essential; divided responsibility for this important function may well lead to a disaster.

Anthrax flares up from time to time, and vaccination is being enforced in infected areas. There is great danger of infection of stock grazing in the vicinity of carcasses or bones of animals that have died of the disease if these have not been disposed of by burning or burying. Suitable quarantine measures should be imposed.

Foot-and-Mouth Disease is well established, outbreaks occurring each year. In 1950, 4,221 cases of the disease were reported from all provinces except Uva. Experience in Mexico during a recent disastrous outbreak has resulted in considerable scientific progress in its control. Ceylon could profit by close contact with the joint Mexican-U.S. Commission dealing with this work and with the Animal Production Branch of FAO.

Tick-borne diseases *(Piroplasmosis* and *Anaplasmosis)* caused by protozoans are being controlled to an increasing extent both by dipping against ticks and by pre-immunization of European stock imported into the island. Young stock from European cattle previously introduced is being pre-immunized on the government farms at the higher elevations.

Of the diseases attacking the commonly used water buffalo, sarcoptic mange is readily curable by Gammaxene spray or paste. In *Paramphistomiasis*, the causal organism uses the snail occurring in channels and irrigation tanks as an intermediate host; control of the snail being impossible, the diseased buffaloes are treated with hexachlorethylene, with reported success.

Dogs are extremely numerous and, on the whole, poorly fed and cared for in the island; hence rabies is frequent. The Division of Veterinary Services has no power to implement the provisions of the Rabies Ordinance, but is doing what it can by vaccinating dogs whenever possible. Thirty-six thousand were so treated in 1950. The danger to human beings inherent in the frequency of this dread disease appears not to be sufficiently realized by the public. Probably the recorded cases are only a fraction of the actual number; it is notable, for example, that in 1950 the Medical Research Institute, Colombo, reported 438 positive samples out of 829 brains of dogs examined. Much stricter control of dogs should be promulgated, and the regulations of the Rabies Ordinance should be more effectively enforced.

The hardy goat has two diseases of some significance: the goat-paralysis which recently caused trouble in Jamnapari goats in the Dry Zone, and pleuro-pneumonia. Poultry has suffered in earlier years through the pseudo-fowl pest (ranikhet disease). Since the introduction of vaccination, however, it has been fairly well controlled. In 1950, 190,216 birds were protected against the disease.

Water Conservation

Wastage of water in Ceylon is notably frequent in irrigation of paddy, but it is also evident in some degree in the irrigation of all other kinds of crops. In the better watered portions of the country, this is partly due to lack of appreciation of the value of water. There is also the belief that water must be kept flowing throughout the operation, and a mistaken concept in the minds of irrigators that the more often water is applied the greater the economic yield. Some wastage occurs because the bund and channels are badly aligned, poorly made or inadequately maintained. There are considerable losses because of seepage in the more porous soils, leakage from distributories, and the tendency to discharge and replace water too soon in the fields.

It is difficult to estimate the average usage of irrigation water per acre in different parts of the island. In some instances this is from two to four acre-feet, depending on the local rainfall, temperature, evaporation and soil conditions. In most others it is appreciably higher than four, ranging up to eight. In many instances the usage on paddy is said to attain 14 acre-feet—a far too heavy volume, resulting in much waste.

Ordinarily it can be assumed that cultivators will take all the water they can get; this is particularly true for paddy. It is understandable, because up to a point (not known to the average cultivator) the yields of paddy do increase with the frequency of irrigation. Beyond that point, however, the additional frequency of irrigation fails to produce a corresponding return in yield. The island's production will benefit when cultivators know these facts.

As Rhind [18] has stated, frequent renewal of irrigation water does improve the oxygen content of the soil, and this is of some importance in the early stages of the paddy crop. Yet where water

---

[18] *op. cit.*

is limited, frequent irrigation means that less acreage can be watered. Hence what may be gained up to a point on a given area may well be lost because the aggregate acreage is reduced accordingly.

Trials in Ceylon suggest that yields of paddy increase as the intervals between irrigations decrease, but not in proportion; water consumption increases as the interval between irrigation decreases, but again not proportionately. Rhind points out that crops on government farms are almost invariably produced with less water than is used by farmers adjacent, and that yields on the government farms are generally two to three times higher.

Obviously there is no royal road to control of irrigation water on so many hundreds of thousands of small holdings and fields. The most that can be expected is that Department of Agriculture officials, representatives of the Cooperative Societies, Rural Development Societies, village headmen and others do all they can by demonstration and exhortation. Demonstration is usually the most valuable method, especially if conducted on private fields with the cooperation of the farmers themselves. Evidence of a successful yield on an official farm is not nearly so effective as a successful demonstration on property owned and worked by the average cultivator.

It is suggested that the Directors of Irrigation and Agriculture, and the authorities responsible for rural development and other activities on the colonization schemes, collaborate in working out plans for such demonstrations and for some form of control. Every field officer—especially those of lower rank actually working on the ground and intimately associated with the cultivator—should receive special instruction in this subject and should be charged with promotion of water conservation methods. It will be pointless for Ceylon to spend great sums on new irrigation schemes while continuing to waste large quantities of water.

Soil Conservation

Natural erosion, resulting in the age-long change in topography and in the alteration, transport, and deposition of soils has operated for millions of years in Ceylon and, of course, still is in action. Man-induced or what might be termed accelerated erosion, however, has increased considerably since the country was first known to the European. It has been responsible for comparatively rapid deterioration in the quality of the soils and for loss in their water-conserving power. There are numerous causes for this wastage in the Ceylonese heritage.

A very common and potent cause is the removal of the natural forest and vegetation on steep slopes, along river valleys or on any ground having an appreciable run-off of water. Here the early coffee planters, as well as tea and rubber planters both past and present must be held responsible, together with Ceylonese peasantry who for many years have cultivated country of this kind. In earlier days the run-off and erosion were worse than they are today; nevertheless, there still is too much loss of soil and too much deterioration of what remains.

Much deterioration occurs through farming, on any land, in such a manner as to fail to conserve the physical and chemical characteristics of the soil, to hold the water in position and to dispose of the excess without damage to the site itself and to country in its vicinity. In other words, low-grade field husbandry results in visible and hidden inpoverishment of the site and of the soil.

Inefficient and careless usage of water in irrigation causes surface and gully wash, leaching of nutrients and general impoverishment. It is a matter of greatest urgency that this wasteful and harmful use of water be stopped. Poor pasture management is also dangerous; and the burning of natural vegetation, followed by uncontrolled grazing, browsing and trampling of livestock, gradually renders both soil and vegetation less productive. And to add to all these, the excessive fragmentation of arable land makes the application of water saving and soil conservation methods exceptionally difficult.

The Soil Conservation Act. Historically the control of water, and thus of erosion of soil, has been given consideration by the government for almost a century. It is only very recently, however, that special legislation has empowered the Minister of Agriculture and Lands and the Director of Agriculture to do something practical about it.

Soil Conservation Act No. 25 of 1951 enables the government, through the Minister and the Director, to take the following steps as may be needed:

(a) To assess, by means of surveys and other methods, the nature and extent of soil erosion and damage to land by floods and droughts; and, on this and other evidence, to determine the localities which should be declared "erodible areas".

(b) To require the owners of land to take measures designed to prevent or control soil erosion, including the afforestation of sources and banks of rivers, reservation of a prescribed width of land free from cultivation along the banks of rivers, conservation of vegetation along such banks, training of streams by means of check dams or otherwise, and erection of contour ridges or terraces.

(c) To prohibit or restrict the "clean weeding" of land, or any other agricultural practice conductive to erosion.

(d) To restrict the use of land for agricultural or pastoral purposes, where deemed essential to the prevention or control of erosion or to the protection of the sources and banks of rivers.

(e) To prohibit or control the exploitation of forest and grassland, as a means of erosion control or to reduce the danger of fire.

(f) To give directions for seasonal or periodical changes in the type or nature of crops cultivated, or for the adoption or alteration of cultivation practices for the purpose of promoting the conservation of soil.

(g) To declare that any erodible areas should be withdrawn from cultivation, or that any measures designed to prevent or

353

reduce erosion should be taken by the Government on such land.

(h) To make regulations in respect of a wide range of matters, such as: measures to be taken by owners for land for its preservation and the promotion of its fertility; measures to be taken by owners to prevent, reduce or remedy the damage by erosion; control of the grazing of livestock where it may induce deterioration or erosion; control of floods and the effects of drought, by such methods as may be considered necessary; prohibition or restriction of burning of grass, and of the spread of fire during the burning of *chena* areas; specification of the times of tillage and irrigation and of the methods of tillage within specified localities, so as to ensure the economic use of water; changes in the type or nature of the crops to be cultivated, or the adoption or alteration of cultivation practices so as to conserve the soil; cambering, drainage and other such treatment of roads and paths; prohibition or control of the scouring of drains and water channels; and any other matters arising from the Act or required to be prescribed.

(i) To take such steps as may be necessary, in the particular circumstances, to assure the legal and practical application of the powers of the Act, so as to conserve water and soil.

Considering the wide powers provided and the wide range of subjects covered, this Act is not only comprehensive but admirably concise.

Appointment of Soil Conservation Officer. In 1950 the government appointed an experienced Soil Conservation Officer to the staff of the Department of Agriculture. As understood by the Mission the duties of this officer are: to report on the detailed conditions of misuse of water, soil erosion and deterioration; to indicate measures to be adopted to control or restrict such wastage and deterioration; to train local staff for the executive and administrative work of conservation; to advise the Minister as to regulations to enable the staff to apply the Act with efficiency and circumspection; and to further in every way possible the development of a "conservation consciousness" on the part of officials, those who farm the land, and the public at large.

Suggestions. It has already been proposed by the Mission that the Soil Conservation Officer prepare a statement of the problems in conservation, the program he envisages over the next ten years, and an estimate of the requirements in staffing, labor and equipment to make such a program feasible. It would be desirable to study such a complete document in the light of local conditions, as a guide to formulation of a realistic program. Ideally there is a great deal that should be done, but to do it all would cost more than the country could afford. A happy medium must be found.

The present staff for Soil Conservation is inadequate to the big tasks awaiting attention. Pending full study of the proposals made by the Soil Conservation Officer, as suggested above, it would be well to recruit several additional skilled specialists to aid in the training of field and other staff. Men with experience in Asia or the tropics would be particularly suitable.

Constant propaganda should be employed to make all groups living on the land increasingly conscious of the menace of erosion and deterioration, and of the economic losses that follow wasteful use of irrigation water. The University, the schools, radio broadcasting, the cinema and other means of instruction should be utilized. Technical details of such a propaganda campaign should be organized by the Soil Conservation Officer, so that nothing but scientifically correct information is given out.

To ensure cooperation from the estates, the middle and smallholders, the colonists and the villagers, their participation through regional or local committees should be considered. This presupposes the guidance and technical aid of trained officers, but it also means putting the local responsibility upon men living in a specified locality. Reporting and advisory duties would be expected of such committees. In due course the larger ones, at all events, would be expected to control their own equipment, implements, tools, and labor and to be guided technically by a conservation officer appointed by the Director of Agriculture. Models of this kind of organization are to be seen in the United States, South Africa and Southern Rhodesia, where the governments have been greatly aided by the interest and support of local farmers banded together in this way.

The Conservation Act is a good step forward. By itself, however, it is useless; it depends upon staff and upon careful application. At this stage the lack of sufficient staff makes it inadvisable to attempt detailed regulations. It would be far better to begin by getting some additional seniors as soon as possible and with their aid to train suitable staff and set up a proper organization of inspection and advice. Strict enforcement could follow later. All phases of the program should emphasize that conservation is best attained by good farming, and that the mechanical or engineering methods have special but limited application. Conservation means prevention, not cure.

A special problem of potential danger in indiscriminate farming of the catchment area of the Gal Oya reservoir is discussed in the general review of the Gal Oya Scheme in Chapter 12.

Dry Farming

In recent years there has been considerable discussion of "dry farming" in the Dry Zone, especially in connection with colonization schemes. Its possibilities and limitations deserve examination because disproportionate emphasis is sometimes put upon irrigation in postwar agricultural development throughout the world.

Dry farming, broadly, refers to nonirrigated arable agriculture, with complete dependence upon rainfall and ground moisture. In this sense it is actually the way most of the world's crops are raised. But there is a more specialized meaning: the term specifically refers to such farming when practiced under somewhat unfavorable conditions which require special techniques to make the most of a little moisture. This is what is meant in Ceylon's

Dry Zone, as it is in parts of India, Pakistan, Australia and other similar areas.

Dry farming is not new; but its success depends upon enlightened crop selection, careful husbandry, and close attention to soil condition, timing, ingenuity and industry on the part of the cultivator. Since time immemorial Ceylonese peasants in chena areas have used dry farming to grow various millets, tubers, pulses and other crops; but their yields and acreage have been low in comparison with what can be achieved in the future.

Governmental Efforts. Preliminary work on dry farming has been in progress for some time at several government centers such as Kurundankulam and Ralapanawa, and more recently at Maha Illuppallama and Olukarande. Research has now been centered at Maha Illuppallama under a specially appointed Dry Farming Research Officer. Meanwhile outside technical assistance has been secured through FAO, which has sent a special team for the subject.

To coordinate the various aspects of dry farming activities, a Departmental Dry Farming Committee has been appointed. A comprehensive series of investigations is to be undertaken to determine how this type of farming could best be carried out in different parts of the Dry Zone, [19] so as to produce good yields with simultaneous soil preservation and improvement.

Springing from the encouraging results obtained at Kurundankulam—where small-scale dry-farming colonization trials have been conducted for 13 years—detailed proposals have been drawn up in cooperation with the Land Development Department for

---

[19] Apart from Department of Agriculture memoranda and reports, two new papers by B. H. Farmer soon to appear will touch on this subject and are worth perusal: *Some Thoughts on the Dry Zone,* to appear in Bulletin of the Ceylon Geographical Society; and *Rainfall and Water Supply in the Dry Zone of Ceylon,* to appear in *British Tropical Lands,* edited by R. W. Steel and C. A. Fisher, for publication by Philip, London.

the establishment of three dry farming colonization schemes. Each of these cooperative schemes will cover about 660 acres. Individual holdings will be of 14 acres per family; of this, 12 acres are to be under crop rotation and ley, with the remaining two for homestead and other purposes. Restoration of abandoned tanks is to form part of the undertaking. Crops to be cultivated will include sorghum, kurakkan and other millets, chillies, dhal, pulses, groundnuts, yams and other tubers, and, if possible, cotton; in the southeast, or Hambantota Dry Zone, tobacco will be tried more fully. Cattle grazing will occupy as much as half the arable area.

Observations. In the Mission's opinion, dry farming is feasible in those parts of the Dry Zone where rainfall irregularities are not too severe. The range of crops which would ensure economic returns to the cultivators, though necessarily limited, is still wide. Among the more reliable crops would be: kurakkan and other small-grained millets; sorghums of the hardier dwarf types; maize of hardy varieties (but only in the most favorable locations); gingelly (sesame); tobacco under some conditions; yams, sweet potato and manioc; dhal and some of the hardier pulses; greengram fibers such as Deccan hemp (Hibiscus), sisal and in some spots cotton. In areas of higher rainfall, or where some irrigation is available in the event of serious drought, the list may include chillies, onions, shallots, cowpeas, bananas, mango, other fruits and green vegetables.

High land colonies and chena probably would be best put to kurakkan, hardy dwarf sorghum, small millets, groundnuts, yams, manioc and dhal.

For dry livestock farming there is probably a less promising future. Colonists can maintain a few working water buffalo, several milk cows, several goats and a few sheep. But dry stock ranching on a large scale without due provision for water, additional fodder, dipping, and local veterinary supervision, would run serious risk of failure.

The Gal Oya Development Board, particularly, should proceed

with care in its livestock project and should not attempt to carry
a large number of cattle too soon. The natural pastures and browse
are poor except for a short period during the rainy season. Ultimately, with Zebu cattle of the right type, adequate water, and
additional fodder in the dry season, good stockmen could undertake livestock production under extensive ranching methods; but
local experience is still far from sufficient to warrant the risk of
large scale development.

Gradual growth of dry farming is advised, rather than sudden
expansion. In this way experience gained from year to year will
prevent large-scale losses. Small practical trials are valuable.
Meanwhile, because of uncertain seasonal variations, upwards of
five years investigation at the Maha Illuppallama Research station
and several other stations will be needed in order to collect the
scientific and practical information required for reasonably secure
dry farming under the range of Dry Zone conditions. Until such
knowledge is in hand, the government should neither plant large
acreages of high land with crops of the kinds mentioned, whether
by traditional or mechanized means, nor encourage colonists to
do so.

Land Tenure

Ceylon's complex forms of land tenure and the laws and customs of inheritance constitute a continuing background of difficulty. They underlie problems of settlement, rehabilitation, soil
and water conservation and progressive replanning of crop production. They engender more primitive—rather than improved—
agricultural methods. By promoting inefficiency, directly or indirectly, they oppose efforts to raise the general standard of
living.

Ceylon is not unique in this. Similar conditions elsewhere in
Asia as well as in Africa have shown the difficulties inherent in
efforts to change old laws and customs relating to land tenure. But
Ceylon is a small country with a fast-growing population, and
the problems appear in sharp relief. Meanwhile experience has

demonstrated that unless certain reasonable changes are introduced, there can never be any hope of a satisfactory land-use policy or true rehabilitation of the areas most affected.

Problem areas, such as Kotmale, Udahewaheta and Walapane in the Central Province, exemplify the complications which already obstruct any efforts to replan in the interests of either the cultivators or the country as a whole, and suggest that the government should lose no time in creating a special body for their investigation.

Fragmentation through Inheritance. Operation of the existing laws of inheritance must be blamed for much irrational fragmentation of one-time larger farms or allotments. Serious situations are created. One of the first and most obvious is overpopulation of the farm. Another is the uneconomic exploitation of the subdivided portions—and thus of the whole farm—making impossible the introduction of any worthwhile pattern of soil and water conservation. Seen in action over an entire district or catchment area, the phenomenon presents a large patchwork of sub-economic units for which agricultural replanning and improvement are impractical.

Fortunately for the future, the Land Development Ordinance has created a new system of tenure so far as crown or "waste" land is concerned. The land is first alienated as a lease, the allottee being required to develop the land and to live on it. Thereafter, he is given a grant by deed. Special rules regulate succession, and prevent subdivision or alienation of the grant outside the particular family. Under these limitations the grantee can name his successor. In certain instances leasing or mortgaging of the land is forbidden, except to the Crown; nor may the owner dispose of it otherwise, except by special authority. And finally, the land cannot be seized and sold by a court of law. This has its advantages, although undoubtedly it impairs the value of the property as security for credit in any form.

Peasant allottees pay annual rent on a basis of 1-2% of the unimproved value of the land, middle-class allottees on a 4%

basis. The allottees must live on the land; but while the peasant must work it himself, the middle-class allottee may employ hired labor. This system also applies to estates taken over by the state for village expansion, subdivision, and allocation in plots, as well as to lands restored to former owners under the Land Redemption Ordinance.

Government policy and mechanism in disposal of crown land is covered by Land Development Ordinance No. 19 of 1935. Under this Ordinance all crown land in a village area has to be "mapped out" before any is alienated. This mapping gives prior consideration to the needs of the local villagers, and is done by a Settlement or Revenue Officer in consultation with them. Land is set apart for more than a dozen different purposes [20]. Once confirmed by the Land Commissioner, such a scheme may not be varied to permit alienation of land mapped out for village needs or peasant colonization without consent of the Minister for Agriculture and Lands.

Fragmentation of Estates. Alongside the new system of tenure for alienations from crown land, there remains the legacy of small sub-economic farms and plots. Where such fragmentation is serious, informed and courageous action by the government will be necessary. In such cases there is no other direct road to real improvement of production.

Yet, unfortunately, a new form of fragmentation has commenced to show itself: the outright purchase and subdivision of larger properties.

---

[20] In order of priority, these purposes are: village expansion, village forest, village pasture, chena, other village purposes, peasant colonization, protection of the source or course of streams, prevention of soil erosion, forest reserves (as contrasted with village forest), government purposes including buildings and roads, preservation of areas of archaelogical and historical interest, development of towns, alienation to middle-class Ceylonese, alienation to persons irrespective of class or race, and any other purpose.

Extreme care will have to be exercised by the government lest, on the sale of larger estates of tea and rubber especially, there be an uncontrolled fragmentation. Units might at first be economic, but later they are likely to lapse in productivity. The buyers of these properties are too often interested either in purchase solely for subdivision and sale, or in purchase for exploitation while high prices obtain, followed by sale in the form of plots. In other instances the government itself has purchased estate land, either planted or suitable for planting, for the purpose of village expansion.

Fragmentation brought about by private or official purchase and subdivision demands a reasonable form of control to ensure proper management and maintenance of subdivisions with due attention to good husbandry of soil and water. Otherwise it can have but one result: deterioration. The government therefore is urged to go into this matter without delay. The longer fragmentation is allowed, the more difficult will become the treatment of the ills that follow it. Human welfare, as well as soil, is at stake.

Insecurity of Land Titles. A problem closely related to land tenure is that of the insecurity of Ceylonese titles to land. The problem is complicated by the existence, side by side, of different systems of law—Dutch, English, and survivals of the Sinhalese feudal period; by the absence of accurate surveys, with resultant indeterminacy of boundaries; by the accumulation, in the long process of fragmentation, of a host of actual or potential claims to a particular piece of land. The result is that property rights, especially on small agricultural holdings, are indescribably complicated and insecure.

This is bad enough in itself. But even more serious are some of the consequences. If the title is not clear the owner cannot sell his property, or else must sell it at a discount. Insecurity of title also means that he will find it difficult or impossible to borrow, even for improvements to his land. Perhaps this obstacle to the establishment of a workable and adequate system of rural credit is the most serious aspect of the problem.

The tenure of land enters intimately into innumerable social relationships and institutions; and any change in the title system must be examined from many viewpoints. Nevertheless, the disadvantages of the present situation are serious enough to warrant vigorous action for the common good. Insecurity of title, just as much as fragmentation, jeopardizes human welfare.

Possible Solutions. In the Mission's opinion the Fifth Report of the Commission to Inquire into the Law relating to Mortgage, Credit Facilities and the Protection of Lands of Agriculturists (Session Paper IV—1946) contains commendable recommendations as a starting point to solve these problems.

Another possible basis for reform is the Torrens system of title registration [21] which has worked well as a solution to similar situations in Australia, New Zealand, and the United States, among other countries.

The essence of the Torrens system is that when the title to a piece of land is registered, the certificate of title establishes an indisputable right of ownership to the estate so registered. Under more common systems of recording the only authoritative title is contained in a complex of instruments, so that any intending purchaser of a property must, on every transfer, institute a time-consuming and costly search of all the records if he wishes to verify the title thoroughly.

When the Torrens system is established, the landowner applies for registration, submitting such documentary evidence of ownership as he may possess. After preliminary examination of this evidence and due notice to any recorded holder of a lien or claim, the registrar advertises the application and appoints a time for a hearing. If there is no objection by that date, the land is registered and the owner acquires a provisional title. If the title is contested, the issue is referred to the courts for decision, special land courts

[21] Niblack, Wm. C., *An Analysis of the Torrens System*, Callaghan & Co., Chicago, 1912.
Yeakle, M. M., *The Torrens System*, Torrens Press, Chicago, 1894.
Hogg, J. E., *Australian Torrens System*, 1905.

having been set up in some countries for the greater convenience of applicants. Provisional titles, granted either by the registrar or by the court, become permanent and indisputable at the expiration of a fixed period of grace, usually from three to five years. For the additional protection of claimants, most countries using the Torrens system have set up an indemnity fund, financed out of small fees charged at the time of registration.

Once a property has been registered, a later purchaser has no need to undertake an expensive and tedious search of title. All claims against the title are recorded on the certificate, except such matters of public knowledge as tax assessments, public highway rights and the like, or rights of possessors not recorded, which are subject to clarification by inquiry.

Without doubt, were such a system instituted, there would be a large volume of cases before the courts during the period of grace. While the interests of legitimate claimants must be protected, shortcuts in dealing with minor claims and claims of doubtful validity would be justified, in the interest both of expediting solution of the tangle and of keeping to a minimum the costs of the proceedings.

If smallholders had to bear the cost of defending their titles, the expense would be insupportable and this consideration apparently caused the Kandyan Peasantry Commission to reject a solution along the lines proposed here. [22] But the situation is so confused, so inimical to sound credit arrangements, and so important to the future of the country's agriculture, that it might well repay the state to bear the cost of legal proceedings for properties below some reasonable maximum size. Other schemes for improv-

---

[22] "We have given much consideration to the possibility of introducing a system of registration of title, but, in view of the tremendous expense involved, we hesitate to do so. We have, however, taken into consideration the peasants' need for credit and have made certain recommendations for improving rural credit facilities, which will, we hope, minimize the consequence resulting from uncertainty of title."—*Report of the Kandyan Peasantry Commission*, p. 107.

ing rural credit facilities—desirable for independent reasons—
are like applying a poultice to a tumor when surgery is needed.

The Mission believes it to be important that proposals for solution of the land-tenure system be worked out as soon as possible, and recommends an immediate further investigation of all possibilities of reform, including the adoption of something similar to the Torrens system as well as the proposals made by the Mortgage Commission mentioned above. It may well be that such investigation will confirm that only drastic changes can remedy the situation. In that event, we believe the necessity of cutting the Gordian knot should be faced. Delay in meeting the urgent need for a remedy will only make the difficulties more serious.

What is needed is some method of clearing the books, as it were, of old and conflicting claims to property, and of getting owners off to a fresh start, clear and unencumbered.

Survey of Land Use Potential

Ceylon needs, for every aspect of her agricultural planning and general development, a thorough-going, detailed survey of land-use potential. This is a task for field work combined with correlation of existing data on such factors as the topography, vegetation, soil, climate, water supply, population, crop adaptability, locally available transport, and so forth. No such survey of the island exists.

The Survey Department has done not only the basic work of triangulation, levelling and topographic survey, but also much detailed work in connection with special engineering block and settlement, land development, town and other surveys—all important basic survey information. In addition, the Irrigation Department has been responsible for certain specific surveys required for planning the alignment of supply channels or irrigation schemes.

At the other extreme, some very general surveys have been made to obtain broad impressions or gross estimates of the existing acreages of given agricultural crops or of land possibly useful for a particular crop. Recently, for example, a survey was conducted to determine very broadly the distribution of additional land capable of carrying coconut, and a committee appointed by the Minister for Agriculture and Lands has reported generally on the availability of crown land for various uses.

None of these, however, neither the basic land surveys of the Survey Department, the special surveys of the Irrigation staff nor the multitude of very general surveys of an agricultural nature, provides the kind of information required with the necessary precision.

Objectives. The kind of survey essential to the proper planning of agricultural and forestry development is altogether different in objective and technique. Its aims must be:

(1) To collect information on the past, present and potential uses of land, and at the same time to obtain and coordinate all relevant information regarding physical, biotic and human resources—either being utilized or capable of being developed and utilized.

(2) To prepare new detailed maps setting out the above information in relation to the past, present and potential future.

(3) To submit recommendations regarding the potentialities of the various regions, sub-regions, vegetation types, classes of soil and water supplies, and to indicate the sociological, health, welfare, transport and other requirements for the development of a particular kind of crop, a particular kind of farming or other land use.

Procedure. Such a survey would need not only existing maps, but also suitably scaled aerial photographs (1: 5,000 to 1: 15,000 depending on the exact details required) and a series of maps prepared therefrom, showing such features as: the distribution of natural vegetation; arable and pastoral land within each particular region; the major soil types; major features of topography in relation to planning of development; irrigation areas actual and potential; conservation of native or induced vegetation; proposed localities for specific crops; and farming practices. Relevant

366

details of population density and distribution, transport facilities both existing and proposed, and other significant matters, should also be shown.

Maps of this type could be produced only through a combination of intensive ground inspection, aerial photography, collaboration with local agricultural and other officers, and study of whatever literature exists. At a later stage such information would be checked, wherever possible, on an experimental basis.

Using these maps in suitable scales as a necessary background, the survey group would prepare detailed sets of recommendations regarding extension of existing agricultural, forestry or other practices and the opening up of new areas for selected purposes. Recommendations would be framed in collaboration with appropriate professional, technical, administrative and business authorities.

Staff. Personnel for a proper land-use potential survey would consist of a variable number of men of diverse training and experience. They would work either in small or large groups or even individually, according to the region and the particular phase of the task involved. A team of four to six good men could cover 750 to 1,000 square miles a year according to the detailed requirements. Less intensive surveys would permit far greater coverage.

Without indicating the total number of men or their exact distribution, it may be said that the survey team should be able to call on agriculturists, ecologists, soils men (pedologists as well as those who know how to assess the agricultural potentialities of soils), foresters, conservationists (who must be trained in either agriculture or forestry), irrigation engineers, road engineers, and officers who have special experience in the growing of certain crops or livestock. The speed of operation depends entirely upon the rate at which the proper types of men can be obtained, and the skill of management.

Comments. Ceylon most courageously is attempting to embark on large developments in land utilization. It is noteworthy that the European countries concerned with the opening-up of undeveloped lands—more especially the British—have been paying growing heed to modern methods of survey of land-use potential. One such survey was carried out in the intermediate stages of the East African Groundnut Scheme with excellent results, and unquestionably the Scheme could have benefitted greatly from it earlier. A government-supported survey is in progress in the great Kilombero valley of the Rufiji river in Tanganyika, while in a part of the Anglo-Egyptian Sudan a leading firm of engineers has recently embarked on another. A survey has just been started in Burma. Consideration is being given to instituting similar studies in several British areas in Central America.

The Mission believes this kind of survey to be of the greatest value to the long-term interests of Ceylon. To date not even the Gal Oya Valley Project has had the advantage of a land-use potential survey, either for the area already cleared of jungle or —what is even more important—for the area proposed for clearing in the future. Such a lack is bound to bring in its train disappointment, criticism, wasted effort and unnecessary expenditure of public funds. The East African Groundnuts Scheme commenced in just this way, and it is well known that this resulted in wrong selection of one major developmental area and detailed errors in the clearing of land in another. It was only after the information obtained by a properly organized survey became available that such errors no longer were made and many millions accordingly were saved.

No matter requires more serious attention from the government in its efforts to improve the agricultural economy and to settle people on the land well and happily, than this one of obtaining basic information on land-use. Necessarily cursory surveys such as those recently undertaken by the Land Utilization Committee may well spell later disappointment and unnecessary financial loss.

The Mission therefore strongly recommends the early undertaking of a complete survey of land-use potential as described. First attention might be given to the Gal Oya Development region, since this project is already so far advanced.

Advice might be sought from the government of Tanganyika regarding the survey in Kilombero, and also from the private organizations now conducting the surveys in Burma and the Sudan. Possibly the Overseas Food Corporation (East Africa Groundnuts Scheme) as well as FAO could help in recruiting staff. For really first-class aerial photography and mapping, one of the better known private companies specializing in this work usually offers the most satisfactory solution.

The Problem of Personnel

Some excellent men are to be found in the various services of the Department of Agriculture and Lands, and in other departments whose work bears upon agriculture and forestry less directly. But the task is large, and officials are well aware of the difficulty in building a staff fully adequate to handle the development program at the desired speed.

In the aggregate, professional, technical and applied knowledge still is far below the standard required for a successful assault upon the forces of ignorance and inefficiency that hold back progress in this sphere. In part, this is due to the enforced preoccupation of a high proportion of the better trained, more experienced senior officers with administrative duties resulting from the increased volume of responsibility falling to the Departments in recent years. It is also due to the failure of the services to attract enough of the most capable, well trained recruits to their ranks.

Their inability to secure enough good people goes back to the failure of the University of Ceylon to draw men to its Faculties of Agriculture and Veterinary Science in large enough numbers. Many Ceylonese suggest that this, in turn, can be traced to those intangible but nevertheless very real forces described as "social and professional status"—in which potential financial advancement and the nature of the dowry likely to be bequeathed at the time of marriage are large elements. An additional reason given locally is the greater attractiveness of "white-collar" professions. The phenomenon is certainly known to exist elsewhere, and it is

369

one that takes wise leadership on the part of University, government service and other authorities to overcome. Most of all, it demands consistent example by the senior officers themselves—the demonstration that the individual is not in any way humiliated by taking off his coat, soiling his hands with mother earth and doing a practical field task.

In this matter, especially, it may be regrettable that the earlier practice of training men overseas has largely fallen away. Coupled with the general shortage of trained men, it must be acknowledged that the attitude and approach developed through training in such places as Britain or the United States comes closer to meeting the practical problem.

For similar reasons too rapid replacement of European staff by Ceylonese personnel will only intensify the problem. Retirement of the more experienced European staff before they can be matched locally helps to bring about a want of clarity in objectives, a weakness in organization and direction, and an insufficiently critical attitude in research and experimentation.

Extension Staff. Because the staff of all grades is limited, while at the same time the additional colonization schemes and other new centers require the attention of extension officers from various departments, agricultural extension is not being conducted with either the coverage or the efficiency necessary. Until this is rectified the standard of farming and production will be lower than that which would be possible under better conditions of advice, guidance and demonstration.

Extension officers, by the very nature of their duties, must be men of good all-round practical knowledge; they should also have the kind of personality that draws the best from the farmers and others with whom they have to work. Particular care should be given, therefore, to the selection of the men themselves as well as to the kind of training they are to be given. Here the University Faculty and the Agricultural School for the Agricultural Assistant grade could certainly make important contributions.

Some form of investigating committee should be set up to

advise the government on the related matters of staffing needs, technical and other qualifications existing and required, stipends, possibilities of recruitment upon a graduated sequence, and similar questions. The authorities responsible for training at the various levels should be asked to submit suggestions for attracting to the service men with the required personality, approach and elements of technical knowledge.

Agricultural Education and Research

Technical knowledge can bring no improvement in agriculture until it reaches the man with the plow. But so far as the farming communities of different kinds are concerned, their instruction in better methods—that is, instruction not only by word of mouth and organized demonstration but also by showing individual cultivators how to improve their practices and yields on their own farms—must largely await the recruitment to the service of more and better trained staff. Education must produce this staff.

University Education in Agriculture. The Mission would much like to see the University provide a more satisfactory course of agricultural education and training for men destined to fill the gazetted posts and the equivalent posts in estate service. Until it is prepared to make a first-rate appointment to the Professorship of Agriculture, however, it is difficult to see how any real progress can be made toward this end.

Owing to the special circumstances of tradition, custom and status, unusual wisdom will be needed to surmount the various obstacles operating against the attraction of young men to the University degree in Agriculture. The problem is particularly acute among young Sinhalese.

To outline in detail the course of study to be presented would be out of place in a report of this kind. The course would tend to produce the right kind of officer only if it combined sound academic training and realistic practical experience. Such a course can be provided once arrangements are made for good staff, suitable field training facilities within reasonable distance, and the necessary periods of student absence from the University at planned intervals.

By agreement with the Department of Agriculture the University could have facilities for training at various government regional centers. This could be worked out in relation to the sequence, so that students could assist on such stations at the same time as they receive practical guidance and experience.

School of Agriculture for Agricultural Assistants. Production of men with the practical knowledge, manual ability, and right approach for demonstration work is the big task awaiting the government's School of Agricultural for Agricultural Assistants. That this kind of training should be correct is as important as turning out the best possible kind of gazetted officer. There is much scope for inspired teaching, training and development of approach in this subordinate grade.

The record of this School is a good one. It is a pity that, owing to new construction needs of the University, the School should have to be moved from its present site at Peradeniya. From limited inspection the nature of the courses given and the attitude of the staff were satisfactory. Training the students in close association with the School Farm and Experiment Station has everything to commend it.

It is suggested that all necessary staff, equipment and other facilities required for continuation of the work of this school be granted on as favorable a basis as funds permit. The Agricultural Assistant is a key man in the Department of Agriculture, as well as in the farming life of the country as a whole.

Kundasale School of Agriculture for Girls. While the objectives of this school are entirely sound, it is believed that the training and the facilities will have to be improved very greatly if the school is to produce women with a realistic approach to certain aspects of agriculture, rural home management and so forth. Even a brief inspection shows many features that call for adjustment in organization, approach, staffing and physical plant. In fairness, however, it must be noted that both the Principal and

Vice Principal have been appointed only recently, and that they realize fully the need for various changes.

Practical Farm Schools. Eleven practical farm schools, at which sons of village cultivators and others are given at least a basic education in agriculture in the vernacular, are reported to be doing useful work. In certain cases some of the staff may not have been fully equipped for their difficult and important task of imparting practical knowledge to potential cultivators. An improvement in this respect, however, is unlikely until the Department of Agriculture has a larger and a better trained junior staff from which to choose such teachers.

General Agricultural Research. For a country as small as Ceylon a commendable amount of attention has been paid to various kinds of investigations and research in the agricultural field.

Among the Department of Agriculture's activities may be mentioned various investigations, trials, and some basic research in the Divisions of Botany, Chemistry, Entomology, Plant Pathology, Horticulture, Tobacco, Agricultural Engineering, Systematic Botany and Soil Conservation. In addition, ad hoc studies are being conducted by the Agricultural Research Officers, North Central and Eastern Divisions respectively, and by the Curators at the Botanic Gardens at Heneratgoda (southwest lowlands region), Peradeniya (upland or hill subregion), and Hakgalla (montane subregion). In animal studies, the Divisions of Veterinary Services and Animal Husbandry are conducting ad hoc investigations. Forestry research, in silviculture and utilization, is financed separately from the budget of the Department of Forestry.

So far only a small contribution has been made by the University, through the Faculty of Agriculture and the Department of Veterinary Medicine.

As already noted, three commodity research centers—the separate Tea, Rubber, and Coconut Research Institutes—are undertaking special investigations and have behind them records of useful service. Especially notable is the work of the Tea Research Institute.

On the whole, therefore, the general coverage is fair to good. In quality of work, there is the inevitable variation according to differences in flair, ability and experience, and availability of staff and facilities. If there is any outstanding fault, it is that a better coordination of objectives, programs and testing of reported results is required. The present overlapping, as well as gaps, could to a large degree be removed by a closer knitting of information, exchange of views and coordination of effort.

Unfortunately, the total number of research officers employed is comparatively small and so are the funds. For the range of subjects being investigated it would not be realistic to expect that the quality of the work could be uniformly good throughout. Some of the more senior staff are overburdened; in the nature of scientific research this means that the quality must suffer. Some of the junior men are still relatively inexperienced in research; others lack fundamental training of the kind requisite to sound investigational approach.

It is time that there was a careful review of the whole position of agricultural research, and of the requirements in men and facilities to meet the growing demands of the agricultural community. If for nothing else, this is needed for the purpose of defining more precisely what is being done and by whom, whether further support is desirable and in what measure and form.

External Technical Assistance

At a number of points throughout this chapter it has been noted that specific outside assistance would be helpful—or in some cases indispensable—for further development in certain lines.

In none of these projects is success likely to be achieved unless the government staff concerned can work in the closest collaboration and fullest harmony with the consultants, advisers, experts and committees who may be provided by the international or other organization for the assistance mentioned.

From the Mission's observations, references in official records and the popular press, it is abundantly clear that the government should instigate more effective machinery for requesting and using scientific and technical assistance from outside organizations and individuals. The many problems in this field are reviewed in in Chapter 19.

Insufficient collaboration between ministries and simultaneous consultation with a number of experts on similar or closely related topics has resulted in duplication, confusion, misunderstanding and sometimes error. A particularly striking example is sugar, on which advice has been sought independently by the Ministry of Agriculture, the Ministry of Industries and the Gal Oya Development Board. Experts have been obtained independently from India and from FAO and a suggestion had been made to get further advice from Australia. Yet the whole complex field of sugar production has not been adequately covered.

The Mission has already suggested (in Chapter 4) that all requests for external technical aid be channelled through the proposed Development Advisory Board.

SUMMARY OF PRINCIPAL RECOMMENDATIONS

Individual Products

Tea. 1. Main government policy should aim at encouraging and assisting the tea estates to maintain and improve efficiency. Expansion of acreage within the limits allowed by the International Tea Agreement should by no means be debarred but opportunities are narrowly limited by physical conditions.

2. To safeguard continuous rejuvenation and prevent fragmentation, government should make a clear statement of policy with regard to requisitioning of tea estates and impose conditions designed to preserve estates when requisitioned or sold privately.

3. Concentration of the smaller tea factories should be encouraged.

4. The smallholders extension service should be expanded.

5. Propaganda for increased tea consumption in Ceylon itself should be undertaken, with a special eye to smallholders' tea.

375

Rubber. 6. Measures to increase yields per acre should have precedence over increase of existing acreage.

7. Assistance to replanting—including planting with other crops—should be expanded along the lines of the existing Rubber Rehabilitation Scheme. Government should influence growers in the better localities only to adopt a steady long-term replanting policy not determined by temporary market influences. Only the best available clones should be used.

8. Expansion of propaganda service among smallholders should have high priority. Special attention is required to methods of tapping, measures against disease and methods of processing.

9. General control, research and advisory work on rubber, now divided between several departments of government, should be brought under more unified control.

Coconuts. 10. The existing coconut area should be surveyed, mapped and more accurately classified according to type of holding.

11. A program of rehabilitation by replanting and underplanting should be drawn up, aiming at the replacement of at least 15,000 acres and preferably 30,000 acres per year. While financial assistance by government to such replanting, e.g. by issue of seedlings at less than cost price, is not ruled out, government efforts should be directed more to persuasion of smallholders to replant and to soil conservation, fencing and other incidental parts of such a program.

12. Surveys should be made of new areas suitable for coconut cultivation.

13. A tax based on either acreage or production should be levied to finance a ten-year program of research based on firm long-term budgeting.

14. Educational work through the extension officers of the Agricultural Department, Cooperative Societies and Rural Development Societies should be intensified to persuade smallholders to

adopt improved cultivation methods as well as adequate replanting practice.

Cacao. 15. Both entirely new planting (in the limited suitable areas available) and underplanting on the better rubber estates should be encouraged; marginal rubber localities should be avoided and the Department of Agriculture should organize further research on the growing of cacao with the help of experts from the Gold Coast or other large cacao-producing area.

Coffee. 16. An attempt should be made to reestablish a more resistant variety (e.g. *robusta*) but thorough trials should precede extensive plantings.

Cotton. 17. Selection, agronomic and field husbandry trials already begun by the Department of Agriculture should be vigorously pursued and aid should be sought from the Empire Cotton Growing Corporation.

Groundnuts. 18. Trials already started should be continued and extended; the lessons to be learned from the experience of the Overseas Food Corporation in East Africa should be drawn upon; and extension of cultivation in Gal Oya and other suitable colonization areas encouraged.

Illuk Grass. 19. Much more extensive trials should be made both of the possibilities and costs of growing this grass and of its paper-making qualities before the proposed paper factory is started. (See also Chapter 15.)

Pineapple. 20. Extension of acreage with a view to canning should be encouraged, with the assistance of experienced growers and canners from outside Ceylon.

Sisal. 21. Intensive and extensive trials should be undertaken in the Dry Zone, with outside advice which might be obtained from the government of Tanganyika and the East African Sisal Growers Association.

Tobacco. 22. The development work of the tobacco officer and his staff should be continued and reinforced by the addition of a specialist in soil conservation; more experimental work is required in the extension of Virginia type cigarette tobacco in the Jaffna region.

Other Commercial Crops. 23. The Department of Agriculture should encourage the cultivation of the following crops, paying particular attention to supply of improved varieties and obtaining advice from countries with special experience (e.g. Zanzibar for cloves); arecanuts; citronella; pepper; nutmeg; cloves; kapok; Deccan hemp; rozelle; sunn-hemp; pawpaw; turmeric; ginger; chillies; gingelly; oil palm; and cashew nut.

Rice. 24. Research work of the Department of Agriculture on all aspects of rice cultivation should be increased, and staff increased accordingly; special attention might be paid to the influence of the length of the day on rice yields.

25. Increased extension work is required to disseminate among smallholders the knowledge of improved methods, strains, etc.

26. The restoration and improvement of a large number of small tanks and irrigation schemes should be expedited, after adequate survey and planning. (See also Chapter 13.)

27. Close study should be made of use of water on paddy lands with a view to avoidance of wasteful or harmful overapplication. On colonization schemes and elsewhere demonstrations should be organized on the farmers' own lands to show the effects of bad use of water.

Other Cereals. 28. The Department of Agriculture should encourage wider use in the Dry Zone of sorghum (on which advice should be sought from the Queensland-British Overseas Food Corporation); kurukkan; and a number of varieties of millet.

Sugar. 29. The trials already made by the Department of Agriculture should be followed up by establishing a small commercial-scale unit of, say, 6,000 acres, as now understood to be proposed by the government at Maha Illuppullama. Larger-scale development should not be planned pending experience of the many complex problems involved in this initial development.

Miscellaneous Food Crops. 30. Additional investigational and extension work, both in the Dry Zone and elsewhere, is recommended on a number of beans and pulses; certain yams, sweet potato and manioc; the ordinary potato; and onions.

Fruit. 31. Additional work should be undertaken similarly on a number of fruits beyond those already mentioned. Citrus and bananas should be especially studied and mango cultivation should be encouraged with a view to canning.

Vegetables. 32. Valuable work by the Department of Agriculture in encouraging cultivation and marketing should be actively continued.

Pastures and Livestock. 33. Trials and investigation of grasses, legumes and fodder plants should be continued and extended.

34. A long-range livestock development policy should be laid down, covering perhaps 25 years and divided into, say, four sub-periods. It should be recognized that unduly rapid action in this field is extremely hazardous.

35. An island-wide survey of livestock population and potential should be organized.

36. Close attention is required to the production of types of cattle suiting the varied requirements (for draft animals, milk and meat) of different owners and the distribution of appropriate sizes for breeding. The milking properties of water-buffaloes should be further developed and used.

37. Livestock research stations should be established in the lower Wet Zone, upland Wet Zone and Dry Zone.

38. Pilot dairy schemes should be established at high elevations (over 5,000 feet).

39. Firm quarantine against rinderpest and other diseases should be maintained; and in view of the existing prevalence of foot-and-mouth disease, information on the latest scientific developments in its control should be sought from the joint Mexican-U.S. Commission dealing with this work.

40. Government should provide technical advice and stock at

cost for large-scale poultry undertakings and should endeavor to secure the production of nonfertile eggs for the Buddhist community.

Forests. 41. The basic policies of preservation and controlled exploitation now pursued by the Department of Forests should be continued and the Department should be strengthened to make them more effective.

42. A good forest survey should be made, based on aerial photographs and reconnaissance and enumeration on the ground.

43. Great care should be exercised in parting with any additional portions of the forest estate as now delimited.

44. Foundation of plantations of indigenous and exotic trees should be intensified.

45. The ban on removal of indigenous forest over 5,000 feet, for the purpose of planting suitable exotic trees, should be relaxed under careful supervision.

46. Planting of teak should be encouraged in the Dry Zone.

47. Further attention is required to forestry education and research, in which assistance might be sought from FAO and other outside agencies.

General Problems

Agricultural Extension. 48. Further considerable expansion is required in extension work generally and the interest and services of Cooperative Societies, Rural Development Societies and others concerned with village welfare should be fully mobilized. Although this work must be mainly directed to the multitude of smallholders, special attention should be paid to the potentially valuable group of middle-class farmers.

Soil Conservation. 49. The Soil Conservation Office should be asked to draw up a ten-year program of work.

50. Additional staff should be recruited, including men with experience in Asia or the tropics.

51. Constant propaganda should be continued to make all concerned aware of the menace of erosion and the measures needed to fight it. The active participation of estate-owners, medium land-holders and smallholders should be organized through regional or local committees.

Dry Farming. 52. Systematic trials and study, as now proceeding with the help of the FAO team, should be continued, with a view to gradual and sound expansion.

Land Tenure. 53. The possibility of applying the Torrens system of land registration should be investigated and proposals worked out as quickly as possible for a solution on this or other basis, of the present problems of land tenure in the island. It may be necessary, to prevent further multiplication of the abuses of insecurity and fragmentation, to take drastic action and government may need to contribute financially either to the compensation of claimants or to the expenses of litigation.

Survey of Land Use Potential. 54. Great importance is attached to the carrying out of such a survey with proper expert advice, as a basis for nearly all agricultural planning. It should collect all relevant historical and present information and prepare maps based on it, and submit recommendations regarding potential uses. Advice should be sought from the government of Tanganyika and from the private organizations which have had experience of such surveys in Burma and the Sudan.

Agricultural Education and Research. 55. Existing provision for special agricultural education in the School of Agriculture, the School of Agriculture for Girls and the practical farm schools should be maintained and developed. Additions to staff are required in most of these institutions.

56. The University should be enabled to make a first-rate appointment to the Professorship of Agriculture as the essential first step in the improvement of higher agricultural education.

57. Existing agricultural research institutes and stations should be fully supported and, in order to allot due priority and ensure

that the necessary staff is available to cope with the immediate new needs for research work, only a portion of which are mentioned here, a careful review should be made of the whole position of agriculture research in Ceylon.

Cost of Recommendations

The major financial costs involved in agricultural development are those of irrigation, jungle clearance and settlement of colonists. These are discussed in Chapters 12 and 13. [23] Recommendations dealt with in this chapter involve, almost entirely, action by the Department of Agriculture and other government agencies by way of research, investigation, survey, education and extension work. The costs involved consist primarily of the salaries and incidental expenses of the additional staff.

These must depend both on the speed with which staff of the quality required can be recruited and on the outcome of some of the investigations proposed, which may affect the direction of the Agriculture Department's activities. Any present estimate is therefore approximate. It is on that basis that the following estimate of costs averaged over the six-year period 1953-59 is submitted.

---

[23] Costs of agricultural development involved in new industrial developments, e.g. sugar, are allowed for under the head of Industry, Chapter 16.

AGRICULTURE

TABLE VIII

ESTIMATED COST OF AGRICULTURAL RECOMMENDATIONS, 1953-59
(thousand rupees)

		Annual Average Cost
1. Additional staff * in Agriculture and other Depts.		1,000
2. Soil Conservation		
(i) Additional Staff**	400	
(ii) Equipment	400	
(iii) Assistance to farmers for soil conservation work	1,500	2,300
3. Advisers (12 at Rs. 50,000 each) assuming half cost is met by FAO, Colombo Plan or other agencies, plus sundry incidental costs		325
4. University Education (grant to University, plus scholarships for foreign study)		325
5. Research and Experimentation (additional staff and equipment)		325
6. Land-use Survey *** (staff and aerial photographic survey)		650
7. Animal Husbandry Survey (one year, average over six-year period)		10
8. Sundry crop trials, etc.		65
Total annual average		*5,000*
Total over six years		*30,000*

---

* To a maximum of 50.
** To a maximum of 20.
*** To a maximum of 4.

12. Colonization

Colonization has been a leading feature of the government's development policy for many years. It is associated especially with the late Prime Minister, Mr. D. S. Senanayake, who started some of the older schemes when he was Minister for Agriculture before the war. The colonization at Minneriya, the first area of organized settlement, and at Polonnaruwa—to mention only the most prominent schemes—can now be regarded as established successes.

Objectives of the policy are simple. On the one hand there are large areas of under-utilized land; on the other there are thousands of families living in congested areas or in otherwise unproductive conditions. Settlement of this population on the idle land holds out bright hopes of giving them a better life, while simultaneously adding directly to the wealth of the nation. But the actual process is less simple. Opening up the land practically always involves the irrigation of some part of it; the jungle must be cleared and the land prepared for crops; houses have to be built; roads and other communal facilities must be provided; and the new settlers have to be able to support themselves during the period before their holdings begin to yield.

The first step—irrigation—is one which can seldom be undertaken without the aid of public authority; it is discussed in detail in Chapter 13. Other phases of the process of colonization are not so automatically the responsibility of government, but the central government has in practice taken a substantial share in them. It is the organization and policies involved in these that we propose to consider here.

General Features. Ceylonese colonization schemes are all based on crown lands—i.e. land in public ownership. No problems of title or acquisition arise. Furthermore the land is retained in public ownership, the colonists receiving long leases rather than freeholds. Apart from this and other common characteristics however, it is convenient to consider separately the "normal" schemes —individually of moderate size and using traditional methods of land clearing—and the more comprehensive development projects involving mechanical methods of clearing.

Normal Schemes. The usual colonization scheme is based on the restoration or enlargement of an old tank, and may involve from a few hundred to one or two thousand settlers. The general procedure follows an established pattern.

A suitable area is first selected on the basis of climate, topography, irrigation possibilities, acreage available, transportation facilities and related matters. The scheme is then planned in some detail before the jungle is felled. The Survey Department completes a topographic and land survey, and produces the necessary maps. With the aid of these and its own special surveys the Irrigation Department plans the irrigation works—the restoration or extension of the tank, the alignment of main and distributory channels, and so forth. The Department of Agriculture meanwhile advises on the suitability of the soils for various crops.

The land is then demarcated into colonist holdings, each containing five acres of irrigated land (normally for paddy) and three acres of nonirrigable, high or dry land. Sites are marked out for houses, wells, etc. Appropriate areas of nonirrigable land are set aside for public buildings, recreation parks, churches, communal pasturage and other public purposes.

While the Irrigation Department is carrying out its necessary works, the Land Development Department organizes and conducts the clearance of land, utilizing for the greater part traditional, nonmechanical methods. It also undertakes or supervises the construction of colonists' cottages, group or communal wells, public buildings of all kinds and other ancillary work.

Colonists are selected by the government agent or his representative (with the advice of agricultural, rural development and other officials) from among applicants all over the country. Preference is of course given to those from congested areas. Normally only men without land are taken. The selected men and their families are brought to the site of the scheme when their cottages and water supply are available. They are given nontransferable leases subject to various agreed conditions as to cultivation, maintenance, etc.

Paddy land is prepared according to an agreed program in which the colonists take part. Financial aid is given the colonists towards the costs of such part of the felling and stumping as has not been done by organized paid labor and is left for them to do. Fencing material is provided for the protection of the cleared land, the colonists doing the actual erection. The remaining preparation of the ground for its first crop is the responsibility of the colonist, although he receives further financial aid towards its cost. Also, advances are made against the expected income from the first crop, so that the colonists may have some free money or credit while they await their first harvest.

Both directly and through cooperative societies, the colonists are assisted by the systematic issue of selected seed or other planting material, tools and implements, work animals, and such incidental items as poultry. Subsequently they are granted certain credit facilities, and are aided in the processing and sale of their produce. Advice and guidance—and where possible, demonstration—are provided the colonists by the appropriate government staff.

It will be seen that much the greater part of the work involved in settling a colonist on the land in these normal schemes is undertaken by, or under the direct supervision of, government agencies. The aggregate cost of the various pieces of assistance provided by government is probably from Rs. 12,000 to Rs. 15,000 per settler, including irrigation costs of about Rs. 3,000-5,000. These are at best, rough estimates, as the work is scattered among a number of departments and to some extent intermingled with other departmental activities.

Special Development Projects. Ceylon's one large-scale scheme, employing mechanical methods to a considerable extent, is the Gal Oya Development. Its basic purpose (to quote the former Minister of Agriculture and Lands) is ". . . to establish, within the area of authority, the maximum number of families of Ceylon citizens that the area can carry at a reasonable standard of good and comfortable living conditions." It operates under a special authority created for the purpose—the Gal Oya Development Board—with wide powers of control and administration in its area and considerable freedom from ordinary government and civil service rules.

Basic to the scheme is the control of the Gal Oya, a river which rises in the central hills and flows through the Dry Zone for some 60 miles to discharge on the East Coast south of Batticaloa. (See Map 3.) The catchment area is about 770 square miles. At a suitable site a dam has been built and a new reservoir created, as described in Chapter 13, with a storage capacity of about 770,-000 acre feet.

The Gal Oya Board contemplates settlement of about 2,500 families annually for 10 years on land ready for cultivation and equipped with houses and other facilities. Assuming an average family of at least five, the project thus aims to provide living requirements for about 25,000 families or from 125,000 to 150,-000 people. As there would be many other persons serving the cultivators and their families (shopkeepers and traders, craftsmen, school teachers and public officials of all kinds) the ultimate total population of the area would be nearer 250,000.

For purposes of irrigated and dry land farming and associated activities, the project will use jungle country in the Gal Oya valley and neighboring lowlands to the extent of about 200,000 acres. Land not needed for roads, channels, towns, etc. will be distributed at the rate of four acres of irrigable and three acres of non-irrigable land per settler. In addition, plans call for:

(a) The possible undertaking of certain large-scale agricultural enterprises under direct operation by the Board, such as livestock production (for which the Board has set aside 10,000 acres as a livestock farm) and, more doubtfully, sugar.

(b) Development of the hydro-electric potential created by the dam construction (see Chapter 14).

(c) Promotion of industries based on the agricultural production of the area and the electric power made available.

Although methods of operation in the Gal Oya scheme are broadly similar to those already described for the "normal" schemes, there are the following important differences:—

(a) The dam construction was entrusted to a firm of American contractors who, working with up-to-date mechanical equipment, have completed the work very rapidly; the responsibility for the remainder of the irrigation works remains with the Irrigation Department.

(b) Clearing of the land is being done mechanically.

(c) Levelling and initial preparation of the soil, as well as clearing, is done by the Board instead of being left to the colonists.

(d) The Board, being vested with all powers of local government, is able to control more effectively the details of village settlement, to exclude "squatters", and to prevent the unauthorized establishment of village shops or boutiques.

In the general comments appearing in the remaining pages of this chapter more will be said about the Gal Oya project, including some observations which may be relevant to other large-scale schemes under consideration.

The Pattern of Land Development. A striking feature of the older schemes, as now operating in Minneriya and Polonnaruwa, is the exact uniformity of the size of holding. A great many factors combine to make uniformity appear desirable: the many conveniences to orderly planning; the desire to prevent, in future years, either the fragmentation of land among a multitude of owners or its concentration in a few hands—in fact, the very abuses from which many of the colonists are being rescued; a strong feeling that equity demands equal distribution of the available land among colonists—a feeling that is all the stronger when the land and so many ancillary constructions are provided virtually free. In view of all these pressures it is very natural that the authorities have tended to say in almost every scheme, "So many acres, so much for paddy and so much for dry farming, for each settler, neither more nor less."

However natural the decision, we feel grave doubts that rigid and permanent uniformity is wise. In the first place the area which can be efficiently cultivated depends on the size of the family unit, including children of working age. However carefully selected originally, the families chosen cannot all have the same number of effective workers; still less can equality in that respect be guaranteed over future years. Apart from mere numbers the ability, skill and industry of individual settlers must vary, and the best may easily be able to manage two or three acres more than the least efficient. Insistence on exact uniformity of holdings must therefore mean wastage of both land and labor; for while some holdings may be only partly or inefficiently cultivated, at the other extreme there will be individual colonists with inadequate scope for their abilities and energies.

It is beyond the intended range of this Mission's work to make a detailed study of possible modifications in present practice in this matter. Yet in principle it does not seem impossible to devise a system of allocation of land which would preserve the merits of present arrangements, guaranteeing a minimum for every settler, but with some degree of flexibility to suit the individual circumstances and to give scope to individual enterprise and energy. For example, it might be possible to give each colonist a somewhat smaller standard allotment (say three acres of paddy and two of high land) and to offer supplementary allotments, at something approaching an economic rental, to those desirous of extending their acreage.

Secondly, and more radically, the Mission doubts that development exclusively on a peasant basis is the best way—much less the quickest way—to secure the opening up of the Dry Zone on which so much of Ceylon's future depends. It would be advantageous if the energies of local men with more capital and with better education could be drawn into the operation. This might be achieved if they were afforded the opportunity of taking up larger blocks of land to develop on a large-farming or estate basis. In the earlier stages of Minneriya (and in other areas not classified as colonization areas) there was provision for allocations of larger acreages to "middle-class" Ceylonese, but for various reasons this practice seems to have lapsed.

We believe that while retaining peasant settlement as the main line of advance, it would be very useful to make a trial issue of leases of suitable length to individuals prepared to take up larger areas, and also to corporations, whether limited liability companies or cooperative societies, prepared to lease even larger blocks of land. Such longer leases would of course be granted on terms fixed at the true economic value of the land. Probably much more, perhaps the whole, of the clearing and preparation of this land could be made the responsibility of the lessee.

It is a mistake to think that leases on such a basis would necessarily contribute any less to the relief of the population pressure. The labor required for cultivation would be substantially the same; the difference would be that it would be employed on a wage basis. If larger blocks were leased closely adjacent to small-holding areas they might offer supplementary employment to the small-holders or members of their families, especially perhaps during the period before the first crop is obtained off the small-holdings, when the additional cash income might be especially valuable.

The Mission believes that many of these views are shared by others who have recently considered this problem. We would emphasize that we have not had the time to make any full study and the ideas we have put forward are merely suggestions. The whole subject of policy in the disposal of crown lands was referred in 1951 to an interdepartmental committee which has recently submitted its report. We urge very strongly that the above suggestions be fully examined in the course of consideration of that report.

Selection of Colonists. If any land is made available for leasing in larger blocks, we think that there should be no criterion of selection for those lessees other than their willingness to pay whatever rent and/or premium may be fixed and to accept whatever necessary conditions may be imposed as to cultivation, soil conservation, use of water, etc. The guiding factor should be enterprise, for the benefit of national development, and there should be no question of selection on any racial, national or occupational basis.

Selection of the peasant holders, who will in any event continue to constitute the vast majority of lessees, is another matter. It is natural that preference should be given to men from overpopulated areas; and it is wise, in order to promote at once an atmosphere of familiarity and cooperation, to try to group together families originating in the same district. We believe, however, that the present policy of drawing colonists almost exclusively from the landless class may be mistaken. It cannot help but mean that the colonists are, on the average, men who are comparatively inexperienced in agriculture and comparatively unsuccessful as farmers. There must tend to be a paucity of natural leaders amongst them.

It may be that men already in occupation of land are less likely to apply for acceptance as colonists. But if they do apply, it is probably because they are more enterprising and they should not be excluded from consideration. The migration of a man who already has land in an old village contributes just as much to the solution of the population problem as does the migration of a landless man, since the land he vacates will naturally be taken over by someone else. The Mission would therefore recommend the maximum of flexibility here also.

The Finance of Colonization. It has already been noted that the cost of settlement in the "normal" schemes is very high. The

391

cost in Gal Oya is expected to be perhaps a little, if not significantly, higher. The cost in the Walawe Ganga Scheme (if, contrary to the Mission's views, that is carried out as now planned) would be about twice as high—upwards of Rs. 30,000 per settler. Even the cost in the normal schemes is so high as to raise the question of whether the government is doing too much for the individual settler.

Historically the matter is understandable. When the first colonization schemes were started some 20 years ago, government was not at first willing to do much more than provide the irrigation and let the colonist do the rest. At that time the region involved was still highly malarial and comparatively inaccessible, and there was great difficulty in persuading men to settle in it. So inducements were added by way of additional free services and financial aids.

Today the situation is entirely different. The areas of colonization are virtually free from malaria or can be made so; modern road transport has rendered them far more accessible; and colonization is an established and accepted operation, no longer a daring and highly risky adventure. The result is that there are many more applicants for allotment of land in the settlement areas. Indeed in the older settlements a major problem is the squatter who moves in and occupies land illegally, with no assistance whatever from the government.

Fully accepting the wisdom of the past policies in past circumstances, the Mission believes that the changed conditions justify and demand a re-examination of the whole scale of assistance to colonists. If something can be saved there, it will make more funds available for other development. This is a matter for detailed examination from the financial, agricultural and sociological points of view, but we make the following specific suggestions:

(a) Reduction of the standard, or minimum, allotment of land to each colonist, as already recommended on other grounds, would mean a lower cost per settler. [1] With the same amount of land, the government might then be able to offer a larger number of families an opportunity to earn a better living.

(b) Clearing assistance might profitably be concentrated on getting the colonist's first two acres ready as soon as possible, including stumping as well as felling, while reducing the amount of help given in clearing the rest of his land.

(c) Housing specifications can be made less expensive to provide the basic requirement of cottages reasonably resistant to weather, termites and other forces of deterioration, without anything unduly elaborate. The colonist could enlarge or modify this to suit his taste, at his own expense and effort. Some saving might be made by the general use of round timber and cadjan instead of squared timber and tiles for roofing, leaving repair and replacement of the thatch after a year or two to the colonist; in any case the use of imported tiles is unnecessary. The alternative of requiring the colonist to make his own habitation is also worth study, although there are obvious and serious objections such as the possibility of long delay in getting families into residence and difficulty in obtaining building materials locally. The materials problem might be eased, however, if government put up part of the cost of materials on some equitable and easy form of repayment.

(d) There should also be a review of the charges made for land, now fixed at comparatively low figures (e.g. in Gal Oya, Rs. 180 per colonist). Rents paid customarily by tenant farmers of paddy land elsewhere in the country are something like 50% of the gross value of the crop. In settlement areas, assuming a paddy yield of 15 bushels per acre for each of two crops per year and a price of Rs. 9 per bushel—if the land charge were only 25% the rate per colonist would be about Rs. 340 or nearly twice as much as the current Gal Oya rate. It is reasonable to hope that

---

[1] The cost per acre would be a little higher, if no other changes were made, as some costs, e.g. housing, vary with the number of settlers.

with improved methods and guidance, yields in the colonization areas will eventually be much better than the average of the island, in which event the 25% formula would produce a still higher revenue and make more funds available for future development. We cannot say with certainty that 25% is the right basis; yet in view of the large amount done for the colonist it seems not unreasonable. In any event the question of rentals to be charged needs re-examination in the light of current prices and costs.

Other Issues of Policy. Officials recognize the urgency of settling as many people as possible, as soon as possible, on newly developed land, so that "living room", a better standard of life and an increase in national food supply may be provided. This urgency is a constant temptation to government to try to carry forward simultaneously more colonization schemes than the available staff can administer. The official staff today is short of both the experienced men and the juniors needed for planning, executing, maintaining and improving the schemes through their various phases.

Progress is not to be judged by the number of acres said to be cleared or in stages of being cleared, nor by the number of families either resident or about to move into a colonization scheme. True progress is to be gauged rather by the economic well-being of the families living in a scheme and the quality and quantity of the crops they produce, with full regard for the maintenance and improvement of the soil and the economic use of water.

The schemes already well advanced and in a postpreliminary stage should be completed. However, we would recommend that, before further schemes of any size are commenced, a schedule of priorities should be drawn up by the officers most closely in touch with conditions and examined by the ministers concerned. From this schedule a systematic program of development should be prepared. Such a procedure would result in better project selection, more sensible planning, and cheaper and better prosecution of the various phases of the clearing, prepar·

ing, building, water supply and other operations. [2] This hard-working and enthusiastic staff would not be taxed almost to the limit, but instead could produce sounder proposals and more efficient accomplishment.

In general, and clearly without prejudice to the results of further study and the experience being gained in Gal Oya, the Mission feels that in the near future better results will be obtained by concentrating on the smaller normal schemes than by embarking on new large-scale projects. With improvements, and with a limited amount of mechanical help, the traditional methods of jungle clearing are likely to yield better results agriculturally and at lower cost. Furthermore the over-all risks, in such matters as erosion, are much smaller in the older style schemes.

The Gal Oya Project. The basic concept of turning into productive use the large areas of valuable soil now lying under cover of the jungle is admirable. The Gal Oya region, moreover, forms an excellent area in which to make a bold new venture in the use of rapid methods hitherto untried in Ceylon; and the Mission, on several visits to the project, was much struck by the enthusiasm of all concerned, from the Chairman of the Board, Mr. H. J. Huxham, and his colleagues, down.

Nevertheless, we were left apprehensive that the proposed rate of development, involving the settlement of some 2,500 families per year after the first year, is too high and may lead to waste and loss. Even the lower target of about 1,500 families for 1952 may be unrealizable without this risk.

In any circumstances the proper synchronization of the supply of equipment for land clearing, for preparation of the irrigation channels and for the agriculture operations would be difficult. In these days of abnormal rearmament programs there is even more danger that supplies will be spasmodic and inadequate, with

---

[2] Planning and the preliminary investigations of specific schemes would be greatly accelerated and improved in quality if a good aerial photographic survey were provided as recommended elsewhere.

serious effects on the rate of land clearing and preparation and of those aspects of production that depend on mechanical farming equipment. The Development Board is also handicapped by the shortage of trained and experienced personnel. The effects of such a shortage in a scheme of this kind were well exemplified by the Tanganyika ground nut project of the Overseas Food Corporation of which a member of the Mission had direct and close experience.

In addition to these two paramount factors of material and staff, there are some other more specific comments and observations concerning Gal Oya which should be noted:

1. Planning has suffered from inadequate topographical, soil and vegetation surveys. We have urged elsewhere the importance of such surveys before further large schemes are undertaken.

2. More jungle has been felled than could receive adequate final preparation for either dry land or irrigation farming in the first season. Consequent dangers include resprouting of the felled but uncleared trash, permanent loss of organic matter and damage to the soil if firing is used to clear the trash after drying, and loss, by erosion, of soil exposed by clearing but given no further treatment or natural cover. As to the first point, several thousand acres of cleared land have in fact had to be left alone temporarily, having strongly resprouted.

3. Correctly, in principle, catch-crops have been sown with the twofold objective of providing some sort of cover against both sun and heavy rain and of bringing in a limited amount of food; but it is feared that these have been selected unwisely and have been put in with inadequate preparation of the soil.

4. Lack of maps or complete planning appears to be hampering the orderly progress of the detailed irrigation, with some ill effects on staff morale.

5. Development of sugar production on some 20,000 acres, optimistically estimated to yield 40 tons of cane per acre, has figured prominently in Gal Oya plans hitherto. These plans may now be

in abeyance if, as reported, the government intends to install a sugar factory elsewhere (see Chapter 11). In any event, bearing in mind the considerations on sugar mentioned elsewhere in this report, the inadequacy of transport and the apparent characteristics of the Gal Oya soil, the Mission feels that very great caution should attend any plans for sugar at Gal Oya at present.

6. Dangers of flood erosion in the catchment area and of early siltation in the reservoir have been very differently estimated by various investigators. The 770 square miles of catchment has not been reconnoitered over its whole area, but for about 350 square miles it is reported to be covered mainly by jungle ($\frac{1}{4}$ of the area), grassy park land (2/5), and jungle in which chena is carried out ($\frac{1}{4}$); a patchwork of village gardens, paddy fields, and other small plots constitutes the balance. The major causes of disturbance appear to be the chena burnings and the severe fires that rush through the grassy portions of the vegetation, exposing the soil to erosion by storms.

So diverse have been the views expressed, and so very severe the damage that has occurred in other countries in somewhat similar conditions, that the Mission recommends to the Board the appointment of an impartial, experienced observer or group to pass expert judgment on this matter and propose appropriate remedies if needed.

7. Although the project is primarily designed for the small farmer, and although the small individual acreages may lend themselves best to farming with hand labor and draft animals, this should not rule out the use of mechanical equipment for bottleneck operations such as initial preparation of the soil. Experience in Africa suggests that the time saved at the outset of the season by getting the land broken up by tractor plough or disc harrow is more than amply justified by the results. It is also worth considering whether sorghum and similar small-grain cereals should not be harvested by machine. Equipment and operators might be supplied through cooperative societies.

Summary of Recommendations

1. Possibilities for more flexibility in the size of holdings allotted to colonists should be examined—e.g., a smaller standard allocation with provision for supplementary allocations at economic rentals.

2. In connection with the recent report of the interdepartmental committee on disposal of crown lands, the government should consider very seriously leasing some larger blocks of land in the Dry Zone development areas to individuals or corporations willing to operate on a large farming or estate basis.

3. Selection of colonists should not be limited to men now landless.

4. The cost of settlement per colonist should be reduced if possible. Suggested measures include reducing the minimum allocation of land (see recommendation 1), limiting the clearing work done by government, and reducing the cost of houses.

5. Annual charges made to colonists for land should be increased, perhaps to 25% of the estimated gross yield.

6. Care should be taken not to overload the administrative and technical services available by undertaking too large a burden of colonization work at once. Pending the result of further studies, work should be concentrated on the smaller schemes and no new "special" or highly mechanized projects should be started.

7. The possible rate of progress in the Gal Oya Development Scheme should be reviewed realistically in the light of a number of technical problems and dangers; if found necessary, the annual target of settlers should be reduced.

8. The Gal Oya Board should organize a land-use potential survey of its own, including an aerial photographic survey and the preparation of large-scale maps.

9. The Board should also seek early outside advice to settle the controversial question of erosion and siltation dangers in the Gal Oya reservoir area.

10. Regular use of tractors for early season ground breaking on colonists' land should be tried, possibly through cooperative societies.

13. Water Resources and Irrigation

This chapter describes the basic water resources of Ceylon and and discusses in detail certain aspects of their utilization and control. Water can be used as a source of power, for irrigation and for drinking and other domestic and industrial uses; water-courses may be useful means of transport; and the disposal of surplus water raises problems of drainage and flood control. To avoid repetition, water power is dealt with in Chapter 14, water transport in Chapter 16, and water supplies to towns and villages in Chapter 17. In this chapter attention is concentrated on the basic situation; on irrigation, flood control and drainage (including salt water exclusion); and on general organizational problems in relation to water. It cannot, however, be too strongly emphasized that no single aspect of water utilization can be properly considered in isolation from the others. The recommendations as to organization made here and elsewhere are specially directed to ensuring the fullest coordination of all water activities.

Physical and Hydrological Background

1. *Geography and Geology.* The features of Ceylon's geography of greatest interest with respect to water resources are the location of the mountainous area in the south central part of the island and the existence of three steps or tiers of land. The mountains form the highest step, while the upland and coastal plains form successive steps on each side. Three peneplains can be seen at levels of 6,000, 1,600 and 100 feet above sea level. Five sixths of the area of the island is at a level lower than 1,000 feet. About three quarters of the area is below the level of 500 feet. Table I shows the area above different levels.

TABLE I

Areas of Land at Different Levels

Elevation Feet	Total Area Sq. Miles	Dry Zone Sq. Miles	Wet Zone Sq. Miles
Above 8,000	15	0	15
″ 7,000	85	0	85
″ 6,000	150	0	150
″ 5,000	275	45	230
″ 4,000	650	250	400
″ 3,000	1,230	300	930
″ 2,000	2,300	600	1,700
″ 1,000	4,140	1,060	3,080
″ Sea Level	25,000	17,300	7,700

Two aspects of the island's geology are of particular importance to a study of water resources. First is the general prevalence in the sub-soil of impermeable crystalline rocks, which themselves cannot retain water, and which are covered by a layer of weathered rocks and soil that is generally too thin to provide good water storage. As a result, in most of the island there is no accumulation of easily accessible underground water and no possibility of obtaining supplies of water from wells. Only in a few limited areas, most importantly the Jaffna Peninsula, is there a limestone sub-soil which makes this possible. In those areas wells are extensively used both for ordinary water supply and for irrigation.

Second, a feature of the coastal areas and the lower parts of the river valleys is the wide extent of alluvial deposits in the flood plains of the rivers, which provide the most fertile paddy-lands and also widen the areas subject to flooding at periods of heavy rainfall.

2. *Rainfall*. The map of the average annual rainfall (Map 5) shows a concentration of rain in the southwest quadrant of the island, generally called the Wet Zone. The other parts of the island, i.e. the north and southeast parts, are called the Dry Zone. The average rainfall for the whole island, based on 40 years' records, is 75.6 inches per year.

The following table shows monthly rainfall for the whole island, and for the Dry Zone and Wet Zone separately.

TABLE II
AVERAGE MONTHLY RAINFALL
(inches)

Month	Whole Island	Dry Zone	Wet Zone
January	8.24	8.96	5.98
February	3.20	3.00	3.81
March	4.78	3.82	7.82
April	6.02	4.82	9.84
May	5.83	3.23	14.06
June	3.48	1.10	11.02
July	2.91	1.28	8.02
August	3.17	2.08	6.64
September	4.50	3.03	9.18
October	9.85	8.46	14.26
November	12.62	12.21	13.89
December	11.00	11.66	8.92
Total	*75.60*	*63.65*	*113.44*

The heaviest rains occur during the southwest and northeast monsoons. The onset and duration of the monsoons, especially the northeast, vary a good deal from year to year but the normal period of the southwest monsoon is from May to September and for the northeast from November to March. During the transitional months, October and April, convectional rains are generated by the difference of temperature between the sea and the land. Generally the coastal areas receive early morning showers and inland areas afternoon showers. In what might be called a normal year the southwest monsoon starts in May, when rains fall mainly on the southwest coast. In June, the rain is inside the southwest quadrant and is very rare in the Dry Zone (less than two inches). In July the monsoon is at full strength, but the heaviest rains are concentrated in the mountainous part of the island. In August the monsoon begins to lessen and the rain increases in the Dry Zone. In September the southwest monsoon disappears and the convectional rains begin, most heavily on the coastal areas. In October there are rains, mainly convectional, on every part of the island but again the heaviest rains are in the mountainous area. In November the northeast monsoon starts and brings rain to almost the whole island, but most heavily on the northeast coast and in the mountains. From December to February the monsoon lessens and the rains are more widespread. In March the northeast monsoon ends and convectional rains begin again. In April the situation is the same as in October, with convectional rains over the whole island.

This theoretical or average regime is, however, rarely realized in so simple a sequence. There are wide differences between one year and another in the timing of the monsoons and in the quantity of rainfall. The rain is often concentrated in areas very much smaller than either the Wet or the Dry Zones taken as a whole and the average rainfall for the island or for one of the two zones cannot give an accurate idea of the mean rainfall on a specific watershed. To gather data that can be used for the study of the regime of the rivers it is necessary to study the rainfall in each catchment area.

3. *Hydrology.* The heavy rains have eroded the mountainous part of the island and carved many narrow and deep valleys occupied by torrential rivers. In many places harder rocks have been less eroded than softer adjacent strata and picturesque waterfalls result, especially in the southern part of the mountainous area where the two steps are more apparent. When the rivers reach the lower peneplain that forms the main part of the island, the grade of the river beds falls rapidly and, when not swollen by floods, the waters flow slowly toward the sea. Generally the profiles of the rivers show a sequence of steps; between the flat stretches there are rapids and falls. In the flat stretches of slow flow are alluvial deposits, forming fertile plains on which paddy is cultivated. Such alluvial plains are formed not only in the low

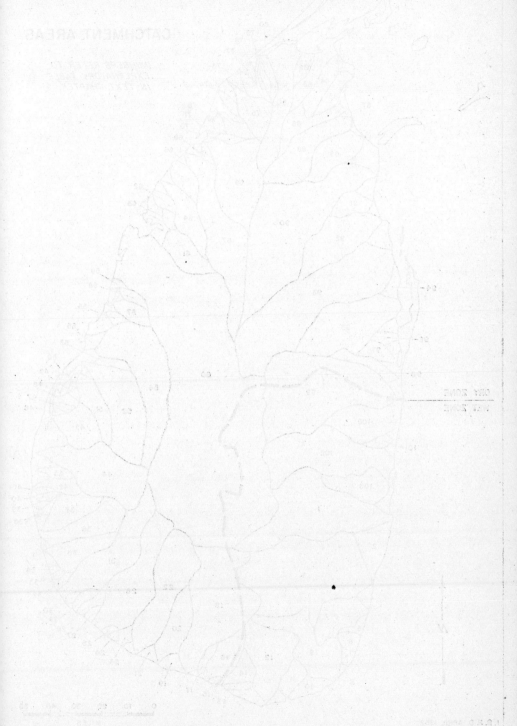

MAP 12

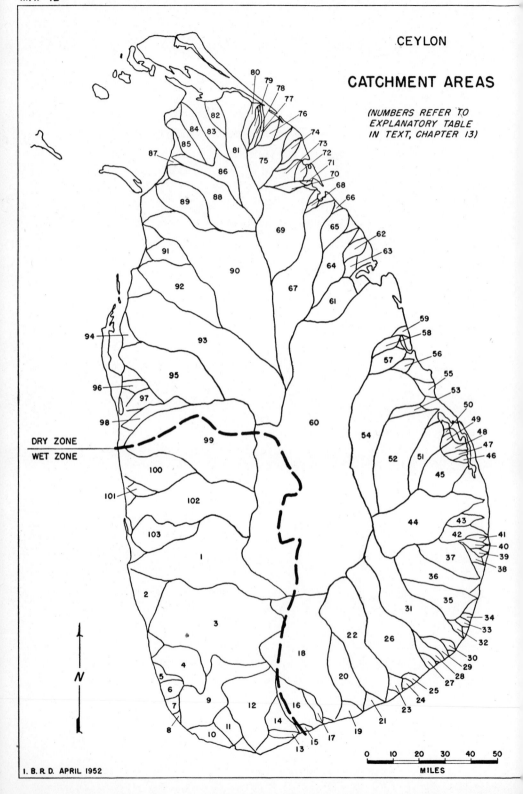

CEYLON

CATCHMENT AREAS

(NUMBERS REFER TO
EXPLANATORY TABLE
IN TEXT, CHAPTER 13)

DRY ZONE
WET ZONE

N

I. B. R. D. APRIL 1952

0   10   20   30   40   50
MILES

part of the island but even in the highlands of the mean peneplain.

Map No. 12 shows the 103 defined catchment areas of the main rivers of the island and Table III gives the main data collected for each river. This table has been prepared by the Hydrologic Section of the Irrigation Department from the most accurate available data on the discharges and the rainfall, but the discharge of about three rivers out of four is computed from rainfall data and by comparison with neighboring watersheds. Only about one fourth of the discharges have been computed from records of gaugings made on the rivers. Gauging records exist for most of the main streams, but the gauging stations have been established at different times. For some, the data have been recorded for 20 or 30 years but for many others the data go back only a few years. The values for the mean discharges computed from the newest gauging stations will require records over a period of several years before they can be considered as reliable. Accordingly, while Table III gives the most accurate picture at present available of the discharge of the various rivers, it must be regarded as still only a first approximation.

The map shows many short coastal rivers with small watersheds. Those in the Dry Zone are generally dry during the dry season. The catchment areas of the 103 rivers listed in Table III total 23,321.9 sq. miles. The remaining area of the island consists

TABLE III

DRAINAGE BASINS & MEAN ANNUAL RUN-OFF

(*The Area of a Basin is the Drainage Area Above the River Mouths*)

No. of Drainage Basin	Name	Area in Sq. Miles	Mean Annual Run-off in Ac. Ft./Sq. Mile		Mean Annual Run-off Ac. Ft. x 1000
			Gauged	Estimated	Estimated
1	Kelani Ganga	885	5600		4956
2	Bolgoda	146		3000	438
3	Kalu Ganga	1050	5600		5880
4	Bentota	243		3500	850
5	Madu Ganga, Randombe Lake	23		2000	46

TABLE III—Continued

No. of Drainage Basin	Name	Area in Sq. Miles	Mean Annual Run-off in Ac. Ft./Sq. Mile		Mean Annual Run-off Ac. Ft. x 1000 Estimated
			Gauged	Estimated	
6	Madampe Lake	35		2200	77
7	Telwatte Ganga, Hikkaduwe Ganga	20		1800	36
8	Ratgama Lake	4		1500	6
9	Gin Ganga	370	5500		2035
10	Koggala Lake	25		1800	45
11	Polwatte Ganga	91		2400	218
12	Nilwala Ganga	375	3200		1200
13	Sinimodara Oya	15		1000	15
14	Kirama Oya	87		1700	148
15	Rekawa Oya	295		500	15
16	Urubokka	136	1700		231
17	Kachigal	86		900	77
18	Walawe Ganga	954	1700		1622
19	Karagan Oya	22.5		300	7
20	Malala Oya	310		800	248
21	Embilikala Oya	23		300	7
22	Kirindi Oya	455	1000		455
23	Bambawe Ara	31		200	6
24	Mahasiliwa Oya	5		150	1
25	Butawa Oya	15		200	3
26	Menik Ganga	497	800		398
27	Katupila Ara	33.5		300	7
28	Kurunda Ara	51		300	15
29	Nabadagas Ara	42		250	11
30	Karambe Ara	18		200	4
31	Kumbukkan Oya	656		750	492
32	Bagura Oya	36		250	9
33	Girikula Oya	6		150	1

TABLE III—Continued

No. of Drainage Basin	Name	Area in Sq. Miles	Mean Annual Run-off in Ac. Ft./Sq. Mile		Mean Annual Run-off Ac. Ft. x 1000 Estimated
			Gauged	Estimated	
34	Helawe Ara	20		250	5
35	Wila Oya	189	600		134
36	Heda Oya	236	1000		236
37	Karanda Oya, Kirimeti Ara	165		700	116
38	Symena Ara	20		250	5
39	Tandiadi Aru	8.6		250	2
40	Kangikadichi Ara	22		300	7
41	Rufuskulam	13.5	650		9
42	Pannel Oya	72	400		29
43	Ambalam Oya	45		350	16
44	Gal Oya	700	1400		980
45	Andella Oya, Nawakiri Aru	204	500		102
46	Tumpankeni Tank	1.5		1000	2
47	Manakada Aru	4.5		1000	4
48	Mandipattu Aru	39		1000	39
49	Pathanthodaphue Aru	39		1000	39
50	Vett Aru	10		500	5
51	Unichchai	135	1200		162
52	Mundeni Aru	500	800		400
53	Miyangolle Ela	88		600	53
54	Maduru Oya	602	700		421
55	Pulliyanpota Aru	20.3		200	4
56	Kirimechchi Odar	30		250	8
57	Bodigoda Aru	64		500	32
58	Mandan Aru	5		200	1
59	Makarachchi Aru	54		400	22
60	Mahaweli Ganga	4034	800		3227
61	Kantalai Basin	174		400	70
62	Pan Oya	56		400	22

TABLE III—Continued

No. of Drainage Basin	Name	Area in Sq. Miles	Mean Annual Run-off in Ac. Ft./Sq. Mile		Mean Annual Run-off Ac. Ft. x 1000 Estimated
			Gauged	Estimated	
63	Palampotta Aru	27		500	13
64	Pankulam Aru	147		800	118
65	Kunchikumban Aru	80		800	64
66	Pulakutti Aru	8		400	3
67	Yan Oya	594	1300		772
68	Mee Oya	35		850	30
69	Ma Oya (Padawiya)	400		900	360
70	Churiyan Aru	29		600	17
71	Chavar Aru	12		600	7
72	Palladi Aru	24		600	14
73	Mandal (Nay Aru)	73		850	62
74	Kodalikallu Aru	29		600	17
75	Per Aru	146		800	117
76	Pali Aru	33		450	15
77	Maruthapilly Aru	16		250	4
78	Theravil Aru	35		300	10
79	Piramenthal Aru	32		300	10
80	Netheli Aru	47		300	14
81	Kanakarayan Aru	350		700	245
82	Kalawalappu Aru	22		250	5
83	Akkarayan	75		300	23
84	Mandekal Aru	116		400	46
85	Pallavarayankadu Aru	62		250	15
86	Pali Aru	176		300	61
87	Chappi Aru, Punkadi Aru	26		125	3
88	Rarangi Aru	325		300	98
89	Nay Aru	219		300	66
90	Aruvi Aru	1268	318		405
91	Kal Aru	82		250	21
92	Modaragama Aru	364		350	127

TABLE III—Continued

No. of Drain-age Basin	Name	Area in Sq. Miles	Mean Annual Run-off in Ac. Ft./Sq. Mile		Mean Annual Run-off Ac. Ft. x 1000
			Gauged	Estimated	Estimated
93	Kala Oya	1044	350		360
94	Moongil Aru	17		125	2
95	Mi Oya	675	350		236
96	Madurankuli Aru	28		300	8
97	Kalagamue Oya	59		400	24
98	Rathambala Oya	84		400	34
99	Deduru Oya	1022	900		920
100	Karambala Oya	230		1000	230
101	Ratmal Oya	84		900	76
102	Maha Oya	590	1600		944
103	Attanagalla Oya	284		3000	852
	Totals	23,321.9			32,159
Area of Jaffna Peninsula including Vadamarachchi Lagoon but excluding islands		393.2		500	197
Intermediate coastal areas between adjoining watersheds		1,464.9		250	366
Total area & run-off for island		25,180.0			32,722
Mean annual run-off in inches of depth over island					24.4"
Mean annual rainfall on island					75.6"
Mean over all ratio of run-off to rainfall					32%

of the Jaffna peninsula, say 393.2 sq. miles, and of coastal areas of 1,464.9 sq. miles that have no definite drainage.

Table IV classifies the watersheds according to size and lists those of most importance.

TABLE IV

CLASSIFICATION OF WATERSHEDS BY SIZE

Area	No. of Watersheds
from 1 to 50 sq. miles	48
from 51 to 100 sq. miles	17
from 101 to 500 sq. miles	25
from 501 to 1,000 sq. miles	8
from 1,000 sq. miles upward	5
Total	*103*

Watersheds over 1,000 sq. miles:—

Mahaweli Ganga	4,034 square miles
Aruvi Aru	1,268 square miles
Kalu Ganga	1,050 square miles
Kala Oya	1,044 square miles
Deduru Oya	1,022 square miles

Watersheds between 500 sq. miles and 1,000 sq. miles:—

Walawe Ganga	954 square miles
Kelani Ganga	885 square miles
Gal Oya	700 square miles
Mi Oya	675 square miles
Kumbukkan Oya	656 square miles
Madru Oya	602 square miles
Yan Oya	594 square miles
Maha Oya	590 square miles

The 38 rivers with watersheds in excess of 100 sq. miles drain a total area of 20,966 sq. miles, about 84% of the whole area of the island.

The catchment areas alone, however, are an insufficient indication of the flow of water in the different rivers. The Wet Zone rivers naturally have a proportionately higher total discharge, and those having watersheds partly located in the mountains have a larger flow during the low water season than those located wholly in the lowlands. Table V gives estimates for all rivers having a discharge in excess of 500,000 acre feet per year. The total

TABLE V

ANNUAL DISCHARGES AT PRINCIPAL RIVERS

Rivers	Yearly Discharge in 1,000 Acre ft.
Kalu Ganga	5,880
Kelani Ganga	4,956
Mahaweli Ganga	3,227
Gin Ganga	2,035
Walawe Ganga	1,622
Nilwala Ganga	1,200
Gal Oya	980
Maha Oya	944
Deduru Oya	920
Attanagalla Oya	852
Bentota	850
Yan Oya	772
Total	*24,238*

yearly discharge of these 12 rivers is about 75% of the total of all the rivers of the island. Twenty-four other rivers with a yearly discharge in excess of 100,000 acre feet have a total discharge of about 6.5 million acre feet. The total for the 36 main rivers is therefore about 95% of the total for all the rivers.

The table sharply illustrates the importance of location. For instance the Mahaweli Ganga, which is mainly located in the Dry Zone and has a north-northeast orientation, has a catchment area nearly four times as large as that of the Kalu Ganga, located wholly in the Wet Zone, but enjoys a discharge only just over half that of the Kalu Ganga. The last named, with a catchment area of about 1,000 sq. miles, has the highest discharge. The Kelani

Ganga, with a catchment area less than 900 sq. miles, is second. Fourth in the classification is the Gin Ganga, with a catchment area of 370 sq. miles, but located in the Wet Zone with a favorable orientation towards the southwest. The Kalu Ganga, Kelani Ganga and Gin Ganga all have discharges of nearly 6,000 acre feet per square mile of catchment, whereas the Mahaweli Ganga has only 800 acre feet per square mile, and the Aruvi Aru, with the second largest catchment area (1,268 sq. miles) and a watershed entirely located in the Dry Zone, has a yearly discharge of 405,000 acre feet, or only 318 acre feet per square mile.

Table VI gives in cubic feet per second the mean monthly discharge, recorded in 10 gauging stations on seven different rivers, over periods varying from two to 26 years. The same data are shown graphically in Chart No. 1.

All the ten stations except that on the Gal Oya show a low water period in February. All without exception show a second low water period in September (in one case the actual minimum is in August), but this is most marked in the Dry Zone rivers.

The main difference between the regimes of the Wet Zone and Dry Zone appears in the period from February to September, i.e., during the southwest monsoon, when the Wet Zone rivers experience high water and floods while in the purely Dry Zone rivers the discharges are steadily falling. Rivers, such as the Mahaweli Ganga, which rise in the Wet Zone and flow through the Dry Zone or which rise on the slopes of the central mountains have intermediary regimes. In the Dry Zone about 80% of the total annual rainfall occurs between the end of October and the beginning of February. Therefore the rivers with a catchment area in that zone have a short period of high water followed by a sharp drop in February and a long period of very low water. In the Wet Zone, where heavy rains occur during both the monsoons, there are generally two periods of high water and floods between the two periods of low water in March and September. The distance between the mountainous area and the sea is short in the south and in the southwest; the regime of the rivers is therefore torrential

CHART I

MEAN MONTHLY DISCHARGES OF SELECTED RIVERS – CEYLON
(IN 100,000 ACRE FEET PER MONTH)

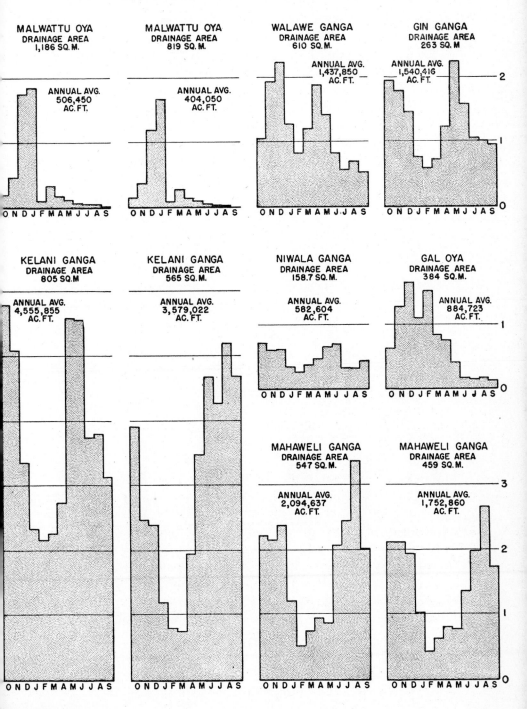

B. R. D. APRIL 1952

with heavy floods. The water runs down from the mountains along sharp slopes, in river beds with a high grade, but when it arrives in the plain it spills out of the river beds and spreads over large areas of the country, then, owing to the flatness of the coastal area, it empties slowly into the sea. In the very flat Dry Zone the heavy rains of the northeast monsoon form large stretches of flood water.

Table III shows the discharges remaining in the rivers after diversion of the water used for irrigation. The total discharge for all rivers is estimated at 32,722,000 acre feet, corresponding to a depth of 24.4 inches on the total area of the island. As the average rainfall is 75.6 inches, the ratio of run-off to rainfall is 32%. This is low for a tropical country, but it is highly influenced by diversion of water for irrigation and by heavy evaporation in the Dry Zone.

The catchment areas of the Wet Zone drain 18,987,000 acre feet, say 58%, of the total run-off on the island with a ratio of run-off to rainfall of 56%. The catchment areas of the Dry Zone (some of them partially located in the Wet Zone) drain 13,735,-000 acre feet with a ratio of run-off to rainfall of 20%. In this zone, part of the water flowing in the rivers is diverted, either via reservoirs or direct, to irrigate about 600,000 acres of paddy fields, but it is difficult to estimate this diversion at all precisely. Part of it is absorbed by the paddy, another part is lost by infiltration and evaporation during storage or conveyance in irrigation channels to the fields, but part does eventually return to the rivers by natural or artificial drainage. The proportion so returning may be large when, as in Ceylon, excessive amounts of water are supplied initially to the paddy fields.

IRRIGATION

Possibilities and Projects

We have stressed the importance of rice as the staple foodstuff of the people of Ceylon and the urgent necessity of increasing output in order to reduce dependence on imports (Chapter 11). While there are large areas in the Wet Zone where paddy can be

TABLE VI

AVERAGE MONTHLY FLOWS IN CEYLON RIVERS

River	Gauging Station	Drainage Area in Sq. Miles	Period of Records	Oct.	Nov.	Dec.	Jan.	Feb.
Kelani Ganga	Nagalagam Street	805	1924-50	580,513	509,443	334,605	233,288	215,829
Kelani Ganga	Glencorse Estate	565	1948-50	392,050	247,849	239,639	119,979	81,416
Mahaweli Ganga	Peradeniya	459	1943-50	212,844	212,947	194,391	101,370	41,981
Mahaweli Ganga	Gurudeniya	547	1944-50	222,698	215,874	237,250	120,564	51,613
Malwattu Oya	Kappachchi	819	1944-50	14,854	35,239	118,673	166,091	7,985
Malwattu Oya	Tekkam	1,186	1945-50	18,004	45,265	174,254	184,840	9,354
Walawe Ganga	Embilipitiya	610	1942-50	104,405	194,448	222,151	125,379	83,239
Gal Oya	Inginiyagala	384	1937-46	63,802	128,584	166,817	111,084	152,395
Gin Ganga	Agaliya	263	1927-50	195,689	180,207	147,381	77,562	59,250
Nilwala Ganga	Bepageda	158.7	1940-51	71,936	61,361	62,901	34,855	26,143

TABLE VI—Continued

Average Monthly Flows in Ceylon Rivers

River	Gauging Station	Mar.	April	May	June	July	Aug.	Sep.	Annual Average Ac. ft.
Kelani Ganga	Nagalagam Street	227,753	276,583	556,775	555,739	373,812	379,295	312,220	4,555,855
Kelani Ganga	Glencorse Estate	74,058	194,778	346,250	468,995	427,220	517,489	469,299	3,579,022
Mahaweli Ganga	Peradeniya	61,707	79,195	77,772	134,586	198,070	264,985	173,012	1,752,860
Mahaweli Ganga	Gurudeniya	76,446	94,572	86,316	207,599	244,092	336,202	201,411	2,094,637
Malwattu Oya	Kappachchi	27,769	13,164	9,389	3,965	3,236	3,146	539	404,050
Malwattu Oya	Tekkam	32,169	16,202	11,161	6,023	4,017	4,013	1,145	506,450
Walawe Ganga	Embilipitiya	118,331	189,500	140,845	83,357	56,601	68,177	51,417	1,437,850
Gal Oya	Inginiyagala	83,052	77,151	40,836	17,597	14,717	15,813	12,875	884,723
Gin Ganga	Agaliya	73,006	122,090	224,042	160,158	104,151	101,800	95,080	1,540,416
Nilwala Ganga	Bepageda	36,502	44,460	66,317	70,443	32,689	32,163	32,834	582,604

grown on the basis of natural water supplies alone, in the Dry Zone and indeed in many places in the Wet Zone, paddy cultivation depends completely on irrigation.

In the Dry Zone, most of which is very flat, large amounts of alluvium have been deposited by the rivers. These deposits make excellent paddy fields, but the rainfall is only about 60 inches per year and badly distributed, about 80% occurring in five months during the northeast monsoon. The ancient inhabitants of the island learned early that life and cultivation in the Dry Zone are only possible if water is stored for the needs of the people, cattle and crops during the dry season. In most of the island wells cannot provide enough water, because of the nature of the subsoil.

In ancient times reservoirs were built almost everywhere by damming the valleys of the rivers with earth levees provided with masonry spillways. The number of such reservoirs or "tanks" is very large. More than 10,000 are known; many are now ruins but more than half are in operation today. Their size varies from a capacity of only a few acre feet to nearly 100,000. Often there are several tanks built on the same stream.

But the ancient irrigation works were not confined to tanks. The tanks themselves were generally on small rivers or tributaries, construction on the main rivers being apparently thought too risky or being beyond the powers of the ancient Sinhalese. In consequence the catchment areas were often inadequate for the size of individual tanks; hence water was diverted from neighboring valleys by overflow dams or anicuts through long canals, called Ela, joining one valley to the other. Some canals are more than 50 miles long, with low grades and excavated very accurately. In the Dry Zone, the hilly area between two watersheds is generally low and the excavation of canals through the hills is not very difficult.

It can be assumed that not all the tanks now known were ever in operation at the same time. Apparently the construction and the decay of many tanks is a consequence of migrations of popu-

414

lation following wars or epidemics. After the collapse of the last great age of the Ceylon kingdoms in the 13th Century, most of the ancient tanks and irrigation works fell into ruins in the course of the next few centuries. When the Portuguese landed on the island at the beginning of the 16th Century very few irrigation works were in operation. The Dutch, coming after the Portuguese in the middle of the 18th Century, were more interested in agriculture and started some irrigation works to encourage it. The British succeeded the Dutch about 1800 and in 1857 undertook a program for the restoration of the old irrigation works.

Work of the Irrigation Department. The Department of Irrigation was created in 1900, becoming part of the Ministry of Agriculture and Lands in 1932. Until 1931 the Irrigation Department was almost exclusively engaged in the repair, maintenance and operation of the ancient irrigation schemes. About 100 main irrigation schemes, called major works, were completed during this period; in 1930 the area of paddy fields sown under these works was 162,797 acres. Besides the major works the irrigation department repaired many small or minor irrigation works, tanks and anicuts. Drainage of land and exclusion of salt water were undertaken in other areas.

Construction, maintenance and operation of the major works is the responsibility of the Irrigation Department. The owner of the irrigated land contributes by an assessed annual rate towards the cost of maintenance. The contribution is generally low, the maximum being theoretically five rupees but actually 3.5 rupees per acre.

About 125 irrigation schemes are classified as major works, among which are 108 tanks, whose capacity varies from a few acre feet to more than 72,000 acre feet. Their total capacity is about 660,000 acre feet; they irrigate about 200,000 acres of paddy land.

The minor or village works include all the small village tanks and some small canals fed by anicuts for the irrigation of a few acres of land. The construction or the remodelling and improvement of these works is done by the Irrigation Department, but the villagers maintain and operate the works under the supervision of government representatives. The Irrigation Department is in charge of the maintenance of the masonry structures.

Village works are numerous; at present 6,524 village tanks are in operation. In the year 1947-48, 648 village tanks were repaired or improved, in 1948-49, 44 and in 1949-50, 37. For the same years anicut schemes repaired or improved numbered 666, 60 and 52, respectively. In 1950-51, 275 village works (tanks and anicut schemes) were under construction or repair. Studies were made on 338 schemes and preliminary investigations on 247.

The area of paddy land irrigated under the village works is about 400,000 acres. The rate of development of the irrigation schemes is given by the following figures showing the acreage of paddy land under irrigation:

Year	Major Works	Minor Works	Total Irrigated Acreage	Rainfed Lands	Paddy Total
1937-38	170,426	370,000	540,426	270,000	810,426
1946-47	181,290	390,000	571,290	361,587	932,877
1949-50	209,027	397,040	606,067	361,587	967,654

Irrigation received a new impulse under the six-year program adopted in 1947, which aimed to provide with irrigation facilities 142,496 acres of land between the years 1947-48 and 1952-53. Table VII shows the details of the program as revised. With the completion of this program, 76,688 acres of new paddy lands will be irrigated under 24 different schemes. Many other more routine works of less magnitude in the major and minor works classes are to be carried out at the same time by the Irrigation Department. Most of the irrigation schemes listed in the first six-year program are of the same kind as those completed before, i.e. remodelling and improvement of old schemes.

The Gal Oya Project. The largest scheme commenced under this program, the Gal Oya project, is different from previous ones

416

both in its magnitude and in the way the construction has been carried out. An earth fill dam 3,600 feet long and 154 feet high (above the lowest level of the foundation) has been constructed, providing a storage capacity of 770,000 acre feet. The volume of the earth fill is about five million cubic yards. At the foot of the dam is a power plant of 10 MW. The irrigable area is 120,000 acres, of which about 86,000 acres are new lands to be reclaimed from the jungle.

On the new lands colonists will be settled by the government, each being provided with four acres of irrigated land and three acres of non-irrigated land for dry farming, together with a house, cultivation implements and an allowance and subsidy to start cultivation. The schedule provides for the settlement of 25,000 families in about ten years. The clearing and levelling of some 200,000 acres of high and low land in the jungle has to be done in the same time. A new organization, the Gal Oya Development Board, with a large degree of autonomy, was set up to carry out the construction, maintenance and operation of this scheme.

The construction of the dam, spillway and power plant was entrusted to an American contractor working with his own staff and with modern mechanical equipment. Construction is now complete and the first two generating units are being installed in the power plant. The excavation of the main canals, the secondary canals and the field ditches has been started. The felling of the trees and the clearing and preparation of the land are progressing.

Costs for the irrigation works alone are estimated at about Rs. 133,000,000. The original estimate of the cost of the works given to the contractor (i.e., the dam, the spillway and the power plant) was U.S. $10.5 million, or about Rs. 50 million, but this has since risen to about Rs. 70 million. No accurate estimate of cost can be given for the excavation of the main canals, the branches, tributaries, field ditches and the construction of the different structures needed to provide the irrigation facilities, because the designs are not completed. A rough estimate is about Rs. 63 million giving a total of Rs. 133 million.

417

TABLE VII

Irrigation Department Revised Program of Works—1947-53

Name of Work	Estimated Cost in Rupees	Total Irrigable Acres Under the Scheme	Total Irrigable Areas Provided with Irrigation Facilities Prior to 1947 or Existing Paddy	Balance Irrigable Area to be Provided with Irrigation Facilities from 1947	Total for six years 1947-53			Balance Irrigable Area to be Provided with Irrigation Facilities after 1953
					Paddy Area	House and Garden Acres	Total Acres	
Giritale Scheme, N.C.P.	500,000	779	—	779	779	232	1,011	—
Parakrama Samudra Scheme, N.C.P.	9,600,000	18,150	4,100	14,050	14,050	7,959	22,009	—
Elahera Scheme, N.C.P.	3,650,000	4,725	389	4,336	4,336	2,612	6,948	—
Raja Ela Scheme, N.C.P.	420,000	1,140	326	814	—	814	814	—
Minneriya, Stages II & III	1,900,000	4,167	—	4,167	4,167	1,708	5,875	—
Kagama Extension Scheme	1,900,000	3,288	1,623	1,665	1,665	882	2,547	—
Nuwerawewa Extension	1,005,000	1,563	907	656	656	528	1,184	—
Bathmedilla Scheme, Uva Province	1,175,000	1,264	—	1,264	1,264	627	1,891	—
Minipe, Stages I & II	895,000	3,425	2,277	1,148	1,148	267	1,415	—
Ridigendi Ela Scheme	3,000,000	5,000	1,693	3,307	2,870	1,060	3,930	437

TABLE VII—Continued

IRRIGATION DEPARTMENT REVISED PROGRAM OF WORKS—1947-53

Scheme								
Dewahuwa Scheme, C.P. & N.C.P.	3,506,000	2,335	—	2,335	2,335	1,412	3,747	—
Gal Oya Scheme, E.P.	133,000,000	120,000	33,000	87,000	21,000	15,600	36,600	66,000
Kantalai Extension Scheme, E.P.	19,500,000	24,000	4,909	19,091	3,000	3,750	6,750	16,091
Allai Extension Scheme, E.P.	14,119,000	18,525	4,025	14,500	4,750	1,750	6,500	9,750
Huruluwewa Scheme, N.C.P.	10,000,000	10,000	—	10,000	4,000	1,600	5,600	6,000
Murapola Scheme, C.P.	1,860,000	578	—	578	578	1,210	1,788	—
Unnichchai Extension Scheme, E.P.	225,000	2,206	—	2,206	2,206	1,055	3,261	—
Welipatanwila Sheme, N.W.P.	150,000	633	—	633	633	—	633	—
Kottukachchiya Scheme, N.W.P.	180,000	850	117	733	733	399	1,132	—
Kattiyawa Tank, N.C.P.	438,000	500	—	500	500	300	800	—
Kumbukkan Oya Extension Scheme, Uva P.	260,000	1,600	782	818	818	310	1,128	—
Karachchi Extension Scheme, N.P.	3,500,000	5,000	—	5,000	2,000	1,500	3,500	3,000
Attaragalla Tank, N.W.P.	780,000	1,200	—	1,200	1,200	600	1,800	—
Kandalama Tank, C.P.	5,800,000	4,000	—	4,000	2,000	1,200	3,200	2,000
	216,363,000	234,928	54,148	180,780	76,688	47,375	124,063	103,278

419

The construction of the works by the contractor was completed in due time, but the construction of the irrigation canals, which are the responsibility of the Irrigation Department, is behind schedule. The main reason given for this delay is that the engineering plans were not delivered in due time by the Survey Department. The Survey Department, in charge of the survey and the drawing of the engineering plans, is overwhelmed by uncoordinated requests coming from every department.

If by 1953, at the end of the first three years, present plans are fully carried out, 77,000 acres of an ultimate 181,000 acres of new paddy land will be provided with irrigation facilities. This will leave roughly 104,000 acres to be cared for in subsequent years.

Future Developments Programmed. A second six-year program is under study and a tentative draft is given in Table VIII. The necessary studies are not complete and the cost figures of new schemes are only rough estimates. This program comprises, first the completion of the irrigation schemes started in the first six year program (Gal Oya, Allai, Kantalai, Hurulawewa, and Iranamadu extension), and second, three new schemes: Padawiya, Pavatkulam, and Walawe Ganga.

The main project in this second six year program is the Walawe Ganga scheme. It contemplates the construction across the Walawe valley of an earth fill dam designed to store about 260,000 acre feet of water that could be used for the irrigation of 53,000 acres of paddy land. Of these 40,000 would be new lands. The construction of the dam would also permit control of floods that each year damage the cultivated lands in the downstream area of the valley. The government estimates the cost to be about Rs. 117 million. Specifications are ready and the construction is scheduled to start in 1953.

Near Embilipitiya, at the dam site selected, the valley is broad and flat. The dam would be 104 feet above the lowest level of the foundation in the river bed, but the extensions of the dam on the two banks would be lower. The total length of the dam would

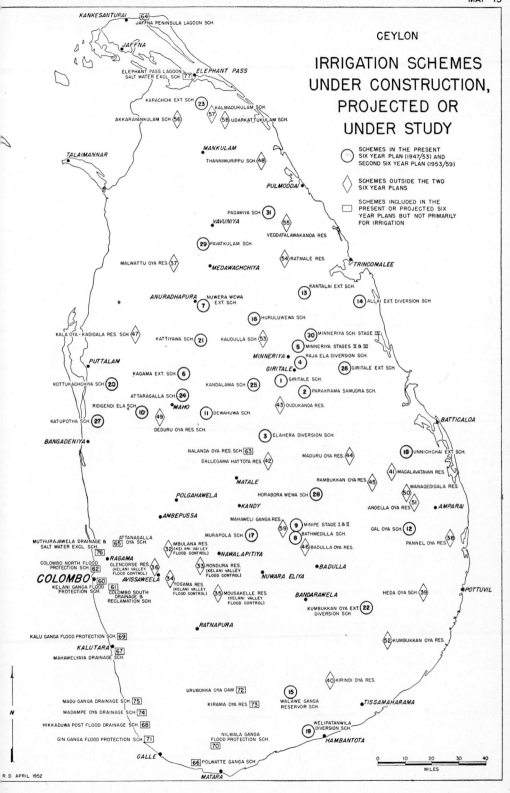

MAP 13

CEYLON

IRRIGATION SCHEMES UNDER CONSTRUCTION, PROJECTED OR UNDER STUDY

SCHEMES IN THE PRESENT SIX YEAR PLAN (1947/53) AND SECOND SIX YEAR PLAN (1953/59)

SCHEMES OUTSIDE THE TWO SIX YEAR PLANS

SCHEMES INCLUDED IN THE PRESENT OR PROJECTED SIX YEAR PLANS BUT NOT PRIMARILY FOR IRRIGATION

KANKESANTURAI 64
JAFFNA PENINSULA LAGOON SCH.
JAFFNA

ELEPHANT PASS LAGOON 77 ELEPHANT PASS
SALT WATER EXCL SCH.

KARACHCHI EXT SCH 23
KALMADUKULAM SCH.
57
AKKARAYANKULAM SCH. 56 58 UDARKATTUKULAM SCH.

TALAIMANNAR

MANKULAM
THANNIMURIPPU SCH. 48

PULMODDAI

PADAWIYA SCH. 31
VAVUNIYA 55
VEDDATALAWAKANDA RES.
29 PAVATKULAM SCH.

MALWATTU OYA RES. 37 MEDAWACHCHIYA 54 RATMALE RES.
TRINCOMALEE

KANTALAI EXT SCH.
13
ANURADHAPURA NUWERA WEWA 14 ALLAI EXT. DIVERSION SCH.
7 EXT. SCH.
16 HURULUWEWA SCH.
30 MINNERIYA SCH. STAGE IV
KALA OYA - KADIGALA RES. SCH. 47 KATTIYAWA SCH. 21 KAUDULLA SCH. 53 5 MINNERIYA STAGES II & III
MINNERIYA 4 RAJA ELA DIVERSION SCH.
PUTTALAM GIRITALE 26 GIRITALE EXT. SCH.
KAGAMA EXT. SCH. 6 1 GIRITALE SCH.
KOTTUKACHCHIYA 20 KANDALAMA SCH. 25 2 PARAKRAMA SAMUDRA SCH.
ATTARAGALLA SCH 24 43 OUDUKANDA RES.
RIDIGENDI ELA SCH. MAHO BATTICALOA
KATUPOTHA SCH. 27 10 49 11 DEWAHUWA SCH.
DEDURU OYA RES. SCH.
BANGADENIYA 3 ELAHERA DIVERSION SCH.
NALANDA OYA RES. SCH. 63 MADURU OYA RES. 44 18 UNNICHCHAI EXT. SCH.
DALLEGAMA HATTOTA RES. 42 41 MAGALAVATAVAN RES.
MATALE RAMBUKKAN OYA RES. 45 50 MANAGEDIGALA RES.
POLGAHAWELA HORABORA WEWA SCH. 28 51
KANDY ANDELLA OYA RES. AMPARAI
AMBEPUSSA MAHAWELI GANGA RES.
MINIPE STAGE I & II GAL OYA SCH. 12 38
ATTANAGALLA MURAPOLA SCH. 17 59 9 BATHMEDILLA SCH. PANNEL OYA RES
MUTHURAJAWELA DRAINAGE & 65 OYA SCH. 8
SALT WATER EXCL. SCH. 76 IMBULANA RES. 46 BADULLA OYA RES.
RAGAMA 32 (KEI ANI VALLEY
COLOMBO NORTH FLOOD GLENCORSE RES. FLOOD CONTROL) NAWALAPITIYA
PROTECTION SCH. 62 (KELANI VALLEY 36 33 RONDURA RES. BADULLA
COLOMBO 60 FLOOD CONTROL) (KELANI VALLEY HEDA OYA SCH. 39
KELANI GANGA FLOOD AVISSAWEELA YOGAMA RES. FLOOD CONTROL) NUWARA ELIYA POTTUVIL
PROTECTION SCH. 61 (KELANI VALLEY
COLOMBO SOUTH FLOOD CONTROL) 35 MOUSAKELLE RES. BANDARAWELA
DRAINAGE & (KELANI VALLEY
RECLAMATION SCH. FLOOD CONTROL) KUMBUKKAN OYA EXT. 22
RATNAPURA DIVERSION SCH.
52 KUMBUKKAN OYA RES.
KALU GANGA FLOOD PROTECTION SCH. 69
KALUTARA 67
MAHAWELYAYA DRAINAGE SCH.
40 KIRINDI OYA RES.
URUBOKKA OYA DAM 72 15
MADU GANGA DRAINAGE SCH. 75 WALAWE GANGA
MADAMPE OYA DRAINAGE SCH. 74 KIRAMA OYA RES. 73 RESERVOIR SCH. TISSAMAHARAMA
HIKKADUWA POST FLOOD DRAINAGE SCH. 68 WELIPATANWILA
GIN GANGA FLOOD PROTECTION SCH. 71 19 DIVERSION SCH.
NILWALA GANGA HAMBANTOTA
FLOOD PROTECTION SCH.
GALLE 70
66 POLWATTE GANGA SCH.
MATARA

N

0   10   20   30   40
MILES

R. D. APRIL 1952

TABLE VIII

Irrigation Department—2nd Six Year Program—1953-1959

Name of Scheme	Approx. Area for Development (acres)	Total Developed by Oct., 1953	1953-54	1954-55	1955-56	1956-57	1957-58	1958-59
Gal Oya	86,000	26,000	10,000	10,000	10,000	10,000	10,000	10,000
Allai	14,500	4,750	1,000	1,000	1,000	1,000	2,000	3,750
Kantalai	18,000	3,000	2,500	2,500	2,500	2,500	2,500	2,500
Huruluwewa	10,000	4,000	2,000	2,000	2,000	—	—	—
Iranamadu Extension	5,000	1,800	1,500	1,700	—	—	—	—
Padawiya	14,000	—	—	1,000	2,000	2,000	2,500	2,500
Pavatkulam	4,500	—	1,000	1,000	1,000	1,500	—	—
Kandalama	4,000	—	1,000	1,000	1,000	1,000	—	—
Walawe	40,000	—	—	—	—	4,000	4,000	5,000
	196,000	39,550	19,000	20,200	19,500	22,000	21,000	23,750

421

be 17,500 feet, including a central concrete section about 530 feet long for the spillway and the intake structures. The volume of the earth fill would be about 5 million cubic yards. The spillway, a concrete structure 412 feet long linked with the dam by two abutments, would be located about 600 feet southwest from the river bed, and equipped with nine radial crest gates, 40 feet long and four sluices. The irrigation outlet and the heads of the penstocks would be in another section 116.5 feet long.

A hydroelectric plant would be built and equipped with three units, only two to be installed at the first stage. Each unit would be a 3,750 kva vertical shaft alternator driven by a 4,700 hp Francis type turbine. The development of the scheme would be entrusted to a Board of the same pattern as the Gal Oya Development Board.

Expenditure Contemplated. We propose here to attempt an estimate of the total capital expenditure envisaged under schemes now under consideration. First, the past expenditure of the Irrigation Department is summarized in Table IX.

TABLE IX

EXPENDITURE OF THE IRRIGATION DEPARTMENT, SELECTED YEARS FROM 1899

Period	Year	Expenditures in Rupees
Crown Colony	1899	373,642
	1909	785,756
	1910-11	838,116
	1930-31	1,636,347
Donoughmore and Prewar	1931-32	1,567,629
	1939-40	3,204,434
Donoughmore and War	1940-41	3,387,709
	1946-47	14,541,791
Independence and Postwar	1947-48	25,446,101
	1948-49	50,099,673
	1949-50	43,818,804
	1950-51	68,000,000 (est.)
	1951-52	66,000,000 (est.)

Table X breaks down expenditures into the main items for the years 1947-48 to 1949-50. The figure for major works in 1948-49 is higher than in 1949-50, because of the heavy outlay needed to start the Gal Oya scheme. On the basis of the estimates for the year 1950-51 and 1951-52, corresponding figures will be respectively Rs. 58 million and Rs. 54 million.

TABLE X

MAIN CATEGORIES OF IRRIGATION EXPENDITURE,
1947-48—1949-50

Years	1947-48	1948-49	1949-50
Personal Emoluments	2,026,511	2,304,926	2,489,117
Maintenance	2,044,657	2,133,594	2,125,084
Other Charges	4,300,503	4,948,413	4,775,670
Total	*8,371,671*	*9,386,933*	*9,389,871*
Village Works	1,387,643	1,931,713	2,488,699
Major Works	14,686,787	38,781,027	31,940,230
Total	*16,074,430*	*40,712,740*	*34,428,933*
Grand Total	*24,446,101*	*50,099,673*	*43,818,804*

Expenditure on the construction of village works is increasing; thus the estimates of expenditure for the year 1951-52 provide more than Rs. 4 million for minor works.

No schedule of expenditure for the years following 1951-52 was available to the Mission. The second six-year program was still in process of preparation and no decision had been taken about it. Estimates are incomplete and the cost figures given are only tentative. Table VII has been presented by the Irrigation Department. Of the irrigation schemes started in the first six-year program, generally the head works are already in operation; the works needed to complete the projects are canals and structures providing the new lands with irrigation facilities.

According to the second six-year program, about 97,950 acres of new lands brought in under the earlier program have to be provided with irrigation facilities. On a basis of Rs. 600 per acre, these will cost a total of Rs. 58.77 million. The estimated cost of the Pavatkulam Scheme, which can be completed in the second six-year program, is about Rs. 6.6 million. Walawe Ganga is estimated at Rs. 117 million. But only 13,000 acres of new lands out of 40,000 could be provided with irrigation facilities in the six-year period. Thus the total cost for those years can be reduced by the cost of irrigation facilities for the remaining 27,000 acres, or by some Rs. 16 million. No estimate for the Padawiya Scheme is available. Assuming an expenditure of Rs. 6 million for the headworks and an average cost of Rs. 600 per acre for the irrigation facilities, the total cost for it would be roughly Rs. 14.4 million. Of this about Rs. 10 million would be spent in the first six years. On the above assumptions the total expenditure for the second six-year program will be:

Schemes	Acreage to be Made Available by 1959	Cost in Rupees
Completion of Schemes Started in the First Six Year Program	97,950	58,770,000
Walawe Ganga Scheme	13,000	101,000,000
Pavatkulam Scheme	4,500	6,600,000
Padawiya Scheme	10,000	10,000,000
	125,450	*176,370,000*

This would mean an average yearly expenditure of about Rs. 30 million for the second six-year program.

Several other classes of capital expenditure not included in the six-year program must be added to this estimate:

a) Village works, which should certainly be encouraged and may need up to Rs. 6 million per year.

b) Improvements classed as major works, Rs. 1 million to 2 million per year.

c) Works designed primarily for nonirrigation purposes (flood control, drainage, salt water exclusion, etc.) which can also be adapted for use in irrigation, e.g. the Nalanda Oya Scheme. This is designed to control the flow of the river through a storage reservoir which could also supply additional water to tanks in an adjacent valley; cost, Rs. 2 million to 3 million per year.

In total, therefore, an expenditure averaging about Rs. 40 million per year over the six year period commencing in 1953 would be needed to carry out all the projects now envisaged. This is for construction of irrigation works only and includes nothing for clearing, levelling and preparing the newly irrigated land or for settlement of colonists.

The settlement of a colonist on a holding of four to five acres of irrigated land and three acres of nonirrigated land is said to cost between Rs. 12,000 and 14,000. Subtracting irrigation expenses of about Rs. 4,000, the minimum expenditure for settlement must be taken as Rs. 8,000 per settler, or Rs. 1,600 per acre of new irrigated land. The second six-year program provides for the development of about 125,000 acres of such land. Settlement cost will run about Rs. 200 million, or, say a yearly expenditure of about Rs. 34 million. The irrigation program will therefor require a yearly capital outlay of about Rs. 74 million. This is not a recommendation of the Mission, but only a summation of the cost of proposed programs.

Problems of Implementation of the Program. It may be seriously doubted whether development could in fact be maintained at such an average rate. One limiting factor is the ability of the administration to carry through the necessary settlement of colonists at a rate of four to five thousand a year. That depends on problems of clearing, levelling, building and organization which are discussed in Chapter 12. Here we are more particularly concerned with the ability of the Irrigation Department to carry out its part of the work. We suspect that the number of schemes at present under investigation, study or construction will exceed its capacity. Starting works in many different locations causes a dispersion of staff and, as skilled and trained staff are scarce, construction must suffer. The normal technique of execution itself causes difficulties and leads to bottlenecks. Works are begun before preliminary studies are completed, sometimes because of political pressures. Later they have to be interrupted for months because of the lack of construction plans.

Sometimes delay in ordering heavy machinery causes interruption in the concrete work because of lack of data concerning the machinery. Studies are particularly hampered by the lack of adequate maps. The design section of the Survey Department is overwhelmed with requests and has insufficient staff to draw promptly the many plans needed. The whole Irrigation Department is kept busy meeting the requirements of construction works already started. No one has time to think about the coordination of the projects into a large program for the rational utilization of water in the island. In actual construction work, the dispersion of limited manpower and construction equipment leads to low efficiency. Means of concentrating work started at the same time need to be investigated.

Almost all the irrigation works have hitherto been constructed by the Irrigation Department with the help of small craftsmen. The Gal Oya Scheme is the first to be undertaken by a large outside contractor.

It is clear that the Irrigation Department labors under a heavy load. Much can be done, however, to relieve that burden. First, the creation of an organization charged with preparing a program for the rational utilization of the island's water resources as a whole would relieve the Irrigation Department of many investigations and studies that take time and staff. Second, increase of staff at nearly all grades is required. Third, a larger use of contractors would speed construction work and provide a large number of technicians and skilled laborers.

Determination of Priorities. Precise recommendations on priorities are difficult to make because so many schemes are projected or under study and too often the main data needed for a decision are missing. It will be the task of the proposed organization to integrate the different projects into a coordinated program. The Mission submits the following general observations and specific suggestions.

Some idea of the total acreage of potential new paddy lands can be obtained from consideration of the amount of water available in the island. We have shown (Section 3) that the total average discharge of the rivers flowing in the Dry Zone is about 13,735,000 acre feet. The losses by evaporation in reservoirs and distribution channels are heavy, because most of the tanks are shallow and offer a large surface of evaporation in proportion to their capacity, while some of the canals are created by building a single levee on the low side so that they are just a succession of shallow pools filling every depression of the ground. For the same reasons the losses by seepage are also heavy. If 30% is allowed for these losses, the water available is reduced to 9,614,500 acre feet. With the present duty of 12 feet, this could irrigate about 800,000 acres of paddy land. But that is a theoretical maximum, unattainable because it is impossible to store all the flood water even with a large reservoir capacity. A large part of the rain falling downstream of the reservoirs cannot be stored and will run straight to the sea. On the other hand, some part of the water can be used more than once. On balance, assuming no reduction of the irrigation duty, the development of new irrigation might reasonably be expected to double the present irrigated area—i.e., provide about another 600,000 acres of paddy land.

This estimate is very rough but shows that the water supplies are limited and that irrigation schemes must avoid the waste of water. It emphasizes the need for a program of rational utilization of water resources. Hitherto, most schemes have been just improvements of the ancient irrigation schemes. The policy of development is the same; tanks are rebuilt on the old locations near the paddy land; and most of the improvements are just increases of capacity which lead to a search for additional water, which has then to be found in an adjacent watershed.

To sum up, present development policy works from downstream to upstream. It should work just the reverse, starting upstream with a proper distribution of the available water. The policy of moving upstream was easy in the past when the irrigated area was small in relation to the available water resources, but as the area increases it will lead to confusion.

A prime necessity is a soil survey which will permit determination of the areas most suitable for irrigation and the amount of water required. Next there must be, in every area planned for new irrigation, a careful study of the irrigation duty appropriate to the local conditions of rainfall, evaporation, permeability of soil, etc. The standard duty used in paddy cultivation in Ceylon is wasteful of water, being five feet in *Maha* cultivation and seven feet in *Yala*. In some places the total is as high as 14 feet, while in others the farmers constantly complain about the shortage of water and ask for an increase of the irrigation duties.

Tests made on experimental farms show that a better yield can be obtained with much less water. If that experience is borne out in field practice, it should be possible both to improve yields and to irrigate more land with a given amount. The determination of the proper irrigation duty in every scheme will certainly take time and patience; authority and firmness will be needed to induce farmers to change centuries-old customs; but it will be work of the greatest value.

Once the areas and the irrigation duties are fixed, the amount of water needed is known and the study of the irrigation schemes can be started. The data about the rivers' discharges are basic for those studies; adequate means must be provided for their collection.

For the distribution of water some general rules have to be followed. The waters of a river should be used first for irrigation on the lands in its own valley, provided they have been ascertained to be suitable. Generally the fluctuation of the rate of discharge in the Dry Zone will require the construction of reservoirs to store the water. Reservoirs built by damming the main valley of the

river, where suitable sites can be found, are most efficient hydrau-
lically.

The construction of reservoirs in tributary valleys involves the
conveyance of water from the main river through anicuts and
feeder canals. The amount of water that can flow in the feeder
canal is limited and the longer the canal, the more limited is the
discharge.

Such canals will divert only part of the high waters, but will
take most and perhaps all of the discharge in low water periods.
Downstream areas will then suffer, because the floods will flow
almost without change, but no water will be left in the river bed
in the dry season. Irrigation schemes of this type will experience
difficulties, since a long time is needed to fill the reservoir. If the
high water period is late, cultivation will be delayed and its
efficiency will suffer. When the high water period is short, the
reservoir will not get filled.

When the reservoir is built in the main valley, it can be used to
control the floods. If its capacity is large enough, it can obviate
or mitigate most of them, especially if forecasts of floods are
available. It can be filled in a short time and will not delay the
beginning of cultivation.

When the storage is in a valley that is not part of the watershed
of the main river the effects are even worse. Generally the canal
will be longer; more water will be lost and the flow will be less.
The main valley of the river will be deprived of most of the
low water discharges and the drought will be more severe because
no drainage from the irrigated land can be expected. In high
water periods the floods will occur almost as before.

Water from one watershed should be diverted to another only
after careful study because it entails the creation of new water
rights that will be difficult to withdraw in the future. Only if
the needs of the main valley are met should a diversion be
made at all and then only to the extent that water is in excess
of those needs. Generally a reservoir will be needed with enough
capacity to store the excess of water during the high water period

for the time needed to convey it to the other watershed. The Nalanda Scheme is an excellent instance of what can be done along this line. It will supplement the flow of the Amban Ganga during the dry season and will spill the excess of the high waters in the Kala Oya watershed during the flood period.

All the above considerations show the need for coordination and the importance of preparing a program for rational water use. Such a study will take several years. Meanwhile it would be advisable to avoid starting new schemes which might be harmful to the program in the future. Under the existing policy of remodelling and improving the capacity of the old tanks, new lands of low grade may be cleared, put in cultivation and irrigated with water at the expense of far better lands discovered by the projected soil survey.

To avoid such lasting damage to future development, increased attention should be given first of all to the remodelling of the village schemes. Generally the amount of water needed is small and cannot seriously disturb a general program. The tanks to be repaired should be selected to avoid waste of water by evaporation and seepage. In some of the small, shallow tanks the loss by evaporation may be as high as half of the stored water. The cost of village works is generally low; they are mainly earth works that can be undertaken by villagers without large construction equipment. No settlement expenditure is involved in the improvement of village irrigation schemes and the lands that can be irrigated are generally already under cultivation in one fashion or another. The efficiency of irrigation is often higher in the village works where everyone is interested in the better use of the available amount of water. When the water is distributed by a national government agency, each farmer cares only about getting as much water as he can, the responsibility of providing it being the government's.

Second, major irrigation schemes can be carried out if they do not involve diversion of water from adjacent valleys. In planning such schemes care must be taken to avoid increasing the area under irrigation beyond the permanent availability of water. A sequence of wet years often tempts those concerned to increase irrigated lands to an extent which cannot be maintained when, in the usual cycle, a sequence of dry years follows and waste and complaints result.

The three new irrigation schemes that are included in the tentative second six-year program—Padawiya, Pavatkulam and Walawe Ganga—raise no problems of possible disturbance of a general program. The Padawiya and Pavatkulam schemes are small and will provide storage for two small rivers in the Dry Zone. We definitely recommend their construction.

The Walawe Ganga project, however, is dubious. Although it will not impair utilization of water in other valleys, grave doubts arise about its intrinsic economic merits. A figure supplied by the government puts the cost of headworks, power system and irrigation facilities at approximately Rs. 117 million. Since this estimate is unsupported by details, it is not clear how it was obtained. The Mission's own estimate, based on experience at Gal Oya and elsewhere, comes closer to Rs. 200 million. Until convincing estimates of costs are available, the Mission has serious reservations as to the economic merits of the project.

Even apart from these misgivings there are doubts about technical aspects of the scheme which point to the necessity of a comprehensive review. The quality of the soil is questionable; the dam site is not a good one; and the valley is broad and flat and thus not suited to a reservoir. The Walawe Ganga runs across the foothills of the central mountains in an area where erosion is said to be high. The capacity of the reservoir is about one-third that of Gal Oya, but twice as much water will flow through it. With an equal ratio of silt per unit the siltation of the Walawe reservoir will be about six times heavier. On the Gal Oya, analysis shows content of silt varying from 70 to 600 parts per million in weight, but the silt content of the Walawe Ganga has not been investigated. With a rate of erosion of 10 tons per acre, found in a neighboring valley, the life of the reservoir will be about 150 years. This figure is given only to show that the question of siltation must be studied to prevent future difficulties. For all these reasons, it is advisable to delay construction of the Walawe Ganga scheme pending the completion of the following studies:

a) a soil survey of the land in the area to be irrigated;
b) a study of erosion in the upstream watershed and of the resulting siltation of the reservoir;
c) an aerial survey of the valley to ascertain that no better dam site can be found.

These studies can be carried out in two or three years. The delay will give an opportunity to study any difficulties that may be encountered in the Gal Oya scheme, and to work out improved techniques for handling large schemes like the Walawe Ganga. It will also permit further consideration of the question whether the large capital sums involved could not be spent to far greater effect on other, more economic irrigation projects. If this recommendation is accepted we urge that, to avoid a reduction in the acreage of new irrigated land to be provided under the six-year program, a number of smaller irrigation schemes be started as soon as the necessary studies and surveys can be made. It should not be difficult to find in the Dry Zone schemes capable of developing say 10,000 to 13,000 acres of paddy land within three years of commencement and, we should hope, more within the six-year period. If this is done, a sum of about Rs. 50 million might be substituted for the Rs. 101 million shown (p. 424) as the partial cost of Walawe, to cover the smaller schemes to be substituted, other schemes which may be begun but not finished by 1959, and any work which may be started later on a modified Walawe project.

Map No. 13 and Tables VII and VIII show the irrigation schemes under construction under the first six-year program, together with those projected for the second six-year program or now under study. The number of projects already at some serious stage of consideration is large and many others could be added.

432

In the largest valleys of the island, especially the Mahaweli Ganga, there are both sizeable areas of land and substantial unused water resources available for irrigation. It is a matter of urgency to prepare a comprehensive program for their rational utilization, on the basis of full surveys as proposed above. In a few years it will be too late, as the water resources will have been put to use in a dispersed and wasteful fashion.

Finance Required for Program Recommended. If the suggestions we have made above are accepted the revised estimate of costs of irrigation works to be undertaken in 1953-59 will be:

	Million Rs.
Completion of Schemes in the First Six-year Program	59
Pavatkulam Scheme	7
Padawiya Scheme	10
Other Schemes to be Completed by 1959	20
New Schemes to be Initiated but Not Finished before 1959 (including possible modified Walawe Ganga Scheme)	30
Village Works	36
Improvements Included in Major Works	10
Nonirrigation Schemes	15
Total	*187*

The connected cost of development clearing, soil preparation, housing, etc. is dependent on the two factors of total acreage and cost per acre. As to the first, the acreage made available under these proposals should be no smaller, indeed we hope it would be larger, than under the proposals listed on page 424. As to the cost per acre we have recommended elsewhere that a reduction be made in the cost of settlement per colonist; but since much of that reduction should, it is suggested, be gained by reducing the standard allocation of land, the cost per acre would not be greatly reduced. We think it should be sufficient to provide Rs. 190 million for development costs, over the six years in place of the Rs. 200 million on page 425.

433

ADMINISTRATION

Organization of the Irrigation Department. The Irrigation Department is under the supervision of the Ministry of Agriculture and Lands. The head of the Department is a Director who is assisted by a deputy director and two assistant directors. The internal organization consists of a central unit and five auxiliaries.

The central unit is concerned with the maintenance, operation and extension of the existing major works and with the restoration and improvement of minor works. It is divided into seven territorial divisions headed by divisional engineers, each subdivided into units headed by irrigation engineers.

The five auxiliary branches are as follows:

(i) *Major construction.* A senior construction engineer heads this branch. Under him are construction engineers in charge of the individual schemes. The construction of the Gal Oya scheme is being carried on by a contractor under the supervision of a resident engineer. A divisional engineer is in charge of the construction of the canals system.

(ii) *Designs and Research.* The research and designs sections are in the charge of senior engineers. The research section includes a laboratory for hydraulic and soil tests.

(iii) *Training technical staff.* Training classes are provided for irrigation learners and cultivation officers.

(iv) *Cultivation and minor works.* These works are in the charge of the cultivation officers and irrigation engineers.

(v) *Plant and machinery.* The mechanical branch, headed by the chief mechanical engineer, is responsible for the maintenance and repair of all mechanical plant and vehicles and the training of mechanics and operators.

The internal organization of the Irrigation Department follows the pattern generally adopted for such a department. Subject to any conclusions which may be reached by the special mission now reviewing the organization of the department, we believe it adequate to carry out the irrigation schemes. On the side of general planning and coordination, however, it needs strengthening. At present the preparation of construction plans and regular duties relating to irrigation schemes require the full attention of the department; no one has any time to think about the general policy of development.

The Director of Irrigation recognizes this weakness and has asked for the creation of a planning section. It has been suggested that a planning section should be provided under one of the international technical aid schemes and that it should consist of seven trained experts; a project planning engineer, a design engineer, a flood control engineer, a hydroelectric engineer, a geologist, an economist and an agricultural economist. The creation of some such organization is highly advisable, but its field of activity would stretch far beyond the normal work of the Irrigation Department. We therefore recommend that it be kept outside of the Irrigation Department and that it form part of a more comprehensive water resources planning organization discussed below.

Staff. The permanent staff of the Irrigation Department numbers about 1,600 people, exclusive of the manpower used in actual construction. About 100 are engineers or assistant engineers, of whom some three fourths work in the territorial divisions and subdivisions. About 15 are stationed at headquarters in the Design and Research and the Plant and Machinery Sections. About 15 are assigned to construction schemes. The recruitment of staff is difficult and there is a shortage of trained people in every category, especially construction engineering. In 1950, on a trip to Europe, the Director of Irrigation tried to recruit 10 construction engineers but secured only three. Engineers with the training and know-how that comes only of long years of experience are particularly scarce. In part the shortage is the result of over-hasty replacement of British engineers who were formerly in the Department by young Ceylonese engineers. The latter, however well educated, do not have the skill and experience of the former British engineers and are in any case, far too few. Recruitment of non-Ceylonese engineers will therefore be necessary for a long time, but it is made difficult by the unattractiveness of the salaries offered. Except for senior construction engineers, who can earn 1,750 pounds, the salaries for construction engineers range from 700 pounds to 1,500 pounds a year (about U.S. $1,960 to $4,200). Even with free housing on construction works and some other privileges, the terms are not good enough to attract engineers with the necessary experience.

The practice of offering only temporary contracts of short duration, generally three years, also hampers recruitment. A well qualified engineer is usually employed in his own country at a good salary and with prospects of improving his situation. To induce him to leave his position he must be offered something materially better than he could normally expect by staying, because he knows that when he returns three or more years later it may be difficult to find a job with equally good prospects. The salary needs to be high enough to allow a margin for saving, and if he is interested in the work he is likely to want and should get a longer commitment. It is worthwhile to improve recruitment of engineers because bad engineers waste money and cannot properly train the people who are working with them. But good salary and adequate contract periods are not enough. Working conditions need to be such that the engineers can find real satisfaction in their work. They must be given responsibility and scope consistent with their abilities, and the means to carry out their tasks. Moreover, a country like Ceylon presents many special difficulties. There is a lack of skilled labor and equipment, and the engineer will sometimes have to supersede the foreman or the skilled laborer when their knowledge is deficient. To compensate for these difficulties, he must not be tied down by rules and red tape or feel that he has no backing behind him.

If Ceylon is unable to make the salaries and prospects sufficiently attractive, some of the international organizations may be able to help in engaging engineers. Even if they cannot provide men for construction jobs they may be able to secure them to train young Ceylonese engineers. They could also help to send the latter abroad for training.

It is not only engineers that are lacking but foremen and, in construction, the foremen are very important. Their training is difficult because they can acquire the needed practical know-how only on the job. Sending foremen to be trained in foreign countries presents a number of problems and is apt to be disappointing. Their training is best provided in Ceylon, where they should be used in construction works as assistants to trained foremen on the job. The international organizations might also be able to provide instructors for local training of Ceylonese foremen, but suitable instructors are not easy to find.

One way of training foremen and skilled labor that ought not to be neglected, is to increase the number of foreign construction contractors working on the island. When a foreign contractor undertakes a construction project in a country like Ceylon, which lacks the needed engineers, foremen and skilled labor, he sends out a carefully picked team of engineers, foremen and technicians. This nucleus recruits and trains the labor and complementary staff needed to carry out the work. When the foreign contractor leaves, there remains behind a corps of people well trained in different specializations. This procedure has a distinct advantage over the importation of instructors. Without elaborate precautions, it is easy to make a mistake in the choice of instructors, whereas the contractor has a direct interest in sending competent foremen who have usually been trained in working with him over a long period. Also, in choosing the complementary staff to be trained, the contractor has more freedom to dismiss and replace incompetent people.

Most young Ceylonese engineers are educated in Ceylon Technical College, a school under the supervision of London University. Engineers for irrigation work are trained in the department itself. Engineering appears not to have much appeal for young Ceylonese.

Most educated youths prefer the life of an office worker in town to that of an irrigation engineer, who must live in the country, often in uncomfortable temporary buildings, and work most of the time in rain and mud. This attitude hampers the development of the country. The educational system can help to develop a greater inclination among the youth for an engineering career. But it will take patience and time because of the barriers imposed by customs and prejudices arising from the long established cultural and religious concepts of the country. (See Chapter 4.)

Operation. The operation of irrigation schemes comes under the Irrigation Ordinance, last revised in 1938. Authority is vested in the Revenue Officer, who determines the distribution of water, the period of irrigation, etc. after consultation with the landowners and the Irrigation Department.

Owners are lax in observing the dates fixed for watering, and cultivation of the different plots of a given scheme is staggered. Hence the watering period is stretched beyond its proper limits and not enough time is left between the two cultivations for maintenance and repairs and for cleaning the canals. Sometimes the water stored in the tanks is insufficient to irrigate all the irrigable land. This is frequently true in Yala but can happen also in Maha in dry years or when the area under irrigation is excessive.

In such a case the Irrigation Department recommends a reduction of the cultivated area and estimates the acreage it is safe to sow. Its advice is not always followed, however, so that in the middle of the cultivation period, the area under cultivation may have to be drastically reduced to save the remainder of the crop. Waste of water, seeds and labor results, with loss to the economy and a reduction in the efficiency of the irrigation scheme. Sometimes a local shortage of manpower causes lands rented from nonresidents to lie uncultivated. This difficulty is increasing with the development of new settlements, which attract laborers by their superior advantages. Everything possible should be done to avoid such a situation. In view of the urgent need for extending paddy

438

cultivation, to leave irrigable lands fallow is intolerable. Obviously it is wasteful to spend large amounts of money on new irrigation schemes and settlements if their development reduces the areas under cultivation elsewhere. The remedies for these defects lie partly in the better enforcement of irrigation rgulations but to some extent they are outside the sphere of irrigation policy.

Maintenance and Revenue. Besides an adequate organization and staff, the financial and material means must be provided to carry out a development program. During recent years the financial provision in the budget for the Irrigation Department has been adequate, but it may be questioned whether it has been spent in the right way and especially whether enough has been devoted to maintenance. There is a common tendency to neglect maintenance for the sake of new works. A new scheme is, of course, far more striking than repairs, often invisible, in schemes already in operation over many years. But in irrigation, maintenance is vital. When maintenance is neglected the water seeps everywhere, efficiency is reduced and soon the schemes are in ruins. These mistakes of the past must be avoided in the future. Small sums spent today in correct maintenance will render unnecessary later expenditure of vastly larger sums to make good the consequences of neglect.

In each of the years from 1947-48 to 1950-51 the expenditure on maintenance was between Rs. 2 and 2.3 million. In the 1951-52 estimates Rs. 3 million are earmarked for maintenance. Contributions from the owners of lands irrigated under the major works are used to pay part of the cost of maintenance. The contributions vary according to the scheme. They are often as low as one rupee per acre and the maximum rate of five rupees per acre is never collected. For 209,027 acres irrigated in 1950-51 the contribution is estimated at 379,380 rupees, or about 1.8 rupees per acre. This is very low when compared with the benefits received and could be increased without hardship. It is impossible to estimate the amount that should be spent each year on maintenance of the widely varying schemes. But in a country with heavy rains, floods

439

and sustained heat, maintenance must receive constant careful attention. In the year 1950-51, for example, maintenance work encompassed some 109 miles of tanks embankments, 50 miles of flood levees, 1,206 miles of canals, and 342 miles of agricultural roads, as well as numerous anicuts and other structures.

We recommend therefore that the funds available for maintenance should if anything be increased. This might have to be at the expense of capital expenditure on new works, but we believe it would be possible and fully justifiable to augment the funds for maintenance by increasing the contributions collected from owners and occupiers of irrigated land.

Mechanical Equipment. Another difficulty encountered in the construction of the irrigation schemes has been delay in deliveries of heavy machinery, such as gates required for certain structures. These delays are very long. If added to the time needed to order the machinery they often total two years. Under present conditions early improvement in delivery dates is not to be expected. But a reduction should be possible in the time lost in red tape before the needed authorizations are given and the machinery ordered.

In some cases matters might be improved by giving the contractors more responsibility. Private concerns are more supple in their organization and often are able to order in a shorter time than a government agency.

The mechanical construction equipment now in operation in the Irrigation Department is in the charge of the Mechanical Branch; it is valued at about Rs. 40 million. [1]

This branch has charge of the maintenance and repair equipment and the training of operators, mechanics and drivers. Its

---

[1] This equipment includes: about 100 tractors, half over 89 hp; 28 excavators (capacity $1\frac{1}{2}$ to 5 cu. yds.); loaders; 60 dumpsters; 17 Euclid trucks (15 cu. yds.); 8 Caterpillars DW10 (9 cu. yds.). Besides other equipment not listed here, the Irrigation Department has 174 trucks and 36 cars or jeeps.

staff comprises about 1,800 people. The main repair shop is located in Ratmalana but temporary repair shops are installed on the site of works using much mechanical equipment. There is a striking diversity in the types of equipment used. Since this requires a large stock of spare parts, the inevitable delays in their delivery reduce the efficiency of maintenance and repair work. Standardization of equipment would meet this difficulty, and would also make it easier to train operators. It can best be approached gradually, by standardizing replacements as old equipment wears out. By this means, it should be possible, for example, to reduce the different types of trucks from 20 to three or four. The Mission recommends that this procedure be followed.

Efficient operation also requires that the equipment be adequate for the work and that the operators be properly trained. At present engineers in the subdivisions may lack information as to what equipment is most suitable or the best equipment may not be available. Often the operators do not have the knowledge and training to use their machinery efficiently and to preserve it. Heavy rains in the wet season and heat and dust in the dry season frequently cause interruptions of work. Therefore it is not surprising that efficiency is often low and cost per unit high. Better training of the operators, facilitated by standardization of equipment, could help materially. Improvement in the procedure for ordering spare parts is also much to be desired. Delays in delivery run as high as 18 months to two years, with expensive equipment lying idle meanwhile.

FLOOD CONTROL

Owing to the physical features of the land, Ceylon is visited by frequent floods which are difficult and expensive or impossible to control. With the mountains concentrated in the center of the island, the water from the heavy cyclonic rains runs off very rapidly into the surrounding flat coastal plains. There the water drains very slowly into the sea; further replenished by local rains, the rivers spill over their banks and flood the surrounding countryside. As the watersheds are comparatively small and subject to the same weather influences, it commonly happens that the whole watershed gets heavy rain simultaneously and control is almost impossible.

Table XI gives the flood records on some of the principal rivers.

TABLE XI

FLOOD RECORDS OF PRINCIPAL RIVERS

River	Location	Average Flow in Cu. Ft. per Sec.	Maximum Flood Discharge in Cu. Ft. per sec.	Date
Kelani Ganga	Colombo	6,292	220,000	17.8.47
Mahaweli Ganga	Paradeniya	2,421	180,000	15.8.47
Walawe Ganga	Embilipitiya	1,985	79,500	15.8.47
Kalu Ganga	Putupaula		99,000	16.8.47
Deduru Oya	Ganewewa		93,000	12.1.47
Nilwala Ganga	Bopagoda	806	88,000	16.8.47
Gin Ganga	Agaliya	2,129	49,000	18.5.40
Aruvi Aru	Tekkam	699	150,000	3.1.49
Gal Oya	Inginiyagala	1,223	86,000	2.2.38
Yan Oya	Pangurugaswewa		85,000	2.1.49

The last three rivers listed are wholly or mainly in the Dry Zone; it will be seen that the flooding there is as serious as in the Wet Zone.

Many studies have been made of possibilities of controlling these floods. The construction of reservoirs large enough to store the surplus water in the heaviest floods is virtually impossible because in the mountains the valleys are too narrow to provide large sites, while in the lower land only shallow reservoirs covering very extensive areas and requiring very long dams are possible. In both areas reservoir construction would swallow up very valuable land now under tea, rubber or other crops. Control by levees is equally difficult; they would absorb strips of the most valuable alluvial soil along all river banks. All tributaries and

442

branches in the coastal plain would have to be similarly treated and new systems of drainage would have to be constructed. Moreover, the prevention of flooding would put an end to the deposit of silt in the fields, which is of great value for the maintenance of fertility and the reclamation of marshes. Particular attention has been given to certain main rivers: the Kelani Ganga which threatens Colombo, the Mahaweli Ganga which threatens Kandy, the Kalu Ganga, the Gin Ganga and the Nilwala Ganga. In practically every case it has been concluded that the only practical course is to concentrate on local protection of the more heavily populated areas involved and in some cases to relocate settled areas and villages on higher land.

Some 20 different projects for Colombo have been studied and rejected in the last 50 years. The main area of flooding lies where the Victoria Bridge and the Sedawatta railway bridge cross the Kelani Ganga. Here the river is confined between two levees, that on the left bank being higher to give better protection to Colombo town. The channel at the Victoria bridge can take only about 60,000 cubic feet per second; the excess spills over the levees into the country north of Colombo to empty into the sea. In 1947, American consulting engineers studied a wide variety of methods of control, e.g. improvement of the existing river bed, excavation of a new floodway, extension of the levees upstream and control of the floods by reservoirs. They investigated seven dam sites and considered 15 different solutions; estimated costs varied from Rs. 44 million to Rs. 400 million. They concluded that the solution open to least objection was the construction at Glencorse of a reservoir with a capacity of more than 3 million acre feet to control a flood of the size of the 1947 flood. A hydroelectric plant was projected for a minimum output of 25.5 MW. Estimated costs were about Rs. 120 million, of which about half was required to buy land and to relocate villages, roads and railroads. More than 40,000 acres of cultivated land, including 16,000 acres of rubber, would be flooded in the reservoir. Villages and small towns like Avisawella would be destroyed.

In spite of many advantages, especially the possible generation of 200 million kwh of hydroelectric energy at low cost, the project was abandoned. Recently the project of excavating a new channel that would drain the floods into the sea in the vicinity of Colombo was revived. This would involve the enlargement or rebuilding of both bridges. Its cost would be quite disproportionate to the normal annual expenditure on flood control, which in 1949-50 was about Rs. 1 million, or to the actual value of the damage done by even the heaviest floods.

The best course would seem to be the unheroic one of accepting the fact that floods will occur, abandoning any idea of preventing them by reservoir construction (which would sacrifice an annual value in agricultural production far greater than the average annual loss by flooding) and concentrating on mitigating the effects of floods in populated areas. To this end, villages especially endangered should where possible be relocated, and protection by levee should be extended. Expenditure on this kind of work might be increased to Rs. 2 million per year. As to Colombo, the studies already made are exhaustive enough to justify a firm decision not to proceed with any major works designed purely for flood control. But if and when it becomes necessary to reconstruct the two bridges over the Kelani Ganga, a simultaneous enlargement of the river channel should be considered. We cannot recommend the inclusion of such reconstruction (estimated in 1948 to cost Rs. 200 million and almost certainly higher today) in a development program for the next six years, in which attention must be rigorously concentrated on investments of direct economic value.

The present gauge-reading stations should be fully maintained and communications from them improved so as to provide effective flood-warning and minimize loss of life and property.

DRAINAGE AND SALT WATER EXCLUSION

The coastal areas are very flat and lie close to sea level. Hence all along the coast there are swampy areas that cannot be cultivated.

444

There are also many lagoons where the sea water enters freely; over a period of time the tides and the floods have salted the land surrounding the lagoons and it has passed out of cultivation. The Irrigation Department has made many studies and prepared a number of reclamation projects, both for drainage of the low lands and swamps and for exclusion of the salt water from cultivable lands, especially in the southwestern and northern areas where pressure of population on cultivable land is most acute.

In the southwest most of the schemes are for drainage. Drainage by gravity alone is difficult, because the land is so low that the excavated drains, while working properly at low tide, cannot empty at high tide. Indeed the flow is often reversed at high tide and unless barred, salt water is poured onto the land. Therefore most of the drains must be provided with gates that open and close with the tide.

Such a scheme is under construction in the area north of Colombo, where about 6,000 acres are located between the two canals which connect Colombo and Negombo. They contain abandoned paddy fields, said to have deteriorated because of the embankment of the Kelani Ganga near Colombo. The levees prevent the silt being deposited in the fields but do not prevent flood damage. A floating plant called Salvina Auricula has developed in this area, covering the rice fields with a layer of peat and making it impossible to grow paddy. Drains have been excavated emptying into the Hamilton Canal; but when the gates at their outlets are closed the flow is reversed, threatening to bring salt water into the drains. This experiment is interesting and will show if the steps taken can arrest the deterioration of the land and secure its reclamation for the cultivation of paddy.

Other schemes of drainage are prepared or under construction south of Colombo along the southwest coast, e.g. the Mahaweli Ganga, Madu Ganga, Madampe and Hikkaduwe Ganga drainage schemes. Each of these schemes provides drainage for some thousands of acres, but so far there has been no general study and estimate of the total acreage of land that can be so reclaimed.

445

A general survey of the area that can be reclaimed should be started, coupled with a soil survey to establish whether the quality of the land is high enough to pay the cost of the works. In most of the areas, the land is so low that efficient drainage can be provided only by pumps. Pumping is expensive unless cheap power is available. Before starting reclamation on a large scale it must be ascertained that the land to be reclaimed will be able to grow valuable crops.

In the north, in the Jaffna peninsula, the situation is different. It is not swamps that have to be reclaimed but land surrounding large lagoons that becomes salted when the level of the lagoons rises with the tide or when floods occur in the wet season. These lands, if protected against the salt, can be washed and provide excellent grazing and arable land.

One scheme of salt water exclusion is already in progress in the Vadamaradchi lagoon, on the northeast coast, where a dam 610 feet long is under construction at Thondamannar. This dam is provided with 34 bays, some of which will be closed by gates and some by stop logs. The dam is intended to prevent the salt water from flowing into the lagoon and will allow the floods to empty into the sea. When completed the scheme will give protection to about 8,300 acres of cultivated lands and enable about 6,700 acres of land that are now useless to be put under cultivation. It is estimated to cost Rs. 1.4 million.

The construction of a similar dam at Elephant Pass, south of the Jaffna peninsula, is under consideration; it would reclaim about the same acreage of land as the Vadamaradchi Scheme.

The Mission recommends:

(a) a co-ordinated study of the numerous schemes already investigated, both in the southwest and in Jaffna, and the preparation of a long-term program of drainage and salt water exclusion;

(b) the completion of the schemes already described for the exclusion of salt water from the lagoons in the Jaffna peninsula;

(c) the deferment of any major drainage and reclamation

446

schemes in the southwest, pending review of the results obtained in those already completed or under construction, and pending also the preparation of a comprehensive program.

In the next few years, expenditures on drainage and reclamation schemes may be put at above Rs. 1 million per year.

PLANNING AND SURVEYS

Planning Section. An organization to prepare a program for the rational utilization of the water in Ceylon is badly needed. No inventory of the potential water power in the island exists. Even where studies have been made of individual watersheds, they have usually been specific in character, and water is taken for what appear to be the most urgent needs without any general plan. The area of the island is not so large as to require piecemeal consideration. If water is to be properly utilized it must be considered as a unit. The monsoon, the concentration of the sources of water in the central mountainous area, and the flatness of the low land are all favorable to the diversion of water from one watershed to another, as was common practice in ancient times.

Preparation of a basic program of development of the island's water resources must be carried out by a single organization. It is not possible in such a study to separate hydroelectric power from irrigation or from flood control. At present hydroelectric power is the responsibility of the Electrical Undertakings Department (EUD) under the supervision of the Ministry of Transport and Works; irrigation and flood control are the responsibility of the Irrigation Department under the supervision of the Ministry of Agriculture and Lands. In the EUD no proper hydroelectric power section exists; the Irrigation Department is fully occupied with the preparation, maintenance and operation of irrigation schemes. The organization to be created must not depend on any of these departments. It must be part of the independent Planning Section which we have recommended in Chapter 4.

The organization to be created might be called the Water Resources Planning Section. It should not be responsible for detailed study and design of particular hydroelectric plants or irrigation schemes, but should have charge of preparing for the whole island a program of development of the water resources.

The program should provide accurate information on:

a) Dams and reservoirs;
b) Hydroelectric plants;
c) Irrigation schemes;
d) Reclamation schemes;
e) Flood control schemes;
f) Water supply schemes.

It should show how the different schemes are linked together and how they must be carried out to provide a rational development of the island's water resources. To prepare such a program the planning section must be provided with all the data already collected by the different departments, especially the Irrigation Department. Maps must be available. For the study of irrigation a soil survey is needed.

The head of the Planning Section should be a man trained in the planning of large valley development schemes, and the Section should further include a project planning engineer, a design engineer, an irrigation engineer, a drainage and reclamation engineer, a flood control engineer, a dam engineer, a water supply engineer, a hydrologist and an engineering geologist. The economist and agricultural economist suggested earlier in this chapter for inclusion in the Irrigation Department's planning section would be better placed in an agricultural section or a general section of the planning department. All the experts will need to be recruited abroad; the international organizations can be of great help in obtaining them.

The preparation of such a program will take a long time because it will require many field investigations. The study of particular valleys requires an accurate knowledge of the sites, that can be acquired only by firsthand investigation, often long and tiring. The planning team must be provided with adequate staff and equipment to carry out the work. Survey teams will be used to make topographical studies of valleys and rivers where needed.

The complementary staff should be Ceylonese. To each foreign engineer should be attached a Ceylonese assistant who will thus obtain a good training and be able in the future to continue the work.

Since the investigations will take time, it is advisable to get started as soon as possible. The specialists needed should be engaged for the period needed to complete the program, say about three years. Until now too many experts have been called in to study particular schemes, remaining in the island too short a time to do an efficient job. A number of reports have been made in this manner and then shelved without bringing the country any benefit.

What is now needed is to design a program of rational utilization of the water resources that will coordinate the different schemes already studied and provided a guide for the better development of the island.

Surveys. As repeatedly shown, the lack of accurate large scale maps hinders the progress of many studies. An aerial survey is highly desirable and would be of great help for many studies, especially those concerned with the utilization of water for irrigation or water power. Very often the design of the works and the construction plans are delayed by the lack of engineering plans, which in Ceylon are on the scale of 4 chains to one inch. The drawing of these plans is the responsibility of the Survey Department, which comes under the Ministry of Agriculture and Lands, but is not subordinate to the Irrigation Department. The Survey Department is overburdened and is unable to prepare promptly the engineering maps needed for the design and drawing of the works.

To improve the situation is difficult, because of insufficiency of skilled staff to enlarge the Survey Department. The best that can be done is to try to reduce the duties of that department.

Preparation of a new large-scale map is imperative. The best map of the island is on the scale of one inch to one mile with contours at a vertical interval of 100 feet. This map is on too small a scale even for preliminary studies; the vertical interval is too large and in the flat area of the island is meaningless.

Today, whenever some idea of the level of the ground is necessary to preliminary study, a special survey must be undertaken. Such work could be saved in a large number of preliminary studies if an adequate over-all map were available on a scale of about one inch to 30 to 32 chains, with contours at an interval of 12 to 18 feet in the mountainous area and 6 to 9 in the flat area. The Survey Department could then concentrate on the larger scale engineering plans needed for the design and layout of the works. Its tasks could be further reduced if aerial survey and mapping were entrusted to a qualified private concern.

Summary of Recommendations

Planning and Surveys

1. A Water Resources Planning Unit should be established, working under the central economic planning organization proposed in Chapter 4 and charged with the study of all aspects of water utilization and control. It should include engineers, concerned with project planning, design, irrigation drainage and reclamation, flood control, dams and water supplies, a hydrologist and an engineering geologist. This Unit would take on the duties proposed by the Irrigation Department for a special Irrigation Planning Section within that department.

2. The present organization for recording the variations in the flow of the rivers should be maintained and extended as the foundation for a systematic survey of the available water resources of the island.

3. For the work of development of water resources as well as for other purposes, an early large scale aerial survey is imperative; for the proper selection of lands to be irrigated a full soil survey is also required.

450

Administration and Training

4. The Irrigation Department should be strengthened at all levels. In particular it is desirable to renew the recruitment on agreement of non-Ceylonese engineers to supplement the scarcity of trained Ceylonese and help in further training. Although the non-Ceylonese will not be employed permanently they will need to be offered attractive terms as regards length of service as well as salary and working conditions.

5. Efforts to train Ceylonese as engineers, foremen and other technicians should be intensified. In particular:—

(a) foreign engineers on agreement should be required to devote part of their time to training local men;

(b) young Ceylonese engineers should be sent overseas for specialized training; the assistance of international organizations should be enlisted for this;

(c) special attention should be given to the training of foremen, which can only be done in Ceylon; if outside contractors are employed on specific works they should be required to devote particular attention to training foremen.

6. To relieve the Irrigation Department while its staff is being built up and to help in training, more use should be made of outside contractors for specific construction jobs.

7. Improvements should be made in the organization of the mechanical equipment available to the department by allowing greater flexibility in the ordering procedure and by standardization of types.

8. Funds for maintenance of existing irrigation works should be increased, if necessary at the expense of new construction.

9. Immediate study should be made of the possibility of reducing the present standard irrigation duties in the established sources, which there is every reason to believe are excessive, wasteful of water and possibly damaging to the land.

Program of Development Works, 1953-59

10. Schemes started under the 1947-53 program should be completed.

11. The proposed Padawiya and Pavatkulam schemes should be undertaken.

12. Accurate cost estimates of the proposed Walawe Ganga project need to be prepared, and its technical merit has yet to be demonstrated by adequate soil surveys and other studies. The Mission strongly recommends that action on this project be deferred until these studies can be completed.

13. The general emphasis should be on the smaller schemes; in place of Walawe Ganga the Mission recommends the undertaking of several smaller schemes, which could make available within the program period as much land as Walawe Ganga and perhaps more.

14. Funds should be provided for continuation of village works, for improvements classified under major works and for the development for irrigation purposes of schemes of water use designed primarily for other purposes, e.g. flood control.

15. No major flood control schemes should be undertaken but increased funds should be made available for local protective works. The re-channelling of the Kelani Ganga near Colombo should be reconsidered if and when it is decided to reconstruct the two bridges over the river. Gauge-reading stations should be maintained so as to provide the most effective warning system.

16. Studies should be undertaken of drainage, reclamation and salt water-exclusion schemes both in the southwest coastal area and in Jaffna peninsula, with a view to drawing up a long-term program of work; and certain schemes already started or planned in the Jaffna area should be completed.

14. Power

Official policy in the field of electric power has been aimed at:

(i)   Substitution of hydro power for thermal power;

(ii) Electrification of areas not yet served; and

(iii) Provision of electric power for new industries and new uses.

Progress has been and is being made towards these objectives but they are to some extent conflicting. They cannot all be attained in a short space of time and the rate of progress towards their full attainment depends on how much of the country's available resources can be devoted to this purpose within the total development program. The problems involved are brought out by the ensuing analysis of present supplies, prospective needs and potential output.

THE PRESENT SUPPLY POSITION

We have to consider separately the areas covered by the Government Electrical Undertakings Department (EUD), the areas covered by municipalities and other public bodies, and the private supplies generated by estates, industrial concerns, etc. The capacity of the various categories of supply is summarized in Table I.

(1) *The Government Electrical Undertakings Department (EUD)* is an organization within the Ministry of Transport and Works but with separate legal personality, which operates the government-owned main thermal and hydro plants in Ceylon. The accounts of the Department have been merged in the central government budget since 1950-51. Accordingly the whole of its revenue is treated as part of general revenues of the government and the

453

TABLE I

INSTALLED ELECTRIC CAPACITY IN KW

Owner	Hydro Power	Thermal Power Steam	Thermal Power Diesel	Total
EUD	25,300	11,500	6,000	42,800
Municipalities and Urban Councils	—	—	10,000	10,000
Government Factories	—	—	3,600	3,600
Other	10,000[1]	—	77,000[2]	87,000
	35,300	11,500	96,600	143,400

[1] Drawn from *Fascinating Ceylon* by S. E. N. Nicholas, The Times of Ceylon Ltd., Colombo, 1950, p. 83. The original figures (13,000 HP) are for direct use of water power, and are here converted to electrical equivalents.

[2] Approximate estimate.

whole of its expenditure, both recurrent and capital, has to be voted by Parliament.

The Department is headed by a Chief Engineer and Manager, responsible to the Minister. He and all other members of the staff are employed under the normal conditions of the civil service in Ceylon. A reorganization of the Department aiming at technical decentralization is at present under consideration.

The responsibility of the EUD now extends to the Western, Central and Uva Provinces, and to the Jaffna Peninsula. This does not mean that the distribution network covers the whole areas of the provinces concerned, nor that all distribution networks in those provinces are directly owned and operated by the Department. Towns such as Kandy, Ratnapura and other small municipalities have their own power plants and distribution networks not yet connected to the grid operated by the Department.

Prior to 1950 the EUD area was served primarily by the

thermal power plants of Stanley, Pettah and Wellawatta with a total capacity of nearly 18,000 kw, against a total load, immediately before the war, in Colombo Town and the surrounding area of about 14,000 kw. With the opening of Ceylon's first important hydroelectric installation at Laksapana in October 1950 the use of the thermal plants was suspended and at the same time plans were made to satisfy an increased demand for power in the area.

This increase derived first from the Colombo area itself, where there had been a sharp increase of some 5,000-6,000 kw. Second, following its general principles of development, the Department arranged to extend its distribution network so as to make hydroelectric power available both to parts of its own area, such as Nuwara Eliya and Diyatalawa, which had hitherto run on diesel power, and to the previously independent municipal areas of Kandy and Ratnapura. This program provides for the construction, inter alia, of a 66 kv overhead line Norton Bridge-Peradeniya, a 33 kv line Avisawella-Ratnapura and distribution branches of the 33 kv overhead lines Norton-Nuwara Eliya and Nuwara Eliya-Diyatalawa-Bandarawela. Some of these overhead lines are still under construction (e.g. Norton Bridge-Peradeniya), while the 33 kv Nuwara Eliya network and the overhead lines Avisawella-Ratnapura and Nuwara Eliya-Bandarawela are planned for the near future. In addition, a number of routine constructions will connect new consumers in the area around Colombo Town.

This short-term program, when fully carried out, will considerably increase the load fed by the EUD power plants. In December 1951 the actual maximum peak load recorded at Laksapana Power Station was already some 22,000 kw. The new load to be shifted from thermal to hydro power new connection lines is about 3,000 kw; additional demand from new consumers in the next two years can be forecast as some 2,000-3,000 kw; and in the first few months of 1952, a power need of 3,000 kw has to be provided for the Colombo Plan Exhibition. Thus within a couple of years the total load to be met regularly by the EUD will reach the level of 28,000-30,000 kw. Power rates were low-ered in late 1951 and this will help to bring about an increase in demand.

From these figures, it appears that the normal capacity of the new Laksapana plant will fall short of requirements by some 6,000-8,000 kw. Moreover, its maximum output during a severe dry season may fall as low as 12,000-13,000 kw. The conclusion is unavoidable that the thermal power plants in Colombo will again be working in the next year, in parallel with the Laksapana Power Station.

Some of the most significant features of existing load graphs are shown in Charts 2, 3 and 4. The main feature of power demand in the areas concerned is a very high peak load during the evening hours, due to the combined load of fans and lights. While the average annual load factor of the Colombo area can be assumed to be 50%, for Ratnapura and Kandy it is only 30%. Interconnection of such towns as these with the EUD net-work will mean a reduction of the total load factor. On the other hand, the fact that prospective new consumers are mainly indus-trial will to some extent balance the negative influence of town loads. On balance, no considerable change can be foreseen for the next few years in the load factor of 50%. The general load curve to be fed in the future by the plants of EUD should increase this figure to a level of roughly 55%. Chart 5 (worked out by EUD) shows the expected load graph in 1956 compared with the present one.

The following figures show the comparative increases during recent years in total output and peak loads:

	Power Generated in EUD Plants (kwh)	Peak Loads (kw)
1948-49	57,075,779	13,400
1949-50	65,749,000	14,000
1950-51	90,000,000 (forecast)	21,000
1951-52	115,000,000 (forecast)	28,000

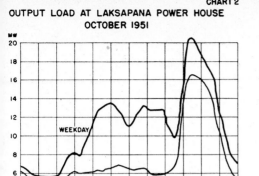

CHART 2

OUTPUT LOAD AT LAKSAPANA POWER HOUSE
OCTOBER 1951

CHART 5

EUD ANTICIPATED LOAD CURVE
1956

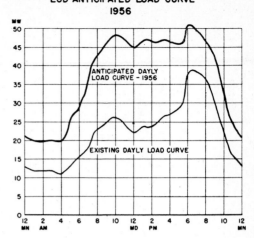

CHART 3

LOAD GRAPH – JAFFNA CITY
OCTOBER 1951

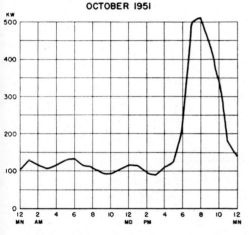

CHART 6

TOTAL LOAD GRAPH –
KANKESANTURAI POWER STATION, OCTOBER 1951

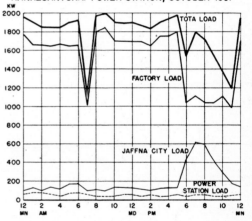

CHART 4

LOAD GRAPH – GALLE
OCTOBER 1951

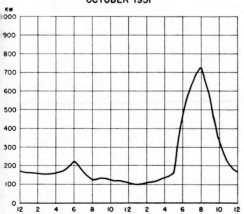

CHART 7

RECENT AVERAGE
CEYLON OUTPUT OF RUBBER, TEA & COCONUT

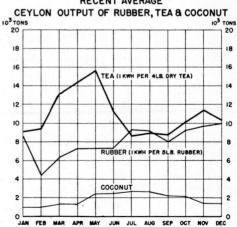

R. D. APRIL 1952

(2) *Municipal and Other Public Supplies.* Some 57 town districts, including Kandy, Galle and Jaffna, have electric power supplies independent of EUD, i.e. directly served by municipalities and urban councils or by private undertakings.

These all operate on diesel generators of different size. As a general rule, they possess a great number of small sets, perhaps as a result of gradual expansion. They serve to make spare plants available, thus avoiding trouble in distribution by breakdowns of machinery. While bigger towns are provided with power for industrial and domestic use and the power station runs all day, most distribution plants in small towns run only during the evening and night for domestic consumption. Operation and maintenance naturally suffer from such a system and generation efficiency is lower than it should be.

The size of the existing power plants and their limited utilization in a large number of towns suggests that power is not in demand and that further expansion and improvement of power production is uncalled for, but after visiting a great number of towns the Mission believes this impression to be erroneous. Small private power plants to supply rice mills, rubber and coconut factories, pumps, etc., operate close to the existing distribution network, and availability of more power would certainly stimulate new installations and the mechanization of equipment now operated by hand.

It is our general impression that the small undertakings are hampered in carrying out new construction either by a natural rigidity in their organization or by the regulations of the Electricity Act 1950, which require any new development to be submitted to the supervisory control of EUD.

Galle, with some small outlying towns, is provided with power by the Municipal Council Electrical Undertakings. A diesel power station of some 1,000 kw installed capacity operates with full load in the evening hours and a new 500 kw set is projected for early installation. In addition to existing demand, which is considerable, a brief inquiry on power needs in this area showed that better distribution facilities would very soon increase power demand all along the coast road from Galle to Tangalla to roughly 6,000-7,000 kw. Galle is a typical example of the limitation of power consumption due mainly to uncertainty of the responsible authorities as to what to do and how to do it.

Trincomalee represents a different kind of weakness. A small power station owned by the Municipality of Trincomalee runs 380 kw diesel sets to meet the peak load of 300 kw. The distribution network is on low tension and no initiative has been taken to meet the growing power demand because the supervisory authority of EUD has not decided on its desirability.

Trincomalee could get ample power from the large station operated by the Navy. This still feeds some parts of the town directly and the Navy could cover all additional power requirements of the town; the main obstacle to be overcome seems to be a difference of opinion with the EUD on the price of power.

Jaffna. Power for Jaffna Town is produced by the power station of the Cement Factory in Kankesanturai, delivered to this municipality by the Electrical Undertakings Department, and distributed by the Municipal Council. Differences of opinion and interests between the three bodies concerned make it impossible to carry out satisfactorily a sound program of development for the pressing needs of this thickly populated area, where power is a vital necessity for agricultural purposes.

Chart 6 shows a graph of the present situation in Jaffna peninsula. The cement factory is overwhelmingly the largest consumer; the needs of Jaffna Town and of agriculture are subsidiary. Considerable additional power could be provided if various factories now in contemplation in the area are constructed. Jaffna peninsula is too far from any hydro power resources to be served by other than thermal power sources.

Public power consumption, i.e. exclusive of power produced by private factories for their own consumption and by Kankesanturai

Power Station for cement production, may be summarized as follows:

Population of Ceylon	7,500,000
KWH generated by EUD, Municipal, Urban Councils and private Agencies	100,000,000
KWH generated per head of population	13
KWH sold per head of population in Colombo Area (1950)	146.5

Table II shows how this compares with some other countries.

TABLE II

AMOUNTS OF POWER GENERATED IN DIFFERENT COUNTRIES

Country	Population (*millions*)	KWH Generated (*millions*)	KWH Generated per capita
Ceylon	7.5	100	13
Korea	29.3	655	22
Turkey	20.9	789	38
Colombia	11.3	746	66
Mexico	25.4	4,428	172
Spain	28.3	6,312	223
Italy	46.6	28,338	610
U.S.A.	154.3	370,233	2,400
Norway	3.3	17,317	5,251

Source of data other than Ceylon and Korea: United Nations, *Monthly Bulletin of Statistics*, April 1952. Data for Ceylon and Turkey, Colombia, Mexico and Spain relate to 1950; for Korea, to 1949; for all others, to 1951.

These figures show that use of electricity is still very limited and point to very large possibilities of expansion of electric facilities.

(3) *Private Supplies.* The area of intensive cultivation as shown

in Map 11 is thickly dotted with power plants—some of considerable size—operated by tea factories, coconut oil mills, mines, rice mills, etc. for their own consumption. Were the distribution network sufficiently developed to reach them, these establishments could be directly fed from EUD supplies.

We have, in cooperation with officials of the EUD, made a tentative estimate of power production in these scattered private plants. Owing to the lack of full records of power consumption in the different factories, this estimate had to be based on data relative to the efficiency of engines, working hours, and the distribution of load in different hours and different seasons. In spite of these inevitably rough methods, it is believed the results approach the real figures fairly closely.

(a) *Tea factories*—In 1950 some 310 million lbs. of dry tea were produced by 950 factories. Our studies show an average power need for the production of dry tea of 1 kwh for 4 lbs. of tea. This indicates an energy production of some 75,000,000 kwh and a total installed capacity of nearly 50,000 kw.

(b) *Rubber factories*—Rubber production in 1950 was 113,000 tons of crepe or about 250,000,000 lbs. Some 5 lbs. of rubber are produced per kwh and gross consumption of energy is therefore some 50 million kwh. Installed capacity is accordingly estimated at 25,000 kw.

(c) *Coconut oil mills*—The difficulty of getting figures on coconut is greater than for tea and rubber, since the proportions of the several commodities produced vary with fluctuations in their market prices, and since the coconut industry (apart from the large oil mill in Colombo) is widely scattered in a great many small factories. Moreover, figures on internal consumption of coconut products are uncertain, and no data are available on output of coir fiber. Hence any estimate of power consumption must be very rough.

The British Ceylon Corporation, leading oil processor, shows a production of 18-19 lbs. of coconut oil per kwh. Figures obtained from a cursory investigation of small plants give the lower value of 14 lbs. per kwh. Taking into account all the difficulties, we hazard the following rough estimate.

Coconut oil production in a year:	250,000,000 lbs.
Energy needed, same period:	18,000,000 kwh
Load:	8,000-10,000 kw

An estimate of power needs for other products such as dessicated coconut, coir, etc., could be made only on the basis of a cautious percentage of the requirements for oil.

Chart 7 (worked out by EUD) shows in graphic form the average output by months of the main products: tea, rubber and coconut. The seasonal maxima of the different crops vary and thus help in evening the load graph.

(d) *Rice mills*—Some rice mills are operated with mechanical power; generally the peasant prefers to mill his rice in little diesel-operated factories or hand-operated mills scattered through the country.

An estimate based on sample data gives a production of some 2 lbs. of paddy (one of rice) for 1 kwh. Assuming an average working time per mill of 2,000 hours a year, with present annual production of approximately 15 million bushels of paddy, the real energy produced can be estimated at 7,500,000 kwh, under a load of some 3,500 kw. Allowing for the fact that some rice is milled by hand and should therefore be excluded from mill production, we may put the figure for power needs of rice mills at 7 million kwh.

(e) *Graphite mines*—The two important graphite mines in the country use some 400 kw. This industry is to be further developed in the near future and a considerable amount of power has been requested from the EUD.

(f) *Textiles, etc.*—Some small plants are also running for little undertakings such as textiles, saw mills, etc. but no specific data are available.

Summarizing, power consumption by existing factories in kwh equivalents is at present as follows:

	Output (kwh)	Installed capacity (kw)
Tea	75,000,000	50,000
Rubber	50,000,000	25,000
Oil	18,000,000	10,000
Rice	7,000,000	3,500
Others *	8,000,000	4,500
	158,000,000	*93,000*

* Including cement factory at Kankesanturai 6,000,000 kwh.

FUTURE TREND OF CONSUMPTION

The main influences on future power consumption in Ceylon will be:

(1) The spontaneous development of existing loads;

(2) Increase of load due to availability of new power; and

(3) Power needs of newly planned industrialization schemes.

(1) *Normal Growth.* Growth of power consumption has long been hindered because the erection of new power plants was delayed by the difficulties of getting materials and machinery after the outbreak of the second World War. In the EUD area the situation did not improve considerably until the end of 1950, when Laksapana began operation, and even today no considerable margin of hydropower is available. The total capacity upon which EUD can rely during an extreme dry season has been shown to be little more than 28,000 kw (12,000 hydro and 16,000 thermal).

Assuming a very low average rate of increase of demand of 6% yearly, in five years the spontaneous growth of load in the existing network of EUD should absorb all the hydro and thermal power now available. New overhead lines to those districts not yet provided with power will need to be planned and carried out in step with the construction of new power plants.

(2) *Availability of New Power.* The optimistic outlook held by some that the additional 25,000 kw installed at Laksapana had resolved the power problem in the south central area for a long period, was proven wrong in only one year's time. Even if new power were available to an amount of, say 30,000 kw and 150,-000,000 kwh, it would be absorbed very quickly by the ever-growing demand of existing consumers and factories now operating on their own resources.

But there are other important considerations. The shift to electric operation of plants now running with other means will be stimulated by the higher efficiency of electric motors and all the improvements such a system entails. Consider for instance the tea industry: data collected by EUD on tea factories already converted to electric energy show a gross average figure of 6 lbs. of made tea per kwh. Previous data collected by ASEA in the electrified Midford tea factory show nearly 5 lbs. per kwh consumption for power and light. But other ASEA figures show that if the firing and withering of tea were done by electricity, much more power would be required. Average data show that, while power and light alone require only 1 kwh for 5 lbs. of tea, withering requires 3.5 kwh and firing 4.5 kwh.

In both the coconut oil and the rubber industry, concentration of production in larger factories appears likely because of the higher efficiency of the larger units. This will hasten electrification since, while concentration improves mechanical efficiency, it also requires technological improvements which absorb further amounts of power. Moreover, merely making power available encourages the setting up of all kinds of new facilities, such as new public lighting and household installations. Experience shows that generation of new electric power automatically creates new demands.

Taking these considerations into account, it is a realistic assumption that demand by consumers in the EUD's present area will increase by a further 75,000,000 kwh. Substantial increases in demand could also be expected if the EUD were able to offer an unrestricted supply to local authorities within or adjoining its area. The present levels of consumption in these adjoining towns are:

	kwh
Kandy	2,500,000
Galle	1,500,000
Ratnapura	400,000
Kegalla	120,000
Diyatalawa	430,000
Kurunegala	550,000
Total	*5,500,000*

Account has also to be taken of losses in distribution and stand-by capacity. In so wide an area, with a medium distance of about 40 miles between the main hydroelectric source (Laksapana) and the gravity center of load, and with a high-tension distribution network (132 & 33 kv) of some 600 miles, experience suggests a loss figure of about 18%, to include losses in low-tension distribution. Stand-by capacity is obviously necessary to cover possible breakdowns and errors in estimates of demand which can easily occur.

Allowing for expanded consumption by municipalities, distribution losses and the need for stand-by capacity, total needs for new power in the EUD area up to the time of completion of the additional power station planned at Laksapana (Stage II A), i.e. in four to five years' time, may be put at 150,000,000 kwh, with a peak load of 35,000-40,000 kw. We presume that thereafter 30,000,000 kwh per annum of additional power will be needed to meet the demands of new customers. On these assumptions a reasonable forecast for the next 10 years is:

	kwh
Existing demand	100,000,000
First 5 years' demand	150,000,000
Next 5 years' demand	150,000,000
Total	400,000,000
Losses (18%)	72,000,000
Generation need	472,000,000

Load = 110-120,000 kw
Installed capacity = 150,000 kw

(3) *New Industries.* This estimate does not take into account the development of large industrial schemes which, if carried out, will require additional power and necessitate the provision of even larger power plants. A number of such projects have been proposed for either government or private execution. In Table III we attempt to evaluate the power requirements of those proposals now being seriously considered.[3]

---

[3] These estimates are based on data from the following publications:

1. National Fertilizer Association of U.S.A.
2. Federal Power Commission, *Power Requirements in Electrochemical, Electrometallurgical and Allied Industries,* 1938.
3. Federal Power Commission: *Industrial Electric Power,* 1939-1946 and *Statistical Abstract of the U.S.,* 1951 (U.S. Department of Commerce).
4. U. S. Bureau of Mines Report.
5. Westinghouse Electrical International Co.
6. U. S. Interstate Commerce Commission Statistics.
7. Quaderni della Guinta Tecnica del Gruppo Edison—Milano.
8. Documentation technique de EDF—Paris—*Consommations Specifiques d'Energie Electrique.*
9. M. de Leener—*L'Influence du Cout de l'Energie Electrique sur le Bilan Economique de la Nation.*

Information has also been supplied by Mr. Peterson of the British Electricity Authority.

TABLE III

CONSUMPTION OF SELECTED INDUSTRIES AND RAILROAD TRANSPORT

Products or Operation	kwh required per unit of output *
Ammonium Sulphate	700-750/LT
Nitrogen—existing synthetic ammonia plants in U.S. at capacity operation	1530/ST
Nitrogen—synthetic ammonia using electrolytic hydrogen	1500/ST
Caustic Soda, electrolytic	3000/4000/LT
Synthetic Ammonia (Fauser process)	13,000/14,000/LT
Cast and Alloy iron	
Duplex	50/115/ST
Batch-cold melt	500/600/ST
Cast Steel	
Duplex	75/150/ST
Batch-cold melt	500/700
Steel ingots	
Duplex	100/210/LT
Batch-cold melt	550/700/LT
Rolling mills (from ingot to structural)	85/100/LT
Sugar (beet)	120-150 LT
Oil extraction (copra)	120/LT
Textiles	
Spinning	0.55-0.63/lb.
Weaving	0.45/lb.
Knitting	0.20/lb.
Ceramics	
Architectural	300/LT
Industrial	730/LT
Paper (newsprint)	1500/LT
Rubber Processing (crepe—Ceylon)	450/LT

* Abbreviations: LT, long tons; ST, short tons.

TABLE III—Continued

Products or Operation	kwh required per unit of output *
Rubber Processing (U.S.A.)	2910/LT
Cardboard (Europe)	300/1000/LT **
Paper and Cardboard (U.S.A.)	820/LT
Acetic Acid (by distillation)	25/LT
Cement Portland	30/100/LT
Cement Average (U.S.A.)	120/LT
Railways	
Freight ⎫ Passenger ⎬ Europe (suburban traffic)	0.065/0.095/LT mile 0.80/passenger mile
Freight ⎫ Passenger ⎬ U.S.A.	0.46/LT mile 0.22 passenger mile

* Abbreviations: LT, long tons; ST, short tons.
** Depending upon thickness of paper and kind of raw material.

These figures give some idea of the large amounts of power that would be needed by the principal industries now being planned. Without data on expected total output, of which only fragments are available, total power requirements cannot be estimated. But one or two illustrations indicate that it would be a very large total indeed.

The Colombo plan for Ceylon included a fertilizer project to produce 80,000 tons of ammonium sulphate a year; this plant alone would need roughly 60,000,000 kwh. A steel mill is projected with electric melting ovens needing 10,000 kw. Normally such plants run with a load factor of 55% and on that assumption, the project would need some 50,000,000 kwh.

These figures bring out strikingly how important it is that any discussion of new industrial plants start with an exact evaluation of the power needs involved. Certainly the availability of power cannot be taken for granted.

(4) *Conclusions on Consumption Trends.* The existing power plants are no more than sufficient to cover for a few years the natural increase of demand in the EUD area and cannot provide any considerable increase of load in the remaining parts of the country. In two years, since no new power resources will be available in that time, a shortage of power is threatened. There can therefore be no possibility in the near future of the complete replacement of thermal by hydroelectric power. On the contrary, in order to reduce as much as possible the period of limitation imposed on the development of the country, it is essential that all existing diesel power plants now out of operation be kept in good maintenance and fit to run in case of emergency.

It is also important to draw up a balance sheet of power availability and power demand over the next few years. Power available will include existing plants, planned new developments at Laksapana on a realistic construction time schedule and multi-purpose schemes such as Gal Oya and Walawe. On the demand side, power needs for normal development in the surrounding areas and especially in the Colombo area should be realistically assessed and the size of industrial plants fixed according to the ascertained availability of power, allowing for seasonal variations.

The multi-purpose schemes are more suited to feed local industries than to be tied up to the EUD grid, as will be shown in more detail in a subsequent section of this chapter.

Jaffna and Trincomalee need special consideration. In the Jaffna area there are plans for DDT, caustic soda, and chlorine factories in the neighborhood of Elephant Pass, and the existing cement factory is to be enlarged. All these will demand increased power. It is evident, however, that the supply to the northern part of Ceylon of hydroelectric power, which can only come from the center or south, will be possible only when large amounts of power are available in excess of the needs of the more southerly area. It will, moreover, have to come over 132 and 220 kv overhead lines, which will be economical only when large quantities of power are available for transmission. The time when such excess will be available from the centers of hydroelectric generation is very distant and the needs of Jaffna must for a considerable period be met by other means, i.e. by generation of thermal power by high efficiency plants erected for such of the development schemes as appear to be economic.

In Trincomalee development plans will be dependent on whether, when and how industrial developments take place, including the possible exploitation of ilmenite. In the short term any such new plants should be provided with thermal power. The well-equipped harbor, the availability of fresh water and the proximity of Indian coal resources, all indicate that steam generation plants would be most suitable for this spot. The hill area, where hydropower plants could be developed in the future, is more than 100 miles from Trincomalee and if only a little power were needed, the construction of very high-tension overhead lines would not pay. A possible long-term plan for providing Trincomalee with hydro power is sketched in below.

How To Meet Power Needs

(1) *Introduction.* As already indicated the aims of current policy include (a) the establishment in the shortest possible time of hydro power plants large enough to dispense with the importation of fuel for power production and (b) the provision of power for industrialization. Are those aims reconcilable one with the other? And if not, which has to give way? If the main purpose is to avoid importation of fuel, any industrialization program will have to be delayed for a good many years; if industrialization is overriding, it will be necessary to construct new thermal plants and accept the necessity of continued import of fuel for a further period.

Leaving aside political and military considerations, the answer to these two questions depends on problems of both time and money, on the allocation of developmental resources best calculated to benefit the people of Ceylon economically.

(2) *Potential Hydroelectric Power in Ceylon.* The potential hydroelectric development in the island has not hitherto been investigated with any accuracy. No inventory of the potential water power that can be harnessed has been made and all the figures given in this field are mere guesses without firm basis. In the reports of the UN Economic Commission for Asia and the Far East (ECAFE) Ceylon is given a potential water power of about 1,000,000 kw. In other reports about 500,000 kw are suggested.

In 1949 the EUD listed the potential water power sources for electrical development as shown in Table IV. (See also Map No. 14)

TABLE IV

ESTIMATED POTENTIAL HYDROELECTRIC POWER

	Power in 1,000 HP
Aberdeen-Laksapana	200
Teldeniya	160
Kitulgala	50
Ulapana	40
Haragama	36
St. Clair Falls	10
Gal Oya	9
Elgin Falls	8
Beliprul Oya	6
Walawe Ganga	6.5
Heda Oya	5
Perawella	4
Unichchai	3
Dunhinda Falls	1.8
Total	539.3 *(say 400,000 kw)*

Few of these schemes have been investigated with any accuracy and detailed information is available only for Aberdeen-Laksapana, Gal Oya and Walawe Ganga.

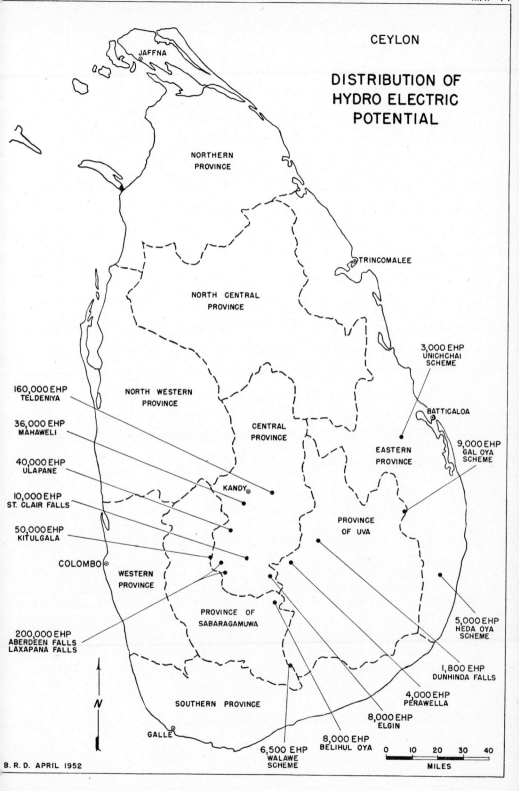

MAP 14

CEYLON

DISTRIBUTION OF
HYDRO ELECTRIC
POTENTIAL

JAFFNA

NORTHERN
PROVINCE

TRINCOMALEE

NORTH CENTRAL
PROVINCE

3,000 EHP
UNICHCHAI
SCHEME

160,000 EHP
TELDENIYA

NORTH WESTERN
PROVINCE

CENTRAL
PROVINCE

BATTICALOA

36,000 EHP
MAHAWELI

EASTERN
PROVINCE

9,000 EHP
GAL OYA
SCHEME

40,000 EHP
ULAPANE

KANDY

10,000 EHP
ST. CLAIR FALLS

PROVINCE
OF UVA

50,000 EHP
KITULGALA

COLOMBO

WESTERN
PROVINCE

200,000 EHP
ABERDEEN FALLS
LAXAPANA FALLS

PROVINCE OF
SABARAGAMUWA

5,000 EHP
HEDA OYA
SCHEME

1,800 EHP
DUNHINDA FALLS

N

4,000 EHP
PERAWELLA

SOUTHERN PROVINCE

8,000 EHP
ELGIN

GALLE

6,500 EHP
WALAWE
SCHEME

8,000 EHP
BELIHUL OYA

0   10   20   30   40

MILES

B. R. D. APRIL 1952

Another list (set out in Table V) is given in the pamphlet, *Fascinating Ceylon*, by S. E. N. Nicholas.

TABLE V

CLASSIFICATION OF HYDROELECTRIC SCHEMES BY HEAD PRESSURE

Head Pressures	No. of Schemes	Estimated Output
		(in 1,000 HP)
2,000 to 1,000 feet	13	307
1,000 to 500 "	18	168
500 to 100 "	5	258
Under 100 "	1	3.5
Total	*37*	*736.5 (say 555,000 kw)*

The mountainous concentration in the center of the island with the higher peaks forming a high peneplain surrounded by a second peneplain at lower level is basically favorable to the development of water power. The schemes with the higher heads are found between the highest and the intermediary steps, the most favorable area being the south of the mountains where the two steps are closer and the slopes steeper. But the total area of the highest step and the catchment areas upstream of the points where development is possible are small as is therefore the discharge in the rivers. In such areas the grade of the river bed is high and the valleys are deep and narrow, so that the reservoirs that can be constructed will need high dams but have only small capacities and will be expensive in relation to the storage provided. Possible sites for the utilization of the rivers can be found in the lower peneplain also, but the head will be low and most of it will have to be provided by the construction of dams. Such plants are generally expensive if the construction is required for hydroelectric purposes only, but in the areas in question the reservoirs so built will have substantial capacity and can be used also (or primarily) for irrigation and/or flood control.

The wide fluctuations in the flow of the rivers (see Chapter 13)

471

create problems of equalization of the output of hydroelectric power. At first glance it might be expected that the different rainfall regimes of the different parts of the island would make it possible to find rivers with watersheds where the period of maximum flow occurs when the water is at the lowest level in other watersheds, so enabling output to be maintained at a steady level by interconnection of the different plants. Unfortunately, as shown in Chapter 13, the two periods of low water, February and September, are substantially the same for all the rivers of the island. Some equalization of output could be provided in February by plants working in conjunction with irrigation schemes when water is needed at that season for irrigation, but in September it is not possible to expect such regulation.

The development of the different hydroelectric schemes will therefore generally require the construction of reservoirs for the regulation of the river flow. To harness a river on the minimum discharge only means a waste of power which Ceylon just cannot afford. Installations designed to utilize the maximum rates of discharge will develop more total power, but the minimum power will be the same unless the flow of the river can be regulated by reservoirs. If regulation by pondage or storage is not possible, the output has to be equalized by thermal plants and the full benefit of the hydroelectric power is not obtained. Maximum use of reservoir storage for regulation of the flow should therefore be planned, subject of course to suitability of dam sites and costs of construction. But one must bear in mind that some years are very wet and some others very dry and there are very large variations in the discharges of the same river from one year to another. Several dry years may occur one after the other and the storage of water from the wet years to the dry years is generally impossible. Accordingly, even with the maximum use of storage, the amount of hydroelectric power available will vary a good deal in different years.

No country can rely wholly on hydro stations for its electric power unless it has potential water power far in excess of its needs or possesses rivers of extraordinarily steady flow. Ceylon is not provided with an excess of potential water power and the flow of its rivers is very irregular. It is therefore not possible to look to meeting all the island's power needs with hydroelectric plants. Thermal plants will continue to be necessary to supplement the output of the hydro plants and assure a steady total output of power at all times. The more reservoirs that can be built for the regulation of the flow of the rivers, the less thermal plants will be needed, but a certain ratio between thermal plants and hydroelectric plants has to be maintained. Experience in a number of European countries which enjoy large hydroelectric potentialities suggests that the economical utilization of hydro power calls for stand-by thermal plants with an installed capacity of 30% of the maximum hydro installation.

(3) *Individual Hydroelectric Schemes.* Apart from small hydroelectric plants on certain tea and rubber estates, before 1950 only two hydroelectric plants had been installed for public use. The first is the Nuwara Eliya plant working under a head of 250 feet, with an equipment of two water turbo-driven alternators, one of 250 kw and the other of 80 kw and a diesel-engine-driven alternator of 225 kw. The plant is very old and of small importance. It is used to meet the needs of Nuwara Eliya and its output in 1949-50 was about 1.4 million kwh. The second was installed in Norton Bridge for the construction of the dam and of the Laksapana Scheme and had four turbine alternator sets of 250 kw. The output of the hydro plants and assure a steady total output of ceased operation since the completion of Laksapana.

a) *Laksapana.* In October 1950 the Laksapana Plant, the first major hydroelectric plant of Ceylon, was put in operation, being the first stage of a larger hydroelectric project. It works on a head of about 1,500 feet, this being the difference between the levels of two rivers, the Kehelgamu Oya and the Maskeliya Oya, which run in narrow valleys parallel to each other but at different levels and separated by a narrow ridge. A gravity dam in concrete has been constructed to bar the Kehelgamu Oya at Norton

473

Bridge. The dam site is in a narrow gorge followed by a stretch with a high grade. The dam is 114 feet high above the lowest part of the foundation and its crest is 2,844 feet above mean sea level. The total storage capacity is 31.9 million cubic feet and the effective capacity is 13.6 million cubic feet. From this small reservoir the water is taken by a tunnel, surge chamber and penstocks to the power station in the Maskeliya Oya valley, flowing eventually into the Maskeliya Oya at a level of 1,240 feet. The station has three units each of 8,333 kw capacity.

The flow needed to generate this total power of 25,000 kw is 250 cubic feet per second and the effective capacity of the Norton Bridge pond, 13.6 million cubic feet, corresponds to about 15 hours of run at full power without any inflow. The Norton Bridge reservoir provides enough pondage to meet the diurnal variation of the load but is not large enough to provide any seasonal regulation. The catchment area of the Kehelgamu Oya is about 52 sq. miles. The maximum flow recorded is 25,000 cubic feet per second but the minimum flow is as little as 32 cubic feet per second. Although wholly in the Wet Zone and enjoying a high total rainfall the variations in the flow of the Kehelgamu Oya are still very great and long dry periods occur when the flow is inadequate to sustain the normal output of the plant. With a load factor of 50%, which is about the load factor of the connected network, the plant is able to meet the requirements of the load curve when the flow is not less than 125 cubic feet per second. At that rate of flow the full capacity of pondage in Norton Bridge has to be used to maintain the plant in full operation at all times of the day. If the flow falls below that level, the help of thermal plants will be needed to maintain output. From December to April the possibility of such an occurrence is high. In 1922, for instance, there were 11 days with a flow of between 58 and 32 cubic feet per second. But the flow of the Kehelgamu Oya during the high water period is enough to provide the water needed during the low water period if that water can be stored.

Accordingly a further stage in the Laksapana development,

CHART 8

CEYLON HYDRO ELECTRIC SCHEME (STAGE IIA)

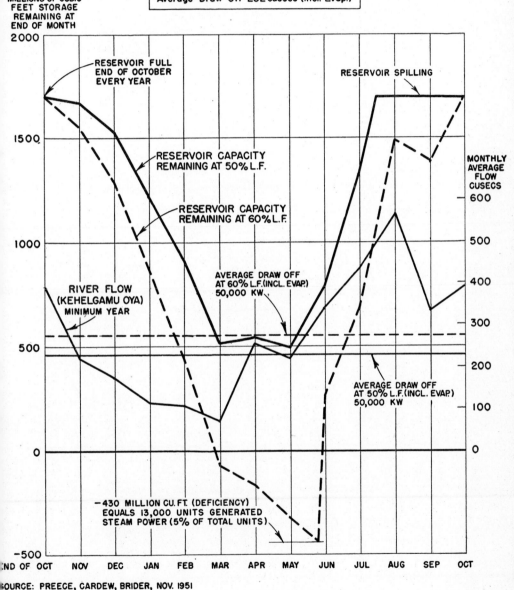

CASTLEREAGH STORAGE RESERVOIR

Absolute Capacity 2,000,000,000 cu. ft.
Effective Capacity 1,700,000,000 cu. ft.
Maximum Output 50,000 KW
Normal Load Factor 50%
Average Draw Off 232 cusecs (Incl. Evap.)

MILLIONS OF CUBIC FEET STORAGE REMAINING AT END OF MONTH

RESERVOIR FULL END OF OCTOBER EVERY YEAR

RESERVOIR SPILLING

RESERVOIR CAPACITY REMAINING AT 50% L.F.

RESERVOIR CAPACITY REMAINING AT 60% L.F.

MONTHLY AVERAGE FLOW CUSECS

RIVER FLOW (KEHELGAMU OYA) MINIMUM YEAR

AVERAGE DRAW OFF AT 60% L.F.(INCL. EVAP.) 50,000 KW

AVERAGE DRAW OFF AT 50% L.F.(INCL. EVAP.) 50,000 KW

−430 MILLION CU. FT. (DEFICIENCY) EQUALS 13,000 UNITS GENERATED STEAM POWER (5% OF TOTAL UNITS)

END OF OCT   NOV   DEC   JAN   FEB   MAR   APR   MAY   JUN   JUL   AUG   SEP   OCT

SOURCE: PREECE, CARDEW, BRIDER, NOV. 1951

B. R. D. APRIL 1952

known as Stage IIA is planned to provide such storage. The dam site selected is at Castlereagh, about four miles upstream from Norton Bridge. A dam about 130 feet high will provide a storage capacity of about 2,000 million cubic feet and an effective capacity of 1,700 million cubic feet. This will make it possible not only to regulate the flow needed for the generation of 25,000 kw with a load factor of 50% but to double the generating capacity of the Laksapana Plant. Tenders have already been invited for this construction.

Chart 8 shows the average draw off curves of Laksapana Stage IIA, assuming 50% and 60% load factors and minimum annual flow for the Kehelgamu Oya. [4] As no exact reference is given to the frequency curve of river flows, the statements which follow are very cautiously framed on the basis of normal experience in hydro power plants of similar size and features. The total output of Laksapana Stage I and IIA is given in Table VI according to varying assumptions.

TABLE VI

LAKSAPANA I & IIA OUTPUT, ASSUMING MINIMUM
RIVER FLOW AND DIFFERENT LOAD FACTORS

Load Factor %	Possible Output kwh x 10^6	Integrated Output by Thermal kwh x 10^6	Total
45	200	—	
50	220	—	
55	240	—	
60	247	13	260
65	247	33	280

The table shows that the projected plants can guarantee, with a 55% load factor, a maximum of 240 million kwh delivered on the spot without constantly using thermal plants. Assuming that

---

[4] As calculated by Consultant Engineers Preece, Cardew & Rider, London.

the records of minimum gauges are valid for many years to come, a higher utilization of Laksapana could be expected by intergration of its output with thermal power during hydrologically normal years. Gaps in hydrological records do not enable us to fix the definite size of the thermal electric plants necessary for this, but Table VI has been worked out on the assumption of the 30% ratio mentioned earlier.

The construction of Castlereagh Dam will also provide an opportunity of developing further generating capacity by utilizing the head between the Castlereagh level and the Norton Bridge level (Stage IIB of the Laksapana development). The mean level of the water in the reservoir as planned will be 3,575 feet above sea level. Between this and the mean level at Norton Bridge, 2,840 feet, there is a head of 735 feet and preliminary study shows that this can be harnessed with a new plant, situated at Norton Bridge, that will be able to generate about 25,000 kw. The construction of this scheme is so closely linked with that of the Castlereagh reservoir that the two might proceed simultaneously. The intake works will be part of the Castlereagh dam and there will be no need either of diversion structures or new pondage, the pondage of Norton Bridge being large enough to compensate the differences between the flow needed in the new plant and the one needed in Laksapana at the beginning and at the end of each load variation.

With a load factor of 50%, that is with conditions of consumption as at present, the yearly output of Laksapana plant is about 100 million kwh. With the construction of the Stage IIA, i.e. the construction of the Castlereagh Dam and the increase of the power installed in Laksapana plant by another 25,000 kw a further 100 million kwh per year will be provided. The construction of Stage IIB, i.e. the harnessing of the head between Castlereagh and Norton Bridge, would add another 100 million kwh.

b) *Gal Oya.* The second hydroelectric plant presently under construction is the Gal Oya scheme. This plant is almost completed with a reduced installed power and is expected to be in operation in the summer of 1952. The head for this hydroelectric plant is provided by the new Gal Oya dam built to provide storage of 770,000 acre feet of water primarily for irrigation. The full supply level is at 260 msl and the level of the water at the head of the irrigation canal is at 150 msl, giving a head available for the generation of power of 110 feet at the maximum but falling to 50 feet or lower as the reservoir is drawn upon for irrigation in the dry season. Eventually the plant will be provided with four turbine alternator units each of 2,500 kw but only two units are being installed initially. From 1937 to 1946 the mean yearly discharge of the Gal Oya river at Inginiyagala was 885,000 acre feet. After allowing for loss by evaporation, infiltration and spill, the amount of water actually available annually may be put at just about the capacity of the reservoir, or 770,000 acre feet. Although the whole of that can be regarded as available for irrigation, not all of it can be utilized for the generation of energy. The turbines cannot work with a head of less than 30 feet, corresponding to the level 180 msl for the water in the reservoir. Under the level 180 msl the capacity of the reservoir is 40,000 acre feet. Therefore the maximum amount of water that can be used for the generation of energy is reduced to 730,000 acre feet. Computations made by the engineers in charge of this plant show that an average of 14 acre feet is needed to generate an output of 1,000 units, the variation of head being taken into account. Consequently the average yearly output of energy obtainable when the plant has its full capacity installed would in theory be about 50 million kwh. For the present the output will certainly be much lower. With the present installed capacity of 5,000 kw the theoretical yearly output is 43.8 million kwh. Obviously, however, there must be interruptions for maintenance and repair and the load factor is unlikely to exceed 60% at best, so that the actual output is likely to be no more than 25 million kwh.

There are, however, further difficulties in making full use of Gal Oya's theoretical capacity. The primary purpose of the scheme is irrigation and the rate of discharge of water from the reservoir will be determined mainly by the needs of irrigation. With an irrigation duty of five feet for the cultivation of paddy in Maha (wet season) the discharge will for some months exceed by about 50% the maximum that can be worked in the turbines, even when all four are installed.

A large part of the water stored in the reservoir, and the most valuable part for the generation of energy because it is stored at the highest level, will thus be released for irrigation without generating energy. If, as is projected, the cultivation of paddy is developed as much as possible in Maha, the Yala (dry season) cultivation being confined to crops that need less water, the bulk of the energy will be generated from November to March and the output will be very low during the rest of the year. Even in the future, with the installation of further units it is doubtful whether the yearly output can be increased to much more than 25 million kwh. This is typical of the difficulties which arise when hydroelectric development and irrigation are associated in a multipurpose scheme.

It has been assumed that, as it will be a long time before local consumption will absorb all the Gal Oya output, the surplus can be used to supplement the main EUD supply by connecting Gal Oya to the central grid. The above analysis shows that this prospect is less promising than might appear at first sight because the excess output from Gal Oya will be available at the wrong time of the year, i.e. November to March, whereas Laksapana output will be at a minimum and will require supplementation between March and June.

An even more serious problem is that the distance separating Gal Oya from Norton (or from Kandy) is too great to be covered by other than 132 kv overhead lines. The cost of a 132 kv connection via Badulla, Nuwara Eliya and Norton, a distance of 90 miles, can be estimated at not less than Rs. 12.5 million including transformers and equipment. Assuming 8% for capital, maintenance and operating costs, total annual costs would be Rs. 1 million. Thus the cost of transmission per kwh would be: for 100 million kwh, one cent; for 50 million kwh, 2 cents; for 25 million kwh, four cents; and for 10 million kwh, 10 cents.

Whether it will be economic to deliver energy from Gal Oya power station to EUD will depend upon: (a) an exact evaluation of the cost of the link; (b) an evaluation of amount of energy which can be useful to EUD; (c) the price which can be paid to Gal Oya Board; and (d) the point of delivery. Our present impression is that however cheaply surplus power may in theory be generated at the point of production, transmission costs will make it more expensive when supplied to the grid than energy produced otherwise.

c) *Walawe Ganga.* Another hydroelectric plant is proposed as part of the Walawe Ganga multi-purpose scheme (discussed in Chapter 13). The proposal contemplates the construction of a dam about 110 feet high to store about 260,000 acre feet of water, primarily for irrigation but intended also for flood control. As in Gal Oya, the generation of energy would be subordinated to the needs of irrigation. The specifications for the construction provide a power plant with three units, two of them being installed in a first stage. Each unit would be a vertical shaft alternator of 3,750 kva driven by a Francis type turbine of 4,700 hp. No detailed estimates are available of the yearly output and the probable seasonal fluctuations but some of the factors involved are as follows:

The upstream catchment area is 610 sq. miles and the mean yearly discharge is about 1,440,000 acre feet. The Walawe Ganga has, like the Dry Zone rivers, two marked low water periods, in September and March, and much of its high rate of annual discharge is concentrated in frequent and heavy floods. The capacity of the reservoir is very small compared with the yearly discharge and much water will be spilt during the high water periods. During the floods the head will be reduced in the power plant by the increase of the level of the water in the tailrace. About 100,000 acre feet are needed each month to generate a minimum output of 10,000 kw. Such a discharge is available with the natural flow

479

from October to May, with the exception of March, when about 17,000 acre feet would need to be drawn from the reservoir. During August and September the shortage of the natural discharge would need supplementing by about 140,000 acre feet, which could be drawn out of the reservoir if the irrigation needs were satisfied. From the power point of view the Walawe Ganga scheme has real potentialities and it would be more favorably placed than Gal Oya for connection with the grid. Its realization is, however, dependent on the economics of the irrigation part of the scheme, doubts as to which have already led us to recommend against its immediate execution. We suggest, therefore, that no reliance be put on the availability of power from Walawe Ganga in the near future.

d) *Other Possibilities.* Other hydro projects have been discussed in Ceylon, but only on a basis of personal appraisal, as designs and regular survey data are not yet available. As an example, the projects described as Laksapana Stage III and IV mentioned in many official papers as the next ones to be built, are so far elaborated only in very general terms. Stage III envisages the utilization of Laksapana Falls on the Maskeliya Oya and Stage IV the construction of a dam to provide for regulation of the flow upstream of the falls. A statement of the EUD handed to the Mission says: "Preliminary investigations have also been carried out on the other sources and among those that show great promise are Teldenya, Kitulgala, Ulapane, Haragama and St. Clair Falls, which five sources will yield 220,000 kw." All these, however, require much further investigation.

Summing up, the hydroelectric position and prospects for the next few years are as follows:

1) Plants now in operation:
   a) Laksapana, Stage I, capacity 25,000 kw and yearly output of about 100 million kwh.
   b) Nuwara Eliya, capacity 330 kw, yearly output 1.4 million kwh.

2) Plant under construction; Gal Oya, capacity 5,000 kw, to be increased to 10,000 kw, yearly output probably about 25 million kwh. Whether this can be economically linked to the main grid and fully used is doubtful.

3) Further projects planned in detail:

   a) Laksapana Stage IIA (construction of Castlereagh Dam); will add 25,000 kw to the capacity of Laksapana and over 100 million kwh to its annual output. The cost is tentatively estimated at Rs. 4.5 million. Tenders have been called for. If construction is started in 1952 the plant can be completed in 1956.

   b) Laksapana Stage IIB (harnessing of head between Castlereagh and Norton Bridge); will add another 25,000 kw of capacity. Construction could be started (after further investigation) in 1954 and completed in 1958.

   c) Walawe Ganga (part of multi-purpose scheme) with installed capacity of about 11,000 kw; dependent on decision about the main scheme and subject to conflict with irrigation needs.

(4) *Proposed Construction Time Schedule*

a) *Thermal and Hydro Plants.* Where power needs are urgent, thermal plants are to be preferred to hydro plants, since the latter require a great deal more time for both planning and construction. For a soundly based hydro project an accurate ground survey is needed. This must be supplemented by thorough hydrological records. Being a "tailor-made" job, the initial plans are hardly ever exactly realized, which means delays for new calculations, drawings, and tests, and for additional discussions with public authorities. All these preliminaries can easily take four to five years or more.

In contrast, thermal plants are not "tailored" to fit a particular location, but can be set up wherever fuel and a market are avail-

481

able. Standard "ready-made" plans can be drawn upon, with only minor adaptations for a particular site. The time required for planning, completion of agreement between customer and contractor, etc., need not be more than a few months to a year.

There is a similar difference in the construction stage. Three years is the very minimum that must be allowed for simple and well-designed run-off river plants, even with normal conditions of transportation, delivery of cement, and availability of man-power. At present delivery of generators and turbines takes not less than two years and may take more. Installation and testing of machinery and equipment, even without complications, takes a further year. When the hydropower plant involves difficult construction such as dams, long tunnels and the like, plus transportation facilities and deliveries of special machinery and equipment, the very minimum construction period is four to four and a half years. Ceylon at present depends entirely on foreign countries for machinery and for contractors and would perhaps need a longer period, even if the construction of dams and the delivery of machinery were carried out by well equipped and trustworthy contractors on the spot. For large thermal plants, on the other hand, delivery of installations and machinery, together with construction, will not take more than two and a half to three years.

The total time of planning and construction is thus strongly in favor of thermal installations. These can be completed in three to four years, whereas hydro plants require seven years on the average and may need as long as 9 to 10 years.

Thermal power has the additional advantage of making possible a better balance between demand and production. Thermal plants can be used to fill in the gap between expanding demand and the delayed appearance of new hydro power.

b) *Planning Schedule for the Main EUD Area*—On the basis of all the above considerations, a tentative schedule for construction of new plants is proposed in Table VII.

The projected layout on capital expenditure refers only to the power stations; capital needs for transmission and distribution network are discussed under costs and rates. Our earlier conclusions on consumption trends indicate clearly that there will not be sufficient power for large industrialization schemes, railway electrification, etc. before about 1960. Total expenditure over the 10 year period is Rs. 185 million. The amount falling within the six year period commencing October 1, 1953 for which the Mission has to program more specifically would be about Rs. 130 million. Having regard, however, to all the claims on available funds the Mission feels that there may have to be some postponement in the commencement of the proposed additional 50,000 kw hydroelectric scheme. Only Rs. 110 million is therefore provided in the basic program set out in Chapter 6.

c) *Planning Schedule for Other Areas*

Jaffna. Assuming that in 10 years to come power needs will increase materially either on account of agricultural or industrial development, the construction of new thermal power capacity has to be seriously considered. Actually the extension of the power station in Kankesanturai has already been provided for; deliveries by the cement factory to Jaffna are both suitable and desirable, and appear to coincide very well with the load graph of the industrial plant.

As yet, however, no clear outline of development for the Jaffna Peninsula has been worked out on the basis of which power requirements can be determined.

A committee or similar group, representative of interested authorities and assisted by experts in agriculture, industry and power is needed to consider the problems involved in the development of this part of the country and to make a survey by which power needs could be fixed. If it should prove that in 10 years to come 10,000 kw or more would be needed, it would be suitable to consider a new thermal plant running with coal and operated by a special authority.

Trincomalee. As no considerable changes in power demand in this town can be expected for many years, it seems advisable to

TABLE VII

TENTATIVE SCHEDULE FOR DEVELOPMENT OF NEW POWER RESOURCES BY EUD

Year	Minimum Hydro Power available kw / kwh x 10^6		Thermo Power Installed Capacity kw	Load Factor Provided %	Maximum Possible Output with Thermo P. Support kwh x 10^6	Schedule for new power plants Construction	Estimated Capital Expenditure Hydro Rs.x10^6	Thermal Rs.x10^6
1952	25,000	100	18,000	50	140	Construction Laksapana IIA begins	5	—
1953	25,000	100	18,000	50	140		10	—
1954	25,000	100	18,000	50	140	Construction Laksapana IIB begins	15	—
1955	25,000	100	18,000	50	140	Enter in operation Laksapana IIA	20	—
1956	50,000	150	18,000	50	170	New Hydro P. plants to be begun	25	—

Additional schedule bars: Laksapana IIA, Laksapana IIB, New 50 mw Hydro, New 25 mw Thermo

484

Year	Minimum Hydro Power available kw / kwh x 10⁶	Thermo Power Installed Capacity kw	Load Factor Provided %	Maximum Possible Output with Thermo P. Support kwh x 10⁶	Schedule for new power plants Construction	Estimated Capital Expenditure Hydro Rs.x10⁶	Thermal Rs.x10⁶
1957	50,000 / 200	18,000	55	220		30	—
1958	75,000 / 230	18,000	55	270	Enter in operation Laksapana IIB. New thermo plant to be begun 25,000 kw	25	2
1959	75,000 / 300	18,000	55	320		20	5
1960	125,000 / 400	18,000	55	420	Enter in operation new hydro 50,000 kw	10	10
1961	125,000 / 500	40,000	55	550	Completion thermo power station 25,000 kw	—	8
					Total:	160[1]	25[2]

Laksapana IIA — Laksapana IIB — New 50 mw Hydro — New 25 mw Thermo

[1] Based on the estimates of Messrs. Preece, Cardew and Rider for Laksapana IIA = Rs. 40 kwh capital.
[2] Based on cost of diesel generators in Ceylon = Rs. 1,000/kw installed.

485

rely on Navy power stations. Though the Navy cannot assure delivery of power under all circumstances because its own needs take priority, reasonably satisfactory arrangements could probably be worked out in discussions with the interested authorities. Since interruptions would be likely only in wartime, special stand-by sets could be established. The ilmenite exploitation project in Pulmoddai, if carried out, should be provided with a power plant of its own, which could fill in when Navy installations fell short and so provide a secure electric supply to consumers in the town.

Galle. It has been pointed out that demand in this area is expected to increase in a short time, and even more rapidly when power limitations are removed. To feed this area with hydro power seems reasonable. The link should run from Norton through Ratnapura district and should be finished to coincide with the opening of Laksapana Stage IIA.

Other minor towns. When the projected hydroelectric schemes are completed, Ceylon will have available a considerable number of idle diesel sets. These could, after overhauling, be re-employed to augment the capacity of plants in towns such as Anuradhapura, Puttalam, Vavuniya, or wherever more power were needed. Power could be sold to consumers at cheaper rates, owing to the lower cost of the installations. Later, when loads reach the level where diesel costs are equal to operation and capital costs of hydro power, the grid of EUD should be extended to them.

(5) *Further Studies of Hydroelectric Development*

Mention has been made of the need for more detailed study of Laksapana Stages III and IV, involving the harnessing of Laksapana Falls and the construction of a reservoir on the Maskeliya Oya. Detailed investigation of both these should be undertaken simultaneously and as early as possible. As to other major schemes mentioned as possibilities, virtually no precise information is available. It is therefore important that an organization should be established to undertake the systematic study of the rivers from the point of view of the development of hydro-electric power as soon as possible. Such a study requires trained and experienced men, the collection of the necessary basic hydro-logical, rainfall and geological data and accurate large-scaled and close-contoured maps for the study of the grade of the river beds. It will need to be carried out in close coordination with the work of the more general Water Resources Planning Unit recommended in Chapter 13.

The study of the rational utilization of the water resources of the island is urgent because by about 1956 a decision will have to be taken whether and where to go on with hydroelectric schemes. The construction of Laksapana Stage II will be finished, but consumption forecasts suggest that additional power of about 50,000 kw will be needed in 1960 and the provision of that capacity by 1960, as provided for in Table VII, will necessitate the commence-ment of new construction in 1956. The study of the harnessing of Laksapana Falls and of the upstream reservoir should therefore be completed by 1956, when it can be decided whether to go on with the construction of Laksapana Stage III and IV or to turn to other rivers.

The area where the major hydroelectric schemes can be pro-jected is limited and in four years it should be possible to select the better sites and to make studies accurate enough to make a choice. Our time in Ceylon was too short for us to collect all the necessary data and examine all the factors involved in selecting specific stretches of the rivers to be studied but we make the fol-lowing general recommendations.

First consideration ought to be given to the highest heads be-cause they need less flow to generate the same power. In the central mountainous area where the rainfall has the better distribu-tion and where the flows are therefore more regular, the most suitable river stretches are found. The catchment areas and the discharges are generally small. Equalization of flow can there-fore be provided with reservoirs of small capacity that are easier to find and less expensive to build. The generation equipment can be of smaller size and less expensive, and can be constructed more easily at a time when the shortage in steel has to be taken into consideration.

Many other considerations will of course have to be taken in account. Often it will be better to extend the development of a particular valley in which reservoirs are already built and some regulation of the flow is provided, than to start with the development of another valley where the regulation of the flow has to be provided by fresh construction of expensive reservoirs. The needs of flood control and irrigation have to be considered at the same time and sometimes projects that would be uneconomic for the generation of energy by itself may be found worth while in combination with one or both of these other functions.

(6) *Development of the EUD Distribution Network*

Parallel to the development program of new power plants indicated in Table VII a program for construction of high tension overhead lines is necessary, including the 132 kv, 33 kv, 11 kv and similar systems.

a) *132 kv System.* Bearing in mind the development program for new power plants, the anticipated steady increase in generation and consumption, and distances separating the power plants from distribution centers, a voltage not lower than 132 kv must be adopted for the main transmission grid. Map No. 15 shows a proposed grid prepared in consultation with the Chief Engineer of the EUD and incorporating features of a scheme annexed to a pamphlet on Laksapana prepared by Mr. G. D. Somasundaram. [5]

The proposed grid covers the area of main population density, where initial development of industrial schemes is expected.

The 66 kv overhead transmission line Norton-Stanley (45 miles), already in operation, is prepared for transformation to the higher voltage. So is the line from Norton to Paradeniya, now

---

[5] G. D. Somasundaram, *The Aberdeen-Laksapana Hydro-Electric Scheme;* The Engineering Association of Ceylon, 1948.

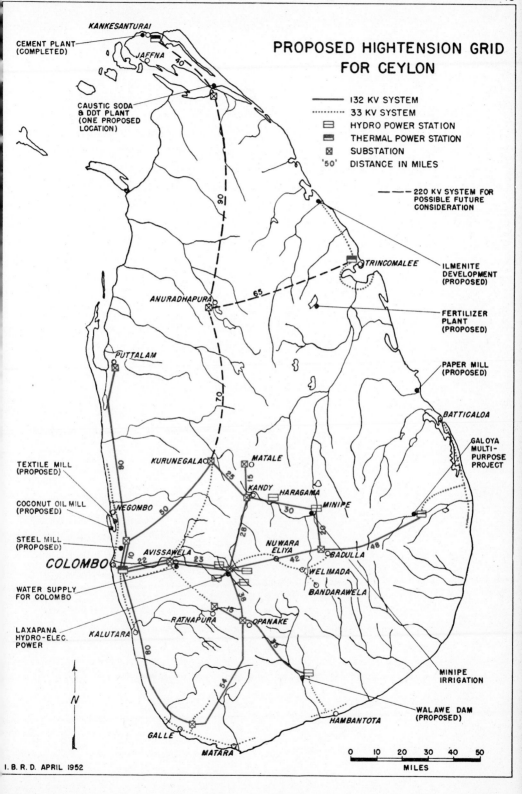

MAP 15

PROPOSED HIGHTENSION GRID
FOR CEYLON

──────── 132 KV SYSTEM
·············· 33 KV SYSTEM
▱ HYDRO POWER STATION
▭ THERMAL POWER STATION
⊠ SUBSTATION
'50' DISTANCE IN MILES

── ── 220 KV SYSTEM FOR
POSSIBLE FUTURE
CONSIDERATION

KANKESANTURAI
CEMENT PLANT
(COMPLETED)
JAFFNA
40

CAUSTIC SODA
& DDT PLANT
(ONE PROPOSED
LOCATION)
90

ILMENITE
DEVELOPMENT
(PROPOSED)
TRINCOMALEE

ANURADHAPURA
65

FERTILIZER
PLANT
(PROPOSED)

70

PAPER MILL
(PROPOSED)

PUTTALAM

BATTICALOA

GAL OYA
MULTI-
PURPOSE
PROJECT

TEXTILE MILL
(PROPOSED)

KURUNEGALA
25
MATALE
15

KANDY
HARAGAMA
30
MINIPE

COCONUT OIL MILL
(PROPOSED)
NEGOMBO
50
80

STEEL MILL
(PROPOSED)

COLOMBO
AVISSAWELA
22
23
28

NUWARA
ELIYA
42
BADULLA
48

20

WELIMADA
BANDARAWELA

WATER SUPPLY
FOR COLOMBO

10

LAXAPANA
HYDRO-ELEC.
POWER
KALUTARA

RATNAPURA
15
OPANAKE
36

MINIPE
IRRIGATION

80

54

WALAWE DAM
(PROPOSED)

GALLE
HAMBANTOTA

MATARA

0 10 20 30 40 50
MILES

N

I. B. R. D. APRIL 1952

under construction. The 66 kv voltage should be considered as transitional and further construction should be provided only for 132 kv.

The link Kandy-Minipe-Badulla-Gal Oya is shown, but without prejudice to the decision whether it will be economic to develop it.

The power stations Minipe and Haragama have been indicated as possible power sources, but without prejudice to any decisions on these projects, which have still to be investigated.

In planning the main lines of the 132 kv grid the Colombo area is assumed to remain the main consuming center. Two rings have been provided, one passing through Kurunegala, and the second through Galle. It is a matter of priorities when to construct them and in what order. Finally, the overhead line Colombo-Puttalam has to be considered as a distant possibility; economic considerations will determine the time for its construction.

The grid as planned involves 55 miles of double circuit lines (Norton-Avisawella-Stanley-Ja-Hela). The total scheme covers 605 miles and is expected to cost nearly Rs. 85 million. (The existing lines are excluded from this estimate.) It also involves setting up 12 substations 132/33/11 kv with a presumed expenditure (including transformers) of Rs. 50 million. For the period under consideration, 1952-1961, total probable expenditure can be put at the lower figure of Rs. 100 million.

b) *The 33 kv System.* Some of the designed overhead lines are still under construction. The scheme does not refer in detail to the entire system projected by EUD; it shows very lightly the lines which can be considered as tie lines connecting several substations such as Norton-Nuwara Eliya-Badulla, Colombo-Avisawella-Ratnapura-Kurunegala. It is not easy to estimate expenditure required for the distribution of the expected power output of 450 million kwh. The more developed the grid, the smaller should be the distribution network. Allowing for 100 miles already constructed, it can be expected that in 10 years to come some additional 250 miles will be set up and 200,000 kva of transformers will be purchased and installed. Expenditure including installations will total Rs. 45 million, based on consumption estimates of EUD.

c) *The 11 kv and 3.3 kv Systems.* In the EUD area it is planned to standardize voltages at 11 kv. As the problem is not urgent, the change-over will not be carried out in any fixed time. Meanwhile the spreading out of loads in the different districts over shorter distances can conveniently be made by 11 kv cables and overhead lines; substations and transformers have also to be provided. We assume that of the total amount available some 50% at this voltage will be sold in bulk or emitted in low tension networks. Transformers of 75,000 kva capacity and 100 miles of cables and overhead lines seem safe reference figures. On this assumption the total expenditure for the 11 kv system is estimated at Rs. 20 million.

Totalling these figures for transmission and distribution overhead lines and cables, including transformer and substations, we get, for the period 1952-1961:

132 kv Grid	Rs. 100 million	
33 kv System	45	"
11-3.3 kv System	20	"
Total	*Rs. 165 million*	

No allocation of the total expenditure between future budgetary years is possible at this stage, its allotment depending upon availability of power and of capital. But it can be expected that as new power plants are constructed, expenditure rates will accelerate from 1955 and for the six-year period 1953-59 the total may be put at Rs. 100 million.

The black dotted line in Map 15 shows a 220 kv grid. That is not a suggestion; it serves to bring out the costliness of a water-power supply to Jaffna and Trincomalee. The 200 mile division between Kurunegala and Kankesanturai is in fact too great. This fact should postpone any conclusion on this problem until loads are so high that reexamination of the point is worth while. In any event, if this situation should arise, the planned 132 kv grid is fit to face it.

TECHNIQUES OF CONSTRUCTION

(1) *Electric Installations*

The technique used in Ceylon for electric equipment is in accordance with British standards and should be continued. Up to now all important projects have been carried out according to suggestions from well-known British consultants. The task of a consultant, however, is to advise on specific problems as requested, while the responsibility for choosing better materials or devices and improving methods of construction, maintenance and operation falls upon the local authority.

Materials, machinery, devices, and apparatus installed in new plants are of good and solid construction. There is a tendency to simplify operation and maintenance and avoid complexities which would require skilled technical staffs, and therefore to design schemes and choose equipment as simple as possible. In consequence, modern techniques, as adopted in highly developed countries, are rather neglected in Ceylon. Improvements in this respect in new construction are at least advisable for the sake of safer and more economical operation and maintenance. For example, in view of the large development of electric utilities expected in Ceylon, we suggest a larger use of electronic tubes, techniques for remote controls, telemetering, carriers, automatic control of breakdowns and operation, etc. A grid as suggested needs a high degree of security; rupturing capacity of switchgears ought to be calculated for the very short circuit current of the grid; fuel oil breakers as now used seem unfit for the purpose. Size and features such as reactance and power factor of electric machinery for the main power stations should be fixed taking into account capacitance and reactance of the whole grid, and on the pattern of a large parallel running operation. Selective protection on main rings should be provided. Finally, schemes of power stations ought to be planned on the assumption that operation will be linked up to a central control board, whose location has to be chosen carefully to ensure the best and the safest operation.

(2) *Overhead Lines*

Overhead lines in Ceylon are very expensive, as all materials needed must be imported. Nonetheless, a better technique in selecting materials and in calculations could bring savings; for instance, the use of aluminum-steel for wires and steel for earth conductors, which is quite usual in the United States and in Europe. High stress steel towers are cheaper in terms of transport and erection.

Use of material locally available should be carefully reviewed. The country enjoys large timber resources; tests have already been made on various wood types, with favorable results for some, e.g. red gum and hiara wood for use in high and low voltage overhead lines. A plan should be worked out with the Forestry Department for regular planting and cutting of those woods so as to insure a regular delivery of poles and due rotation of cutting.

Large employment of concrete poles is usual; in view of the very great number of poles needed for the development program, every effort should be made to get them cheaper by improving construction methods and by better calculation. Installation of modern machinery (on a centrifugal or vibration system) and the establishment of a factory seem advisable to this end.

Reliance upon contractors from overseas, although it may be necessary at present, is likely to be expensive. An efficient local organization headed by a responsible high-level officer with skilled engineers and well trained workers should be developed as soon as trained men can be obtained in order to speed up work and reduce costs.

(3) *Communications*

It is vital for hydro power industries to enjoy rapid means of long-distance communication: it saves time, money and all kinds

492

of trouble. This is particularly true in Ceylon, where power is generated far away from consumption centers, and where the operations of the Department, which will in time be extended to Kandy, Galle, Ratnapura and elsewhere, can be efficient only with good and sure telephone communication.

Communication facilities in Ceylon are at present poor. EUD is well aware of the need for improving these services. Use of carriers or high frequency transmissions, as aids to normal wire communications, should be seriously considered and a complete project should be studied with a broad view of possible future needs.

In addition, with the increase of loads and therefore of revenue possibilities, the problem of transportation means should be considered more thoroughly. Trucks, cars, and motorcycles ought to be stored in sufficient number to respond promptly to any need which might arise.

COSTS AND RATES

(1) *Costs*

It is important for a farsighted program of exploitation of Ceylon's hydroelectric potential to estimate future costs of power realistically. There is a widespread impression among both the general public and government circles in Ceylon that hydro power will be much cheaper than thermal power. As a result certain rates have recently been reduced in the EUD area involving a probable decline in revenues. The reductions are already reflected in the Department's estimate of gross revenue for 1951-52 of only Rs. 9.5 million, against Rs. 10.7 million for 1950-51.

Are these reductions justified by a real decline in cost, or are they rather the effect of a very approximate appraisal more approaching a state of mind than any concrete estimate? We believe that EUD should reconsider the basic assumption of its cost calculations, taking into account the following considerations.

Unless there is some powerful overriding reason, an electrical undertaking should be managed as a commercial venture. Like

493

any other commercial enterprise, it produces a service for which it incurs costs. These costs must be recovered from someone. If the users of electric power do not pay in full for the service they receive, the taxpayer must shoulder the burden. Of course, the rates will vary for different categories of users. But if over-all loss is to be prevented and if, better still, the undertaking is to yield a surplus to be allocated to expansion, charges must be relatively high for those who can bear them. In general, this means those commercial customers for whom power is a minor element in cost.

Hydro power can be cheaper than thermal power if plants are well designed and favorably located in respect to consumption centers, if money is cheap and if operation and maintenance are economical. In any event, the cost of hydro power should be related to the pattern of distribution of consumers, as it includes customers who use different kinds of facilities and different amounts of power. Hydro power is, generally speaking, cheaper at its source but it is not cheaper to the consumer everywhere and at every time.

(i) *Capital costs*, i.e. interest, amortization, and depreciation. In Ceylon it is customary for the government to finance undertakings by means of loans raised by public subscription, at different rates of interest, generally 3% and on 25 year terms. This appears to be an arbitrary rate rather than one which would attract investors in a free money market. From the information given to the Mission it appears that the interest charge should be raised. Considering present rates of interest in the United Kingdom and other countries, the Mission considers that the interest charges for further loans to commercial undertakings such as EUD should be raised to not less than 4-4½%. Furthermore, loans to EUD are made without obligation to pay interest during the period of construction (see Appendix A footnote, Administration Report of EUD, 1950). This is not the rule in commercial financing and means that the money is lent at a rate of interest which cannot be exactly calculated, but is certainly lower than that nominally charged depending upon the time for construction of the works.

Amortization provides the reimbursement of the loan at maturity, but as the life of the physical assets is generally longer than the term of the loan, it is the usual thing here, as elsewhere in government financing, to convert the expiring loan into a new one, possibly at a different rate of interest. This means that loan charges are spread over the whole duration of the assets and enter in a fixed percentage into the cost of the delivered power.

The annual payments to be made into depreciation and obsolescence funds should be very conservatively calculated. Experience is that the life of electric plants tends always to be shorter in practice than initially assumed [6] and depreciation rates ought to be set accordingly. Ceylon might well adopt for accounting purposes the following conservative estimates of the life of various items in a hydroelectric installation.

TABLE VIII
Hydroelectric Plants

		Years
1.	Civil engineering (dams, channels, etc.)	50
2.	Buildings	40
3.	Power plants and machinery (turbines, generators, etc.)	25
4.	Substations and ancillary	25
5.	Transmission lines	25
6.	Transformers	25
7.	Switchgears	25
8.	Miscellaneous (network, cables, etc.)	15

Moreover, in assessing the capital value of existing investments in generation and distribution facilities, the present actual value of the installations should be taken. Their original costs may have been lower, but the trend is for costs to increase continuously.

---

[6] A clear example in Ceylon is the obsolete and now abandoned Power Station of Norton Bridge.

Finally, any investment made for development of the network should be counted as capital investment. In Ceylon this rule is not followed, owing to the application of a Treasury regulation set out in a memorandum issued in 1938 (No. 18) and still in force. This provides that any expenditure for extension of distribution network of 33 kv or less is made on condition that when the estimated revenue from the proposed extension is less than 20% of the capital cost of the work involved, the consumer will be required to contribute toward the cost of the extension, or to guarantee a minimum annual revenue, or both, at the option of the Department. Such a rule might be justified for a small-scale enterprise. But application to larger and more farsighted schemes, such as the EUD development program of 33-11-3.3 kv, is illogical and hampers their construction.

ii) *Costs of Operation and Maintenance*

These vary from time to time with the prices of labor and materials, but are relatively higher for hydro than for thermal plants, since the former require more personnel. Automatic control devices greatly reduce labor costs, so much so that the modern trend in every country is to substitute automatic equipment for labor wherever possible. The economy of labor thus obtained is so great that this substitution may pay even where, as in Ceylon, wages are relatively low.

EUD is not at present in a position to adopt modern techniques of this type, since they require skilled and well trained operators and high-level technical staff who have to be adequately paid. But as the level of training of staff is raised (a necessary preliminary to the installation of new plants discussed later), it will become increasingly possible to substitute automatic controls for the generally less efficient labor-using methods. As that time approaches, EUD should study the problem carefully considering the advantages to be obtained from introducing the most modern automatic control devices in the light of labor costs. In the meantime, costs of operation and maintenance can be lowered by improve-

ments in organization and staff, especially by giving responsibility and authority to the best men and relieving them of routine
duties and paper work which now make too heavy demands on
their time.

(2) *Rates and Tariffs*

Electricity rates vary widely, reflecting both large differences
in efficiency of plants and in the principles according to which
charges are determined for different categories of customers.
Table IX summarizes the data on average charges for the main
towns.

TABLE IX

AVERAGE RATES

(*rupee cents per kwh*)

Year	Town	A	B	C	D	E
1950	Colombo	18.8	25.4	8.75	13.6	16.29
1950	Nuwara Eliya	12.7	24.4			21.83
1949	Kandy	25.42				33.71
1949	Galle	31.55	21.80			39.30
1949	Trincomalee	40.80	31.30			45.35
1949	Jaffna	31.10	18.10			44.65
1949	Ratnapura	41.80	19.95			39.10

A—Private supply
B—Public lighting
C—Traction
D—Bulk
E—Total supply

Source: Appendix O of the Administration Report for 1950, EUD.

Peak prices are as follows:

	Cents Rs.
Private supply in Baruwala-Alutgama	88.72
Public light in Kotte	77.10
Total supply in Pusselawa	88.50

For purposes of comparison, we show in Table X the rates charged three different categories of users in four large cities overseas and in Colombo during 1950. Rates are expressed in U.S. cents, and refer respectively to small light consumers (15 kwh consumption per month), small industrial consumers (6,000 kwh per month), and large industrial consumers (75,000 kwh per month).

TABLE X

COMPARATIVE PRICES OF POWER

(U.S. cents)

Town	Light 15 kwh/month	Industrial power 30 kw 6,000 kwh/month	Industrial power 3,000 kw 75,000 kwh/month
New York	6.33	4.19	2.40
Zurich	8.15	2.35	1.27
Paris	4.65	3.60	1.56
London	5.8	1.79	1.59
Colombo	8.3*	1.80	1.30

* EUD rates Nos. 2 and 3, two-part tariffs and bulk tariff No. 6, Ceylon Government Gazette Extraordinary No. 9872, June 8, 1948.

Although conditions of generation and distribution are generally more favorable to economical operation in these overseas cities than in Colombo, it is noteworthy that rates in Colombo for both classes of industrial consumers are next to the lowest. Only with respect to light consumers are Colombo rates relatively high. At some time in the future, when Ceylon's electric power potential is more fully developed, low rates may be justifiable. Today, however, when the country is faced with heavy demands from all sides for developmental expenditures, it is surely a wise policy to tap every available source of investment funds. If a government establishment like EUD can, without serious injury to the customers it serves, run at a profit and build up a substantial surplus, it can make an important contribution to the country's development. By obtaining an annual surplus it ensures the availability of funds needed for the expansion of the electrical network, and by providing these out of its own resources, it frees the limited amounts in the general budget for other more pressing uses.

There is no reason to believe that an increase in rates to industrial users would impose any hardships commensurate with the benefit gained from having more ample funds for future electrical development. In few if any of the industries now using power is it more than a minor element in their total costs, so that a rate increase would have an inappreciable effect on the prices of their products. Of course, for very heavy users of power such as a chemical industry, where the cost of electric current is an important item in total costs, a low rate would be essential and would follow the established principle in electricity rate-making of charging what the traffic will bear. But this same principle would justify some increase in rates to other consumers.

For the reasons just given, the problem of electricity rates should be carefully reviewed in the light of the following considerations:

a) For most of the southern area, rates should be standardized and constructed on a uniform pattern.

b) Rates charged should cover all costs which can be specifically allocated to a particular use, such as depreciation and interest on transmission lines, current operation and maintenance of the lines and local installations, and the like. Common costs, such as that of generating electricity at the plant, should be completely covered out of revenue, but the share borne by any user should be allocated in terms of what the traffic will bear. Exceptions, properly counterbalanced, can be made in justifiable special cases.

c) Low rates for off-peak periods may be used to stimulate two- or three-shift operations in industrial establishments, thus ameliorating the load factor.

ORGANIZATION AND PERSONNEL

The present electricity organization in Ceylon is inadequate to deal effectively with the operation and maintenance of a large high-tension grid switching in parallel hundreds of mw, let alone the large development program. Strict control by the Ministry, together with subordination of EUD to Treasury regulations, seriously hampers the organization whenever major decisions have to be taken promptly. The heavy bureaucratic control makes it impossible to give sufficient responsibility and autonomy to capable people so that they may display their full capacities. This renders evaluation of the higher-level staff difficult, but the Mission believes that if greater autonomy and responsibility were given to the managerial staff, initiative would be encouraged and managers would have a better chance of allocating the right men to the right places.

One test of efficient management is employment in relation to output; another is the allocation of work. On both counts, the EUD needs to improve. Employment (3,384 employees in 1951) appears excessive in relation to 100 million kwh output. Among this large number of employees, an insufficient number of well-trained and willing officers do their best to speed up work and make operations efficient. But it is a common complaint in EUD that the best men are overloaded with work, most of which consists of paper battles, while far too many minor employees look on government employment as a form of unemployment insurance and do not exert themselves on the job.

These difficulties could be remedied, partly by changes in organization, partly by an improvement in personnel. The Mission believes that EUD should be transformed into an Authority with full responsibility for the development program and for operations within its defined area. This Authority might be patterned on the British Electricity Authority, which should be studied, and consulted for information and suggestions.

The area under the Authority's control need not embrace the

500

UNIVERSITY COLLEGE OF WALES LIBRARY ABERYSTWYTH

whole island; on the contrary, we believe that limiting its area would improve organization. It might be well to restrict it within the borders of the southern and central hills districts, where agreements between the Authority and Municipal and Urban Councils could transfer to the Authority the necessary properties and responsibility for organization and operation.

The areas centering in Jaffna, Trincomalee and Batticaloa, face quite different problems; distinct agencies could be provided. Jaffna and Trincomalee for example, will be fed for a long time by thermal power without any tie with the grid of EUD. Jaffna peninsula in particular has its own development problems and needs, and a very peculiar electric economy and operation technique, based on the overwhelming needs of the cement factory; it is too far away from Colombo to be satisfactorily controlled by a central organization. On the other hand, Batticaloa district ought to be fed by Gal Oya power resources. The major problem here is agricultural development, and responsibility for electricity supply rests with the Gal Oya Board, as provided by the Gal Oya Act of 1949. A branch of this board could be given full technical responsibility for the development of the electric network and delivery of electric energy to customers in and outside the boundaries of the Authority's area along the south eastern coast.

Personnel

The present shortage of qualified personnel will be aggravated in the near future, when newer and more modern plants will be installed. Steps should be taken at once, under the guidance of experienced technical advisers, to obtain for the Department high-level officers and technicians, skilled in the techniques and operations of modern electric plants. The Mission makes the following suggestions for action:

a) Promising young engineering graduates should be recruited by the Department and instructed in operation and construction activities. Care should be taken to place the new employees under

501

only the most capable chiefs of staff; if available, low-current specialists should be recruited.

b) A restricted number of the best qualified higher officials should be sent overseas for training. The main topics to be studied might be: very high voltage systems, interconnection grid and parallel systems, automatic controls, breakdown protection, and hydroelectric plant techniques. We are well aware that the main obstacle to carrying out this suggestion is the shortage of higher-level personnel in the Department. This difficulty might be met by rotating officials on duty and in foreign training. Those remaining on duty and taking over part of the responsibilities of absent colleagues should in fairness be compensated with extra pay.

The government should also check the possibility of calling in the competition of private organizations, as a means of speeding up the planned projects and of carrying out construction on a sound economic basis. This is, however, a matter of general policy; we indicate it only as a possibility.

RECOMMENDATIONS AND SUGGESTIONS

The principal recommendations and suggestions contained in this chapter are summarized here.

Recommendations reflect an opinion based on thorough examination of the main factors involved. Suggestions, on the other hand, deal with matters on which the Mission was unable to obtain sufficient data to form a decided opinion, and which should be more carefully investigated before a decision is taken.

1. *A Reform of the Electrical Undertakings Department* is recommended. It is suggested that it be transformed into an authority exerting its power within boundaries restricted to the central and south-west area of the island. Information and suggestions should be solicited from the British Electricity Authority.

2. *Separate Authorities or Agencies* of a technical and economic character are recommended for Jaffna peninsula and

Batticaloa district. Setting up of a Trincomalee district authority is suggested as a possibility for the future.

3. *Technical Assistance.* It is recommended that a high level technical adviser be employed to assist in the development of better techniques in construction and operation. The adviser should work with the Manager responsible for the Department (or the Authority), advising on all questions involving important or special technical problems and checking projects prepared by consultants and offers of major importance.

4. *Training of Ceylon Technical Personnel* in overseas countries is recommended; a rotation of officials to be sent abroad is suggested.

5. *Recruitment of Young Engineering Graduates* is recommended: special care in training them is suggested.

6. *Study of a General Scheme* for development of power resources is recommended. Exact data and surveys made by good consultants under control of the technical adviser are necessary. Hydro power should be integrated with thermal power plants to be constructed in the locations and of the size indicated by the results of the survey.

7. *A Time Schedule for a Medium-term Development Scheme* is suggested.

8. *A Transmission Grid* must be studied as soon as possible as a whole and in detail; it should be carried out in step with the construction of power stations with a close consideration of power needs. Map 15 outlines a suggested grid. A normal transmission system of 132 kv for the grid is recommended.

9. *The Distribution Network* should be developed to make power readily available and to meet future growth of loads. Expenditure for this purpose should be counted as capital investment.

10. *Gal Oya Power Station.* It is recommended that the output of this station be used in the Gal Oya Board Authority's area and environment until the amounts of power needed by the

EUD grid are such to justify the construction of a 132 kv link to Norton.

11. *Jaffna Peninsula.* Thermal power generation is recommended, as a 220 kv tie line would be necessary to feed this district with hydro power. As power demand increases, installation of a coal power station is suggested.

12. *Trincomalee.* It is suggested that this area be fed entirely by Navy power plants until growth of demand justifies either a link to hydro power plants or the installation of a new thermal plant on the spot.

13. *Other Districts,* such as Anuradhapura, Vavuniya and Puttalam, could acquire additional power by installing reconditioned diesel sets released by the delivery of hydro power to other parts of the country. Increasing the autonomy of their authorities is suggested as a means of stimulating the development of their electric facilities.

14. *Rates for EUD* should be based on a more exact calculation of cost of hydro power. Careful accounts should be set up to permit accurate calculation of the cost of new power, which will be the predominant part of the total available in the future. The policy should be adopted of setting electricity rates so as to yield a surplus of revenue, this surplus to be used as a fund for the further development of electrical undertakings.

15. *Private Development of Power Resources* might be considered as a means of supplementing the efforts of the government, provided more rapid provision of power facilities is regarded as highly desirable. This would require changes in legislation.

16. *Capital Costs* over the program period 1953-59 are estimated at Rs. 140 million for new installations and Rs. 100 million for development of the distribution network.

15. Industry

With good reason, Ceylon recognizes that her balanced development requires industrial advance along with the more urgent agricultural improvement and extension. If this advance is to contribute to real economic progress, it will require a cool evaluation of industry's role, a realization that industrialization is not an end in itself, a critical selection of industries for real benefit, and realistic choice of efficient operating methods.

TODAY'S INDUSTRIAL PICTURE

Viewed in proper perspective, manufacturing—even large-scale industry—is not new to Ceylon. What is new is industrial diversification. Until the last decade most of the island's major industry was concerned with the processing of tea, rubber and coconuts, and the manufacture of machinery for these industries. It is only recently that any serious effort has been made to establish factories processing other agricultural products or making finished goods from the other natural resources of the island or imported raw materials.

The popular belief that Ceylon is virtually without industry probably stems from familiar association of its existing major industries with agricultural production. As everywhere, it is the novel that attracts attention. Thus the prospect of a comparatively small new sugar mill or a factory to make paper from illuk grass—either one equally dependent upon an agricultural crop—is heralded as a notable industrial advance. Meanwhile there is a tendency to overlook even such large producers as the island's 950 tea factories, to say nothing of a multitude of rubber mills and the large and small factories producing coconut oil,

505

desiccated coconut and other products. When we consider these, the hundreds of thousands of workers they employ and the 156,-000,000 kwh of power they consume, it is probable that Ceylon is proportionately far more industrialized than many another "underdeveloped" country today. The real pressure, then, is not merely for an industrial payroll but for channeling local energies and resources into economical production of a wider variety of finished goods.

Closely related to the industrial processing of the three main income producers of the island is a substantial and long-established machinery manufacturing business, supplying much of the equipment for the local tea and rubber industries and lately beginning to export as well. Moreover, characteristic of the transition of a country in Ceylon's present stage of development, there has been a gradual growth of small factories producing such consumer goods as matches, textiles, shoes, beer and soft drinks. These, like the principal ones already named, are mainly private enterprises. Some are new, others quite old: the first textile mill was established in 1883, and the brewery in 1884.

But of the major industries, all except the machine shops are too specialized to have built much in the way of broad industrial experience, trained labor and technical know-how for expansion into new industrial fields. Most of the others, taken together, are still too small to have done so despite their greater diversity.

During the Second World War the government itself set up a dozen small industries to supply such articles as plywood, paper, drugs, glassware, ceramic ware, acetic acid, wood products, and re-rolled steel. Most of these were emergency affairs, merely intended to alleviate local wartime shortages. In the absence of competition some of them at first showed a profit. Yet at the time of their establishment proper equipment was not available, and most of them were technically unsound and uneconomical at the outset. This fact became apparent immediately after the war, as soon as competing foreign goods re-entered the market. Reluctant to release employees and anxious to give these ventures a longer trial once they were started, for years the government attempted to keep them alive through such heroic measures as the Industrial Products Act, virtually compelling buyers to take their wares. Enormous annual losses continued, however, and most of them were finally forced to close for "reorganization." Of the lot, the only important one still operating is a plywood factory supplying about 10% of the island's tea chests.

As a newer addition, in late 1950 the government put into operation a modern cement plant currently providing about one third of the local requirements of that material. Today the government has nearly a dozen medium and large-scale industrial projects in various stages of preparation. These include factories for textiles, coconut oil, sugar, steel, paper, fertilizers, caustic soda, DDT insecticide, and concentrated ilmenite. New products of comparable size being contemplated by private industry are limited to two—a tire factory and a flour mill—and even these are contingent upon some form of government participation.

Today's situation is the result of two extremes. On one hand, for a number of reasons which we shall examine, private capital alone has not done its share. On the other the government, coming to the rescue, has not tried to "help private industry to help itself," but has tried to do the whole job unaided. One consequence is that private capital—its interest now stirring a little—feels actually excluded and afraid. Another is that the government is deprived of the advantages of commercial know-how and business management so necessary to successful production.

GOVERNMENT INDUSTRIAL POLICY

Sympathetic understanding of this condition requires a brief review of circumstances and events which led up to it.

Modern organized production in Ceylon began with the plantations established by non-Ceylonese initiative. Capital invested in productive and commercial enterprises by 1939 was 85% external. It was directed first to production for export, and the economy developed on the basis of specialization in primary

507

agricultural products. Most of the time the three main products were sufficiently lucrative—for Ceylonese and outside investors alike—to leave little incentive to branch out into other lines. The Ceylonese themselves lacked the technical background for other types of production. Non-Ceylonese investment funds found full employment in tea, rubber and coconuts—or, alternatively, in the complementary import trade in manufactured goods and other consumption needs of the island. Only in periods of general depression did these lines decline—notably in the thirties, for example—and these were poor times to expect new kinds of investment anyway.

Disruption of supplies during the first world war brought little immediate change, but it underlined the inherent shortcomings of the system. And in the years that followed Ceylon, in common with many other areas, realized how difficult it would be to achieve a higher level of living while continuing to concentrate on the production of raw or primary materials involving a low average productivity of her people.

The trouble was that while Ceylon's need for industrial diversification was apparent to many, nothing had occurred to alter the individual's conservative outlook toward change on his own part. That is, he saw no advantage to himself in being the first to try something new; in fact, he does not today.

Birth of a Ministry

In a move to call public attention to the possibilities of industrial development, a Ministry of Labor, Industry and Commerce was established under the 1939 Donoughmore Constitution. Government activity in this field was intensified in 1938 with the creation of a separate Department of Commerce and Industries, whose functions included the actual establishment and maintenance of factories, industrial centers, workshops, training schools and facilities for industrial research. Under this arrangement at least two of the government factories (coir and plywood) were set up by 1941.

Events surrounding the establishment of the plywood factory are significant, and appear to have had great (possibly disproportionate) influence upon later governmental industrial policy. As recorded in an official publication, [1] the project was first prepared by the government and offered to private enterprise for initiation. Says the report:

> "Private enterprise was, however, not responsive. The suggestion was then made that the Government would underwrite the full issue of shares. This suggestion again met with no response. The Executive Committee then decided that the Government should establish the factory on its own account."

On the basis of what happened, it is easy to understand the decision of the executive committee in this case. Whether the episode by itself was enough to justify a subsequent strong leaning toward government factories, as opposed to private enterprise, is another question. Perhaps the same thing would have occurred had the issue been a shoe factory or a soap plant instead of a plywood mill. Yet in some respects the incident was a special case. Ceylon's chief market for plywood is in the making of tea chests. Hence the large tea planters would have been among the most likely prospects for private financing of a plywood mill, since it would have been to their advantage to have control of their source of supply. But, today at least, many of the large planters are also shareholders in the company which supplies them with foreign-made tea chests, and it is not unreasonable to suppose that this was true in 1941. Perhaps other conditions too— such as the shortage of trained workmen, or lack of information on available supplies of logs for the mill—were influential in discouraging private investors or operators. Whatever the facts, the episode powerfully reinforced the government's inclination to take a direct hand in industrial production.

---

[1] Sessional Paper XV. *Report on Industrial Development and Policy* by the Executive Committee for Labor, Industry and Commerce, Ceylon, September, 1946.

509

Early Efforts. Government efforts toward establishment of new industries then began in earnest. Funds were provided for the training of Ceylonese technical specialists aboard. In principle, certain industries (examples: textiles, quinine and cement) were selected as basic and necessary to the island's progress. In his 1940-41 Budget Speech, the Minister for Labor, Industries and Commerce issued a statement on industrial policy in which he recommended among other things, that:

1) Industrial surveys should be conducted for the establishment of major industries in Ceylon.
2) The Department of Commerce and Industries should carry out research into potential industries of the country.
3) Demonstration centers should be established throughout the country as a part of the policy of imparting technical advice and instruction in cottage industries.

It was in the period immediately following this declaration that the government undertook the creation of nearly a dozen assorted small factories. The original spirit behind the policy of the 1940-41 Budget Speech was, "to open up avenues of economic industrial exploitation which private enterprise had hitherto generally not attempted to traverse." At the time, however, all criteria had to be tempered by the urgency of meeting immediate shortages under World War II conditions. As a matter of record, many of the industries established at this time were not expected to survive the return of more normal conditions.

New Policy. A more exhaustive report and statement of governmental policy on industrial development was issued in 1946. [2] Early in this report the Executive Committee for Labor, Industry and Commerce declared: "With the end of war and the gradual return of normal conditions. . . . a more comprehensively planned industrial policy should be determined for this country. It is our considered opinion that industrial development must be a

---

[2] Op. cit.

part of the general economy of this country if we are to achieve a higher standard of living for our people, and if we are to make any serious attempt toward the goal of full employment. We are aware that Ceylon is, and will continue to be, mainly an agricultural country, but we realize that there certainly is a place in it for industrial development as well." The report advocates that the state undertake certain fundamental functions to this end, enumerating the following in particular:

1) Providing competent technical advice;
2) Creating and sponsoring institutions that offer long-term and mid-term credit facilities at cheap rates of interest;
3) Providing opportunities for technical training to insure a ready supply of skilled labor;
4) Providing adequate marketing facilities.

Although it is true that these services have developed adequately in some countries with little or no intervention by the state, there is no doubt that Ceylonese conditions do require government assistance in these matters. The 1946 Report recognized that the government had created mechanisms and institutions for them, but called attention to numerous inadequacies in their performance. The present mission finds them still inadequate in 1952, and elsewhere in the present report offers suggestions for their improvement.

On the major question of the extent to which the government itself should engage in manufacturing, the 1946 Report offered arguments at length both for and against government ownership of industries. The text gives the impression that the Committee was somewhat biased at the outset in favor of government enterprise. In the end, however, it recommended division of industries into two categories—*basic* and *nonbasic.* It recommended that the former be nationalized and be the exclusive monopoly of the state, and that nonbasic industries be left to private enterprise. Where nonbasic industries had already been established by the government, it was recommended that these be offered to the public for purchase by private investors.

Basic Industries. No clear definition of a basic industry was offered then, nor has one ever been formulated since. However, it was pointed out that basic industries would occupy positions of strategic value in the development of industrial resources; that they were ones which might become monopolies; and that they required a large capital outlay, which it was thought best that the state should provide. In this category the Committee definitely placed: (1) power; (2) heavy industries such as iron, steel and cement; (3) heavy chemicals, including fertilizers; (4) specified drugs and pharmaceuticals; and (5) cotton spinning.

In justifying these initial selections, the Committee stated that the first three supplied capital goods and were therefore basic. Drugs and pharmaceuticals were included because of their importance to health and the undesirability of any private monopoly in this field. Cotton spinning was named as basic because the hand-loom industry of the country could benefit from a cheap supply of yarn. With these as precedents, it must be acknowledged that the way was open for declaring almost anything a basic industry. [3]

Current Policy. It is the Mission's impression that the general policy of the Ministry of Industries has not particularly favored private enterprise. It has entered—or announced plans to enter —a great many unrelated lines of manufacturing; by doing so it has discouraged private capitalists from launching at least some ventures that they had planned. It has opposed private exploitation of incidental resources such as ilmenite, and has reserved for itself other types of production which by no stretch of the imagination

---

[3] It is easy to understand why the Committee could not crystallize its definition of a "basic" industry. In the Mission's view, any attempt at rigid classification of specific industries in this way is unsound, and entirely different criteria must be used to decide the government's role. Elsewhere, similar attempts to define "essential" industries in wartime have shown that a persuasive argument can be made for inclusion of even the most frivolous ones, if such be the desire.

could be considered basic. [4] Until very lately it has attempted to keep in operation most of the original group of uneconomical wartime factories, sometimes in competition with private ones. The government tannery not only competes with sixteen struggling small private tanneries, but forces them to relinquish the best of their raw material instead of purchasing its own in the open market.

Finally, the government is entering fields of industry already widely established on the island by numerous private companies. An outstanding example is the making of coconut oil, for which the island's installed plant capacity already exceeds the supply of coconuts. In this case the government's contention is that it plans to install a more efficient plant using solvent extraction, and that it will also make secondary products from the oil. Yet these things could be accomplished at less expense without adding to the mechanical milling capacity. In fact, several private millers are planning solvent extraction on their own account, and government assistance to these might be more advantageous as well as cheaper.

Within recent months there has been a noticeable swing in government attitude toward private capital. It would not be accurate to interpret this as a movement in favor of private enterprise; rather, it is a greater willingness to allow the investing public to participate in government industrial schemes. It may have been influenced by the growing public protest against the losses and inefficient management of these enterprises, and the demand for a more businesslike operating formula. But it coincides with a crystallizing opinion of local private investors that they must accept some form of partnership with the government

---

[4] For example, when a small Ceylonese tea manufacturer asked the Ministry for advice from its laboratories on making of caffeine from tea waste, he was told that this was confidential technical information being reserved for a government project. Caffeine is used principally in soft drinks.

513

if only to avoid its competition and the force of its superior economic weapons.

We cannot escape the conclusion that the Ministry of Industries, intent on building big factories of its own, has had its attention diverted from more fundamental areas of public service such as training technologists and skilled workers, affording technical and other aid to existing industries, and encouraging enlistment of private capital and energies toward development of a sounder pattern of diversified small industries which the country needs.

Apart from these aspects, it should be observed that in general the government's industrial development policy appears to be directed inward, mainly toward a mere reduction in imports, rather than toward outward expansion into new markets. The Mission has seen very little effort in any line toward exports of new finished goods. Thus, except in tea, rubber and coconuts, the aim seems to be one of curtailing international trade rather than expanding it. Retreat into self-sufficiency offers a more dependable market in troubled times, of course; but it also limits development of industries, in terms of both size and diversity, to the absorptive capacity of the home market.

Factors Influencing Industrial Development

Capital

While no complete figures are available, there is evidence [5] that local private capital would be able to handle an appreciable growth in industrial investment if it could be encouraged to do so. True, it would not be enough for all of the large schemes now planned by the government; yet it is notable that the government itself contemplates eventual public sale of up to 80% of the shares in some of these, [6] which must presuppose existence of such funds.

---

[5] Chapters 5 and 9.
[6] *Ceylon Daily News*, Feb. 4, 1952.

Central Bank figures on the flight of external capital during 1950 and 1951—representing chiefly the sale of tea estates to Ceylonese—may be interpreted to mean that no less than Rs. 30 million in each of these years could have been diverted to new private industrial capacity if the investors had so elected; and this amount is not the total available, but only that which came to light in this way.

Investment Trends. Preference for investment in land is almost invariably encountered in underdeveloped countries. In Ceylon it is unusually strong; there is a sentimental attachment that goes much deeper than the mere security of real estate. Land values are high, often out of all proportion to their yielding capacity when farmed for paddy. And in tea and rubber no sentiment is necessary, for estate shares may pay 20% or more.

If the local capitalists do not choose to buy land, they can import merchandise or else participate in rice speculation and similar activities. These things they understand and consider reasonably secure, and they offer a quick turnover. One banker estimates the average return from such transactions at around 10%, although they yield up to 70% at times.

Against this, Ceylonese investors know that modern industries can pay only modest annual rates of return if they are to remain competitive. With luck, they may be able to secure heavy protection or subsidy from the government in certain cases. Otherwise, if their owners insist on extracting quick returns, they can do so only by such measures as adulteration, progressive lowering of the quality of the product and inadequate plant upkeep—all of which impair the security of the investment.

The Ceylonese say that their own countrymen will do these things, and that therefore they seldom care to buy shares in a Ceylonese industrial concern. If they buy shares at all, they prefer those of a foreign company with established technical standards. Thus the promotion of local joint stock companies is difficult; of those that exist, many are really family-held.

It is only in recent years that Ceylonese investors have started

515

to buy industrial shares, whether foreign or domestic. Companies whose securities have been available on the open market for over half a century find that even today only 5% to 10% are held by Ceylonese.

External Capital. Outside capital has considered Ceylon an excellent place for investment in the past. A partial study in 1947 showed foreign investments (mainly British) totalling Rs. 411 million, of which Rs. 145 million was invested in local companies. Today, however, this capital is beginning to move out. During 1950 Rs. 36.2 million left, while less than half this amount entered as new foreign capital. The net flight accelerated in 1951, when in the first six months alone Rs. 38.6 million was withdrawn and only Rs. 14.6 million came in; total flight in 1951 was Rs. 78.6 million. No dollar capital entered at all in 1951, despite attempts to attract it.

This is an undesirable trend, at a time when the total resources available for investment are already insufficient to cover the island's hopeful plans for rapid economic development. The government must accept a share of the blame for this, for its failure to adopt a clear-cut policy toward external capital and for numerous incidents giving the impression that such capital is unwelcome. The rest is due to uncertainty—the investor's fear that a new government might bring even greater unfriendliness and expropriation—and to the fact that opportunities for investment elsewhere compete for this capital more enthusiastically.

Something more than mere statements by individual government officials will probably be necessary before the confidence of private investors can be restored and the flight of capital reversed. For there have already been such statements, but they lack demonstrated performance. The 1948-49 Budget Speech stated that "the Government . . . would welcome the investing of money, whether it is local or foreign, in the development of our resources, provided the most modern methods are used in such development." Yet, whatever the reasons, foreign capital had great difficulty in bringing in a modern canvas shoe factory, while one using more antiquated methods was given support. Both the Prime Minister and the Minister of Finance have repeatedly emphasized the need for foreign capital; but meanwhile certain others have opposed it and encouraged public sentiment against it. Too hasty and overzealous prosecution of the Ceylonization program—in employment, finance, trade and culture—has resulted in a confused and cautious attitude among all investors, especially non-Ceylonese.

A cabinet committee was appointed in August, 1950 to investigate the whole question of foreign capital, as well as to recommend the terms on which it should be brought in. Unfortunately, by early 1952 the committee had not yet met. On the other hand, at least the dual taxation of British capital has been substantially eliminated by recent amendment of the income tax ordinance, and other incentive measures are either on the books or contemplated.

Suggested Course. In view of the rate of progress in development for which Ceylon is striving, the Mission feels that every effort should be made to call into play such private capital resources as can be reached, whether domestic or foreign. In particular, since so many other parts of the program demand public funds by their very nature, government money should be saved for these by encouraging private capital to enter the types of activities to which it is best suited. Industry is certainly one of them. While the government must help industry, it must remember that every rupee of public funds invested in industrial plants is a rupee withheld from education, health, irrigation and similar essentials.

Industrial Credit

Development of private industry has been retarded by inadequate facilities for medium- and long-term credit. Although the problem was recognized publicly in the 1946 Report on Industrial Development, there has been little improvement to date.

Establishment in 1943 of the Agricultural and Industrial Credit Corporation (Chapter 9) was expected to offer some relief. This organization was given the specific function of promoting industrial ventures by underwriting share capital and even undertaking management. The Mission finds, however, that it has failed to discharge this function. Entrepreneurs who have solicited credit from it for capital equipment and expansion have found it impossible to arrange acceptable security and terms.

Branches of British and Indian commercial banks on the island tend to limit their lending to short-term import-export transactions, especially financing the tea, rubber and coconut trade. Local factories are granted short overdrafts for raw materials and the like at $3\frac{3}{4}\%$ or higher, but funds for plant development must come from their own earning or the private pockets of their owners.

To a manufacturer buying production machinery, credit for 90 or 180 days is of little use. He cannot hope to repay such a loan out of earnings from the equipment. Especially in Ceylon, where most machinery must come by long overseas shipment and where installation may proceed slowly, it is likely that the loan will fall due even before the new equipment is ready to run.

One institution which has helped—although not enough—is the Bank of Ceylon. This bank has sometimes lent as long as 25 months for purchase of new machinery. Such financing is done by successive renewals of six-month loans at interest rates ranging from 3% (on government securities) to 5% or 6%. Mortgages may be taken on plant equipment, but in such cases the loans are then further secured by the personal notes of the borrowers. Thus if the equipment offered as first security disappears (as has happened) the courts give the bank recourse to the personal possessions of the guarantors. As one might expect, the bank avoids loans on new enterprises unless its officials are personally well acquainted with the individuals involved.

The net result is that the island now has no agencies whatsoever from which a local industrial operator can get the long-term credit he needs. This is one of the major reasons for the Mission's proposal of a Ceylon Development Corporation, which is described in Chapter 4.

MANAGEMENT

Lacking a broad industrial background which is only now being built, it is only natural that for the moment Ceylon has few persons of general industrial management experience.

Private Industries. Among private plants, distinction between the functions of ownership and management is less frequent in Ceylonese-owned enterprises than in the others. As larger units are built, however, it it becoming clearer to the investors that ownership does not automatically confer management ability. In some cases trained foreign managers are being hired, at least until local personnel can gain experience. This is more common in technical positions, for Ceylonization pressure has made it extremely difficult to import skilled administrative personnel.

Where management and ownership are distinct, it is noted that maintenance and replacement of capital equipment are often better. But as a rule Ceylonese factory owners tend to take out large profits at the expense of maintenance, reinvesting these (if at all) in other ventures or in land. Efficiency then suffers through deterioration, and so does the psychological incentive for good performance.

Reports from different factories show a wide variation in the output of workers, even with the same equipment. Similar variations are noted in the history of individual plants. All evidence indicates that such differences are largely attributable to the choice of managers and supervisors, their qualities of administration, initiative and leadership, and their understanding of the worker as a fellow individual.

Government Factories. The management problem in government-operated industries is a very acute one. It is now acknowledged by all that their present administrative structure is hopelessly unsatisfactory.

To their credit, it must be said that officials have been quick to recognize the need for experienced industrial managers and have imported them. But these managers are unable to give their best performance while virtually all administrative authority is retained by the Ministry. Inevitably, the very decisions for which their skill and judgment were sought are made for them by government officials instead. Hiring, firing, production planning, accounting, purchasing, distribution and sale are all handled through the inherently cumbersome mechanisms of government, and a resulting large overhead is charged against production costs.

Some very competent managers have been obtained; but delays, veto and frustration have caused a number to resign. This, and the fact that governmental salary limitations have not kept pace with the industrial world, now make it difficult to replace them with the best men.

A solution probably lies in conversion of these enterprises to ordinary corporations (Chapter 4) where responsibility for efficient management can be left to competent managers chosen by a board of directors, and where the government can limit itself primarily to the role of stockholder and recipient of dividends.

Some progress is being made in discussions toward this goal. However, it is felt that current local thinking has not yet fully evaluated the real essentials of the problem. One proposal, disclosed in a memorandum released to the press in February, 1952, would create government-owned corporations but would actually leave all final operating authority in the hands of the Ministry of Industries, where it is now. We fear that this would merely continued the present system under a new name, and would solve nothing. Further consideration will show that the key to good management and protection of investment is to delegate authority to competent personnel with a minimum of restriction, and to hold them responsible for performance.

INDUSTRIAL TECHNOLOGY

As with general factory management, industrial technology in all its forms is deficient in Ceylon for historical reasons.

What is not yet fully appreciated is that application of technical knowledge is the very essence of industry, extending all the way from top planning and administration down to the daily duties of supervisors and skilled workmen. Probably no single factor has so much influence upon the rate of successful industrial growth.

Although its importance—in name—has been recognized in Ceylon's multitude of requests for foreign technical assistance, one fears that in some quarters its true meaning has been misunderstood. As the topic is a broad one and affects not industry alone but every phase of development, it is reserved for separate treatment in Chapter 19.

LABOR

Availability. At the moment Ceylon has neither a shortage nor a surplus of industrial labor, although skilled labor of all kinds is scarce. There is, indeed, widespread underemployment on the island, but this is chiefly among the agriculturists who fail to use their land and time to best advantage.

With current population growth outrunning production, the situation in another decade may be changed; but today unemployment, in the ordinary sense, is not present. Nowhere in Ceylon has the Mission found any large group of employable persons actively seeking work and unable to obtain it. Official employment exchanges have only about 70,000 registered as unemployed; informed opinion places the real total at around 200,000, including those in remote villages who might register if they were closer to an exchange office.[7] Of the 70,000 registered, investigators of the International Labor Office estimate that 25% are really employed, and that a total of 85% (including those employed) are simply using the registry as a means of seeking government jobs. Rather than jeopardize their chances of such a position, it is claimed, many of the registered persons refuse private employment. Thus, in relation to the population, the

---

[7] Labor exchanges are maintained only in the larger centers. It has been found that the outlying workers are seldom willing to travel 20 or 30 miles to register, since they would not care to accept work that far away if it were offered.

actual number unemployed but willing to work amounts only to normal fractional unemployment—i.e. enough to prevent inflationary bidding for workers.

In past years Ceylon has had a large Indian labor force. Over 80% of the workers on the tea estates (whose factories constitute Ceylon's largest industry) have been immigrants from southern India. Some have brought with them special skills. Many others have found employment in occupations not favored by Ceylonese. The current campaign of Ceylonization has stopped the immigration and is rapidly diminishing this Indian labor supply, however, leaving vacancies which are not easily filled.

Thus, for example, when the government distillery at Seeduwa was ordered to deal only with Ceylonese toddy tappers, it was thereafter unable to obtain more than a third of the supply of raw material needed to keep it in operation. A Jaffna pottery factory, now losing its Indian workers, plans to close by next year because it cannot get Ceylonese replacements. Local workers are unwilling to learn the necessary skills, while available potters 20 miles to the south refuse to move that far to work in the factory.

Immobility. The comparative immobility of industrial labor is, in fact, something of a problem. It was one of the original reasons for importation of Indians; hence Ceylonization intensifies its effects. The Ceylonese worker wants to remain where he is—usually the village or town where he was born and reared. Prospects of government employment may attract a small excess of workers to the capital and to a few of the larger municipalities. Yet even in these, new enterprises and construction projects frequently must use special inducement to persuade laborers to move in from nearby villages. The larger industrial projects of the government, often seemingly located without regard to the labor supply, find it necessary to provide costly colonization schemes at the factory sites.

From one occupation to another, mobility of labor is restricted for a different reason. Although the caste system is seldom acknowledged, vestiges of it definitely exist. Some of the older occupations are identified with certain castes. If tradition has labeled a certain activity a "low-caste" one, it is difficult to find willing workers for its expansion. The same problem sometimes arises even within the existing labor force of a single factory, when it becomes desirable to shift workers from one department to another in response to changing market demands. Yet while this resistance to shifting is a nuisance to employers, in truth it does not seriously hamper industrial production.

Productivity. Opinion of employers on the output of Ceylonese labor varies. A few find it equivalent to Indian labor, but most of them report it from 20 % to 30% lower in productivity. They say that the workers generally respond to ordinary economic motivation such as incentive pay, but only within limits. The local worker likes to spend his pay as soon as he gets it, so that when there is money in his pocket absenteeism is not uncommon. Factories granting a specified number of paid days of sick leave per year find that the workers usually manage to take advantage of all of it; on the other hand, some factories have cut this lost time in half through payment of extra wages for any days of sick leave not actually taken.

All employers interviewed—both Ceylonese and foreign— agree that the Sinhalese is not naturally inclined toward hard physical labor. [8] On light work calling for finger-dexterity his output can sometimes be remarkably high; but generally, in the Ceylonese climate at least, he prefers a moderate pace with a minimum of physical exertion. Some types of work that are merely distasteful he will do when suitably compensated; yet even when desperately in need of employment, if given a job such as moving heavy barrels he will not stay with it under any circumstances. To get such work done regularly, employers claim that they have had to resort to foreign (usually Indian) labor. The same has been true of those occupations which,

---

[8] His willingness to clear chena land by hand would seem to belie this.

523

though not physically exhausting, are commonly regarded as "low caste".

Strong preference for government employment is an outstanding characteristic of the Ceylonese worker. At the higher occupational levels there is a traditional dignity attached to government service, probably arising out of the former authority of the colonial government official. Now the preference extends even into the ordinary unskilled occupations, and must be attributed in some degree to the easy-going policy of the government toward its workers. A government job is soft, secure, and pensionable, even if the wages are low.

Attributes. The Ceylonese worker acquires skills easily. Once satisfactorily placed, he prefers to remain in his job a long time, and so becomes proficient. Security of tenure is more important to him than personal advancement. This has a tendency to stifle the ambition to learn techniques beyond the requirements of his immediate task, and thus interferes with the upgrading process upon which industry normally counts to produce its foremen and supervisors. On the other hand, one good effect is that labor turnover is low.

An attribute worth a good deal is the pleasant and receptive disposition of most Ceylonese workers. Because of it, harmony is not difficult to maintain. Plant managers here—as anywhere else —must be fair, understanding and sympathetic to get the best results from their labor force. But they are not constantly faced with organized defiance, unreasonable demands, resistance to modern improvements, and similar bugbears that plague employers is less fortunate areas. This fact alone may go far in aiding Ceylon's future industrial and economic development.

RAW MATERIALS

Nothing in potential economic development can more easily lead to false conclusions than the question of available raw materials.

In the first place, local occurrence of a raw material is not a necessary condition for the establishment of an industry. It helps, but it is only one factor among many. Where other conditions are highly favorable a sound industry frequently can be built upon imported materials. For instance, it is improbable that Ceylon can ever be a good wheat-growing area; but local milling of foreign wheat would save on exchange, shipping and unloading costs, would minimize storage problems under tropical conditions, and would make valuable by-product animal feeds available locally instead of somewhere else.

As for what domestic materials are at hand, in the absence of adequate research and measurement the most expert opinions on this subject are nothing more than educated guesses. In Ceylon, as in most underdeveloped countries, the optimists talk of "vast untapped resources," while the pessimists conclude that the potentialities for anything new are insignificant merely because the materials in plain sight do not provide an obvious foundation for immediate expansion of large-scale industry.

Possible Ceylonese raw materials for industry include agricultural crops, livestock, forest products, minerals, marine life, and the atmosphere. For the first two, the ultimate variety and supply are certainly not limited to what is available at the moment; they can be decided by Ceylon herself, subject only to the liberal bounds of acreage, soil and climate. Under proper management this is equally true of forest products. There is even some choice in marine life, to the extent that such things as oysters, pearls and fish can be cultivated.

For the rest—in marine and forest products, minerals and the atmosphere—the island must accept what there is. But what is that? Fisheries are only now being studied. Whether we choose to regard the forests as something to be depleted or cultivated, it is certain that they contain many valuable products other than just timber and firewood. What research has been done to find and industrialize them? Mineral resources are only partially explored; the rest must be found by geological prospecting. In fact, of the various categories of existing or potential raw material resources, only the composition of the atmosphere is well-known.

Among the established or partially known raw materials available now are tea and tea waste; copra, coconut oil, poonac, coir fiber and waste; rubber; tropical woods; forest plants bearing tannins, fibers, dyes, drugs and extracts; seeds containing oils for soap, paints and cooking uses; rice hulls; tobacco and its wastes; cacao; assorted spices, fruits and grains; essential oils; animal hides and skins, blood, horns, hooves, bones and wastes; sea salt; gems, graphite, silica sand, ilmenite, monazite, thorianite, mica, clays, kaolin and iron ore; fish shells, pearls and other marine products. Those which definitely could be made more available through agricultural effort are too numerous to mention, but prominent among them for industrial use are the oil seeds, tannins, hard fibers, lighter tobaccos, sugar cane, cotton and milk.

A few of these materials are already in partial use. Others—notably tea, rubber, coconut derivatives and graphite—are mainly exported in the raw or semi-processed state. Many are not exploited at all. Several—such as rice hulls—are systematically thrown away, or burned without even recovery of their heating value.

But enumeration of these diverse raw materials does not mean that the Mission recommends immediate industrialization of all of them. Just as the presence of a local material is not always a requisite for establishing an industry, neither is it a complete justification for doing so. There must be other elements, and there must be proper timing. To return to the example of rice hulls, these may be extracted for oil at the moment when the continuous supply in one locality can justify a solvent extraction plant; until then they should be fed to cattle or else burned as fuel for the rice mills.

Among the minerals, the time is not ripe for local conversion of more than a few to finished products. Silica sand, kaolin and clays can be industrialized readily, for example, and to some extent are. Ilmenite could be concentrated now for export, but its manufacture into white paint in Ceylon is considered premature. Regions containing thorianite should be re-explored with a Geiger counter at once, as a likely source of dollar exchange if as much as 40-50 tons can be extracted annually. The known deposits of iron ore are appreciable but badly scattered, and probably should be held in reserve pending a major change in the fuel and energy situation.

Of the rest of the materials listed, some need only technical advice and market education for profitable utilization. Others may need more elaborate research before economic uses can be found for them. A number are agricultural products requiring lengthy trials and cultivation experiments before they can be grown in quantity. Finally, there are the many materials not now known to exist which may lie buried under the soil or be capable of cultivation if introduced.

Indeed, by far the most important thing that can be said of Ceylon's raw material resources is that a great deal more should be known about them. Intensification of the Geological Survey, experiments in new crops, and more effective industrial research as proposed in Chapters 4 and 19 are major steps to be taken toward this end.

CRITERIA FOR SELECTION OF INDUSTRIES

THE ROLE OF INDUSTRY

Ceylon seeks industrialization as a means for improving her level of living. In a purely materialistic sense industry may do this. But there are other ways to raise the level of living, too, and many ways to measure it. In the end it will always be determined by the extent to which a people's individual efforts can carry them toward health, comfort and happiness—whatever they themselves mean by these goals. We have sought to understand what the Ceylonese mean by them, and to estimate the particular contribution which industrial activity can make at this time.

The role which industry should play in Ceylonese economic development over the next few years is fairly clear. It emerges as a question of what will be the most effective utilization of available resources to satisfy the wants and needs of the Ceylonese people. There is competition for these resources. There are priorities among the wants and needs. Since industrialization cannot supply all of them, it is not a panacea for economic ills. In Ceylon the role of industry need not be minor; yet, in view of other local factors, it must remain secondary so long as the land is not well utilized and the island cannot yet feed its own people.

BASIC ELEMENTS

To suggest criteria for the selection of industries in an orderly development program, then, the Mission has first examined the available physical resources: capital, labor and raw materials. Elsewhere in this report we have considered the availability of power, which for most industries is a means of increasing the productivity of labor; and we have touched upon the scarcity of fuel, which may represent either power or raw material. These are the physical elements which must be put together in varying proportions as ingredients of industrial production.

Initiative and enterprise determine whether they will even be put together at all, and for what purposes. Technology must provide the correct method for putting them together, without which the resources themselves might be useless. And how effectively, economically and harmoniously the whole process is carried out depends upon the intangible quality of management. Therefore it has been necessary to attempt an evaluation of these elements too. Industries chosen for development should be, first of all, those whose requirements of the several resources—both physical and intangible—can be met most satisfactorily.

False goals should be avoided if progress is the aim. An outstanding example is the popular error—no more common in Ceylon than elsewhere—of calling for more industry as a means of providing employment. Of course it provides employment; but this is not its primary objective. If it were, then the most

528

inefficient and unproductive industries would be the most desirable. Certainly it is better, as a guide to development, to regard labor as a resource to be utilized profitably rather than as a public charge to be disposed of in some way.

Suggested Criteria

As indicated earlier, under appropriate conditions an industry based upon imported raw materials can be very successful. Ordinarily these cases are in the minority, however, unless there is a local surplus of some other component—such as skilled industrial labor, or perhaps cheap power. And until such a surplus exists in Ceylon, industrial development based primarily upon local materials is to be preferred. But in no sense is this a fast rule; in fact several exceptions are offered elsewhere in the present report.

We have noted, too, that existence of a local raw material does not necessarily justify its immediate utilization. For various economic reasons it may be better to leave it alone for the moment. Perhaps the market for the product is not yet large enough; or perhaps the people's needs can be satisfied from a cheaper source, to their benefit; or it may be that the country simply cannot afford to do everything at once, and must make a choice. Thus, for instance, there is no advantage to Ceylon in depleting her own future iron ore reserves merely because she has them; they will keep very well underground until later. To meet her present small requirements of steel, the island can ill afford the extra drain on her capital, power and other resources which a local steel mill would cause at this time.

Whenever possible, Ceylon should choose industries which do not require large amounts of fuel. [9] Coal or petroleum must be imported; there is no natural gas; local peat deposits are disappointing; and the use of firewood as industrial fuel elsewhere has almost invariably led to wanton destruction of forests.

---

[9] Exceptions to this are such industries as sugar mills, which use their own waste products as fuel.

Some few electrochemical industries and other heavy power users need not always be barred if otherwise suitable. It should be remembered, however, that such industries are the logical users of off-peak (low rate) hydroelectric power. Therefore their establishment should be timed to correspond reasonably with development of the island's limited hydroelectric potential; and above all, they should be situated where they can use it as early as possible, even if circumstances force initial dependence upon fuel.

Industries which demand huge volumes of fresh water may be acceptable, if local surveys positively assure such a supply continuously and without harm to surrounding agriculture. A great deal of water falls on Ceylon, but only seasonally and not uniformly (Chapter 11). Where wells are to be used, adequate continuous-pumping tests must be made; in many parts of the island salt water enters the wells as soon as large volumes are pumped.

Until vocational training has been greatly expanded and improved, the country should lean toward industries whose requirements of skilled labor are moderate, or whose techniques are simple enough that workers can be trained rapidly in the plants themselves.

As a governing policy the aims and circumstances of Ceylon, including the nature of her known raw materials and the immobility of her labor, favor development of numerous small industries rather than a few large ones. New discoveries may change the picture later; meanwhile, such a course is the shortest route to diversification in any event, and offers the greatest opportunity for wide participation in the benefits of industrialization.

As much as possible, new industries should be chosen so as to improve the economic stability of each other and of existing ones. This means absorbing materials from each other, supplying the market with complementary products, alternating any seasonal labor demands, furnishing return cargo for otherwise empty transport vehicles, etc. When industries are allowed to spring up by themselves, they tend automatically to form an intricate pattern of mutual dependence and assistance. When, as in Ceylon, a government feels that it must supply an initiative that is otherwise lacking, it must make a conscious effort to follow such a pattern. Random development of individual industries without thought of their interrelationships can be very wasteful of resources, and can sometimes place burdens upon the people greater than if they had no industries at all.

SOME PRESENT AND POTENTIAL INDUSTRIES

In the following pages the Mission reviews briefly the experience, needs and possible improvement of existing industries and offers some observations on the feasibility of a number of specific new ones. Much more could be said on each one of them. The Mission has tried to limit itself to presentation of the main problems, omitting unnecessarily detailed historical descriptions and academic discussion.

Potentialities of individual industries have been assessed on the basis of the general criteria already discussed and the particular facts as currently ascertainable. The short period of the Mission's visit did not permit complete engineering and economic analysis of all the numerous projects; however, earlier reports of persons retained by the government as experts have been studied, existing projects examined physically, and supplementary information obtained from as many sources as were available within the time allowed.

We have thought that it will be most helpful to the government if we express a frank and definite judgment based on the information available, whenever this is possible. We therefore recommend for some industries, including some not hitherto considered closely, and against others, even though they are included in current government plans. But there are some projects in which we have felt that the existing technical information was inadequate either to form a positive opinion or to justify immediate large investment. In such cases we have attempted to suggest

531

the lines of further study which sound caution requires. In some other cases we can do no more than indicate the desirability of original research, as existing information is not sufficient even to frame a concrete project.

To have expressed precise and definite views in every case reviewed would have been to ignore the lesson of all industrial experience: the necessity of research and close individual study before taking firm decisions about new possibilities. Our remarks on each industry will perhaps serve their most useful purpose if they provide pointers to practical studies to be made in due course by the proposed Institute for Applied Research and the Development Corporation.

Arrangement of products within this section is alphabetical. Occasionally, under the various heads, a few facts and figures may be restated to serve more than one purpose—a circumstance which in itself illustrates the interrelationships between industries.

BEER

Brewing has been conducted by a private corporation at Nuwara Eliya since 1884. The site, although removed from the principal market of Colombo, was originally chosen to provide a cool climate where less refrigeration would be needed. The local beer has a good market acceptance, and enjoys export throughout this part of the world. In the island it is preferred by many over the various imported brands.

Ceylonese beer at present is made entirely from imported materials—flaked corn, sugar, barley, hops, etc.—some of which may eventually be produced domestically. Carbon dioxide for recarbonation is brought from Colombo, where it too is made from imported fuel; the brewery could recover its own CO_2, which is now wasted. By-product yeast is all sold in Colombo. Spent grain and similar refuse is recovered for sale to nearby farmers as cattle feed and roughage.

Production, now at 44,000 gallons per month, is soon to increase to 60,000 upon completion of new installations now in progress. The increased demand is chiefly for bottled beer, which now accounts for more than half the output. Recently another corporation, with 51% Ceylonese capital, announced its intention to erect a second brewery to make up to 1,000,000 gallons per year. The plan is excellent, but we feel that the government should be prepared to give full cooperation in expanding the export of beer in this event; for the new installations in the existing brewery alone will bring domestic volume up to 80% of the island's present annual consumption of 900,000 gallons.

BOTTLE CAPS

Current production of bottled mineral water, carbonated beverages and other soft drinks is about 6,000,000 bottles per month, with an estimated potential market for 750,000 more of certain types. Bottled beer output is about 144,000 bottles monthly, soon to increase to 240,000. All of these use crown-type bottle caps. In addition, unknown amounts of milk, oil and other liquids are similarly bottled.

All of the island's bottle caps are now imported, sometimes with difficulty. The number consumed would, under Ceylonese conditions, approximately balance the output of a single hand-fed press of the type commonly used in forming these caps. This could be the start of a small local industry, and by interchange of dies it could expand into various other lines of sheet metal stamping as well. Lithographing and cork cutting would be involved as supplementary activities.

The principal objection offered by those approached by the Mission on this subject has been the problem of buying tinplate—which is as hard to get as the bottle caps. Yet today some candies, bakery goods and tobacco products made in the island for local consumption are packaged in tinplate, more as a carry-over from earlier days of overseas shipment than because of actual climatic necessity. Such tinplate could be diverted to more essential use, and with a saving in cost to the present users.

Stamping of small bottle caps affords a complete recovery of

533

the sheet, for the residue emerges as a bright perforated sheet often used in other countries for poultry fencing and highly effec· tive "scarecrows."

Buttons

For some time Ceylon has exported seashells, usable for making buttons and ornaments. Plans for a 1952 pearl fishing program are expected to yield an extraordinarily large supply of oyster shell, of a type especially suited to button manufacture. Authorities are already considering this activity.

After cutting out the discs of shells which are split and drilled for buttons, residual shell may be ground for use in poultry feed.

Canned Goods

Industrial canning and preserving of foods has not developed as rapidly as would be expected. Export, except for occasional gift packages, has not developed at all. The chief reason is lack of marketing effort; but behind this lies the failure to centralize the industry into economical production units and to bring about the uniformity of product which the buying public demands.

Experience shows that a significant canning industry cannot be built on anything resembling a cottage industry basis. It is true that "home-canned" products enjoy a certain sale everywhere; but for continuous bulk orders the central cannery, under close technical supervision, offers the only system capable of insuring the desired quality, sanitary standard and uniformity.

Canneries can seldom expect to operate economically on a single commodity. Mangoes ripen in a given district more or less at the same time, for example, and must all be canned at once. The cannery cannot afford to shut down thereafter until the next mango season; it must shift to other crops in succession through the year, keeping its equipment and staff busy as long as possible in order to lower its costs. To do this economically requires careful thought in locating the plant, for many fresh

534

fruits and vegetables will not stand long shipment or extra handling.

With these principles as a guide, the Mission believes that this industry could be greatly expanded. Apart from the commoner items for local consumption there are opportunities for specialty exports—notably several varieties of chutney for the dollar area. Shortage of tinplate need not offer a serious deterrent, as an improvement in local glass manufacture would provide containers of the type used increasingly in the trade. Standardized metal "press-on" closures would provide an additional line for the bottle-cap plant already suggested, and rubber sealing rings can be lathe-cut from locally-made rubber tube as is often done elsewhere.

CEMENT

Ceylon's cement plant, located atop the Kankesanturai limestone deposits on the Jaffna peninsula, has been the first of the government's modern factory projects to go into operation. Started in August, 1950, the plant uses the dry process and a single kiln equipped with a preheater. Its rated capacity is supposedly about 300 long tons per 24-hour day.

Although frequent press references give the present output at 250 tons per day, the records of the factory indicate that on very few days has the production exceeded 225 tons. These records also show that from January to October, 1951 the plant was shut down a total of some 50 days, in periods ranging from a day to several weeks, because of various troubles. Hence an actual output approaching rated capacity is still far from being achieved. Reasons for this are, in the main, inherent in the administrative structure.

Investment in the cement plant is now about Rs. 21 million for an annual production of not more than 60,000 tons. While the management hopes to make certain mechanical changes to raise the output of present equipment another 15,000 or 20,000 tons, total investment (by then Rs. 22.5 million) will still be disproportionately high. Accordingly, it is now planned to install a second kiln to raise production to 180,000 tons by the end of 1952, at an additional investment of Rs. 4.5 million. Such an output would approximately equal the island's consumption, as 113,503 long tons were imported in 1951 to supplement the present Kankesanturai production.

Consumer Reactions. Locally-made cement sells for Rs. 7.5 per bag at the plant, and for Rs. 9 in Colombo with transportation cost included; in small retail lots the Colombo price is Rs. 9.8. British cement is landed in Colombo, duty-paid at Rs. 9, but is often retailed at Rs. 11 or more because of its greater market acceptance. Duty-free buyers, such as the Gal Oya Board, can get cement delivered at Batticaloa from England at Rs. 6 per cwt. bag, or from India at Rs. 7—in either case cheaper than from Jaffna.

Preference for foreign cement is general, despite the fact that the Kankesanturai plant attempts to hold its product within British standard specifications. Consumers claim that the imported product consistently exceeds these specifications by a wide margin, while the local cement just meets them. Investigation discloses that the local plant control laboratory has never made comparative tests on this point. In any event, engineering and construction firms in Ceylon find that without the extra safety factor, use of local cement requires greater care in designing of structures. Large consumers such as the Colombo Port Works reportedly refuse to rely upon the Ceylonese product for this reason. Some users also complain of occasional substandard quality and shortweight bags; these charges, however, were not substantiated to the Mission.

Deliveries. Actually, the cement plant enjoys orders for much more cement than it can supply. The government has ruled that requests should be filled in the following order of preference:

(1) Charitable institutions
(2) Direct consumers (not dealers or contractors)
(3) Cooperative stores

(4) Government enterprises
(5) Small dealers
(6) Large dealers

At the time of the Mission's visit new orders were arriving at the rate of 700 to 800 tons daily. Outstanding orders in mid-November totalled 7,000 tons, and buyers were asked to limit new individual orders to 26 tons each—representing two railroad carloads. Meanwhile, not only was the effective plant capacity limited to a third of the demand, but the shortage of railroad cars prevented movement of more than 60-70% of the output. Thus, until the transport difficulty is removed, installation of a second kiln will not solve the problem.

Difficulties. Mechanically, the plant is a fairly good one. Initially a poorly constructed roof collapsed; since then the preheating system has given some trouble; the limestone crane is overworked through unnecessarily repetitious handling of material; and the sacking and carloading operations could be improved to reduce losses through breakage of bags. But these defects will soon be corrected.

Most of the shut-downs and troubles can be attributed, directly or indirectly, to the difficulties of outright government operation of the plant, and are so recognized. Replacement parts have been slow in arriving because of lengthy government purchase methods; and constant official intervention in management has made it difficult for the plant to retain competent technical help for more than short periods. As for operating costs, it appears that the factory employs from two to three times the number of workers that it needs.

The Mission believes that removal of the management functions from government offices will alleviate at least 90% of the cement plant's troubles, and will permit it to make a real contribution to the island's development as a soundly based industry.

CHEMICALS

Caustic Soda. Annual consumption of caustic soda is about

1,500-2,000 tons, now imported chiefly from England and to a smaller extent from the United States. It is presently used almost exclusively in soap making. The island's largest and most modern soap factory in Colombo consumes around 1,000 tons, the remainder going to numerous smaller plants in Colombo, Kandy and elsewhere. Consumers at present receive the caustic in the solid form, storing it in the original shipping drums until used.

Initial contracts have already been let by government for erection of an electrolytic caustic soda plant to be located close to the Elephant Pass saltern at the base of the Jaffna peninsula. Projected cost is in the neighborhood of Rs. 8 million.

It is understood that the factory will produce annually 1,500 tons of caustic soda, with an expected 1,200 tons of by-product chlorine and 15,000,000 cu. ft. of hydrogen. Raw solar-evaporation salt from Elephant Pass will be refined and electrolyzed by the usual methods. Power required will be around 6,000,000 kwh per year, which will have to be supplied by a new thermoelectric plant using imported fuel. The caustic soda will be shipped to Colombo and other consuming centers in water solution, at approximately double the tonnage of the dry material.

The location of the plant is not the best. It is as far as possible from any potential source of hydroelectric power—so far that connection with an island-wide power grid cannot be visualized for at least a decade or more. Likewise, it is as far as possible from its main market; this means an unnecessarily high transport cost, using special railroad cars or containers to handle the corrosive caustic solution. Fuel, if imported through Colombo, will also have an unnecessarily high rail transport cost; yet if fuel can be discharged in the north, the remaining transport load (product) will be southbound only, over the same line already carrying an uncompensated southbound cargo from the cement mill and thus aggrevating the car shortage. Only about 25% of the chlorine can be utilized in the associated DDT plant (discussed below), so that whatever of the remainder is saleable will have to be transported also, either as chlorine in very expensive cylinders or as bleaching powder at increased tonnage. There is no immediate prospect for utilization of the hydrogen at Elephant Pass, except for a small amount which would be burned with chlorine to form hydrochloric acid; most of the hydrogen will be wasted, unless a further investment in pressure cylinders is contemplated.

Availability of salt is given as the reason for placing the plant near Jaffna. But the Mission observes that salt of equivalent quality [10] is available at Palavi, less than half the distance from Colombo and Kandy, and closer by rail to the projected paper mill at Valaichchenai where some of the caustic and chlorine may be used. Palavi, furthermore, is within reach of hydroelectric power through development of the power grid shown in Map 15. and would permit utilization of surplus power at certain times. An Elephant Pass factory, with little or no prospect of hydroelectric connections, will be forced to remain dependent upon fuel from abroad.

Relocation of the plant at Palavi would not, of course, eliminate the need for special shipping containers. Yet it would shorten shipping distances, reducing both freight costs and the total investment tie-up in containers or cars. With the proposed restoration of the rail extension to Puttalam (Chapter 16), we believe that this location would provide caustic soda to Ceylonese users at a lower price and with smaller capital outlay.

One further suggestion, whose costs should be studied at once, is the temporary utilization of Gal Oya power for making caustic soda. For some years it seems probable that much of this power will be wasted unless very expensive transmission lines are built (see Chapter 14). The electrolytic cells are small self-contained units which can be installed there and moved later, and most of the auxiliary equipment can be similarly recovered; a temporary building at Gal Oya would be usable for some other purpose later, remodelling only its floor.

---

[10] For electrolysis all of it will have to be purified further, regardless of source.

Naturally, this presupposes the transport facilities which Gal Oya must have anyway. Also, it means hauling salt in and product out, and it entails extra moving and installation costs later. To offset this, it eliminates an extra power plant at this time as well as several years' purchase of fuel, and would recover a large percentage of Gal Oya power on which investment charges are already being incurred. How these factors balance will depend upon a careful and realistic cost accounting, which we strongly recommend as the first step.

DDT Insecticide. Consumption of DDT on the island in recent years has approached 325 tons per year, [11] and is expected to increase with extension of the antimalarial campaign. UNICEF has offered to donate the equipment and initial technical personnel for a Rs. 2 million plant making 500 tons of DDT annually, provided that Ceylon assures supplies of the necessary alcohol, benzene, chlorine and sulphuric acid.

It is planned to install this plant at Elephant Pass, close to the caustic soda plant. Counting losses, it would then absorb about one fourth of the electrolytic chlorine available. Sulphuric acid, alcohol and benzene will have to be imported, although it has been planned that ultimately the sulphuric acid and alcohol will be made on the island.

As with the caustic soda plant, the DDT factory would benefit in shipping costs by placing it in a more central location such as Palavi. Materials will have to be transported from a seaport— at present Colombo or possibly Trincomalee. The DDT will be distributed to various parts of the island, in smaller lots which can be sent either by rail or highway.

Sulphuric Acid. Several proposals have been made for the manufacture of sulphuric acid. The soundness of any of them is debatable. The island has no known commercial deposits of

---

[11] As Technical DDT equivalent, representing some 70% of this amount as pure DDT compound. The crude product also contains other chlorinated compounds formed by side reactions in the process.

sulphur, pyrites, or other standard sulphur sources; nor are these things easy to obtain. One current scheme is to make the acid from gypsum; it has even been proposed that this be obtained from the local salterns. It should be pointed out that the amount available from salterns is only trivial (see *Salt*), that the supply would probably have to be imported from India or Egypt, and that to make sulphuric acid from gypsum under any circumstances is a costly and uneconomic process to be resorted to only in emergencies.

Of the various plans, the most recent is the announced intention of the government to build a sulphuric acid plant at Elephant Pass, in order to supply acid to the DDT plant just discussed. This cannot be justified on economic grounds. The smallest feasible contact-process plant would produce at least six times as much acid as the DDT process would require, and there is no other major use for sulphuric acid in that region. Furthermore, the small amount of acid used in making DDT can be regenerated, for its serves as a coupling and dehydrating agent and is not actually consumed in the process. In view of the general shortage of sulphur, it is predicted that this re-use of acid will soon become standard practice in DDT plants. In any case the needs of this plant can be met easily with an occasional small rail shipment.

If sulphuric acid production were at all feasible in Ceylon, it would be preferable to make it either at the proposed fertilizer factory (but see further remarks under *Fertilizer*) or else near Colombo where it can serve the various smaller consumers— but under no circumstances at Elephant Pass. Under present conditions Ceylon's prospects for buying acid from existing foreign plants are probably better than her chance of acquiring its raw material.

Acetic Acid. Both acetic and formic acids are imported for the coagulation of rubber, as well as for minor uses. Imports in 1951 totalled 6,710 cwt. of acetic acid valued at Rs. 543,598, and 7,639 cwt. of formic acid worth Rs. 769,344.

Interesting experiments during 1940-41 indicated an unusually high yield of acetic acid obtainable by destructive distillation of coconut shells. On the basis of the first rough laboratory tests a pilot plant was erected by the government at Madampe in 1942, and an attempt was made to operate it commercially.

It appears that the action was premature at each stage. Preliminary laboratory work was not carried far enough, the pilot plant was built without adequate data, and promising side-reactions were not properly investigated. Available technical advice was overruled, perhaps because of undue administrative enthusiasm and haste. The project was a failure.

Ceylon's need for acetic acid will continue, and there are two possibilities for its local manufacture. One is by the controlled oxidation of molasses alcohol. For the other, a full scientific review of earlier destructive distillation experiments—to be made by the proposed Institute for Applied Research—may suggest a renewal of this experimental work on a more critical chemical engineering basis.

Clay Products

Pottery is made on the island, both in small factories and as a cottage industry. Brick and tile are manufactured on a somewhat larger scale, although the output cannot satisfy local needs. Imports in this class are chiefly tiles from India, of which over 20 million were purchased in 1951.

From 1943 until recently the government operated a ceramic factory for pottery and semi-porcelain articles. Using obsolete methods and lacking proper technology, its rejection rate on manufactured ware ran as high as 95%; its financial losses were among the highest of all government factories—averaging each year 4.46 times the invested capital. It is now being demolished and replaced with a new one to be run as a cooperative. The government has also announced intentions of opening six new brick kilns in various locations.

In every respect there is room for improvement in these industries. The Jaffna Museum exhibits bricks, taken from ancient tanks, which are superior to many made and sold locally today. Colonists have protested against the use of domestic roofing tiles on houses provided to them free, and have asked the government for Indian-made tiles.

Actually, there is scant justification for continuing to depend on imports for good quality bricks, tiles and ceramic ware. The island has workable clays, some of which need modified processing. Kaolin, potentially the basis for a chinaware and porcelain industry, occurs widely in large deposits; near Colombo, one deposit alone is estimated at 10 million tons. Inadequacy of funds for research in this field can be blamed at least partially for the lagging development.

Pottery-making suffers from a shortage of skilled workers. In its cottage industry aspect, a little inexpensive modernization of the wheels and kilns would be of great help. More critical standards of production would benefit the larger factory operations, as is true also in the making of bricks and tiles. The use of local firewood and coconut husks for firing presents certain problems of uneven heating and fuel loss, which careful experimentation could correct.

Some technical progress in these matters has been made by government ceramists. It is disappointing that so little effort has been made to publish and disseminate their findings for the benefit of the industry. We recommend that this be done—not once but continuously—and that such experimentation also continue for constant improvement. Work of the government ceramics laboratory may be supplemented later by related studies in the proposed Institute for Applied Research.

Coconut *(Desiccated)*

A very substantial industry exists in the manufacture of desiccated (shredded) coconut. Export shipments of its several grades have grown steadily over recent years, exceeding 100,000,000 lbs. in 1950. Production methods are improving slowly, and it is not improbable that more rapid advances could result from an industry-wide technical study. However, a good many factories will be able to reduce their costs at this stage merely by emulating the more progressive ones in choice of equipment and handling procedures.

COCONUT OIL

As the only vegetable oil yet to achieve importance in Ceylon, coconut oil is not only one of the principal exports but also the island's main cooking oil, the basis for the local soap industry, and almost the sole standby for a hundred domestic purposes calling for an oil of this type.

Production and Consumption. In terms of oil (or oil content) annual exports of oil and copra in the last decade have averaged about 87,000 tons; this was approximately the level for 1950, after a high of 138,830 tons in 1943. Local consumption cannot be determined as accurately, but for some years the trade has estimated it at 100 tons daily, or about 36,500 tons per year. On this basis the portion of Ceylon's coconuts destined for oil purposes represents the equivalent of 123,500 tons of recovered oil.

Actual exports are made only partly as oil, and partly as copra to be processed elsewhere. But especially over the last ten years, the proportion of oil expressed on the island has grown from 26% to over 85%. The shift has received added impetus recently through preferential export duties designed to encourage local processing.

Extraction Methods. By far the greatest part of the oil is processed through expellers; of these there are at least 154 units on the island, with a combined capacity of 835 tons per day. Anderson expellers predominate in number, although a few of the larger new ones are of other types. In addition, a comparatively small amount of oil is extracted in crude stone and steel *chekkus* (little primitive mills) whose output is all consumed domestically.

Tests of the poonac (spent cake) from various expellers on the island indicate a probable average residual oil content of 7-8%, representing about 5% of the original oil in the copra. The chekkus, of course, are much less efficient and yield a poonac containing 15% or more residual oil; on the other hand, they represent very little of the total production. The Mission emphasizes this distinction to correct a misunderstanding, for there has been a good deal of publicity suggesting that Ceylon's poonac averages 15% oil, whereas in fact only a small portion of the poorest grade reaches this figure.

Milling Capacity. Ignoring the chekkus, the known installed capacity of modern expellers could produce 250,500 tons of oil per year of 300 working days. Reducing this conservatively to a 250-day year, to allow for holidays, short crop seasons and repairs, would still give a capacity of 208,750 tons, not taking into account any intended new installations.

Actual oil output is much less. The highest export of processed oil, in 1951, was about 104,800 tons; to this we may add estimated domestic consumption of 36,500 tons, giving a total of 141,300 tons. Thus it would appear that in the best year to date total output was less than 68% of available capacity. Stated another way, the supply of copra reaching the existing mills is only enough to keep these units running at capacity for 169 days per year. Furthermore, if the remaining copra now available for export (after meeting other local needs for coconuts for food, etc.) were all supplied to these mills, it would be used up in another 15 days.

Government Plans. According to information supplied by the Ministry of Industries, the government intends to install its own oil processing plant at Seeduwa. This will have an expeller capacity to handle 200 tons of copra daily, followed by a continuous solvent extraction unit. There will also be a batch extraction plant to take 50 tons per day of poonac, groundnuts or other oil-bearing material.

Cost of the project is announced as Rs. 12 million. Its justification is given as the desire to recover the final 4-5% of the original oil now left in the poonac. It is also reported that the plant will engage in a series of secondary processes such as oil refining, hydrogenation, and manufacture of fatty acids and glycerine. The Mission understands that engineering designs are now being made with outside technical help, and presumes that this will lead to certain reductions in the original ambitious plan.

Comments. We feel that in principle the introduction of solvent extraction will be a definite step forward. Several of the larger private companies on the island are also contemplating it—which raises a question as to the need for the government to do it. What is alarming, however, is the government's plan to increase the total expeller capacity of the island when present units are greatly under-utilized. Such an act could not be characterized as anything less than an outright waste of public funds, and it is hoped that plans will be changed on further study.

If the solvent extraction method is introduced, it should be in connection with existing expellers. These could then be operated at a somewhat lower optimum extraction rate, the remaining oil being removed by solvent. But to install a plant to absorb raw copra into new expellers will draw scarce raw material away from present plants; some will undoubtedly be forced out of business.

These facts imply that any government participation in the coconut oil industry should be by way of financing the use of solvent extraction in existing plants. This may be done through the proposed Development Corporation, enlisting private capital also and encouraging private or cooperative—rather than governmental—operation of such plants. Any further assistance to the development of the oil industry might well take the form of encouraging farmers to produce other types of oil seeds.

COIR FIBER

Although a number of hard fibers are potentially important in Ceylon (Chapter 11), that of the coconut husk will continue to be a major product so long as copra and coconut oil are among the island's main exports.

The fiber is obtained by retting the husks for three to six weeks in lagoons, then combing it out on revolving spiked drums. Short (mattress) and long (bristle) fiber is separated in this process. Mattress fiber receives little more treatment except for removal of coarse vegetable matter by tumbling and screening. The better grades of bristle fiber are later hackled and bleached (SO_2).

Commercial fiber extraction is carried out as above in about 300 small factories in a small area north and east of Colombo. Their product supplies most of the exported fiber, whose grading and final processing is done by large exporters in the capital. In addition, however, there is an appreciable cottage industry in fiber extraction, rope and yarn spinning, and mat weaving; this is scattered, but an important area of concentration extends along the entire west coast south of Colombo.

Utilization. An overwhelming percentage of Ceylon's commercial fiber is simply baled and exported, without manufacture into finished articles. Mattress fiber—and to an appreciable extent bristle fiber also—finds use in purchasing countries as upholstery stuffing; in this application only a small amount can be absorbed in Ceylon manufactures, as there is slight hope for export of upholstered furniture. On the other hand much of the bristle fiber eventually goes into brushes, door mats, and other products which could be made locally for export.

Governmental interest in development of coir manufactures has lagged. At one time a small factory was installed at Katunayake, but in common with other government-operated industries it was not a commercial success. Since then attention has been concentrated upon the cottage industry aspects—which indeed merit it —but further prospects of large-scale mechanized manufacture apparently have not been considered.

From questioning, it appears that some officials feel that factory-made coir goods would interfere with the cottage industry, although admittedly there exists a very special market for hand-made yarn. Others feel that exclusive export of baled fiber must be accepted as the natural order, and that local manufacture into finished goods will not be economically successful; failure of the Katunayake factory is cited in support of this view and it is claimed that Ceylon cannot compete with the labor costs of the Cochin coast of India.

We believe that this illustrates one inherent danger in hastily conceived factory projects; for such enterprises, handicapped from the first, should not be taken as a guide, lest they discourage sounder ones. In this case one must reflect that the exported fiber is indeed manufactured into articles elsewhere, or it would not be sold; and this manufacture is often done under wage rates much higher than India's or Ceylon's, but compensated by efficient methods. The case of copra was once similar, yet now the island manufactures oil and even soap.

Suggestions. A concerted drive should be made to determine potential foreign and domestic markets for finished coir goods of uniform manufactured quality. Buyers' specifications should be obtained, and plans made to meet them by commercially managed production. Simultaneously, thought should be given to new uses for coir, as in the manufacture of rope-soled shoes described elsewhere in this chapter.

Wall board, siding and panels for building construction can be made in several ways by bonding coir fiber with cement, shellac or other materials. A Ceylonese inventor has recently made such board from the waste coir dust which accumulates at fiber mills. These, and many other possible uses for both fiber and dust, should be subjected to practical trials by the proposed Institute for Applied Research.

CONFECTIONERY AND CHOCOLATE

Candy of various kinds is made by at least 118 commercial manufacturers as well as by numerous householders who offer it for sale. Total volume, to judge by sugar consumption, is nearly 10,000 tons yearly; a further 650 tons are imported. The industry is said to employ 5,000 persons.

Plants range in size up to about 50 workers. The larger ones are semi-mechanized and make as many as 300 varieties, with no large volume of any single type. It is at once clear that greater economies could be realized in individual plants by concentrating on continuous production of fewer varieties. Present investment in rolls, dies, etc. is high in proportion to output, and during much of the time machinery units are now idle or shut down for the frequent conversion and interchange of dies.

Candy consists almost entirely of sugar. Manufacturers complain that the government adds a mark-up of about 80% to the cost of the sugar it sells them, while customs duties on imported confectionery have been lowered from 60% to 25%. Under these circumstances imports of confectionery doubled between 1950 and 1951. The foreign tonnage is still not large enough to have hurt domestic production, and its competition is helpful in holding down retail prices. At the same time, the local industry appears to be unnecessarily penalized and is not encouraged to expand. The Mission believes that this situation may merit some adjustment—through a lowered sugar price, if possible, rather than a more protective tariff.

Some standard types of local candy are packed in tins, whose cost represents 20% of the wholesale price. The custom apparently originated in imitation of British confectionery packed for long ocean shipment to Ceylon. For local consumption, however, it should be unnecessary; plenty of similar candy is sold in cardboard boxes or paper wrappers, and is preserved satisfactorily. Considering the high cost and the shortage of tinplate, the tinning of confectionery may well be abandoned.

Chocolate. As a specialized branch of confectionery manufacture, the chocolate industry on the island has suffered more than the rest—partly through its own fault. Of the several chocolate factories once operated, most have now closed and the largest remaining one has reduced its staff from 150 to 40 workers. This is unfortunate, since cocoa is a domestic crop.

Chocolate production is subject to the same problems of sugar prices and customs duties as affect the rest of the industry. But in addition, techniques of manufacture are much more critical and consumer-preference has a greater effect on sales. Also, the distribution and sale of chocolate in a hot climate requires extra precautions to prevent loss. Thus only the most alert local manufacturers have survived in competition with carefully made imports.

For development in this line, the real key is not fiscal protection but a greater quality-consciousness on the part of the local industry, plus enterprise and salesmanship. Present chocolate candy can be made smoother, less crystalline and more homogeneous. New products such as baking chocolate, breakfast cocoa and syrup can be added to the output. The basic technology of chocolate preparation is described in standard reference books; hence technical improvement, in all but the highest refinements, presents no unusual problem.

DAIRY PRODUCTS

Health authorities recognize that the local milk production and consumption of dairy products is far too low (see Chapter 17). While it is difficult to separate cause and effect in this instance, a number of definite influences can be recognized.

Government efforts to create dairy industries must aim at making the primary milk production profitable to the private farmer. Maintenance of government milk producing centers (Chapter 11) is helpful; but since the government cannot hope to milk all the cows, its breeding experiments, stud centers and extension education are of greater significance. Dairying will not attract more farmers so long as a Ceylonese cow gives only a few quarts of milk per day.

An equally important government task is to assure the public a safe and healthful product. There is no dairy inspection service. So far as the Mission knows only two private dairies [12] are

---

[12] One of these uses an exceptionally modern milking machine, of a type only now being installed in the more advanced countries. Milk runs directly from the cow to processing equipment, through steril-

producing milk by methods fully satisfactory in health standards, although conceivably there are some others. Ordinarily, the island's milk is produced under filthy conditions. Moreover, in a recent experiment adulteration was found in 60% of the cases tested.

Milking and handling conditions on the government farms—which supply hospitals—are fair but not perfect. There are no coolers, although a fundamental of good dairy practice is to cool the milk immediately after milking to arrest bacterial growth. To date, at least, the milk is not pasteurized; it is merely placed aboard the night train for Colombo, to arrive in the early morning.

Processed Milk. Production of butter, cheese, casein and secondary dairy products cannot become significant until the general milk supply is greatly increased. On the other hand, maldistribution of milk might be relieved by use of the latest concentrating process. In this the milk is first pasteurized and homogenized, after which two thirds of the water is removed in a standard stainless steel vacuum pan. The resulting concentrated liquid is then again pasteurized, homogenized and bottled. In this state it can be shipped or stored under refrigeration for a month or more. It is reconstituted by the user, who adds more or less water to make milk or cream as desired. In flavor it is considered by many to be superior to fresh milk, and users often prefer to add more water than was originally removed.

Similar advantages can be obtained through manufacture of dried milk powder, which Ceylon now imports. However, this is not always as popular with individual domestic users. Further-

ized stainless steel pipes, registering its weight enroute. It is pasteurized, cooled by refrigeration, and shipped to Colombo in insulated trucks. There it is mechanically bottled by an independent food company, and distributed to consumers. The entire operation is a model to be studied, although not all dairies need such elaborate equipment to produce good milk.

551

more, spray-drying equipment is expensive and limited in application, while the standard equipment for the liquid concentrating process could be recovered readily for other use if for any reason the process were later abandoned.

Drugs

A small factory for extraction of quinine from local cinchona bark was opened by the government in early 1943. At various times later, we are informed, this plant undertook production of strychnine, pyrethrum, caffeine, and shark liver oil.

At the end of 1951 the drugs factory was closed, owing to a drop in demand for quinine and for other reasons. It performed a useful service in alleviating wartime shortages, but was not a financial success. At that, its average annual loss (22% of invested capital) was one of the smallest of all the operating deficits of the various government factories.

Shark oil production has been transferred to the Fisheries Department. Quinine extraction is stopped. Production of caffeine and some other drugs will be continued by the Laboratory of the Ministry of Industries.

The Mission suggests that more economical caffeine production could be handled by one or more private tea factories, and that the remaining drug production of this original enterprise be suspended until more urgent need or a wider market develops. Meanwhile, research in preparation for future new drug products from local materials should be continued.

Fertilizer

Plans now being pushed by the government call for the erection of a small factory at Kantalai (southwest of Trincomalee) for the annual production of 80,000 tons of ammonium sulphate and possibly 40,000 tons of superphosphate. This will involve burning 300 tons of firewood per day, local production of sulphuric acid, and importation of gypsum and phosphate rock. The probable investment has been guessed locally at Rs. 50 million.

At least two independent engineering reports were submitted on this project in 1949. The first was rejected because its recommendations were based upon a similar Indian project which has not proven as successful as hoped. The second is being used with some modifications as a basis for still a third, now in preparation by a new specialist. The wood-burning feature is common to all of them, however, and the Mission finds that the troubles experienced in India were to a large extent due to underestimating the difficulties and costs of providing this material.

In Ceylon it has been assumed that a 25,000-acre forest tract adjoining the plant can supply 300 tons of wood daily on a sustained 50-year cycle (most of the 800 workers to be employed are for forest work). However, informed local estimates as well as foreign experiences in similar tropical forests indicate that not more than one quarter to one third of the required wood will be forthcoming. We fear that in practice this circumstance will inevitably lead to clear felling. Also, if our estimates are correct, within 12 to 14 years the entire wood supply of the tract will be exhausted, leaving the factory dependent upon more distant and costly sources.

As already mentioned, manufacture of sulphuric acid will be handicapped from the first. With world supplies of sulphur short, it will be difficult for Ceylon to obtain its needs at the expense of existing plants; it would be safer to count on purchasing the acid. Regardless of whether the island buys sulphur or acid (or the fertilizer itself), it will remain dependent upon imports.

Fertilizer consumption, even if it doubles or trebles within the next few years, will remain comparatively small. Ordinarily the supplies are ample. If there are occasional difficulties in obtaining it from abroad, it is only because of shortages of the very raw materials which Ceylon would have to import for her own factory. Thus there seems to be little justification for Ceylon to make such a large factory investment for fertilizer within the next 10 or 15 years. It is recommended that the project be postponed and the funds diverted to more urgent needs.

FISH

Development of the fishery industry has been the subject of considerable technical study in recent years. [13] While it has been estimated that in view of other food supplies domestic consumption should be at least 35 lbs. per capita per year (Japan consumes over 60 lbs.) actual consumption is only about 20 lbs. Even so, nearly half of this is imported from India, the Maldive Islands and elsewhere.

Fishing occupies some 120,000 persons, distributed about the entire coast but chiefly on the northern half of the island. One government trawler is in operation; other than this most fishing is conducted on a small scale on or near shore, using beach seines, catamarans and outrigger canoes. The catch includes various edible fish as well as some sharks, lobsters and assorted mollusks. Shells are exported. Pearl diving—suspended for the last 25 years—is being reopened under government supervision this year.

Problems. Traditionally the individual fishermen have been financed by middlemen. The terms have left the fishermen very little return for their efforts; many of them, in fact, have found themselves permanently in debt. Abuses of this kind have led increasingly to formation of fishermen's cooperative societies, and these together with various types of government assistance in marketing are improving the situation.

Since the bulk of the catch is in the north, while the largest market is Colombo, transport is a major problem. Only two refrigerated railroad cars are reported to exist, and as of December 1951 their working order had not been substantiated by the Mission or by the FAO fisheries team.

Neither is there adequate refrigerated storage. At present fish

---

[13] Principal studies, except the current one being conducted through FAO, are presented in detail in a government publication, *Ceylon Fisheries—Recommendations of Experts on Fisheries Development, Research, Socio-Economic and Industrial Problems;* Sessional Paper VI (1951).

must be sold without fail the day it reaches Colombo. Canny buyers, aware of this, often are able to delay purchase until the price crashes at the end of the day. Four new ice plants, to be built by the Fisheries Department at (or near) Jaffna, Mannar, Puttalam and Colombo, may afford some relief; their combined capacity will be only 25 tons, however, sufficient for only a portion of the catch. Another proposal calls for small portable ice plants to be used at seasonal fishing centers. Mechanically refrigerated trucks and central cold storage depots at consumption points do not appear to have been considered to date.

Regarding the basic need to enlarge the catch, there is no easy solution. The government has hoped to purchase more trawlers, but to expect a large increase by this means is to ignore the real problem: traditionally the Ceylonese are neither fishermen nor seamen. Experts, judging from their experience with the present trawler, estimate that it may take a generation to train enough personnel to operate such boats without excessive risk. Furthermore, local fishermen today do not care to use the new types of gear being introduced; they dislike abandoning their old nets, which in fact are quite good for their original purposes.

Prospects. Under these circumstances the best that can be expected is a very gradual increase in catch, through small successive improvements, and a better economic position for the fishermen to be achieved by improved financing, handling and marketing. Meanwhile, ocean research is needed to provide more knowledge of the profitable fishing areas, quantities and types available, and seasonal movement. The research, at least, can be accomplished if the government is prepared to pay the salary scale generally accorded to competent specialists in this field.

Until the catch is much larger, more centralized and more regular from day to day, there is no prospect of an economic fish cannery. For the same reason no large supply of fish meal (for feed or fertilizer) is in sight for the near future—although small amounts are made by scattered individuals today. Any significant production of shark liver oil will require more sharks than have been caught to date.

Potentially important as the fishing industry is, then, two main points emerge concerning its expansion: (a) the catch can be enlarged somewhat at this time by increasing the effective fishing time of present personnel and equipment—using such means as towing the small boats to and from the grounds; (b) for the rest, any substantial increase must await the training of many more seamen and fishermen. Ceylon cannot expect a large catch—even by buying new trawlers—until this last is done. It may take many years.

GLASS

Two factories—one private and one operated by the government—produce a limited amount of glassware on the island. Both use local glass sand and cullet and imported supplementary materials. Principal products are tumblers, lamp chimneys and paperweights. A few specialties such as ink bottles and jars are also made. All of the glassware is hand-blown.

Ceylonese glass sand is of fair quality, but contains traces of ilmenite which impart an undesirable dark color to the product. This can be removed, but attempts to do so have only just begun.

Locally made glassware is protected by the Industrial Products Act, requiring purchase of a fixed percentage of the domestic product with all similar importations. But much of the local material is unsaleable, particularly that from the government factory, with the result that dealers must charge the public more for the desired imported ware in order to cover the expense of these forced purchases.

Government Glass Factory. Existence of the government glass factory in its present form and location is difficult to explain. The Mission has taken into account the fact that it was built under wartime conditions, but this hardly justifies its extreme inefficiency even with its primitive methods. Its flow lines could hardly be worse. Its location has little to commend it expect the proximity of sand, which could be shipped cheaply in bulk; everything else, including fuel, must be hauled in, and the fragile product must be shipped at higher rates back to Colombo. Its financial losses have been great, averaging annually more than twice the invested capital.

Plant layout is fundamentally bad from the first. Blowers walk as far as 40 ft. from the pot to the mold for each article blown. Annealing is done by wood fires, unevenly and by guesswork. Finished ware is carried in boxes, over a tortuous circuit of several hundred feet, to a separate building for sorting; rejects (for cullet) are carried all the way back—and the rejects amount to 60-70% of the total blown. [14] Cut-off and fire polishing are done in still another building.

To do these things the plant employs 315 men—several times as many as should be needed for a hand-blown production of this size. Plant capacity has been rated at 850 tons per year, now reduced to 400 tons since one furnace has been torn down; but with shut-downs and various organizational troubles the 1950-51 output was only 98 tons. The highest ever reached was 216 tons in 1946-47, and the eight year average is only 126 tons.

Aside from poor factory design, which must be attributed to deficient technical advice in the beginning a basic trouble lies in the method of management. Although a skilled foreign manager has been retained, his authority to act is inadequate for proper discharge of a manager's functions. It is reported that no less than 29 different government officials direct his actions by signed orders. Many of the shut-downs are for lack of supplies, caused by delays in approval of recommendations and the cumbersome purchasing mechanism of government. Staff morale is low; the manager lacks even the power to hire, promote or discharge workers in accordance with his best judgment. These and similar

---

[14] In an attempt to reclaim rejected glass, cullet runs as high as 70-80% in the molten glass batch, to the detriment of quality; it should not exceed 30% for this type of product.

problems, common to the various government-operated plants, have already been discussed earlier in this chapter.

From a technical standpoint, the Mission can see nothing to do with this factory except to abandon it. Attempts to reorganize it are futile; if the government feels that a glass factory of its own is actually necessary it will be cheaper in the long run to build an entirely new one—properly designed, better located and under independent management. To put more money into the present one will be, in our opinion, a continuing waste of development funds.

Private Glass Manufacture. Commercial production of glassware under private management has been more successful, and has shown a profit. Methods used at present are somewhat more advanced, although not the most modern. For example, the ware is hand blown, but annealing is done in an automatic lehr and is more uniform. Rejection is low, so that cullet admixtures are within normal limits and the glass is of a more controlled quality.

Private installation of new automatic bottle-making and flat glass machinery is being contemplated.

Prospects for Bottle Manufacture. Breakage and nonrecovery of soft drink bottles on the island is estimated at 10% of monthly beverage production, or around 180,000 per month. Beer bottle replacements currently average 5,000 monthly, and will shortly increase to about 8,000 with expanded brewery output.

At present most replacements are purchased from second-hand dealers, who collect bottles originally brought to the island as containers for imported beer and other liquids. Large-size beer bottles, not used in Ceylon, are exported to India; but mixed with these are some 8,000 to 10,000 small bottles each month. This loss to the local beverage industry is made up by direct importation of new bottles at a landed cost of about 30 cents each.

Local beverage bottlers express the view that they would welcome domestic manufacture to meet their growing bottle needs. Such bottles, however, must be made to very exacting standards in order to function in modern capping machinery and to withstand the high gas pressure required. The Mission emphasizes that poorly made bottles for beverage use would be a genuine public menace, and the cause of many serious accidents. Establishment of local bottle manufacture must be predicated on very competent and authoritative technical management and the use of modern automatic machinery.

On the basis of past and current performance, the Mission feels that an attempt at government manufacture of beverage bottles would not give the Ceylonese public the required safeguards. By the same token, application of the Industrial Products Act to this class of goods would be to invite the loss of children's eyes, disfigurement and worse, as well as to jeopardize growth of the local beverage industry.

LEATHER

Manufacture of leather is not yet an important industry. Animal slaughter is small, and even then only a part of the available supply of hides is processed on the island. Local tanning is done in 16 small private tanneries and one operated by the government in connection with its shoe factory. Except for the latter and a few handicraft shops, fabrication of leather products is almost negligible.

Varying in size but not in methods, the private tanneries each handle 3,000 cattle hides or less per month. Processing is primitive. Actual tanning is done in vats, without control, usually by a 40-day immersion in mimosa (wattle) extract followed by three or four days treatment in a bath made from gall nuts to improve the color.

After the tanner has obtained his hides, government agents come and select the best from his stock. These are purchased at fixed prices for shipment to the government tannery. [15] The re-

---

[15] Private tanners permit this, claiming that if they did not they would be refused export permits for their finished products. Prices paid in December, 1951, were Rs. 0.375 per lb. for cattle hides and Rs. 1.16 each for goat skins.

mainder are then tanned, and the best of these ordinarily exported to England as low or medium grade leather. Those which are too poor for export are sold on the local market for whatever they can bring.

The government tannery handles about 2,500 cow hides, 5,000 goat skins and 100 buffalo hides per month. About 25% of its output is chrome-tanned in drums and is believed to be the only leather of this type made in Ceylon. The remainder is ordinarily vegetable-tanned for six weeks in vats of pure mimosa extract, without rocking, rotation or control. Handling and processing methods in this plant are a little better than those in the private tanneries but leave room for improvement. The number of workers is considerably larger than in the private plants handling nearly the same output.

Tannins used on the island are mostly imported. Oils employed for finishing include coconut, gingelly, groundnut, olive and linseed.

Hides. Ceylonese hides are generally purchased from the butchers at the various municipal abattoirs about the island by collectors who salt and ship them. Most of them go to the Colombo area, which contains the majority of the tanneries as well as the port.

The hides are small, and not of very good quality. Tick damage is not serious, but flaying is often done carelessly and there are numerous butcher cuts and holes. The worst damage, however is from branding.

Animals and hides examined by the Mission usually were found to have a great many brands, often extending over most of the usable portion of the hide. Customarily only one brand is for identification of ownership, even when the animal has changed hands, for an altered brand is looked upon with suspicion. But this brand is made with a running iron, frequently right on the flank, and may be a foot in diameter. In addition the rump, flanks and other parts may be decorated with an assortment of brand marks designed to bring good luck, ward off evil, etc.

Prior to 1936 branding was compulsory. This is no longer true, but a Cattle Ordinance of 1943 has since attempted to prescribe the location of the identifying brand. Enforcement is difficult, however, and superstition continues to cause serious defacement of the hides.

Export of raw cow and ox hides has been prohibited for the past two years, but after tanning they may be exported under permit. During the first nine months of 1951, 5,467 cwt of these tanned hides were sent to the United Kingdom. In the same period exports of buffalo and other hides in the raw or salted state, chiefly to India, totalled 5,627 cwt. Recorded imports of hides and leather were very small. From these figures it is apparent that some expansion of both tanning and leather goods industries is possible even now, and that there will be a greater potential when present efforts to enlarge the cattle population begin to yield results. Special attention should be given to the prospects for developing leather-working as a cottage industry, using attractive tooled designs based on such historic patterns as the Anuradhapura moonstones.

MACHINERY AND SHOPS

Vital to the industrial development potential of Ceylon is the existence of well-equipped shops capable of manufacture, repair and maintenance of capital equipment. For example, such shops will be an asset to the projected sugar industry, which will need annual refacing of crushing rolls and occasional fabrication or rebuilding of gears, bearings, evaporator parts and other items. Large sugar-producing countries having numerous mills commonly send these parts to centrally located shops rather than maintain duplicate machining facilities at each sugar factory.

At least five major private engineering firms operate excellent shops on the island. Among other things, these manufacture annually about Rs. 6 million worth of capital machinery for the tea and rubber industries. Ceylon is said to produce 30% of the world's supply of certain types of tea machinery and 50% of

561

that used locally. Some machinery is exported to India, Africa and Australia.

In addition, the large railway workshops at Ratmalana, employing 4,000 men, are equipped for all but the very largest of fabricating jobs. Under special conditions these shops have sometimes served private industries for essential needs.

Although shortage of steel and other materials is sometimes a problem, the principal handicap to expansion of shop activities is the scarcity of skilled machinists. Virtually the only school for these is maintained by the railway shops, which absorb the whole output. Private firms train their own men, but lose a part of them to government service. Increased public training facilities will be the soundest impetus which the government can give to shops and manufacturing industries requiring this type of skilled worker.

Meat and By-Products

Because of tradition as well as religious influence, meat consumption has never been very high. The cattle population is small (Chapter 11). Total slaughter recorded for 1950 included only 147,458 cattle, 10,453 buffalo, 36,497 sheep and 114,657 goats. This was supplemented by imports of about 10,000 cwt. of various meats, for there is a limited specialized market for foreign cuts, sausages and tinned meats.

Localized meat shortages are chronic. Small as the demand is, it often exceeds the supply. The native cattle are undersized (slaughter weight probably averages only 400-600 lbs.) and it takes many to make much meat. For sentimental reasons the villagers are often reluctant to sell their animals for slaughter. There is a general prejudice against refrigerated meat, since its history cannot be traced easily and there is no assurance that it has been killed in the special manner demanded by custom. Consequently meat does not move appreciably between cities, but is generally sold fresh in the local retail markets within a few hours after butchering.

Slaughter. Abattoirs are provided by the principal municipalities throughout the island. Most of them are simple concrete killing floors, roofed and built within a walled enclosure. Killing is done by independent butchers, who buy the live cattle from the farmers and pay the municipality a small fee per head for use of the facilities. Inspectors are provided in some of them, either by the municipal or central government, and these certify the condition of the meat by first approving the live animal and later stamping the carcass. Rejection is rare.

Killing is done in the morning hours, usually before 9:00 a.m., sometimes only on certain days of the week and seldom on Fridays. To permit free passage of the soul at death, the animal is not tied; it is merely thrown down on the floor and killed by sawing through the jugular vein and trachea with a large knife. The blood usually flows to waste through gutters; in a few cases, as in Jaffna, it is accumulated with manure and other offal for monthly sale as fertilizer.

Although killing floors are washed daily, sanitary conditions are not good. Smaller animals are suspended for cutting, but much of the butchering is done on the common floor and parts are left lying about during the process. In some abattoirs large numbers of carrion birds cover the carcasses and peck at the meat at will.

By-Products. All parts of the animal are the property of the butcher. Except for the hide, there is little economic recovery of meat by-products. They are not all wasted, for entrails and similar parts are sold as cheap meat and lose their identity in piquant curries. Bones, feet, etc. are sometimes sold at about 5 cents per lb. for conversion to bone meal. But the special by-product value of certain parts is lost.

It is not generally appreciated that profitable recovery of by-products is essential if the public is to be supplied meat at acceptable prices. As a rule 40% of a steer, 50% of a sheep and 25% of a hog must be converted to by-products or lost entirely. Some of this weight represents low-priced bulk commodities such

563

as fertilizers; other products, such as glandular extracts, account for little volume but are extremely valuable.

Small, dispersed abattoirs and prevailing methods of operation create special problems in the assembly and processing of meat by-products. Although the low slaughter volume of the island would rule out some possibilities for the present, technical study, perhaps through the proposed Institute for Applied Research, should result in economic recovery of an appreciable portion. Possibilities in wool, hair, bristles, gut, sausage casings, poultry feeds, liver extract, neatsfoot oil, pancreatic enzymes, glue, gelatine and exportable pharmaceutical bases should be investigated, as well as increased tankage and bone meal.

MINERALS

Any statement of Ceylon's mining potentialities must be tempered by the fact that little is really known about them yet. Present activities are based upon earlier chance discoveries of outcrops, plus some sporadic geological work done since 1903.

Production today is mainly confined to graphite and gems. There is some utilization of limestone (see *Cement*), quartz sand (see *Glass*), and clays (see *Clay Products*). Salt (see *Salt*) is not mined, but is obtained by solar evaporation of sea water. New projects now contemplate exploitation of deposits of iron ore (see *Steel*) and ilmenite. A number of other minerals are known to exist.

Graphite. For high grade graphite, Ceylon is the world's leading producer. Although exports today are from 12,000 to 14,000 tons per year, output during the recent war years rose easily to twice this level.

Workable deposits are found over a large part of the island, from Vavuniya southward. The largest mines are in the southwest, especially near Ruwanwela and Kurunegala, and extend to depths of 600 to 1,600 feet. Many of the others are shallow pits; over a thousand were in operation during the war, but in not more than one in ten were the methods economical enough to survive any but the highest prices, and most of them are now dormant.

A half dozen or more of the largest mines use some mechanized methods, or at least mechanical haulage. On the whole, however, output per man-hour is low, and many production economies could improve Ceylon's competitive position and rate of return.

Similarly, mining methods have created dangerous hazards, and at the same time have been wasteful of reserves. Half-mined deposits have been left in such a way that it is unsafe to reopen them later. The optimistic belief that the island's graphite reserves are inexhaustible may have contributed to this practice. What may be forgotten is that even with vast resources, the most economically exploited ones tend to be exhausted early and the others incur higher costs.

Very little of Ceylon's graphite has been used locally in manufacturing. Domestic consumption of most graphite products has been too small to warrant factory production. With the advent of the new caustic soda plant, however, the possible manufacture of anodes for the electrolytic cells may offer a nucleus for some slight expansion into dry batteries and other lines.

Gems. Few parts of the world produce a greater variety of gemstones than this island. Centered about the Ratnapura district, the deposits include sapphires, rubies, beryl, alexandrite, cat's eyes, aquamarine, tourmaline, topaz, zircon, garnet, moonstone, spinel and others.

Most of the stones are washed from alluvial gravels, using primitive but fairly satisfactory methods. Conversion to hydraulic mining—often discussed—is not recommended for numerous reasons. The industry is conducted by small operators and individuals who are perfectly able to meet the demand, and no great advantage to the country would accrue from introduction of large-scale methods at this time. Some losses could be eliminated, however, by devising simple improvements in washing techniques.

Gem cutting, also done by simple home-made and hand-powered equipment, is surprisingly acceptable. Two main shortcomings are noted: (a) facet angles are not always uniform, and (b) the custom of cutting for greatest weight does not always give the stone its greatest value. More than a few exported gems, especially of the most expensive varieties, are recut for greater value later.

Ilmenite. Ilmenite ($FeO.TiO_2$) occurs widely in the island's sands, and even as a troublesome impurity in most available glass sand. Two valuable beach sand deposits exist at Pulmoddai, north of Trincomalee, and at Tirukkovil, south of Batticaloa. These have highly concentrated areas of about 4 million and half a million tons of ilmenite respectively, plus extensive zones of poorer material varying from 10% to 60% purity. The highly concentrated tonnages are roughly 75% ilmenite, 10-12% rutile and 8-10% zircon. Ilmenite from these areas is reported to contain over 52% TiO_2. [16] Further quantities, of untested composition, extend from the beach out under the sea.

Buyers from the United States, United Kingdom and Japan have shown interest in these deposits, although no firm orders have resulted to date. Several private concerns have requested mining concessions with royalty payments to the government, but these have been refused on the ground that they planned to ship the ore for refining elsewhere. There are indications that a concession might have been granted to an acceptable private company if one had been willing to refine the sand in Ceylon in financial partnership with the government.

However, the government now plans to install its own separating plant at Pulmoddai, to treat up to 100,000 tons of the raw sand annually. Cost of the plant is estimated at Rs. 7 million. A second call for tenders was made in March, 1952—the first call having failed to attract a response. Earlier plans to process the mineral

---

[16] Other important sources of ilmenite, with their TiO_2 content for comparison, include those of Travancor, India (60%), Quebec, Canada (ore 35%), Senegal (concentrate 55-58%), New York (ore 19%), Florida (ore 6%) and Brazil (washed 71.6% ilmenite, TiO_2 content probably about 52%).

into white paint pigment have been wisely abandoned, and the new project will be limited to ore concentration.

In whatever way it is done, there is no doubt that this Ceylonese mineral should be developed. It is to be hoped that the government will attempt to secure enough advance orders to indicate the size of the available market, for the projected plant is large in relation to world consumption.

A more cautious approach would be to sell and ship crude sand at first from the smaller Tirukkovil deposit where highway transport facilities already exist. This would establish market connection prior to launching the new plant, and would also get a return for this southern deposit whose refinement would otherwise call for expensive intermediate shipment to Pulmoddai.

Meanwhile, there is no satisfactory access to Pulmoddai. An existing crude road is broken by small ferries, and is incapable of carrying a truckload of sand to the port of Trincomalee. In Chapter 16 the Mission proposes relocation of a portion of available narrow-gauge railway to serve this route.

Thorianite. Although a few tons of thorianite were exported before 1910, interest later ceased. Subsequent investigations have shown the mineral to be more widely distributed on the island than at first believed. Because of increased demands for radioactive materials, we believe that it will now be worth while for mineralogists of the Government of Ceylon to open discussions of this subject with the United States Atomic Energy Commission.

Monazite. New market inquiries should be made with respect to the monazite-bearing sands of the southwest coast, from which 3,000 tons were taken between 1918 and 1922. These sands are high in monazite (15%) which in turn averages 10% thoria. Changes in the market value of associated minerals, including ilmenite, have occurred since these workings were abandoned.

Mica. Prospects for development of the known deposits of mica are slight, unless a substantial market for flaked or ground mica can be secured. The local mica is of good quality but sheet sizes are very small. Possibilities for use as paint or plastic fillers and thermal insulation should be investigated.

Geological Survey. Ceylon's first mineral survey was made between 1903 and 1918, with a view to development of what were then considered economically important minerals. Thereafter until 1938, although a few assorted studies and traverses were made, very little actual geological work was done, and at times none at all.

A systematic geological survey has been in progress since 1940. Geological mapping is being done gradually, on a scale of one inch to the mile. The task is under very capable direction and could be expanded into a real asset to Ceylon's development. But it suffers from shortage of funds and personnel, aggravated by distraction of the technical staff with administrative paper work.

The Mission feels that this activity is being seriously overlooked. It is not even mentioned in the research budget of the Colombo Plan, for example. Some of the funds now absorbed in less promising activities of the Ministry of Industries could be directed more profitably to these mineral studies. It is recommended that the annual allocation for the Geological Survey be increased by Rs. 500,000 at least.

PAPER

Construction of a novel Rs. 17 million paper mill at Valaichchenai, north of Batticaloa, has been started by the government. It is to produce annually 2,500 tons of printing and writing paper from illuk grass, using a soda process, and 2,000,000 cement sacks (500 tons) from imported Kraft pulp.

Much of the technical and economic background of this project is obscure. A report upon which it is based was supplied to the Mission by the Ministry of Industries; but apparently the report is being followed in some matters and not in others. Where present procedure departs from the recommendations, we have not seen what technical counsel may have called for such action.

Neither is it fully clear why certain other parts of the report have been accepted as sound.

The abovementioned report recommends illuk grass and paddy straw as the only local materials suitable, but rejects citronella grass which is actually used successfully elsewhere (e.g. Guatemala City). The cost of illuk grass is admitted to be a complete guess (see Chapter 11) and the few simple tests reported cannot be considered as more than a preliminary hint of its feasibility as an industrial raw material. This, together with some inconsistencies and a prediction that newsprint from illuk would be more costly [17] than the imported variety, raises a serious question as to whether the government has protected itself adequately with technical advice on paper-making.

While the recommendation to base a large investment on the commercially untried illuk has been accepted, other recommendations more easily checked have not fared as well. The report analyzes transportation costs and says, "We found these costs in favor of manufacturing the paper in the Colombo district." There the investigator also found a suitable site, the paper market, the necessary water supply, purchasable standby power, transport facilities, repair shops, labor, housing, and other requisites. But the plant is now being built almost as far from Colombo as possible, in a virtual wilderness, where all of these auxiliaries must be separately provided and where a labor colony must be brought in from elsewhere. This, of course, is responsible for the greatly enlarged cost of the project.

The Mission's recommendation in this case must depend upon how far construction has already gone. While in favor of experimentation, it is our belief that the commercial success of illuk as an industrial crop for paper-making is at best questionable, and that eventually the factory may find itself using another raw material. In any event, if a review of transportation costs at

---

[17] It is highly improbable that newsprint paper (as customarily defined) could be made from illuk grass at all, because of the type of pulp obtainable from this class of material.

today's levels agrees with earlier calculations, the factory should not be located in Valaichchenai but near Colombo. Finally, paper consumption in Ceylon is so small and varied that the competitive commercial success of a local paper mill is doubtful. Costs will be high.

The first step, therefore, is to obtain a really competent technical review of the project, arresting further expenditure meanwhile. Private services such as those of the Paper Institute of Appleton, Wisconsin, in the United States, may be sought. Full-scale cropping of illuk should be tried, costs analyzed, and the material subjected to more complete pilot tests in a paper mill. Local "spent" citronella grass also should be tested.

If results so indicate, and expenditure has not gone too far, present buildings at Valaichchenai should be preserved for some other future purpose and the paper project moved to a more economical location. If the project is shown to be unsound, it should be abandoned now at a small loss rather than later at a large one.

RICE

Hulling, milling and parboiling of rice is a widespread industry. In addition to an unknown number of private units, in recent years the government has built and operated at least five full-scale mills and about 400 hulling plants. The combined capacity of the government units is said to be 2,750,000 bushels of paddy, of which 1,800,000 bushels represent complete milling installations.

In the better mills the polishing and rough dust are recovered for cattle feeding. Hulls, however, are seldom utilized as elsewhere. In general the mills are operated by diesel power instead of steam, while the hulls are hauled away and dumped at extra expense; in at least one government mill they are even sacked for this journey.

Occasionally some hulls are burned to raise steam for parboiling, but most of the Ceylonese mills spend extra money for firewood for this purpose instead. We suggest that all of the major mills should eventually be equipped with standard hull-burning steam boilers, to use steam as much as possible for both operating power and parboiling. This step will curtail the use of firewood and imported engine fuel, while simultaneously saving the present cost of hull disposal.

RUBBER GOODS

Although production of smoked sheet and crepe rubber has long been a major export industry (Chapter 11), it is only recently that local manufacture of finished rubber goods has begun. In addition to rubber-soled shoes (see Canvas-and-Rubber Shoes) during 1951 these included various toys, dolls, balls, balloons, heels and soles, garden hose, floor and table mats, brake blocks, surgical gloves and specialties.

In this line there is much opportunity for expansion and for creation of successful small industries. Whether for molding or latex dipping, equipment can be comparatively simple and lends itself to any scale of operations. The market is wide; export of some items has already started, while many domestic needs remain to be satisfied. The variety of possible rubber manufactures is limited only by observation, ingenuity and salesmanship.

Plans are nearing completion for a small tire factory, to be privately operated with mixed public and private capital. Technical guidance will be supplied through arrangements with a leading foreign tire manufacturer. Although the Ceylon market is small and the competitive export opportunities limited, we believe the enterprise to be soundly based. Tire production involves much hand work, even in large factories, and the process can be successful in small units.

If the Mission has any suggestion to make on tire production, it is to concentrate the enterprise upon the most common types and sizes of tires. Special types, needed only in smaller quantities, should continue to be imported until demand increases; for each one requires a separate investment in capital equipment. The government should take this into account when contemplating tariff adjustments or other related measures affecting the industry.

SALT

All Ceylonese salt is produced under government control, by solar evaporation of sea water. Main salterns are operated directly by the government at Elephant Pass, Mannar and Palavi, whose combined output is about one third of the total production. Other salterns—at Puttalam, Hambantota and various localities—are operated either by the government itself or by private harvesters who sell the salt to the government. The Hambantota saltern is worked by the government through private contract labor.

Elephant Pass has the largest output, averaging 200,000 cwt.; next is Palavi, with 70,000 cwt. in 1951. The island's consumption, from these and the others, is estimated at 800,000 cwt. per year. Another 40,000 to 45,000 cwt. will be needed for projected caustic soda manufacture.

In the larger salterns gypsum is separately precipitated first. Only small amounts of gypsum are available from this source, of course (3,500 cwt. from Palavi, for example), but enough for small-scale manufacture of blackboard "chalk" and some plaster of Paris. Thereafter, in a system of crystallizing ponds, salt is separated between liquor densities from 25° to 30° Baume. The remaining bittern is discharged to the sea, at points removed from the intakes.

In most cases the salt, harvested by hand, is not washed at all; in a few places it is rinsed with saturated brine. After the harvest it is stored in piles lightly covered with palm fronds, where rain is expected to clean it.

All salt inspected by the Mission in Ceylon was unnecessarily high in magnesium impurities, hygroscopic, and therefore perpetually moist and bitter. There are two reasons for this: (a) the crystallization is continued just a little too far—to 30° instead of a safer 28-29° Be., and (b) the salt is not properly rinsed. For this last, either fresh water or at least clean sea water should

572

be used after coarse "washing" with saturated brine. [18] Ordinary good practice in solar evaporation will yield non-hygroscopic salt of at least 99.5% purity.

With some redesign of ponds, production of by-product chemicals from the waste bittern of the larger salterns may be considered eventually, but we do not recommend this step at present.

Very small amounts of refined table salt are made locally, but the product is still impure. By ordinary practice, truly economic production of this commodity is difficult unless the market can justify a plant capacity of 25-50 tons per day.

SHOES

Three factories are making shoes on the island, with a combined output of 8,000-9,000 pairs per week. There are also numerous small shoemaking establishments doing custom work. Nearly ten times this number of shoes are imported, principally from India and the United Kingdom. Thus, although shoes are not worn by the whole Ceylonese population, the domestic market justifies a much larger production even now.

Leather Shoes. With a maximum output of 125 pairs per day, the government shoe factory is the only major manufacturer of leather shoes. About 40% of the production is for military or other governmental use; the remainder is sold on the open market. The enterprise is not successful. Losses of the plant are difficult to break down, because the shoe factory and tannery are operated together. Jointly, however, they have averaged an annual loss of over five and a half times the invested capital. Many reasons for this are readily apparent.

In the first place, the equipment is badly out of balance. While a few "bottleneck" units limit output, much of the machinery is antiquated or in bad repair or both. Under present lines of

---

[18] Upon suggesting these steps to the local management, the Mission learned that earlier specialists had advised the same thing, but no action had been taken.

command, the factory management has been powerless to make the obvious adjustments and changes.

Workers in this plant produce only from one third to one half of what would be expected in a British factory. Even so, the 97 workers are too many—although they have been reduced from an earlier 230. Moreover, for its small output, the plant attempts to make too many different types of shoes.

Reorganization of the factory to give responsibile authority to its management would probably make economical operation feasible. This would call for a more independent form of control, however, and would also entail some capital expenditure for new or rebuilt equipment. Refinancing through the proposed Development Corporation is suggested.

Canvas-and-Rubber Shoes. A new factory, member of an international chain, opened in Colombo in March, 1951, to make "tennis" shoes. Now producing 3,000 pairs per week, this plant uses modern, high-speed vulcanizing equipment and mechanized operations throughout. Its product is of good quality, is sold locally at advertised standard prices (Rs. 4.90 per pair, men's sizes), and has been well received. In November, 1951, a first foreign order of 2,000 pairs was exported.

Present output can be doubled by using two shifts on certain operations. In all probability this will be done as orders expand, for the comparatively low productivity of local labor necessitates greater use of the capital equipment as a cost compensation.

Another factory, Ceylonese-owned, makes the same type of shoe at Ratmalana. Three months after starting in February, 1951, output was brought up to 1,800 pairs per day. However, by comparison the methods of this plant are somewhat crude, slow and inefficient, and the resulting product is visibly poorer in quality as well as uniformity. The market reacted to this fact quickly, forcing an early cutback to 1,000 pairs per day. No export orders had been obtained by the end of the Mission's visit, nor were any likely unless quality could be improved.

Although the first-mentioned factory is able to sell on its quality,

574

the second now depends heavily upon the recently applied Industrial Products Act. (Buyers must now purchase five domestic pairs for each one imported.) Herein is apparent one of the less favorable effects of such protective legislation. For the less efficient plant is now expecting to expand, using the same antiquated methods to produce a product not wholly satisfactory to the market. We believe that it would be far better for this plant to use any new capital to improve its methods. Industrialization based upon expanded inefficiency will not help Ceylon's economy in the end.

Both of these factories use domestic fabric, although it appears to be of lower grade and higher cost than the imported types. Its imperfections are said to increase rejections and to cause various production troubles, raising shoe production costs further. Also, both factories experience unusually high labor costs through low worker productivity.

If these problems can be at least partially corrected, there is a good future for this local industry. At the same time, it should be noted that rubber shoes are perhaps not the most satisfactory for Ceylon's climate, and that efforts to produce other types cheaply will be rewarding.

Rope-soled Shoes. One promising type is the rope-soled shoe sometimes known as "alpargatas." [19] Although not yet made in Ceylon, some of these were imported during the war and enjoyed a good sale. Such shoes are cheap and have remarkable wearing qualities.

In making this shoe, a rope is first spun from a coarse fiber. This is wound flatwise into the shape of a sole, using a metal form, and is then stitched crosswise with heavy thread. To this sole is sewn an upper, which may be of light canvas as in the rubber-soled

---

[19] Properly the trade name of the largest South American manufacturer of these shoes, the term is frequently used in the generic sense. Such shoes are made in various countries by large and small manufacturers.

type, or may be only a few open straps as in the Mexican *huarache.* An inner sole of heavier canvas or other material may be added to protect against any discomfort from the fiber-ends in the rope sole.

Various fibers have been used successfully, from soft jute to the coarser sisal, henequen, palm and others. In Ceylon the abundant coir should be tried. If desired, coir soles could be made to specifications through cottage industry. These could then be purchased by a factory for addition of the uppers and finishing by machinery, and for commercial distribution and sale.

SOAP

As nearly as can be ascertained, a yearly 11,000 tons of soap are manufactured locally. Over 70% of this comes from one large foreign-owned factory, employing 400 workers and selling its entire output on the island. A few of the smaller firms are applying for export permits, but most of their production is also for local use.

The largest factory and two or three others blend coconut oil (65%) with other oils, tallow and rosin to obtain a soap of exacting specifications. The remainder use only coconut oil, generally in the cold or the semiboiling process. Only the leading plant recovers glycerine, of which 500 tons annually are shipped to South Africa for refining.

Soap manufacturers are bothered mainly by supply problems. The worst shortages have been in the necessary oils other than coconut (see Vegetable Oils) and in caustic soda for which domestic manufacture will ultimately afford relief. The industry also suffers from adulteration of the local citronella oil, of which it consumes nearly half the output.

SOFT DRINKS

Trade and other informed sources report a rapidly expanding local market for soft drinks. Many are now made although the cola types are absent.

While most of the needs of this industry could be supplied domestically by properly organized manufacture, almost everything except water is now imported. This includes flavoring syrups, sugar, coloring, bottles, and caps. Even a part of the carbon dioxide is shipped from Singapore.

Flavoring extracts could be made in Ceylon now, under imported technical supervision. Domestic manufacture of bottles and caps is discussed elsewhere. For certain beverages the island can also supply caffeine and papain.

STEEL

Ceylon's first venture in steel production was started by the government in 1941. It consisted of a small rolling mill assembled from used equipment and miscellaneous available parts, and was intended to reroll old railroad rails and imported billets.

For various reasons—including the technical difficulties characteristic of rerolling old rail steel—the project was a failure. Reportedly the steel was poorly rolled, weak, nonuniform, and had a tendency to split. Buyers tried to use it when imported steel was unobtainable, but avoided it when they could. Moreover, for such a small plant, too many different shapes and sizes were made; costs were disproportionate, and in postwar years the government product was priced higher than the imported material. Sales naturally dwindled. In an effort to move its stock, the government invoked the Industrial Products Act and required importers to take one ton of local steel for every three tons imported. [20]

But while the government thus forced fabricators to buy its steel, the government departments themselves recognized its poor quality and refused to accept products made from it.

Under these circumstances unused local steel began to accumulate in customers' warehouses. The buyers, finding the material

---

[20] Under pressure from consumers this ratio was later reduced from 1:3 to 1:5.

quite useless, finally ceased to take delivery of it. Requirements under the Industrial Products Act still remain in force, although the mill has finally closed down with Rs. 2 million worth of unwanted product on hand. Today, while importing good grades of steel at Rs. 30 per cwt., users comply with the law by depositing money for the required amount of government steel at Rs. 42.5 per cwt., but prefer to leave the local material where it is. Since it has no value except as scrap, local steel users fear that eventually—when it has all been sold at Rs. 42.5 per cwt.—they will then be required to sell it back to the government at the prevailing scrap price.

New Plans. Ceylon's annual requirement of steel, of all types, amounts to around 30,000 tons. The Ministry of Industries now plans to provide 20,000 tons of this by erection of a new steel mill at an investment of Rs. 24 million. To be located at Ragama, near Colombo, the new mill expects to use local ore and scrap in the production of steel by the costly electric furnace process. Rolling and fabricating are to be included. Among the announced final products are to be: 6,250 tons of merchant section; an equal amount of bar stock and rods; 2,000 tons of hoop iron; 420 tons of bolts and nuts; 100 tons of rivets and washers; 80 tons of wood screws; and small quantities of agricultural hand tools. For the small tonnage involved, these will require a highly complex plant and very probably a much larger investment than has been provided for.

Scrap now available on the island has been estimated at 60,000 tons, with annual accretion of about 3,000 tons. Some of this, however, is in nonrecurrent forms, so that in all probability the new plant will have to seek imported scrap after a few years. Local ore deposits are said to total 6,000,000 tons, but are chiefly limonite nodules and boulders— even the larger masses extending only a few feet below the surface; the better grades average 49-50% iron content. The deposits are scattered over wide, discontinuous areas, and the Mission believes that mining costs will be higher than anticipated.

Electric power requirements will be about 50 million kwh per year, calling for installed generating capacity of 10,000 kw. It is announced [21] that this much power has been earmarked for the project out of Stage One of the current hydroelectric development scheme. If so, this would dispose of fully half the 100,000 kwh of additional power expected for 1956, and apparently overlooks the fact that the full amount will be needed to meet existing deficiencies and normal expansion by that date. It should be noted, also, that the characteristics of this heavy steel mill load may be such as to cause serious line fluctuations throughout Colombo.

In reality, then, if this mill is built it will be necessary to install still another 10,000 kw capacity somewhere. The Mission estimates that for hydroelectric power this will mean a delay of five to six years and an additional investment of Rs. 30 million, including transmission lines. A thermoelectric plant at the mill would cost about Rs. 9 million and could be ready to run in two and a half to three years' time; this would therefore be the logical choice under the circumstances. But a thermoelectric plant would have to use imported fuel, thus negating all or most of the expected advantage of the electric smelting process, for the island's steel would remain dependent upon imports of critical materials.

Recommendations. These observations suggest that the government may be proceeding prematurely on this project. In the absence of sufficient preliminary engineering, it is probable that the full impact of the proposed steel mill upon the island's economy has not been calculated. The Mission strongly recommends that before going further the government seek a complete technical and economic evaluation from a large and experienced commercial steel company—preferably one which does not ordinarily export steel to Ceylon, and would therefore be unbiased. Meanwhile we must state that, from available evidence, it is our

---

[21] *Ceylon Times*, November 9, 1951.

considered opinion that this project will imperil other more urgent developments and should be long deferred. [22]

SUGAR AND BY-PRODUCTS

As indicated in Chapter 11 (where cane-growing is reviewed) the Mission agrees in principle that an attempt should be made to develop a sugar industry. Because this is an entirely new and complex activity, we hope that no more than one mill will be installed at first to provide a background of local experience for later expansion of the industry. Although some good agricultural work is being done on cane, to date there is no evidence of adequate planning by persons fully acquainted with the factory side of sugar. Additional outside technical help for this phase will be needed. There will also have to be closer attention to the special problems of cane transport, for which some suggestions are made in Chapter 16.

By-products potentialities must be examined with realism. Contrary to predictions in the press, Ceylon cannot hope to make wall board from her cane bagasse; it will be needed as the cheapest fuel to run the sugar mill itself, and only a very efficient mill has any surplus. Power alcohol can be made from molasses; but it must be realized that synthetic alcohol is produced at half the cost, and that many of Cuba's wartime fermentation alcohol plants are now shut down. This is said not to discourage alcohol production, but merely to suggest that the government must feel fully justified in paying the higher price which may result.

At the same time, other by-product opportunities have not been considered adequately. If alcohol is made, carbon dioxide will be available in quantities sufficient for making dry ice, and also to replace present imports of liquid CO_2 for beverage plants. Molas-

---

[22] For further significant discussion of this topic see especially an article by Prof. E. Stuart Kirby, *Comparisons of Progress*, in the Far Eastern Economic Review (Hongkong), Vol. XII, No. 14, April 3, 1952, pp. 440-442.

ses can serve as a substrate for production of high-protein yeast food, valuable as a supplement to Ceylon's protein-deficient human diet, or as a cattle feed. Molasses can also be fed to cattle directly (as much as four pounds per day per head) or mixed with other prepared feeds. Cachaza should be put back on the fields as fertilizer, unless the market justifies prior extraction of the wax; but small-scale wax extraction seldom pays, and this might better be deferred until a larger mill is built.

Sugar technology is well advanced in a great many parts of the world. There is no need for Ceylon to proceed with so little of it as is now available on the island. The type of advice now needed will be best obtained from experts associated with the commercial sugar industry itself.

TANNINS

Almost all tannin used on the island is imported. Not only is this a hazardous situation for the leather industry and a needless expenditure of foreign exchange, but growing world demands for tannins offer Ceylon an opportunity for the creation of a small new industry and a new export product. In particular the Argentine *quebracho*, long a leading world market item, is becoming scarce and must be replaced with similar types.

Most promising are the tannins obtained from fruit or seeds, rather than from wood or bark; for the former are annual crops while the latter require the killing of the trees for tanning extraction. Field research and laboratory development will be needed to select the best commercial tannins for production in Ceylon.

TEA

Many aspects of tea production, including its economic prospects, have been discussed in Chapter 11 and elsewhere in this report. Treatment here will be limited to a word about its factory production side.

As the island's largest industry, its 950 factories account for about half the country's total exports. At an average factory

581

production cost of Rs. 0.51 per lb. of made tea [23] (out of an over-all cost of Rs. 1.65), annual expenditure in this phase amounts to Rs. 153 million. Thus it is seen that, to offset rising agricultural production costs, there is considerable leeway for regaining these through more efficient factory methods.

Technical development of the industry is the responsibility of the Tea Research Institute. Its experimental factory at St. Coombs conducts complete processing and makes trials of new types of equipment. In the main, however, work of the Institute is concentrated upon agricultural problems of the crop; factory improvement is relegated to a very minor position.

One good reason for this is the shortage of technical research staff, especially in the fields of chemical and mechanical engineering which are essential to factory processing studies. Another is the industry's general hesitancy to try new methods, in the fear that they may affect the delicate flavor of the tea. The possibility of this last cannot be denied, and tea is a commodity which sells on an intangible flavor basis. It does not follow, however, that the market will tolerate no changes. For the common assumption that all changes will be for the worse is without foundation; it is just as possible that a given modification in processing might increase the percentage of higher-value grades produced.

Actually, there are some improvements which could reduce costs without danger of altering the flavor. For example, more often than not the plucked leaf is carried by hand to the top floor of the factory. There, most laboriously, it is spread out by hand on withering racks. After withering, it is even more tediously removed. These operations could be mechanized without change in the actual withering process.

Withering itself is admittedly a sensitive operation. Attempts to hasten it artificially to date have disturbed the traditional appearance unfavorably. Yet this process is long, and ties up

---

[23] Includes Rs. 0.46 operating cost plus Rs. 0.05 plant upkeep and depreciation.

investment in both tea and equipment. Initial failure should not interfere with persistent research toward its improvement.

Research should continue also in the processes of rolling, sifting, rerolling, fermentation and firing, as well as in conveying, storage and packaging. Particular attention should be paid to methods for increasing the productivity of the worker, which can then justify wage increases; stated another way, this can mean lowered labor cost per pound of made tea. Similarly, an objective should be more efficient machinery, representing lower capital investment in relation to output. By-product utilization of tea waste—not only for caffeine but in other outlets—should not be overlooked as a source of supplementary income.

In Ceylon's tea factories, opportunities for such improvements are apparent on the briefest inspection. The Mission feels that both the Tea Research Institute and the individual factory owners should exert more effort in this direction, as fast as funds and personnel become available. In the island's tea production, a factory saving of Rs. 0.01 per lb. of product can mean Rs. 3,000,-000 to the industry.

TEXTILES

Consumption of cotton textiles is placed at nearly 100,000,000 yards annually. Most of this is imported, with India the chief supplier.

Private Production. Commercial spinning and weaving has been practiced on the island since 1883, in a single mill at Wellawatta. Owned by Ceylonese but under British technical management, this mill still operates all of its original looms. Expansion ceased in 1923, except for the later addition of some 3,000 spindles, bringing the present capacity to around 25,000 yards of cloth per day. The plant employs 1,200 workers, operates 23,000 spindles, and uses 7,000 pounds of cotton daily. The bulk of its raw cotton is imported from West Africa. It also operates the island's only cotton gin, processing the entire local crop of about 700 bales (raw, 320 tons) and returning the seed to the farmers.

There is also a fairly significant handloom industry, with about 3,000 looms active and an estimated annual output of 3,500,000 yards. It is claimed that another 5,000 looms are idle for lack of yarn, of which the supplies from the Wellawatta mill and elsewhere are inadequate. Development of this cottage industry is one of the objectives of the government, which hopes to get 10,000 such looms into production within the next two years.

Commercial incentive for growth of local textile manufacturing has been poor. Ceylonese textiles workers have not performed up to Indian standards; local cotton-growing has failed to develop; imported cotton has been expensive or scarce; and foreign-made cloth has enjoyed a better demand because of its quality and price.

While it is not generally appreciated, the Mission feels that the quality factor has been especially influential; other local industries using textiles (e.g. canvas shoe factories) are dissatisfied with the domestic fabric, so that the mutual support between industries is lacking in this case. Correction of this can come about only through improved quality and economy of production. Attempts to solve it by protective measures or other "shortcuts" will only aggravate it, as experience has amply shown elsewhere.

Government Textile Projects. Plans for two new textile plants have been announced by the government. One, for which Rs. 17 million has already been voted to the Ministry of Industries, is to be located near Negombo. The other, calling for a Rs. 6 million government loan, is to be built near Colombo by the Cooperative Wholesale Establishment.

Each of these mills is to employ 1,000 workers, using modern textile machinery. That of the Ministry of Industries is to have 25,000 spindles and 500 looms, making 10,000,000 yards of material and half this equivalent of handloom yarn; the CWE mill will have 10,000 spindles with room for more, and will produce 2,000,000 yards. The obvious discrepancies in expected employment and investment costs merely indicate premature announcement and incomplete technical preparation.

Textile specialists hold the view that increased Ceylonese

textile manufacturing can be sound economically if the island can grow more of its own cotton. Otherwise, it is feared, the projects will not be competitive with foreign sources. Since the present Wellawatta mill is already prepared to absorb much more local fiber, we believe that emphasis upon new mill construction is disproportionate at this time. Unquestionably at least one such project should be pursued, so as to begin the early training of workers. Meanwhile, however, there should be a more vigorous scientific agricultural study of local cotton-growing (see Chapter 11) to develop firm raw material sources.

It is possible, in fact, that provision of more economical raw cotton would encourage private mill expansion, with much greater operating economy and a saving of public investment funds. Outright government operation of textile mills will undoubtedly be costly and unsatisfactory, and should be avoided, although this need not preclude government financial participation under experienced commercial management.

Tobacco Products

The island not only grows tobacco (Chapter 11) but both imports and exports tobacco and its manufactured products. Local manufacturers include well known domestic and English brands of cigarettes, made in modern factories, and a type of rough hand-made cigar popular among Ceylonese. The principal export item is chewing-type leaf tobacco sold to India, while major imports consist of Indian beedies and two thirds of the country's requirements of light cigarette leaf. Largely because of this last item, obtained from the United States and India, Ceylon is a net importer of tobacco.

Cigarettes. Local manufacturers produce an average of 150,-000,000 cigarettes per month, of which the largest factory makes about 80%. Actual manufacture is fully mechanized, although certain handling and packaging operations are done by hand. The principal plant employs about 650 workers, all Ceylonese but with foreign technical supervision.

Main problems of the cigarette industry are those of supply. Ordinary Jaffna tobacco is not satisfactory for cigarettes, and the manufacturers have extended various aids to local growers in an effort to reduce their dependence upon imported Virginia types. Some other material problems have been created by the current "Ceylonization of Trade." For example, German or Japanese viscose film is used for moisture-proof wrapping; recent government regulations required this to be imported only through Ceylonese dealers, none of whom was prepared to furnish it.

Packaging is done both in tins and in paper. The largest company operates its own can-making machinery, but only at half capacity because tinplate supply is short. Despite the humid climate, it is probable that cigarettes are tinned more as an imitation of British export packing than as a necessity. Informal trials made by the Mission over a two-month period indicated that modern paper packaging methods preserve cigarettes satisfactorily under Colombo conditions.

As suggested earlier the can-making machinery and tinplate could better be diverted to the production of tins needed for food canning and other more essential uses, and all cigarettes packed in the type of paper, foil and viscose film wrapper so commonly used throughout the world.

Cigars. The characteristic Jaffna cigar is consumed only in Ceylon and the Maldive islands; it is hand-rolled, black, and not much bigger than a cigarette. Makers state that it was once large, but that through efforts to hold the traditional retail price in the face of rising costs it has gradually shrunk.

Cigar factories in Jaffna alone are now said to number about 100. In reality they are little more than thatched sheds, with mat-covered earthen floors on which from 20 to 100 workers sit cross-legged and make the cigars. All operations are done by hand, with virtually no mechanical equipment of any kind more complex than a knife.

There is no shortage of workers. Almost all are Ceylon Tamils. There is a limited amount of specialization among them; some prepare the leaves, some roll, some cut, and others pack. They are paid piece rates, at around Rs. 6.5 per 1,000 cigars. A worker produces about 500 cigars daily, or occasionally as high as 1,000 and works 20 days per month.

Members of this industry seem chiefly disturbed at the competition of new entrants, and would like legislation to shut them out. Many of these are apparently workers who have left older factories to start their own. Officials and established manufacturers state that the new entrants are manufacturing inferior cigars which find no market; if this is true, the older factories have nothing to worry about. What is more likely, in the Mission's opinion, is that workers have simply been dissatisfied with their wage earnings at existing rates, and that older manufacturers are quite naturally unhappy that they cannot retain both the market and workers without altering wages and prices.

One possible help to this technologically stagnant industry might lie in by-product recovery. The aggregate waste of mid-rib tobacco in these factories has been estimated at more than 30 tons per month—sufficient for preparation of nicotine insecticides. A small Jaffna insecticide factory, cooperatively owned by the cigar manufacturers, could enlarge its raw material supply by purchase of wastes from the Colombo cigarette companies as well. After extracting the nicotine, the residue would be valuable as fertilizer. [24]

VEGETABLE OILS *(other than coconut)*

Preoccupation with coconut oil may have led Ceylon to overlook the potentialities of other vegetable oil sources. At the present time several other oils are needed locally and must be imported; yet the island's climate and natural vegetation suggest that several could even be produced for export, and existing

---

[24] Some tobacco waste is already sold as fertilizer—but without prior recovery of nicotine.

industrial processing equipment has excess capacity available to handle them.

Soap can be made from coconut oil alone, and is in fact so made by various small local manufacturers. But to get the quality of soap demanded by the market, the largest soap plants (representing 80% or more of the total output) must limit themselves to 65% coconut oil. Procuring the other oils needed is one of their greatest problems. Some mee [25] is obtained locally from wild growth, as is also a little kapok oil. Mowrah oil is imported from India. Groundnut and palm oil were once obtainable from India, but now the former must be secured from South Africa and the latter is scarcely available at all.

Proposals have been made to use rubber seed oil, but this is not likely to be available in commercial quantities. In any event, it has a high iodine number and is less suitable for soap than for paint.

Gingelly (sesame) oil is processed locally in primitive fashion. Although in other countries this is a very important food oil, its popularity in Ceylon seems to be chiefly in other applications such as medical, pharmaceutical and cosmetic preparations.

There is no doubt at all that investigations in this field by the proposed Institute for Applied Research can disclose numerous undeveloped potential sources of oils native to Ceylon, and which can serve variously in the manufacture of soap, paints, foods and other products. Moreover, efforts to increase production of certain well-known oils such as groundnut (Chapter 11) should assist in supplying present industrial needs.

Wheat Flour

Although in prewar years Ceylon imported only about 16,000 tons of wheat flour annually, shortages of rice have stimulated its use until in recent times an established consumption of at least

---

[25] *Bassia longifolia*, and *B. latifolia*.

170,000 tons seems certain. (Imports in 1951 exceeded this greatly, reaching 214,181 tons, but the year was probably abnormal.)

It is the conclusion of the 'Mission that wheat should be milled in Ceylon, now that a regular demand is assured. The island will probably never become a wheat-growing area, yet there are distinct advantages to local milling of imported wheat in the existing circumstances. It may be added that several other tropical countries have found this so in late years and have encouraged the growth of a domestic milling industry.

Advantages. Wheat can be shipped, unloaded and stored in bulk. Flour, on the other hand, must be handled in sacks or other containers; this adds appreciably to the handling costs, in addition to which shipping is more expensive. Because of its perishability, flour requires rapid transport and cannot conveniently take advantage of the slower vessels. Once landed in Ceylon, it must be distributed and consumed fairly soon to avoid spoilage. Wheat can be held for much longer periods—even years, with proper precautions—thus smoothing out irregularities in supply from the sources.

Cost of milling represents value added by manufacture. In the purchase of foreign flour this means, of course, an extra expenditure of foreign exchange for an operation which could be performed by Ceylonese labor and capital.

Moreover, the milling of wheat yields products other than flour. A normal extraction rate of 72% gives, from 100,000 tons of wheat, about 72,000 tons of flour [26] and 28,000 tons of livestock feed (bran and shorts). Wheat germ oil and vitamin B-1 are included in the feeds at this extraction rate, and do not reach the country if only flour is imported. With domestic milling, these

---

[26] Wheat is tempered by the controlled addition of moisture before milling. Purchased wheat contains some unavoidable foreign matter which is removed in the milling process, but its weight is approximately compensated by the higher moisture content of the product.

products are available for local use. The vitamin B-1 can be included in the flour by using a higher extraction rate (perhaps 85%) which also means more flour and less feeds. Germ oil is a valuable product by itself or as a constituent of the animal feeds; extraction rates must not be so high as to include it in the flour, where it would cause rancidity and spoilage.

Recommendations. The Mission has ascertained that a syndicate of leading Ceylonese investors would be willing to undertake local flour milling in participation with the government, under conditions which appear to be reasonable and beneficial to the country. Such a procedure is recommended, with commercial management in private hands.

A mill capacity of 50 sacks (of 280 pounds) per hour would supply about one third of the normal wheat flour consumption in recent years. It is believed advisable to start with a mill no larger than this, to allow for unpredictable consumption shifts and other intangible factors. At present costs, such a unit would involve an investment of about Rs. 9.2 million including between £250,000 and £300,000 sterling exchange for the machinery and equipment.

We feel that this should be one of the first enterprises to be considered by the proposed Development Corporation, in cooperation with the interested private investors. Partial government financing could be supplied most favorably through this agency. Government cooperation would also be needed in providing a site in the Colombo Port area, to permit economical pneumatic transfer of wheat from ship to silo. Finally, provision would have to be made for a guaranteed supply of wheat if its importation remained under government control, and for subsidy if the government wished to continue selling flour below cost as at present.

WOOD PRODUCTS

Material Supply. Studies of Ceylon's timber resources and utilization have been initiated recently with the cooperation of FAO (see also Chapter 11). It is too early for concrete findings from this work. Nevertheless, there are already reasons for believing that commercial timber supplies are none too plentiful. Sapu, preferred by boxmakers, appears to be running low. So does jak, wanted by the sawmills but now cut only on special permit. Builders have trouble getting lumber, while sawmills must import a part of their logs and squared timber. Even curio makers complain of difficulty in obtaining the ebony and other woods upon which their business depends.

Whether those shortages are real, or merely the result of under-exploitation and maldistribution, remains to be seen. Also, it is quite possible that laboratory research on physical properties can point to new species suitable as substitutes for sapu, jak and others for specific uses.

Firewood. Throughout the island many fuel needs are met with firewood. If limited to small, nonindustrial uses the practice may continue indefinitely; however, the almost unbelievable loss of forest resources that has been observed in numerous other countries where wood and charcoal are the traditional domestic fuels must not be overlooked.

In particular, the Mission is alarmed at the various current proposals for large-scale firewood consumption. The projected fertilizer factory, for example, is to use 300 tons per day. The railways are testing firewood as a locomotive fuel for the second time, and contemplating a demand equal to the output of 20% of the island's forest reserves. Many factories are already consuming this type of fuel. The danger, as we see it, is that each new proposal of this kind is considered by itself alone, without proper realization of what the aggregate implies.

In view of the ultimate loss of soil and agricultural production that characterizes unnecessary forest cutting, the Mission urges a general policy of avoiding projects demanding large volumes of firewood wherever possible.

On the other hand, it is observed that huge quantities of firewood are being wasted in land clearing, logging and other operations. Merely because it can now be had a few rupees cheaper somewhere else, great volumes of felled wood are piled and burned on the spot. In some cases even valuable saw-timber is being lost in this way. We suggest that this waste of resources, wherever it occurs, should be of national concern while still remediable.

Lumber. Most of the lumber for neighborhood use in the island is cut by hand pit-sawing. The enterprises are small family affairs; the boards are comparatively cheap, and remarkably uniform considering the method of cutting.

Power sawing was once more general, but a great many small mills have ceased operation. At present there are only four or five sawmills of importance, including especially those in Colombo and one attached to the government plywood factory. The largest mill handles 500 cubic feet per day when timber is available.

Local logs are scarce, high priced, and often of poor shape for commercial sawing. The main sawmills import a large share of their logs and squared timbers from Canada, Africa and elsewhere. Slab, edgings and similar waste is recovered as much as possible for the production of mouldings and small shapes.

Little or no Ceylonese lumber is well seasoned. Large sawmills have tried to hold stocks for air-seasoning, but the demand siphons it off too rapidly. Smaller mills are reluctant to meet the heavy investment in inventory which seasoning requires. One leading mill has considered kiln-drying.

Veneer and Plywood. Originally established without a technical study and with only a token vote of Rs. 10, the government plywood factory at Gintota has gradually been organized into an acceptable plant whose investment is now Rs. 2.8 million. Under experienced technical management its efficiency has continued to improve. For example, in 1944 it recovered only 19 square feet of 3/16" 3-ply from two cubic feet of timber; by yearly increments the recovery has risen to about 33 square feet at present, and will probably reach 40 when new edge-glueing machines are installed. [27] Volume recovery on sawn logs (in the associated sawmill) is 75%. Virtually all wood waste is burned to raise steam. Personnel has been reduced from 350 to 238, with greater production from the same machinery.

Tea chests are the main product, accounting for 75% of the output; these are competitive in price and quality with imported Japanese chests. Other products include assorted panels for construction and special uses. New plans call for installation of a hot-resin bonding press to make moisture-resistant plywood, and a slicer for production of figured decorative veneers to be exported.

The plant has had the usual difficulties due to the limitations of government management. Its output fell off in 1951 because of glue trouble, attributed to the fact that in 1947 the governmental offices purchased a huge supply of perishable casein glue —enough for many years; when it began to spoil in May, 1951, a new supply was ordered through the proper governmental channels, but it had not been obtained in December.

Actually, it appears that if freed of direct government administration this plant would be profitable. Apart from losses caused by delays, etc. as above, 18% of its current production cost is extra overhead of Colombo officials while the wage bill at the plant is only 12%. A further 1% sales commission is incurred because the product must be sold through government distribution offices.

Furniture and Woodenware. Numerous small enterprises make furniture, carved wooden curios and other articles.

A most extensive furniture undertaking is the series of government carpentry workshops, originally launched as a temporary scheme to provide work for numerous unskilled or semiskilled carpenters released from wartime jobs. Continued ever since, these workshops have been disappointing. Costs have been unusu-

---

[27] Theoretical maximum is 64 sq. ft., but because of unavoidable losses this is never reached.

ally high and the product is of such low quality that it has no market demand. Government offices have purchased the furniture for their own use, but at prices sometimes twice as high as for equivalent (or better) merchandise available on the open market.

A recent wise official decision recognizes that the present method of operation is uneconomical, and will convert these workshops to cooperatives. By this move the carpenters will have the responsibility of improving their own efficiency and workmanship, and will be relieved of a permanent state support which was never intended for them in the first place. Government loans will be available when needed.

Ceylon's carved curio industry shows considerable art and skill. We feel that the export market for these items could be encouraged. Also, we believe that an unexploited market exists for lathe-turned wooden bowls and similar articles which can be made from the island's unusually decorative woods.

COTTAGE INDUSTRIES

Throughout this chapter are various references to cottage industries. Their potential importance in Ceylon springs from the considerable amount of agricultural underemployment in the island, and accordingly the subject deserves the full attention which it has been receiving from the government and specialized international agencies. The limited space accorded it here is no index of its significance, but rather emphasizes that it is a most detailed topic in itself, by its very nature calling for extensive and minute separate study. One such study—although controversial—has been made recently by the International Labor Organization. Much more remains to be done.

Among the cottage industries and handicrafts practiced or attempted in Ceylon are the making of handloom textiles, pottery, reed mats, baskets, coir yarn and woven products, lace, tortoise-shell articles, carved wood, lacquer ware, brass ornaments, costume jewelry and Kandyan silverware. To encourage these and others, government assistance has been provided increasingly in the form of schools and training centers, community workshops, loans to individual craftsmen and to cooperatives, marketing facilities, and even subsidized supplies of raw materials.

The Mission believes that efforts to develop these activities should continue, always keeping in sight the primary objective of utilizing part-time energies of underemployed producers. In this respect the authorities should note that the low production overhead of the home is the factor which can make such handicrafts economically competitive in a mechanized world. The observed tendency to convert cottage industries into centralized "factories," offering full-time wage employment and incurring separate industrial overhead while attempting to retain the inherently less efficient production methods, is not sound. Such measures are the product of well-intentioned enthusiasm, but we fear that they jeopardize the movement itself. Also, in providing full-time employment which draws underemployed agriculturalists away from agriculture altogether, they tend to defeat their own purpose.

Similarly, care must be taken in any attempts at fiscal protection of cottage industries, lest such action actually inhibit the modern industrial growth which is equally a part of the development program. Instead, continued assistance in training, extension of credit, formation of cooperatives, standardization of quality, and marketing should be emphasized. In certain cases we believe that the proposed Institute for Applied Research will be able to contribute to the improved design of inexpensive home production equipment for these crafts.

MISCELLANEOUS INDUSTRIES

In this report no attempt is made to deal with every existing or potential industry in Ceylon. Apart from those already discussed, however, there are some others which may be mentioned here.

One of considerable interest and importance is a composite factory at Kandana, privately operated by a local joint-stock company and manufacturing glassware, matches, match boxes, soap, molded plastic articles, flashlight batteries, hard candy, disinfectants and ink. This is an unusually progressive enterprise employing about 600, and has generally paid good dividends while continuing to expand and modernize its production.

In some ways this factory serves as an example of principles urged by the Mission. Its glass manufacture, for example, is commercially successful while that of the government glass factory is not. It does not rely upon the Industrial Products Act and it pays wages higher than those specified by the Minimum Wage Law. Its match manufacture is not yet the most economical on the island, but the company is preparing to solve this problem by installing new machinery while a dozen match factories in similar condition have depended upon quotas, protection and price-fixing by the government.

Arrack, the island's distilled liquor, is produced by a government distillery and by nine others who sell their product to the government. Consumption, which before the war was about 350,-000 gallons per year, reached over two million gallons in 1950-51 and represented an expenditure of more than Rs. 121.6 million. Thus the industry is significant, if locally controversial. Output during the last year was severely curtailed by a somewhat hasty attempt to Ceylonize the toddy tappers who provide its raw materials; failure of Ceylonese tappers to replace Indians in this occupation forced stoppage of the government distillery until the Ceylonization ban was modified.

Among the products of industries capable of establishment or expansion—and not already mentioned elsewhere—are fiber bags, high-grade furniture, margarine and cooking fats, prepared animal feeds, and various light manufactures in wood or metal. In this category are many which lend themselves to small private operation, which the Mission sees as the natural backbone of the island's industrial development in the next decade or more.

Summary of Principal Recommendations

Broad Industrial Policy

Objectives

1. Development of industry should be encouraged as an important productive activity, but secondary to agriculture for the present.
2. The aim should be to develop a broad industrial base for future growth, through diversification of small and medium-sized industrial units, rather than concentration upon a few large factories of special types.
3. Greater emphasis should be placed on export possibilities for manufactures, to avoid limiting potential production to the small needs of the local market.

Ownership and Operation

4. Attempts to distinguish between *basic* and *nonbasic* industries should be discarded as unsound.
5. Government financial participation in industrial development should continue where necessary, but every inducement should be used to call forth private capital in order to conserve public funds for other important uses.
6. The government should not undertake further industrial projects under its own management. It should participate in the role of shareholder—even up to 100% if necessary—but should leave the function of management to boards of directors and competent industrial executives. Recently announced plans to create separate government industrial corporations—if actually considered—should be modified to give genuine rather than nominal control to officers of the corporations.
7. Present government industries should be reorganized in accordance with the principles of the preceding recommendation.

8. Insofar as possible, government participation in industrial ventures should be through the medium of the proposed Ceylon Development Corporation (Chapter 4).

9. Clarification of official policy toward new foreign capital is desirable. We believe that such capital should be attracted if possible.

Public Service

10. Work of the Ministry of Industries should place greater emphasis on service and help to the industrial community, instead of competing with it. Personnel of the Ministry should become better acquainted with the many existing industries on the island and their common problems.

11. The Ministry should encourage and support the training of many more skilled workers and technologists, not merely for government service but for employment in all branches of industry.

12. The Ministry should give greater financial support to basic studies of resources, and to publication of findings for the information of the citizens who pay the bill. Especially, the geological survey should be allocated at least an additional Rs. 500,000 per year to intensify its work.

13. The government should support more effective industrial research through the proposed Ceylon Institute for Applied Research, as well as fundamental studies through other agencies such as the University of Ceylon when they are prepared to undertake them.

TYPES OF INDUSTRIES SUITABLE

General Criteria

14. Under present conditions—with no surplus of local industrial labor, special skills and power—most new industries should be based on local raw materials. Exceptions occur in certain unusual cases.

15. An industry should not necessarily be created at once merely because a raw material is available. Production should begin only when economically justified.

16. In general, industries chosen should be those which do not demand large amounts of power, fuel or fresh water. If any heavy power-users are built, they should be located within early reach of the central power grid.

17. Until training facilities are greatly improved, new industries should be either those not calling for unusual amounts of skilled labor, or ones employing techniques which can be learned easily and rapidly.

18. Industries should be chosen to fit into a natural pattern of mutual assistance—using each other's products and by-products, balancing the load on the country's transport system, manufacturing complementary products for the market, etc.

Cottage Industries

19. Development of cottage industries should continue to be encouraged as a means of utilizing the productive potential of underemployed agricultural workers.

20. More intensive technical and market studies of the island's cottage industries should be made, toward improving their economic soundness.

21. If cottage industries are to exist, they should remain true cottage industries. To attempt to transform them into any semblance of factory operations while retaining the less efficient cottage methods is economically unsound.

22. As one test of the soundness of a given industry, the government should determine whether its overhead is low enough to enable it to exist without fiscal protection. If any protective measures are used, care should be exercised that they do not hinder equally important industrial developments.

INDIVIDUAL INDUSTRIES

Beverages

23. Manufacture of soft drinks should continue to expand, with efforts toward domestic production of more of the necessary raw materials.

24. Export of beer should be encouraged.

25. A small sheet metal stamping industry should be started, to make bottle caps, jar closures and such other articles as may be feasible. Complementary operations should include cork-cutting, gasket-making and lithographing.

Canning and Preserving

26. Canning of foods should be developed, not as a scattered cottage industry, but in well-situated modern canneries where quality and sanitation can be controlled to market specifications.

27. Uniform chutney production should be encouraged for export.

28. Use of tinplate for packaging cigarettes and confectionery should be discontinued, and the limited supply of the material diverted to more essential use.

Cement

29. The cement plant should be enlarged and improved as planned, but provision should be made for better railway car service to move the product.

Chemicals

30. The electrolytic caustic soda factory should not be built at Elephant Pass, but at a more economical location such as Palavi, within range of the power grid. Its temporary installation at Gal Oya should be studied from a cost standpoint, as a possible means of utilizing power there during the first few years.

UNIVERSITY COLLEGE OF WALES LIBRARY ABERYSTWYTH

31. DDT, like caustic soda, should be made at Palavi, or a similar location.

32. Sulphuric acid manufacture is not recommended at this time. If the government elects to proceed nevertheless, location of a sulphuric acid plant at Elephant Pass is in no way justified. The use of gypsum as a raw material for this product cannot be recommended under normal conditions. Purchase of the acid is more secure than purchase of standard sulphur source materials in present circumstances.

33. Acetic acid should be produced eventually, either by controlled oxidation of molasses alcohol (if available) or by destructive distillation of coconut shells (after more complete research).

34. Salt evaporation should be adjusted to standard technical practice to produce a more acceptable salt.

35. Manufacture of by-product chemicals from salt bittern should be considered later, but not now.

Coconut Products (see also Oils)

36. Factory production of high-grade exportable coir fiber articles should be stimulated.

37. Makers of desiccated coconut should compare notes and examine their own operations for opportunities for small improvements.

Fertilizer

38. The government fertilizer project should be postponed.

Fisheries

39. Gradual improvements of the fishing industry should be continued through such aids as towing small boats to sea and back, provision of refrigerated storage and transport, education, financing and marketing assistance.

40. Ocean research on profitable fishing areas should be undertaken, with the best technical assistance obtainable.

41. Purchase of additional trawlers should be deferred until there are at least enough skilled local seamen and fishermen to man the present one without outside help.

42. Button manufacture, with a by-product of ground shell for poultry use, should be considered.

Glass

43. The present government glass factory—regarded as irretrievably inefficient—should be abandoned without further investment or loss of public funds.

44. Bottle manufacture should be encouraged; but as a public safeguard against dangerously defective bottles this should be done only under true competitive conditions with modern automatic bottle-making machinery.

Leather

45. Tanning of leather should be improved by dissemination of basic technical information and by greater governmental cooperation with the island's tanners.

46. Production of hand-tooled leather goods should be developed, possibly as a cottage industry.

Meat

47. Sanitary conditions in the island's abbatoirs should be improved through more rigid health regulations and inspection.

48. Commercial recovery of more secondary products of slaughter should be studied.

Milk

49. Sanitary regulations on milk production should be improved and enforced, beginning with the government farms themselves. Manufacture of the newest form of liquid

concentrated milk should be considered for safer distribution.

Minerals

50. Possibilities for local production of graphite anodes and similar articles should be studied.

51. Ilmenite separation at Pulmoddai should proceed, but rail access to Trincomalee should be provided. Meanwhile the government should encourage export of raw ilmenite sand from the more accessible Tirukkovil deposit in order to establish market connections.

52. Thorianite deposits should be discussed with the United States as a possible dollar export. Markets for monazite and ground mica should be reinvestigated in the light of changed markets.

Oils

53. Solvent extraction of coconut oil should be encouraged, but preferably in participation with private millers through the agency of the proposed Development Corporation. If the government erects its own plant, it should not under any circumstances contain additional mechanical oil milling equipment, but should be built adjacent to existing private mills.

54. Any funds which the government had planned to invest in oil milling equipment should be diverted to encouragement of local cultivation of oil seeds other than coconut, to meet requirements of local soap factories.

Paper

55. A more thorough and competent technical review of the illuk paper project should be made before any more major funds are spent on it. Better pilot tests should be made on illuk, and the same should be done with spent citronella grass. (See also Chapter 11). Technical help of the Paper Institute at Appleton, Wisconsin, U. S. A., is suggested.

Rice

56. Rice mills should recover the fuel value of their waste hulls, by installation of hull-burning steam boilers for motive power and parboiling.

Rubber

57. Diversified rubber goods manufacture should be encouraged.

58. Tire production should concentrate on the most common types and sizes. The remainder should be imported. Government tariff policy should take this into account.

Shoes

59. The shoe industry should be expanded; manufacture of low-cost rope-soled shoes is proposed.

60. Reorganization of the government shoe factory should provide for independent management and adjustment of equipment for more balanced production. Fewer types of shoes should be made.

Steel

61. Production of steel should be deferred as costly and entirely premature in relation to power and other developments.

Sugar

62. Additional experienced technical help on factory production of sugar should be obtained to supplement present agricultural studies.

63. To encourage local production of confectionery, soft drinks, and similar industries, the government should lower its profit on the sugar which it sells to industrial consumers.

Tea

64. The Tea Research Institute should devote more attention to studies of tea factory improvement, for which it is un-

usually well equipped. Lower production cost should be the major aim.

65. Caffeine production by one or more tea factories rather than by the government should be encouraged.

Textiles

66. In expansion of local textile manufacture new mills should be built only one at a time, preferably under private management or with government participation through the Development Corporation. Moreover, the economic soundness of these mills is likely to be dependent upon increased local cotton growing.

67. Textile quality should be more carefully watched, to assure its acceptability in secondary industries and the competitive market.

Tobacco

68. Jaffna cigar manufacturers should attempt a small cooperatively-owned factory to make nicotine insecticides from their tobacco wastes.

Wheat Flour

69. A modern flour mill, using imported wheat, should be established under private management with government capital participation through the proposed Development Corporation. It should be situated in the Colombo Port Area. Initial capacity of 50 sacks per hour is recommended.

Wood Products

70. Industrial use of firewood should be avoided wherever possible. In particular, large new industries should not be based upon its use.

71. The government plywood mill should be placed on a paying basis by giving it independent management and removing the excessive government overhead.

605

72. Local manufacture of lathe-turned woodenware and carved curios should be encouraged, with an effort to develop export markets.

73. Laboratory investigations should be conducted to determine the physical properties of various native woods not now commercialized.

16. Transportation

By comparison with many other countries of the world Ceylon has been fortunate in the development of extensive transportation media during the past century. The basic pattern has already been set and today's problem is one of improvement in detail, not of development from scratch.

Unfortunately, in Ceylon as in many more fully developed countries, natural growth and improvement were retarded during the depression of the thirties and the war period; and the increased tempo of economic development experienced during the war and postwar years has superimposed a greater demand for all types of transportation.

Except for the Jaffna peninsula at the northern end of the island, population, production, commerce and industry are centered in the southwestern or wet zone which is served by the only major port of Colombo. Here is the seat of government and finance, most of the existing commerce and industry, nearly all the export-import trade and by far the most populous city. The one port, one city and one zone economy arose from geographical and related conditions and from the comparative ease of developing the country's natural resources in this area. The mountain ranges in the south-central region also form a natural barrier to easy surface transportation. Consequently most of the existing transportation facilities and the main lines of communication lie in the western half of the island, while comparatively sparse facilities are found in the eastern half.

The main port, Colombo, has been called upon to handle an ever increasing volume of traffic, far beyond its present design capacity, with consequent major congestion. This has resulted in an ocean freight surcharge and higher costs generally to all concerned. Major development works are now in hand which should relieve this congestion for many years to come. The minor ports of the island are as yet undeveloped but it is time for one or two of these to receive attention.

During the war the railroads were worked to maximum capacity, with excessive wear and tear of trackage and rolling stock and a minimum of betterment and renewals. It was even deemed advisable to lift the track between Bangadeniya and Puttalam on the west coast to obtain material for the maintenance of more strategic routes.

During the same period the only important roads constructed or improved were those of military importance while general maintenance and new construction were reduced to the barest minimum. In the postwar years much of this backlog has been made up, but further improvements are necessary to meet present day requirements.

Air transportation within the country is still in its infancy but is capable of a steady natural growth, assisted by the construction of airports during the war.

Telecommunications internally are extensive but there is considerable room for modernization and expansion, particularly in the rural areas.

Maps Nos. 19 and 20 show the more important present media of surface transportation as well as some major changes and developments recommended for their expansion and integration.

Ports and Harbors

The commercial ports of Ceylon today comprise the one major port of Colombo, and some half dozen minor ports of the open roadstead type strung around the coast. The more important are Galle on the south coast, Batticaloa on the east, and Kankesanturai, Kayts and Jaffna in the extreme north.

An important naval base is located at Trincomalee harbor on the northeast coast which, by agreement with the Government of Ceylon, is under the control of the British Admiralty. Trincomalee has not hitherto been put to commercial use.

(1) *Colombo*

History. Between 1874 and 1912 the port of Colombo was developed into the major seaport of Ceylon with a water area of some 640 acres protected by concrete breakwaters, but no deepwater alongside berths except oil tanker piers had been constructed up to the end of 1951. Ships of deep draft are moored in midstream and all freight and passenger traffic between ship and shore are handled by harbor craft.

Shore facilities include large and small graving docks, bulk coconut oil tanks, bulk petroleum and fuel oil terminals, coal yard, barge repairing basin, small naval yard, mechanical workshops, patent slipway of 1,000 ton capacity and boat repair yard, shallow water piers and wharves for passenger and cargo craft and a number of warehouses and transit sheds scattered over the area.

A canal and locks connect the harbor basin with a system of lakes known as Beira Lake, east and west, which are in turn connected with the main canal system of the west coast.

Map No. 16 shows the layout of the port of Colombo and also certain new development works in hand and proposed. Briefly, the project calls for the construction of about 7,000 linear feet of deep water quays and complementary facilities at a cost of about Rs. 80 million; it is scheduled for completion by the end of 1953.

Administration. The Port of Colombo (Administration) Act No. 10 of 1950, was brought into force on January 1, 1951. The Act set up an Advisory Board known as the Colombo Port Commission presided over by a Port Commissioner. Under the general direction and control of the Minister of Transport and Works, the Port Commissioner is responsible for the day to day administration and operations of the port's undertakings assisted by a staff, all of whom are public servants under the Civil Service Code. The Commission is also responsible for the construction, maintenance and operation of coastlights and navigational buoys for the whole of Ceylon. Total personnel of the Commission now exceeds 5,000.

There are a number of deficiencies in the functioning of the Port Commission. Most important is the shortage of qualified technical officers and staff essential to the proper administration and working of the port. This situation arises from the Commission being subject to treasury and civil service regulations, and from the lack of suitable local personnel. Government regulations have also added to formalities and delays in administration, especially in the purchase of equipment and machinery.

TABLE I

PORT UTILIZATION COMPARISON
Tonnage of Vessels Entering Ports 1947-50
(*to nearest 1,000 tons*)

Port	1947-48	1948-49	1949-50
Colombo [1]	8,732,000	11,748,000	12,344,000
Bombay [2]	7,909,000	14,947,000	7,715,000
Calcutta [2]	3,698,000	4,386,000	4,728,000
Madras [2]	3,063,000	3,488,000	3,763,000
Cochin [2]	1,823,000	2,170,000	2,221,000
Rangoon [3]	3,225,000	2,679,000	2,649,000
Singapore [4]	5,559,000	6,980,000	8,205,000

[1] Figures for year ending December 31
[2] ,, ,, ,, ,, March 31
[3] ,, ,, ,, ,, September 30
[4] ,, ,, ,, ,, June 30

Source: Colombo Port Commission.

MAP 16

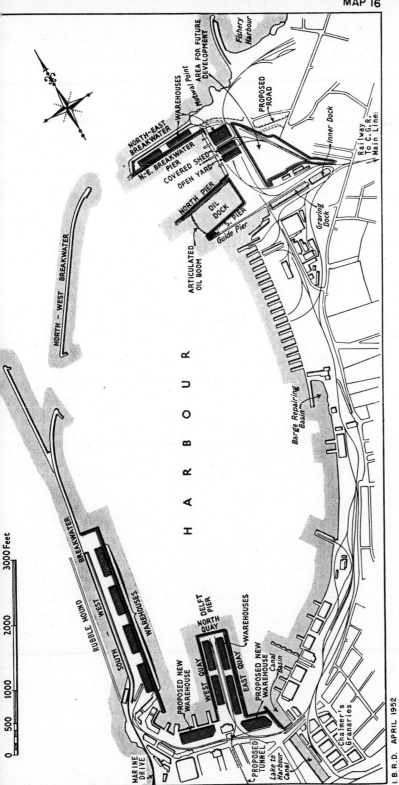

PORT OF COLOMBO

DEVELOPMENT PROJECT

1950 - 54

I.B.R.D.   APRIL 1952

The Commission has also had to follow the broad governmental policy of "Ceylonization" of labor at serious cost to efficiency, particularly in man-hour output.

Traffic. Its geographical location on the main sea routes to the Orient and Australasia makes Colombo an important port of call. It stands at or near the head of port utilization compared with other ports in Southern Asia. Although many of the vessels carrying intransit passengers call at Colombo for only a few hours to a day, they occupy berthage space and utilize other facilities. Table I shows this comparison.

The number and tonnage of ships handled at Colombo has greatly increased since 1940, and since 1947 has more than doubled, as shown in Table II.

TABLE II

COLOMBO SHIPPING

(merchant ships, hired transports, hospital ships)

Year	Number	Registered Tons
1940	1,848	7,350,937
1941	1,661	5,542,324
1942	1,230	3,549,539
1943	1,074	3,380,257
1944	1,155	4,353,807
1945	1,039	3,958,101
1946	1,352	5,168,465
1947	1,561	6,127,904
1948	2,054	8,732,381
1949	2,584	11,747,518
1950	2,700	12,344,074
1951	2,766	12,312,699

Source: Colombo Port Commission.

Import cargo tonnage, shown in Table III, has grown somewhat less but since 1946 the increase has been substantial.

TABLE III

Colombo Imports

(*tons*)

Year	General Cargo	Coal	Bulk Fuel Oil	Total
1940	1,048,343	500,807	487,618	2,036.768
1941	1,008,556	296,004	344,394	1,648,954
1942	951,865	333,479	389,487	1,674,831
1943	1,106,210	218,188	475,511	1,799,909
1944	1,356,296	286,002	744,313	2,386,611
1945	1,443,111	375,924	1,033,053	2,852,088
1946	1,119,580	342,966	508,694	1,971,240
1947	1,244,430	319,668	336,532	1,900,630
1948	1,302,074	347,622	444,858	2,094,554
1949	1,509,427	378,737	668,850	2,557,014
1950	1,550,100	362,892	711,586	2,624,578
1951	1,770,767	290,374	714,384	2,775,525

Source: Colombo Port Commission.

Export cargo figures, given in Table IV, also show a rise, especially since 1946.

The over-all increase in port traffic and its nature have given rise to serious problems in the working of the port, due chiefly to physical conditions, but also in part to the nature and incidence of shipments.

Finance. The annual revenue from the port has increased over the past decade with the increased traffic, but annual working expenditure has also increased and actually exceeded revenue in 1947-48. In March, 1949, a 60% surcharge on port charges was introduced to offset higher working costs. Revenue substantially exceeded expenditure in 1949-50 and 1950-51.

No statement of over-all capital expenditure on the port appears to be available nor is any method of amortization used. If the port accounts were to be commercialized they would undoubtedly show an annual loss. The excess of revenue or expenditure is absorbed into the general budget of the government. Table V shows the annual revenue, expenditure and loan fund expenditure since 1940-41. No charges are included for services rendered to or by other Government departments.

The major item under Recurrent Expenditure is personal emoluments amounting to Rs. 2,055,990, Rs. 2,433,084 and Rs. 2,552,491 for the three periods of the table above. Under Special Expenditure the major item is Cost of Living Allowance of Rs. 3,283,826, Rs. 3,424,076 and Rs. 4,065,000 (which are really a permanent addition to Personal Emoluments) for the three periods and an item for new machinery and equipment of Rs. 1,094,960 (1951-52 estimated).

TABLE IV
COLOMBO EXPORTS
(*tons*)

Year	General Cargo	Coal Bunkers	Fuel Oil Bunkers	Bulk Coconut Oil	Total
1940	585,935	223,670	321,055	—	1,130,660
1941	549,232	252,847	324,323	—	1,126,402
1942	601,057	164,175	187,725	—	952,957
1943	709,960	102,840	190,582	—	1,003,382
1944	552,834	147,421	294,085	—	994,340
1945	574,898	134,672	586,597	—	1,296,167
1946	484,282	137,944	286,205	—	908,431
1947	540,186	97,160	293,428	—	930,774
1948	701,305	115,233	370,922	66,507	1,253,967
1949	683,863	111,064	563,992	55,024	1,413,943
1950	711,665	87,019	558,434	47,144	1,404,262
1951	705,606	73,179	570,766	71,585	1,421,136

Source: Colombo Port Commission.

TABLE V

COLOMBO PORT—ANNUAL REVENUE AND EXPENDITURE

(*rupees*)

Year	Working Revenue	Working Expenditure	Excess of Revenue Expenditure (—)	Loan Fund Expenditure
1941-42	5,883,333	3,263,231	2,620,102	—
1942-43	6,348,518	4,489,599	1,858,919	—
1943-44	6,299,260	5,499,912	799,348	84,712
1944-45	7,950,773	6,630,978	1,319,795	470,119
1945-46	7,730,173	7,317,219	412,954	2,645,416
1946-47	8,838,835	8,215,719	623,116	192,215
1947-48	9,992,961	11,792,666	(—)1,799,705	396,433
1948-49	13,685,312	11,721,531	1,963,781	1,641,554
1949-50	17,483,910	12,173,387	5,310,523	1,264,099
1950-51	21,052,560	13,279,453	7,773,107	6,535,331*
1951-52 (est)	21,000,000	16,427,781	4,572,219	30,652,200*

Source: Colombo Port Commission.

* Includes expenditures on Port Development Scheme of Rs. 5,195,393 for 1950-51 and Rs. 23,200,000 (estimated) for 1951-52.

For general budget purposes the annual working expenditure is broken down into Recurrent Expenditure and Special Expenditure. Table VI shows these totals for 1949-50 (actual), 1950-51 and 1951-52 (estimated).

TABLE VI

COLOMBO PORT—ANNUAL RECURRENT AND SPECIAL EXPENDITURES

(*rupees*)

Expenditure	Actual Expenditure 1949-50	Estimates 1950-51	Estimates 1951-52
Recurrent	7,392,808	8,117,084	8,605,991
Special	4,780,579	5,879,136	7,821,790
Total	*12,173,387*	*13,996,220*	*16,427,781*

Source: Government Estimates, 1951-52.

Loan fund expenditure on capital account, proposed or in hand, is indicated in Table VII.

TABLE VII

COLOMBO PORT—LOAN FUND EXPENDITURE

(*rupees*)

	Amount Chargeable	Est. Exp. to 30 Sept. 1951	Est. Exp. 1951-52
Coal handling equipment	1,434,000	1,184,000	250,000
Housing C. P. C. employees	8,250,000	—	1,000,000
Extra high tension supply	3,555,000	600,000	800,000
Diesel locomotives	1,800,000	—	900,000
		(*)	1,000
14″ pipeline to K.O.D.	900,000		900,000
Salvage of S. S. *Soli*	850,000	—	850,000
Dock pumps, etc.	620,000	— (*)	100
Twenty-ton travelling crane	200,000	— (*)	100
Port Development Scheme	79,270,000	10,250,000	23,200,000

Original estimate 77,920,000
Marine Drive   750,000   (*) To place indents
York St. Tunnel 2,600,000

            81,270,000
Less charged to
   Loan Scheme
   1937   2,000,000

   Balance   79,270,000

Deepening lake and locks	450,000	—	175,000
Purchase of lighters etc.	1,700,000	—	1,600,000
Diesel repair shops	1,348,000	—	356,000
Suction dredger	900,000	700,000	200,000
Totals:	*101,277,000*	*12,734,000*	*30,232,200*
			12,734,000

Estimated expenditure
1950-52   42,966,200   42,966,200

Balance est. exp. 1953-? 58,310,800

Source: Government Estimates, 1951-52, Vote No. 11.

The Colombo Port Commission has now commenced to carry out a continuing internal audit of its accounts. A staff of eight persons was requested but only four positions were approved by the Treasury. Valuation of the assets of the Commission is also under way. This is expected to be completed during 1952, when it could be used as a basis in commercializing the accounts.

We consider that the accounts of the Colombo Port Commission should be commercialized as soon as possible. The present accounting practice makes no provision for the amortization of loan fund expenditure on capital account and consequently does not truly reflect the financial operations of the port.

Port Congestion. The increase of traffic in recent years to levels far beyond those for which the port was designed has caused serious congestion and slower ship turnaround. This, in turn, has brought about a special freight surcharge of 25% and generally higher costs for landing and shipping cargo. The chief causes of this congestion may be summarized as follows:[1]

(a) Inadequate and outdated port facilities, principally the lack of alongside deep-water berths, lack of sufficient transit shed warehouse accommodation, the inadequate and diverse nature of land transportation methods for the clearance of import cargo and poor accessibility to the port area and transit sheds. As a result cargo handling cannot be mechanized to any appreciable extent.

(b) Uneven flow of bulk food purchases of the government.

(c) Less skilled labor and lower output as a result of the national policy of Ceylonization.

(d) Increase in number of importers and delays in effecting clearance of cargo.

---

[1] For details see recent annual Administration Reports and the *Report of Committee on Handling of Ships in the Port of Colombo.* (Millbourn Report), published as Sessional Paper XXV, October 1951.

(e) Shortage of qualified technical staff employed by the Port Commission.

(f) Labor employment conditions and lack of incentive to greater output.

(g) Excessive number of stevedoring contractors and poor supervisory control.

Of these by far the most important cause of congestion is the inadequacy of the port facilities for the handling of the increased traffic. Consequently, most of the present difficulties will be greatly alleviated upon completion of the port development works now in hand. That congestion and attendant difficulties have not been worse is a tribute to the work and ingenuity of the officers and staff of the Port Commission.

We therefore recommend that everything possible be done to speed up construction and completion of port development scheme, Stages I and II. The work under construction is, we understand, behind schedule. Both contract work and complementary departmental work should be speeded up, as well as the completion of any additional engineering, plans and specifications. Formalities in the placement of orders for necessary material, machinery and equipment should be reduced as early delivery dates are becoming more and more difficult to obtain.

The construction and completion of ancillary works proposed by the Port Commission should be similarly expedited. These works include the rubble mound breakwater, the marine drive, the York Street railway tunnel and the Beira Lake development projects. The engineering, preparation of plans and specifications and the placing of contracts for construction and materials should be expedited so as to obtain full and immediate value of Stages I and II of the port development scheme as each part is brought into use. As a corollary, no new construction for other departments or outside concerns should be allowed in the affected areas, unless it forms part of the project. Immediate steps should be

617

taken to acquire the necessary land and rights of way where this has not already been done.

We further recommend the coordination of plans and construction to improve port accessibility and inland transportation now being carried out by the Port Commission, Colombo Municipality, Government Railways and the Public Works Department.

Access to the port area by means of road, rail and canal is inadequate. This causes much of the traffic congestion and delay in moving import cargo. The authorities concerned should draw up coordinated plans and proceed with constructive measures to improve all round accessibility to the various quays, transit sheds and warehouses within the port areas.

On the other hand, we advise the postponement of construction work under Stages III (extension of southwest breakwater quay) and IV (outer breakwaters) of the Port Development Scheme. Engineering studies for those works should continue.

With the completion of Stages I and II of the port development scheme most of the present port congestion will be relieved. The traffic of the port is not likely to increase sufficiently within the next ten years to justify the expenditure of funds on either Stage III or Stage IV; but as conditions at that time cannot be foreseen with any certainty, engineering studies of both stages should be continued so that Stage III may be put into operation the moment that conditions warrant. The engineering of Stage IV, consisting of outer breakwaters to the north of the harbor, is a more complex and difficult matter on account of the proximity of the mouth of the Kelani River and the unknown characteristics of the ocean currents in the area. Consequently, it will be necessary to carry out careful surveys and long-term model experiments in determining the most efficient and satisfactory layout. Our recommendations with regard to Galle Harbor should be closely associated with these surveys and the relative merits of further developing Colombo or Galle should be carefully analyzed from the over-all economic point of view.

We concur fully in certain recommendations for the improvement of the administration and operation of the port contained in the Millbourn Report, insofar as conditions have not greatly changed in the meantime. The recommendations we have in mind are:

(a) Every effort should be made by government departments and shipping companies to regulate the flow of vessels bringing full cargoes of all classes of goods into the port.

(b) Arrangements for the clearance of food cargoes direct from lighter to road and rail transport to destinations outside the port area should be made well in advance of the arrival of ships. There should be maintained at all times the closest liaison between the various responsible persons, in order that the fullest use may be made of all transport facilities.

(c) The unloading of lighters should be maintained on a 24-hour basis.

(d) Mobile handling equipment should be introduced to the maximum practicable extent at the earliest possible moment.

The Port Commission, with government backing, should further aim at:

(a) Reduction of the number of stevedoring companies to one, or at most two, by amalgamation or reorganization.

(b) Improvement of labor output by various means, including the introduction of piece-work rates or incentive bonuses, and instruction in port operations for all grades of staff and labor.

(c) Maintaining at all times a complete staff of qualified and experienced technical and administrative officers to insure that all departments function at maximum efficiency.

We do not concur in the suggestion that a port warehouse be constructed on the site of the present Chalmers Granaries, situ-

619

ated adjacent to the lake-to-harbor canal, for the following reasons:

(a) The existing buildings cannot be spared during the period of new construction.

(b) The time required for construction would be too long to be of any immediate value.

(c) Such construction would tend to perpetuate already serious traffic congestion in the area.

(d) Long-term planning as proposed above should aim at the elimination of the Chalmers Granaries completely for better use of the site. (For a possible use see under Colombo City in the section on Roads and Highways).

The possible formation of an autonomous Port authority is discussed in the section on Regulation and Development of Transportation.

Pilferage. Cargo losses, damage, pilferage and theft have become very serious. The subject has been exhaustively investigated by a Colombo Port Commission Sub-Committee of Enquiry which submitted its report on July 19, 1951 and we recommend that its findings receive prompt attention and that its recommendations, or improvements thereon, be carried out to the maximum extent practicable.

Labor and Welfare. Port labor management is both complex and difficult. The Port Commission has made much progress in improving working conditions in the way of emoluments, security and frequency of work, recruitment, registration and general welfare. In spite of this there is a regrettable tendency for labor to reduce output in inverse ratio to the improvement in working conditions. The general policy of Ceylonization of labor has proved uneconomic, resulting in lower output and higher costs to exporters and importers alike. Such higher costs are eventually passed on to the consumer with a snowballing effect, increasing the cost of living while reducing profits on exports.

(2) Galle

History. Galle Harbor, situated on the south coast about 75 miles from Colombo, lies between the headland known as Watering Point on the east and the headland on which is built the Fort of Galle on the west. These headlands are about 6,000 feet apart; the available depth of bay back to Gibbet Island is about 3,300 feet. The bay faces south and is exposed to the full force of the southwest monsoons, but is protected from the northeast monsoons. Much of the entrance and area within the bay is covered with reef and rock shoals as shown on Admiralty Chart No. 819. It is the cost of dealing with these reefs and shoals which has delayed development of the port.

Galle was used as a port of call for ships prior to the development of Colombo and various proposals have been made from time to time since 1858 for its improvement by heavy breakwater construction and dock dredging. In each case the schemes were dropped on account of cost. The most recent estimate of cost was that given in a Report of the Minister of Communications and Works to the State Council, dated August, 1935. The scheme consisted of three breakwaters, a western, an island and an eastern breakwater, estimated to cost Rs. 17 million, plus dredging and rock removal at a cost unknown because of insufficient survey data.

Accidents to shipping have occurred on several occasions and with the increasing size of ships, owners are becoming greatly concerned for the safety of vessels calling at Galle. Consequently, if it is desired to continue its use as a port, conditions will have to be improved.

Administration. The Port of Galle is administered by the Colombo Port Commission through an Assistant Master Attendant, who also acts as pilot, with a staff of about 50 persons.

Traffic. Between 1924 and 1935 the number of vessels calling at Galle increased from 96 to 123 and the net tonnage rose from 259,426 tons to 337,413. Since 1946, all rice imports for the whole of Ceylon have been handled at Colombo and the number of vessels calling at Galle has fallen to an average of 35 per year, with an average net tonnage of 132,270 tons. For the three year period, 1949-51, import cargo averaged 25,000 tons and export cargo 22,000 tons per year.

Finance. The annual revenue from the port of Galle is small and fairly stationary. In 1949-50 the amount was Rs. 72,239 while the estimates for 1950-51 and 1951-52 are Rs. 75,000 for each year. Annual expenditure for the port is considerably higher. For 1951-52 annual recurrent expenditure is estimated at some Rs. 70,000 and special expenditure at about Rs. 150,000, including about Rs. 45,000 for cost of living allowance and about Rs. 105,000 for maintenance, repairs, inshore dredging and small jetty reconstruction.

Future of Galle Harbor. Galle is the principal town of the highly productive Southern Province. Because of the limitations of the port, most of the region's imports and exports are routed through Colombo, 75 miles away. If any appreciable volume of trade were to be diverted to Galle there would be a corresponding decrease through Colombo. Undoubtedly, it would be more convenient and economical for more of the overseas trade of the region to pass through Galle. This trade is increasing; to it will be added the trade emanating from the regions to the east as these become developed under the various current and future development schemes.

There appear therefore to be three possible policies for the future of Galle Harbor, namely:

(a) Allow present conditions to continue indefinitely with the probable result of diminishing overseas trade (as ships tend to increase in size and draft) and the slow decline of Galle as a port of call.

(b) Carry out partial improvement from time to time, of relatively limited scope and cost, but as part of a master plan which could be used as the basis for the full future development of the port.

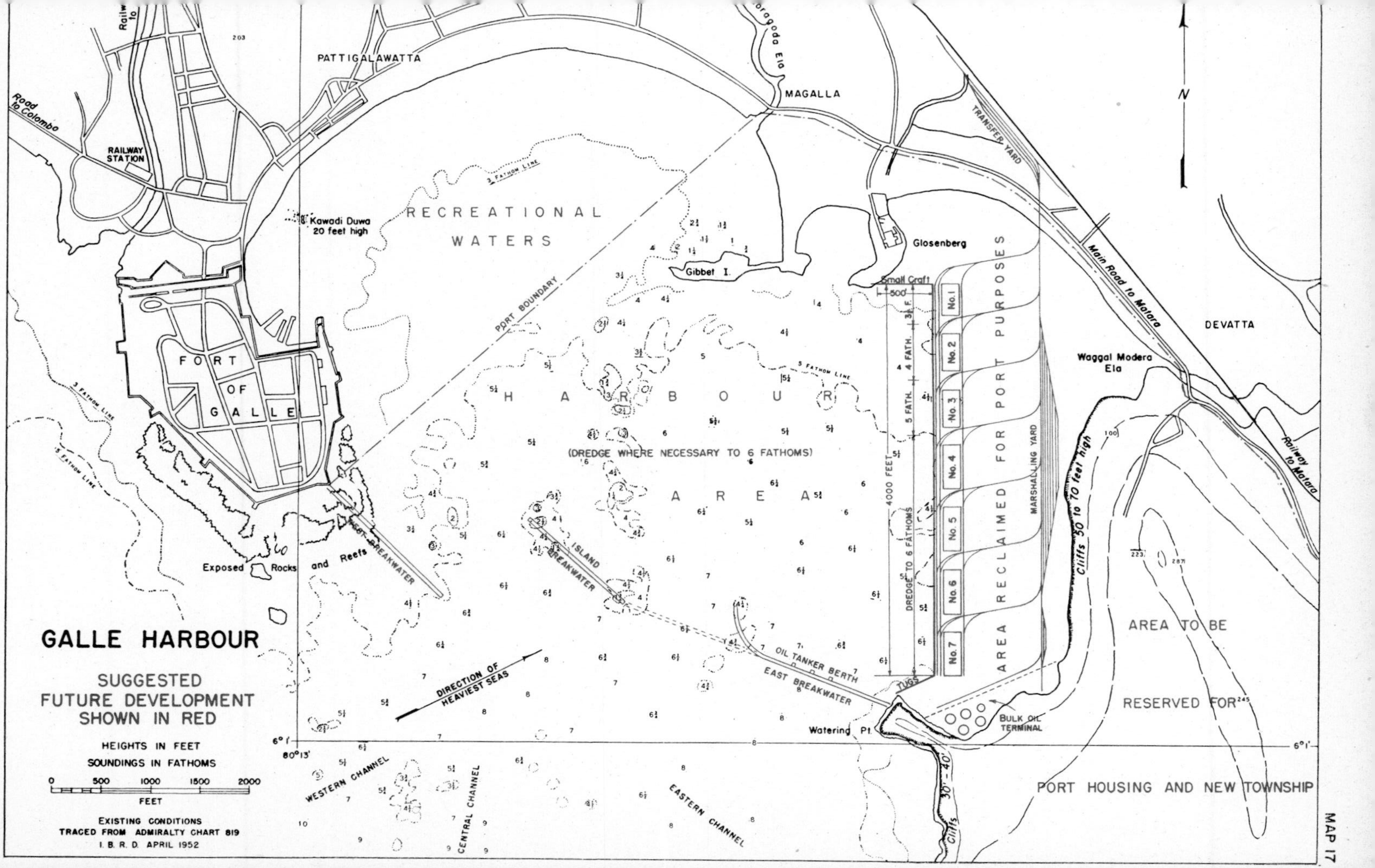

MAP 17

GALLE HARBOUR

SUGGESTED
FUTURE DEVELOPMENT
SHOWN IN RED

HEIGHTS IN FEET

SOUNDINGS IN FATHOMS

0   500   1000   1500   2000
FEET

EXISTING CONDITIONS
TRACED FROM ADMIRALTY CHART 819
I. B. R. D. APRIL 1952

(c) Embark upon a full-scale port development project over the next few years.

The Mission feels that the second policy offers the best answer to the problem. By this means Galle can become a useful satellite port to Colombo, and encourage and assist local trade and industry without making too great a call on the country's present financial resources. We accordingly recommend partial improvement of Galle harbor by dredging and removal of hazardous rocks in the proximity of the berthing areas. This could be the first stage of a long-term master plan for the ultimate development of the port. In the meantime, the work would have useful results. It will first be necessary to complete a detailed hydrographic survey of the harbor bottom in the areas selected for dredging and rock removal. With these data, proper engineering plans and specifications can be produced and a contract placed for the work.

The existing anchorage equipment at the harbor is on the light side and should be improved by increasing size and weight of lines, chains and anchors, so as to provide a greater degree of safety to ships using the port. The use of heavily anchored mooring buoys should also be investigated and, if found feasible, they should be provided as an interim measure.

At present all the island's rice imports are handled through the port of Colombo, thereby increasing the congestion there as well as on the inland transportation systems. This practice arises because the necessary fumigation of the rice requires facilities available only at Colombo. We recommend that facilities be provided to land at Galle rice imports required for distribution in the southern and southwestern regions. Construction of a fumigatorium at Galle would relieve congestion at Colombo and reduce the cost of transportation to the southern and southwestern regions of the island. The dearth of warehouse space also makes storage of the grain a problem in the Colombo area. At Bussa, some five miles west of Galle, there are several valuable buildings constructed for a prisoner-of-war camp. With a railway siding taken off the nearby Galle-Colombo main line, and with rice fumigation facilities at Galle Harbor, these could be used to store rice.

Selection of a fumigatorium site at Galle presents some difficulty, but there are several possibilities that should be investigated in detail. One is Kawadi Duwa and another is on the lee side of Gibbet Island. Both would require some land reclamation and the construction of a small lighter wharf. At Kawadi Duwa the wharf could take the form of solid fill to form a small protected basin, but this site has the disadvantage of being fairly close to the town. The lee side or north shore of Gibbet Island is well segregated and offers greater construction possibilities. A short access road would be required to join the main Galle-Matara highway, while a railway siding taken off the nearby Galle-Matara line should also be investigated and installed if possible.

For both strategic and economic reasons, the long-term development of Galle harbor into a modern port providing safe anchorage in all weathers ought, we believe, to be continuously borne in mind. Colombo city will become increasingly congested and Galle offers a good location for the development of a second major city and port for the island. When the time arrives for seriously considering the expansion of Colombo harbor under Stage IV (outer breakwaters), it might well be found that the money could better be expended on the development of Galle harbor in accordance with the master plan mentioned above. As an example of such a master plan we have prepared Map No. 17. Along with the new port would go a new township laid out on modern lines and located on the headland to the east of the harbor. Steps should be taken now to reserve the entire area for such use. A new water supply scheme may then be necessary, but electric power should have been made available by linking Galle to the island's hydroelectric grid system.

(3) Trincomalee

History. The harbor of Trincomalee, used as a naval base since 1795, is situated on the northeast coast of Ceylon, about 175 miles

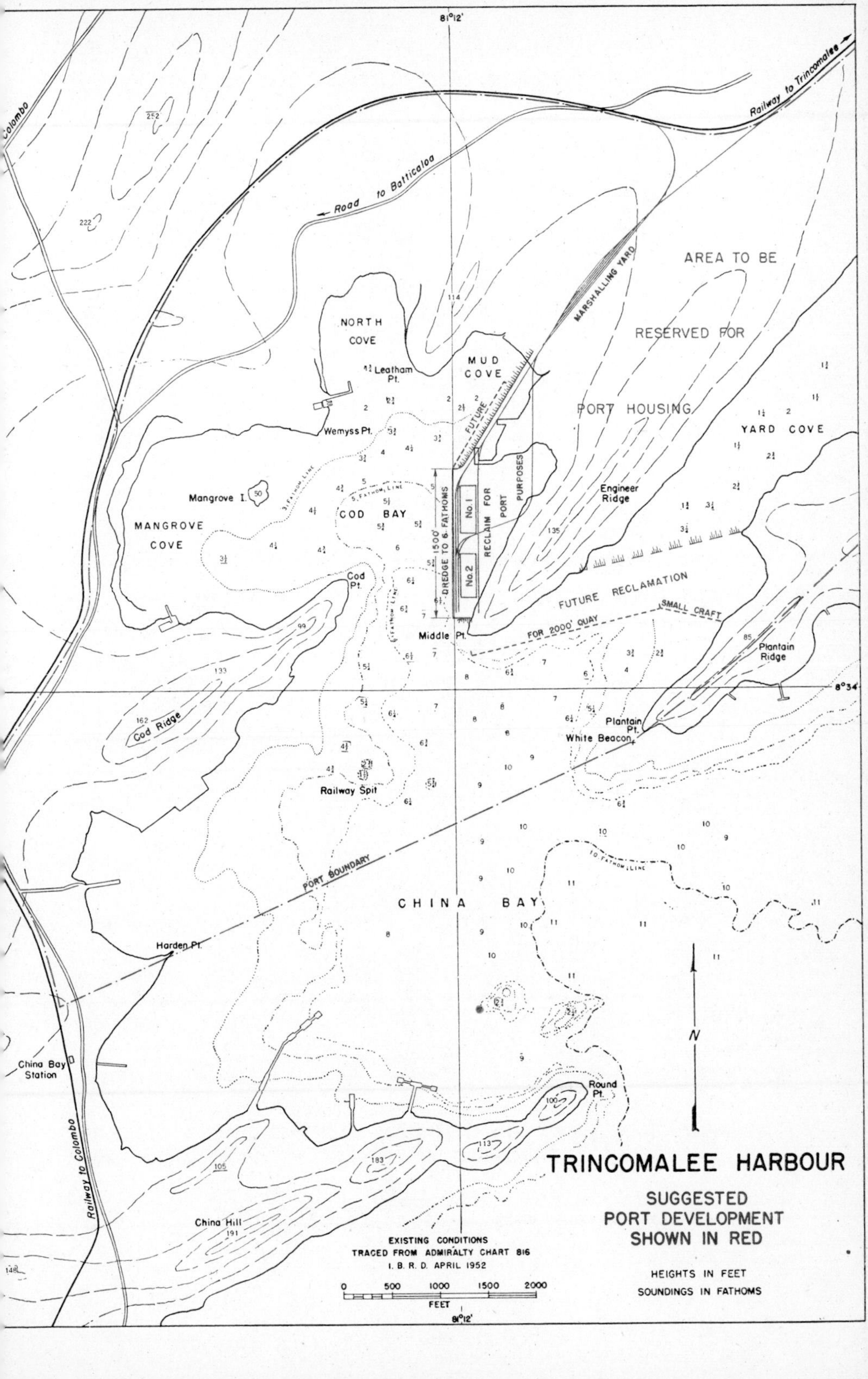

MAP 18

TRINCOMALEE HARBOUR

SUGGESTED
PORT DEVELOPMENT
SHOWN IN RED

HEIGHTS IN FEET
SOUNDINGS IN FATHOMS

EXISTING CONDITIONS
TRACED FROM ADMIRALTY CHART 816
I. B. R. D. APRIL 1952

0   500   1000   1500   2000
FEET

by road northeast from Colombo. The inner harbor consists of a wide expanse of deep water, landlocked except for a narrow entrance from Koddiyar Bay, which is open to shipping throughout the year. Thanks to its sheltered position no seas can be generated by either the southwest or northeast monsoons. In every way it may be termed an ideal harbor.

Land communications between Trincomalee and the rest of the country comprise the railroad link from Maho Junction on the main Colombo-Jaffna line, the main road from Colombo via Dambulla, a minor road from Anuradhapura, a coastal road from Batticaloa to the south and a minor road of some 35 miles connecting with the village of Pulmoddai on the north coast (the site of extensive deposits of ilmenite sand).

Administration and Finance. Trincomalee is at present purely a naval base controlled by the United Kingdom Admiralty under agreement with the Government of Ceylon. It is used as a commercial port only to a very limited extent, as shown by the figures of annual port revenue, which were Rs. 12,606 in 1949-50 and Rs. 15,000 (estimated) in 1951-52.

Future Prospects. Except for the Jaffna peninsula, most of the northern and eastern regions of the island are comparatively undeveloped. However, this situation is changing with the progress of agricultural development projects and, to a lesser extent, industrial schemes. The valley of the Mahaweli Ganga should undergo further development. The Gal Oya project to the south is well under way, while numerous smaller projects are already in operation or are being planned. The Mission feels that the general development of the eastern and northern regions of the country would be assisted and accelerated if a sea outlet were to be established at Trincomalee, which is nearer and more accessible than Colombo.

It is understood that a working arrangement can be made with the Admiralty for developing Trincomalee as a commercial port and that surplus Admiralty electric power and water supplies could be made available for such a development. Other existing facilities include a large bulk oil storage tank farm which could also be used for mercantile bunkers.

We recommend that a beginning should be made in providing commercial port facilities at Trincomalee by arranging for the detailed engineering investigation and the construction of a modern marginal quay, complete with transit sheds and other appurtenances, forming the first stage of a master plan for the development of the port. General requirements are that the commercial establishment should be well removed from the naval establishments, that the area and depth of water be sufficient, that the necessary land area be available, that road and rail communications be easy to provide, that electric power and water supplies be available and that there be ample space for future development. These requirements can be secured at the inlet known as Cod Bay on the extreme west of the inner harbor. Subject to detailed engineering investigation, we believe that a suitable quay could be constructed with its face located approximately on Longitude 81° 12′ running due north from "Middle Point" to a point opposite the existing Mud Cove Pier. Fill for reclamation purposes behind the quay wall could readily be obtained from the west side of "Engineer Ridge," thereby adding extra space for warehouses, railroad tracks, etc. Map No. 18 shows the general arrangement we suggest.

(4) *Northern Ports*

History. The northern peninsula, commonly called the Jaffna district, is populated largely by Tamil stock, a particularly hardworking and energetic people. Unfortunately the area has no natural harbors and most of its export-import trade is routed through Colombo over a 250 mile railway connection. A comparatively small amount of maritime trade passes through the small ports of Jaffna, Kayts, Kankesanturai and Valvedditurai, all of which are of the open roadstead type and extremely exposed to the various monsoons. Only small craft of shallow draft can approach the shore, while loading and discharge of cargo has to be done by means of smaller craft which can be beached.

Administration and Finance. These northern outports are administered by the Customs Department assisted by the Public Works Department. Operation and maintenance of coastal lights and navigation marks are under the control of the Colombo Port Commission.

Revenue from port, harbor, wharf, warehouse and other dues accruing from the northern outports for 1951-52 is estimated as not exceeding Rs. 80,000.

Future of Northern Ports. Of the four northern ports mentioned, Kankesanturai offers the best prospects for development. Although exposed to the northeast monsoon, it is protected from the heavier southwest monsoon. Other advantages include close proximity to the Government Cement Factory with a potential yearly output of 200,000 tons, electric power supply from the cement factory power plant, the adjacent railhead of the railway system and proximity to Kankesanturai airport.

The visible and potential maritime trade do not, however, justify at present any major port development schemes for the northern peninsula. It is likely to be more economic to concentrate on the development of Trincomalee which can serve both the northern and eastern regions of the island.

We therefore recommend deferment of any major development of a northern port but recommend an engineering survey of Kankesanturai to obtain basic data for possible future development. It would be comparatively easy and economical to include the survey at Kankesanturai under the same contract as that for surveys at Colombo, Galle and Trincomalee. If and when the time comes to develop this port such a survey would greatly assist the determination of the final layout as regards nature of ocean currents, degree of shoaling and erosion, etc. It would also provide a basis for closer estimates of cost.

(5) *Capital Requirements for Ports and Harbors*

Capital requirements for port and harbor development recommended by the Mission during the six-year period 1953 to 1959 are shown below in Table VIII. Stages I and II of the Colombo Port development are assumed to be completed by 1953-54, the ancillary works by 1954-55 and the port access improvements by 1956-57. The recommended port development works at Trincomalee are assumed to be completed by the end of 1958. The Mission has considered possible requirements at other outports not discussed in detail here, but has concluded that no major development of any of them can be justified on economic grounds within the period with which it is concerned.

TABLE VIII

ESTIMATED COST OF RECOMMENDATIONS, PORTS AND HARBORS
(*million rupees*)

Particulars	Estimated Cost
Colombo—commercialize accounting	—
Colombo—port development scheme, Stages I & II	65
Colombo—ancillary port works	
Colombo—port access improvements	13
Colombo—engineering survey for Stage IV	0.1
Colombo—improved administration and operation	—
Colombo—reduction in pilferage and cargo losses	—
Galle—hydrographic survey and partial dredging	4
Galle—improvements to anchorage equipment	0.3
Galle—provision of facilities for importing rice	0.5
Trincomalee—provision of commercial port facilities	25
Kankesanturai—engineering survey	0.1
Total	*108*

Average yearly expenditure is Rs. 18 million, but yearly variations will be wide with the major expenditure occurring during the next two or three years. Chart 9 shows the general priority rating of the Mission's recommendations with respect to ports and waterways. In addition to the above, it will be necessary to provide, say, Rs. 10 million for additional equipment of all kinds.

628

CHART 9

MISSION RECOMMENDATIONS	FISCAL YEAR									
PARTICULARS	1952-1953	1953-1954	1954-1955	1955-1956	1956-1957	1957-1958	1958-1959	1959-1960	1960-1961	1961-1962
Colombo Port Comm. Commercialize Accounts	▨									
Colombo Port Dev. Stages I and II	▨▨ (IN HAND)									
Colombo Port Ancillary Works	▨▨▨ (PARTIALLY IN HAND)									
Colombo Port Access Improvements	▨▨▨▨▨▨									
Colombo Port Survey for Stage IV	▨ (SURVEY)									
Colombo Port Improved Operation and Working	▨▨▨▨▨▨▨▨▨▨									
Colombo Port Reduce Cargo Pilferage, Etc.	▨▨▨▨▨▨▨▨▨▨									
Galle Harbor Survey and Partial Dredging	▨ (SURVEY)		▨							
Galle Harbor Improved Anchorage	▨									
Galle Harbor Rice Import Facilities	▨									
Trincomalee Port Development		▨ (SURVEY)			▨▨▨					
Kankesanturai Engineering Survey		▨ (SURVEY)								
Canals, Waterways Improvements	▨▨▨▨▨▨▨▨▨▨									

GENERAL PRIORITY RATING
FOR PORTS AND WATERWAYS PROJECTS

R. D. APRIL 1952

Inland Waterways

History. The canals and inland waterways of Ceylon are partly man-made and partly natural waterways such as rivers, lakes and lagoons. The most important canal system is on the west coast. Together with intervening lakes and lagoons, it extends over some 96 miles from Puttalam in the north via Colombo to Galpotta and Kalutara in the south. The more important lagoons and lakes are those at Puttalam, Mundal, Chilaw, Negombo, Colombo (Beira Lakes), Bolgoda, Koggala, Batticaloa and Jaffna. Rivers also play a small part in water transportation but floods prevent their year-round use.

The canals are mainly a legacy of the Dutch occupation and are gradually diminishing in importance as transportation media. However, they still provide the cheapest form of transport where time is of minor importance.

Administration and Finance. Maintenance is the responsibility of the Public Works Department, while the collection of tolls and rents falls to the Revenue Department. In 1950 some 146 miles of waterways were maintained at a cost of Rs. 252,000. Annual revenue was about Rs. 10,000.

Traffic. In 1949 a rough survey of canal traffic showed that about 600 *padda* boats transported about 9,000 tons of goods over the system. Traffic density was negligible while rates averaged 10 to 20 cents per ton mile. It is understood that the canals are also used a good deal by local people for the transport of their own crops and goods. Some 4,000 persons are said to be engaged in canal transport.

Future of Canals and Waterways. While the inland waterway system is a useful adjunct to the transportation media, no case exists for any major development programs. Maintenance and minor improvements might continue with particular attention being given to increasing controlling depths from the present minimum of three and a half feet to a minimum of five feet in the canals and channels. Annual expenditure on maintenance and improvement of canals and waterways might reasonably be increased to some Rs. 500,000, half of which would be on capital account.

The Gal Oya Project centered at Amparai on the east coast makes the Batticaloa Lagoon of special interest. Pending the full development of railway and highway communications between the Amparai area and Batticaloa, the lagoon could be used for water transport, particularly of building materials required for the project.

The channel depth at the Batticaloa Lagoon from Chavalankadai to Batticaloa, a distance of some 23 miles, should be increased to a minimum of five feet in the controlling sections. We also recommend the construction of a small barge marginal wharf located on the north side and adjacent to the west approach of the Lady Manning Bridge at Batticaloa. This location is on the alignment of the existing railway track, which could be extended to serve the proposed wharf. A bulkhead, with retained backfill, some 200 feet long and 45 feet wide would provide for a transit shed 20 feet wide, as well as a 25 foot apron for the installation of a rail siding adjacent to the transit shed and a roadway along the wharf face. To be of real value these facilities on the Batticaloa Lagoon should receive top priority and be undertaken by the Gal Oya Development Board with the assistance of the Railway Department and Public Works Department.[2] At Chavalakadai and intermediate points small barge discharge facilities would also be required.

Capital Requirements for Inland Waterways are estimated at Rs. 2 million over a six-year period.

RAILWAYS

(1) *Description and Administration*

The Ceylon Government Railway plays an important part in the country's transportation system. For many years, from 1867

---

[2] This proposal was suggested by the Mission while in Ceylon and may be already in hand.

MAP 19

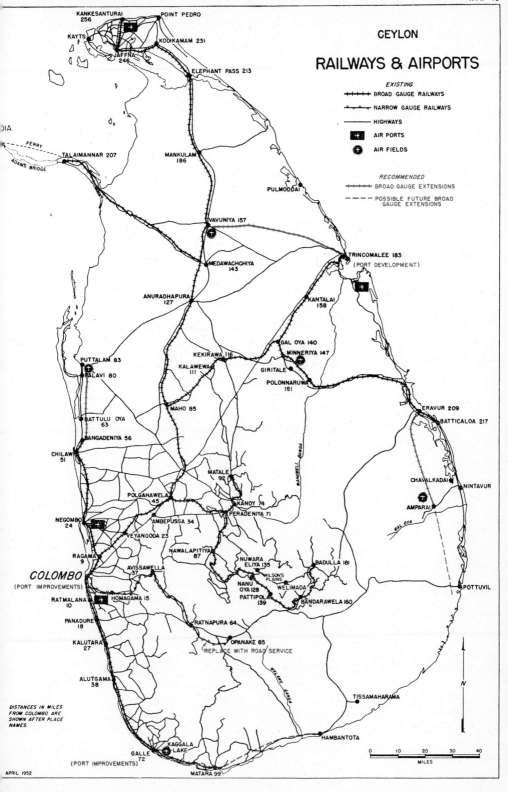

CEYLON

RAILWAYS & AIRPORTS

EXISTING

├┼┼┼┤ BROAD GAUGE RAILWAYS

╫╫╫ NARROW GAUGE RAILWAYS

──── HIGHWAYS

◼ AIR PORTS

● AIR FIELDS

RECOMMENDED

├┼┼┼┤ BROAD GAUGE EXTENSIONS

──── POSSIBLE FUTURE BROAD GAUGE EXTENSIONS

KANKESANTURAI 256
POINT PEDRO
KAYTS
KODIKAMAM 231
JAFFNA 246
ELEPHANT PASS 213

DIA
FERRY
ADAMS BRIDGE
TALAIMANNAR 207
MANKULAM 186
PULMODDAI

VAVUNIYA 157

TRINCOMALEE 183
(PORT DEVELOPMENT)

MEDAWACHCHIYA 143

ANURADHAPURA 127

KANTALAI 158

PUTTALAM 83
PALAVI 80

KEKIRAWA 116
GAL OYA 140
MINNERIYA 147
KALAWEWA 111
GIRITALE
POLONNARUWA 161

MAHO 85

BATTULU OYA 63
BANGADENIYA 56

ERAVUR 209
BATTICALOA 217

CHILAW 51

MATALE 92

CHAVALKADAI
NINTAVUR

POLGAHAWELA 45
KANDY 74
PERADENIYA 71

AMPARAI

NEGOMBO 24
AMBEPUSSA 34
VEYANGODA 23

GAL OYA

RAGAMA 9
NAWALAPITIYA 87

NUWARA ELIYA 135
BADULLA 181

COLOMBO
(PORT IMPROVEMENTS)

AVISSAWELLA 37
WILSON'S PLAINS
WELIMADA

RATMALANA 10
HOMAGAMA 15

NANU OYA 128
PATTIPOLA 139
BANDARAWELA 160

POTTUVIL

PANADURE 18

RATNAPURA 64

KALUTARA 27

OPANAKE 85
REPLACE WITH ROAD SERVICE

ALUTGAMA 38

N

TISSAMAHARAMA

DISTANCES IN MILES FROM COLOMBO ARE SHOWN AFTER PLACE NAMES.

HAMBANTOTA

0 10 20 30 40
MILES

KAGGALA LAKE

GALLE 72
(PORT IMPROVEMENTS)

APRIL 1952

MATARA 99

MAHAWELI GANGA

WALAWE GANGA

to 1930, the railway returned a handsome working profit, but the growth of road transportation competition has converted the railway into a financial liability requiring subsidization from general revenues.

As a government department, the railway has had to act as a model employer without the flexibility of private enterprise to meet competition in its various forms. Of recent years governmental policy has purposely maintained low fares and rates with increases few and far between.

In a small country with comparatively short distances, a railway is severely handicapped as it cannot undertake long hauls of bulk commodities such as maize, wheat, coal and ores. Ceylon possesses neither the long haulage nor the bulk commodities. Nevertheless, the railway must be considered a valuable material asset which should be maintained in a constant state of efficiency for trade, economic development and strategic purposes.

Railway Network. The extent of the railway network of Ceylon is shown on Map No. 19. Lines radiate out from Colombo to Galle and Matara in the south, Bangandeniya and Talaimannar on the west coast, Jaffna and Kankesanturai in the north, Trincomalee and Batticaloa on the east coast and Kandy, Matale and Badulla in the hill country. The first rails were laid in 1865 as a government undertaking and the railway has throughout been owned and operated by the government. The network falls into two types, with about 750 miles serving the low and comparatively flat country and about 150 miles serving the central mountain area. All the main lines are broad gauge of five and a half feet; there are also 86 route miles of two and a half feet narrow-gauge line in the low country area, from Colombo via Avissawella and Ratnapura to Opanake in the foothills of the central massif.

Feeder road services of about 400 route miles are also operated by the Railway Department. These include the passenger, parcels and goods service between Bangadeniya and Puttalam, and the service between Nanu Oya and Ragala via the mountain resort of Nuwara Eliya. Parcels and goods services are operated between

Matara and Tissamaharama on the south coast and also between Kodikamam and Point Pedro in the north. A collection and delivery service is operated within the Colombo Municipality.

Lines abandoned since 1937 include 27 miles of broad gauge between Bangadeniya and Puttalam, and 30 miles of narrow gauge.

Existing broad gauge mileage consists of 809 route miles, 62 duplicate track miles, 907 running line miles and 1,043 total track miles including sidings. Existing narrow-gauge mileage consists of 86 route miles, 91 running line miles and 102 total track miles including sidings.

Management, Staff and Labor. The Ceylon Government Railway is administered under the Railway Ordinance (Chapter 153 of Legislative Enactments of Ceylon) as a government department under the general direction and control of the Minister of Transport and Works. The General Manager is the chief executive officer of the department.

Staff and labor employed by the railways has increased by more than 50% during the past decade, rising from 14,290 in 1940-41 to a high of 22,076 in 1948-49. Since then there has been a slight decrease to 21,547 in 1950-51. Employment costs have increased even faster, from under Rs. 14 million in 1940-41 to over Rs. 44 million in 1949-50, or a 226% increase. Chart No. 10 illustrates this growth. A further increase in employment costs is anticipated for 1951-52 when the cost of living and special living allowances are due to rise by Rs. 5.5 million. For the year 1949-50, salaries, wages, allowances, pensions and gratuities accounted for about 60% of railway working expenditure.

Individually, many of the executive and staff are performing their duties efficiently under the greater workload of increased traffic and services, but from such observations as the Mission was able to make in the short period at its disposal, there appears to be considerable room for improvement in the over-all efficiency of management, operation and maintenance.

With the tremendous amount of detail involved in the manage-

CHART 10

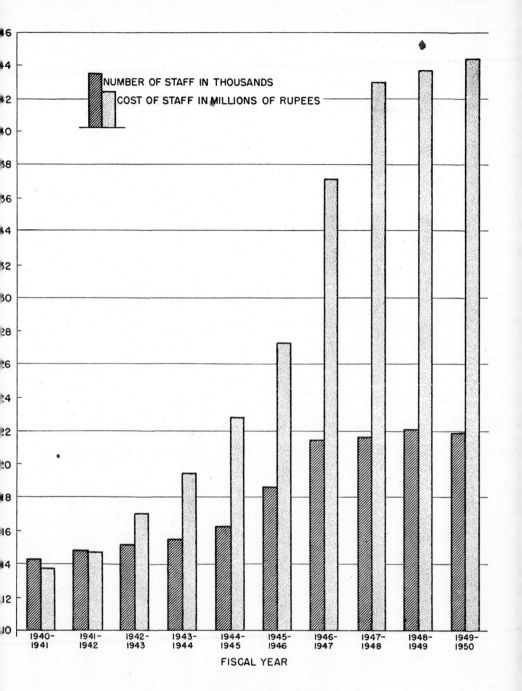

CEYLON GOVERNMENT RAILWAY

TOTAL NUMBER AND COST OF STAFF

ment and operation of a railway it is not possible to put forward precise and detailed recommendations for improving efficiency. That requires detailed investigation and research which can best be done by a firm of consultants specializing in railway management and operation. We accordingly recommend the appointment of a firm of railway management consultants to investigate all phases of management and operation of the railways with a view to introducing more modern methods and incentives to increase efficiency. With a working expenditure of Rs. 75 million, a reduction of a mere 1% in costs would mean a yearly savings of Rs. 750,000. There is no doubt that such an investigation would more than pay for itself. It would add to the department's own commendable efforts the fresh objective viewpoints and broad experience of such an outside organization.

The executive railway personnel are handicapped by having gained their experience almost entirely locally, and having had little or no opportunity of becoming familiar with the business and technical advances made in other countries of the world. To remedy this state of affairs, the Mission recommends that periodic overseas visits should be made by department heads and potential heads in order to study the latest techniques in railway management, operation and maintenance. To avoid language difficulties, the United Kingdom and the United States would offer the best ground for these visits. A month or two spent in each country during the summer season should prove highly beneficial to the efficiency of the railway. Detailed advance planning of each individual trip is essential to its maximum usefulness.

Traffic. Table IX shows the annual results of railway operations since 1940. All types of traffic increased substantially. Passenger traffic was greatly stimulated during the war years and reached a record high in 1950-51 with an increase of 148% over 1940-41. Only 0.3% of passenger traffic is first class travel, 2.7% second class, while 97% is a low-fare third class. Available coaching stock has not kept pace with this great increase in passenger volume, resulting in much overcrowding and discomfort. Chart No.

633

11 shows passenger and goods traffic in graphical form. Allowing for expected growth, the graph has been projected to 1960, indicating a probable volume of passenger traffic of 30 million and goods volume of 2 million tons per year.

TABLE IX

RAILWAY TRAFFIC, REVENUE AND OPERATING EXPENSES *

Year	Length of Line in Miles	Capital Outlay	Number of Passengers	Number of Season Tickets	Goods Traffic in Tons
1940-41	951	222,939,032	11,088,385	212,001	1,137,594
1941-42	940	222,277,165	14,646,041	254,952	1,172,904
1942-43	913	222,127,208	18,872,120	342,148	1,312,704
1943-44	913	218,169,753	20,933,180	412,777	1,552,584
1944-45	913	218,170,685	24,920,215	463,145	1,691,055
1945-46	913	218,311,377	25,952,928	472,189	1,369,211
1946-47	913	222,172,672	26,004,880	471,032	1,110,342
1947-48	893½	231,598,011	26,478,943	453,649	1,199,523
1948-49	896	236,108,947	26,418,119	445,602	1,267,936
1949-50	896	242,414,034	24,316,510	476,032	1,280,891
1950-51***	896	247,314,000	27,525,000	513,000	1,514,000

Year	Earnings Coach Traffic	Earnings Goods Traffic	Earnings Livestock Traffic	Miscellaneous Receipts	Total Earnings
1940-41	7,670,980	10,085,373	129,220	704,352	18,589,925
1941-42	13,046,522	14,285,611	146,209	824,094	28,302,436
1942-43	19,383,269	18,604,524	230,502	1,475,657	39,693,952
1943-44	26,252,471	23,516,834	240,525	2,000,941	52,010,771
1944-45	30,517,053	26,385,305	183,122	2,533,561	59,592,041
1945-46	30,418,767	22,928,279	236,417	2,725,225	56,308,688
1946-47	27,308,145	18,910,891	181,185	1,948,849	48,349,070
1947-48	28,154,554	21,864,123	232,704	2,216,974	52,468,355
1948-49	28,447,780	24,324,355	217,587	2,088,609	55,078,331
1949-50	29,756,989	25,117,527	243,018	2,532,605	57,650,139
1950-51***	33,000,000	30,000,000	370,000	2,610,000	65,980,000

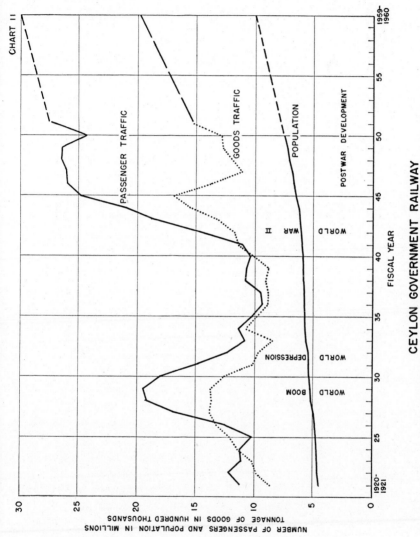

CHART II

CEYLON GOVERNMENT RAILWAY

PASSENGER AND GOODS TRAFFIC AND NATIONAL POPULATION

I. B. R. D. APRIL 1952

TABLE IX—(Continued)
RAILWAY TRAFFIC, REVENUE AND OPERATING EXPENSES *

Year	Operating Expenses and Renewals	Paying Train Miles	Percentage Expenses to Gross Revenue	Operating Profit	Operating Loss
1940-41	22,943,972	4,502,014	123.42	—	4,354,047
1941-42	24,681,923	4,215,293	87.21	3,620,513	—
1942-43	29,288,670	3,491,393	73.79	10,405,282	—
1943-44	33,022,005	3,559,925	63.49	18,988,766	—
1944-45	43,285,516	3,754,570	72.64	16,306,525	—
1945-46	52,472,305	4,155,972	93.19	3,836,383	—
1946-47	65,018,922	4,442,970	134.48	—	16,669,852
1947-48	73,075,518	5,111,453	139.28	—	20,607,163
1948-49	73,729,299	5,533,597	133.86	—	18,650,968
1949-50	74,250,153**	5,714,933	128.79	—	16,600,014
1950-51***	72,760,000	5,990,000	110.28	—	6,780,000
Total				53,157,469	83,662,044

* All monetary figures are rupees.
** Includes renewals met from Loan Funds, Rs. 2,977,632.
*** Estimates.
Source: Ceylon Government Railway.

Goods traffic over the decade 1940-41 to 1950-51 has shown a less spectacular rise of some 33%, the latest figure still being below the war record in 1944-45. The increase during 1950-51 has severely taxed the available wagon stock, causing some diversion of goods traffic to the highways, which have already captured most of the natural increase since the end of the war. Comparison of the increase in goods traffic with the increase in total tonnage of exports and imports, shown in Tables II and III, indicates that the railway has shared less fully in the postwar boom as regards goods than in its passenger traffic.

The recently adopted Motor Traffic Act No. 14 of 1951 is aimed, inter alia, at assisting the railway to meet highway competition by reserving longhaul traffic as far as possible to the railway. Some time must elapse before it can be seen how far the railway will benefit, but some increase of traffic is certain and this, coupled with the natural growth and economic development of the island will throw an increasing load upon the railway. It is therefore very necessary for the management to expedite proposed improvements, not only to meet existing demands but also to be in a position to meet increasing demands of the immediate future.

(2) *Finance*

From 1867 to 1930 the railway consistently made profits. Between 1930 and 1951 there have been some years of gross profit before interest and annuities and some of loss. The accumulated gross profit in this period amounted to Rs. 57 million (Rs. 53 million accruing during the booming war years), while accumulated loss in bad years amounted to about Rs. 104 million, leaving a net loss of Rs. 47 million.

Table IX shows the financial results of railway operations since 1940-41. Excluding annuities and interest on capital, the accumulated operating loss amounts to some Rs. 30.5 million. What is perhaps more important is the postwar development. During the past five years, with rapidly rising costs of labor, material and equipment, accumulated operating losses amounted to Rs. 79.3 million. For the year 1950-51 the operating loss is estimated at Rs. 6.78 million; when interest and annuities of about Rs. 5.7 million are added, gross loss is approximately Rs. 12.5 million.

Looking into the immediate future, 1951-52 revenue is estimated at Rs. 65 million and operating expenses approximately Rs. 79.5 million, leaving an estimated deficit of Rs. 14.5 million on operations. On this basis the gross deficit, including interest and annuities, will amount to some Rs. 20.5 million. With no reserve funds upon which to draw and with the annual deficits forming a charge against the general revenues of the island, the operation of the railway is being heavily subsidized by the general public.

There are circumstances in which financial support to railway operation from general tax funds is justifiable. This is true if the continued maintenance of the railway is essential for strategic reasons or for the basic economic development of the country, and if the users of the railway, whether passengers or shippers of goods, cannot bear additional charges or will switch to other means of transport if rates are raised. But subsidization is not justified if it merely provides transportation below cost and benefits railway users at the expense of the general public. We strongly suspect that it is this which is happening in Ceylon today. The pressure of demand on railway facilities both for passengers and goods is strong prima facie evidence that users could afford to pay higher fares and freights and would accept moderate increases without any significant additional switch-over to road transport. In the interests of the general budget and therefore of the funds available for general development, railway finances should without delay be brought closer to a balance by increases of rates.

Passenger Fares. Basic fares per passenger mile and rates for other coach traffic have not kept pace with increased operating costs, which have risen 340% since prewar. Table X shows the 1938-39 fare structure compared with 1949-50. It will be noted that third class fares have been increased only 29% for low country lines and 71% for the high country lines. This class provides 97% of the passenger traffic and most of it is in the low country. In the same period, comparable fares, plus tax, in the United States have more than doubled.

Constant complaints are heard from the travelling public with regard to the quantity and quality of railway services offered. If it cannot afford to pay enough to cover the cost of services of a given kind, then they must be decreased. On the other hand if it demands more and better services, it must pay accordingly; otherwise the general public will be subsidizing the travelling public. For this there appears to be no serious strategic or economic justification. Certainly the burden of present passenger fares is far from excessive. In 1949-50, the average receipt per passenger was only 86 Ceylonese cents.

TABLE X

CEYLON GOVERNMENT RAILWAY

Comparison of Prewar and Postwar Coaching Fares and Rates

	Prewar (1938-39)		Postwar (1949-50)		Percentage Increase	
	Low Country (cents)	High Country	Low Country (cents)	High Country	Low Country	High Country
1. Passengers						
1st Class	7	10.5	11	16	57	52
2nd Class	4.6	7	7	10*	50	43
3rd Class	2.3	2.3	3	4*	29	71
2. Parcels						
According to weight and distance (except perishables)	1 cwt for 100 miles Rs. 3.20		Rs. 4.80		50	

* Limit under Railway Ordinance.
Source: Ceylon Government Railway.

The Mission is satisfied that the situation requires an increase of third class low country fares, season tickets and selected coaching traffic rates. We suggest increasing third-class passenger fares by 16.6% to bring the fare up to 3.5 cents per mile, and also increasing monthly ticket fares for all classes by 25%. With the buoyant passenger traffic being experienced and the better service being offered by the railway, we do not believe that the increases will cause less travelling. They should improve revenue by an estimated Rs. 2.5 million yearly. Parcels and HC & D traffic could bear a 15% increase to improve revenue by an estimated Rs. 500,000 yearly.

Freight Rates. Table XI compares current with prewar freight rates. Increases have amounted to 25-54% according to classification. Like passenger fares, freight rates have not kept pace with increased operating costs, but unlike passenger traffic, goods traffic has failed to share in the postwar upsurge. The highways have captured most of the increased goods traffic, but the facts suggest that this is due more to convenience and greater speed of delivery than to an advantage in rates. Lorry transport rates for the low country are now about 25 to 30 cents per ton mile and about 55 cents for the high country, i.e. higher than the railway average. If greater attention is paid to speeding up delivery of freight, the railway ought to be able to compete even at increased rates, particularly with the assistance of the recently adopted Motor Traffic Act.

The Mission therefore recommends various increases in freight rates for classes one through five for both low country and high

TABLE XI

CEYLON GOVERNMENT RAILWAY

Comparison of Prewar and Postwar Goods Traffic Rates Per Ton Mile

| | Prewar (1938-39) | | | Postwar (1949-50) | | Percentage Increase | |
Class	Low Country	High Country (cents)	Class	Low Country	High Country (cents)	Low Country	High Country
1	8	12	1	10	15	25	25
2	9	13.5					
3	10	15	2	14	19	47	33.3
4	11	16.5					
5	12	18	3	17	23	48	33.3
6	13	19.5					
7	14	21	4	20	27	48	33.3
8	15	22.5					
9	17	25.5	5	24	32	50	33.3
10	19	28.5					
11	21	31.5	6	30	40	50	33.3
12	24	36	7	36	54	50	50
13	39	58.5	8	60	80*	54	34

* Limit under Railway Ordinance.
Source: Ceylon Government Railway.

country to raise estimated revenue by some Rs. 7 million annually. Class 1 should be increased most and Class 5 least.

If our recommendations for increased passenger fares and freight rates are adopted, the revenue of the railway should improve by some Rs. 10 million annually. This would go a long way to offset the anticipated operating loss of Rs. 14.5 million in 1951-52. It would give management, staff and labor an incentive to try to close this gap by greater all round efficiency and individual output.

(3) Equipment

At the end of September, 1951, the Railway owned 216 broad gauge locomotives of sixteen different types and sub-types. Details are shown in Table XII. There has been very little replacement during the last 20 years because of the depression of the thirties and, later, the war. With the increased traffic of recent years the locomotive position has steadily deteriorated despite commendable efforts to keep old locomotives in working condition. This has proved costly in upkeep and repairs as well as uneconomical in operation. A program for the purchase of new locomotives was commenced in 1943-44 but deliveries have been very slow. How-

TABLE XII

RAILWAY ROLLING STOCK, SEPTEMBER 1951

Years Old	Locomotives		Coaching Stock		Wagon Stock	
	Broad Gauge	Narrow Gauge	Broad Gauge	Narrow Gauge	Broad Gauge	Narrow Gauge
Less than 10	27	4	24	3	899	—
10-20	4	—	90	9	223	—
20-30	95	7	345	36	1,038	29
30-40	62	9	178	33	596	130
40-50	21	4	70	16	233	58
Over 50	7	—	—	—	—	—
Total	*216*	*24*	*707*	*97*	*2,989*	*217*

ever, three new main-line steam engines and four new diesel-electric shunting engines were placed in commission recently, while three more steam engines and four more diesel-electric engines will be put into service shortly. Twenty-five main line diesels together with five other diesels are now on order, to cost around Rs. 22 million.

The Railway Department proposes to reduce the types of broad-gauge locomotive to four of steam and two of diesel. This is all to the good as it will reduce the number of spare parts and special tools necessary. The introduction of diesel-electric traction appears sound in principle, but the ratio of steam to diesel should be carefully checked from time to time. While both coal and oil fuel have to be imported, the source of coal in India is nearer and less likely to be cut off in the event of war. There is also the long-range factor of hydroelectric power development now under way. It may be another 20 or 30 years, however, before this form of traction can be economically applied to the railway outside of the Colombo area, and then probably only in the southwest and in the central mountainous regions.

Broad gauge coaching stock of all descriptions at the end of September 1951 numbered 707 units. Compared with 1937-38, the number of coaching vehicles has changed little while passenger traffic has increased 250% from 10,859,072 in 1937-38 to 27,-525,000 in 1950-51. Consequently, locomotives and coaching stock have been greatly overworked while the overcrowding and general discomfort to passengers has become serious. This state of affairs has naturally driven much traffic to the highways, not so much by choice as by necessity. Orders have been placed for 187 new units of broad gauge coaching stock, of which 47 unit bodies are to be built locally. Until a substantial portion of the total order has been delivered, conditions will remain unsatisfactory.

Broad gauge wagon stock of all descriptions at the end of September 1951 numbered 2,989 units. Compared with 1937-38 the number of wagons available for freight traffic has increased

641

about 20% while freight conveyed had increased 67% by 1950-51. This shortage of freight wagons has caused considerable operational difficulties to management and delays to users, again causing diversion of traffic to the highways. Orders for 486 broad gauge units of various types have been placed, of which 25 wagons and six van bodies are being built locally. These will relieve much of the wagon shortage but additional procurements will still be necessary.

Narrow gauge locomotives numbered 24. Five new diesel-electric locomotives costing Rs. 2.2 million have been ordered for the narrow gauge line. The Mission recommends, however, that this order be cancelled, if possible, and no further orders placed for this gauge, which, as specifically recommended later, the Mission considers should be discontinued.

Narrow gauge coaching stock of all descriptions numbered 97 units. Orders for 13 underframes and bogies have been placed overseas and 13 bodies are to be built locally, all at a cost of roughly Rs. 700,000.

Narrow gauge wagon stock of all descriptions numbered 217 units. Orders for 13 wagons have been placed for local construction at a cost of some Rs. 600,000. Pending a final decision on the future of the narrow gauge line, the Mission does not favor any new purchases of either coach or wagon stock.

Railway Workshops. The extensive railway workshops at Ratmalana, 10 miles south of Colombo, occupy a fenced-in area of 52 acres of which about 12 acres are under roof. They were commenced in 1934, have thoroughly proved their value and were able to meet demands for a number of years. The shops were planned on a basis of 450,000 loco miles per month, but this has now increased to 600,000. With fewer spare parts available the current work-load cannot be met satisfactorily. Further extensions, with additional machine tools and equipment, are required to attain greater self-sufficiency. The department proposes to erect a new carriage building shop at Ratmalana estimated to cost Rs. 2 million. Items to provide for annual replacement for worn-out and for new machine tools are included in the annual government budgets. Considering the various difficulties, the shops appear to be well run. Improvements in detail are possible (for example, the application of "Brightness Engineering" or color conditioning of machine tools, etc.) but these can best be left for study and report by the previously recommended consultants.

The shops also provide a valuable training establishment. After a one year course at the Basic Training Institute some 250 workers are apprenticed for four years in the workshops. In addition, a program of lectures has been instituted for the past two years.

Apart from normal railway work, the shops turn out many articles for use by other government departments and for approved private orders. It has become essentially an industrial undertaking and its further development should be encouraged. The shops currently employ about 2,500 persons in all categories. Normal day shift is from seven a.m. to four p.m. from Monday through Friday; with a five and a half hour morning shift on Saturday, the total work week amounts to 45 and a half hours.

It has been found in industrialized countries that the short Saturday morning shift is uneconomical. The Mission believes that an important improvement could be made by the introduction of a five-day work week. Since the workshops are a technical undertaking, the change need not be considered as a precedent for other government departments, where conditions are totally different. We suggest a five day week of nine hours each on the main production lines, with workshop maintenance carried out on Saturdays at straight time instead of on Sundays at overtime rates. Apart from operational economies, workers would have a two-day rest period each week with a consequent improved man-hour output during the work week. Emergency and breakdown work could be performed as necessary. In due course, when the overload of maintenance and repairs is reduced by the scrapping of worn-out equipment, the daily hours could be cut to eight and a half and perhaps eventually to eight hours.

(4) Extension of Railway Network

Various proposals for extensions of the railway network will be examined individually. Suggestions emanating from the Railway Department are as follows:

a) Relaying Bangadeniya—Puttalam Section

This section of about 30 miles of track was removed during the war in order to use the material on more strategic sections of the railway system. The land, buildings and bridges, etc. are intact but require minor repairs. To place the section in operation again would cost about Rs. 8 million.

The Motor Traffic Act reserves for the railway, under certain conditions, long distance traffic being hauled 60 miles or more. Whether or not this figure is justified on general economic grounds remains to be seen. It may be noted that the present railhead at Bangadeniya is 56 miles from Colombo while Puttalam is 83 miles so that it might pay the railway to extend the line at least to Battu Oya (63 miles), if not to Puttalam, to come within the Act. Much will depend upon how the Act is administered and whether or not an extension of the line beyond the 60 mile limit will qualify for preference under the Act. If the caustic soda plant now projected is relocated in the Palavi area near Puttalam, as recommended in Chapter 15, it would reinforce the proposal to relay the section.

The Mission therefore recommends the relaying of the Bangadeniya-Puttalam section when funds become available and, in the meantime, the maintenance in good condition of the existing structures. Meanwhile, full statistical records should be kept of the passenger, parcels and goods road-feeder service between Bangadeniya and Puttalam, as well as records of the potential railway traffic now being carried privately.

b) Kelani Valley Narrow Gauge Line

This feature of the railway system presents a constant problem which sooner or later will have to be solved. The department has suggested converting the line to broad gauge from Colombo to

Avissawella, with the Colombo-Homagama section double tracked, while retaining the narrow gauge line from Avissawella to Opanake for goods traffic only.

The line serves the important tea and rubber area lying between the central mountains and the southern coast. Although rising to no great height, it suffers from extreme curvature and consequent slow speeds of travel, particularly beyond Avissawella, 37 miles from Colombo. The 85 mile run between Colombo and Opanake takes from seven and a half to eight and a half hours by mixed goods-cum-passenger train.

No separate traffic records for this line have been kept since 1943. This is most unfortunate, as the value of the line to the railway as a whole cannot now be correctly determined. This should be immediately remedied by maintaining separate records to assist in the final solution of the problem.

To obtain the preference given under the Motor Traffic Act the line must remain at least as far as Ratnapura (64 miles from Colombo), so that continuation on a part broad-gauge, part narrow-gauge basis will mean trans-shipment, additional delay, double handling and possible damage or loss of goods at Avissawella. Furthermore, the country would still be left with an even shorter and less remunerative section of narrow-gauge line. The department's suggestion would cost about Rs. 50 million to complete and the essential problem would still remain unsolved.

Since the relatively short haul of 85 miles from Opanake to Colombo lends itself to road transportation, the Mission recommends instead replacing this narrow gauge line by equivalent road transport services. The track bed should be converted into an express highway and the track and equipment used elsewhere for industrial purposes.

Bus and lorry road service, to be operated by the Railway Department, should be substituted for the present narrow-gauge facilities. The service must be of sufficient quality and quantity to meet all traffic demands, run strictly to schedule and operated with maximum efficiency. The time required for the Opanake-

Colombo run would be cut by more than half, to about three and a half hours, enabling a bus and driver to make a round trip in one eight-hour shift. Shorter intermediate distances out of Colombo could be run at higher frequencies in line with the present railway schedules, with more round trips per bus. Similarly, lorry transport could be scheduled to obtain maximum traffic. Where shippers offer full lorry loads, delivery could be made at final destination without extra cost to the Railway and at reduced cost to the shipper. The Rs. 3.5 million proposed expenditure on new diesels, coaches and wagons for the narrow-gauge line would be much better spent on road transport equipment; it would provide about 100 buses and lorries. The Mission further recommends that the narrow-gauge track bed be converted into a three-lane express highway restricted to motor traffic only. During the conversion period the transport services replacing the railway could use the highways paralleling the line. Existing station buildings and goods sheds should be used as main halting points to pick up passengers and freight.

All the narrow-gauge assets in trackage, material and equipment could be used to better advantage for industrial development, for example in the sugar or ilmenite projects. [3] These are located in the northern half of the island and are self-contained, requiring no raw material trans-shipment to the broad-gauge system.

At Maha Illuppallama, situated south of Anuradhapura, or at Giritale south of Minneriya, it is proposed to cultivate 6,000 acres under sugar cane. Some 25-30 miles of narrow-gauge track could be installed in the cane fields for transport of the cane to the factory. Factory output should be railed by means of a short spur taken from the broad gauge track in the vicinity of Ihalagema between Kalawewa and Kekirawa on the Maho-Trincomalee line in the case of the Maha Illuppallama site, or from

---

[3] See Chapter 15. Some of the narrow-gauge equipment and about 30-35 miles of track could also be useful in the fertilizer project if, after re-examination, that is decided to be sound.

646

the track between Minneriya and Polonnaruwa in the case of the Giritale site.

At Pulmoddai, situated on the east coast about 35 miles north of Trincomalee, it is proposed to develop the ilmenite sand deposits for overseas export. At present the coast road between Trincomalee and Pulmoddai is mainly of gravel or dirt construction and crosses over four ferries which cannot carry heavy loads. Costly road and bridge construction would be necessary for heavy road haulage. The construction of a narrow-gauge line on an inland route would probably cost no more than a good road. If the potential export volume is sufficient, then the railway offers a good means of bulk haulage to dockside at the commercial port recommended for development at Trincomalee. The remaining 40 miles of track to be re-used could be allocated to this project. If this line should become redundant in the future owing to depletion of sand deposits or other causes, it could be converted into a highway.

Existing narrow-gauge equipment could all be allocated to these three sample projects. Wagon stock could be used as it is, or converted to the needs of the industry. Likewise, the bodies of coaching stock could be removed and the underframes converted. Maintenance and overhaul of equipment would be far less than that required for main-line operation and most of it could be done locally. Since the three projects are in relatively close proximity, interchange of equipment would be comparatively simple by means of well-bogies running on the broad-gauge line.

These combined recommendations of the Mission, as we have noted, should cost under Rs. 25 million, of which about Rs. 12 million would be on highway account, about Rs. 8 million on industrial account and under Rs. 5 million on railway account for the purchase of road transport equipment and cost of track removal. They would bring simultaneously a permanent solution to the narrow-gauge problem, assistance to industrial development, and benefits to the railway and the general public.

647

c) *Extension from Matara to Hambantota*

This would carry the railway line some 52 miles along the route of the present railway-operated goods and parcels road service. The trace has already been run on a preliminary survey. The total cost would be in the region of Rs. 35 million.

The Mission does not see sufficient economic justification for the extension within the foreseeable future but it might be justified later. To assist in a future decision, records of passenger, goods and parcels traffic over the route should be maintained, whether carried by the department or by private carriers. In the meanwhile the right of way and necessary land areas should be reserved for possible railway use.

d) *Double-tracking Panadura-Alutgama Section*

This is designed to improve traffic speeds and operation. About 21 miles of track is involved, with an estimated cost of some Rs. 15 million exclusive of two major bridges. At present the line is double-tracked from Colombo to Panadura. To extend the double track would require major new bridges at Panadura and at Kalutara, unless single track operations can be continued at these points until the existing bridges have to be replaced on account of age. While the Mission feels that the proposal has merit, unless traffic increases more rapidly than now expected, the construction should be delayed for a few years.

e) *Extension from Batticaloa to Nintavur*

This would carry the line down the east coast, crossing the Batticaloa Lagoon by the Lady Manning Bridge, originally built for the railway but now used as a highway bridge. The distance is about 30 miles and the whole project is estimated to cost about Rs. 16 million. The major development taking place south of Batticaloa in the Gal Oya project and the possibility of other schemes provide a prima facie case for a rail extension to tap this southern area. Considerable quantities of construction materials are being imported from other parts of the island and through the port of Colombo, while general imports to and exports

648

from the area will increase with time. The development of a commercial port at Trincomalee and the extension of the railway would permit overseas freight to be transported directly from the docks to the southern area, thereby eliminating the long haul via Colombo. The road transport serving the Gal Oya area is expensive and unreliable, as it is a private monopoly and is subject to delays from flooded roadways. The railway would give reliable competitive service and assist in the economic development of the area.

We therefore recommend extending the railway to Amparai. But instead of keeping to the coast it should follow a more inland route from Eravur, just north of Batticaloa, and serve any industrial projects on the way. As additional development occurs south of Amparai the line could be further extended. The inclusive cost of the Eravur-Amparai extension is estimated at about Rs. 30 million.

f) *Extension from Vavuniya to Trincomalee*

This proposal is put forward by the Mission to enable the proposed new port at Trincomalee to serve the northern region more advantageously and to assist in the development of the hinterland through which the railway would pass. The distance by rail from Kankesanturai in the north to Colombo port is about 260 miles. A rail link from Vavuniya to Trincomalee would reduce the distance to a major seaport to about 160 miles. The Mission sees no economic justification for the development of two northern ports and believes that it would be preferable to spend the money on the Vavuniya-Trincomalee railway extension rather than to spend it on a new port at Kankesanturai, the cost of the two being about equal.

The route of the extension would of course have to take account of terrain, areas of future development (such as the Padawiya Scheme) and the maintenance of the shortest possible length of line. The estimated inclusive cost of this extension is Rs. 40 million.

(5) *General Improvements to the Railway System*

The Railway Department either has in hand or proposes to undertake a number of continuation works and new proposals to improve all-round operation of the railway system. Financially, current and forward commitments are large and must be taken into account in scheduling future development and allocations on capital accounts. Table XIII shows railway estimates for 1951-52 in condensed form.

TABLE XIII

RAILWAY ESTIMATES, 1951-52—LOAN FUND

(rupees)

	Continuation Works	General Works	New Proposals	Total
Renewal (estimated)	37,612,948	1,096,330	2,776,624	41,485,902
Capital (")	68,715,254	2,718,670	16,619,996	88,053,920
Total (")	*106,328,202*	*3,815,000*	*19,396,620*	*129,539,822*
Actual expenditure to 1949-50	19,357,050	—	—	19,357,050
Estimated spent 1950-51	15,530,524	—	—	15,530,524
Estimated spending 1951-52	14,358,480	3,815,000	1,826,520	20,000,000

Source: Government Estimates, 1951-52.

It is also proposed to expend the balance standing in the Deferred Maintenance Reserve Account, namely Rs. 9,773,180 in 1951-52.

Of the total estimates of Rs. 129 million under all heads, actual expenditure to the end of 1949-50 was Rs. 19 million, leaving a balance of Rs. 110 million. The estimated amount spent during 1950-51 is probably high. If we take this as Rs. 10 million we have a figure of around Rs. 100 million to be met. Add to this the Rs. 10 million from Deferred Maintenance Reserve Account and we obtain Rs. 110 million in commitments for 1951 onwards. During 1951-52 it is proposed to spend Rs. 20 million, reducing the forward commitments to Rs. 90 million from 1952-53 onwards. This figure may be increased by at least 10% due to rising prices or to underexpenditure. We thus arrive at a figure of Rs. 100 million committed for general improvements to the railway system from 1952-53 onwards.

The Mission recommends continuance of general improvements to the railway system to the extent that funds can be made available.

This is a general recommendation, as it may be that improvements of a more urgent nature will arise which will have to be substituted for those having a lower degree of priority. Of particular importance is the strengthening of the permanent way of the Maho-Trincomalee and Gal Oya Junction-Batticaloa sections and the replacement of the existing lightweight rails with heavier rails. This work should be scheduled for completion by the time that Trincomalee commences to function as a commercial port.

(6) *Electrification of Colombo Suburban Service*

This suggestion by the Railway Department involves the overhead electrification of the Colombo suburban area between Veyangoda in the north and Panadura in the south. The project would include the laying of about 23 miles of new double track between Colombo and Veyangoda, and the construction of a new double-track bridge over the Kelanai Ganga together with about 170 smaller bridges, additional signalling installations, substations, highway overpasses, protective fencing of the route and other miscellaneous work. There would be, of course, the major construction of overhead electric lines for power take-off. The cost as estimated by the Department would run in the neighborhood of Rs. 85 million, including 24 three-car train sets.

The scheme has not yet been worked out in technical or economic detail. Current traffic density is relatively low for electrification, though it is more than can be managed satisfactorily

651

with the present steam traction. The press has reported [4] that preliminary work will commence in the near future and that the project is expected to be complete in five years.

The Mission strongly recommends that the scheme for electrification of the Colombo suburban service should be deferred for the present because:

(a) The necessary hydroelectric power to operate the proposed electrified section will not be available until about 1960, if then.

(b) The funds available for major capital projects are severely limited in view of other more urgent railway improvements and the various high-priority development projects.

(c) Procurement of material and equipment will be difficult and costly during the next few years on account of rearmament programs.

(d) The current introduction of diesel-electric traction will largely relieve the present shortage of locomotives.

The whole question could be studied and a detailed economic and technical report obtained from consultants appointed when there appears to be a prospect of the necessary hydroelectric power becoming available, so that the project could be commenced and scheduled for completion at the appropriate time. Much useful work could be done in the meantime by the Railway Department and by other authorities. As an example, to relieve congestion in Colombo and to provide a greater traffic potential, suitable areas of land adjacent to the railway should be acquired for the development of townships laid out on modern lines.

When the island's power resources permit, the Colombo area should be first considered in a long-range program looking toward partial electrification of the railway system and a gradual reduction in steam and diesel-electric traction (now dependent on imported fuels).

Capital Requirements for Railway. Taking into account rec-

---

[4] *Ceylon Daily News* January 8, 1952.

CHART 12

MISSION RECOMENDATIONS	FISCAL YEAR									
PARTICULARS	1952-1953	1953-1954	1954-1955	1955-1956	1956-1957	1957-1958	1958-1959	1959-1960	1960-1961	1961-1962
Report by Consultants	▨									
Overseas Visits by Railway Personnel	▨▨▨▨	▨▨▨	▨▨▨	▨▨▨	▨▨▨	▨▨▨	▨▨▨	▨▨▨	▨▨▨	▨▨▨
Fare Increases	▨									
Rate Increases	▨									
Five Day Week at Ratmalana Shops	▨									
Relay Bangadeniya – Puttalam Line	▨▨									
Replace K.V. Line with Road Service	▨									
Extend Matara – Hambantota Line				POSTPONE FOR FUTURE CONSIDERATION						
Duplicate Panadura – Alutgama Section				▨						
Extend Eravur – Amparai Line		▨▨								
Extend Vavuniya – Trincomalee Line					▨▨					
General Improvements to Railway System	▨▨▨▨	▨▨▨	▨▨▨	▨▨▨	▨▨▨	▨▨▨	▨▨▨	▨▨▨	▨▨▨	▨▨▨
Electrification Colombo Section								▨▨	▨▨	▨▨

GENERAL PRIORITY RATING
FOR CEYLON GOVERNMENT RAILWAY PROJECTS

ommendations of the Mission, capital requirements for the railway
during the 10-year period 1952-53 to 1962-63 are shown below.
It will be noted that average annual expenditure is about Rs.
25 million, but yearly variations will be wide. Chart 12 shows
the general priority rating of the Mission's recommendations with
respect to the railways.

Particulars	Estimated Cost (million rupees)
Investigation and report by consultants	0.2
Periodic overseas visits by personnel	0.5
Increase in coach fares and rates	—
Increase in freight rates	—
Five-day work week for Ratmalana workshops	—
Relaying Bangadeniya-Puttalam section	8.0
Replacing Kelani Valley line with road services (Re-use of track and equipment will be a charge to the projects taking possession and a credit to the railway)	4.3
Extension of Matara-Hambantota line deferred	—
Duplicating Panadura-Alutgama section	15
Extension of Eravur-Amparai section	30
Extension of Vavuniya-Trincomalee section	40
General improvements to railway system (allowing 25% for additional requirements)	125
Electrification of Colombo suburban section (part cost; balance to be expended in later years)	27
Total	*250*

Bearing in mind other claims on the budget, we have assumed
expenditure over the program period 1953-59 to total Rs. 150
million, as distributed in Table II C, Chapter 6.

ROADS AND HIGHWAYS

(1) *Present Position and Administration*

Ceylon is fortunate in possessing a relatively large system of
roads and highways. Many of the roads are paved, are in com-

paratively good condition and carry a fair volume of diverse traffic. Map No. 20 shows how the main trunk roads generally radiate from Colombo and reach into all the main regions of the island. A network of major and minor roads supports these trunk roads, but is much less developed in the east and north than in the populous southwestern area. It is estimated that there are over 30,000 miles of roads of all categories in the country, but about 40% of these are merely natural tracks and bridle paths traversing the forests, hills and jungles.

In the flat country, particularly in the undeveloped regions, trunk and major roads are fairly straight but on the narrow side and subject to flooding in certain low lying areas. In the hilly and mountainous regions, roads are both narrow and extremely curved, usually following the profile of the topography. The main roads are well served with bridges and culverts but these vary greatly in loading capacity and width. Most of them are single-lane roads and cause traffic bottlenecks at certain points. Prior to the war the density of motor and other traffic was such that the road system generally could meet demands. But the postwar period has brought a large increase in motor vehicle traffic; in the more populous areas road congestion has become serious. Ribbon development and the narrow streets through towns and villages aggravate it. Outside of Colombo and its suburbs there are no wide roads of the modern speedway type, but improvements to existing roads and new construction are in continuous progress.

Administration. Responsibility for construction and maintenance of roads falls under four administrative heads. The Public Works Department, under the Minister of Transport and Works, is responsible for about 11,000 miles of major and minor roads. This work comes under the Director of Public Works Department, who is the chief executive officer. The work is decentralized to various subordinates on an area basis. Cost of all public highway work is borne by the central government.

Village committees control about 8,000 miles of village paths

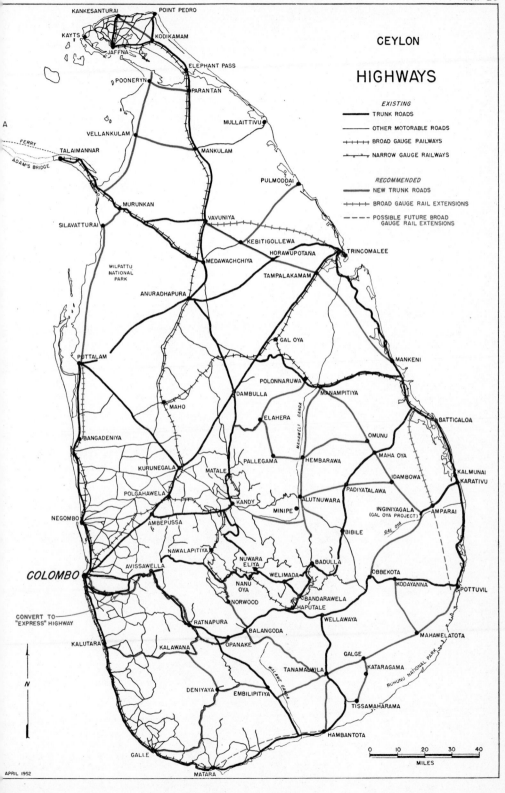

MAP 20

CEYLON

HIGHWAYS

EXISTING
TRUNK ROADS
OTHER MOTORABLE ROADS
BROAD GAUGE RAILWAYS
NARROW GAUGE RAILWAYS

RECOMMENDED
NEW TRUNK ROADS
BROAD GAUGE RAIL EXTENSIONS
POSSIBLE FUTURE BROAD
GAUGE RAIL EXTENSIONS

APRIL 1952

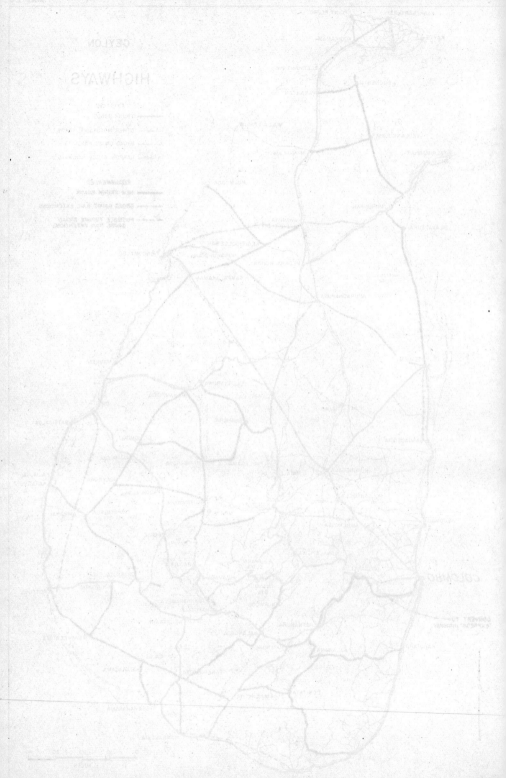

and cart tracks. They are financed out of village funds, assisted occasionally by grants from the central government. Municipalities, Urban and Town Councils control about 800 miles of streets and roads within their respective administrative limits. The Department of Irrigation, using departmental funds constructs and maintains certain roads required for various irrigation projects.

Operational. In addition to the maintenance and construction of roads and bridges, the Public Works Department is responsible for a large number of other works, including buildings of all kinds and improvements to buildings, water supply projects, sewerage projects, government factory projects, and a considerable amount of miscellaneous work. In 1949-50 total expenditure by the Department was Rs. 82 million.

Decentralization of the work is accomplished by means of six Divisional Superintending Engineers in charge of divisions and 33 Executive Engineers in charge of districts. They are assisted by various assistant engineers, inspectors, supervising-overseers and overseers. For road maintenance purposes, funds are allocated to the Superintending Engineers to be applied at their discretion. This system appears to be working satisfactorily and should be continued.

The actual work of maintenance and new construction of roads is performed mainly through the overseers who appear to take the place of regular contractors. They are paid on a predetermined unit cost basis and are left to hire labor and perform the work, which is mostly done by hand with hand tools. Up to the end of 1951 the department possessed practically no modern road construction equipment. Imported road materials, such as bitumen, bridge steel, etc. are supplied by the department, but all local materials such as hand broken stone, must be produced by the overseer along the way. As may be imagined, the rate of progress is extremely slow. It is said that a rate of three miles per year is the average for the construction of a narrow 10 foot third-class road following the topographical profile in hilly country.

Bridge construction and maintenance is under a subdepartment in charge of the Executive Engineer, Bridges. Here again, shortage of plant and equipment seriously retards the increasing volume of work.

The Mission recommends that the department should procure a steadily increasing quantity of modern construction plant and equipment for road and bridge construction. There is a dearth of road construction companies having the necessary facilities in Ceylon. Although contractors registered with the department number 150 for road works and 80 for bridge work, most of them merely supply labor and depend upon the department for equipment and technical supervision. With the greatly increasing cost of labor and materials, the employment of selected modern equipment will produce a much greater volume of work at lower unit cost.

Technical Staff. The Public Works Department suffers from a severe shortage of professional engineering skills in all fields. The department is handed an ever increasing workload which it cannot hope to accomplish in the time usually desired. Surveys, planning and design work are retarded by shortage of staff. In 1949-50 only 172 detailed drawings were produced and many projects had to be postponed. This deficiency will take a number of years to overcome in spite of the effort being made by the government to foster technical education. If real progress is desired the Mission feels that some means must be found to attract foreign technical and professional personnel to Ceylon.

For example, local engineering firms should be encouraged to expand their facilities and staff to handle Public Works Department contracts from the investigation stage right through to completed drawings and specifications for the various categories of work. Sources for top grade personnel include the technical assistance agencies under the United Nations, the Colombo Plan and the United States technical aid program, but procurement from these and similar sources will most certainly be insufficient and slow. Another and quicker method which could be applied simultaneously is to arrange for one or more foreign firms of consulting engineers to establish offices in Ceylon, if necessary for a limited number of years. Staff would consist of a nucleus of key foreign personnel in all grades and specialities, supported by a number of Ceylonese. By employing such highly skilled personnel utilizing the most modern design techniques, the work would be greatly expedited, while at the same time the Ceylonese personnel would receive intensive training.

Labor. The supply of unskilled labor is generally adequate for all types of construction work. On the other hand the supply of skilled and semiskilled labor is insufficient to meet present and future demands. Particularly is this the case in the operation of mechanical road construction equipment. The Gal Oya project at Amparai has shown that Ceylonese can readily be trained in the operation of mechanical equipment. This process should be continued.

We recommend intensified training of PWD personnel in the operation and maintenance of modern road construction plant and equipment. Pending the arrival of the recommended modern equipment, arrangements should be made for them to be trained at Gal Oya and elsewhere to operate this type of machinery.

Highway Classification. Until very recently, PWD roads have been classified in accordance with maintenance costs at so much per mile. Obviously, this method of classification is unsatisfactory and we were glad to learn that a new system is to be introduced, shown in Table XIV. This method will take into account both the road width and the load bearing capacity.

This proposed reclassification is an improvement on the previous method, but road widths are still very narrow. However, provided a sufficient width is reserved in the first place, future widening of the road may be carried out easily and economically. The policy has been to reserve a width of 66 feet, but the Mission regards this as inadequate.

TABLE XIV

Proposed PWD Highway Classification

Road Type	Load Capacity tons	Width of Paving feet	Width of Platform feet	Remarks
Trunk and	10	14	24	Traversing uninhabited areas.
major		16 to 20	30	Traversing other areas. (Within
(Class I)				urban areas widths to be greater)
Minor	6	12 to 14	24	Traversing general areas.
(Class II)		20	30	Within urban areas.
Rural	2½	10 to 12	20	Traversing general areas.
(Class III)		20	30	Within urban areas.

The Mission considers that future highway policy should provide for:

(a) New road classification.

(b) Reservation of 100 feet minimum width of land.

(c) Initial construction of all culverts and major bridges to a width of 32 feet minimum on all Class I and Class II roads.

With regard to land reservation, a width of 100 feet will permit the ultimate development of four traffic lanes, one median strip, two sidewalks and two marginal strips for drainage ditches and embankments. In urban areas the marginal strips may be used partly for sidewalks and partly for an extra parking lane on each side. We have prepared Chart 13 showing a three-stage system of economical road development from one lane to four traffic lanes.

Construction Specifications. Ceylon roads are generally of four types as regards construction, i.e. metalled roads, track metalled roads, gravel roads and natural tracks. Metalled roads form the main highways and usually consist of a base course of hand-packed six-eight inch stone (rubble), and a wearing surface of

CHART 13

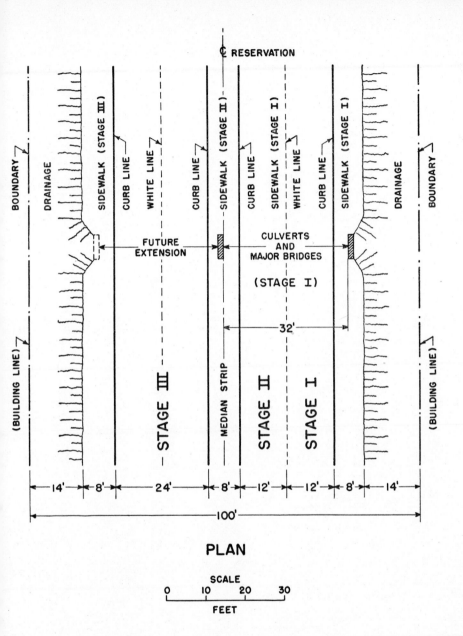

PLAN

SCALE

0   10   20   30

FEET

EXAMPLE OF HIGHWAY DEVELOPMENT IN STAGES

I. B. R. D. APRIL 1952   J. L-J.

two to three inches of crushed stone chocked with .75 inch stone and impregnated with a surface coat of hot bitumen. This general specification has been used extensively in the past, but in view of the considerable advances in modern road design and construction methods the Mission is of the opinion that the PWD highway specifications should be re-examined and brought up to date. In particular, the use of the hand-packed rubble base course appears now to have become over-costly and far too slow for general application.

Road construction material of good quality in the form of granites, gneisses and schists, is widespread except in the north and northwestern coastal belts where limestone predominates. Such an abundant store of natural construction material should be put to better advantage by the use of more modern techniques in design and construction.

Mechanically crushed stone should be used to a far greater extent. This would permit construction and maintenance of a greater highway mileage at lower unit cost. Stone crushing plants of both fixed and mobile types should be included in the modern equipment to be procured. Central crushing plants should be established at strategic points in the island where major highway and other new construction is proposed or in progress. Crushed stone of suitable size could then be produced in large quantities to meet PWD requirements as well as for sale to other departments (railway ballast for example) and private concerns. Major quarry sites should be located so as to permit access by short spurs of broad-gauge railway track for distribution.

Ceylon roads are notable for the large number of culverts. Many of these could be replaced in new construction by larger single culverts with connecting drainage ditches which can be easily built with modern earth moving equipment.

Bridge construction, until recently, has been to no standard loading specifications, but current and future construction is being designed to British Ministry of Transport loading. This should suffice for Ceylon's requirements.

(2) *Highway Improvements*

Apart from new road construction, the PWD has an extensive program for the widening and improvement of existing roads. This program will take many years to complete, as new work will be continuously added with the general economic development of the island. It is not possible for the Mission to suggest a priority listing, since requirements will vary from year to year. In 1950 some 4,400 miles were taken over from the District Road Committees and added to the 6,670 miles now being maintained by the PWD. It is proposed to bring these former DRC roads up to standard, but shortages of various kinds, together with responsibility for other public works and new roads construction, will slow down progress.

Traffic bottlenecks occur along both major and minor roads, usually in the towns and villages where the road areas are often used as meeting grounds for the village populace and resting places for domestic animals. The Mission feels that such bottlenecks, particularly on the main highways, should receive special attention.

Apart from Colombo, which has its own special traffic problems, much can be done to ease the flow of traffic through small towns and villages located on the main highways. Where road widening is impracticable or too costly, bypasses should be constructed. Surveys for bypasses should be made without delay and the necessary land reserved while the towns and villages are still relatively small and land values comparatively low. Delay in reserving land will only cause increased and more costly transportation problems in the future. White traffic lines should be painted along the more congested roads and off-street parking bays constructed at bus stops.

Funds. Government estimates for 1951-52 allocate Rs. 55.5 million to the Public Works Department for all works activities. Additional work to be carried out for other departments will boost this total to about Rs. 80-90 million for the year. Table

XV shows in condensed form figures for bridge and highway continuation works, new proposals, loan fund expenditure and maintenance.

If all estimated expenditures are actually made, forward commitments will amount to Rs. 61.5 million. It is certain, however, that the PWD by itself cannot hope to accomplish a volume of work amounting to an annual expenditure on roads and bridges of Rs. 36 million (Rs. 39 million less Rs. 3 million for new plant and vehicles) employing only its present resources in manpower and equipment. If the department manages a total of Rs. 25 million annually it will be doing well.

TABLE XV

PWD HIGHWAY ESTIMATES, 1951-52

(*rupees*)

	Estimated Total Cost	Actual Exp. to end 1949-50	Est. Exp. to Sept. 1951	Estimated 1951-52
(a) Continuation Works				
Bridges	10,431,450	1,986,033	3,165,700	1,001,800
New roads	9,096,686	1,699,541	2,462,486	849,200
Additions and improvements	3,377,750	541,385	1,472,550	880,200
Total	*22,905,886*	*4,226,959*	*7,100,736*	*2,731,200*
(b) New Proposals				
Bridges and strengthening	3,855,500	—	—	3,250,000
New roads	70,000	—	—	70,000
Additions and improvements	4,100,000	—	—	4,100,000
New plant and vehicles	3,000,000	—	—	3,000,000
Preliminary investigations	250,000	—	—	250,000
Total	*11,275,500*			*10,670,000*

TABLE XV—Continued

PWD HIGHWAY ESTIMATES, 1951-52

(*rupees*)

	Estimated Total Cost	Actual Exp. to end 1949-50	Est. Exp. to Sept. 1951	Estimated 1951-52
(c) Loan Fund Expenditure				
Bridges and roads	12,965,150		6,801,550	3,392,450
DRC and PRC roads	50,000,000			5,000,000
Total	*62,965,150*		*6,801,550*	*8,392,450*
Total (a), (b), (c)	97,146,536		13,902,286	21,793,650
				13,902,286
Est. Exp. to Sept. 1952	35,695,936			35,695,936
Balance commitments	61,450,600	from 1952-53 onwards		
Expenditures under (a), (b), (c) for 1951-52				21,793,650
Bridge and road maintenance (11,095 miles) for 1951-52				17,260,000
Total				*39,053,650*

Source: Government Estimates, 1951-52.

With the addition of nearly 4,400 miles of DRC roads taken over by the PWD in 1950, it is obvious that maintenance costs alone will soon hit the Rs. 20 million mark and go on increasing, leaving little scope for continuation works, new proposals and improvements. More rapid progress will depend upon outside assistance.

The Mission recommends, therefore, that the PWD should obtain the services of local or foreign consulting engineering firms possessing adequate facilities to carry out surveys and the preparation of detailed designs, drawings, specifications and estimates covering a substantial volume of highway improvement and new construction located in the low country areas. As these surveys are completed, contracts could then be let out to major highway construction contractors possessing the necessary plant and equipment and capable of completing work to the value of about Rs. 15 million per year. We specify the low country areas for this procedure as the Mission believes that in general, highway improvements and new construction in the mountainous estate areas are best left to the PWD. The proximity of tea bushes to the roads renders the use of heavy earth moving equipment inadvisable, as potential damage to the tea is great.

(3) *New Roads and Highways*

The basic highway pattern has already been largely established but a few gaps remain, mainly in the less developed areas of the north and east. On Map No. 20 the Mission indicates a recommended network of roads to close the more important gaps in the basic pattern. Initial construction of new roads should generally be to Class I or Class II specifications, the latter to be improved to Class I as and when future traffic requires.

Feeder roads are not shown on the map but should be located to best advantage to serve both the main highways and the railroad. As a general policy, main highways should not be located so as to parallel the railways closely. The two systems should be well apart with a network of lateral feeder roads serving the areas between them.

Priority of new construction will be governed largely by the needs and progress of other projects for development. A second factor affecting priority is method of construction. For short feeder roads and roads located in hilly estate areas, the present hand methods of construction could be employed. For long distance work in flat country, mechanized methods should be adopted. If our recommendation to replace the narrow-gauge line with a road service is carried out, top priority should be given to the conversion of the track bed into a three lane express highway restricted to motor traffic.

Colombo City. The city of Colombo has its own special problems with regard to streets and roads. Increasing motor vehicle traffic, combined with bullock carts and other older forms of transport, is engendering considerable congestion. Of necessity, the whole problem requires thorough and detailed engineering investigation, planning and design. It is understood that the Colombo Municipal Council, in co-operation with PWD and other authorities, is working on this problem. Proposals to date include the expenditure of about Rs. 70 million for new throughways and other improvements. With the proposed new highway bridge over the Kelani Ganga, total expenditure would be in the neighborhood of Rs. 100 million. Although the Mission has not studied these proposals in any detail, they appear generally sound in principle but much will depend upon the engineering details.

One important decision involves the location of the coastal railway track on the southern route. This matter affects several of the proposals for Colombo as well as possible future electrification of the railway. If our recommendation for the removal of the narrow-gauge line is approved, the broad-gauge track might be relocated along the abandoned line from Colombo Fort to Nugegoda. From here the line could run south to Ratmalana and rejoin the coastal route. This possibility should at least be investigated as to advantages and disadvantages, feasibility and probable cost.

A private suggestion was made to construct a marine drive along the submerged reef running between the Galle Face and Mount Lavinia. After careful consideration the Mission cannot recommend the proposal as being either feasible or economically justified.

We referred earlier to Chalmer's Granaries in connection with Colombo port congestion. This site is far too valuable to be allowed to remain permanently a warehousing area. The buildings themselves are of outdated design. The Mission recommends that they be replaced on another and better site by improved types of building to provide greater storage space, and that the present site be utilized for traffic and municipal purposes.

Possible alternative sites are the Beira Lake area, the northern area of the port, or the Weragoda area in the vicinity of the port railway connecting with the main line, the St. Sebastian Canal and the network of existing and proposed trunk roads in the Grand Pass-Weragoda area. The construction of the York Street railway tunnel and the existing port-Kolannawa line would render unnecessary the line passing through the Chalmer's Granaries area to Fort Station. The area thus made vacant by the removal of the buildings could be put to a number of important uses. One of high value would be a modern bus terminal and a large parking area. Roofing over a portion of the harbor-to-lake canal is a further possibility for improving the area and utilizing it more effectively.

(4) *Capital Requirements for Highways*

The Mission will not attempt to make a detailed analysis of the capital requirements for roads and highways since the work is of a continuing nature. Annual expenditure will be determined mainly by (a) funds available and (b) ability to expend the funds allotted.

Maintenance appears to be approaching Rs. 20 million yearly, while continuation works and new proposals will have a backlog of at least Rs. 70 million at the start of 1952-53. It would take the PWD about ten years to work off the backlog without incurring additional new highway works. Given outside engineering and construction assistance, progress could be stepped up to a point where a combined total of about Rs. 20-25 million of new works and improvements could be completed annually. On this basis we estimate that about Rs. 40-45 million could be expended yearly to cover both maintenance and new construction, excluding Colombo City requirements.

The proposal put forward by the PWD to improve and construct nearly 10,000 miles of roads and highways over a 50 year period at an estimated cost of Rs. 1,200 million is an ambitious undertaking, involving an average yearly expenditure of Rs. 24

million. As the mileage of new improved roads increases so will the total annual cost of maintenance. Having regard to other expected calls on available funds as well as difficulties of physical achievement, we have thought it advisable to provide for an average annual expenditure of Rs. 17.5 million in the basic program proposed for 1953-59, or Rs. 105 million in all.

ROAD TRANSPORTATION

(1) *General*

History. Since the first automobile was imported in 1902, the number of motor vehicles of all catagories has risen to about 60,000, or about one vehicle to every 130 persons. During the twenties and thirties, motor bus operation was uncontrolled and the business mushroomed as numbers of small-scale operators entered the field. After intense competition the stronger concerns were able to consolidate and expand their activities, but conditions had become so chaotic by 1937 that the government requested the Hammond Commission to report on the matter. Ordinance No. 45 of 1938 resulted. This aimed at greater control and integration, but it still failed to provide adequate control of road transportation. In 1942, Ordinance No. 47 was introduced. This established a system of exclusive road service licensing. Finally, [5] Parliament passed the Motor Traffic Act No. 14 of 1951. Its purpose is to control and integrate all forms of highway transportation as well as to give a limited degree of protection to the railways.

Administration. Highway transportation control is a function of the Ministry of Transport and Works, with the Department of the Commissioner of Motor Traffic as the executive agency.

Funds. In 1949-50 and 1950-51 expenditure by the Traffic Department amounted to about Rs. 450,000 yearly. For 1951-52 the estimated expenditure is about Rs. 900,000. The increase is

---

[5] Based on the recommendations of the Nelson Report of 1944 and the Putnam Report of 1949.

due mainly to higher cost of living allowances and greater responsibilities assumed under the new Traffic Act.

(2) *Passenger Transportation*

At the end of 1950 registered cars and cabs numbered 34,212 and registered buses 3,145. Of these 2,000 buses were licensed for operation by 67 companies during 1951. The biggest company operated 242 buses, three others operated over 100 and 19 companies operated between 25 and 100 buses. For the month of March 1951, the total bus mileage was about 5.7 million miles with the total number of passengers carried about 19.2 million. Non-scheduled operators to the number of 149 had 207 buses registered in their names. For cab service (nontaxi) a further 91 vehicles were licensed to 34 operators who totalled 150,000 miles and carried 230,000 passengers during March 1951.

Public road transportation is characterized by its inability to meet current demand and by the age and worn condition of many vehicles, 35 to 40% being unfit for continued service. Consequently, complaints by the travelling public are frequent and justified. There are not enough buses. Long waits and overcrowding are common. Operation is irregular and schedules are not maintained. Overcharging of fares has been reported, and the behaviour of drivers and conductors is offensive. In spite of great improvement compared to prewar days, much still remains to be accomplished.

Fares. The present fares per passenger-mile vary from three to five cents according to the operating area. Low-country authorized bus fares are between three and four cents, mid-country four cents and up-country five cents per passenger-mile. Cab fares are 7.5 cents for low-country and 10 cents per passenger-mile for up-country operation. These fares have not been appreciably increased since 1943 and appear to be among the lowest in the world.

In the early days bus operation was extremely profitable but highly risky. Dividends were high for those concerns that survived the competition. The position has since changed considerably as the result of greater control and sharply increased costs of equipment, fuel and labor. Financial records of a number of bus companies now indicate much more modest returns. Some show net operating losses. It is of course recognized that these financial returns are submitted for official scrutiny and are not necessarily designed to show the most glowing picture of company finances. Depreciation rates are high (usually 25%), and other expenditure items might not survive careful investigation. Many concerns suffer from earlier policies of paying out high dividends without making provision for income taxes and replacements; they now find it difficult to renew or increase their fleets of buses to meet public demand. Yet the financial data available do not support the view that current bus company profits and operating margins are excessive by Ceylonese standards. To remedy the shortcomings of the road passenger services would squeeze existing margins and raise costs closer to or even above operating revenues. If there is to be any real progress in meeting public demand for adequate and satisfactory road transport services, it appears to the Mission that fares must be increased.

The average bus passenger would probably be willing to meet a small increase in fares in return for improved and adequate transport service. Bus fares might therefore be allowed to rise by not more than one cent per mile. Along with such fare increases should come stricter control and inspection as provided for under the new Traffic Act.

As an interim measure, a dual fare structure might be imposed. The higher fares might be allowed only on newer vehicles or those being operated fully up to standard. These would be nominated as first class buses; they should meet a specified standard of comfort, of maintenance of schedules, and of civility of personnel. Vehicles not meeting these standards would be nominated as second class buses; they would be penalized by not being permitted increased fares until brought up to first class standard. Thus an incentive would be provided for well managed concerns to offer high quality services. Furthermore, the travelling public could select the class of service for which it was prepared to pay.

(3) *Freight Transportation*

At the end of 1950, there were 11,827 registered lorries, vans, trailers, tankers, etc. Licensed vehicles (i.e. vehicles actually in use) included 7,125 private, 1,772 government and 194 semi-government. Of these, lorries and vans accounted for the great majority.

Conditions of freight haulage have been more orderly and stable than in passenger transport. Nevertheless, in the earlier periods competition was strenuous and rates were sometimes forced below operating costs. The ordinances mentioned previously attempted to bring the freight haulage industry under better control by licensing vehicles for operation only in approved areas and/or on specific routes.

Of recent years the issue of licenses has reflected the following policies:

(a) *Long distance haulage competing with railroad:*
Applicant, whether private or for hire, must prove that existing facilities, including the railroad, are inadequate or unsuitable.

(b) *Local transport for private work:*
Applicant must show potential usage for at least 20 days or 75-100 tons per month.

(c) *Local transport for hire:*
Applicant must prove that the area is not adequately or suitably served.

(d) *Advertising and distribution:*
Small vans of 10 cwt capacity are freely licensed for large areas.

Freight Rates. Although a schedule of "reasonable" freight haulage rates has been promulgated, operators usually charge what the

669

traffic will bear. Table XVI shows the promulgated rates per ton-mile for different vehicle capacities.

TABLE XVI

SCHEDULED AND NONSCHEDULED HIGHWAY FREIGHT RATES

(*rupees*)

Distances	Scheduled Highway		Non-scheduled Highway
	Vehicle not exceeding 2 tons capacity	Vehicle exceeding 2 tons capacity	Vehicle of any capacity
Miles			
0-1	1.6	1.5	1.5
1-2	1.1	1.0	1.0
2-5	1.0	.9	.75
5-10	.8	.7	.6
10-15	.7	.6	.45
15-25	.6	.5	.4
Over 40	.4	.3	.25

These "reasonable" rates are not legally obligatory and are usually undercut either due to competition or the desire to obtain return loads for empty vehicles. Typical rates currently being charged for freight haulage are shown in Table XVII.

TABLE XVII

TYPICAL HAULAGE RATES FOR ESTATES AND LARGE SHIPPERS

(*cents per ton mile*)

Distances	Low-Country	High-Country
Miles		
0-3	40	75
3-10	32	60
10-25	25	55
Long distance (150 miles)	20-27	30-35

The operating cost of a three ton capacity vehicle is reported as about 60-70 cents per mile or 20-30 cents per ton-mile, fully loaded. Overloading by as much as 50-60% is common, to the detriment of both vehicles and highways. A typical, well managed, large road haulage company currently makes about 15% net profit after taxes. But increased operating costs together with a stricter enforcement of the regulations under the Motor Traffic Act will soon call for higher rates for road haulage. Efficient management and operation of the road haulage industry will assume even greater importance than heretofore.

Motor Traffic Act No. 14 of 1951. This Act amends and consolidates existing laws relating to motor vehicles and their use on the highways. It also regulates passenger and freight services and provides for the regulation of traffic on the highways. The Act continues as an interim measure the policy of controlled private monopolies. Later the present firms will be required to convert themselves into a smaller number of public utility companies. Unless the road passenger services are nationalized, these companies must continue to remain in operation. Apart from the road transport services now being operated by the Railway Department and the Colombo-Opanake road service recommended to replace the narrow gauge line, the Mission does not favor nationalization of highway transportation.

The Motor Traffic Act is the result of previous reports on highway transportation and of careful study by the Ministry of Transport and Works assisted by various other departments, authorities and associations. The Act and the regulations under the Act cannot but have a beneficial effect on highway transportation. However, much will depend on administration and enforcement; the regulations themselves appear to conform well with the requirements of modern highway usage. Although amendments and additions will doubtless become necessary, the Mission is of the opinion that the broad policies underlying the Act are sound and well suited to present-day conditions.

CIVIL AVIATION

History. Civil aviation has been largely a development of the war and postwar years. In 1939 all civil aviation activities were suspended and the existing airfield at Ratmalana (Colombo) and the emergency landing ground at Puttalam were placed under military control. The impact of the war resulted in major improvements to Ratmalana airport and the rapid construction of airfields at Negombo, Kankesanturai, Trincomalee, Minneriya, Vavuniya and Koggala. When peace returned Ceylon was in the happy position of being able to acquire some valuable airfields at comparatively little cost to the country. Map No. 19 shows the location of airports and airfields.

In 1946 the Department of Civil Aviation was set up under the Minister of Transport and Works to control and develop all aspects of civil aviation, both local and international. Ceylon became a member of the International Civil Aviation Organization and is a party to the International Air Services Transit (two freedoms) Agreement. Bilateral agreements are made where necessary with other governments on the international routes to cover the remaining three basic freedoms of the air.

The Government next proceeded to finance and operate an airline known as "Air Ceylon". Over the following years there were developed scheduled services, classified as local (Ceylon), regional (India and Pakistan) and international (United Kingdom and Australia) routes. The last category, more accurately described as intercontinental, was commenced in 1949, and was undertaken with the help of Australian National Airways Pty. Ltd., with operational management under ANA.

Development of civil aviation has stressed regional and international rather than local operations. This policy, while courageous, quite naturally encountered technical and financial difficulties which led to annual operating losses and some curtailment of regional services. Yet there has been progress, though at considerable cost.

Air Ceylon. In 1946 three DC3 Dakota aircraft were purchased from war surplus stocks in India, at a cost of Rs. 270,000 each. They were not placed in scheduled service until a year later when, in December 1947, Air Ceylon commenced operations on the Colombo-Kankesanturai-Madras route with 3 trips per week in each direction. After the purchase of a fourth Dakota aircraft in 1948, flights on this route were increased to five a week, Trichinopoly was served twice a week via Kankesanturai, and a weekly flight went from Colombo via Trichinopoly and Bombay to Karachi. There followed a period of trial and error, culminating in the current regional and local schedules:

(a) Colombo-Kankesanturai-Madras: daily.

(b) Kankesanturai-Trichinopoly: daily—connecting with (a).

These services are now being operated with only two of the original four aircraft, as one was destroyed in a crash at Trichinopoly in December 1949 and a second was sold during the latter half of 1951.

In the international field Air Ceylon, with the assistance of Australian National Airways, commenced operations in March 1949, using two DC4 Skymasters supplied on a charter basis by ANA. Initially, a weekly service was flown from Colombo to London and to Singapore. By arrangement with the Australian Government, a special monthly flight was permitted to Sydney from January 1950, later increased to a fortnightly service. In 1951 this became a scheduled service. According to the agreement between the Ceylon Government and the Australian National Airways, the latter act as operating agents and assume charge of the general management of the airline's international operations. Currently, Air Ceylon's round-trip international schedules are as follows:

(a) Colombo-London: weekly (via Bombay, Karachi, Cairo, Rome).

(b) Colombo-Singapore-Sidney: fortnightly (via Djakarta, Darwin).

Air Ceylon Ltd. To assist the development and organization of its air transport, the government decided to convert Air Ceylon into a statutory corporation and by the Air Ceylon (Incorporation) Act, No. 7 of 1951, the corporation was authorized to take over and manage the airline for a period of 10 years. Authorized

673

capital of the corporation is Rs. 15 million, to which the government made an initial contribution of Rs. 1.02 million inclusive of the value of the assets transferred from Air Ceylon. The Corporation may call up further contributions of capital from the Government with the approval of the Minister of Transport and with the concurrence of the Minister of Finance. Section 33 of the Act also provides for a possible participant in the corporation (currently ANA). Its capital contribution is to be maintained on a 49:51 ratio with that of the government.

Section 47 of the Act requires the Corporation to give preference in employment to qualified Ceylonese personnel so that at the expiration of a 10 year period its undertakings will be staffed by citizens of Ceylon. Under an Agreement with ANA, the latter

TABLE XVIII

CEYLON—CIVILIAN AIR TRAFFIC

Year	Number of Passengers	Mail in tons*	Freight and Excess Baggage (tons)
1938	161	42.75	n.a.
1939	237	39.35	n.a.
1940	1,794	39.51	10.91
1941	3,054	44.13	15.44
1942	2,816	99.90	19.72
1943	3,123	150.85	25.33
1944	6,632	118.90	127.20
1945	9,949	226.75	162.19
1946	32,856	296.60	389.70
1947	54,662	313.93	895.74
1948	73,521	412.09	1,431.40
1949	41,601	99.05	961.36
1950	46,419	89.20	536.53
1951			

* Long tons of 2240 lbs.

n.a.=not available.

Source: Department of Civil Aviation statements.

undertakes to afford reasonable opportunity for the employment of Ceylonese personnel in management and in the operation of aircraft.

Control and management of the corporation is vested in the hands of five members of whom three, including the chairman, are nominated by the Ceylon Government. The other two members, including the general manager, are nominated by the participant (ANA).

A more detailed analysis of air traffic on the various airlines for the years 1939 and 1946-48 is given in Table XIX, and for the years 1949 and 1950 in Table XX.

TABLE XIX

CEYLON—TOTAL AIRLINE TRAFFIC

Year	Airline	Number of Passengers	Mail (lbs.)	Freight and Excess Baggage (lbs.)
1939	Tata Air Lines *	601	88,054	n.a.
1946	Tata Air Lines	10,713	51,827	n.a.
	BOAC and Quantas	1,388	n.a.	n.a.
	Charter and non-scheduled	45	n.a.	n.a.
		12,146		
1947	Air India Ltd.	14,047	106,340	4,642
	Air Ceylon	693	n.a.	n.a.
	Charter, etc.	103	n.a.	n.a.
		14,843		
1948	Air India Ltd.	9,790	127,793	311,705
	Air Ceylon	10,803	n.a.	109,884
	BOAC	2,006	66,973	52,765
	Charter, etc.	1,934	n.a.	n.a.
		24,533		

* Predecessor of Air India, Ltd.

Source: Department of Civil Aviation Administration Report, 1946-48.

TABLE XX

CEYLON—TOTAL AIRLINE TRAFFIC

Airline	Number of Passengers		Mail (lbs.)		Freight and Excess Baggage (lbs.)	
	1949	1950	1949	1950	1949	1950
Air Ceylon	28,146	28,296	43,613	49,341	480,915	552,328
Air India Ltd.	9,002	10,594	112,560	99,533	294,560	246,741
BOAC	2,155	3,034	56,000	32,026	156,800	36,674
Quantas E. A. Ltd.	n.a.	224	n.a.	2,820	n.a.	5,999
Charter & non-scheduled	1,275	3,112	n.a.	6,600	n.a.	19,230
Total	*40,578*	*45,260*	*212,173*	*190,320*	*931,375*	*860,972*

Source: Department of Civil Aviation Administration Report, 1949-50.

Foreign Air Lines. Foreign air lines operating to or through Ceylon include British Overseas Airways Corporation, Air India, Ltd., and Quantas Empire Airways Pty., Ltd., all on scheduled services. Non scheduled services have been operated in the past by Australian National Airways Pty., Ltd., Alaska Airlines Inc., Skyways International Inc., KLM Royal Dutch Airlines, Air France and the Tiger Line.

Traffic. Table XVIII shows total civilian air traffic including passengers, mail and freight transported to and from Ceylon for the period 1938-1951.[6] There appears to have been a major decrease in traffic in 1949 and subsequently compared with the two previous years, but this may be due to a change in compilation methods.

---

[6] It will be noted that there is some disagreement between these figures and those in subsequent traffic tables, due possibly to method of compilation.

Table XXI gives the traffic statistics for the Dakota aircraft (regional and local) services of Air Ceylon for the years 1948-50.

TABLE XXI

CEYLON—AIR CEYLON "DAKOTA" TRAFFIC

	1948	1949	1950
Passenger (number)	10,835	24,856	26,255
Mail (lbs.)	n.a.	25,581	19,965
Freight and excess baggage (lbs.)	116,569	480,015	519,753
Passenger—miles flown	3,437,396	10,617,745	6,215,820

Source: Department of Civil Aviation Administration Report, 1949-50.

Unfortunately, the Department's administration reports give no separate traffic statistics (except for mail) covering Air Ceylon's international services. But by a process of subtracting the figures in Table XXI from those in Table XX we obtain the figures shown in Table XXII as possibly applying to the international services operated with Skymaster aircraft.

TABLE XXII

CEYLON—AIR CEYLON "SKYMASTER" TRAFFIC *

	1949	1950
Passengers (number)	3,289	2,041
Mail (lbs.)	18,032	29,376
Freight and excess baggage (lbs.)	0**	32,575

* Table XX less Table XXI.
** Cannot be correct but is obtained by the subtraction method.

The administration reports of the Department of Civil Aviation up to now have not contained full and properly analyzed statistics as regards traffic and financial results of its undertakings. The Mission strongly recommends that this omission be rectified in the future and would point to the excellent statistics given in the reports of the Port Commission, the Railway Department and the Department of Posts and Telecommunications.

Fares and Rates. The passenger fares on the Ceylon-India services have remained steady at about 20 to 21 cents per passenger-mile. Freight and excess baggage rates are in accordance with tariffs laid down by the International Air Transport Association.

Finances. Table XXIII shows expenditure incurred on behalf of the Department of Civil Aviation since 1946. These amounts are exclusive of various capital and loan fund expenditures on construction or improvements to airports.

TABLE XXIII

ANNUAL EXPENDITURE BY DEPARTMENT OF CIVIL AVIATION
(*rupees*)

Year	Expenditure
1946-47	1,216,684
1947-48	446,401
1948-49	615,180
1949-50	809,190
1950-51 (est.)	1,585,436*
1951-52 (est.)	1,967,166

* Includes Rs. 300,000 for acquisition of Kankesanturai airfield.
Source: Government Accounts and Estimates.

Annual financial results of Air Ceylon for the period 1947-48 to 1949-50 are given in Table XXIV. These figures cover all services so that the actual results of the individual routes (internal, regional and international) cannot be determined.

Ceylon Air Academy. In November 1950 the Department of Civil Aviation inaugurated the Ceylon Air Academy as a training school for civil aviation personnel. The training of personnel has progressed satisfactorily. The Academy is now developing a new internal service, employing aircraft which carry three and nine

TRANSPORTATION

TABLE XXIV

AIR CEYLON FINANCIAL RESULTS

(rupees)

Year	Traffic Revenue	Incidental Revenue	Total Revenue	Total Expenditure	Loss
1947-48	818,397	62,243	880,670	1,309,660	429,020
1948-49	1,403,983	7,766	1,411,749	2,084,222	672,473
1949-50	1,715,975	121,920	1,837,895	2,437,647	599,752

Source: Department of Civil Aviation statements.

persons including crew. In September 1951 they became regularly scheduled services, changing from tri-weekly to daily service in January, 1952.

Routes connect Colombo (Ratmalana), Minneriya, Trincomalee and Jaffna (Kankesanturai) with a line between Minneriya and Amparai. A southern route connects Colombo with Galle (Koggala). The Department intends eventually to set up these internal services under a new agency within the Department to be operated on a commercial basis. It will utilize personnel trained in the Air Academy but will be under entirely separate management and will maintain its own accounts.

Development Program. Over the period, 1952-59 inclusive, the Department of Civil Aviation hopes to put into effect a development program covering ground facilities, communications equipment, aircraft and training. The over-all cost, as estimated by the Department, amounts to nearly Rs. 32 million for the eight year period. (See Table XXV.)

The Mission is of the opinion that this is a desirable program. As a general policy, priority should be given to improvement of ground facilities and communications, with the aim of developing Colombo into a first class international airport, and to the further development of internal and regional rather than intercontinental services. We doubt if more than Rs. 20 million can be allotted to this in the basic program put forward for the six years 1953-59. The civil aviation program will therefore have to be spread over a

TABLE XXV

Civil Aviation Development—Estimated Cost

Year	Ground Facilities	Communications Equipment	Aircraft	Training Equipment	Training Personnel
1952	Rs. 165,000	Rs. 50,000 $ 67,950 £ 2,904	— £ 17,000	— £ 6,300	Rs. 115,500
1953	Rs. 6,250,000	Rs. 52,000 $ 61,745 £ 5,194	 £ 40,000	 £ 6,300	Rs. 131,000
1954	Rs. 5,350,000	Rs. 54,000 $ 78,220 £ 3,514	 £ 44,000	 £ 6,800	Rs. 146,000
1955	Rs. 4,450,000	Rs. 56,000 $ 90,440 £ 3,865	 £ 50,000	 £ 6,800	Rs. 150,000
1956	Rs. 2,550,000	Rs. 58,000 $ 99,486 £ 4,251	 £ 11,000	 £ 6,800	Rs. 157,500
1957	Rs. 1,000,000	Rs. 60,000 $ 189,434 £ 4,677	 £ 13,000	 £ 7,000	Rs. 158,250
1958	Rs. 1,000,000	Rs. 62,000 $ 120,375 £ 5,144	 £ 13,000	 £ 7,000	Rs. 159,500
1959	Rs. 1,000,000	Rs. 64,000 $ 132,415 £ 5,658	 £ 54,000	 £ 7,000	Rs. 160,250
Total:	Rs. 21,765,000	Rs. 456,000 $ 840,065 £ 35,207	 £242,000	 £ 54,000	Rs. 1,178,000

Grand Total: *Rs. 23,399,000*   *$840,065*   *£ 331,207*

Grand Total when converted* to local currency (approx.) Rs. 31,814,300
   * $ 1.00 = Rs. 4.762   £ 1 = Rs. 13.33.
Source: Department of Civil Aviation.

slightly longer period unless supplementary funds are forthcoming.

Future of Ceylon Civil Aviation. Following the establishment of Air Ceylon's international service, London-Colombo-Singapore-Sydney, the tendency has been to protect it against competition from other airlines. Being in the business itself, the government has hesitated to encourage the increased use of Colombo as a port of call or junction point, despite the considerable trade advantages which would flow from such use. It is thus possible that Ceylon's "chosen instrument" policy may be running counter to its national interest in developing traffic through Colombo. Ceylon's geographic position and its remarkable scenic and historic attractions might be made to yield considerable foreign exchange. This could come from increased use of its ground facilities by foreign airlines, from tourist stopovers, as well as from commercial improvement which should result from increased knowledge of the country. Developmental policy over the next few years should take account of this basic geographical factor.

It appears unlikely that the present charter procedure can be made the basis for a permanent international service for Air Ceylon. While little capital investment is required, current expenditures are too high for the very slight advantages obtained. Ceylon captures a small share of the available traffic over this well-travelled route, but its aviation gets little stimulus. Technical experience gained by Ceylonese personnel has been minimal, and it is doubtful whether anything is added to Ceylon's international trade or to traffic for the airline itself. It employs administrative personnel and current appropriations which could be used more effectively in the development of internal and regional services.

Under these circumstances it is probably unwise either to continue this device of chartering aircraft or to undertake a heavy investment in equipment to operate a service over the London-Sydney route. A policy of developing internal and regional services should bring superior results in the cultivation of new traffic and the training of flight and ground crews and administrative personnel. Ceylon already possesses pilots in sufficient numbers to operate such services on a modest scale and to train additional crews with little, if any, foreign assistance. As the international (transcontinental) service has shown, it is difficult to combine a training program with such an operation until extensive experience has been gained in the local field. The agency (ANA) owning and operating the aircraft has not taken any significant step toward introducing Ceylonese personnel into the flight crews or toward training them.

Probably the best approach to effective Ceylonese participation in international air transport would be to begin the intensive cultivation of the regional field. While the entrance into the Ceylon-Pakistan service may have been premature, some type of service between these two countries might be feasible for Air Ceylon, possibly on a Colombo-Cochin-Bombay-Karachi route. Another possibility inviting study is the establishment of direct services between Colombo-Calcutta-Chittagong-Colombo, and Colombo-Rangoon-Bangkok-Colombo. This would afford travellers on any of the international airlines an interesting choice of routes and give Colombo a better opportunity of attracting round-the-world travellers and businessmen.

The internal services possess good growth possibilities and should be expanded. The Colombo-Galle service might eventually be extended to Tissamaharama and even on to Amparai. With regard to the central mountainous area the possibility of using Nuwara Eliya as a stop has been investigated, but weather conditions and terrain make this undesirable. In place of Nuwara Eliya the Mission recommends that Wilson's Plains be investigated as the site of a possible airfield to serve the Nuwara Eliya-Bandarawela areas.

TELECOMMUNICATIONS

History. Telecommunication services are a monopoly of the Department of Posts and Telecommunications. Earlier there were a large number of licensed manually-operated private telephone systems in estate areas, but most of these have been taken over by the Department.

In 1935 the Government considered but rejected the alternative of handing over the system to private companies. It then initiated a long-range development program to modernize the existing antiquated system. By the end of 1939 the worn-out Colombo Exchange had been replaced with a modern automatic system and 97 small automatic exchanges had been installed in various parts of the country. The war interrupted this program but it was resumed thereafter. However, progress has been slow because of the difficulty in obtaining materials and equipment from foreign manufacturers.

Overseas Communications. Ceylon is relatively well served by overseas communications. Telephone service to India is obtained by submarine cable via the Palk Straits between Talaimannar and Rameswaram to connect with the Indian Telephone network. Radio telephone service is also available with most of the world.

Telegraph service to India is also via the Talaimannar-Rameswaram submarine cable. From Colombo radiate other submarine telegraph cables to provide access to most other parts of the world. Until recently, Cable & Wireless Ltd. owned and operated the overseas cables from Colombo as well as a radio telegraph circuit, but the Company's assets in Ceylon have now been taken over by the government and are being operated by Cable & Wireless personnel pending permanent arrangements. Direct radio and telegraph facilities are also available between Colombo and ships operating in the Indian Ocean.

Domestic Communications. Telephone service exists between the principal towns and most of the rural districts. As of the end of September 1951, there were approximately 17,672 telephones in the country, of which 11,040 were connected to the three Colombo exchanges. Map No. 21 shows the extent of Ceylon's telephone system. Before the war the net annual increase in subscribers was under 400, of which about 55% were on the Colombo exchanges. In 1939 there was a total of 5,810 subscribers in Ceylon and by 1945 this had increased to 7,698, representing an average growth of about 320 per year. By improvisation and using up existing stocks of equipment over 2,000 new subscribers were added during the war years, but demand continued to grow and by 1949 there were 6,277 waiting applications. As of October 1951 there were 5,387 waiting applicants of whom 2,825 were in the Colombo area. According to latest reports it is expected to clear the Colombo waiting list by the end of 1952.

The majority of trunk circuits are run overhead on pole routes. Carrier circuits are in operation over some of the longer routes, such as Colombo to Galle, Diyatalawa, Nuwara Eliya, Anuradhapura and Trincomalee. There is also a 27-mile trunk cable between ·Colombo and Kaltura on the south coast.

The telegraph network is as widespread as the telephones, in that telegrams handed in at subpost offices are transmitted by telephone. The more important offices are provided with separate telegraph circuits worked by morse code or teleprinter. Map No. 22 shows the extent of the telegraph system. Table XXVI gives domestic communications plant statistics for the years 1947 to 1951.

Despite the relatively extensive telecommunications network

TABLE XXVI

DOMESTIC COMMUNICATIONS PLANT

	1947	1948	1949	1950	1951
Overhead routes (miles)	4,732	4,765	4,836	5,236	5,516
Overhead wire (miles)	35,265	35,995	37,705	39,828	41,162
Underground wire (miles)	46,779	46,911	47,408	53,536	60,538
Telegraph sets (morse)	117	117	120	128	137
Teleprinter sets (combined)	53	57	60	85	98
Telephones	13,323	13,568	14,160	15,834	17,672

Source: Department of Posts and Telecommunications.

and facilities provided by government, the existing system is seriously overloaded, resulting in long delays in completing telephone calls or effecting delivery of telegrams. Faults occurring on the trunk lines are also numerous and of long duration; many are caused by bad weather or depredations by elephants and other wild animals. The frequent faults of short duration were mainly due to worn out equipment. Table XXVII shows the number and duration of faults for the period 1938-49.

TABLE XXVII

FAULTS ON TELEPHONE AND TELEGRAPH TRUNK LINES

Year	Faults No.	Average Duration Hrs.	Mts.
1938	3,204	3	21
1939	4,624	3	10
1940	4,565	3	49
1941	5,135	3	20
1942	5,572	3	42
1943	6,040	3	38
1944	6,868	3	46
1945	6,275	3	46
1946	6,433	3	48
1947	7,093	4	00
1948	7,839	3	12
1949	9,416	3	29

Source: Posts and Telecommunications Department Report, 1948-49 (Pub. Feb. 1951).

Finances. In common with some other though not all countries of the world, Ceylon's postal and telecommunication facilities are operated with a consistent annual deficit. Table XXVIII shows the position with regard to the telephone and telegraph services for the period 1946-47 to 1950-51. Telephone and telegraph rates were increased in April 1949, but with the heavy capital expenditure being made to improve and increase communication services

it appears that the time has come when further slight increases in selected rates are in order. The 1949 increase has not affected the buoyant traffic and the strong demand for more and better services.

TABLE XXVIII

TELEPHONE AND TELEGRAPH OPERATING RESULTS *

(*rupees*)

Year	Telephone Deficit	Telegraph Deficit	Total Deficit
1946-47	1,530,295	1,191,556	2,721,851
1947-48	1,317,881	1,574,038	2,891,919
1948-49	1,159,421	1,434,093	2,593,514
1949-50	315,093	1,225,105	1,540,198
1950-51 (est.)	nil	1,300,000	1,300,000

* Excludes reserve for deferred maintenance.
Source: Department of Posts and Telecommunications.

Expert Study. At the request of the government a detailed report on the telecommunications system of the island was submitted on May 14, 1951, by Mr. B. Bradley, a retired telecommunications engineer of the British Post Office. While the report presented no broad quantitative proposals or estimates regarding additional facilities, it covered much ground in operation procedures. The report is most commendable and in view of its very recent origin the Mission will not attempt to cover the same ground again.

The Mission is of the opinion that most, if not all, of the recommendations contained in the Bradley Report should be implemented to the maximum extent practicable. The report suggests many economies and improvements which could be effected in the interests of the Department and the public alike.

Future Development. The six-year modernization program for the period 1947-53 was originally computed to cost about Rs. 14.5 million but has since been revised upwards to Rs. 19.35

million. Up to the end of 1950-51 actual expenditure totalled some Rs. 9.5 million while estimated expenditure for 1951-52 is about Rs. 4.5 million. This leaves Rs. 5 to 6 million to be expended in 1952-53 to complete the program.

TABLE XXIX
TELECOMMUNICATIONS DEVELOPMENT PROGRAM, 1953-59
(*rupees*)

Head	Estimated Cost	Imported Materials	Local Labor and Materials
Trunks and junctions	3,000,000	2,000,000	1,000,000
Sub post offices	5,000,000	3,500,000	1,500,000
Underground lines	5,000,000	3,000,000	2,000,000
Underground trunk cables	12,000,000	7,000,000	5,000,000
New exchanges	6,000,000	5,250,000	750,000
Acquiring private exchanges	3,000,000	2,000,000	1,000,000
New Colombo exchanges	20,000,000	18,000,000	2,000,000
Central: 10,000 initial			
20,000 ultimate			
Satellites: 4 x 5,000 initial			
4 x 10,000 ultimate			
Telephones to subscribers	8,000,000	6,000,000	2,000,000
Laboratory	500,000	400,000	100,000
Workshop machinery	300,000	275,000	25,000
Telegraphs and teleprinters	1,000,000	800,000	200,000
Transmitting, monitoring and frequency checking stations	6,000,000	5,000,000	1,000,000
Radio telephone services	1,000,000	800,000	200,000
Radio trunk services	3,000,000	2,250,000	750,000
Training school	300,000	200,000	100,000
Totals:	*74,100,000*	*56,475,000*	*17,625,000*
Percent of total		76%	24%

CLASSIFICATION OF IMPORTED EQUIPMENT AND MATERIALS

	Rs.
Overhead line including copper wire	13,000,000
Underground cables, loading coils, repeaters	10,000,000
Telegraph equipment	800,000
Telephone equipment	22,925,000
Batteries and charging equipment	3,500,000
Radio equipment	6,000,000
Workshop machinery	250,000
	56,475,000

Source: Department of Posts and Telegraphs Statement, Nov. 1951.

For the future development of the telecommunications system the Department has drawn up a program to cover the period 1953-59. Table XXIX shows the main heads and estimated cost of this program.

The Department also plans development of overseas telecommunications along the lines laid down by Cable & Wireless Ltd., prior to the acquisition of its assets by the government. The estimated cost was Rs. 3.5 million, but the program has not been started nor has it received expert appraisal.

New buildings are also required, including an extension to the present Central Telegraph Office, a workshop in Colombo and smaller buildings in the rural centers. These items may cost in the neighborhood of Rs. 12 million. The whole program may be tabulated as follows:

Head	Estimated Cost	Imported Materials	Local Labor and Materials
Telecommunications (domestic)	74,100,000	56,475,000	17,625,000
Overseas telecommunications	3,500,000	2,525,000	975,000
Buildings	12,000,000	2,400,000	9,600,000
Total	Rs. 89,600,000	61,400,000	28,200,000

688

The execution of such a program requires a yearly average expenditure of Rs. 15 million as compared with a current expenditure of about Rs. 4 million to 5 million. Although the department expects to have completed a major phase in the technical training of staff by 1953, thereby removing one of the most serious obstacles to an increased pace of development, the envisaged program represents a threefold increase in yearly expenditure. The Mission believes that such rapid expansion within the six-year period will be very difficult; the development period will probably have to be extended over a much longer span of, say, 10 to 12 years. In the basic program for 1953-59, therefore, only Rs. 35 million has been included for this purpose.

The Mission believes in any case that it will be wise to obtain external assistance to plan and coordinate details of the development program and, if further funds should become available, to aid in construction and installation. The preparation of a completely integrated technical plan is a complex undertaking, requiring highly qualified telecommunications experts who are abreast of the most modern technical advances in the field. Outside assistance to expedite building construction may also be required if valuable equipment is not to deteriorate from long periods of storage.

VHF Radio Relay Systems. Subject to expert detailed investigation on the spot, the Mission believes that Ceylon offers a fertile field for wide use of the VHF radio relay system of communications. The large areas of flat country studded with islands of abruptly rising hills provide ideal terrain for this type of communication. Relay towers erected 25 to 50 miles apart provide point-to-point communication. Microwave transmission networks cost about half as much as the conventional telephone and telegraph lines and the relay equipment may be installed at locations which are inaccessible for periods of several months. Maintenance costs are low, since there are no poles and wires to be blown down in storms or to be damaged by wild animals.

We therefore advise that expert technical advice be secured

689

regarding the possibility of installing extensive microwave transmission systems of telecommunications.

Although radio telephone services already connect certain points (such as Colombo-Inginiyagala), Ceylon lacks extensive experience with VHF radio relay systems. The Mission is of the opinion that, before sanctioning comprehensive development of telecommunications, expert advice should be sought as to the suitability of such systems for possible extensive use.

Sea Transportation

For some time past the government has been considering the establishment of a Ceylonese shipping line, either as a completely national undertaking or in association with an established operator. The idea of a national merchant marine naturally appeals to all Ceylonese who would like to see the Ceylon flag flying at sea and the commerce of Ceylon carried in home-owned ships. There is also the thought that a national fleet could be used for bargaining purposes and would reduce ocean freights, particularly on the Burma-Ceylon rice run.

Before any steps are taken to establish a national merchant marine, the following facts should be carefully weighed:

(a) Capital requirements would be extremely high because of the inflated current cost of new and even secondhand ships.

(b) Ceylon at present has no trained officers or seamen to man the ships. To employ any considerable number of overseas personnel would be costly, even if they were available.

(c) Ceylon lacks men with experience in the management and administration of a merchant marine.

Apart from the foregoing there are many other factors directly and indirectly affecting a venture of this nature. It is common knowledge that the operation of a shipping line requires long experience and tradition if it is to be conducted on a profitable basis.

A high enough price will command almost anything, but Ceylon can get much greater value from investment in its internal development. Establishment of a national merchant marine cannot, at present, be justified on any economic grounds.

An alternative proposal of entering into an association with an established foreign shipping line should also be examined with great care. It has been suggested that a corporation be formed on the lines of Air Ceylon Ltd., with the government putting up a large share of the capital and then accepting the ships on a charter basis. Unless the presumed reduction in freight rates (which cannot be guaranteed) is more than sufficient to offset the capital expenditure plus interest there is no point in entering into such an arrangement. Furthermore, the cost of this type of venture should be weighed against the actual returns to the government, and therefore the taxpayer. More often than not it is the charterer who makes the actual gains, leaving mostly expectations to the other partner. As in the case of Air Ceylon Ltd., despite agreement by the participant to train Ceylonese personnel, such training cannot be carried out very extensively— certainly not to the degree warranted by the expenditure incurred.

Entry into a charter association would, in practice, curtail Ceylon's freedom of action in taking advantage of the highly competitive freight markets. Except in time of war or a similar emergency, Ceylon possesses the advantage of a buyer's market. The current freight surcharge to Colombo is chiefly due to inadequate port facilities and will disappear when the new development works are completed. Furthermore, the recommended construction of a fumigatorium at Galle could avoid much of this freight surcharge by diverting large rice imports through the port of Galle.

Coastal Shipping Service. Sight must not be lost of the fact that Ceylon is an island and is therefore largely dependent on its seaborne commerce. The Mission is of the opinion that Ceylon should, in the course of time, acquire a modest merchant marine but one that is founded on first hand experience and suited to her particular type of economy.

The best approach to this objective would be to establish a small coastal shipping service which could be gradually developed into a regional and eventually into an ocean service. The financial and managerial experience gained with the coastal service would be of great value when the time came for expansion into broader fields. At the same time Ceylonese officers and crews would be trained to take on larger ships at a later stage.

The Mission would therefore support the establishment of a coastal shipping service as a preliminary to the eventual creation of a small national merchant marine. We have in mind the pro-

TABLE XXX

RECORDED SALES OF VESSELS
(July 1951 to January 1952)

Name of Vessel	Year Built	DWT	Sale Price	Approximate Price per DWT
		tons	(rupees)	(rupees)
Liberty Type				
M/S *EMPIRE CONRAD*	1942	10,300	8,200,000	795
M/S *SCOTTISH PRINCE*	1944	10,100	8,850,000	875
S/S *TROPIC*	1943	10,713	7,750,000	725
S/S *DAYBEAM*	1944	10,850	6,750,000	625
S/S *PORT ALBANY*		10,439	7,650,000	735
Coastal Type				
M/S *LUTZ*	1933	2,470	1,730,000	700
S/S *SHEAF FIELD*	1942	2,825	2,330,000	825
S/S *SPRUCELAND*	1942	2,750	1,200,000	440
S/S *SVIDBY*	1943	2,820	1,200,000	425
S/S *KINDU*	1947	3,074	3,000,000	980
M/S *BENVEG*	1949	1,320	1,870,000	1,420
S/S *VILLAVICIOSA*	1950	2,928	4,000,000	1,365

692

curement of two or three ships of about 1,500 to 2,000 deadweight tons suitable for coastal service between the ports of Ceylon and for short runs to the South Indian ports as traffic develops. As an indication of the recent cost of secondhand merchant ships built since 1930, some recorded sales are given in Table XXX, both for Liberty ships and for vessels suitable for coastal traffic.

Before embarking on any shipping scheme involving heavy capital expenditure, (or even of limited expenditure as in the case of a coastal service), a complete and thorough investigation must be carried out by qualified persons and a full report produced covering all its aspects. The time and cost required to complete the investigation would be amply rewarded. Current reports indicate a surplus of certain categories of shipping tonnage which could be purchased at lower than prevailing prices for use in coastal service.

Capital Requirements. The cost of establishing a state-owned coastal shipping service including the capital cost of two vessels, training of ships' personnel, administrative and other incidentals, is estimated at Rs. 5 million. An operating subsidy would certainly be necessary, at least for a few years; this might amount to half a million rupees a year for two vessels. This, as a commercial enterprise, would be very suitable for financing through the proposed Development Corporation.

REGULATION AND DEVELOPMENT OF TRANSPORTATION

Elsewhere in our report we have recommended the establishment of a Development Advisory Board to review all projects relating to Ceylon's economic development, to make suggestions on its own account, and to formulate recommendations to an Economic Committee of the Cabinet with respect to both long-range plans and the annual components thereof. Since transportation is intimately connected with all aspects of Ceylon's progress, its regulation and expansion should receive the special attention of the Development Advisory Board. If a well-conceived pattern of development is to emerge, plans for transportation must be integrated with those of other Departments.

Ceylon Ports Authority. In an earlier section we detailed some of the defects which are inherent in the present Colombo Port Commission. With the continued growth of Colombo port, the problems of the Commission will undoubtedly multiply, while administration and operation of the recommended commercial port at Trincomalee will further add to the Commission's responsibilities. Additional administrative and technical staff will soon be required for Trincomalee, and possibly for Galle in the more distant future.

Consequently, the Mission recommends that Ceylon's port authority should be reconstituted as a semiautonomous body with responsibility for the administration of all ports. A number of autonomous and semiautonomous port authorities and port trusts exist which experience has shown to be the type of body most suited for major port operation. The government should retain broad control through the Minister of Transport and Works and the government-appointed Chairman of the Authority.

SUMMARY OF RECOMMENDATIONS

PORTS AND HARBORS

1. *Development of the Port of Colombo*

a) Stages I and II of the harbor development scheme should be completed as rapidly as possible; Stages III and IV should be deferred for the present, but engineering studies of them should continue.

b) Various ancillary proposals by the Port Commission (including the rubble mound breakwater, the marine drive, the York Street railway tunnel and the Beira Lake development) should also be expedited.

c) The various authorities concerned with road, rail and canal access to the port (the Port Commission, Colombo Municipality, Government Railways and the PWD) should draw up coordinated plans for improvements.

694

2. *Administration of the Port of Colombo*

a) The accounts of the Port Commission should be commercialized, so as to make proper provision for amortization of loan fund expenditures.

b) The recommendations of the Millbourn Committee for administrative and operational improvements, and certain other suggestions put forward by the Mission, should be implemented.

c) To check the serious increase in pilferage and other cargo losses, effect should be given to the recommendations made in 1951 by a sub-committee appointed by the Port Commission.

3. *Galle*

Certain partial improvements to the harbor, designed to form part of a larger master plan of development, should be carried out and studies initiated with a view to more extensive improvements later; the anchorage and buoy equipment should be improved; and facilities provided, including a fumigatorium, for the import of the rice requirements of the Galle area, so relieving congestion at Colombo.

4. *Trincomalee*

Commercial facilities should be provided, probably at Cod Bay in the inner harbor, subject to the agreement of the British Admiralty; the exact timing of the construction will depend on the rate of new development in the surrounding area.

5. *Northern Ports*

New port development in the north should be postponed for the present, priority being given to Trincomalee; but an engineering survey might be undertaken at Kankesanturai.

6. *Ports Authority*

The Colombo Port Commission should be reconstituted as a semiautonomous Ceylon Ports Authority with responsibility for all the ports in Ceylon.

WATERWAYS

7. Increased expenditure of Rs. 2 million over six years, on maintenance of inland waterways is recommended.

RAILWAYS

8. *Administration and Operation*

a) An experienced firm of consultants should be engaged to advise on details of operational practice and methods.

b) A regular series of training visits to overseas railways by Ceylon railway personnel should be organized.

c) The railway workshops at Ratmalana should adopt a five-day work week in order to improve operational efficiency.

9. *Railway Rates*

The Mission is not satisfied that the present operating deficit, and consequent subsidization by the government, is necessary and recommends increases of passenger fares and certain freight rates.

10. *Railway Extensions and Improvements*

a) The existing programs of general improvement and rehabilitation of track and rolling stock should be carried out; total cost is put at Rs. 125 million but this will have to be spread over more than six years.

b) The remaining narrow-gauge section in the Kelani valley should be taken up; the road-bed converted into a motor road, on which more efficient road services could be provided; and the track used in industrial projects requiring extensive local transport facilities, such as the proposed sugar cane development.

c) The track on the Bangadeniya-Puttalam Section (taken up for re-use elsewhere during the war) should be relaid.

d) New extensions should be constructed from Eravur to Amparai and between Vavuniya and Trincomalee.

e) The line between Panadura and Alutgama should be double-tracked.

11. *Electrification*

Since sufficient hydroelectric power is not expected to be available before 1960 at earliest, the proposed electrification of Colombo suburban services should be deferred. Studies should be undertaken in a few years' time so that a firm decision as to the economics of the conversion can be taken when the power outlook is more promising.

ROADS

12. *Equipment*

The Public Works Department should acquire a steadily increasing volume of modern road and bridge construction plant and equipment for use by the department itself and local contractors.

13. *Administration and Technical*

a) Increased attention should be paid to the training of operational personnel.

b) There should be increased use of consultants and contractors on specific works, to relieve the PWD; if so employed they should be required to pay special attention to training of a Ceylonese subordinate staff.

c) Suggestions are made for a new classification of highways, for changes in highway standards and specifications and for improved construction methods and use of local materials.

14. *Program of Development*

a) A general program of improvement and development, including certain new road links, is recommended, to cost an average of Rs. 17.5 million per year over and above current maintenance expenditure.

b) Special attention should be given to the removal of bottlenecks in towns and villages on main routes.

697

c) In the city of Colombo a scheme is suggested for the removal of Chalmer's Granaries near the canal to Beira Lake, and the use of the site for a modern bus terminal, parking facilities and other public purposes.

15. *Road Passenger Services*

No change in the present basic system of operation of bus services by controlled private enterprise is proposed but permission to increase fares is recommended, at least for those bus operators prepared to comply with improved service standards.

CIVIL AVIATION

16. A detailed program of development of ground facilities and extension of Air Ceylon's internal and regional services is recommended.

TELECOMMUNICATIONS

17. The detailed proposals for reorganization made in the recent report by Mr. B. Bradley should be implemented.

18. A program of improvements and extensions estimated to cost about Rs. 90 million in all is recommended; expenditure within the period 1953-59 is estimated at Rs. 35 million. Outside advice in the planning and coordination of the details of this highly technical operation will probably be necessary.

19. Expert advice should be sought on the possibility of installing extensive microwave transmission systems of telecommunications in Ceylon.

SEA TRANSPORT

20. The Mission does not favor any attempt in the near future to establish a national shipping line operating ocean services. Development of coastal shipping should be attempted first and might be undertaken by the proposed Development Corporation.

TRANSPORTATION

SUMMARY OF CAPITAL REQUIREMENTS, 1953-1959
(*million rupees*)

Section	Head	Cost
II	Ports and harbors (with addition for equipment)	118
III	Inland waterways	2
IV	Railways (part of Rs. 250 million over 10 years)	150
V	Roads and highways (excluding maintenance)	105
VI	Road transportation (non-capital)	—
VII	Civil aviation	20
VIII	Telecommunications (part of Rs. 90 million over 12 years)	35
X	Regulation and development of transportation (non-capital)	—
	Total	*430*

17. Public Health

INTRODUCTION

"Of all gains, the gain of health is the highest and the best."
Buddha.

In the calculation of a country's resources for economic development health is a primary factor. The standard of living of a people, the conditions under which they live and work and the food they eat—all affect health. Economic improvement or progress will be illusory if the health of the people is not improved. In the ultimate analysis the true wealth of a nation is its people. But mere masses of substandard humanity are more of a liability to the state than an asset. The strength and prosperity of a country depend rather upon the quality of its population, upon its standard of health, intelligence and industry.

Economic and social progress has always been hindered by the prevalence of disease. Those countries which have not applied modern scientific knowledge to the solution of their community problems have lagged behind. A vast majority of their people live in ignorance and superstition under unsanitary and overcrowded conditions of life—they merely exist in poverty and misery.

The poverty of the people in such conditions itself impedes the provision of better medical and public health facilities as well as the growth of the environmental conditions which are fundamental to healthy living. To establish adequate curative and preventive medical services, obviously essential as they are, is not enough. Hygienic housing, adequate nutrition, protected water supply for drinking and domestic purposes, underground drainage, health education, recreational and cultural facilities for

700

UNIVERSITY COLLEGE OF WALES LIBRARY ABERYSTWYTH

leisure—all are equally, if not more, important requirements for any substantial improvement in the health and welfare of the people.

At present, the people of underdeveloped countries are caught in a vicious circle. Because of adverse economic conditions their health is poor and because of poor health their economic output and efficiency are low. This vicious circle has to be broken.

Ceylon is far from being at the lowest level. Its people are better off economically than those of most other countries in Asia, and they have a well-organized curative and preventive service. They have every reason to congratulate themselves on the successful control of malaria, formerly their enemy number one, and on the significant improvement in mortality rates. They should be grateful to the pioneers who have set up so admirable a basic administration. But, although the death rates have fallen, the same cannot be said of the sickness rates of various diseases. Concerned as this report is with the steady continued improvements of the present level of health, it will necessarily deal more with the defects in the current health program and the ways in which it can be improved than with the results already achieved.

Ad hoc measures to prevent and control epidemics, and to provide the minimum of curative and preventive services while half-heartedly dealing with environmental hygiene and sanitation, will at best maintain the present level of health. If the country is not to continue to trail behind the countries of the West indefinitely, the wide gap between sanitary conditions in Ceylon and in advanced countries must be bridged. Ceylon must apply the most modern scientific methods of disease prevention taking advantage of other people's experience, and strive to get on a par with the West within the twentieth century.

THE STATE OF PUBLIC HEALTH

1. VITAL STATISTICS

Whereas the birth rate in Ceylon has remained as high as ever, at 40.4 per 1,000 of population in 1950, the death rate has come

701

down to 12.6 per 1,000, which is the lowest on record and com-pares very favorably with most countries.

This reduction and the similar fall in infant and maternal mortality rates is shown by the following table, as well as in Charts Nos. 15 and 16.

TABLE I

BIRTH AND DEATH RATES, 1945-1950

(per 1,000)

	Birth Rate	Death Rate	Infant Mortality Rate	Maternal Mortality Rate
1945	36.7	22.0	140	16.5
1946	38.4	20.3	141	15.5
1947	39.4	14.3	101	10.6
1948	40.6	13.2	92	8.3
1949	39.9	12.6	87	6.5
1950	40.4	12.6	82	5.6

The number of premature births, however, is still as high as 31% of all live births and is the cause of nearly 50% of neonatal deaths. Premature births in Western countries range between 5% and 12% only.

Another feature of note is that although the total number of deaths under five years of age has shared the spectacular decrease in the general death rate, its ratio to the total number of deaths has remained high. In fact, as shown by the following figures, it has increased slightly, although that may be due to the higher proportion which the age group 0-5 now forms of the total popu-lation.

Year	Percentage of Deaths under Five Years to Deaths at all Ages
1945	40.5
1946	43.0
1947	43.1
1948	45.5
1949	45.3
1950	46.3

Source: Reports on Vital Statistics.

702

CHART 14

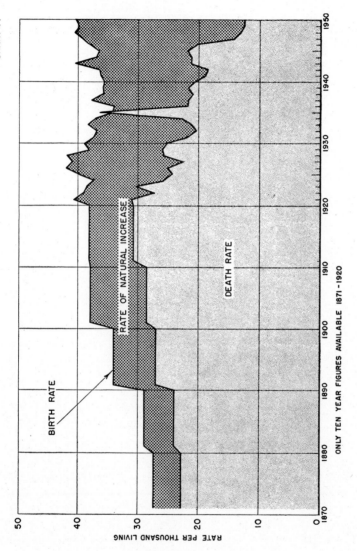

RATE OF BIRTHS, DEATHS AND NATURAL INCREASE – CEYLON

PER 1000 LIVING

ONLY TEN YEAR FIGURES AVAILABLE 1871 - 1920

I. B. R. D. APRIL 1952

The corresponding ratio in the United States is 9.1, in Japan 27.3 and in India 37.7 (see Table II).

It is recommended that as a preliminary to remedial action sample surveys be undertaken to determine the causes of such a high percentage of deaths in this age group. It may well be found that it is closely associated with malnutrition.

Table II compares birth and death rates per 1,000 of population of certain countries with those of Ceylon.

TABLE II

COMPARATIVE BIRTH AND DEATH RATES OF VARIOUS COUNTRIES

Country	Year	Birth Rate (per 1,000)	Death Rate (per 1,000)	Natural Rate of Increase Per Year (%)	Percentage of Deaths under Five Years to Deaths at all Ages
United States	1945-49	23.4	10.1	1.3	9.1
Canada	"	26.7	9.3	1.7	14.7
United Kingdom	"	18.6	12.3	0.6	6.5
France	"	20.1	13.9	0.6	—
Germany	"	13.1	10.9	0.2	—
New Zealand	"	25.0	9.6	1.5	7.6
Japan	"	29.9	17.0	1.3	27.3
India	"	27.1	18.8	0.8	37.7
Uruguay	1948	21.1	8.3	1.3	16.5
Chile	1950	32.4	15.7	1.7	31.1
Ceylon	1950	40.4	12.6	2.8	46.3

Recent United States figures show what can be achieved by the application of improved medical knowledge, especially through public health measures. Thus:

in 1900 there were 17.2 deaths per 1,000; in 1948 there were 9.9;

in 1915, the infant mortality rate was 100; in 1948 it was down to 32;

703

in 1935, maternal mortality was 5.8 (about the same as in Ceylon in 1950); in 1948 it was only 1.2;

in 1900 life expentancy was 47 years (about the same as in Ceylon today); about 20 years have been added to it—in 1948 it was 67 years.

2. MORBIDITY *(Sickness)* RATES

All diseases and illnesses do not end in death, nor do they take the same time to kill. Some are acute, others tend to become sub-acute and still others become chronic and debilitating. Therefore a study of mortality figures alone does not give the true picture of a nation's state of health.

Health has been defined by WHO as "a state of complete physical, mental and social well-being, not merely the absence of disease or infirmity." Many persons without any definite signs of disease are so devitalized as to be incapable of efficient work. It is hard to measure ill health at all precisely, but the scale of attendance at hospitals and dispensaries gives at least an indication, even though the figures reflect only diseases with obvious signs and symptoms for which the patient sought skilled or tech-nical treatment. The scale of hospital attendances is shown in Table III (see also Chart No. 17).

TABLE III
HOSPITAL PATIENTS, 1945-50

		In-patients		Out-patients	
	Population	Total	Rate per 1,000 Population	Total	Rate per 1,000 Population
1945	6,496,000	511,177	78.6	7,107,642	109.4
1946	6,695,000	502,012	74.9	7,498,522	112.0
1947	6,879,000	540,768	78.6	7,172,724	104.3
1948	7,086,000	662,433	93.5	8,332,086	117.6
1949	7,297,000	741,202	101.6	9,420,091	129.1
1950	7,550,000	846,001	112.0	11,444,206	152.5

CHART 15

INFANT MORTALITY RATE
(PER 1000 LIVE BIRTHS)

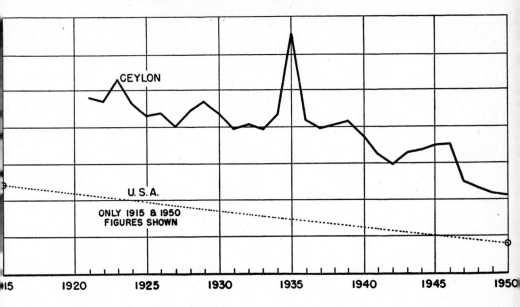

CEYLON

U. S. A.

ONLY 1915 & 1950
FIGURES SHOWN

15   1920   1925   1930   1935   1940   1945   1950

CHART 16

MATERNAL DEATH RATE
(PER 1000 LIVE BIRTHS)

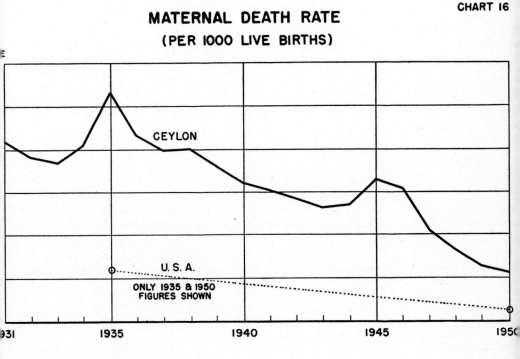

CEYLON

U. S. A.

ONLY 1935 & 1950
FIGURES SHOWN

931   1935   1940   1945   1950

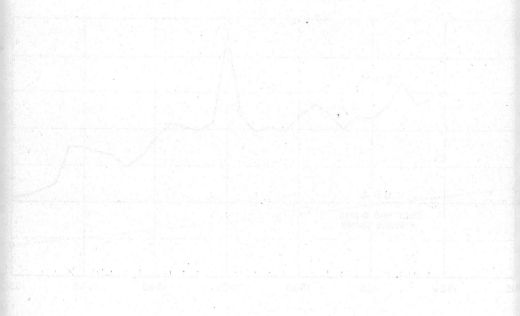

In 1950 of every nine persons in the island one was an indoor patient, receiving free treatment and free food for an average of 8.6 days.

It is very likely that the numbers of visits have risen because of greater public inclination to resort to hospitals. Nonetheless the increase in the rate is very striking, the more so because the number of cases of malaria has been brought down from over 2.5 million in 1945 to about half a million in 1950.

Professor H. Cullumbine of the University of Ceylon has examined the hospital morbidity data for the years 1945 and 1949. His calculations show the following approximate percentages of increase in hospitalization in various groups of diseases in 1949 over those of 1945.

Circulatory system	60%
Respiratory system	90%
Digestive system	52%
Genitourinary system	40%

Moreover, in rural areas many of the sick among the poorer classes and especially the children and the aged are treated by trained indigenous medical practitioners, of whom there are some 500 in the island. Figures for these patients are not available but in Colombo, which is comparatively well served by up-to-date hospitals, the number of patients treated at the Hospital for Indigenous Medicine increased from 61,780 in 1942 to 422,803 in 1950, indoor cases increasing from 981 to 3,197.

As already noted, this increase in recorded sickness is very probably due not, or at least not wholly, to there being actually more illness, but to greater inclination on the part of the people as a whole to take advantage of the facilities offered. Many classes of the population and many types of disease which were not treated in hospitals previously are now being dealt with there. But however much the apparent increase is discounted it remains obvious that there is a great deal of sickness in Ceylon, that there is no evidence that the real rate of sickness is showing any tendency to decline as fast as the rate of mortality and that the country continues to suffer a grave economic loss from consequent impairment of productivity.

Certain major causes of both sickness and mortality, in particular malnutrition, malaria and tuberculosis, are discussed later in this chapter. But as a cause of morbidity special mention must be made of hookworm, a disease prevalent throughout the island. In spite of the campaign against it started in collaboration with the Rockefeller Foundation over 35 years ago and despite the reduction through regular and systematic treatment of the intensity of individual infection, its effect upon health in general is still serious. Hookworm treatment was given by various agencies during 1949 and 1950 to as many as 1,902,055 and 1,861,403 people respectively. Its extent and significance are summarized in the following quotation from a paper by Dr. C. T. Williams, formerly Assistant Director of Ceylon Medical and Sanitary Services (Health):

"It is estimated that 88% of people in Ceylon harbor hookworms. Though we do not come across advanced cases of hookworm disease at present thanks to the Rockefeller Foundation which started a campaign in Ceylon in 1915 yet the infestation is still fairly high in remote areas to cause physical and mental retardation of children. Along with hookworm, round worms play an important part in lowering the health of the school-going population in rural areas. After worm treatment administered in schools, I have seen masses of round worms passed by children.

I have not the shadow of doubt, that round worm infestation in pre-school children is one of the most important causes of the high mortality in that age group."

This emphasizes the need for improvement in environmental sanitation, which is the weakest link in the set-up for prevention and control of communicable diseases.

CHART 17

TOTAL NUMBER OF INDOOR HOSPITAL CASES - CEYLON
(IN THOUSANDS)

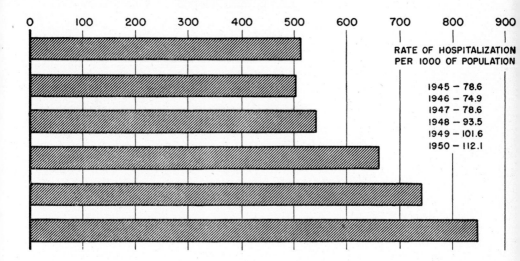

RATE OF HOSPITALIZATION
PER 1000 OF POPULATION

1945 — 78.6
1946 — 74.9
1947 — 78.6
1948 — 93.5
1949 — 101.6
1950 — 112.1

CHART 18

ESTIMATED POPULATION GROWTH — CEYLON
(IN MILLIONS)

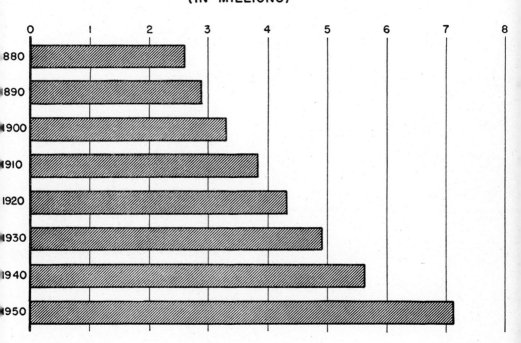

The Population Problem of Ceylon

The Natural Increase

Chart No. 14 shows the rates of natural increase from 1871 to 1950, and Chart No. 18 shows the steady growth and a tripling of the population during the period, the numbers rising from 2.5 million to 7.5 million. In earlier years part of the increase was due to immigration. In the last few years the rate of growth has risen higher still on the basis of natural increase alone. Table IV shows the natural increase for the years 1945 to 1950.

TABLE IV

Natural Increase of Population, 1945-50

Year	Estimated Population	Natural Increase (Births minus Deaths)	Rate of Natural Increase per 1,000
1945	6,496,000	95,563	14.7
1946	6,695,000	120,949	18.1
1947	6,879,000	172,647	25.3
1948	7,086,000	193,984	27.4
1949	7,297,000	199,302	27.3
1950	7,550,000	209,358	27.7

Source: Official report of Division of Medical and Sanitary Services.

The estimated population at mid 1952 was 7,870,000. If the current rate of increase is maintained, population will be just under 10 million in 1962 and 12.7 million in 1972 [1].

The island-wide average density of population has risen from 98 per square mile in 1871 to 298 today, but the increase has been greatest in the Western, Central and Southern Provinces, which have densities today of 1319, 495 and 450 respectively. The implications of those densities—and of the prospect of further

---

[1] These figures are based not on the crude over-all rate of 2.8 but on current reproduction rates allowing for calculated changes in the age distribution, but for no further fall in death rates.

707

increases—for overcrowding and general sanitation and therefore for the rate of sickness are obvious.

The following table compiled from the League of Nations
Statistical Year Book 1942 to 1944 gives comparisons with certain other countries of the world. (Figures for India and Ceylon
are brought up to date.)

TABLE V

COMPARATIVE DENSITY OF POPULATION IN VARIOUS COUNTRIES

Country	Large Countries	Density per sq. Mile
Australia		2
Canada		3
Brazil		13
U. S. S. R.		23
United States		41
Greater China		105
India Union		292 (1950)
	Intermediate Countries	
Chile		18
Mexico		26
Turkey		59
France		194
Pakistan		194
Germany		352
Japan		496
	Small Countries	
England & Wales		718
Holland		717
Ceylon		298 (1950)
Korea		285
Switzerland		269
Hungary		221

Densities are naturally higher in industrial countries, but it
will be seen that Ceylon's density of population is higher than that
of any other predominantly agricultural country in the table.

Ceylon has not hitherto had to face the problems of general
over-population, despite the very great pressure of population in

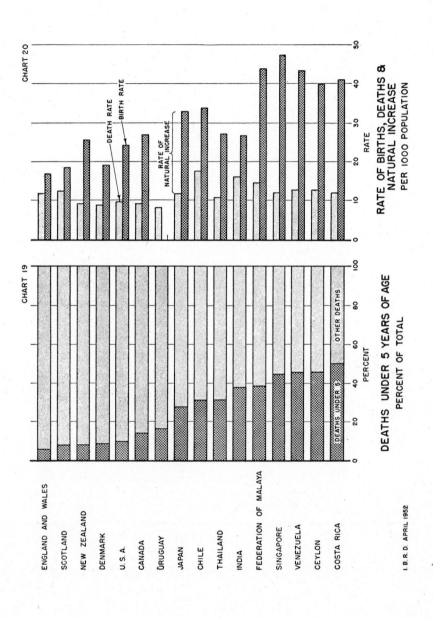

CHART 20

RATE OF BIRTHS, DEATHS &
NATURAL INCREASE
PER 1000 POPULATION

CHART 19

DEATHS UNDER 5 YEARS OF AGE
PERCENT OF TOTAL

ENGLAND AND WALES
SCOTLAND
NEW ZEALAND
DENMARK
U.S.A.
CANADA
URUGUAY
JAPAN
CHILE
THAILAND
INDIA
FEDERATION OF MALAYA
SINGAPORE
VENEZUELA
CEYLON
COSTA RICA

I.B.R.D. APRIL 1952

some areas. But if the present rate of increase is not checked it will be only a few years before the population problem will be felt very keenly and very obviously. The new land available for cultivation, although considerable, is limited; and the development of new resources and means of employment through industrialization is bound to be slow. The economic developments which are in sight can take care of the natural increase of population for only a very few years, after which continuation of that increase can only be at the expense of the health and the standard of living of the people. Unless serious attention is paid at once to the population problem, the next generation will be living under worse, not better sanitary conditions and will be worse, not better fed than the present.

The countries of the world may be divided into three categories. [2] First are those like the United States and Western European countries where birth rates and death rates have both been reduced by the conscious application of scientific knowledge. Second there are those like most of the African countries where births are not controlled, but death rates also have been reduced only a little and population growth is still slow. Ceylon, like India, falls into the third category where the application of modern science is keeping down deaths, but where practically no family planning is practiced. Consequently, while the death rate has been brought down from 31.2 in 1921 to 12.6 in 1950, the birth rate has remained as high as ever, between 34 and 41 per thousand of the population. As a result of this high fertility rate and comparatively low death rate the population has continued to grow rapidly, with a high percentage of child population.

In due time the children will become an economic asset, but they have first to be fed, clothed, housed and educated. The conclusion is inescapable that something must be done to check the rapid growth of population before it becomes the menace in Ceylon it has already shown itself to be in certain other countries.

---

[2] Charts 19 and 20 show comparative birth and mortality rates for Ceylon and various other countries.

Family limitation is most necessary and desirable in the interests both of the parents and of the children if they are to have a reasonable chance of survival and a better start in life. It is a sphere in which the individual has by far the greatest responsibility and a special contribution to make. But government action is necessary if individuals are to be brought to realize their responsibilities and enabled to discharge them.

The experience of Europe and the United States is often cited to show that social and economic advance will "automatically" reduce death rates. Many take comfort in the belief that when living standards have been raised through education, improved methods of agriculture and industrialization, that will happen in Ceylon also. But before such a balance was struck in Europe the population had multiplied three times as a result of social and industrial revolution. Only then did both birth and death rates drop concurrently. Moreover those were days of expansion and colonization when many new countries were opened up and tremendous resources became available from the new world. No such windfall is likely to benefit Ceylon or other countries in the East or West today.

Some object to family planning as an interference with nature. But in all our developmental schemes, when we harness electricity, when we control rivers, and when we postpone death by modern drugs and surgery, we are interfering with nature. Some again consider it immoral to interfere in the ways of God. Is is not more immoral to raise children one is unable to feed and clothe properly and must sentence to chronic malnutrition?

Some well placed people no doubt avail themselves of the knowledge and facilities to prevent conception, but such knowledge should also be made available to the community at large. Health education from elementary classes onward and sex education from the level of high schools upward should be encouraged.

GOVERNMENT POLICY

The government of India has realized the necessity of family planning to raise the standard of the people and has given a bold lead in accepting family planning as government policy. The Mission believes it would be desirable for the government of Ceylon to adopt a similar policy.

It is therefore recommended that the government take advantage of the present psychological moment and declare boldly in favor of family planning in the interest of both parents and the coming generation. Information on and facilities for family planning should be made available at headquarters of provincial and district hospitals for the present, and in due course at all government hospitals, dispensaries and centers. Advice should be given to those for whom it is considered essential on medical grounds, e.g. women for whom conception would be dangerous because of deformities of the pelvis and other specific diseases, and to others who may ask for it.

Ceylon is in a very fortunate position to make this project a success; it has a very fine network of maternity homes which are very popular with the people. Both the medical and auxiliary staff such as nurses, midwives and health educators should be adequately trained in the technique of family planning as well as in the social and economic aspects of the problem.

The medical authorities should keep themselves abreast of the latest knowledge and research work which is being done in the western countries and in India. Ceylon may make some contributions of its own on the subject.

Cooperation of voluntary organizations like the Red Cross Society, Ceylon Tuberculosis Association, and especially women's organizations like Lanka Mahila Samiti should be enlisted and the government should help them with adequate grants-in-aid.

Administrative Services and Training of Personnel

1. Departmental Organization .

The Department of Medical and Sanitary services is one of the largest government departments, its staff numbering about 16,000 or one eleventh of the total public service. Expenditure of the

711

department, which has doubled since 1945, is nearly Rs. 100 million per year, or nearly Rs. 13 per head, a much higher figure than for most Asian countries.

History. The present organization of the medical and public health services of Ceylon evolved from a military and state medical service, some traces and traditions of which can still be seen. The Civil Medical Department was established in 1859 primarily for the care of the sick; the only type of public health work that received any attention then was the control of large-scale epidemics, particularly smallpox. The Contagious Disease Ordinance of 1866, one of the first public health ordinances, laid special stress on this disease. Its prevention was then as much a police function as a public health activity.

The Medical Department continued its activities with a single type of medical officer engaged primarily in the treatment of the sick and attending to any immediate public health need of the country until 1913, when a sanitary branch of the Department was created. Public health work was still confined to the district type, including the sanitation of urban and semiurban areas and the control of outbreaks of communicable disease.

An important landmark in the public health services was the inauguration of the hookworm campaign in 1916. This demonstrated the need for incorporating personal hygiene in the health program and sowed the seed which grew into the present Health Units, covering both curative and preventive services. These are discussed in detail later.

Next came the amalgamation in 1926 of the curative and preventive services under one head, the Director of Medical and Sanitary Services. In 1931 Health and Local Government Departments were combined under one ministry, which gave a great impetus to curative as well as preventive work. Thus the present-day objective of combining the curative and preventive services was achieved well in advance of many other countries. Unfortunately, as will be shown, the benefits which should have accrued from such foresight have not fully materialized.

712

Headquarters Staff. The Director of Medical and Sanitary Services Headquarters has two Assistant Directors, one for the Medical Services in charge of curative work, and the other in charge of the preventive work. There are various other senior officers at headquarters on both curative and preventive sides and in charge of special divisions, such as malaria, tuberculosis, leprosy.

Provincial and District Staff. The supervisory organization in the provinces is different for the curative and preventive sides. On the former, eight divisional Medical Superintendents exercise general supervision over all the district medical officers. The officers in the field doing curative work comprise 554 medical officers, 20 dental surgeons, 334 apothecaries, 1,165 matrons, sisters and nurses, 409 midwives, and hundreds of male and female attendants and other minor employees. On the preventive side five provincial Medical Superintendents of Health supervise the work of 76 medical officers of health, 707 sanitary inspectors, 64 public health nurses, 969 public health midwives, 342 public health apothecaries in rural hospitals and dispensaries, 66 vaccinators and 20 dispensers for hookworm treatment.

Amalgamation of Curative and Preventive Services. For purposes of general administration the island is divided into nine provinces, each under a provincial officer termed a Government Agent.

The provinces are divided into 19 districts and further subdivided into 108 Divisional Revenue Officers' areas, and finally into 3,800 Village Headmen's Divisions.

It is through the provincial administration machinery that the government reaches the people; and it is through this structure that rural development schemes in particular are carried out. The great asset of this organization is that its officers and subordinates deal directly with the people in intimate, workable units. It is therefore essential that the medical and health services should work in the closest cooperation with the general administrative authorities participating in rural development, as elabor-

713

ated in the section on Environmental Sanitation. But as there are eight medical and five health superintendents the two branches do not cover identical areas and much of the advantage of working in close cooperation with the Government Agent appears to be lost.

At many points, some of which will be noted in later sections of this chapter, coordination between the two branches of the Health Services appears incomplete and the advantages of amalgamation at the top seem to pass down only partially to the lower levels in the Department.

It is therefore recommended that instead of 13 provincial superintendents (eight on the medical and five on the health side) there should be nine superintendents, one for each province, in charge of both curative and preventive work. They should be delegated adequate powers to deal with both the services.

By having only one representative of the Director the advantages which accrue from amalgamation of medical and sanitary services at the top will be retained at the provincial level and the policy, as directed from above, will be carried out by one agency both in letter and spirit. The present difficulties in getting men to serve on the health side, which are discussed below, should be easier to overcome.

Relations with Local Government Authorities. Every village and town (except those under the Gal Oya Board) is covered by some local self-government unit. There are seven municipal councils, 36 urban councils, 36 town councils and 400 village committees for rural areas, upon whom various ordinances conferred powers and duties in regard to public health and sanitation. They raise funds by local taxation, supplemented by aid from the central government, which gives quite liberal grants and loans for water supplies, drainage and housing schemes.

The Department of Medical and Sanitary Services assists in the supervision, control and development of these schemes. For each municipal council and important town council a medical officer of health is appointed; for other areas the medical officer in charge of the respective Health Unit acts as an adviser and

714

supervisor; but these officers have not been able to give as much attention to environmental sanitation as it deserves.

To accelerate the development of the rural areas the island is divided into 12 Local Government Regions, each in charge of an Assistant Commissioner for Local Government, and it will serve a very useful purpose indeed to have 12 parallel medical officers of health to work under the nine Provincial Superintendents.

It is therefore recommended that 12 regional medical officers be appointed, one for each Local Government Region, to work under the proposed Provincial Superintendents in the supervision of both curative and preventive services and as liaison officers with the local administrations.

Medical Officers of Health. A special feature of what we believe to be an underemphasis of the preventive side is the position regarding the appointment of Medical Officers of Health. The present policy of recruitment is to invite the medical graduates to indicate their preference for service either in the curative or the preventive branch. During the last three years only four out of nearly 150 graduates selected the preventive branch. Present practice is to assign permanently to the medical branch those graduates in the topmost 75 percent of the final examination. The lowest 25 percent are assigned permanently to the preventive branch. Inevitably this leads to a sense of inferiority and permanent dissatisfaction in the preventive branch.

In addition, the shortage of sufficient permanent Medical Officers of Health has necessitated the appointment of a number of medical officers, i.e. officers on the curative side, to act as medical officers of health. These officers are commonly spoken of as "conscripts." The system works badly as shown by the following quotation from the Administrative Report of the Director of Medical and Sanitary Services, 1950. "In spite of a short intensive course of training in public health, and in spite of being supervised by Senior Medical Officers of Health, the work of these latter officers has been disappointing. Being compelled to do this work temporarily these curative Medical Officers have merely marked time

715

and what is even worse, become traducers of preventive medicine as such." The last sentence of this quotation is of course particularly disturbing. The officers concerned may have expressed a preference for curative work but their terms of service include an obligation to serve for at least two years on the preventive side, for which purpose they are given additional training in public health.

Part of the solution of this problem is to be found in the procedure for the initial recruitment of medical officers of health. Some at least of the best men should be assigned to the preventive branch and adequately compensated for any loss of remuneration that might have accrued if they had been assigned to the curative branch.

It is therefore recommended that the assignment to curative or preventive branch should be decided not by the result of the final examination only, but by the Director of Medical and Sanitary Services (who is in charge of both the branches) in consultation with the principal and the professor of public health administration under whom the officer was trained, taking into consideration the record, aptitude and general behavior of the student.

But it is also necessary that the importance of preventive work should be more fully stressed at all levels of the departmental organization. Hence the importance of the recommendation for the amalgamation of the preventive and curative services in the provincial and regional set-up.

Apothecaries. In 1950, out of a total of 240 central dispensaries established in rural areas, as many as 229 were in the charge of apothecaries. Their work is supervised by the health officers, but for the purposes of provision of drugs and equipment and for promotion and transfers they are under the medical branch. This dual control blurs the sense of responsibility and does not promote efficiency. So far as the curative work in general is concerned the apothecaries appear to be performing their duties quite satisfactorily but their knowledge of medicine is extremely limited. They are in an excellent position to stress the importance

716

of prevention of disease and to promote the health education of the public, and suggestions are made below for improvement of their training in the public health field.

2. TRAINING OF PERSONNEL

The efficient administration of existing hospitals and the extension of medical facilities will be impossible without an adequate number of doctors both in the curative and preventive branches and of nurses, midwives and other auxiliary personnel.

In the course of time doctors and nurses may become available for private practice to treat people in their own homes and at private nursing homes but for the present practically every doctor, apothecary or nurse who qualifies goes into the State Medical Service.

There is today an extreme shortage of personnel when measured against the population. Figures are given in Table VI below. Any plans for the future must provide for the needs of a population which at the present rate of increase will be at least 12.5 million in 20 years time. A long view is essential because it takes a minimum period of five years to train a doctor, plus another year or two for a postgraduate qualification in public health; and three years to train a nurse, plus six months for a public health qualification.

Target. The following table suggests targets for recruitment, determined not by what is ideally desirable but by what may be possible with the training facilities which could be provided. It gives an idea of the magnitude of the task.

The target for nurses is particularly low but it is recommended in view of the very limited facilities likely to be available for their training.

Doctors. The training of doctors is the function of the University of Ceylon. There is only one medical school at Colombo, working at full capacity. It has over 600 medical students in training and it turns out nearly 100 qualified graduates every year, nearly all of whom go into government service. Education

717

in Ceylon is entirely free even at the university level. A medical student obtains free tuition throughout his training. After his admission through an entrance examination he is allowed a number of failures at the first, second and final professional exams. Thus some take a much longer time to qualify than the minimum period prescribed and consequently there is some wastage of medical manpower.

It is therefore recommended that after the first examination for admission there should be a second screening after the first year.

An average of 25 graduates per year is required today to fill vacancies caused by death and retirement. Thus every year 70 to 80 graduates become available as net additions to the medical service of the country. A second medical school at Kandy has been planned. If this is built in the next year or so there should be available from about 1960 an additional hundred or so graduates per year. Bearing in mind that as total numbers go up the replacement of normal wastage will absorb a larger proportion of the output of graduates, the output from these two medical schools seems the minimum which can hold out any prospect of attaining the target of over 4,000 doctors within 20 years.

An early increase in training facilities is therefore recommended. The new medical school should be started as soon as

TABLE VI
MEDICAL PERSONNEL TARGETS

	No. Available	Approximate ratio to present population In Ceylon	In U.K.	Ratio suggested be attained for a population of 12.5 million	No. Required in 1972
Doctors	1,100	1: 6,800	1:1,000	1:3,000	4,167
Nurses	1,500	1: 5,000	1: 300	1:1,000	12,500
Midwives	1,500	1: 5,000	1: 600	1:3,000	4,167
Dentists	30	1:25,000	1:2,800	1:6,000	2,083
Apothecaries	800	1: 9,400	—	1:5,000	2,500
Sanitary inspectors	707	1:10,000	—	1:5,000	2,500

practicable and meanwhile the existing facilities should be extended and used to their maximum.

Nurses. There is an acute shortage of nurses in the hospitals. Fortunately it is not difficult to get students for training. For the 50 vacancies offered every six months for admission for training as many as 500 applications are received. This is remarkable not only for an Asian country, but for any country in the world.

An excellent detailed note on the training of nurses and midwives has been submitted by Miss D. T. Pederson, WHO regional adviser. She makes the valuable recommendation, among others, that a large number of nurses be trained at various hospitals and institutes.

We hope that her recommendation to extend training facilities for nurses will be given effect as soon as possible.

Dentists. It will not be easy to reach the target of over 2,000 qualified officers unless special efforts are made.

It is therefore recommended that additional facilities be provided at the Colombo Dental Institute; that a second institute be started at Kandy along with the proposed medical school there, and that scholarships be offered to attract a suitable number of candidates for this branch of medicine.

Apothecaries have no exact equivalent in most other countries. They combine a full course in pharmacy with an elementary training in medicine and surgery and serve largely as substitutes for fully trained medical practitioners. Of the nearly 700 apothecaries in state service more than half are in independent charge of dispensaries and rural hospitals. This is necessary because of the shortage of qualified doctors. In addition the apothecaries serve very usefully as medical assistants in the rural areas. However strong the arguments for a single standard of minimum qualifications for medical practitioners, the apothecary class will be required for a long time to come. If it were abolished in the near future it is not to be expected that fully qualified medical graduates would replace them in out-of-the-way places; a vacuum would be left for quacks to step in.

Recently the period of study of apothecaries has been increased from two to three years, which is a step in the right direction. This should enable them to be given additional training in medicine, surgery and public health.

It is recommended that facilities be provided to train double the present number of apothecaries for the next 10 years. In their training special emphasis should be laid on the preventive aspects and for those in service refresher courses should be organized.

When the number of fully qualified doctors becomes adequate, the apothecary will have to revert to his legitimate place as a qualified pharmacist and assistant to the doctor in charge of rural institutions.

Sanitary Inspectors. The special emphasis that must be laid on environmental hygiene and other public health developments necessitates not only an increased number of sanitary inspectors, but also steps to engender greater interest and enthusiasm among these officers. The sanitary inspectors today are well qualified but they have no special incentive to make the extra effort that is so badly needed for their arduous duties, for once a sanitary inspector always a sanitary inspector. Some prospect of advancement is required to maintain their interest and enthusiasm. In addition there is an important task of coordination of the sanitation activities of other departments, such as Revenue, Rural Development and Local Government. The interests both of public health work and of sanitary inspectors point to the desirability of establishing a superior cadre of sanitary inspectors, appointments to which should depend rather upon efficiency, initiative and powers of tactful coordination than on seniority.

It is therefore recommended that a cadre of 12 regional sanitary inspectors, one for each local government region, be created and filled by selection from existing sanitary inspectors.

HOSPITALS AND MATERNITY HOMES

Medical care is provided as a national health service by the central government, which has assumed the obligation to provide

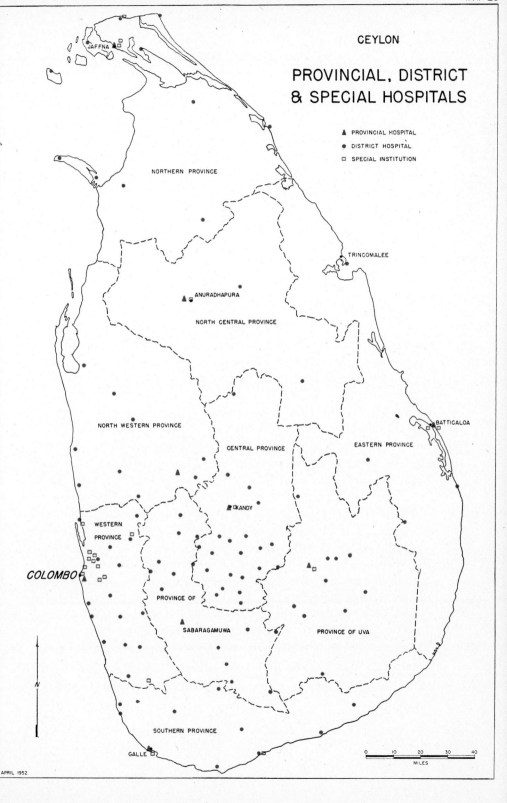

MAP 23

CEYLON

PROVINCIAL, DISTRICT
& SPECIAL HOSPITALS

▲ PROVINCIAL HOSPITAL
● DISTRICT HOSPITAL
□ SPECIAL INSTITUTION

JAFFNA

NORTHERN PROVINCE

TRINCOMALEE

ANURADHAPURA

NORTH CENTRAL PROVINCE

NORTH WESTERN PROVINCE

BATTICALOA

CENTRAL PROVINCE

EASTERN PROVINCE

KANDY

WESTERN
PROVINCE

COLOMBO

PROVINCE OF

SABARAGAMUWA

PROVINCE OF UVA

SOUTHERN PROVINCE

GALLE

0   10   20   30   40
MILES

APRIL 1952

hospitals, dispensaries and ambulance service free or at a nominal charge to the patient. The only other medical service is that furnished by the hospitals for indigenous medicine and by a few nursing homes run by private practitioners in Colombo and other big towns. Map No. 23 shows the distribution of hospitals throughout the island.

1. GENERAL HOSPITALS

Hospitalization. Indoor treatment is provided free to all patients with an income of less than Rs. 50 per month. A patient with an income of between Rs. 50 to Rs. 83.33 per month pays 30 cents (US $0.06) per diem. Those whose income is over Rs. 83.33 pay 50 cents per diem. There are also a few paying wards at higher rates in some of the hospitals.

The total number of beds in all hospitals under the Medical and Sanitary Department in 1950 was 19,959, including 5,922 in special institutions and distributed as shown in Table VII.

Figures of the recent increase in the number of patients, both indoor and outdoor, have already been given. During 1950, 846,001 cases were treated as in-patients. Generally speaking, every patient who needs hospital treatment gets it, but there is

TABLE VII

HOSPITAL BEDS, 1950

	Beds	
104 Hospitals	11,646	
14 Cottage hospitals	249	
114 Rural hospitals	2,142	
		14,037
Special institutions including tuberculosis hospitals		5,922
		19,959

a great deal of overcrowding and in certain cases lack of staff and equipment. The bed strength in the tuberculosis hospitals was 1,333, but the number actually accommodated at the end of 1950 was 1,880. Similarly there were 3,179 cases in the mental hospital with a bed strength of 1,800 only. Much the same state of affairs exists in most of the provincial and district hospitals. Overcrowding up to 100% is tolerated and indeed officially recognized as a normal feature, having become a necessity with the increase of in-patients from 511,177 in 1945 to 846,001 in 1950. As a result hospital staffs are unable to give full attention to the serious cases for which the hospitals were intended.

The overcrowding of hospitals is enhanced by the admission of many who could be treated as out-patients, such as cases of incurable illness, the debilitated and the ill-nourished. The Commission on Social Services roughly estimated that only about 60% of cases really deserved to be admitted as in-patients. Better screening of patients could reduce overcrowding to some extent. The temptation to seek admission as in-patients may arise from dissatisfaction with the attention available at the out-patient departments and from the attraction of free diet in addition to free treatment, which may lead also to attempts to stay longer than may be absolutely necessary. This appears to be particularly the case in tuberculosis institutes where the patients require and get a much better diet than is served at the ordinary hospitals.

Out-Patients. Ordinarily treatment is also free at the out-patient department of all hospitals and dispensaries. A small charge, however, is made in respect of certain specialized treatments, and persons with higher incomes pay fees at the rate of 50 cents (US $0.11) per visit for incomes between Rs. 50 and Rs. 100 per month, Rs. 1 (US $0.22) for incomes ranging up to Rs. 200 per month, and Rs. 2 for incomes above Rs. 200. During 1950, 11.5 million cases (first visits 6, 677,914) were treated at the outdoor dispensaries.

A person needing outdoor treatment can always get it, but the numbers seeking relief are very large and many hours of waiting may be necessary. The out-patient departments of the provincial and district headquarters are extremely overcrowded. In order to deal with the vast numbers, the attendant physicians have to deal with patients at the rate of one per minute. Obviously this is not enough for proper diagnosis and treatment.

It is recommended that the number of doctors assigned to the out-patient departments be at least doubled, the facilities for diagnosis and treatment improved, and a home treatment service developed as soon as possible.

To some extent at least this would decrease the demand for admission as indoor cases since a proportion could be treated under home conditions.

Bed Strength. The present overcrowding, the increasing demand of the population for indoor treatment and the growing population combine to make a strong prima facie case for more beds. The precise extent and timing of any increase, however, need careful consideration in the light of a number of factors.

Ceylon has today 2.6 beds per 1,000 of population. By comparison with other predominantly rural countries in the tropics it appears to be well served, particularly as malaria is under control and the country is practically free from cholera, plague and smallpox. Although precise comparison is difficult owing to the different extent of medical service by private practitioners in urban areas, there can be no doubt that Ceylon is a good deal better served than India.

There is a natural tendency to make comparisons with the most advanced countries, especially the United Kingdom and the United States, where the hospital bed ratios are nine and 10 per 1,000 of population respectively. But it should be borne in mind that these figures include the beds provided in special institutions such as mental hospitals, where the same bed remains occupied for years by the same patient. Of the total bed strength in the United States five per 1,000 of population are provided for mental cases.

In the United States it is considered adequate to provide beds for unspecialized cases, i.e. in general hospitals, at the rate of two to 2.5 beds per 1,000 population in rural areas and 2.5 to 4.5 per 1,000 in the smaller towns. Even then as a rule nearly 75% to 80% of beds remain occupied. The bed strength today in Ceylon, excluding special institutions such as tuberculosis and mental hospitals, is about 1.9 beds per 1,000. Most of the population live in rural areas and the majority of cases admitted to general hospitals are for acute diseases, the average duration of stay being only 8.6 days per patient.

Environmental sanitation is emphasized in a later section of this chapter and it is recommended that preference be given to preventive measures. These measures should markedly improve the sickness rates but it will be some time before that happens. Preventive measures are like long-term investments—they take time to bear fruit. Some immediate relaxation of the pressure on hospital accommodation can be secured by proper screening of admissions. In the special case of the tuberculosis hospitals, an increase in home treatment of patients will especially contribute to relaxing this pressure. Later it is to be hoped that more private practitioners will become available to attend patients in their homes.

A final consideration affecting the scale of expansion of hospital accommodations, and particularly its timing, is the availability of medical personnel to staff new hospitals. As already shown there is at present an acute shortage of doctors and nurses and the training of additional numbers takes a long time. Bearing in mind our conviction of the greater immediate importance of public health work and of the desirability in the curative field of increasing the number of doctors engaged in treating outdoor patients (itself a means of easing the pressure on hospital beds), we feel that it will be impossible for several years to make any large numbers of doctors and nurses available for hospital extensions.

In all the circumstances we feel that an ultimate target might be set (for the time being) at an over-all bed strength of 3.6 per

1,000 of population excluding special institutions, but that over the next 10 years it would probably not be possible to do more than increase the total by 50%, i.e. from 14,000 to 21,000 beds in general hospitals and from 6,000 to 9,000 in special institutions.

We accordingly recommend a provision of Rs. 90 million non-recurring expenditure spread over 10 years to provide 10,000 beds, and recurring expenditure for maintenance rising from Rs. 2 million to 20 million. The actual timing of construction must be related not only to the availability of building materials and workers, but also to the availability of medical personnel.

2. Health Clinics

Map No. 24 shows various institutions, such as central dispensaries, rural hospitals, maternity homes and health units, which are connected with both the curative and preventive branches of the Department of Medical and Sanitary Services. These are fairly well distributed in the rural and semi-urban areas according to the density of the population. Each of these institutions has a specific function to perform, but they work in coordination and are physically linked by ambulance services.

It is understood that the various institutions, curative and preventive, were developed as and when the need arose, and that their location was determined by the Minister of Health at the time in the light of local pressures for medical services. A few, even now, can be and are grouped to form a unit or a clinic, but an island-wide master plan for the development of completely coordinated units, at places selected only for their utility to the community, is lacking. Such a plan would of course have to be modified from time to time but it would serve to keep in the forefront the main objective of grouping and coordination.

It is recommended that an all-Ceylon plan should be drawn up to integrate the various rural and district medical health institutions into single all-purpose clinics.

3. MATERNITY HOMES

Ceylonese women are less bound by custom and caste restrictions than their sisters in India and are usually ready to seek the aid of modern medicine. In 1950, 33,739 women were delivered in hospitals, 21,551 in maternity homes, and 77,143 in homes under the supervision of public health nurses or trained midwives. Another 12,000 odd were delivered in rural and cottage hospitals. Thus out of total births of about 300,000 in 1950 nearly 50% were supervised by the Public Health Department.

Beside the maternity beds in hospitals, there are 113 maternity homes in the rural areas, sometimes located in out-of-the-way places. These have a bed strength of 1,168; 99 of these, with 1,039 beds, are run by the central government. These maternity homes are usually associated with a rural hospital or a central dispensary. They are visited once a week by the medical officer of health. Others are located at places perhaps five to 10 miles from another medical institute and are visited by the district medical officer of health, as a rule weekly.

In 1950, 31,093 cases were admitted to all these maternity homes and 21,551 women were delivered. The difference of 9,542 between the admissions of maternity cases and the deliveries is immediately striking; it appears to be a regular feature as in 1949 there was a similar excess of about 8,000. The only explanation available is that many cases were admitted prematurely and were discharged without being confined, but such a margin of error requires explanation.

These maternity homes are very popular indeed and it is good to see Ceylonese women taking full advantage of this facility. Practically everywhere one goes, be it to a provincial, district, or rural hospital or maternity home, there are a large number of waiting maternity patients and like other hospital cases they are fed and treated free of charge. Most of them come in an anaemic condition and are treated for it. They are also given treatment for hookworm as a "measure of routine," although reinfection is unfortunately practically certain when they return to their homes.

726

MAP 24

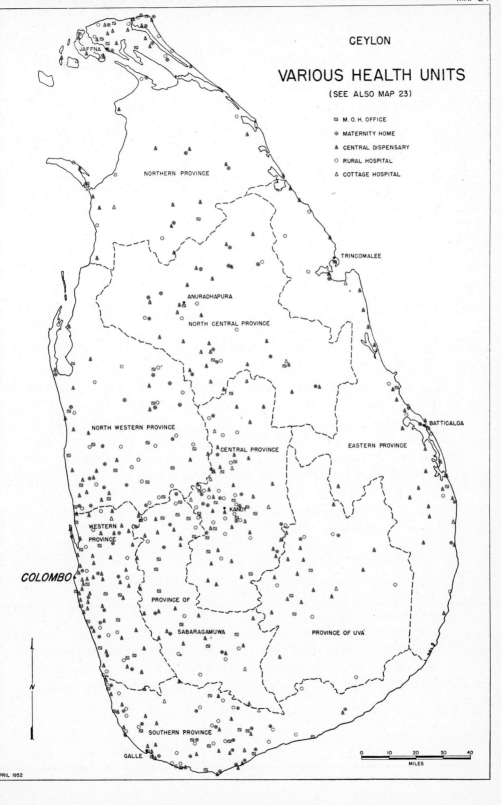

CEYLON

VARIOUS HEALTH UNITS

(SEE ALSO MAP 23)

⊠ M. O. H. OFFICE
⊕ MATERNITY HOME
▲ CENTRAL DISPENSARY
○ RURAL HOSPITAL
△ COTTAGE HOSPITAL

JAFFNA

NORTHERN PROVINCE

TRINCOMALEE

ANURADHAPURA

NORTH CENTRAL PROVINCE

NORTH WESTERN PROVINCE

CENTRAL PROVINCE

EASTERN PROVINCE

BATTICALOA

WESTERN
PROVINCE

KANDY

COLOMBO

PROVINCE OF

SABARAGAMUWA

PROVINCE OF UVA

SOUTHERN PROVINCE

GALLE

N

0   10   20   30   40
MILES

APRIL 1952

Some of these women guessed their time incorrectly and came several days and even weeks before the actual time. Some who had already had one or more deliveries in a maternity home perhaps subconsciously made a mistake in their calculations, having perhaps looked forward to this as a holiday from their homes where they had, as a rule, to work right up to the day of delivery and soon after. Maybe they came to avoid the wrath and displeasure of their mothers-in-law.

The demand for maternity beds is particularly heavy at provincial and district hospitals. In Jaffna for instance, where there are only 34 beds, the Religious Sister in charge stated that 230 deliveries had been cared for in the month of November, 1951. The very next day after delivery, the mother and child had to vacate the bed and be transferred to the category of "floor cases" to make room for other deliveries. They had to vacate even this floor space and be discharged after four or five days; 10 waiting cases had to be discharged unattended during the month. Conditions at the maternity homes in the rural areas, however, are very much better and the atmosphere is more congenial for the women to wait and gossip.

The popularity of confinement in the hospitals and maternity homes is increasing like a snowball. The day may not be distant when as many as half of the total number of deliveries may be expected to take place at these institutions. Instead of 55,000 as at present, 150,000 expectant mothers would then have to be cared for, clothed, fed and housed for a period which has recently averaged a little over 19 days for each delivery. Another 250 maternity homes would be required plus another 3,000 maternity beds at the provincial and district hospitals, with a corresponding number of doctors, nurses and midwives. In view of the acute shortage of personnel, such a demand could not be met for many years to come.

The present cost of a maternity home of 10 to 20 beds (with a double quarter for the nurse and the midwife and with equipment) ranges between Rs. 70,000 and Rs. 100,000. The cost of 250 maternity homes would be well over Rs. 20 million and the additional 3,000 maternity beds in hospitals would cost an equivalent sum. Such additional expenditure and the necessary allotment of medical personnel to provide more and more normal cases of delivery with care at the public expense, does not appear to be justified.

Provision for 10,000 additional hospital beds in all during the next five to 10 years has already been recommended and any additional maternity beds needed at provincial, district and other hospitals should be met from that provision.

It follows that it must be the aim of the health service to encourage the delivery of normal cases at home under trained supervision of nurses and midwives. To discourage and minimize normal cases who come for confinement weeks beforehand, a small fee should be charged, of 30 cents (US $.05) per day for those whose monthly family income is less than Rs. 80, fifty cents for those whose income is between Rs. 80 and 200 and Rs. 1 for those above that limit. Such a charge would ensure that about 50% of the patients partially paid for their stay. Its duration might be curtailed to a week or 10 days, with a corresponding reduction of cost.

Perhaps simple and cheap women's hostels constructed near the hospitals (instead of maternity homes) would be found useful. Here the expectant mothers could cook their own meals, wash their own clothes and keep the place clean themselves.

In principle the Department of Health has aimed to keep the expectant mothers busy by giving them some instruction both in handicraft to improve their family economy and in simple rules of infant care and home hygiene. But except in a very few cases, this aim was not realized. Perhaps an effort in collaboration with the cottage industries section of the Industrial Department would help to make the stay of the mother not only peaceful but also useful.

Dr. S. F. Chellappah, Deputy Director of the WHO Regional Office for South-East Asia, advanced the excellent idea of presenting a sapling of a mango or an orange tree to the outgoing mothers, to create a sentimental bond between the mother and the maternity home. This gesture also was expected to afford an opportunity for the sanitary inspector to visit the home and to do some useful health education and environmental hygiene work. The practice is said to have been short lived however, for want of adequate facilities from the Agriculture Department to supply the required saplings free of cost.

It is recommended that sufficient saplings of a mango or some other suitable plant should be supplied to permit realization of Dr. Chellappah's suggestion.

The Health Unit System

Preventive health work is based on the "Health Unit System," started in 1926 and embracing all the activities which constitute Personal Hygiene and Social Medicine. The objective was to have a complete system of health centers with an adequate staff to supervise specified urban and rural areas. For this purpose the island was originally divided into 63 health units, since increased to 91. Each unit contains one or more hospitals and dispensaries. The personnel consists of a trained full-time medical officer of health with a staff of five or six sanitary inspectors, five or six public health nurses and 10 to 12 public health midwives, each responsible for a definite area and a definite population. These units originated as models to look after a population of 40,000 to 50,000. But the malaria epidemic of 1934-35 created a problem of dealing with a very large number of sick people in the rural areas. The then Minister of Health, who had great faith in their usefulness, secured financial provision for 55 additional Health Units. This was most welcome to those interested in the public health movement, but it left unsolved the major problem of providing the necessary trained personnel for so large an undertaking.

Dr. J. H. L. Cumpston, the late Director General of Health Services of Australia who was specially invited by the Ceylon

729

Government to report, inter alia, on the relationship between and the coordination of the curative and preventive work of the Department, severely criticized the Health Unit System, considered it well nigh a failure and recorded his opinion that "the question is whether the present Health Unit has enough value to justify its retention."

Dr. Cumpston's most important recommendation about the Health Unit is that "the work of maternal and child health is almost entirely clinical and should be transferred to the control of the curative section of the department." He emphasized that the medical officers of health should concentrate on sanitation, nutrition and education.

Since the Health Unit is the foundation on which the preventive health work of the whole of the island is based, and since maternity and child welfare are its most important and popular activity, changes in its organization require very careful thought. Maternal and child welfare clinics offer a great opportunity, if properly used, for health education not only in the care of the mother and child but for the whole family. Preventive inoculation and measures for the control of epidemic diseases can be linked with the problems associated with the mother and the child. In maternal care work one may also win the confidence of the mother and thus gain entrance into the home to inculcate the principles of home hygiene and environmental sanitation. It should also be realized that the work done at the Maternal and Child Welfare Clinic is mostly antenatal and that all abnormal cases are referred to the hospital, becoming the responsibility of the physician there. In principle and in practice maternal and child welfare work is definitely concerned with the prevention, not the care, of disease. We cannot agree with Dr. Cumpston that it should be transferred to the curative section. It is therefore recommended that maternal and child welfare work should remain part of the functions of the Health Unit.

How far the Health Unit may have failed to achieve the expected results and why, is quite another matter. The functions of a Health Unit fall into three categories: (1) maternal and child welfare work; (2) environmental sanitation, control and prevention of infectious diseases including epidemiological studies; (3) health education of the public.

Maternity and Child Welfare Work. There are 701 health centers. At these centers 24,890 clinics were held by the health officers during 1950. They were assisted by 64 public health nurses and 1,063 trained midwives. There were 320,513 expectant mothers, 238,769 infants and 160,579 pre-school children under their care. Under the fixed programs of medical officers of health they devote four full days a week to conducting these clinics. Another day each week is devoted to medical examination of school children in their respective areas, leaving only a day or two each week for other functions of the Health Unit.

It is claimed that concentration on this particular activity accounts for the decrease in the infant mortality rate from 141 in 1946 to 84 in 1950 and in the maternal mortality rate from 15.5 to 5.7. This activity of the health unit must have played a part, but it is probable that the control of malaria has also made an important contribution. Malaria has always been considered as an important contributory cause of high infant and maternal mortality rates and has been known to be the villain of the piece whenever these rates did not respond to more general health measures. Moreover, although Health Units have been operating for the last 15 to 20 years, both maternal and infant mortality rates showed little net reduction up to 1946. The significant decreases occurred simultaneously with the spectacular decrease in malaria cases from 2.5 million to half a million. On the other hand the maternal and infant mortality rates also improved, though not so sharply, in several areas in the island where malaria had never been a public health problem. The improvement must therefore be taken to have been due to a variety of causes in which both the control of malaria and the welfare work of the department played large but not exclusive parts. Accordingly, although maternal and child welfare should, as already recom-

731

mended, remain a responsibility of the Health Unit, the medical officer of health should not devote four days a week to these clinics and the centers should not be treated as outdoor dispensaries for women and children.

It is therefore recommended that the other activities of the Health Unit should receive greater attention and the present over-emphasis on maternal and child welfare should definitely be abandoned.

Environmental Sanitation. There has been a great deal of good work in sanitation: a number of wells have been made sanitary, and many public, private and school latrines have been constructed as the result of strenuous efforts by the public health personnel. Nonetheless if the health officers had devoted more time and attention to this important branch of their activities a much smaller proportion of the latrines actually installed, and especially of the school latrines, would have been found defective. Therewith cases of intestinal infections, hookworm, diarrhoeas and dysenteries might have been more drastically reduced. Hookworm cases coming for treatment have alone ranged year after year between a million and one half to nearly two million. Improved sanitary conditions in general and in the home might be expected to have a powerful influence among children under five years of age.

Dr. Cumpston has rightly stressed the objective: "The total abolition of intestinal infections and parasites must be the goal and the road is through the prevention of soil, water and food pollution, with routine or spasmodic inoculations or medications as auxiliaries only." Such a goal may be far, far away, but it does need restressing. It is recommended that every medical officer of health should devote at least half of his time to this activity.

Health Education is the third important activity of the Health Unit. As early as 1936 the Director of Medical and Sanitary Services stated in his official report:

"The first Health Unit was started as a demonstration of the value of modern public health measures in safeguarding the

732

health and well being of the people. The result of over a decade of health unit work has clearly proved its value and the feasibility of carrying out public health measures successfully in rural and semirural areas.

"An indirect effect of inaugurating and working Health Units in different centers has been the impetus it has given to health work throughout the island which has increased in quantity and improved in quality. It has also roused keen public interest in health work and in this way has proved to be a valuable means of health propaganda."

Dr. Cumpston comments on this: "That was 13 years ago; I have been unable to form any reliable opinion as to whether all that was then claimed is still true, but the persistence of diseases due to pollution of soil, water and food suggests that the health propaganda has not been completely successful."

Health education is rightly considered as an integral part of health activities both in rural and urban areas. Undoubtedly it is a difficult task to change the habits of the people and one cannot expect spectacular results. But the potentialities are so great as to justify the utmost perseverance. Therefore policy should be reoriented to lay special emphasis on the child and the mother and above all on the million and a quarter of school-going children, nearly one fifth the total population. The health officer should spend more time away from his office and clinics and seek every opportunity in his field work of influencing education in the schools.

It is recommended that health education be given not only in the clinic, but also extended to the school and to the home, where mother and child can be reached amongst the environments in which they study and live. Health habits should be developed at the impressionable age and children should be made to practice a regular routine so that the remark, "they did not learn it in their youth," cannot be used as an excuse.

The Medical Officer of Health should be able to leave the actual running of health centers to the public health nurse and the midwife, who are fully trained for the purpose and who already run maternity homes independently. He should act only as a supervising officer, to be consulted in exceptional cases. One visit a month to each clinic may be sufficient. The health officer is primarily a field officer. Except for the minimum time that he may be required to spend at the office, his place is in the field to inspect the work of the sanitary inspectors, public health nurses, midwives, etc. He should devote special attention to the local government authorities in his area, prevailing upon them to provide protected water supplies and adequate drainage and encouraging them to undertake housing schemes.

Some authorities hold the view that if a medical officer of health concentrates on sanitation, nutrition, and education "it will remove the last vestige of attraction for a medical officer to do any health work." We suspect that if an officer requires such attraction he would be unlikely to do much environmental sanitation work. Public health work is the work of a missionary and to him no attraction or temptation is necessary. A health officer is a preventive man first and last and if he has not the missionary spirit and the urge to undertake prevention of disease, his rightful place is on the curative side, be it in the service of the state or outside it.

In sum the Health Unit System is certainly not to be condemned as a failure, but it has not achieved all that can be expected from it. One important cause of poor achievement, the fact that so many health officers are "conscripts," should become less important if our recommendations on recruitment are adopted. For the rest it is a matter of steadily shifting the emphasis to preventive and field activities.

SPECIFIC PROBLEMS—NUTRITION, MALARIA AND TUBERCULOSIS

1. NUTRITION

The nutrition problem in Ceylon, as everywhere, is a combination of problems in economics, agriculture and social conditions and habits. Naturally, economic status mainly determines the quantity and quality of the food eaten. Economically, Ceylon is better off than many underdeveloped countries. There are no obvious signs of famine, but with the universal prevalence of hookworm and the deficiencies in the diet mentioned hereafter, a great many people are in a state of malnutrition. The signs of chronic malnutrition—that is, low weight, anaemia and diarrhoea amongst children and impairment of the function of the liver and diarrhoea amongst adults—are not confined to the lowest income group, but are found even in the higher groups as the result of lack of knowledge of a well-balanced diet.

Food Stuffs. The staple food of the Ceylonese is rice. With this are taken yams, dhals, and a little fish and meat by those who have no objection on religious grounds. Those who live near the coast eat fresh fish. Although rice contains proteins of good quality they are hard to extract because of the bulk which has to be taken; rice is also deficient in calcium, iron, phosphorus and Vitamin A and B-1.

Milk, cheese, bread, butter, eggs, fruits, nuts and green vegetables enter the main meal solely as luxuries or delicacies. Only among the higher income groups are they part of the normal diet. But proteins, in which many of those foods are rich, are essential for the growth and repair of the body. Those of animal origin are preferable and are of particular importance to the vulnerable groups of the population, namely nursing and expectant mothers, infants and growing children.

Milk Supply. In the development of feeding programs for undernourished infants, children and expectant mothers, multivitamin tablets and mineral preparations are useful to make good the deficiencies, but greater emphasis should be placed on such foods as cod and shark liver oil, milk, fresh vegetables and fruit, all of which contain these essential elements.

Although Ceylon is an agricultural country it is one of the poorest milk producing and consuming countries in the world. The consumption of milk is extremely low, about two ounces per day per person as against seven ounces in India and more than 35 ounces in the United States and the United Kingdom. The production and distribution of milk should receive special attention. The government should ask the suggested Animal Husbandry Survey (see Chapter 11) to consider the advisability of establishing cooperative farms for the provision of dairy and meat products. A lesson may be learned from Bombay where the government undertook to supply pure milk of standard quality and in only four years has increased the numbers supplied from 50,000 to 500,000.

It is recommended that a sum of Rs. 1 million per year be provided to develop milk supply schemes.

One would like to see sufficient quantities of milk produced in the country as soon as possible. But until that goal is reached, dried whole milk and dried skimmed milk should be imported to supplement the local supply and distributed through maternity homes and schools at the midday meal. Steps should also be taken to encourage poultry keeping. The question of unfertilized egg production should be considered for orthodox Buddhists, whose principles debar any diet involving the taking of life.

Balanced Diet. The outstanding feature of the wartime diet was the replacement of rice by wheat flour. The substitution of flour for rice, to which the people had been accustomed from time immemorial, was achieved by a successful education campaign. The imports of wheat flour rose very substantially and although they have fallen somewhat since the war they are still many times higher than before, as the following figures show:

	Rice		Wheat Flour	
	000 cwts.	Rs. per Person*	000 cwts.	Rs. per Person*
1938	10,449	9.35	314	.32
1945	3,577	2.9	4,400	4.1
1950	9,808	6.76	3,310	2.63

* Rs. per person calculated at constant (1938) prices.

736

Generally speaking a Ceylonese home is not equipped for baking bread or making *chapatis*. Methods of cooking wheat preparations in a palatable form need to be greatly publicized.

Addition of yeast would fortify the protein deficient diet. The production of yeast from molasses, if and when a sugar factory is established, should be kept in mind. Similarly, edible vegetable oils might be fortified with vitamins A and C.

Cases of endemic goiter have been found in the southwest sector of the island, due presumably to the deficiency of iodine. As salt manufacture is a government monopoly, it should not be difficult to iodize salt and supply it through maternity homes and centers where necessary.

Whereas the nutritive value of imported foodstuffs needs to be publicized, there is a still greater need to publicize the importance of locally produced foods, methods of storage and preservation, and the value of a well balanced diet. A great deal of research should be undertaken in the nutritive values of the foodstuffs that could be produced locally. The possibility of producing protein rich items like soya beans and groundnuts should be explored in conjunction with the research workers of the Agriculture Department.

A short course in dietetics for matrons, nurses and midwives would serve a very useful purpose.

It is recommended that an intensive educational campaign through press and radio be launched and that the advantages of essential foodstuffs and of a well balanced diet be effectively stressed. Attractive and easily understandable charts, posters, leaflets, etc. in Tamil and Sinhalese as well as in English should be published.

2. MALARIA

Malaria has existed in Ceylon for many centuries and must have been one of the important causes of the decay of the ancient Sinhalese civilization. Together with malnutrition it ranks as one of the two foremost problems of public health in the country.

The most severe epidemic of malaria in recent times was that of 1934-35, which took a toll of 80,000 lives. Its immediate cause was the prolonged drought followed by late arrival of the south-west monsoon, which created ideal breeding grounds for the mosquitoes. But the high mortality and morbidity figures reflected not only the severity of infection, but also the undernourishment of the people. The drought caused a failure of crops. The consequent shortage of food supplies aggravated the undernourishment already made severe by the depression of the early thirties.

Control. The most remarkable achievement of recent years has been the spectacular reduction in the death rate of malaria from 1,315 per million in 1945 to 215 in 1950 and the reduction in the number of cases from over 2.5 million to about one million in the same period. The following table shows the malaria morbidity for the island.

TABLE VIII
MALARIA MORBIDITY 1936-1950

Year	Estimated Population	Number of Cases	Morbidity Rate per 1,000
1936	5,631,000	2,947,555	523
1937	5,712,000	2,398,976	404
1938	5,810,000	2,053,079	353
1939	5,897,000	3,210,795	544
1940	5,951,000	3,413,618	574
1941	6,020,000	3,220,360	535
1942	6,021,000	3,225,477	536
1943	6,134,000	2,141,329	349
1944	6,276,000	1,672,478	266
1945	6,496,000	2,539,949	391
1946	6,695,000	2,768,385	413
1947	6,879,000	1,350,521	196
1948	7,086,000	775,276	109
1949	7,297,000	727,769	100
1950	7,550,000	610,781	81

This remarkable reduction is due to the use of DDT as a residual spray. It has not only reduced the mortality and morbidity figures, but it has actually reduced the endemicity of malaria. This is shown by the simultaneous reductions in the spleen rate from 21.2 in March 1938 to 2.7 in March 1949 and in the parasite rate from 415 to 0.6. Along with this reduction in the incidence of malaria since 1946, total deaths and infant and maternal mortality rates have fallen markedly, although deaths due to diarrhoea, enteritis, bronchitis and pneumonia remain unaffected.

Outlook. This quick and marked success has led the specialists to say: "If the present methods could be continued for a period of five years the vector (*Anopholese culicifacies*) would be reduced to still lower levels. There is no reason to consider that the present scheme of anti-malaria work carried out in Ceylon will not lead to malaria eradication within a reasonable period of time at a cost which this country can afford without serious financial embarrassment." [3] Another Ceylonese authority states: "There will never be an epidemic of malaria in Ceylon. With the present organization, it can safely be assured that there will never be this danger. This organization will never permit of a situation such as the one which arose during the previous epidemic." [4]

It is good to be optimistic of ultimate eradication of malaria and consequent saving in funds as well as men and material. But one should be rather cautious in predicting future trends, particularly when the important predisposing factors, malnutrition, undernourishment and hookworm infection, continue as before to sap the vitality of the people. Moreover, as *A. culicifacies*, the only known vector, has recently been found to breed in thick jungles well away from any human habitation, the danger con-

---

[3] Joint Report for 1950 by the Superintendent, Anti-Malarial Measures, and the Chief Entomologist.

[4] Director of Medical and Sanitary Services, as reported in *Ceylon Observer*, 30th November, 1950.

tinues to lurk. Consequently, there should be no premature relaxation of the effort in the name of economy.

It is therefore recommended that the DDT spray measures should be pursued with vigor and extended to newly developing areas of colonization.

Legislation. The Mosquito Borne Diseases Regulations (Ceylon Gazette, June 21, 1946) were prepared to facilitate the anti-larval program of the Malaria Services. These regulations now need to be amended in view of the new effective weapon, DDT residual spray, which is directed against the destruction of *adult* mosquitoes inside the houses.

It is recommended that the regulations should be so amended as to give anti-malaria personnel authority to enter all buildings or man-made shelters for the purpose of disinsectizing all rooms. A penalty should be provided against those who habitually leave their houses closed on the day of the malaria unit's visit. Furthermore, in the land development system it should be made obligatory in the contract of the colonists that they carry out or permit the public health authorities to carry out all anti-malaria measures the latter may specify.

Full cooperation and coordination of efforts between the Department of Agriculture, Development and Public Health should be assured so that all houses built by the Department of Development and Agriculture are well sprayed with DDT *before* they are occupied by the colonists.

The large irrigation and other public works under way are likely to create a number of potential breeding places for mosquitoes. The public health authorities will do well to take special interest in these schemes and get proper drainage provided in the very first instance. This would prevent the appearance of waterlogging and breeding grounds for mosquitoes—the so called "man-made" malaria conditions.

DDT Supply. In the near future Ceylon is expected to have a DDT plant of its own with a capacity of 500 tons. It will be put up in cooperation with UNICEF. Efforts are being made to guarantee availability of the alcohol, benzine, sulphuric acid and chlorine required. A new drug, Dieldrin, is gaining favor as a possible improved substitute for DDT; it is claimed to be a double purpose insecticide, equally efficacious against flies as well as mosquitoes. The possibilities of its use in Ceylon should be investigated.

3. TUBERCULOSIS

Incidence. Tuberculosis is such an insidious disease that it is extremely difficult to get an accurate idea of the number of people suffering from it, but it was estimated in 1944 at 40,000 and is generally believed to have doubled since.

Attendance at the various chest clinics was as follows:

1949	38,414
1950	48,747

The increase in clinic attendances is probably due to (i) increasing awareness of the modern facilities provided at the clinics in the big towns; (ii) discovery of cases as a result of examination of persons known to have been in contact with patients; and (iii) mass radiography both at the clinics and through the mobile unit presented by UNICEF. But there may well be also a real increase in the incidence of the disease, as most of the predisposing causes—malnutrition, overcrowding, unsanitary conditions, ignorance and poverty—are found in many densely populated areas. But while tuberculosis is said to be the disease of the poor, it is also the cause of poverty; if it appears in a middle class family it makes them poor and thus starts the vicious circle of poverty and tuberculosis, tuberculosis and poverty.

Bed Strength. The total bed strength in various institutions is 1,658; the following number of cases of pulmonary tuberculosis were treated as in-patients in recent years.

1948	10,114
1949	10,646
1950	11,454

As improved diagnostic facilities discover more cases, there is a continuously increasing demand for beds in the various hospitals. Institutional treatment is certainly better than treatment at home, even if medical treatment were available there. It is in the interest of the family as well as the patient himself to remove the source of infection, particularly from the children. Moreover, in the sanitarium or the hospital the patient can more easily be taught sanitary habits so as not to spread the infection when he returns to his own home.

Home Treatment. Although the need for more beds is obvious and some additional ones must be provided, it is as yet impossible to provide free hospitalization to all cases of tuberculosis, for a tuberculous patient continues to occupy the same bed for many months. Therefore as an alternative, home treatment must be given its proper place and must be supplemented by an intensive educational effort in the home of the patient. At present only the health visitors go to the home and coax contacts to come to the clinic for examination. If fully trained doctors could follow up the health visitors' work, and provide treatment not only at the clinic but also at the home of the patient in selected cases, pressure on special institutions would decrease.

Voluntary Effort. In a country where long established custom places practically all the responsibility for medical work on the government, it was heartening to learn of the energetic Ceylon National Association for Prevention of Tuberculosis. This society has aroused a great deal of public interest in the problem and is even building a children's 50-bed tuberculosis ward at Welisara. The educational campaign of the association deserves the wholehearted support of public health authorities at all levels, particularly of the Medical Officers of Health in charge of the Health Units.

It is therefore recommended that the Medical Officers of Health should try to establish branches of this association in their respective areas.

In collaboration with WHO an intensive and comprehensive Anti-Tuberculosis campaign has recently been launched. The BCG campaign (vaccination with Bacillus Calmette Guerin) is being enthusiastically conducted and so is the diagnostic drive by mass radiography. Home visits and examinations of contacts have also received great impetus.

ENVIRONMENTAL SANITATION

1. GENERAL

At Anuradhpura are to be seen in a fair state of preservation three open bathing tanks, constructed about 2,000 years ago. They are fed by a stream and built at different levels. The one at the highest level was said to be reserved for drinking water, the one at the next level for bathing and the lowest for washing and for cattle. This indicates that the ancients understood the importance of the pollution of water. This impression is corroborated by the practice of constructing drinking wells in the temples, which the priests were charged to safeguard against pollution, and by the requirement of bathing before prayers. Similarly, in the old buildings evidence is to be found of the construction of drains to dispose of wastewater and drain it away from human habitations. The people in those times therefore must have been familiar, if only empirically, with the importance of personal hygiene and sanitation.

Modern scientific knowledge tells us how and why environmental sanitation is necessary for the prevention of disease and the preservation of health. We can demonstrate that cholera, typhoid, paratyphoid and dysenteries are water-borne and, by practical application of this knowledge, we can completely eradicate these diseases not only in a small community but in an entire nation. There can be no better demonstration than the complete eradication of typhoid in such a vast country as the United States. Only 50 years ago, typhoid killed as many as 40 persons out of every 100,000 in several states. Today, it is unknown. As waterworks spread, typhoid declined.

743

Sickness rates in Ceylon have not fallen with death rates. Sickness is higher where unsanitary conditions and overcrowding are the worst. In the densely populated Colombo district the death rate from tuberculosis is 10 times that of Nuwara Eliya district, where the density of population is about one quarter that of Colombo. Environmental sanitation has been the weakest link in the prevention of disease and the preservation of health. In the succeeding paragraphs, attention is drawn to the important subjects of water supply, drainage and housing.

Although the solution of these problems depends primarily upon the availability of adequate funds and upon the execution of engineering projects, yet the responsibility of stressing their importance remains with the public health workers. They must emphasize and reemphasize that the government should follow a bold and well-planned policy in the interest of the health of the people, which will, in turn, improve their productivity and economic status.

At present the expenditure through the Medical and Sanitary Department on the curative services is about Rs. 96 million and on preventive services about Rs. 20 million. Expenditure is also incurred through the Local Government Department in the form of assistance towards various activities of local authorities. The allotments for sanitary services for 1951 through this agency were:

Village wells	Rs. 1,000,000
Sanitation in village committee areas	75,000
Maternal and child welfare	400,000
Slum clearance	2,000,000
Housing	3,000,000
Drainage	350,000

All these are steps in the right direction and the expenditure on preventive schemes will certainly pay in the long run by saving money which would otherwise be required to expand hospital facilities.

Interdepartmental Cooperation. As nearly 85% of the population lives in rural areas, the role of the Rural Development Department is of great importance. Besides its many other activities, the Department is devoting special attention to rural sanitary work. This program includes health drives, clean-up campaigns, construction of latrines, wells and drains. Also included in the program are milk marketing schemes to supply milk to pre-school children at the feeding centers and to school children at their midday meal. These activities afford many opportunities for the district health officer to come in direct touch with Rural Development officers and with the 5,000 odd Rural Development Societies.

Ceylon's local government structure for rural areas consists of 36 town councils and 400 village committees, whose elected members have certain powers and duties with regard to public health and sanitation. Here is a field where a sanitary inspector can show his initiative and enthusiasm; if his work is adequately supervised by the district medical officer of health, much avoidable sickness may be prevented. This, however, can only be done if that officer spends less time at his desk and gets out into the field where he belongs.

With so many departments such as Revenue, Local Government, Rural Development, Cooperative and even Social Services taking keen interest in the improvement of sanitary conveniences, overlapping is bound to occur.

It is therefore recommended that the Medical and Sanitary Department should take the initiative in channeling the efforts of these departments to prevent overlapping and to maintain intimate liaison and cooperation at all levels between its staff and the staffs of these departments.

2. WATER SUPPLY

General. Unfortunately the geological formation of Ceylon is such that most of the rain water drains away rapidly to the sea. Some of it does percolate to supply underground sweet water in a few pockets of limestone in the northwest coastal belt (Jaffna

Peninsula to Puttalam) and in narrow coastal tracts elsewhere. Generally speaking these pockets are only about 20 to 30 feet deep, supporting only shallow wells with small yields. Typical artesian conditions are unknown. Even in Jaffna Peninsula the lower layers of limestone are charged with salt water and the wells cannot be dug beyond 30 feet.

As a consequence securing water for drinking and domestic purposes in Ceylon has always been difficult. Mostly it has to come from shallow wells, springs, rivers and streams and tanks, not only in the rural areas but also in those of the urban councils. Out of seven municipal councils five have piped water while two do not; but barring Colombo, the supply is neither adequate nor satisfactory from a public health point of view. Even most of the hospitals have to depend upon wells, springs and streams for their water supplies. Various new schemes are in hand but their execution is very slow for want of technical staff and contractors.

Water-Borne Diseases. In these circumstances the large numbers of admissions to hospitals from water-borne diseases is not surprising. Figures for recent years follow.

	Outdoor	Indoor	Total
1948	2,133,706	75,414	2,209,120
1949	2,828,408	94,489	2,922,897
1950	2,845,496	107,445	2,952,941

This group of diseases includes dysenteries, diarrhoeas and enteric fevers most of which are known to be water-borne; it also includes hookworm. The sickness caused by water-borne diseases is fully realized by the public health administration and, of the five items of the rural sanitation scheme, "boiled water for drinking" has received first consideration. However, less than 1% of the total number of houses are reported to use it.

Individual Supply Schemes

(a) *Colombo.* The water supply system of Colombo was established in 1889, based on a reservoir constructed in Labugama

746

about 30 miles to the east. An extension of the scheme is under construction. A second main pipe of 30 inches has been laid and a new reservoir together with a filtration and purification plant is being built in Kalatuwawa a few miles from the first. The construction work is the responsibility of the Colombo Municipality, finance having been provided by loans from the central government totalling Rs. 16 million.

(b) *Other Areas.* Some of the other water supply schemes are also old, like that of Kandy completed in 1879, and that of Galle completed in 1892; they are now inadequate. In Kandy some improvements have been completed but a general remodelling and extension of the scheme is under consideration. In 1945 there were 31 other water supply schemes in operation; only a few have been added since.

(c) *Further Schemes under Study or Construction.* The Public Works Department has about 43 town water schemes and 87 village water schemes on its priority lists but development is slow. In the second quarter of 1951, five of the town schemes and only one of the village schemes were under construction. Some schemes were under study and estimates for about five for towns and 18 for villages were available. To remedy the lack of permanent staff which is delaying these studies, the investigation of three town schemes has been entrusted to a British company and the study of a scheme for the suburban area south of Colombo to a French company. This last scheme is of substantial size, being intended to provide water to about 250,000 inhabitants scattered over an area extending about 27 miles south along the coast from Colombo to the Kalganga. The estimated cost of a project prepared a few years ago was Rs. 46.5 million. It is said four alternatives have been proposed by the French company but no details are available.

Proposed Further Developments. The sanitary engineering section of the Health Ministry has put forward an ambitious program for the development of water supplies, drainage and sewerage on the island. Estimated to cost in all nearly Rs. 300 million spread over five years, the program is divided as follows:

	Number of Schemes	Cost (million rupees)
Municipalities	3	66.
Urban councils	15	180.
Town councils	25	37.5
Villages	50	13.5
Total		*297.*

Central Responsibility and Organization. Sanitary wells and springs can supply water for small villages and out of the way habitations, but for piped water supplies catchment areas will have to be demarcated. Dams small or big will have to be built, maybe at different levels on the same stream; reservoirs and storage tanks, filtration beds and the like will have to be provided. In certain cases several miles of main pipe lines will have to be laid; the opportunity could be taken to supply water enroute to bazaar areas and village communities. In the very nature of things the problem of design and supply will have to be a central responsibility, although regional boards may need to be created for detailed operations. Local distribution could be entrusted to the local authorities, but even here central control will be necessary to prevent waste.

The Ministry of Public Works already has a section in charge of studying water supplies, with a staff, on paper, of about 100. In fact only a skeleton of this section exists. At the time the Mission was in Ceylon, the former head, a water supply expert, had left and his successor had not arrived. The acting head was a senior engineer, but he was almost alone, without a construction or investigation engineer. Of 10 district engineers provided in the budget only one was actually serving and of 21 draftsmen 21 were missing. It is not surprising that the study of the schemes already mentioned is going so slowly.

In the Health Ministry there is a Sanitary Engineering Section

748

in charge of the sanitary works in the towns and villages. Its staff is no larger than that of the Waterworks Section of the Public Works Department. The division of the activities of the two sections is not quite clear, but the tendency of the Sanitary Engineering Section is to deal with the village works and to leave the larger projects in the towns to the Waterworks Section.

Recommendations for Development. Normally water supplies must be drawn from the rivers and will be closely connected with other uses of water, especially irrigation. A first requirement is, therefore, an all-Ceylon survey of all possible sources of water supply, as part of the general survey of water resources recommended in Chapter 13. It may be desirable to call in the services of an outside engineering firm with experience of big water supply schemes, following the precedents already set in the study of certain individual projects. Such a survey will of course also have to take into account the provision of water-carriage systems of sewerage and drainage which are discussed further below.

Any general plan of development of water supplies must clearly await such a general survey as well as detailed studies, but it is possible to indicate an order of magnitude of expenditure which may be justified in this field in the next few years. The quarterly report of the PWD waterworks section shows an average cost of Rs. 50,000 for village schemes and Rs. 500,000 for town council schemes; an average of Rs. 2 million for urban council schemes can be assumed. For the municipalities Rs. 10 million might be allowed and a special allowance of Rs. 30 million included for the suburban area south of Colombo. A reasonable program would then be:

	Number of Schemes	Cost (million rupees)
Southwest suburb of Colombo	1	30
Municipalities	3	30
Urban councils	15	30
Town councils	25	12.5
Villages	50	2.5
Total		*105.0*

The yearly expense, spread over five years, would be about Rs. 20 million. But water supply schemes need much steel pipe and heavy machinery; it is likely that the execution of such a program would take much longer than five years, perhaps as long as 10 to 15 years. On a 10 year basis the yearly expenditure would be about Rs. 10 million. Completion of the program even in that period is unlikely to be possible, however, unless the departments concerned get help from outside in its preparation and planning. Hence the importance of the proposal to extend the practice of engaging the services of specialized companies that have the trained staff to carry out such studies in a short time. The waterworks section and the sanitary engineering section will be relieved of the heavy burden of detailed planning and can be used with advantage to control the work of the companies. The coordination of the different schemes and their integration in a general program of water development must remain with the organization in charge of the central planning of development.

3. CONSERVANCY, DRAINAGE AND SEWAGE SYSTEMS

The provision of protected water supplies alone will not be sufficient to control the gastro-intestinal diseases. The removal of human excreta without pollution of soil and water is equally important to public health.

Latrines. The Medical and Sanitary Department is fully alive to the necessity of satisfactory disposal of human excreta. It has evolved a simple type of latrine which, if used with ordinary care, is quite satisfactory. As many as 350,000 houses, out of nearly a million, have been provided with latrines. Efforts are also being made by Revenue, Local Government, Rural Development, Cooperative, and Social Service Departments to improve water supplies and to construct latrines to cover most of the island. An intimate liaison to avoid overlapping should be maintained through the provincial and regional offices of the Medical and Sanitary Department.

Unfortunately, the latrines are quite often misused and become defective, as is shown by the following table taken from the Administrative Report for 1950.

TABLE IX

PROVISION OF LATRINES

	1948	1949	1950
Existing Latrines			
Public	1,741	1,826	1,836
Private	282,697	293,523	313,825
School	7,609	7,806	8,171
Latrines Found Defective			
Public	707	723	664
Private	66,216	57,110	73,776
School	3,066	3,298	3,942

The latrines in the schools, both government and state aided, are built by the Education Department. It is obvious that adequate attention is not paid to keeping them in good order. It is essential that the Public Health and Education Departments cooperate fully with each other to keep this sanitary convenience in the schools in good condition. There it serves an object lesson to the pupils who need to be taught health habits in their impressionable age.

Emphasis on the proper use of latrines in schools is particularly important in view of the very high prevalence of hookworm infestation, which accounts both for a high percentage of ill-health and anaemia and for physical and mental retardation of children.

Drainage and Sewerage. A drainage system to dispose of the sewage water, human excreta and other community wastes by a water-carriage system is the most satisfactory method. Every urban area, particularly municipal and town councils, ought if possible to be served by underground sewers. As in the case of water supply, here again, with the solitary exception of Colombo City, none of the major towns, and still less the bazaar areas, which are fast developing along the roads as ribbon developments, has any drainage system worth the name. In Colombo itself, although the water-borne drainage scheme was started as early as 1902, not more than 20,000 out of 60,000 houses have proper sewerage systems.

In view of the rapid growth of urban areas and the rapid increase in population, drainage and sewage schemes should form an integral part of any development program. Adequate disposal of human excreta should receive priority over the disposal of sullage and storm waters. Separate systems of disposal will be found cheaper than a combined one. Sewerage system and water supplies must be coordinated and the former should not be installed without an adequate water supply. As already recommended, therefore, drainage and sewerage requirements should be taken into account in any general planning of water development on an all-Ceylon basis.

4. Housing

Although Ceylon is fortunate at present in not having very many slum areas in towns, there are a few where the density of population is as high as 100 to 250 persons per acre. Slum conditions are being created by dividing and subdividing houses which were originally built for a single family. The low rate of house building during the war years and subsequently has resulted in an acute shortage of houses, and materials are also short and labor is scarce; consequently building costs have gone up considerably in recent years. In spite of the Rent Restriction Act, it is said that in big towns, where there has been an influx of population from rural areas as well as a rapid natural increase of population, hundreds of families are paying exorbitant rents and many more are without proper accommodations.

The adverse effects of such overcrowding are reflected in the marked increase in respiratory diseases; cases of pulmonary tuberculosis are believed to have nearly doubled from 40,000 to 80,000 since 1944.

The number of outdoor and indoor hospital cases classified as "Affections of Respiratory System" has increased since 1948 as follows:

	Outdoor	Indoor	Total
1948	841,582	62,197	903,779
1949	919,402	72,596	991,998
1950	1,187,023	90,754	1,277,777

Moreover, in crowded households the common infectious diseases show an earlier age incidence. In Ceylon this is reflected by the continued high proportion (43-45%) of deaths amongst children under five years of age to the total number of deaths.

The need to improve housing conditions, particularly cross ventilation, is all the greater in Ceylon where, except in the hills, there is very little variation between day and night temperatures and between one season and the other. Therefore in poorly ventilated houses the air remains stagnant and vitiated. The occupants do not lose latent heat from the surface of their bodies and thus feel uncomfortable, exhausted and unwell. Coupled with malnutrition these conditions predispose people to tuberculosis.

To improve these conditions new houses will have to be built to meet the shortage, and schemes for slum clearance will have to be pushed with vigor. There is an excellent Housing Ordinance which authorizes the improvement of existing unsanitary buildings and the demolition of those unfit for human habitation. Under the Housing Loan Act, the government can make grants and advance loans to Local Authorities as well as to Cooperative Societies and individuals. But in spite of the good intentions of the government and of local bodies, little progress has been made. There have been many political and social obstacles as well as the great scarcity of architects, engineers and draftsmen which handicaps all building and all the activities of the Public Works Department.

The delay in pushing the housing drive energetically is likely to cause conditions to worsen. The magnitude of the housing problem is such that it needs a completely new approach if the problem is to be solved successfully.

We believe that a vigorous effort is needed to try to solve the problem of scarcity of materials by the discovery of new methods and types of building and by promoting the use of local materials.

In India the Forest Department has been conducting a great deal of research in cheap building material which may be developed from local products. Ceylon appears to have a similar potential which should be explored. A WHO team has recently been investigating the best type of house for tropical and subtropical climates and their report should be useful. Many firms in the West are undertaking research and have found cheap building materials with which buildings could be constructed quickly and with a minimum of skilled labor. Outside help from such sources may be very valuable; by combining foreign know-how and local material, quicker and cheaper construction may be possible.

The whole field of research into building material and techniques appears a very suitable activity for the industrial research unit which the Mission has recommended elsewhere. If that recommendation is accepted, we hope that research in building will be given a high priority. Such research may well eventuate in proposals for local manufacture of materials which would be a useful contribution to industrial development.

We recommend also that to coordinate the work of various agencies interested in the building program, a Housing Commissioner under the Commissioner of Local Government be appointed. It would be one of the main duties of such an officer to consider what further central government assistance towards housing might be proper.

It is extremely difficult to assess the expenditure it is reasonable to provide for publicly assisted housing schemes. The potential cost is very high indeed. Having regard to other calls on the public purse we would recommend the earmarking of a sum of Rs. 5 million a year for housing schemes.

5. LEGISLATION ON PUBLIC HEALTH MATTERS

There are several ordinances which deal with public health and various Ministries play a part in it. Thus the Ministry of Labor and Social Services deals with Vital Statistics, the Ministry of Education with the provision of spectacles and feeding of children, the Ministry of Home Affairs with fairs and festivals and Local Government with slaughter houses.

Legislation which was before Parliament at the end of 1951 designed to reorganize the Health Services would, if enacted, certainly be a great advance and should serve a very useful purpose. But the feasibility of a comprehensive Public Health Act should be investigated, aimed, inter alia, at better enforcement of sanitary provisions. It may be argued that the organization of public opinion should precede legislation. Such a dictum may possibly be true for Western countries today, where people generally are both educated and disciplined, but it has certainly not always been true of those countries and in Ceylon, as elsewhere in Asia, it remains very necessary for legislation to be somewhat ahead of public opinion. Better legislation would make people conscious of their responsibilities and obligations, and if the penalties were imposed without fear or favor, sanitary habits would certainly improve.

THE AYURVEDIC SYSTEM OF MEDICINE

Popular Support. On the second day of the session of the Ceylon Assembly which opened on November 21, 1951, a resolution was moved asking the government to open Ayurvedic hospitals and dispensaries in important towns and places on the same lines as those set up for modern medicine. The unanimity of the praise given from both sides of the House to the system and the demand for extending these facilities was impressive. Government spokesmen accepted the importance of Ayurveda as a system of medicine

755

for Ceylon and promised to give further grants-in-aid to any local body which would set up Ayurvedic institutions but did not agree to establish parallel government hospitals and dispensaries based on the indigenous system.

Leading articles in such important English-language newspapers as the *Ceylon Times* and *Ceylon Observer* have strongly supported revival of the system and urged the government to provide adequate funds and machinery for the purpose. The following quotations from an official publication, *The Health of the Nation*, issued for the Ministry of Health and Local Government on the occasion of the Third South-East Asian Session of the WHO held at Kandy in 1950, reflect prevailing opinion on the indigenous system:

"A system that has stood the test of time in spite of neglect must have something good in it, otherwise a large percentage of the population will not resort to it in times of illness."

"When Ceylon became a subject country the medical systems of the conquerors were developed and supported to the utter neglect of the indigenous systems. State aid declined and ceased altogether. Hospitals maintained by the Sinhalese kings were replaced by hospitals and dispensaries of Western medicine. Though bereft of state aid, the indigenous system of medicine continued to exist side by side with the Western system and ministered to the needs of the great majority of the population."

Professor H. Cullumbine in the Ceylon *Journal of Medical Sciences* for December 1950, records: "It is difficult to assess the value of these systems or to compare them with Western medicine. Many of the inhabitants have great faith in them and there seems to have been a considerable increase in the number of patients seeking these forms of treatment. The indigenous hospital, for example, has increased the number of out-patients attending per year by over 500% since 1942.

The Ayurvedic system does not recognize surgical methods of treatment, but many practitioners do not hestitate to prescribe and to dispense the latest synthetic drugs from the West. Others have faith only in the ancient remedies, though all are handicapped by the difficulties of obtaining these in sufficiently large quantities and by the lack of an Ayurvedic pharmacopoea."

It has therefore to be conceded that the indigenous system has at the minimum a very strong sentimental appeal to the people of Ceylon and that there is a genuine demand for it. Our examination of its position has therefore been dispassionate but sympathetic.

History. A brief historical sketch and description of the system appears to be necessary as a background for its understanding and for evaluation of its usefulness.

Ayurveda or "the knowledge of life" developed in the dim and distant past and is claimed to be of divine origin. It was introduced into Ceylon by the followers of Vijaya who came from India in the fifth century B.C. The two great exponents of the system in India were Charak and Sushrata who lived almost 2,000 years ago. Charak was a physician who arranged his teaching in the form of dialogues with his pupils. These deal with the duties of the physician, diets, drugs, diseases and death, improvement of health and vigor, enjoyment of life and the nature of the soil and its relation to the body.

Sushrata was a surgeon with some knowledge of anatomy. He insisted on dissection of the human body as necessary both for theory and practice. To the Ayurved practitioner of today surgery is only of academic interest, as its practice fell into the hands of the low caste barbers after Buddha preached against the taking of life.

Theory. Ayurveda assumes that the body is composed of three elements—wind, phlegm and bile—from which seven primary constituents of the body (blood, flesh, fat, bone, marrow, bile and semen) originate. According to this belief the *Vital Force,* the regulator of the body, is composed of all the seven constituents and disturbance in their composition produces disease. But such a disturbance is not the sole cause of the disease; climatic conditions, heredity, poison, accidents, over-eating and "karma" also play a part in its production. "Karma" is the law of retribution: "As you sow, so shall you reap." Disease is considered a manifestation of and a punishment for all deeds not only in this life, but also in the previous one.

Not only the derangement of wind, phlegm and bile, but sometimes also demoniacal possession, the anger of supernatural powers or the sins of the parents are thought to cause disease. Signs and portents which have no bearing on the disease sometimes enter into its diagnosis, prognosis and treatment, including even the personality of the messenger who summoned the physician. As a parallel it may be mentioned that there was a time even in England when medicine was applied to the spear and not to the wound.

So far as they concerned public health, earlier sanitary practices were closely associated with religion. Bathing before prayer was enjoined, drinking from the same cup was prohibited. Wells for drinking water were often constructed as a part of the temples, and the priests were commanded to prevent their pollution. Arrangements were made to drain away sullage water, and disposal of filth was entrusted to people of low caste. The caste system itself is the precursor of modern eugenics.

Candidates for the study of Ayurveda were carefully selected and had to be of high mental caliber and character. The physician was to be chaste and abstemious, to wear a beard and to speak the truth. He was to eat no meat. He was required to treat gratuitously teachers, preachers, the poor, the pious and the orphans.

It was with such ideals that in the days gone by the kings of Ceylon, like the kings of India, built hospitals and asylums for the sick, including animals. This system, because of its history, tradition and practice, remained attached to religion and consequently became dogmatic and static. All progress was looked at askance, so much so that a true exponent and devotee of the system even today is not prepared to accept what he calls the "germ theory." To him it is still a theory and he discounts the discoveries of Jenner, Pasteur, Koch and others whose application has saved millions of lives.

There is no doubt that through centuries of trial and error a wide variety of herbal and other preparations have been developed, many of which help to relieve symptoms of various minor ailments and even give temporary relief in diseases of serious nature. The claims made are often vague and sometimes exaggerated. The drugs as a rule are mostly used in their crude form and are cheap and easily obtainable. As such they have a great appeal to the people.

Official Recognition. In Ceylon the indigenous system received its first official recognition in modern times in 1928. A Board of Indigenous Medicine was established and in 1929 a college and hospital were opened with 72 students on the roll and a government maintenance grant of Rs. 50,000.

The Indigenous Medicine Ordinance, No. 17 of 1941, provided for the continuance of the College and the Hospital of Indigenous Medicine as Government institutions. Since then they have expanded considerably. By 1950 state expenditure on these institutions had risen to Rs. 778,276. Since its inception the College has turned out over 500 practitioners of indigenous medicine, the majority of whom have settled down in the rural areas to minister to the needs of the rural population.

The hospital and the out-patient department have been popular institutions. The number treated in the out-patient department has increased from 61,782 in 1942 to 422,803 in 1950, and in-patient cases increased from 981 to 3,197 during the same period.

As there has been difficulty in getting reliable Ayurvedic remedies the government has established a pharmacy to manufacture medicines. The Board of Indigenous Medicine has been entrusted with the task of registering practitioners. More than 5,000 applications have been received.

Training. Although the indigenous system has rendered valuable services in giving medical relief to a large number of people both in the urban and rural areas, neither in India nor in Ceylon

759

has there been, broadly speaking, any carefully controlled study to evaluate the principles on which the system is based. In fact, the indigenous institutions, wherever set up, have by themselves accepted an inferior position which has been all the more emphasized by their admitting students of much inferior basic qualifications. Thus the training and the general standard of education has been of an inferior type.

Although in Ceylon the College and the Hospital for Indigenous Medicine are under the Ministry of Health, the Director of Medical and Sanitary Services has no control whatsoever over them. The institutions are therefore segregated and work in a watertight compartment.

It is recommended that in their own interest these institutions should be placed, like any other institution dealing with preventive and curative medicine, directly under the Director of Medical and Sanitary Services.

Such supervision and guidance will enable the system to develop on scientific lines and will give it an opportunity to make its own contribution to the modern knowledge of medicine. The indigenous system should develop shoulder to shoulder with the Medical College for modern medicine. An Ayurved practitioner must be prepared to change his outlook. He must not continue with obsolete methods and usages; if these are retained merely on traditional or emotional grounds progress will be indefinitely retarded. Equally, the contribution of traditional methods worked out over the centuries should be welcomed by practitioners of modern medicine when their value is proven by objective investigation.

The following detailed suggestions as to training are made:

(1) The standard of admission should be the same as in the Medical College for modern medicine, namely, intermediate science with physics, chemistry, botany and zoology as compulsory subjects.

(2) Teaching in anatomy, physiology and pathology should be improved.

760

(3) Sufficient knowledge of minor surgery should be required to enable the practitioner to be in a position to call in a surgeon when necessary.

(4) Teaching should be reoriented to impart knowledge in up-to-date diagnosis and nomenclature of diseases.

(5) Special training in bacteriology and in the causes, prevention and control of infectious diseases should be provided.

(6) Adequate training in midwifery and maternity and child welfare work should be instituted.

(7) Training should also be given in the technique of vaccination, inoculation, and prevention of diseases.

An Ayurved so trained will be much better equipped to serve the community and to take his legitimate place beside the doctor trained in modern medicine.

Research. Simultaneously with such training, facilities for research work should be provided. Such work should be done in collaboration with fully trained medical graduates, familiar with modern methods of investigation. The discovery of even a few useful drugs will be well worth the money and time spent. But it must be re-emphasized that the efficiency of the drugs and their purity and standardization should conform fully to present-day standards for any modern drug.

A section for research in indigenous medicine should accordingly be started in the present Medical Research Institute. The efficacy of the drugs should be evaluated at the General Hospital, Colombo.

Many of the 500 qualified Ayurvedic physicians make use of sulpha-drugs, penicillin and other modern medicines. As they have no knowledge of their action, they should not be allowed to prescribe them. Special courses should be organized, however, to teach them the techniques of vaccination, inoculation, and disinfection. Thus equipped, they could be usefully employed in the rural areas where other facilities are not readily available.

The 5,000 applications for registration referred to previously should be very carefully scrutinized. Probably only a very limited number will be found qualified for registration as practitioners of indigenous medicine. The others should be completely debarred.

In upgrading the Ayurvedic College and Hospital well-qualified and trained staff will have to be employed. Ceylon is short of teachers, particularly for nonclinical subjects such as anatomy, physiology, pharmacology and pathology and for this as well as other extensions of training may have to turn to outside help. The cost of upgrading and of equipment and research facilities will vary with the progress made. It is recommended that a sum of Rs. 200,000 should be provided in the first year of the development program rising to Rs. 500,000 in the sixth year.

SUMMARY OF RECOMMENDATIONS

Family Planning

1. The Government of Ceylon should take advantage of the present psychological moment and boldly declare in favor of family planning in the interest of both parents and the coming generation. Information on family planning and facilities for it should be made available at provincial and district hospitals for the present, and in due course at all government hospitals, dispensaries and centers. Advice should be given to those for whom it is considered essential on medical grounds and to others who may ask for it.

Mortality among children

2. Sample surveys should be undertaken to determine as far as possible the causes of the high percentage of deaths among children up to five years.

Administration

3. Instead of 13 provincial superintendents (eight medical and five health) there should be nine superintendents, one for each province, in charge of both curative and preventive work. They

should be delegated adequate powers to deal with both the services.

4. Twelve regional medical officers should be appointed, one for each Local Government Region, to be in charge of both curative and preventive services.

5. The assignment to the curative or preventive branch should be decided not by the result of the final examination only, but by the Director of Medical and Sanitary Services in consultation with the principal and the professor of Public Health Administration under whom the officer was trained. Consideration should be given to the record, aptitude and general behavior of the student throughout his medical career.

Training

6. For additional facilities for training of doctors the sum of Rs. 2 million should be provided as recurring expenditure and another Rs. 1 million toward the cost of additional buildings and equipment.

7. After the first examination for admission of medical students, there should be a second screening after the first year.

8. The suggestion of Miss D. T. Pederson, WHO adviser, to extend training facilities for nurses should be made effective as soon as possible.

9. Additional facilities should be provided at the Colombo Dental Institute for training of dentists. A second institute should be started at Kandy along with the proposed medical school there and scholarships offered to attract a suitable number of candidates.

10. Facilities should be provided to train double the present number of apothecaries for the next 10 years. In their training special emphasis should be laid on the preventive aspect. For those in service refresher courses should be organized.

11. A cadre of 12 regional sanitary inspectors, one for each Local Government Region, should be created and filled by selection from existing sanitary inspectors.

Hospitals, etc.

12. The number of doctors assigned to the out-patient departments should at least be doubled, facilities for diagnosis and treatment improved, and a home treatment service developed as soon as possible.

13. Provision should be made, spread over 10 years, of Rs. 90 million non-recurring expenditures to provide 10,000 beds with a consequential recurring expenditure from Rs. 2 million to 20 million for maintenance.

14. An all-Ceylon plan should be drawn up to integrate the various rural and district medical health institutions into single all-purpose clinics.

15. The aim of the Health Service should be to encourage the delivery of normal maternity cases at home under trained supervision of nurses and midwives. It is further recommended that to discourage and minimize normal cases who come for confinement weeks beforehand a small fee should be charged of 30 cents (US $.05) per day for those whose monthly family income is less than Rs. 80, 50 cents for those whose income is between Rs. 80 and 200, and Rs. 1 for those above that limit. A supply of saplings of mango or some other suitable plant should be made available to create a sentimental bond between the maternity home and the outgoing mother and the baby.

Health Units

16. Maternal and child welfare work should remain part of the functions of the Health Unit.

17. Although the goal of total abolition of intestinal infections and parasites may be far away, it needs restressing. It is recommended that every medical officer of health should devote at least half of his time to the necessary prevention of soil, water and food pollution.

18. Health education should be given not only in the clinic,

but should also be extended to the school and home to build good health habits in impressionable children.

19. Activities of the Health Unit other than maternal and child welfare should receive greater attention from the officer in charge. Health Centers should be run by the public health nurse and the midwives who are fully trained for the purpose.

Nutrition

20. A sum of Rs. 1 million per year should be provided to develop milk supply schemes. The proposed animal husbandry survey should consider the advisability of establishing cooperative farms for the provision of dairy and meat products.

21. An intensive educational campaign through press and radio should be launched and the advantages of essential food-stuffs and of a well balanced diet should be effectively stressed. Attractive and easily understandable charts, posters, leaflets, etc. in Tamil and Sinhalese as well as English should be published.

Malaria

22. The use of DDT spray measures should be pursued with vigor and extended to newly developing areas of colonization.

23. Regulations should be so amended as to give antimalaria personnel authority to enter all buildings or man-made shelters for the purpose of disinsectizing all rooms, and a penalty should be provided against those who habitually leave their houses closed on the day of the malaria unit's visit. In the land development system colonists should be obliged by their contracts to carry out or permit the public health authorities to carry out all anti-malaria measures the latter may specify.

24. The possibilities of the use of Dieldrin as an antimalaria insecticide should be investigated.

Tuberculosis

25. The medical officers of health should try to establish branches of the Ceylon National Association for Prevention of

765

Tuberculosis in their respective areas and support an intensive educational campaign.

General Sanitation

26. The Medical and Sanitary Department should take the initiative in channeling the efforts of the several departments concerned to prevent overlapping and to maintain intimate liaison and cooperation between their staff and the staffs of these departments at all levels, provincial, district and rural.

Water Supplies

27. The Central Planning Development Board when constituted should be requested to prepare as soon as possible an all-Ceylon master plan for drinking and domestic water supplies as well as sewage.

28. A sum of Rs. 10 million a year should be earmarked for the purpose of providing water supplies and drainage schemes according to this plan.

Housing

29. To coordinate the work of various agencies interested in the building program a Housing Commissioner under the Commissioner of Local Government should be appointed.

30. Research into new building materials and methods should be undertaken by the Industrial Research Unit, when established.

31. A sum of Rs. 5 million a year should be provided for publicly assisted Housing Schemes.

Ayurvedic Medicine

32. Institutions for indigenous medicine should be placed directly under the Director of Medical and Sanitary Services like any other institution dealing with preventive and curative medicine.

33. The scope of the training of Ayurvedic practitioners should be extended as suggested in the section on Ayurvedic medicine.

34. A section for research in indigenous medicine should be started in the present Medical Research Institute and the efficacy of the drugs evaluated at the General Hospital, Colombo.

35. A sum of Rs. 200,000 should be provided in the first year of the development program rising to Rs. 500,000 in the sixth year for upgrading the Ayurvedic College and Hospital.

18. Education

PRESENT SYSTEM

All children are required to attend school until the age of fourteen. Normally this means that they complete the work of the Primary School (through the fifth standard or grade) and the Junior Secondary School (through the eighth standard or grade). Those who are qualified may go on to Senior Secondary School for an additional two years, possibly even to a Higher School or to the University. Education at all stages is free, even up to and including professional training at the University level.

A peculiarity of Ceylon's school system derives from the use, side by side, of three languages—English, Sinhalese and Tamil. Although most of the population understand only Sinhalese and four fifths of the children attend vernacular schools, the best schools in the island use English as the medium of instruction. Partly this results from the way in which the educational system has developed, partly from the dominant role of English in government, business and the professions. Changes now under way aim to replace this language as the teaching vehicle by Sinhalese or Tamil.

The educational system did not develop according to a carefully worked out plan, but grew haphazardly. Hence it is characterized by a number of defects. Of these the most serious are a lack of close relation between the knowledge imparted to the pupils and their needs in later life, stress on memory rather than on ability to use the knowledge acquired, and a teaching staff that by modern standards is inadequately prepared for its job. We propose to discuss these deficiencies in turn, evaluating re-

768

forms now in progress and making suggestions for further improvement.

CURRICULUM

There can be no quarrel with the subjects now actually being taught. Preparation for life, on the part of any future citizen, must include some competence in reading, writing, and the use of numbers—the traditional "three R's." History, geography, and nature study—the remaining principal subjects of study in the primary grades—are also certainly either directly or indirectly relevant to the present and future activities of the pupils. This is equally true of the subjects now taught at the secondary level.

Ceylon's deficiency in this respect is one of omission—it lies principally in the failure to pay adequate attention to certain other fields of knowledge of at least as great, or even greater, relevance. The arts and crafts, and health and hygiene, though by no means completely overlooked, receive far less attention than is needful. As the Special Committee on Education stated in its Report in 1943: "A . . . major defect in our educational system is its excessive uniformity . . . our system of education . . . is purely academic in character and bears little relation to the practical aspects of life."

Several distinct factors account for this neglect of practical subjects in Ceylon's educational system. When schools were first established in the island by various religious denominations, they were modeled on those of the United Kingdom, which were academic in character. Although the British system has since been changed, the expansion of educational facilities continued on this older pattern. Probably more important, however, is the exceptionally strong social prejudice against manual labor, reinforced by traditions of caste. Because of these deep-rooted cultural influences, parents do not want their children trained in manual skills, the children reflect the bias of their parents in their own attitudes (there is virtually no interest in hobbies requiring manual skills), and the schools mirror established tradition in their curriculum. Finally, as the next section shows, stress on various attainment examinations has tended to stifle the introduction of subjects of study not directly related to these tests.

For Ceylon, much greater emphasis on practical subjects is particularly important. The economy of the country has been, and will long continue to be, predominantly agricultural. Life for most Ceylonese must inevitably be spent in agricultural pursuits or in closely associated occupations. Therefore most children of this country need to be made ready, so far as the schools can make them ready, for life as farmers or as auxiliaries for farmers. This means that they will have to become acquainted with the reasons for and the methods of combatting unsanitary conditions, malnutrition, soil erosion, with the importance of the right choice of seed and of efficient methods of cultivation. In sum, their education should give appropriate emphasis to science with a rural accent, and to practical work in cultivation. Strongly reinforcing the need for this practical type of work for the majority of school children is the low productivity of the country's agriculture, especially of that sector which employs the bulk of the nation's indigenous population. The schools can become the vehicle, not only of a training appropriate to the life the pupils will lead, but also of badly needed agricultural improvement.

Other pupils, who are to take their place in industry or in certain government departments need to become acquainted with the use of woodworking and metalworking tools, with simple carpentering or elementary mechanics. Industrial development is held back, as we have noted many times in this report, by an exceptional shortage of industrial skills. But it is not therefore to be concluded that specific industrial skills, or vocational training, should be introduced in the primary or even the secondary grades. That would mean overspecialization. Yet familiarity with at least the more common tools and some skill in their manipulation are essential to future industrial workers and useful to everyone. Provision of basic manual training would thus establish firmer foundations for future industrial development at the same time that it performed, especially for urban pupils, the function of preparing them to lead useful and happy lives.

In addition to the case based on their relevance to life, the teaching of handicrafts especially, but also of arts and of health education, can be urged as essential parts of a rounded education. Man has hands as well as brain. A balanced education will not be attained without manual as well as mental training. Stated in other terms, the pupil cannot achieve complete self-expression without work in the crafts and in the arts.

KNOWLEDGE IN ACTION

Ceylon's educational system is also weak in training children to apply their knowledge. The teaching of the subjects in the curriculum is bookish and academic. Pupils learn by reading and listening, not by doing. Instead of emphasizing, as the test of thorough knowledge, ability to use it, stress is laid on reproduction of what has been learned. The result is the accumulation by the pupil of a large store of facts. But because he has had little practice in marshalling these facts purposefully, he can answer specific questions, but cannot solve problems.

This situation probably in the main results from the fact that methods of education as well as the content of the curriculum have in considerable part been dominated by examinations, in particular by examinations which originally were meant to be tests of fitness for further education and have come to be, instead, tests of educational attainment. Thus the London Matriculation examination, originally intended to determine fitness of students to proceed to university study, came to be adopted by employers as a measure of competence or attainment and became thereby the main goal of secondary education. As a consequence, the standard of the examination inevitably fell, and it ceased to serve as a suitable university entrance qualification.

In addition, this examination came to dominate the school curriculum, subjects to be taught being chosen with respect to their relevance to this examination and not to the needs of the

771

students. Other examinations, such as the Junior School Certificate and the Senior School Certificate, were modeled on this prototype. As summarized by the Special Committee on Education, "It is not too much to say . . . that the whole of secondary education in Ceylon has been dominated by London Matriculation." Furthermore, since tests originally meant to determine merely "fitness-for-further-study" came to be regarded as tests of attainment and used as criteria for employment, great emphasis has been laid on obtaining a good grade—with, consequently, a "cramming" attitude toward education.

Solution of these difficulties calls for various measures. Ideally, it would probably be well to abolish all "fitness" tests until the university level is reached. There, a qualifying entrance examination, taken only by those desiring to attend the university, would probably still be needed. As for the great majority of pupils, their fitness to proceed with further education, as well as the degree of their attainment, could be measured perfectly adequately—as it is in many other countries—by their record in school.

To transform knowledge into understanding, mere ability to reproduce knowledge into ability to use it, a thorough reform of teaching methods is needed. Most generally, cramming the pupil with facts should give way to training him in orderly thinking. He should be given facts, of course, but above all he should be shown how to assemble and use them to some purpose. Facts can be stored in handbooks; reasoning ability cannot.

But just to set as the goal of education the development of the capacity for independent thought itself involves a reform in education that is absolutely basic. It must start with the training of teachers. Teachers imbued with the importance of using rather than storing knowledge can then realize this objective in the classroom. This will mean the introduction of different methods of instruction, and of examinations which test not just what the pupils know but what they can do with their knowledge.

Techniques which will be helpful in developing reasoning ability are numerous. Thus in all subjects, recitation from memory can be replaced by discussion, even in the early grades. Besides being thought-provoking, by introducing personal experience this method increases the relevance of instruction to the student's life and suggests applications; at the same time, it heightens interest in the subject matter. Science teaching should invariably be accompanied by laboratory work, or at the very least by demonstrations. Widespread use of problems, carefully chosen for their realism and interest, can also be very helpful. This technique, for long regarded as essential in the teaching of arithmetic, can be applied in all fields if some ingenuity is called into play. Field trips can relate schoolroom study of citizenship, geography, biology, and rural science to the facts of real life.

As a means of invigorating teaching, the arts and crafts also have a high value. These subjects constantly pose problems of an individual character, not capable of being solved by reference to a textbook, but requiring the exercise of some originality or ingenuity. Information must be used, not merely memorized. An important by-product of craft teaching, especially in Ceylon, can be the preparation of simple but effective laboratory equipment for their own and other classes by workers in wood and metal.

EDUCATION AND ENTERPRISE

We have already noted the lack of enterprise in Ceylon. Although there are some notable exceptions, there are far too few business men with that initiative, resourcefulness, and daring which leads to the search for new productive opportunities and to their successful exploitation. Recent government policy has not encouraged private initiative, but the main cause is much more fundamental

Especially important as a cause of deficiency in enterprise is family and social tradition with respect to the rearing of children. Parental discipline is firmly established and generally unquestioned, submission to this authority taken for granted. Especially among the more prosperous classes, children are excessively sheltered and looked after by *ayahs*. Initiative, experimentation,

773

inquiring habits of mind are thereby discouraged. The submission of child to parent carries over into the school, where the teacher replaces the parent as the symbol of authority.

Lack of interest in manual skills we have also traced in part to social traditions, and have recommended greater stress on the teaching of arts and crafts as a means of getting the student to apply his knowledge. So here too, more extended teaching of these subjects can help combat deficiency in enterprise. Because of the individuality and variety of the problems raised in these fields, they arouse the curiosity, resourcefulness, and initiative of pupils.

Yet what is really needed is a fundamental alteration in the attitude and approach of the teacher. This should involve a change from past insistence on his authority and on the submission of the pupil to emphasis on the participation of pupils in a common experience of learning, especially of learning to think, with the teacher acting as guide and counselor rather than the fount of all wisdom. This amounts to a revolution in the attitude of teachers. It cannot be accomplished by mere changes in the curriculum, and it cannot be realized overnight. It will require constant emphasis by the Director of Education, by each of the training college principals, and, in view of the long tradition of educational authoritarianism, may and probably will necessitate the leavening of the staff of teachers' colleges with teachers from abroad who are experienced in modern methods of education.

So far we have dealt with the kind of subjects taught and the methods used in teaching them. These are of course vital. But even the combination of an ideal curriculum and the most scientific methods of instruction can be nullified if it is entrusted to a poorly trained teaching staff.

As the Ministry of Education is well aware, school personnel in the island are not, considered in the aggregate, adequately trained to do their job well. There are at the present time some 38,000 teachers in the school system. Of these only 12,600 or one third are "trained"—that is, graduated from one of the two-year teachers' training colleges—or in possession of a university degree. Even the trained group, before proceeding to a teachers' college, had in the main progressed only through a senior school, or to the level of the tenth standard or grade. The other two thirds of the nation's teachers stopped its basic formal education at this point, or at approximately the age of 16, although about half had received some additional training in pedagogy or special subjects. Thus the great majority of Ceylon's teachers are poorly prepared, many of them quite immature. Naturally, of those who have seen many years of service, a considerable proportion have matured and have learned much from the school of experience. For the future, however, reliance must be placed on new recruits to education, and it is important that they should be adequately prepared.

Aggregate figures conceal as well as reveal. Thus they fail to show the marked distinction between different categories of schools with respect to the quality of instruction. It is best, and sometimes excellent, in the English schools, especially in the secondary grades. It is much poorer in the Sinhalese and Tamil (or "vernacular") schools, and worst of all in their primary grades.

Originally, the distinction between these schools derived from their sponsorship. English schools were founded and run by various denominations. Their teachers were comparatively well trained and their standards relatively high. Most of the vernacular schools were government establishments. Since facilities for training their teachers were poor and salaries low, the quality of instruction was bad and standards were depressed. Today the fundamental distinction between these two types of schools rests on the language used as the medium of instruction. Some of the English schools have been taken over by the government, some ("assisted") depend heavily upon government support, while a few remain completely in private hands. Yet the difference in quality continues, perpetuated by the fact that, to teach in an English school, the teacher must understand the language and

775

thus must have undergone some training in one of these superior schools.

A few simple statistics may help to sharpen the picture. Only a small minority of the country's 1,365,000 school children—19% in all—have the advantage of attending English schools. The great majority—75%—go to vernacular schools, the remainder (6%) being scattered among estate schools, *pirivenas*, and small "unaided" private schools.

Some idea of the relative quality of the teachers in English and vernacular schools may be obtained from the following tabulation:

Extent of Training of Teachers, 1950*	Number of Each Category in:		Percent of Each Category in:	
	English Schools	Vernacular Schools	English Schools	Vernacular Schools
University graduates	1,495	—	15.3	—
Graduates of teachers' training colleges	3,086	8,022	31.6	28.3
Certificated	2,153	14,294	22.1	50.4
Probationary or uncertificated	2,367	5,796	24.3	20.5
Other	651	222	6.7	0.8
Total	*9,752*	*28,334*	*100.0*	*100.0*

* Included are all teachers in government, assisted, and estate schools; those excluded are teachers in training colleges (201), unaided schools (317), and pirivenas (526). Among graduates of teachers' training colleges are listed a relatively small number (426) who, though not actually "trained", have passed the intermediate examination of the University. "Certificated" teachers have a senior school education, plus some special instruction in pedagogy. The category "Other" comprises teachers with some special training in drawing, music, handicraft, etc.

Table derived from figures in Tables V to VIII, Administration Report of the Director of Education for 1950.

Especially noteworthy is the fact that only in English schools are there teachers who are university graduates. The proportion of graduates of training colleges is closely similar in the two types of schools, but while just over one fifth of English-school teachers are of the relatively immature "certificated" type, half of the vernacular-school teachers fall in this category. Another striking fact is the large proportion, nearly one fourth, of English-school teachers who are the thoroughly immature and untrained probationers and uncertificated, with nothing more than a secondary school education. These are, of course, new and untried recruits.

The picture suggested by the more general data is confirmed. It is that of a school system in which only a minority of the teachers are trained for their jobs—about half in the English schools and less than a third in the vernacular. The remainder are little or no better than graduates of what in the United States are called Junior High Schools. Moreover, only a small minority of all school children, the 19% who attended English schools, ever come in contact with the relatively small number of best qualified instructors. The majority of the four fifths who attend vernacular schools are, in general, inadequately taught by poorly prepared teachers; since most of the 28% of "trained" teachers are in secondary vernacular schools, those whose education ends at the primary stage receive, with few exceptions, the ministrations of amateurs.

EDUCATIONAL REFORMS

To remedy some of the major educational defects spotlighted here—as well as a few others—Ceylon has just embarked upon a program of educational reform. If successfully carried through, it should go at least a long way toward correcting some of the basic problems.

PRIMARY AND SECONDARY EDUCATION

Under the vigorous leadership of Dr. H. W. Howes, the Director of Education, greatly increased attention is to be given to practical subjects. In the primary grades, workshops of a simple type are to be made universal, and in the words of the government's White Paper on Educational Reform, "the curriculum should be thought of in terms of activity and experience rather than of knowledge to be acquired and facts to be stored." At the junior secondary level, in addition to the traditional core program, practical subjects such as handicrafts, carpentry, gardening, weaving, domestic science and the like are to be included.

All pupils will be required to take some practical work, but there will be two principal groups, one with predominantly practical interests and aptitudes, another with tastes and capacities more inclined toward the academic. The former group will stress the practical studies, the latter the more conventional academic work. Likewise in the senior secondary schools, there will be two streams of pupils, one with a practical, the other with an academic bent; emphasis in studies will be placed accordingly. All will have some training in crafts and the like, and this group of studies will be expanded to include commercial training and the elements of agriculture.

Special provision is to be made, if plans are fulfilled, for additional manual work of a more vocational character for pupils of various ages. Those who fail the fitness test at the end of the junior secondary course may drop out, or alternatively, they may go to vocational schools to be set up by the Ministry of Education and by the Ministries of Agriculture and of Industries.

Some relief from the pressure of examinations is afforded by the abolition of the previous fitness test at the end of the primary grades. Progression of pupils from primary to junior secondary schools is to require no special test, but only completion of the work of the fifth standard. A fitness test is retained, however, at the end of the junior secondary stage, and the senior school certificate examination will also be continued. Without doubt the latter will also constitute, as in the past, an attainment test. To avoid its tendency to force the secondary curriculum into a narrow mold, it is proposed to include a wider range of subjects in this examination, including a number that will vary with the pupil's preparation.

Present plans also call for the coordination of all craft work in the schools under an Assistant Director of Technical Education in the Department of Education. He will be aided by a small staff and by a foreign technical adviser engaged for a term of two years. This Assistant Director will act as liaison officer with the two ministries with regard to the vocational training to be jointly established.

All of these steps are good ones. Special commendation is due the authorities for continuing practical and academic work side by side at the senior secondary level, rather than establishing separate schools for the two aspects of training. At the same time, the plan to stress one side or the other of the pupil's program, in terms of his own interest and abilities, is excellent. Broadening the scope of the senior school certificate examination is welcomed, as is also elimination of the fitness test at the end of the primary grades; it is to be hoped that the test at the end of the junior secondary stage will be the next to go.

Perhaps the most serious hurdle for the educational reform program is its timing. Only a beginning has been made so far in the introduction of practical work into the schools. Although at least one craft is now taught in 117 secondary schools, the remaining 238 have none. In the entire school system there are but 267 handicraft and vocational teachers, and at the rate at which they are being trained it will be decades before there are enough. [1] On a more hopeful note, considerable progress is observed in the preparation of other types of teachers: those in training increased

---

[1] At Ceylon Technical College 45 teachers are in craft training and a like number at the School of Arts. The training is of the simplest sort only, and not what would normally be considered teacher-level; but as new candidates arrive with prior instruction in their earlier grades, they will be able to absorb a more advanced quality of training.

from 1,246 in 1947 to 2,773 in 1951 and over 3,000 in 1952. It is estimated that about 1,550 will now be graduated each year.

School workshops and accommodations for arts and crafts are still sadly lacking, and equipment is quite inadequate. Proper attention to the physical facilities will speed up the program and make it more effective. Early relief could be provided through more generous funds for these essentials. There is, of course, no use in training craft teachers if they are to be turned loose in an empty schoolroom.

VOCATIONAL TRAINING

Under the current program, those who complete the senior secondary course and pass the qualifying examination may go on to higher courses for two years, or to a polytechnic institute. The only one of these at present is the Ceylon Technical College, but it is expected that others will be set up at Kandy, Galle, Jaffna and Batticaloa.

The Ceylon Technical College is an unusual institution. Originally more of an engineering school, it has turned over its regular engineering courses to the University of Ceylon. It now concentrates upon training men at the supervisory level, as distinguished from engineers above it and skilled workmen below. The course is of two years, and has been described locally as "academic work with a practical slant." There are laboratories in hydraulics, physics and chemistry, with another in chemical engineering soon to be added. Shops for wood and metal working were installed about five years ago. Instructions in these practical arts is much less advanced than the equipment would suggest; the aim is merely to give the students a brief working knowledge of them, with neither the skill of a workman nor the fundamental understanding of an engineer.

What is unusual is the concept that a man can omit experience and be trained solely and specifically for the job of foreman or technical supervisor in production, to guide and answer the questions of men who know their work (and the foreman's) better than he does. Unquestionably there is a great need for intermediate supervisory personnel, but one must question why more of them cannot be upgraded from among the more experienced skilled workers. Perhaps in time this will be done, by providing the most promising workers a later opportunity to study supplementary courses in preparation for more responsible duties.

Regular vocational training is offered by the Basic Technical Training Institute at Ratmalana. Founded in 1946, this school is the only significant one of its kind on the island, and prepares machinists, carpenters and electricians specifically for service in the railroad shops of the Ministry of Transport.

Enrollment capacity is about 300, for a one-and-a-half-year course, hence the school can graduate around 200 per year. Students receive six months' training in basic mathematics, measurement, reading of instruments and general subjects, followed by a year of shop work in one of the fields. Because of the school's location it is necessary for all students to live in dormitories. They bring their own bedding, but are furnished free tuition, bed, meals, a suit of work clothes and 16¢ per day for pocket money. Over-all costs of operation, based on present full enrollment, are given as Rs. 300,000 annually.[2]

Applicants are admitted by examination, and now greatly exceed the school's capacity; recently there were 200 candidates for 40 openings. Their fields of specialization are chosen on the basis of faculty opinion alone, after the first few months of work. Since the student is not consulted about his preference, we fear early performance may be misleading and that more than a few misfits may be trained. It is suggested that more attention be paid to the students' personal ambitions, on the ground that he who is happy in his work does best at it in the end.

Nevertheless, fundamentally this is an excellent school, and it will improve. Its head has shown, by personal example, that a

---

[2] The Administration Report for 1950 showed expenses of Rs. 206,-536.90, without depreciation, for an average enrollment of 150.

man with a science degree can profit from ordinary shop experience; and as one result, this year five more university graduates have discarded tradition and entered the railroad shops for practical manual work. It is hoped that others may follow, and that some of them will become instructors later, for shortage of qualified teaching staff is one of the chief problems of the Ratmalana school. This situation, incidentally, is not helped by the fact that instructors are paid less than a routine shop foreman; salary adjustments should be made as better instructors become available.

In one of the school shops is a prominent sign reading: "If the student hasn't learned, the instructor hasn't taught." There may be truth in this, yet it represents an unfortunate philosophy which pervades much of Ceylon's entire educational system: the teacher is expected to drive learning into the heads of perfectly passive pupils. We submit that good teaching requires the full cooperation and effort of the student; that the sign encourages the students to be passive; and that it—and all like it—should be taken down and burned.

With improvements along the lines suggested, it is the Mission's conviction that vocational training facilities of this kind are among the most urgent needs of the country's development program. There should be more of them, and they should supply trained workers equally to private industry—not exclusively to the government as at present.

However great the need, expansion must be governed by the personnel available. We recommend installation of a new physical plant to the extent of Rs. 1 million in 1953 and a like amount in 1954. Additional operating funds should be provided at the rate of Rs. 500,000 in the first year, Rs. 800,000 in the second, and Rs. 1 million annually thereafter through 1958.

TEACHING STAFF

Even with the output of trained teachers stepped-up to 1,550 a year, the rate at which the untrained two thirds of the educational staff can be replaced by well prepared instructors will be tiresomely slow. We may approach this problem by first establishing the number of training college graduates required to take care of normal losses of present staff from marriage, death, or retirement and to keep pace with normal growth in numbers of pupils.

It is reasonable to suppose that, since the existing staff of 12,600 trained teachers is relatively young and has invested time and money in training for a teaching career, the rate of wastage from these causes will be abnormally low, say not over 2% for the next decade or two. The untrained group of 25,400, however, consists both of older teachers and of young probationers or others to many of whom teaching is merely a stopgap form of employment. A higher rate of losses must be applied, and a figure of 4% per year seems conservative.

As for the growth in numbers of pupils, unless classes are to become intolerably crowded, [3] additional teaching staff will be required. Population is now increasing at a rate of approximately 3% a year. But to be on the conservative side, we shall take a figure of only 2% as the addition to staff needed to maintain approximately the present teacher-pupil ratio. On these assumptions, annual requirements for trained teachers may be calculated as follows:

To replace losses from the present trained staff, 2% of 12,600:	252
To replace losses from the untrained staff, 4% of 25,400:	1,016
To maintain the existing teacher-pupil ratio, 2% of 38,000:	760
Total number of trained teachers needed each year:	2,028

---

[3] The average number of pupils per teacher is now 27 for English schools, about 38 for vernacular schools and 55 for estate schools.

At such a rate of graduation from teachers' training colleges, all untrained teachers would be replaced, as their number diminished from natural causes, within a period of 25 years, the existing staff would be maintained, and provision would be made for the growing numbers of pupils.[4] Clearly the present rate of graduation of 1,550 trained teachers a year will fall considerably short of this goal. It will mean either that provision for growth will have to be neglected, with increasing crowding of classrooms and more inefficient teaching, or that untrained teachers will continue to be recruited, with the realization of a fully trained staff postponed for an additional two decades.

By utilizing to the full the existing physical equipment of the training colleges, the annual output of trained teachers could be raised to 1,800. Even this higher figure would be inadequate—if growth were fully covered, provision of a trained teaching staff would take at least 29 years.

In view of the importance of education to Ceylon's plans for development, in particular of instruction revamped so as to develop needed manual skills, this is too long. The aim should be to reduce this period to not more than 20 years. To do this will require the graduation of some 2,300 trained teachers each year. This rate of graduation would provide 272 teachers a year to accelerate the rate of replacement of untrained teachers. It would not necessarily involve the discharge of present staff, but only a reduction in the number of untrained teachers recruited each year.

Realization of this higher rate of graduation is not too ambitious a project, in view of its importance. True, physical facilities at

---

[4] These calculations are only approximate, in that they do not allow for cumulative growth. This would apply both to the numbers of pupils and to wastage of staff from natural causes, and would mean that the figures given, though accurate for the beginning of our period, would be too low as time went on. Taking account of cumulative growth, therefore, would reinforce the argument presented.

teachers' training colleges will have to be expanded by about a quarter, and more staff for these colleges will be essential. The school building program can and should allow for the necessary construction. Additional faculty for the training colleges (some 100 in all) could be prepared without undue strain over the next few years by the Education Department of the University of Ceylon. In the interim some additions to this staff could be recruited from abroad.

Finally, a word about salaries. This is a highly complicated subject, as it requires consideration not only of actual money payments in relation to training and length of service, but also of such matters as conditions of work, length of vacations, and the like.

Superficial comparison indicates that trained graduate teachers obtain salaries which are comparable to Grade I of the clerical service, and considerably lower than Divisional Revenue Officers. Trained teachers fall into pay categories that are about on a par with Grade II clerks or Grade III shroffs, while the certificated group in vernacular schools is comparable with assistant clerks. Although certificated teachers and assistant clerks are subject to identical educational requirements (a Senior School Certificate), and while it must be borne in mind that promotions in the clerical services depend upon in-grade examinations, length of service, and efficiency, it would appear that trained and graduate teachers receive pay that is low in relation to the training required and the duties involved, not to mention their vital responsibility for shaping the mind and the character of coming generations.

Owing to the complexity of the problem, as well as the limitations on its time, the Mission does not feel competent to reach a definite judgment on this matter. It recommends, however, that in view of the importance of attracting young people of ability and character into the ranks of the teaching profession, the Salaries Commission give careful consideration to the question of teachers' salaries.

University Education

Ceylon has only one university, [5] the University of Ceylon. Founded in 1942, it absorbed the older University College and the School of Medicine, and later the engineering courses of Ceylon Technical College. Today it offers courses in Arts, Oriental Studies, Law, Science, Agriculture, Medicine, Veterinary Science and Engineering. Something over 2,000 students are in residence, nearly a third taking Arts degrees and almost another third taking degrees or diplomas in medicine (including dental surgery). The University is still largely housed in buildings in Colombo taken over from the two institutions it absorbed, but it will in the future occupy a very attractive site at Peradeniya, near Kandy. A number of buildings are already completed there and are in use. Others are under construction or planned. The Medical School will remain in Colombo so as to be near the main hospital, but a second medical school is projected at Kandy.

It needs no demonstration that a flourishing and active university life is an integral part of a sound educational system for Ceylon. The higher training given by the University should be one of the essential contributions in the creation of a larger corps of trained engineers, doctors and scientists of all kinds, as well as administrators and managers, so necessary to future progress. It contributes vitally, directly and indirectly, to the training of teachers for the primary and secondary schools. Perhaps most important of all is the indirect contribution which a university can make in the molding of the mental attitudes of the natural leaders of the country. A good start has been made, but Ceylon has still a long way to go to attain the proportions of university-trained population of more advanced countries. Today

---

[5] However, certain private institutions of more limited scope provide instruction in specific fields at the university level. Noteworthy among these is Jaffna College, whose training in some of the sciences is at least equal and perhaps superior to that of the University at its present stage of development.

Ceylon has about one man or woman in full-time university training for every 3,500 population, compared with about one in 77 in the United States, one in 600 in the United Kingdom and one in 1,400 in India.

Today the University depends almost entirely on government grants for its maintenance and extension. With much of the tuition free, income from fees is small, while the University's endowments are negligible. It is therefore necessary to include provision for university capital expenditures in the development program. The mission has no hesitation in recommending continued support for the University. The expenditure which might be incurred if all plans of extension were executed is very difficult to estimate and the mission has not felt able to do more than earmark a total of Rs. 40 million over the six-year period 1953-59, exclusive of the second medical school which is provided for separately under the head of medical expenditures.

Examination of the details of the university organization and its future lines of development are clearly outside the scope of the Mission's task. It follows, however, from our general conclusions on the immediate needs of Ceylon that we should like to see further development of the Faculty of Engineering which was established in 1950 and of the teaching in agriculture. In these and other faculties there may be a special need for continued recruitment of teaching staff from outside the country, with consequent necessity to pay salaries higher than those normally paid to local recruited men. The possibility of assistance from international bodies in solving this problem of foreign staff should be explored.

RECOMMENDATIONS

On the basis of the foregoing analysis, the Mission has the following recommendations to make:

1. Every effort should be devoted to carry out the present plans for expansion of practical work at both primary and secondary levels and the introduction of vocational work for those

leaving school at the end of the junior secondary stage. It would appear advisable, during each of the next few years, to send abroad for special training in craft work a small number of carefully selected craft teachers or trainees. Upon their return, these teachers could become the staff of the proposed new polytechnic institutes, concentrating at first upon preparing additional numbers of craft teachers.

2. Additional funds should be allocated for the purchase of the tools and equipment these teachers will need as they take their places in the schools.

3. Modernization of teaching methods, already under way at the teachers' training colleges, should be carried' through as rapidly as possible. Stress should be laid on cultivating the ability to apply knowledge rather than mere reproduction thereof. To assist in realizing the teachers' role as leader in a cooperative venture rather than as a disciplinary taskmaster, it is recommended that the faculty of training colleges be supplemented with competent foreign staff.

4. To ensure the reasonably early attainment of a trained corps of teachers, the physical and human facilities of training colleges should be enlarged to permit the graduation of approximately 2,300 trained teachers each year. This will require the expansion of physical plant by about a quarter, and a gradual increase in staff of perhaps 100 (50%). These new faculty members could be made available partly by expansion in training activities by the Education Department of the University, partly by the employment of foreign personnel.

5. Additional vocational training institutes, along the lines of the one at Ratmalana, are needed. The Mission recommends installation of physical plant to the extent of Rs. 1 million in 1953 and a like amount in 1954. Additional operating funds should be provided at the rate of Rs. 500,000 in the first year of operation, Rs. 800,000 in the second and Rs. 1 million annually thereafter through 1958.

6. The salary scale of teachers should be surveyed by the Salaries Commission, to ascertain what changes are needed to make teaching as attractive to able young people as an administrative or professional career in government service.

7. The planned development and equipment of the University of Ceylon should be continued with special attention to the expansion of the Departments of Engineering and Agriculture.

19. Technology

BACKGROUND AND NEEDS

Ceylon's desire for rapid progress in agriculture, industry, transport and so many other fields at once has highlighted—as never before—her need for technically trained people. While retaining as much as possible of her own rich tradition and spiritual background, she admittedly seeks material development through an extension of numerous useful Western methods. It has become clear to all that there is no real short-cut to this goal —that technological advance can occur only through the agency of technical personnel. And lots of them.

In most fields, the rate of development is actually limited less by finances than by lack of local technology at all levels. To carry out the various projects there are not enough research scientists, designing and operating engineers, agricultural or manufacturing specialists, or construction engineers. Equally scarce are technical supervisors, draftsmen, control chemists, field foremen, tractor operators, and even skilled workmen. To remedy this must be one of the first tasks.

It is true that the island's trade in past years has offered few posts for technically trained men. The colonial system is usually blamed, and it may be partly responsible. But Ceylonese tradition itself has not particularly favored the practical technical professions, other than medicine. Caste, dowry rights, religious conflicts and the retreat to the security of government service have all tended to discourage the study of applied science or the skilled trades.

As a corollary, we have seen that Ceylonese educational facilities in these fields are almost negligible, even in agriculture.

790

There is no local fountainhead of industrial technology. Research —the essential growth hormone of all production—is extremely limited. Without these things Ceylon's progress is greatly handicapped. We feel strongly that she must start to build her own sources of them; for she can borrow only the bare framework of what she needs, and she should not count on borrowing even this forever.

EXTERNAL TECHNICAL ASSISTANCE

For its many development schemes of recent years the government has quite naturally relied upon imported specialists. Large numbers of these have been sought and brought to the island for periods varying from a few days to several years. Some have been engaged directly by the government; others have been secured through the Colombo Plan, FAO, WHO, UNESCO, ILO and similar agencies. Nearly half of all the experts requested through the Colombo Plan offices by various countries during 1951 were for service in Ceylon.

Coordination. On the whole this form of assistance has been helpful; but it has been attended with considerable confusion. Government officials have been a little too ready to ask for "experts" without a clear-cut definition of the real needs. The international agencies have perhaps been insufficiently insistent upon precise specifications. Because of poor coordination on both sides, identical requests have been made to several specialized agencies. The result has been appreciable duplication and overlapping. Two or more experts may be working independently on the same problem for different government offices—or even for the same office. Recently two appointees arrived from different countries halfway around the world, both to be principal of the same training school.

Selection. There is wide variation in the competence of outside specialists brought to the island. Some of this is merely the result of misinterpreted needs, for a man may be fully qualified in one branch of a subject and find himself asked to advise on a different

791

branch instead. When experts are requested of outside agencies, and the specifications must be framed by nontechnical officials unaided, mistakes are inevitable.

With offers of technical help being made by so many international organizations, it is logical to turn to them first. But both Ceylon and the agencies concerned should recognize that not all of the best technical personnel can be obtained in this way. In such cases it may be necessary for the government to find and engage specialists directly, either as individuals or as members of firms with which they may be permanently associated. For certain types of industrial projects it may be found that the real "know-how" is only in the hands of similar manufacturing concerns elsewhere, and that a special arrangement with such a firm would be the most advantageous.

While the government has already hired some experts directly, and often excellent ones, there are cases in which it has been unwilling to pay for the best. This, we are convinced, is false economy. The cost of a top-grade specialist—whatever his salary —is as nothing compared with the expense of a misstep in designing or locating an expensive industrial plant. It is penny wise, pound foolish to be willing to risk tens of millions on an uncertain project, and at the same time try to save a few thousand on the essential technical advice.

Perhaps this error is one reason why some contemplated projects have had a succession of experts, whose reports contain conflicting recommendations. But another reason for conflicting advice is that more than a few of the specialists have had something to sell, either in equipment or in later services. If any of their reports ever recommended actual abandonment of a project, however uneconomical, the Mission did not see them.

Cooperation. Technical specialists brought to Ceylon by the government often meet unnecessary obstacles which prevent them from doing their best work. All of them interviewed by the Mission told similar stories. Some continue to struggle against difficulties, but a number have simply packed up their belongings and left. We feel that a frank review of their troubles may be helpful in planning future work.

The worst problem—at the root of many others—is failure of officials to delegate authority. This refers not only to such limited and temporary authority as the specialist himself needs, but equally to delegation of local authority from one level to the next within a department. Too often, before action can be taken, minor matters must be referred all the way up to a busy cabinet minister in person. Departmental chiefs enthusiastic over the promotion of their own development programs, are reluctant to hand over the reins to their assistants to carry them out. Thus there is a tendency to overlook three cardinal rules for making good use of an expert, which are: (1) hire the man who knows best how to do the job; (2) give him what help he needs; and (3) let him do it.

Instead, specialists presumably entrusted with the designing of complex processes are disturbed to find their technical decisions made for them by nontechnical government executives. Similarly, managers of government factories cannot plan their operations efficiently because of official intervention in matters which should be under their undisputed control.

Procrastination and organizational delays constitute another serious problem. Experts arrive when requested, then find that adequate preparations for their work have not yet been made. One man claims to have wasted his first four months for this reason; nor would the ministry authorize the small expenditure which would have allowed him to proceed with other portions of his task during this time. A team of specialists, expected to train Ceylonese nationals to carry on their work after their contract expires, are well into their three-year program but are still awaiting the trainees to be selected by the government. The work of some has been delayed by red tape in procurement of ordinary supplies. Still others have had to mark time while interdepartmental jurisdictional disputes were settled.

On occasion—but fortunately rarely—a few government officials have attempted to bring public discredit upon invited specialists whose views did not coincide with their own. The policy is a poor one, regardless of the actual competence of the specialists. Its effect upon Ceylon can be very injurious, for other men, of unquestionable competence, will weigh their desire to serve against the risk of having to suffer such attacks or compromise their principles.

It would be unfair to blame individual officials for all of these troubles. Much of the fault lies in misunderstanding on both sides. A great deal of it would be eliminated if Ceylon herself possessed a well-informed technical agency capable of interpreting between the scientific specialists and the lay government officials. Lacking this, it is even difficult for nontechnical departments to specify precisely the kind of specialized assistance wanted from outside agencies. Above all, then, Ceylon needs *technical help in dealing with technical help*. This should be one of the functions of the proposed economic planning secretariat, aided by such technical institutions and individuals as it can call upon for cooperation and assistance.

Understanding. There is also a mistaken idea of what a single specialist can accomplish. In many a nontechnical man's mind, each project is neatly packaged as a complete unit—fisheries, cottage industries, sugar production, a steel mill, a caustic soda plant, etc. There is a tendency to think that it is only necessary to secure an expert for each of these projects and all will go well.

But the training and experience of specialists is not divided in this way. Ordinarily several different experts, working together, will be needed for one project. When it comes to detail, there is no such thing as a "steel expert" who, by himself, can answer technical questions on every aspect of steel manufacture from ore mining and power transmission to the making of bridge girders and small screws, with production costs and business management thrown in. We believe that international technical agencies should stress this fact more than they do now.

Moreover, operation of a factory requires more than just one

794

expert at the top. Technical understanding and vocational skills are needed in the various echelons all the way through the factory organization. Failure to recognize and provide for this can only result in a succession of production troubles, inferior products, and financial loss.

Finally, we must question seriously the real value of most short-term technical counsel. Unquestionably there are certain very specific needs which can be filled by the service of an outside expert for a few months, or even a few weeks. But where there is a general deficiency of domestic technology, more often what is needed is day-by-day technical guidance over a period of years.

It is especially important that every advantage be taken of outside specialized help to train local men, so that a permanent benefit will accrue to the country. Such training seldom can be accomplished in a short time. The imported expert may have spent from five to twenty years or more in acquiring his particular specialized knowledge. In passing it on to another, it is difficult to speed up the process without omitting something. Thus to assign a Ceylonese to work with a visiting expert for two or three months may be helpful, but it can hardly be expected to make an expert of him. Such collaboration in terms of years would be more useful.

Domestic Technologists

We have dwelt upon the shortage of technically trained Ceylonese, and on the various educational and psychological influences at fault. It is proper, therefore, to emphasize that Ceylon is not entirely without such people, some of them equal to anything the West can offer.

In the last ten years especially, more and more Ceylonese have been sent abroad for advanced training. This is as it should be; for even if the local facilities for technical education were brought up to Western standards, there would still be the need for constant international exchange of scientific knowledge. Under present conditions, the number of these students is still too small.

We believe that a more forward-looking policy would call for greater emphasis upon preparation of Ceylonese technologists in comparison with the number of foreign experts requested.

For really practical training in most lines the periods of study should be longer. Of 80 trainees sent abroad under the Colombo Plan up to March 31, 1952 more than half were sent for one year or less, and a third went for studies ranging from a few weeks to six months. The average period for all of them was only slightly more than a year.

There is room to improve the policy of recruitment of these men. Local candidates for foreign training are now chosen only from the rolls of government, while applications for scholarships from the public at large have been rejected. There is no reason to believe that all the most brilliant and promising Ceylonese are working in government departments.

Up to now, however, most of the jobs available to local technologists after their training have been governmental. This at once suggests two things which the government can do to encourage more candidates for advanced technical preparation. One is to pay them what they are worth. The other is to make better use of them in their work.

Today a scientific officer in Ceylonese government service is penalized for his special training. His salary advancement is slower than that of persons in purely administrative posts for which qualification are less exacting. After a number of years he may find that nontechnical companions who entered the service with him are drawing twice his pay, and that his only road to a corresponding material improvement is to abandon his technical work for something less vital to Ceylon's progress.

With respect to utilization, the Mission observes that some excellent men have been trained—at government expense—in specialties connected with the national development program; yet too many have been employed in entirely different lines, and have never been given an opportunity to serve as intended. Had they been so employed and found wanting, the situation might be more easily understood; but to fail to provide the chance is to question the purpose of the training.

RESEARCH AND DEVELOPMENT

Progress in all lines of production depends upon research, for this is the very source of knowledge. It is no accident that the countries with the most effective research are usually the ones farthest ahead economically.

Present Activities. In the field of agriculture, at least, Ceylon conducts a limited amount of good research. Most of it is done in the special institutions created for work on tea, rubber and coconuts, and has been described in Chapter 11. Scattered work is done elsewhere on specific matters of agriculture and forestry, but the whole falls very short of the country's needs. Outside of agriculture research is almost nonexistent.

Some years ago the government attempted to initiate a form of applied research for the development of industries, and the activity was officially recognized in the name of the Ministry of Industries, Industrial Research and Fisheries. Laboratories were opened in Colombo under the supervision of this ministry, and are still operating. Unhappily they conduct no research, but are occupied with routine analytical matters.

This result might have been anticipated. The laboratories are handicapped by all the problems inherent in bureaucratic control, and have faced difficulties identical with those of the government-operated industries. [1] Furthermore, their services for referee work and routine analysis have been so urgently needed in connection with ordinary processes of government that they have had little or no time for scientific investigation. There is no doubt that Ceylon needs applied technical research, but in our opinion she will never get it through this channel. It has been wisely said that the main job of a research director is to protect the research

---

[1] See under Cooperation, Section II, of this chapter; also Management, Section II of Chapter 15.

men from those who want to direct them. But to make this principle workable requires a different set of conditions.

We believe that the present laboratories of the Ministry of Industries should continue operation, but should be more appropriately designated as the government's Testing and Standards Laboratories. They should expand their service to meet the analytical and testing needs of other government departments as well, unifying these functions as much as possible for the sake of economy. If now and then they find it possible to carry on a little research too, so much the better, but research should not be expected of them.

Encouragement and promotion of research should be expected of all ministries in the interests of progress. Each branch of government deals with problems demanding some kind of investigation—agricultural, industrial, hydraulic, economic, demographic or whatever it may be. The responsibility is always implied, and each ministry should support studies pertinent to its field of service to the public. This does not mean that it must do the work itself; often it is better and cheaper to enlist the aid of independent facilities, by means of contracts or cash grants. We hope that elimination of the term "Industrial Research" from the title of the Ministry of Industries indicates a recognition of the broader role of research in Ceylon's development.

The Real Need. How to make a good local beginning in applied laboratory research and development where it does not yet exist is a special problem. A summary of Ceylon's particular conditions bearing on it would include: insufficient knowledge of local raw material sources; lack of practical experience in finding out about them; shortage of scientific curiosity about them; the general shortage of local technical personnel; underutilization of existing technical staff; inadequate training facilities; insufficient provision for technical review of proposed projects; and lack of facilities to help solve the technical problems of existing productive enterprises. To these must be added the fact that applied research is a course never offered by any university in the world, but calls for development of a certain state of mind and involves techniques learned only in practice.

Yet this combination of problems is not unique, and we find precedent for a successful attack upon it. The mission believes that Ceylon can profit by the experience of Mexico in the creation of an independent technical research institute designed for simultaneous research and practical training.

The Mexican Prototype. Mexico's technological barriers to progress were much the same as those of Ceylon, and were equally appreciated by her government. But her program, which began in 1944, was not a government project. It was initiated and supported by the *Banco de Mexico.* As the nation's central bank, this institution recognized its unusual position and its responsibility to promote the country's development by whatever effective means lay within its power. Its officials rightly reasoned that where information and techniques were deficient, only research and training would provide them.

Since suitably detailed surveys were not available, work had to begin with a nation-wide study or "technological audit," concentrated at first on selected lines of production and later extended to others. The target was not just another set of broad generalities, but down-to-earth findings on: (1) specific ways to improve the existing production through known or new technology; (2) new industries and activities capable of establishment and resources capable of development; and (3) application of practical scientific research to problems hindering local development or endangering retention of markets for local products.

To organize and lead this program through its early years the Banco de Mexico imported a director and several additional outside technologists of his selection—all of them specifically experienced in the kind of task before them. The rest of the staff was recruited in Mexico from among the best available Mexican engineers and specialists. Since one of the primary objectives was to instill in Mexican technologists the spirit of research and to

799

train them in the methods used, preference was given to younger men who could serve their country for a longer future period.

The technological audit phase culminated in a report, prepared jointly by the Mexican and foreign personnel and containing hundreds of concrete suggestions for technical improvement. This was published in two languages and has continued to serve as a guide to many enterprises in the fields covered. Before it was published, however, some of the earliest findings were reported informally and were acted upon. Laboratory research and development programs were started on the industrialization of cascalote tannin, domestic extraction of antimalarial drugs, production of oils for treating and finishing leather, development of by-products of the henequen industry, and others. It is significant that, by this early start, some of these specific developments were almost completed before the formal technological audit report was issued.

At first, to save time, the laboratory research problems were sent north to the United States. Sometimes Mexican technologists were sent with them, to help in their solution and to receive the practical training thus afforded. Yet exporting problems for solution elsewhere could never be a permanent answer; in fact it was often impossible, especially when dealing with agricultural materials which had to be handled fresh from the field. Very early, therefore, efforts were begun to develop Mexico's own research facilities.

Although there were certain local governmental institutions, these had other more appropriate functions and were not adaptable to the type of imaginative research and technical service envisaged. Furthermore it was recognized that private producers in any country are reluctant to bring their problems to a purely governmental institution. A more independent research organization was required.

For this the group made a small beginning by converting a vacant dwelling into a laboratory. The job was done at very little expense, chiefly by the technical men themselves. And in the process young Mexican engineers, already well versed in

UNIVERSITY COLLEGE OF WALES LIBRARY ABERYSTWYTH

theory, learned to use tools and became practical technicians as well. At first some persons questioned the economy of using well-paid scientific men for such work instead of hiring skilled labor; but actually this break with the traditional aversion to manual work on the part of highly educated Mexican specialists was regarded as one of the most important training aspects of the whole program.

Research problems still in progress in foreign institutions were now transferred to this simple but effective Mexican laboratory for completion. Here the young local technologists learned for themselves that such research problems are solved mainly by people working with their hands and minds, and that glittering apparatus and modernistic laboratory buildings are not the most important factors, however useful they may be.

On the side, during this stage the group began to lend its services to the overseas scholarship program of the Banco de Mexico —assisting in selecting candidates to be sent abroad for training, advising on the most appropriate foreign schools or industrial plants to furnish each kind of training, and at times helping to make the necessary arrangements for the students to be accepted.

Participation in this activity brought to light a familiar problem which influenced the next stage of the work. One of the most difficult aspects of a foreign training program for an under-developed country is that too often the technologists return home to find no suitable job ready for them. The country may plan to encourage a certain industry, for example, and may send one or more men abroad to learn its technology. Yet various factors may delay the establishment of the industry. The men come back prepared, but must seek employment in another line for the moment. Sometimes they get buried in desk work and stay there, and the country loses the great value of their training. Seeing this, others are discouraged from technical study.

This was true in Mexico. It was apparent that one remedy would be to provide practical research facilities large enough to receive some of these trained men upon their return, putting them to work side-by-side with imported specialists to solve technical problems of importance to the country until they could be utilized in production itself. In this way their training and experience would increase, instead of withering for lack of practice. There was plenty of work to be done.

Toward this end it was arranged that the Banco de Mexico should invest in a new, larger and properly planned laboratory building. The technical staff designed a structure of wide utility, based on research experience, and even capable of being transformed into an economical factory building if for any reason the laboratory program should be moved in the future.

Once again much of the special interior installation and erection of equipment was done by the technical staff. Newly added Mexican engineers vied with the others in acquiring the practical techniques of welding, pipe-fitting, carpentry, machining, electric wiring, etc. which come into the daily work of a research and development engineer. By this time these men were glad to work with their hands. This was know-how, and there was dignity in it. Some of them began to bring their automobiles to the laboratory's shop to repair them in the evenings; others used the tools to build articles of furniture for their homes in their spare time. Latent ingenuity was released, and found immediate application in their practical investigations.

As research projects were completed, others were started. Among them were the development of a new commercial tortilla flour to help solve certain problems of food supply, a survey of Mexico's fluorspar resources both for export and for the creation of new domestic chemical industries, work on local utilization of meat by-products to curtail unnecessary imports, investigations of 15 unexploited indigenous sources of vegetable oils for food, soap and paint manufacture, and others.

Simultaneously, technical advice was made available to Mexico's development bank—the *National Financiera*—and to local private firms for solution of their individual problems. During the first year of the new laboratory, for example, these included companies making glass, textiles, matches, salt, maguey products, vitamins and corn products.

Cooperation and assistance were exchanged freely with other Mexican institutions. The laboratory soon became a hub of national technical development. It sponsored an important international research conference, among whose direct results were the creation of new government standards laboratories, the *Laboratorios Nacionales de Fomento Industrial,* and several new control laboratories in large industrial plants. Research fellowship funds were supplied to the University of Mexico to encourage interest in applied research as contrasted with pure theory. A wealthy local citizen agreed to donate a fund for the university technical library. A defunct laboratory in Yucatan was revived and staffed, and made some extremely valuable discoveries which will benefit the economy of the entire Yucatan Peninsula.

At the end of five years the program had created a full-grown institution with a reputation for performance. It had also trained a staff of skilled research workers, not only for itself but for service elsewhere. It was found at this time that the value of resulting new exportable products alone, when in full production, would provide foreign exchange annually equal to 60 times the total five-year cost of the program. Moreover, royalty agreements and payments for private service were well on the way to making the program self-sustaining.

After the fifth year the major foreign staff was withdrawn, leaving only one (by local request) to advise during the subsequent transition period. Now known as the *Instituto Mexicano de Investigaciones Tecnologicas,* the laboratory is currently in its second year of independent operation and has some 19 research projects in progress for Mexican private enterprises and government agencies.

Proposed Institute for Ceylon. We have described the Mexican research program at some length because it offers a tangible demonstration of what the mission proposes for Ceylon. The basic pattern has now been worked out in practice, and with a few adjustments can be adapted to Ceylonese conditions and needs. However, Ceylon does not have to retrace all of the evolutionary steps. We recommend the immediate establishment of a Ceylon Institute for Applied Research, along similar lines, and initially under the most experienced external assistance obtainable.

To give the Institute the required independence we propose that it be sponsored locally by the Central Bank, as was done in Mexico. Perhaps, if deemed advisable after the first few years, it might become a direct affiliate of the proposed Development Corporation, but we do not suggest this at first. The Central Bank is already an established institution with the requisite prestige, functioning well, and suitably charged under the Monetary Law Act with the "promotion of the full development of the productive resources of Ceylon." An excellent future is expected of the Development Corporation, but it does not yet exist; and if created it will have its own early problems of organization to work out over a period of time before it will be ready to assist another institution.

Experience has shown that for success a project of this kind has certain fundamental requirements, and that modifications to suit local conditions cannot invade these basic concepts. Therefore we emphasize that competent advice should be obtained as the very first step, before the Institute is created. In this way it should not be difficult to avoid the pitfalls which, through misunderstanding, have brought failure to some hasty attempts elsewhere. We suggest asking assistance of the International Bank for Reconstruction and Development as the agency best equipped to offer experienced counsel on this matter. [2]

Among its functions the Ceylon Institute for Applied Research would make practical field and laboratory studies of local raw

---

[2] The mission has discussed this project with the International Bank for Reconstruction and Development and believes that they would be receptive to the suggestion that they serve as co-sponsors with the Central Bank of Ceylon.

materials and their utilization; it would work on the problems of all kinds of local productive enterprises, test their products, improve quality, find by-products, cut production costs and losses; it would render technical advice to various government departments, the Development Corporation, the Cabinet Economic Committee, and private enterprises as requested; it would aid agriculturalists in problems of equipment, handling and storage of crops; it would propose and develop processes for new industries, build and operate pilot plants, and also design simple cottage-industry equipment.

Publication of technical information and developments of broad value would be an important function. One major service would be to study and solve problems found to be common to a large number of producers in a certain line, and to publish the results for the general benefit of all. This could be done either with the general funds of the Institute, or with special funds supplied by the government or an association of producers, as individual circumstances might dictate. In this way a single well-equipped research laboratory would make unnecessary the wasteful establishment of numerous small, scattered, narrowly-specialized and inefficient "research institutes" constantly being proposed for individual crops or industries. [3]

Large industrial firms would be encouraged to submit their special problems to the laboratory, at their own expense, for confidential solution. Although they may not do this within the first year or so, the Mexican experience indicates that they will support work on this basis once the Institute has demonstrated its ability through actual accomplishment. It would be an aim of the Institute to develop such sources of income through service, eventually becoming as self-sustaining as possible.

---

[3] As an extreme illustration of this, one visiting expert recommended the creation of two separate research institutes to study jaggery (palm sugar) because the jaggery is obtained from two types of palm trees.

TABLE I

ESTIMATED COST TO CEYLON OF FIVE-YEAR PROGRAM FOR INSTITUTE FOR APPLIED RESEARCH

(rupees)

	1st Year	2nd Year	3rd Year	4th Year	5th Year
Personnel [1]	250,000	290,000	350,000	350,000	300,000
Cooperative Research and Training Expense [2]	120,000	100,000	100,000	80,000	80,000
Laboratory Equipment	200,000	250,000	150,000	150,000	200,000
Other Equipment	50,000	30,000	30,000	30,000	30,000
Consumable Supplies	30,000	30,000	50,000	50,000	50,000
Travel & Field Expense	70,000	30,000	50,000	50,000	50,000
Miscellaneous	30,000	20,000	20,000	40,000	40,000
TOTAL CEYLONESE FUNDS [3]	Rs. 750,000	750,000	750,000	750,000	750,000

[1] Assumes specialized technical assistance through International Bank, UN agencies and others. Ceylonese staff to be enlarged gradually as sufficiently trained men become available. Foreign staff to be reduced progressively over last two years, in preparation for completely Ceylonese operation at end of 5th year.

[2] Includes support of selected projects in cooperation with other Ceylonese institutions, especially during early years before full facilities of program are in operation.

[3] Exclusive of long-term investment of approximately Rs. 375,000 in properly designed research laboratory building, to be completed in second year.

We visualize a program of five years with outside help, but with a majority of Ceylonese staff. It would be expected thereafter that the local staff would be prepared to operate the entire program, and that they would continue to train others in the research, educational and administrative techniques of the work. It is through measures of this kind, we believe, that Ceylon must build the foundations of her own technology; for outside help now will be of no real benefit unless her continued development can rest ultimately upon her own efforts.

On the assumption that foreign technical assistance will be available through existing agencies, projected annual operating costs for the Institute total Rs. 750,000 (Table I). This includes equipment purchases; but one additional item is the laboratory building, to be constructed in the first or second year at an estimated cost of Rs. 375,000. The total five-year investment is therefore Rs. 4,125,000. Provision for this is made in the Mission's program of development expenditures, together with a margin of funds to continue operation for the sixth year of the 1953-59 period.

Creation of the Ceylon Institute for Applied Research need not await the formal commencement of the new six-year program. Rather it should be undertaken as promptly as possible. Research takes time, and the sooner it is started the sooner its fruits will be available for the national benefit.

Index

Abbatoirs: 563, **602**

Aberdeen-Laksapana hydroelectric plant: 37, 470

Acetic acid: 44, 506, 541-42, 601

Aerial photography: 30, 340, 366, 369

Africa: 5, 258, 275, 277, 283, 292, 296, 304, 397, 562, 592, 709; *see also* East Africa, South Africa, West Africa

African oil palm: 281-83

Agriculture: 1 ff., 40-41, 209-383; credit facilities for, 59, 162, 198 ff.; and dairy production, 327 ff., 550-52; development of, 23, 114-15, 123-25; education for, 26 ff., 60, 108, 123, 371-74, 381-82, 770, 778, 786 ff.; foreign assistance in, 130, 225, 374-75, 378; fruit cultivation, 9, 13, 310-16, 358, 379, 581, 735; and health, 735-37, 740; and Industrial Credit Corporation, 86-87, 162, 189, 517-18; and industry, 505-506, 525; labor for, 13-14, 31, 33, 369-72; machinery for, 29; Ministry of, 20, 29 ff., 64, 71, 108, 120 ff., 209-383, 385, 415, 434, 447, 449, 598, 740, 778; overseas training in, 370; pests and diseases, 341-50; and population increase, 224-26, 710; private ownership and, 21; production data for, 69; Production and Marketing Societies, 202 ff., 287; products, 226-316; research in, 31, 63, 108, 124-25, 371-74, 797, 805; recommendations for, 375-83; School of Agriculture for Agricultural Assistant Grade, 372, 381; School of Agriculture for Girls, 372-73, 381; supplementary development program, 117; taxation of, 178; technical training in, 55, 62, 130, 214, 225, 370, 372; university degree in, 371-72; *see also* beans and pulses, cacao, cattle, chena cultivation, cinnamon, citronella, coconut, coffee, coir, colonization, cooperative societies, cotton, deccan hemp, dhal, drainage, Dry Zone, estate farming, extension, fertilizer, Food and Agricultural Organization (FAO), fragmentation, ground-nuts, irrigation, jungle clearance, land, livestock, middle class farming, paddy cultivation, peasant farming, rainfall, rice, rubber cultivation, rural development, soil conservation, sugar cultivation, tea, teak, trade, tobacco, vegetables, villages, water supply, and Wet Zone

Air Academy, Ceylon: 678-79

Air Ceylon: 50-51, 672-77, 681-82, 691, 698; finances, 673-74, 679; incorporation of, 673-74

Air France: 676

Air India: 50, 676

Air transport: 45, 128, 608, 671-82, 698; Air Academy, 678-79; air line traffic, 675-76; airports for, 51, 608, 627; civil aviation expenditures, 678; Dakota (DC-3) aircraft use, 672-73, 677; development of, 128, 679-81; fares and rates for, 678; finances, 678-80; foreign air lines, 676; future of, 681-82; International Air Services Transport Agreement, 672, 768; International Civil Aviation Organization, 672; Skymaster (DC-4) aircraft use, 673, 677; traffic, 674, 676-78; and tourist trade, 681-82; *see also* Air Ceylon; Civil Aviation

Alaska Airlines: 676

Alawwa: 348

Alcohol: 284, 540, 601, 741

Alcohol, power: 303, 580

Allai: 420

Alluvial deposits: 400, 414

Alutjama: 48, 128, 468, 696

Amban Ganga: 430

Ambawela: 330

Ammonium sulphate: 467, 552

Amparai: 48, 128, 630, 649, 657, 679, 682, 696

Anaemia: 726, 735, 751

Anaplasmosis: 344, 349

Anatomy, courses in: 760, 762

Animal feeds: 44, 322, 596

Animal husbandry: 29, 125, 327-29; Division of Animal Husbandry and Veterinary Services, 323 ff., 373; survey, 736; *see also* livestock

Anthrax: 325, 348

Anuradhapura: 315, 347, 486, 504, 625, 646, 684, 743

Anuradhapura moonstones: 501

Apothecaries: 713, 716 ff., 763

Appleton, Wisconsin: 470, 603

Aradian Aru: 319

Arecanuts: 136, 258, 378

Arrack: 596

Artificial insemination: 324-25

Arts courses, University of Ceylon: 62, 786

Aruvi Aru: 410

Asia: 11, 258, 275, 278 ff., 611

Assets: Colombo Port Commission, 616; and development, 93; external, 91, 110, 144-45, 156, 176, 190; foreign, 154; surplus, 91; table of, 92, 145

Australia: 45, 141, 257, 294, 324, 357, 363, 375, 562, 672-73, 729; air service to, 50; assistance promised by, 91; tea consumption, 232

Australian National Airways: 51, 672-76, 682

Automobiles: 666-67; *see also* road transportation

Aviation: *see* air transportation

Avisawella: 443, 455, 489, 631, 645

Axonopus compressus: 318, 320

Ayurvedic (indigenous) medicine: 68, 705, 766-67; Board of Indigenous Medicine, 759; College for Indigenous Medicine, 760,

INDEX

Fisheries: 9, 12, 15, 44, 56, 58, 127, 222, 525, 552, 554-56, 601-602, 735; imports, 209; marketing societies, 200

Fish meal: 322, 555

Flood control: 35, 37, 397, 400, 410, 420, 424-25, 430, 441-44, 447, 450, 452, 471, 629; in Dry Zone, 217; forests and, 30; and power, 488; rivers, 442; and road transportation, 654; *see also* irrigation

Flour: 16, 137-38, 605, 736-37; mill for, 42, 127, 507; *see also* wheat flour

Flour, tortilla: 802

Fluorspar: 802

Food and Agricultural Organization: 29, 124, 286, 292, 297 ff., 323 ff., 338, 343, 349, 357, 369, 375, 380-81, 554, 590, 791

Food and foodstuffs: 2 ff., 23 ff., 65, 100; food crops, 285-316, 379; government purchases, 616; imports, 10, 16, 23 ff., 137-38, 148-49, 185-86, 209, 619; Ministry of, 72; subsidies, 123, 170, 184-86; *see also* agriculture

Fodder: 316-22

Fodder plants: 320-22

Foot-and-mouth disease: 348-49, 379

Forbes and Walker, Lt.: 167

Foreign assistance: 27-28, 52, 55, 75, 91; in agriculture, 130, 225, 374-75, 378; in cigarette manufacture, 585; in cloves cultivation, 263; in cotton cultivation, 270; in credit arrangements, 87; in finance, 79; in forests, 342-43; at Gal Oya, 388, 417; in groundnuts cultivation, 281; in housing, 754; in industry, 77; in irrigation, 130, 435, 448-49, 451; in land use potential survey, 369; in livestock survey, 328; in paper manufacture, 603; in power development, 130; in railway planning, 696; in research, 130; in road construction, 656, 697; in sisal growing, 274; in soil conservation, 355; in sorghum manufacture, 294; in steel manufacture, 579; in sugar manufacture, 580-81; in teacher training, 61, 774, 787-88; in technology, 62-63, 81, 130, 521, 791-97; in telecommunications, 689-90, 698; in tire manufacture, 571; in water supply survey, 749

Foreign contractors: and dam construction, 482; and irrigation projects, 37, 130, 437, 440, 451; and power transmission, 492; and public works, 130; and road construction, 655; and water supply, 747

Foreigners, discrimination against: 77; *see also* "Ceylonization"

Foreign exchange: *see* exchange, foreign

Foreign Investment: 76, 90, 516-17

Foreign ownership: 54; in agriculture, 12, 308; of airlines, 676, 681-82; of banks, 158-59; of industry, 507-508; of insurance companies, 163; and investment, capital, 515; of shoe factory, 574; of soap factory, 576; tax on, 177; of tea estates, 229, 235

Foreign trade: *see* trade, export; trade, import

Foremen: shortage of, 437; training of, 451

Forestry: 9, 30-31, 221-22, 331-43; and coconut replanting, 25; commercial, 332-34; 525; conservation, 125, 330, 332; cooperative afforestation, 335-36; deforestation, 125, 361; Department of, 30, 125, 308, 311, 331, 337, 339-42, 369, 380, 492, 754; Dry Zone management, 334; Field Training School, 336; flood control and, 30; fuel forests, 342; history, 331-32; Ordinance, 331; protection forests, 332-33; Ranger College, Coimbatore, 336; recommendations, 380; research, 330, 373, 797; and soil conservation, 30, 352-53; survey, 122; taungya system, 308, 334, 337; *see also* wood products

Formic acid: 541

Fort of Galle: 621

Fort Station: 665

Fragmentation, of farmland: 31, 53, 125, 359-65, 375, 381, 388-89; and paddy cultivation, 287; and rubber cultivation, 238; and soil conservation, 352; and tea cultivation, 229; *see also* land tenure

Freight rates, railway: 48, 89, 123, 638-40

Freight wagons, railway: 641-42, 647

Frogeye: 267, 313

Fruit cultivation: 9, 13, 310-16, 358, 379, 581, 735

Fuel: 333, 579, 591; fuel oil, 609; imports of, 38, 100; for industrial use, 44, 126; supplies of, 44; *see also* coal, firewood, petroleum, power

Fumigatorium, rice: 623-24, 691

Fungus, coffee rust: 211, 277

Furniture: 44, 311, 547, 593-94, 596; tariff on, 146

Fusarium oxysporum cubense: 313

Gadd, C. H.: 345

Galle: 47, 220, 310, 457-58, 464, 489, 493, 608, 618, 621-24, 631, 679, 682, 684, 691 ff., 747, 780; air service, 50; harbor development, 122, 127, 622; power needs, 486; ship traffic, 621; tea cultivation at, 227

Galle Face: 664

Gal Oya River Valley project: 17, 29, 33-34, 123, 126, 200, 224, 270, 281, 297 ff., 356, 368, 377, 387-88, 392 ff., 410, 416 ff., 426, 432 ff., 470, 477, 481, 489, 501, 539-40, 600, 625, 630, 648 ff., 657, 714; air service to, 51; colonization and, 32; dam, 32; development board, 34, 358-59, 375, 422, 536; irrigation of, 36; power needs, 468, 476-79; power station at, 503; rail service for, 48, 128; survey of, 398

Galpotta: 629

Gammaxene: 347-49

Ganewatte: 264, 348

Garden hose: 241, 571

Gauge-reading stations: 444, 452

Gems: 564-66

General Hospital, Colombo: 761

Geography, of Ceylon: 399-400

815

INDEX

Herbs: 759

Highways: *see* Road transportation

Hill (Montane) region: 311, 320; description of, 224; trees in, 333

Hikkaduwe Ganga: 445

Hingurakgoda: 265, 312, 347

Gomagama: 645

Home Affairs and Rural Development, Ministry of: 206, 755

Hookworm: 65, 706, 712, 726, 735, 739, 751

Horse-radish tree: 315

Horticultural Div., Peradeniya: 312

Horticulture, research in: 373

Hose, garden: 241, 571

Hospitals: 129, 324, 551, 704-705, 717, 721-29, 764; Ayurvedic hospitals, 705, 756 ff., 767; bed strength, 721-25; finances, 764; health clinics, 725; increased demand for, 65, 67-68; maternity homes, 726-29, 764; mental, 723-24; out-patients, 722-23; patients, 704; personnel, 724; tuberculosis, 722, 724, 741-42; *see also* health

Housing: 10-11, 65, 67, 714, 734, 741, 744, 752-55, 766; colonization and, 124, 393; commissioner, proposed, 67, 129; credit facilities for, 162; finances, 100, 129, 766; at Gal Oya, 32; and health, 66; increase in production of, 100; and irrigation personnel, 436; Ordinance, 753; supplementary development program, 118; and taxation, 181

Howes, Dr. H. W.: 777-78

Hullaitiva: 222

Hurulawewa: 420

Husbandry, animal: *see* animal husbandry

Husbandry, soil: *see* soil husbandry

Huxham, H. J.: 395

Hydraulics: 780

Hydroelectric power: 15, 18-19, 34 ff., 49, 100, 118, 125, 422, 443 ff., 453-504, 538, 579, 624; Aberdeen-Laksapana plant, 37; classification of projects by head pressure, 671; colonization, 388; development of, 109, 126; equipment, 482; estimated potential, 470; Gal Oya needs, 332, 339; and railways, 641, 652, 697; sites for, 122; total capacity for, 37; *see also* power

Hydrogen: 538-39

Hydrology: 402-11

Hygiene, personal: 729-34

Ice plants: 555

Ihalagema: 646

Illuk: 284-85, 377, 568-570; Farm, Punanai, 284-85; paper, 603

Ilmenite: 469, 486, 507, 512, 526, 556, 564 ff., 603, 625, 647; concentrated, 41, 97; factory, projected, 127, 646; sands, 15

Immigration: 65

Imports: *see* trade, import

Income, national: 2, 11, 15, 79, 88, 97-99, 109, 188; effect of investment on, 104; governmental, 15; investment, 95; labor, 100; from overseas, 12; per capita, 17, 97-98, 105; statistics, 74

India: 3 ff., 15, 45, ff., 62, 66, 135, 141-42, 158, 213, 227, 258 ff., 270 ff., 304, 309, 321, 324, 336, 343, 348, 357, 375, 469, 518, 522-23, 536, 541 ff., 548, 553-54, 561 ff., 573, 583 ff., 596, 641, 672, 683, 693, 703, 709-10, 723, 726, 736, 754, 757 ff.

Indian Forest Service: 334, 342

Indian Telephone Network: 683

Indigenous medicine: *see* Ayurvedic medicine

Indonesia: 141, 227, 231, 236, 244, 262, 273

Industrial Products Act: 43, 149-51, 507, 556, 575 ff., 596

Industry: 1 ff., 40-44, 79, 185, 468, 492-93, 505-606, 805: "Basic" and "non-basic", 512; beer, 532-33, 600; beverages, 600; bottle caps, 533-34; buttons, 534; canned goods, 534-34; cape gooseberry preserving factory, 314; caustic soda, 537-42; cement, 535-37; chemicals, 600-601; cigars, 605; clay products, 542-43; coconut products, 601; coconut oil, 544-46, 603; coconut, desiccated, 543-44; coir fiber, 546-48; confectionery and chocolate, 548-50; colonization and, 388; composite factory, 596; cottage industry, 12, 25, 44-45, 79, 127, 200, 510, 535 ff., 543, 547, 561, 576, 584, 594 ff., 599, 602, 605, 805; credit facilities for, 162, 517-18; dairy products, 550-52; development of, 21, 44, 76, 109, 527-531; drugs, 552; and education, 790; fertilizer, 552-53, 601; finances, 82, 171; fisheries, 554-56, 601-602; glass, 556-59, 602; government policy toward, 76, 507-14; investment, capital, 514-17; labor and, 521-24; and land development, 109; leather goods, 559-61, 602; machinery and shops, 561-62; management, 519-20; marketing societies, 200; meat products, 562-64, 602; milk, 602-603; minerals, 564-68, 603; Ministry of, 71, 120, 284, 303, 375, 508, 510, 514, 520, 545, 552, 568, 578, 584, 728, 778, 798; national income and, 84; paper factory, 377, 568-70, 603; population and, 709-10; power for, 458 ff., 483, 498-99; raw materials for, 524-27; recommendations, 44, 126-27, 597-606; research and, 103, 121, 766, 805; restriction on imports, 149-51; rice, 570-71, 604; rubber goods, 571-72, 604; salt, 572-73; selection criteria for, 527-31; shoes, 573-76, 604; shops and machinery, 561-62; soap, 576; soft drinks, 576-77, 600; starch factory, 308; steel, 577-80, 604; sugar mill, 302-303, 397, 580-81, 604; supplementary development program, 118; tannins, 581; taxes, 178, 605; tea factories, 375, 581-84, 604-605; technology and, 520-21; textiles, 583-85; timber impregnation factory, 338; tobacco products, 585-87, 605; vegetable oils, 587-88; wheat flour, 588-90, 605; wood products, 590-94, 605-606; *see also* entries under individual categories

817

INDEX

Karadian Aru: 272, 284
Karagoda Uyangoda: 319
"Karma": 757-58
Katunayake: 547-48
Katugastola vegetable seed station: 315
Katupotha: 264
Kawadi Duwa: 624
Kayts: 608, 626
Kekirawa: 646
Kegalla: 258, 348, 464
Kegame: 348
Kehelgama Oya: 473-75
Kelani Ganga: 409-410, 443, 452, 618, 651, 664
Kelani Valley: 48, 128, 644, 696
Kelinochchi: 319
Kenya: 273
Kew, Royal Botanic Gardens at: 211
Kilombero Valley, Tanganyika: 368-69
Kindesale: 373 ff.
Kirby, E. Stuart: 580
Kitulgala: 480
KLM Royal Dutch Airlines: 676
Koddiyar Bay: 625
Kodikamam: 632
Koggala: 629, 672, 679
Kolannawa: 665
Kraft pulp: 284
Kudawewa: 265
Kundasale: 347
Kurakkan: 213, 224, 269 n., 292-93, 295-96, 322, 348, 358, 378
Kurundankulam: 357
Kurunegala: 237, 244, 306, 315, 464, 489-90, 564
Kutmale Oya: 333, 360

Labor: 17, 56-57, 519, 521-24; agricultural, 13-14, 31, 33, 369-72; and cement production, 537; and cigar production, 586-87; and Colombo Port, 616 ff.; and colonization, 390; employment for, 100; equipment for, 97; industrial, 14, 40, 109, 126, 511; for jute cultivation, 270; manual, 769; Ministry of, 508, 755; and power development, 496, 500; railway, 632-33, 643, 696; road construction, 657; in rural areas, 58-59; and shoe manufacture, 574; and sugar cultivation, 298, 301; supply of, 53-54; technical training for, 44, 58; and tea cultivation, 231; and tea manufacture, 583; utilization of, 189; in villages, 206-207; wages, 157; see also personnel; technical training
Laboratorios Nacionales de Fomento Industrial (Mexico): 803
Labugama: 746-47
Lace: 594
Lacquerware: 594
Lady Manning Bridge: 630, 648
Laksapana Falls: 480, 486-87
Laksapana hydroelectric project: 37-38, 125, 455-56, 462-64, 468, 473 ff., 486 ff.
Lakes, artificial: see reservoirs; tanks
Lamp chimneys: 556

Land: 1 ff., 18, 23; and agriculture, 12 ff., 34, 65-66, 210; area and altitudes table, 400; and coconut cultivation, 248; and colonization, 33, 124, 384-98; corporation grants, 20; as credit security, 82, 162; development, 1, 40, 108 ff., 123; Development Department, 59, 203, 357, 385; Development Ordinance No. 19 (1935), 360-61; in Dry Zone, 27-28; forests and, 30, 332-35; and investment, capital, 515; and irrigation, 35-36, 124, 438-39; land use potential survey, 122, 365-69, 381, 398; Land Utilization Committee, 368; pasture, 210; and pineapple cultivation, 279; and population, 709; and port development, 618; reclamation, 32, 34, 170-71, 318, 443, 450, 452; Redemption Ordinance, 361; and rice cultivation, 26-27; for road construction, 658; and soil conservation, 25, 353; surveys, 103; taxation of, 181-82; and tea cultivation, 229; tenure, 19, 25, 31, 64, 125, 229, 238, 287, 359-65, 381; titles, 59, 204, 362-65,' 381; tobacco acreage, 263; Torrens titles, 31, 125, 363-65, 381
Lanka Mahila Samiti: 206, 711
Latrines: 732, 745, 750-51
Law, courses in: 786
League of Nations Statistical Yearbook: 708
Leather manufacture: 44, 559-61, 602, 800; shoes, 573-74
Legumes: 264, 318
Life expectancy: 704
Licenses, road freight: 669
Life insurance companies, position table: 164
Life-saving equipment, 268
Lime, soil: 215
Limestone: 15, 564
Linseed oil: 560
Liquors: 145; see also arrack
Lithography: 533, 600
Liver extract: 564
Livestock: 29-30, 213, 221-22, 304-305, 322-31; and agriculture, 326; biological problems, 348-50; cattle, 358; and colonization, 388; coordination in production, 328; development, 125; feed for, 589; and industry, 525; pasturage, 316-31, 379-80; policy, 325-28; Production Station, 329; Research Station, 329; and sugar cultivation, 298; survey, 328; and ticks, 344
Living standard: see standard of living
Loans: power development, 494-95; see also credit
Lobsters: 554
Local government: and health, 67, 714-15; and initiative, 123, 206; loans and development, 162; Ministry of, 67, 129, 720, 744, 750, 754-55, 766; and taxation, 190; see also villages
Locomotives, railway: 640-42, 652
London: 51, 281, 673, 681
London Matriculation Examination: 771-72
London, University of: 437

819

824

INDEX

Thermal power: 37 ff., 100, 125, 455 ff., 468 ff., 481-83, 493 ff., 501, 504, 579; at Colombo, 37; at Kankesanturai, 126; *see also* power, electric

Thondamannar Dam: 446

Thorianite: 44, 527, 567, 603; market survey, 127

Ticks: 344, 349, 560

Tiger Line: 676

Tiles: 542-43

Timber: 15, 311, 335 ff., 525, 590-94; exports, 332; for farm use, 341; government consumption of, 332; and power lines, 492; requirements, 336; road transport of, 338; volume extracted, 332

Tin plate: 549, 586, 600

"Tip burns," onion: 309

Tire, automobile, production of: 507, 571, 604; *see also* rubber

Tirrukovil: 566-67, 603

Tissamaharama: 632, 682

Tobacco: 5, 9, 13, 44, 213, 222, 263-67, 358, 377-78, 605; acreage, 263; American Broadleaf, 265; chewing, 263, 585; cigar, 16, 263, 265, 585-87; cigarette, 14, 213, 263-65, 585-86, 600; Dumbara, 265; pipe, 265; tobacco officer, 265; research in, 373; prices, 266; products, 585-87; Virginia-type, 265

Topography: 3, 366; of Dry Zone, 28; and flood control, 37; and road transportation, 654; and soil conservation, 351-52; survey of, 31, 33, 35; *see also* land

Torrens titles: 31, 125, 363-65, 381; *see also* land

Tourist trade: 128, 691-92

Trade, export: 2 ff., 9-12, 15 ff., 90 ff., 109 ff., 135-51, 158, 171, 185, 526, 648-49, 690-93; African oil palm, 281-83; agricultural products, 2, 5, 12, 23, 41, 124, 209, 227-84, 378; arecanuts, 258; beer, 532, 600; bottles, 558; cacao, 212, 255-57; canned goods, 534-35; cardamoms, 211, 261-62; cashew nuts, 283-84; chillies, 276; chutney, 600; cinchona, 211; cinnamon, 257-58; citronella, 258-59; cloves, 262; coconuts, 25, 96, 124, 135, 212, 243, 252-53, 543-44; coconut oil, 245, 544-46; coir fibre, 547; copra, 544-46; cotton, 269-70; credit facilities for, 518; curios, 594, 606; deccan hemp, 271-72; development program for, 100; duties on, 146, 173-74, 186, 188; finances for, 82; Galle and, 622; gems, 565-66; gingelly, 277-78; ginger, 276; government policy on, 514; graphite, 564-65; groundnuts, 279-81; hides, 559-61; illuk, 284-85; ilmenite, 526, 566-67, 603, 647; and industry, 507, 597; and inflation, 157; kapok, 268-69; leather goods, 559-61; licenses for, 148-49; lima bean, 305; litchi, 313; machinery, 506, 561-62; manioc, 307-308; nutmeg, 260-61; ox hides, 561; papain, 274-75; pepper, 260; pharmaceutical, 564; pineapple, 279; price fluctuation, 15-16, 93-94, 135, 139-40, 155, 168, 170, 188; rice 690; rozelle, 272-73; rubber, 95, 124, 135, 236, 241, 571-72; salt, 221; sea shell, 534; shoes, 574; sisal, 273-74; soap, 576; sunn-hemp, 273; tannins, 581; taxes on, 89; tea, 94-95, 124, 131, 232, 581-84; thorianite, 567, 603; timber, 332; tobacco, 213, 263-67, 585-87; turmeric, 275; to United Kingdom, 259; to United States, 259; vegetable oil, 587-88; *see also* Colombo Port; Galle; Trincomalee; and entries under individual categories

Trade, import: 2 ff., 9-10 12 ff., 23, 90 ff., 99-100, 109, 135-51, 158, 171, 188, 577, 648-49, 690-93; acetic acid, 541-42; beer ingredients, 532; bottle caps, 533; bottles, 558; building materials, 648; confectionery, 549; cargo congestion and, 616; cargo tonnage, 612; carbon dioxide, 580; caustic soda, 538; ceiling on, 148-49; cement, 536; coal, 469, 529; coffee, 277; consumer goods, 95, 135; credit facilities for, 518; currystuffs, 209; development projects and, 97; with dollar area, 147; dried milk, 551; duties on, 145-46, 185; fertilizer, 552-53; finances for, 82; fish, 209; foodstuffs, 2, 185-86, 737; fuel, 37, 469, 579, 641; glassware, 556-58; government policy on, 514; grains, 135; inflation and, 102; licenses for, 148-49; livestock, 326, 348; lumber, 591-92; machinery, 482; manufactured goods, 23, 506, 508, 515; meat products, 562; onions, 309; per capita consumption of, 138; petroleum, 529; price structure of, 139-40; pulses, 209; ratio of investment goods, 101; restrictions on, 149; rice, 26, 209, 287, 411, 621-24, 695; shoes, 573, 575; steel, 577-80; sugar, 297; sulphuric acid, 541; tannins, 560, 581; tea chests, 509, 593; telecommunications equipment, 688; textiles, 583-85; tiles, 542; tobacco, 585-87; turmeric, 275; vegetable oils, 587-88; wheat, 209, 525, 588-90, 605, 736; *see also* Colombo; Galle; Trincomalee; and entries under individual categories

Transporation: 9, 12, 18-19, 45, 127-28, 607-699; and agriculture, 45; development, 109, 116, 693-94; and education, 781; finances, 699; and fisheries, 554-55; and industry, 45; and land development, 109, 210; and mining, 19; Ministry of, 71, 120, 447, 453, 609, 632, 654, 666, 671 ff., 694; and power transmission, 493; recommendations, 497-99; and sugar cultivation, 302 supplementary development program for, 118; *see also* air transport, inland waterways, ports and harbors, rail transport, road transport, sea transport, and telecommunications

Travancora: 346, 566 n.

Treasury: 153-54, 168, 496, 500, 616; bills, rates on, 168, 189; cash balances in, 155; *see also* finance

Trees: 331-343; *see also* forestry

Trichinopoly: 51, 673

Trincomalee: 39, 45 ff., 126 ff., 219 ff., 244,

827